Real Essays

with Readings

Writing Projects for College, Work, and Everyday Life

SECOND EDITION

Real Essays

with Readings

*Writing Projects for College,
Work, and Everyday Life*

Susan Anker

Bedford / St. Martin's
Boston ◆ New York

For Bedford/St. Martin's
Senior Developmental Editor: Beth Castrodale
Senior Production Editor: Karen S. Baart
Senior Production Supervisor: Joe Ford
Senior Marketing Manager: Rachel Falk
Editorial Assistant: Christina Gerogiannis
Production Assistants: Amy Derjue and Kristen Merrill
Copyeditor: Janet Renard
Text Design: Claire Seng-Niemoeller
Cover Design: Billy Boardman
Cover Art: Businessman Writing at Table © Stone/Getty Images; *Girls Studying* © Photonica; *Woman Telecommuting* © Photonica
Composition: Stratford Publishing Services, Inc.
Printing and Binding: R.R. Donnelley & Sons Company

President: Joan E. Feinberg
Editorial Director: Denise B. Wydra
Editor in Chief: Karen S. Henry
Director of Marketing: Karen Melton Soeltz
Director of Editing, Design, and Production: Marcia Cohen
Managing Editor: Elizabeth M. Schaaf

Library of Congress Control Number: 2005927795

0   9   8   7   6   5
f   e   d   c   b   a

For information, write: Bedford/St. Martin's, 75 Arlington Street, Boston, MA 02116
(617-399-4000)

ISBN: 0–312–44900–3   EAN: 978–0–312–44900–1
ISBN: 0–312–44026–X (Instructor's Annotated Edition)   EAN: 978–0–312–44026–8

Acknowledgments

Barbara Lazear Ascher. "On Compassion." From *The Habit of Loving* by Barbara Lazear Ascher. Copyright © 1986, 1987, 1989 by Barbara Lazear Ascher. Used by permission of Random House, Inc.
Dave Barry. "The Ugly Truth about Beauty." From the *Miami Herald*, February 1, 1998. Originally titled "Beauty and the Beast." Copyright © 2003 Dave Barry. Reprinted by permission.

Acknowledgments and copyrights are continued at the back of the book on pages A-16–18, which constitute an extension of the copyright page. It is a violation of the law to reproduce these selections by any means whatsoever without the written permission of the copyright holder.

Brief Contents

Contents

READINGS

Thematic Contents

(Essays listed in order of appearance)

Preface for Instructors

Too often, students perceive their writing course as something they must put up with in order to move on to "content" courses that will help them get a good job. The aim of *Real Essays,* as indicated by its subtitle, *Writing Projects for College, Work, and Everyday Life,* is to show students that the writing course is a crucial gateway to success in every arena of their lives. To achieve this aim, *Real Essays* casts writing and editing skills as practical and valuable. Further, it sends the message that strengthening these skills is worth the effort because all the roles students will play in their lives—college student, employee, parent, consumer, community member—require that they write often and well.

Real Essays shares an overarching purpose with its companion, *Real Writing: Paragraphs and Essays for College, Work, and Everyday Life*—to put writing in a real-world context. Both books link writing skills to students' own goals in and beyond college. What's more, these books motivate students by introducing them to other people who have struggled with writing, have wondered why it is important, and are learning that good writing is not a mysterious, elusive gift but a skill that can be learned by anyone who is willing to pay attention and practice.

Maintaining a strong connection to the real world, the second edition of *Real Essays* does more to build the skills that are essential for success in the writing course and for other college-level work. Expanded coverage of close, critical reading and new advice and assignments on writing about readings give students practical preparation for college success.

Features

Real Essays presents the information that students need and also shows them how and why writing is relevant to them. Many popular features of the first edition have been carried over to the second edition, with revisions based on suggestions from vast numbers of instructors and students.

Motivates Students with a Real-World Emphasis

- **Profiles of Success show that success is within reach.** Each of the nine chapters in Part Two includes interviews with and photographs of former students who have achieved success in the real world.

- **Real-world models of writing give students practical examples.** Unique to *Real Essays*, all the assignment chapters include three essay-length samples — one each from college, work, and everyday life. One example is by the person featured in the chapter's Profile of Success.

Presents Writing in Logical, Manageable Increments

- **A focus on the "four basics" of each type of essay keeps the writing instruction simple.** Each of the assignment chapters opens with a list (indicated by this symbol: ▪▪) of four basic features of the type of writing covered. These lists are followed by model passages that are annotated to show these crucial elements.

- **Step-by-step Writing Guides offer real help.** The Writing Guide in every assignment chapter breaks down the process of writing each type of essay into a series of manageable tasks. Each step is accompanied by clear advice for completing the task.

- **Two chapters help students tackle essay exams, timed writings, summaries, and reports.** Chapter 19, on writing summaries and reports, offers helpful writing guides for these tasks and shows one student's process for writing a book report (on Toni Morrison's *The Bluest Eye*).

- **A thoroughly updated chapter presents ten steps for writing research essays.** This chapter follows one student through the research process and culminates in her paper (new to this edition) about the benefits of mandatory school uniforms.

Presents Editing in Logical, Manageable Increments

- **The editing section helps students overcome the four most serious errors — and more.** In addition to thoroughly covering all standard grammar, punctuation, and mechanics topics, *Real Essays* concentrates first, with fuller coverage and plenty of practice, on the errors identified by teachers across the country as the most serious: fragments, run-ons, subject-verb agreement problems, and verb form problems.

- **References to Exercise Central provide ample opportunities for skill practice.** Marginal references throughout the editing section direct students to Exercise Central for additional exercises. The largest online bank of editing exercises (with more than eight thousand items), Exercise Central offers two levels of skill practice, immediate feedback, and instructor monitoring tools.

- **Review charts at the end of each grammar chapter present key information visually.** For students who are visual learners, the editing section presents concepts and strategies in chapter-ending flowcharts for quick comprehension and practical application.

New to This Edition

We have included an array of new features to help students become better readers and writers throughout college and beyond.

More Help with College-Level Reading

- **A new introductory chapter details essential reading skills** and shows how they can be applied in college and beyond. Accompanying the advice is a wealth of examples—from textbooks, syllabi, tests, and more—as well as exercises that help students identify the main idea and support of anything they read.

- **Readings (79 percent new to this edition) strike a balance between composition classics and engaging topical selections.** Part Eight, Readings for Writers, introduces students to class-proven selections by writers such as Langston Hughes, Nancy Mairs, Brent Staples, and Amy Tan, while also offering newer selections on hot topics like the debate over reinstating the military draft and marketers' controversial attempts to reach ever-younger audiences.

- **Questions in the margins of essays encourage an active approach to reading.** These questions help students take in key information as they read, consider important features of the writing, and learn a process of critical reading that they can apply to other situations.

- **A new mini-casebook of readings gets students to think critically—and write analytically**—about two engaging themes: "Fitting In" and "Expanding Our Horizons." Writing assignments ask students to draw on multiple readings from *Real Essays,* getting students ready for academic assignments.

More Help with College-Level Writing

- **A stronger emphasis on main point and support—two of the biggest challenges for developmental students—fosters effective writing.** Each assignment chapter now offers full coverage of developing a main point and support for the type of essay at hand.

- **New coverage helps students with writing about readings.** A section in the new Chapter 1 helps students summarize, analyze, synthesize, and evaluate readings, providing tips and examples for each of these tasks. New academic writing assignments in Part Two ask students to apply these strategies while writing about multiple readings from the book.

- **New coverage of writing a report.** Chapter 19 now includes writing a report about a book, along with an annotated student report on Toni Morrison's *The Bluest Eye*.

- **More writing-assignment options engage students and encourage critical thinking.** New options include Writing about an Image, based on new color photographs and other visuals; Writing to Solve a Problem, posing real-world challenges for students to address in writing; and Writing about Readings. Assignments based on college, work, and everyday life have been carried over from the first edition.

- **Improved grammar chapters complement the strengthened writing coverage.** The chapters on verb problems and ESL concerns have been expanded, and new ESL notes throughout the grammar chapters offer extra help for students who do not speak or write formal academic English.

- **New writing and research exercises on Exercise Central** cover choosing an effective main point, supporting that point, organizing supporting details, and more. An additional set of exercises deals with integrating source material and documenting sources according to MLA style.

Easier for Students to Use and Understand

- **A clean, new full-color design helps students navigate the book more easily on their own.** *Real Essays* has been redesigned to make key information easier to find and to highlight important elements.

- **Redesigned Writing Guides make it easier for students to work through the writing process on their own.** These guides are now presented as streamlined checklists; students can check off the tasks to keep track of their progress.

- **Visuals in the research chapter clarify important processes.** The research chapter visually models the processes of summarizing, paraphrasing, and quoting from a source to support a thesis. In addition, the MLA documentation section shows students where to find the information they need from key sources to document these sources correctly.

Ancillaries

Print Resources

- **Instructor's Annotated Edition of *Real Essays*, Second Edition.** Gives practical page-by-page advice on teaching with *Real Essays*, including discussion prompts, strategies for teaching ESL students, and ideas for additional classroom activities. It also contains answers to all exercises and suggestions for using the other ancillaries.

- *Practical Suggestions for Teaching REAL ESSAYS,* **Second Edition.** Contains information and advice on working with basic writers, bringing the real world into the classroom, building critical-thinking skills, using computers, teaching ESL students and speakers of nonstandard dialects, and assessment. Also includes tips for new instructors and ideas for making the most of *Real Essays*.

- *Additional Resources to Accompany REAL ESSAYS,* **Second Edition.** Supplements the instructional materials in the text with a variety of transparency masters and other reproducibles for classroom use. The second edition includes new exercises—as well as new diagnostic and review tests—on key writing and research topics.

- **Quick Reference Card.** Offers tips on writing, editing, word processing, and Internet research. Students can prop up this handy three-panel card next to their computers for easy reference while they're writing.

- *From Practice to Mastery* (study guide for the Florida Basic Skills Exit Tests in reading and writing). Gives students all the resources they need to practice for—and pass—the Florida tests in reading and writing. It includes pre- and post-tests, abundant practices, and clear instruction in all the skills covered on the exams. A new chart in the *Practical Suggestions for Teaching REAL ESSAYS* shows how students can use *Real Essays* to brush up on skills covered by the test.

- *The Bedford/St. Martin's ESL Workbook.* Covers grammar issues for multilingual students with varying English-language skills and cultural backgrounds. Instructional introductions are followed by illustrative examples and exercises.

- *Teaching Developmental Writing: Background Readings,* **Second Edition.** Offers thirty-five professional essays on topics of interest to basic writing instructors, along with editorial apparatus pointing out practical applications for the classroom.

New Media Resources

- **Book companion site at <bedfordstmartins.com/realessays>.** Provides additional tools for instructors as well as resources that help students with writing and research. New practices on Exercise Central for *Real Essays* address how to choose an effective main point, how to support that point, how to organize supporting details, and more. An additional set of exercises covers integrating source material into writing and documenting sources according to MLA style.

- **Re: Writing at <bedfordstmartins.com/realwriting>.** Collects the most popular and widely used free online resources from Bedford/St. Martin's in an easy-to-navigate Web site. Offerings include research and documentation advice, model documents, exercises, and instructor resources.

- ***Writing Guide Software for REAL WRITING and REAL ESSAYS.*** Leads students step-by-step through the process of writing each type of essay covered in the text. Also includes critical reading guides and grammar tutorials.

- ***Exercise Central to Go: Writing and Grammar Practices for Basic Writers.*** This student CD-ROM includes hundreds of practice items to help basic writers build their writing and editing skills and provides instant feedback. Drawn from the popular Exercise Central resource, the practices have been extensively class-tested. No Internet connection is necessary.

- ***Testing Tool Kit: A Writing and Grammar Test Bank.*** This CD-ROM allows instructors to create secure, customized tests and quizzes from a pool of nearly two thousand questions covering forty-seven topics. Ideal for assessing students' writing and grammar competency, the test bank can also be used to create practices that are tailored to course goals. Charts at the end of the *Practical Suggestions* and *Additional Resources* print ancillaries correlate topics from *Testing Tool Kit* with chapters in *Real Essays* so that you can use the CD to support your teaching with the text.

- **Comment.** This Web-based peer-review tool allows instructors to respond to student work quickly and easily. Students can also use Comment to respond to each other's work.

WebCT and Blackboard Content is also available for *Real Essays.*

Ordering Information

To order any of the ancillaries for *Real Essays,* please contact your Bedford/St. Martin's sales representative, e-mail sales support at **<sales_support@bfwpub.com>**, or visit our Web site at **<bedfordstmartins.com>**.

Use these ISBNs when ordering the following supplements packaged with your students' books:

Real Essays with
- Quick Reference Card — 0–312–44683–7
- Writing Guide Software — 0–312–45027–3
- *Exercise Central to Go* CD-ROM — 0–312–44678–0
- Comment — 0–312–44681–0
- *From Practice to Mastery* (for Florida) — 0–312–44684–5
- *The Bedford/St. Martin's ESL Workbook* — 0–312–45269–1

Acknowledgments

This edition of *Real Essays* represents the voices and hard work of many individuals joined in an effort to make a practical, motivational book even more compelling for students and instructors. I am, as always, grateful to all of these people.

Reviewers

A large group of reviewers helped to develop and fine-tune the second edition of *Real Essays*. I would like to thank Kathy Bell, Douglas College; Donna Beverly, Montgomery Community College; Marcia J. Booth, Marshall University; Tom Bowlus, Hawaii Community College; Larry Breslauer, Edmonds Community College; Jon Byrne, Itasca Community College; Geneva Chao, Art Institute of California; Stephen Cline, Hawaii Community College; Julie Cote, Houston Community College; Janet Cutshall, Sussex County Community College; Emy DiMattia, Lackawanna College; David Elias, Eastern Kentucky University; Mike Eskew, Chaffey College; Naomi Gallant, University of Massachusetts; Elaine Herrick, Temple College; Sharon Hollis, Lamar Institute of Technology; Kevin Hunt, Goldey Beacom College; Florence Johnson, North Dakota State College of Science; Billy P. Jones, Miami Dade College; Craig Kleinman, City College of San Francisco; Pavla Landiss, St. Louis University; David B. Levy, Housatonic Community College; Pat Mathias, Itasca Community College; Mary D. Mears, Macon State College; Virginia Nugent, Miami Dade College; Carolyn Parks, Union County College; Leslie L. Prast, Delta College; Lorrie Ross, Mt. San Jacinto College; Beverly Schellhaass, Lakeshore Technical College; Rob Senior, Allan Hancock College; Wallis J. Sloat, Harper College; Drema Stringer, Marshall Community and Technical College; Sandra Torrez, Texas A&M University at Kingsville; and Joyce Zymaris, Massasoit Community College.

The following instructors gave us valuable insights on the previous edition: Leigh Adams, Southwest Missouri State University–West Plains; Mary Alexander, University of Phoenix; James Allen, College of DuPage; Cathryn Amdahl, Harrisburg Area Community College; Mark Amdahl, Montgomery County Community College; Mary Ann Bernal, San Antonio College; Jan Bone, Roosevelt University; Carol Ann Britt, San Antonio College; Lorraine Page Cadet, Grambling State University; Nandan Choksi, Art Institute of Fort Lauderdale; Sandra Chumchal, Blinn College; Laurie Coleman, San Antonio College; Nancy Davies, Miami Dade College; Rick Dollieslager, Thomas Nelson Community College; Karen Eisenhauer, Brevard Community College; Linda Elaine, College of DuPage; Eileen Eliot, Broward County Community College; Melanie

Fahlman-Reid, Capilano College; Katherine Finch, North Shore Community College; Anne Gervasi, DeVry University; Laura Gray-Rosendale, Northern Arizona University; Barbara L. Hamilton, Jones County Junior College; Earl Hawley, College of DuPage; Suzanne R. Hess, Florida Community College at Jacksonville; Lesa Hildebrand, Triton College; Kaaren Holum, University of the District of Columbia; Lennie Irvin, San Antonio College; Gail Lighthipe, Bloomfield College; Jose Macia, Broward County Community College; Patricia A. Malinowski, Finger Lakes Community College; Gerald McCarthy, San Antonio College; David Merves, Miami Dade College; Terrance Millet, Linn-Benton Community College; Katona Mulholland, Blue River Community College; Kimme Nuckles, Baker College; Amy Penne, Parkland College; Verlene Lee Pierre, Southeastern Louisiana University; Peggy Riley, Las Positas College; P. C. Scheponik, Montgomery County Community College; Tamara Shue, Georgia Perimeter College; Jeff Siddall, College of DuPage; Norman Stephens, Cerro Coso Community College; Denton Tulloch, Miami Dade College; Pricilla Underwood, Quinsigamond Community College; Gail Upchurch, Olive Harvey College; Paul Vantine, Cameron University; Maria C. Villar-Smith, Miami Dade College; Dorothy Voyles, Parkland College; Ted Walkup, Clayton College and State University; Michael Weiser, Thomas Nelson Community College; and Peggy Wogen, Kishwaukee College.

Students

Many current and former students have contributed to *Real Essays*. The nine "Profiles of Success," who also offered examples of their real-world writing, are (in order of their appearance in the book) Patty Maloney, Rosa Fernández, Daigo Fujiwara, Maureen Letendre, Giovanni Bohorquez, Gary Knoblock, Salvador Torres, Jolanda Jones, and Wayne Whitaker. These individuals are truly inspiring.

Other students and former students who contributed model essays to the book include Florence Bagley, Emma Brennan, Jordan Brown, Traci E. Carpenter, Roberta Fair, Danny Fitzgerald, Cecilia Guillen, Messelina Hernandez, Derek Johnson, Larry Lane, Vidhya Murugesan, Liliana Ramirez, Susan Robinson, Janine Ronzo, Tiffany Shale, Katie Smith, Karron Tempesta, Brenda White, and Carson Williams.

Several students helped us by reviewing readings for the second edition. They were Masataka Aita, Marietta Alston, Maurice Barnes, Sara Bechtel, Corinne A. Cacicuzza, Megan Cleland, Tailynn Collins, Nakia Cooper, Jeremiah DeVote, Shawnta Gladden, Margo Houtz, Chris King, Anthony Lucier, Angelo Madrid, Jessica Marsh, Christina McCune, Kristen Myers, Travis Peters, Wyking Richardson, Ryan Rimmey, Bridgett Runyon, Robert Slautterback, Courtney Thompson, and Shernia Winston.

Contributors

I was incredibly lucky to again work with Janet Renard, whose extraordinary copyediting is unparalleled. She continues to amaze me with what she is able to see and solve. Mark Gallaher, an old friend and talented all-around editor/writer/actor, crafted wonderful questions, prompts, and ideas for the readings. Bruce Thaler contributed exercises on a wide range of topics to the main text and to Exercise Central. Carol Sullivan of Delaware Technical and Community College supplied additional tests and exercises for *Additional Resources to Accompany REAL ESSAYS*, and Billy P. Jones of Miami Dade College contributed icebreaking tips to the *Practical Suggestions* manual. Claire Seng-Niemoeller, who designed the first edition, redesigned the book in four colors with her usual flair. Jason Reblando found compelling visuals and cleared permissions for them, and Sandy Schechter and Diane Kraut persistently maneuvered the maze of securing text permissions.

Bedford / St. Martin's

At the risk of repeating myself ad nauseam, let me say once again that the people at Bedford/St. Martin's are marvels of intelligence, grace, tenacity, and wit. I can never thank them sufficiently.

Two editorial assistants contributed substantially to this edition of *Real Essays*. Stefanie Wortman researched readings, wrote headnotes, and ran the review programs. Following Stefanie's well-deserved promotion, Christina Gerogiannis fell right into step, keeping countless tasks moving in the right direction. Production assistants Kristen Merrill and Amy Derjue pitched in cheerfully at a later stage, assisting ably with the book's production.

Coleen O'Hanley created the book companion site for this edition, managing a myriad of details from site design to production. Nick Carbone, director of new media, and Katie Schooling, senior new media editor, helped to oversee the book's new media program and contributed helpful suggestions throughout. Additionally, Rae Guimond, new media associate editor, has helped to make Exercise Central a more useful resource for both students and instructors. Tari Fanderclai, new media editor, and Nick Carbone were instrumental in developing the Comment resource for peer response.

As usual, this second edition benefited from the sage advice of Karen Melton Soeltz, director of marketing and mother of the miraculous Alexandra. Rachel Falk, senior marketing manager, developed a sound marketing plan for the book and enthusiastically contributed suggestions. Kevin Feyen, marketing manager, was a great and appreciated advocate for the book.

Billy Boardman, consummate dapper fellow, designed another fine cover, and Shelby Disario designed a brochure that presents copious information in a visually appealing way.

The brilliant insights and vision of Joan Feinberg, president of Bedford/St. Martin's; Denise Wydra, editorial director; and Karen Henry, editor in chief, fundamentally shape every Bedford/St. Martin's product, including *Real Essays*. There is none better than this team.

Once again, I worked with Karen Baart, who deftly managed the near-impossible challenge of overseeing the production process. As a colleague pronounced recently, "Karen is super-fabulous!" Yes, indeed.

And then there's Beth Castrodale, senior editor, the Energizer bunny with a brain—the brain behind this and other books. I reel at both the quality and quantity she modestly contributes. I am incredibly fortunate and grateful to work with her.

My every association with Bedford/St. Martin's is a learning expedition, a triumph of teamwork, problem solving, and commitment to do our best—just what we hope to instill in students. I am lucky to share this same type of journey with my husband, Jim Anker, whom I admire absolutely.

Thanks to all of you and anyone else whom I have forgotten to mention.

—Susan Anker

Introduction for Students

How to Use Real Essays

Why Should You Read This Introduction First?

These few pages will explain how to use this book. You've just spent a fair amount of money to buy it, so make sure you get your money's worth. This brief introduction will describe how *Real Essays: Writing Projects for College, Work, and Everyday Life* is organized, how to find information in it, and how to use certain features that will help you improve your writing.

Why This Course Should Be Important To You

Your life is busy. You attend school, and you may even work full time while taking classes. Maybe you're also a parent or have other pressing family or community commitments. You have bills to pay and goals to achieve.

And then there's this writing course.

You may be tempted to think of the course as just something to get through with a passing grade. However, it may be one of your best opportunities to develop the writing skills you need — whatever your current obligations or future plans are.

Here's a true story. When the first book in this series, *Real Writing*, was published, I proudly distributed my author copies to a few friends and relatives. I never thought they'd do much more than look at the pictures and think, "That's my daughter" or "That's my best friend." In fact, they did say these things, but soon I started getting e-mails from people who had seen the book, had actually looked through it, and wanted to know how they could buy a copy. The first request I took as a fluke and wondered why anyone would want to buy this book when they were out of college and already employed in a good position. But the requests kept coming — from people in various occupations, ranging from a police officer to a manager at Verizon to a marketing specialist at IBM to a high-level computer whiz who tests government security programs. Each of them said basically the same thing: "Everyone in this office needs to write, and we're never sure whether what we're writing is right. We're dying for something that will help us, and we like this because it's not just about college writing but about the kinds of writing we really do."

How This Book Is Organized

Real Essays is organized into eight parts:

- Part One (Chapters 1–8) discusses the importance of reading and writing in college and beyond and describes the process you use to write any kind of essay.

- Part Two (Chapters 9–17) gives concrete instruction about how to write nine common types of essays — the ones most often assigned in college courses — and guidance about how to apply those same skills to work-related and everyday writing tasks.

- Part Three (Chapters 18–20) presents strategies for completing other kinds of writing tasks, such as taking tests, writing summaries and reports, and writing from sources.

- Part Four (Chapters 21–25) includes chapters on each of the four most serious grammar errors, the ones that people most often notice: sentence fragments, run-ons, subject-verb agreement problems, and problems with verb forms.

- Part Five (Chapters 26–32) gives you instruction and practice in other areas of grammar.

- Part Six (Chapters 33–35) includes chapters about words: choosing the right word, not confusing words that sound or look alike, and spelling words correctly.

- Part Seven (Chapters 36–40) covers punctuation — using commas, apostrophes, and quotation marks, for example — and capitalization.

- Most of Part Eight (Chapters 41–50) consists of readings that follow the patterns of the nine types of writing covered in Part Two. These readings give you models and ideas for your own writing and help you become a more critical reader. Chapter 51 is a mini-casebook of readings on two themes that will get you thinking about personal growth and education.

How to Find Information in *Real Essays*

Information is easy to find in *Real Essays*. Knowing where to look is a key first step.

Table of Contents

If you want to find a particular chapter, use the brief table of contents (pp. v–vi). If you're looking for specific information within a chapter, try the detailed table of contents (pp. vii–xv), which lists chapter titles and major headings.

Index

If you want to find a particular topic, you can also use the index (p. I-1). Topics are listed alphabetically. To find information on using apostrophes in contractions, look under "apostrophes" and find the subentry "in contractions." The page number will direct you to the right information.

Anthology, citing, 316
Apostrophes, 571–579
   in contractions, 574
   definition of, 571
   editing for, 577–579
   with letters, numbers, time, 576
   to show ownership, 571–572
Appositives

Chart of Correction Symbols

If your instructor uses symbols to indicate grammar, spelling, or punctuation errors in your writing, you can use the chart at the back of the book to get the meaning of each symbol and a chapter reference for more help.

Headings at the Tops of Pages

When you want to know where you are in the book, look at the headings that run along the tops of the pages. The left page gives you the name of the part of the book you're in (for example, Part Seven • Punctuation and Capitalization), and the right page tells you which chapter you're in (for example, Chapter 37 • Apostrophes).

References in the Margins

Real Essays includes helpful tips and references printed right in the margin. These direct you to additional information or resources in the book or on the book's companion Web site.

■ For more practice correcting run-ons, visit Exercise Central at <bedfordstmartins .com/realessays>.

    _____ 9. There are differenc[

    and listening to mu[

    tion from the driver[

    _____ 10. Drivers who love ma[

    strictions many othe[

List of Useful Charts and Reference Tools

Turn to the inside back cover for a list of all kinds of review and summary information in the book, with page numbers given so that you can easily access what you need—a checklist, a diagram, a reference chart—without flipping through the whole book or reading the whole table of contents.

How to Use the Features of *Real Essays* to Improve Your Writing

Real Essays is designed to help you to become a better writer. Here are descriptions of charts, checklists, and other helpful features—some with samples from the book.

Four Basics of Writing

Each of the chapters in Part Two, Writing Different Kinds of Essays, starts off with a list of the four basic features of the kind of writing covered in the chapter. Each list is followed by a model paragraph that is highlighted to show these features. As you read how a particular kind of writing is developed, keep these four basics in mind. As you do the writing assignments, you can refer to these four basics before, during, and after you write. Focusing on just four key elements for each type of writing will make the assignments easier to manage.

> **⬛ FOUR BASICS OF GOOD NARRATION**
> 1. It reveals something of importance to you (**main point**).
> 2. It includes all of the major events of the story (**primary support**).
> 3. It uses details to bring the story to life for your audience (**supporting details**).
> 4. It presents the events in a clear order, usually according to when they happened.
>
> In the following passage, each number corresponds to one of the four basics of good narration.

⬛ IDEA J
Write abo
important
happened
week.

> **1** My guardian angel made sure I got to the interview that changed my life. **2** I went to bed early on the night before the most important job interview I have ever had. I felt that getting this job would be the
> ~~best thing I would ever do, and I wanted it with all my heart. 3 I had~~

4 Events
chronolo

Writing Guides

Each chapter of Part Two ends with a Writing Guide, a helpful checklist that includes the main steps for writing the kind of essay covered in the chapter and details for completing each step. You can follow these checklists as you complete your essays, checking off each step as you go.

WRITING GUIDE: NARRATION	
STEPS IN NARRATION	**HOW TO DO THE STEPS**
Focus.	❏ Think about who will read your narration and you want your readers to understand.
Prewrite to explore your topic. See Chapter 3 for more on prewriting.	❏ Determine your purpose for writing. ❏ Decide what story you want to tell. ❏ Use a prewriting technique to explore your th what happened; how it affected you or others the story shows, explains, or proves.
Write a thesis statement. Topic + Main point = Thesis My father has become a complete stranger.	❏ Decide what is important to you about the sto reader saying, "So what?" ❏ Specify the point you want your readers to un ❏ Write a thesis statement.

Profiles of Success

Each Part Two chapter also includes a Profile of Success, a brief interview with a former student who struggled with writing. Now successfully employed — one is a nurse, one is an attorney, one is a small-business owner, and so on — these individuals tell what they write at work and how their work requires the type of writing covered in the chapter. Later in the chapter — next to a photograph of the interviewee — is an example of the profiled person's on-the-job writing.

Profile of Success

Daigo Fujiwara
Online Art Director

(See Daigo's Description at Work on p. 157.)

BACKGROUND: Daigo came to the United States fro change student when he was a senior in high sch he wanted to attend college in the United States. language test scores were low, so he took writing second language at Becker Junior College and the

EMPLOYER: *The Christian Science Monitor*

COLLEGE(S)/DEGREES: Becker Junior College (A.A.), N (B.A.)

TYPES OF WRITING ON THE JOB: Summaries of articles to illustrators, follow-up letters to illustrators, not tions for interns, forms describing necessary chang

HOW DAIGO USES DESCRIPTION: Daigo has to write d what he needs for the newspaper's art program. T called specifications, are written for freelance arti

TEAMWORK ON THE JOB: Daigo works with editors a *Monitor* to develop a concept, to decide whether illustrations for each article, and to make individu

Quick Review Charts

The chapters in Parts Four, Five, and Six end with review charts that enable you to see, at a glance, what to do when you are editing your own writing for a particular type of grammar problem. These are like flowcharts in a how-to manual.

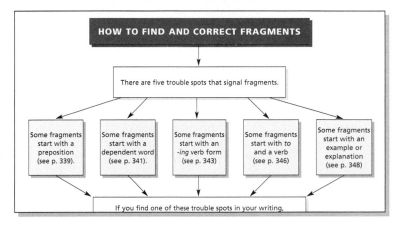

HOW TO FIND AND CORRECT FRAGMENTS

There are five trouble spots that signal fragments.

| Some fragments start with a preposition (see p. 339). | Some fragments start with a dependent word (see p. 341). | Some fragments start with an *-ing* verb form (see p. 343) | Some fragments start with *to* and a verb (see p. 346) | Some fragments start with an example or explanation (see p. 348) |

If you find one of these trouble spots in your writing,

Useful Appendices

At the end of the book are two practical appendices: one on solving problems (p. 725), the other on giving a good oral presentation (p. 728). The problem-solving advice is referred to in writing assignments in Part Two, but you can use it when developing a solution to any problem. Two additional appendices, on writing e-mail and memos and on writing a résumé and a letter of application, appear on the *Real Essays* companion Web site at <**bedfordstmartins.com/realessays**>.

Remember the Number Four

Sometimes when you are writing, it may seem as if there is just too much to remember. To make things a little easier on you, remember the number *four;* it's important in this book. Part One covers *four* basic steps in the writing process: prewrite, draft, revise, and edit. Part Two includes a list of *four* key features, called the "Four Basics," for each type of writing. Part Four presents the "*Four* Most Serious Errors" (fragments, run-ons, subject-verb agreement problems, and verb-form problems), the most noticeable and potentially damaging errors. *Real Essays,* in an effort to give you practical help, focuses your attention first on the most basic and important issues.

What Do You Want from This Course?

As I said earlier, this course is for you: You need the information and practice it provides if you want to pass the course, succeed in other courses, get a job, or be able to stand up for yourself in your everyday life. As you begin the course, decide what you want to gain from it.

First, what are some of your real-world goals? For example, what kind of job or career do you hope to have? What do you want to do in your everyday life: Find a nice place to live? Buy a car? Travel? Get your money back when you've been overcharged? Make new friends?

Do some thinking about your real-life goals and list at least five, the more concrete and specific the better. ("To be happy" may be too general, for example.) Once you have some real-world goals in mind, particularly the job or career ones, try to link those goals to the writing skills you want to learn or improve in this course. Carefully complete the worksheet that follows.

WRITING QUESTIONNAIRE

NAME _____ DATE _____

COURSE _____

Real-World Goals

Use the spaces below to list at least five specific goals you have set for yourself.

_____

_____

_____

_____

_____

Course Goals

Think about your writing and comments you have received about it in the past. What do you think your major problems with writing are? What should you work on improving? List a few answers to these questions in the spaces that follow.

_____

_____

_____

_____

When you have jotted down a few ideas, list three writing skills you want to learn or practice. Be as specific as possible. For example, "Learn to write better" is too general to mean anything much or to help you focus on the areas you want to improve. Expanding on your answers to the questions above, write three specific skills you want to address and improve during this course.

1. _____

2. _____

3. _____

Real Essays

with Readings

Writing Projects for College, Work, and Everyday Life

Part One

How to Read and Write in College

1

Reading and Writing in College and Beyond

What You Need to Know

Reading carefully and purposefully can boost your chances of success not only in college but also on the job and in everyday life. Good readers can find solid, practical information about anything they are interested in: making money, investing, starting a business, finding a job, treating an illness, protecting themselves from unfairness, buying a car at the best price, and so on.

In college, you have the opportunity to learn and polish reading skills that may be more sophisticated than those you used in high school. This chapter will preview those skills and also show how they are linked to good writing.

Why You Read in College

In college, reading involves not just taking in facts but also figuring out what those facts add up to. To succeed in college (and elsewhere), you need to be able to read carefully and deeply for a variety of reasons.

- **To understand and fulfill course goals.** At the start of a course, your instructor will hand out a syllabus that includes a variety of important information. Often, the goals or objectives of the course are on the first page of the syllabus. They may include the following:

  - Recognize key ideas.
  - Read and think critically.

■ For an example of a syllabus, see page 9.

- Read, evaluate, synthesize, and apply information from a variety of sources.

- Understand and demonstrate the stages of the writing process.

- Develop clear thesis statements.

- Develop clear ideas in paragraphs and essays.

- Write complete, grammatically correct sentences.

Note that several of these goals specifically relate to reading. Make sure that you read the course goals very carefully because *you will be graded on how well you achieve them.*

- **To participate in classroom discussions based on the reading.** Often, instructors don't go over the facts of an assigned reading in class. Instead, they will expect students to have done the reading and will build on the facts from the reading in class discussions. Many instructors base part of your grade on the quality of your participation in such discussions.

- **To complete writing assignments based on the reading.** When instructors assign writing based on reading, they want you to do more than list facts from the reading. Typical assignments will ask you to draw your own conclusions about readings by **summarizing**, **analyzing**, **synthesizing**, or **evaluating** their central ideas.

■ For more on summarizing, analyzing, synthesizing, and evaluating, see pages 16–20.

- **To pass tests.** Many of the tests you will take in college will gauge your basic comprehension of readings and class discussion. Beyond this, tests may require you to take a position about course material, including readings, by drawing on evidence from it. Or you may be asked to relate the course material to other information. Advice on taking tests is in Chapter 18.

How to Read in College

In college, you will read a variety of materials: course syllabi, handouts, textbooks, articles, essays, literature, e-mail, discussion boards, and more. While you will read these materials in slightly different ways, they all require you to be able to read closely and critically.

Close reading means paying attention to every word and every point. Closely read course syllabi, tests, and textbooks, taking in every word and highlighting important points. **Critical reading** requires both close reading and more: asking yourself why the author has made these points in this way, what they mean, and whether you agree. You will apply critical reading to textbooks, articles, essays, and literature.

Critical reading requires an active reader who doesn't just passively look at the words. To help yourself concentrate, find a comfortable place that is relatively free from distractions and interruptions. Mental and physical alertness is important: For most people, reading while lying down or slouching causes sleepiness. Instead, try sitting at a table or a desk with a good light source nearby. For many people, reading aloud is an excellent way to absorb the information.

The following basics will help you understand and respond to the reading you will do in this course and others.

▪▪ FOUR BASICS OF CRITICAL READING

1. Preview the essay, article, or chapter.
2. Find the main point and the support for that point.
3. Take notes on paper or in the text.
4. Review and respond to what you have read.

Preview the Reading

Before carefully reading any piece of writing, skim or preview the whole thing, whether it is a chapter or an essay assigned in college, a memo at work, or any agreement you sign in everyday life. The following steps of previewing should be done quickly, before reading the piece for meaning.

Read the Title, Headnote, and Introductory Paragraphs Quickly

The title of a chapter, article, or other document usually gives you some idea of what the topic is. Often, an essay or a chapter is introduced by a headnote, a paragraph (or more) that gives information about the author and the reading. Headnotes can give you background for understanding what you are about to read. Whether or not there is a headnote, writers often introduce their topic and main point in the first few paragraphs, so read those and note what you think the main point might be.

Read Headings, Key Words, and Definitions

Textbooks and magazine articles often include headings to help readers follow the author's ideas. These headings (such as "Preview the Reading" above) tell you what the important subjects of the writing are. As you preview, highlight the major headings.

Any terms in **boldface** type are especially important. In textbooks, writers often use boldface for key words that are important to the topic. Read the definitions of key words as you preview the writing.

Look for Summaries, Checklists, and Chapter Reviews

Many textbooks (such as this one) include features that summarize or list main points. Review summaries, checklists, or chapter reviews to make sure you have understood the main points.

Read the Conclusion Quickly

Writers usually reiterate their main point in their concluding paragraphs. Read the conclusion and compare it with the note you made, after reading the introduction, about what the main idea might be.

Ask a Guiding Question

As the final step in your preview of a reading, ask yourself a **guiding question**—that is, a question you think the reading might answer. Sometimes, you can turn the title into a guiding question. For example, read the title of this chapter and write a possible guiding question. As you begin your close reading, try to answer your guiding question. Having a guiding question gives you a purpose for reading and helps keep you focused.

Find the Main Point and the Support

After previewing a reading, begin reading carefully for meaning. Critical to understanding meaning is identifying a writer's main point and the support for the main point.

Main Point

■ For more on main points, see Chapter 4.

The **main point** of a reading is the central idea the author wants to communicate. Writers usually introduce their main point early, so read the first few paragraphs with special care. After reading the first paragraph (or more, depending on the length of the reading selection), stop and write down—in your own words—what you think the main idea is. If the writer has stated the main point in a single sentence, double-underline that sentence, but also try writing the main point in your own words, which will help you understand it better.

PRACTICE 1   FINDING THE MAIN POINT

Read each of the following paragraphs. Then, write the main point in your own words in the spaces provided.

1. Neighbors who are too friendly can be seen just about anywhere. I mean that both ways. They exist in every neighborhood I have ever lived in and seem to appear everywhere I go. For some strange reason these people become extremely attached to my family and stop in as many as eight to ten times a day. No matter how tired I appear to be, nothing short of opening the door and suggesting they leave will make them go home at night. (I once told an unusually friendly neighbor that his house was on fire, in an attempt to make him leave, and he still took ten minutes to say goodbye.) What is truly interesting about these people is their strong desire to cook for us even though they have developed no culinary skill whatsoever. (This has always proved particularly disconcerting since they stay to watch us eat every bite as they continually ask if the food "tastes good.")
   — From Jonathan R. Gould Jr., "The People Next Door"

   _____

   _____

■ For online exercises on main points, visit Exercise Central at <**bedfordstmartins** .com/realessays>.

2. Relief from depression may be a mouse click away. Australian researchers have developed Web sites to fight depression. In a study of 525 people, those who visited a site designed to reduce anxiety and develop coping skills (moodgym.anu.edu.au) showed a 25 percent improvement in depression symptoms. Those who visited a site offering information about depression (bluepages.anu.edu.au) improved by 20 percent. A control group who participated in weekly phone discussions improved by only 8 percent. The sites are available online for public use.
   — From Kate Dailey, ed., "Health Bulletin," _Men's Health,_ June 2004

   _____

   _____

3. Entrepreneurs have certain traits, such as being creative innovators, moderate risk takers, independent, and determined to achieve success. Also, previous experience in managing a business often helps to make a successful entrepreneur. However, a person who has these characteristics

may not be motivated to use them to launch a business until a precipitating event occurs. A **precipitating event** is a change in the environment that spurs an individual to take action. Such events can take various forms. They may be part of an individual's personal life, such as a change in health, family makeup, or financial status. They may be technological innovations that enable a new type of work or work in a new location. Or else they may be job-related events beyond the individual's control — layoffs, mergers, changes in corporate management, market changes, or even a sudden entrepreneurial opportunity.

—From Kenneth H. Blanchard et al.,
Exploring the World of Business, 1996

_____

_____

4. Class attendance and participation are essential since we do many in-class writings and group work, which are part of a student's grade in the course. If you must miss a class and know that in advance, please contact me so that we can discuss work and assignments that you will miss. Certain absences are considered excused absences: student illness, a death in the family, an accident, and religious holidays. You must arrange to make up work missed, and that work must be submitted within a week. Other absences will be considered unexcused absences unless discussed with me. Any student who has more than three unexcused absences will be asked to drop the course.

—From a syllabus for a writing course

_____

_____

Support

Support consists of the explanations and evidence provided in a piece of writing. In essays and articles, support is essential for backing up the writer's main point. Other documents (like syllabi and test directions) may not necessarily state a main point, but they do include explanations and examples to help the reader.

The type of support provided depends on the purpose of a piece of writing.

• The support in a **course syllabus** is the explanation of things such as course objectives, grading policies, classroom rules, and when assignments are due. The example on page 9 shows part of a typical course syllabus.

Syllabus
Course name and number
Meeting days and hours

Instructor information
Professor name
Phone number
E-mail address
Office hours

Course description: This course focuses on expository writing.
Students will use the writing process and will read, write, and edit
effectively as well as use and document library resources.

Course objectives:
- Use a variety of writing strategies.
- Recognize and correct grammar errors.
- Read and think critically and apply information.
- Develop ideas in paragraphs and essays with clear theses.
- *Etc.*

Read carefully;
your grade will
depend on how
well you achieve
these objectives.

Course materials:
Susan Anker, *Real Essays with Readings,* Second Edition

Grading policies (*percentage of grade*):

Papers	60%
Tests	25%
Homework	10%
Class participation	5%

Explanation of
grading policies

Grading scale for tests and papers:

A	90–100%
B	80–89%

Etc.
See handout with grading rubric and examples.

Explanation of grading criteria

Course policies:
- **Attendance:** Class attendance is required. Students who miss more
  than one week . . . *etc.*
- **Classroom rules:** Arrive on time, turn off cell phones, . . . *etc.*
- **Late or missed work:** No late work is accepted without my
  consent . . . *etc.*
- **Academic integrity:** This course adheres to the college handbook, which
  defines the following criteria: . . . *etc.*   Explanation of course policies

- The support in **test** instructions tells you specifically what you need to do. Often, students do not read the complete directions closely; as a result, they end up either doing less, or sometimes more, than what is required. Following are directions from some typical tests.

ELECTRONICALLY SCORED TEST TAKEN ON A COMPUTER

To select an answer, use the mouse to click on the circle next to the answer. Once you have selected an answer, click on the Next button to move on. A message will appear asking you whether you want to confirm your answer or change it. If you want to change your answer, . . . *etc.*

ESSAY EXAM

Read the essay that follows and respond to one of the writing prompts. You will have 50 minutes to plan, write, and revise your response, so allocate enough time for each step. Your score will be based on your ability to express your main idea, develop support for the main idea, present that support in a logical order, and . . . *etc.*

GRAMMAR TEST

The sentences below may have problems in grammar, usage, word choice, spelling, or punctuation. Each underlined section corresponds to a possible correction. Choose the lettered option that corrects the error. If the original sentence is correct, choose D.

                                 A   B   C

EXAMPLE: Neither Ellen nor Rosa like to get up before eight in

the morning.

A. or   **C.** at

B. likes [This is the correct choice.]   **D.** no error

As you answer each question, make sure the number of the test item matches the number on the answer sheet. You have 50 minutes to complete the test.

- The support in a **textbook** consists of the explanations of topics or concepts in a chapter. (For more on reading textbooks, see pp. 14–15.)

- The support in an **essay** consists of the details, facts, and examples that help you understand the author's main point.

■ For more on support, see Chapter 5.

- The support in a **short story** consists of the details that reveal the characters and situations.

PRACTICE 2   FINDING SUPPORT

Go back to Practice 1 (p. 7), where you identified the main point of each passage. Now, underline the support for each main point.

■ For online exercises on support, visit Exercise Central at <**bedfordstmartins .com/realessays**>.

Take Notes

Another way to read actively and critically is to take notes. Taking notes can help you understand a reading and keep you alert. You can write notes in the margin (if the copy of the reading is your own), in a separate reading journal, on notecards, or on a computer. Using check marks and other symbols, underlining, or highlighting can also make important parts stand out. Here are some ideas about how to take notes:

- Note the <u><u>thesis statement</u></u> (double-underline it).
- Note the major <u>support points</u> (underline them).
- Note ideas you agree with (put a check mark ✔ in the margin).
- Note ideas you don't agree with or are surprised by (put an **X** or ! in the margin).
- Note points or words you don't understand (put a **?** in the margin).
- Note information that answers your guiding question (write "guiding question" in the margin).
- Note thoughts or reactions you have while reading (write them in the margin).

Review and Respond

Often, your instructor will ask you to answer questions about a reading or to write about it. To do either, you may need to skim the reading again, looking at your notes and highlighting before developing a response to what you have read. First, try to answer your guiding question. Also, use the following Critical Thinking guide.

CRITICAL THINKING: READING CRITICALLY

FOCUS
- Review the reading selection.

ASK
- What is the author's main point?
- What evidence and explanations does the writer use to back the main point?

---

continued

- Does the support actually help me understand the main point, or am I left with questions and doubts?
- Has the author convinced me of his or her point of view? How has the piece changed my feelings about the topic?
- What do I think about the author's message? Why?
- How does what I've learned connect to other things I know? How does it relate to experiences I have had?

WRITE

- Based on the answers to your questions and your assignment, write a response to the reading selection.

Later in this chapter, you will learn some specific kinds of writing you may be asked to do in response to an assigned reading.

An Active Reader at Work

Before moving to the section on reading college textbooks, read the following piece. The notes in the margins and within the text show how one student, Tom, read an essay assigned in a writing course. You may want to use this sample as a model for the reading you do in the following chapters. Note that some of Tom's comments in the margin relate to "Why You Read in College" (pp. 3–4). Many of his comments show how he read critically by thinking about how the writer's points related to his own experiences. Additionally, he noted points that are probably important for a class discussion or writing assignment.

Deborah Tannen

It Begins at the Beginning

Deborah Tannen is a professor of linguistics at Georgetown University in Washington, D.C. Linguistics—the study of human language—reveals much about people and their culture. Part of Tannen's research in linguistics has focused on differences in the ways women and men use language and the effects of those differences on communication. The following excerpt, taken from her book *You Just Don't Understand,* describes how girls' and boys' language and communication patterns differ from a very early age.   *Will piece focus on differences?*

GUIDING QUESTION

How do boys and girls differ in their play and the language they use in their play?

This must be a key idea, like my teacher talked about.

Even if they grow up in the same neighborhood, on the same block, or in the same house, girls and boys grow up in different worlds of words. Others talk to them differently and expect and accept different ways of talking from them. Most important, children learn how to talk, how to have conversations, not only from their parents, but from their peers. [. . .] Although they often play together, boys and girls spend most of their time playing in same-sex groups. And, although some of the activities they play at are similar, their favorite games are different, and their ways of using language in their games are separated by a world of difference. *?*

Thesis stating main point. Everything else should relate to this.

✔ I can see this with my nephew and niece. Teachers, too.

Language in games? What does that mean?

Boys tend to play outside, in large groups that are hierarchically structured. Their groups have a leader who tells others what to do and how to do it, and resists doing what other boys propose. It is by giving orders and making them stick that high status is negotiated. Another way boys achieve status is to take center stage by telling jokes, and by sidetracking or challenging the stories and jokes of others. Boys' games have winners and losers and elaborate systems of rules, and the players frequently boast their skill and argue about who is best at what.

But they play in teams together, even though there's a leader.

Support answers guiding question. Probably going to be part of discussion or quiz.

Girls, on the other hand, play in small groups or in pairs; the center of a girl's social life is a best friend. [. . .] In their most frequent games, such as jump rope and hopscotch, everyone gets a turn. Many of their activities (such as playing house) do not have winners or losers. Though some girls are certainly more skilled than others, girls are expected not to boast about it, or show that they think they are better than the others. Girls don't give orders; they express their preferences as suggestions, and suggestions are likely to be accepted. Anything else is put down as bossy. They don't grab center stage—they don't want it—so they don't challenge each other directly. And much of the time, they simply sit together and talk. Girls are not accustomed to jockeying for status in an obvious way; they are more concerned that they be liked.

! Hadn't thought of that.

This is a big difference between boys and girls. Think about my experience as a kid.

I wonder how this affects how people act in business. What about computer games? The same for boys and girls?

—Adapted from Deborah Tannen, *You Just Don't Understand*, 1990

Restatement of main idea: From the time they are very young, boys and girls talk and play differently. Note to myself: Think about how that affects how men and women work together and live together.

Reading College Textbooks

Textbooks usually have many special features to help students find and understand key information. Some of these features (chapter summaries and reviews, checklists, headnotes, headings, and boldface words) were discussed earlier under "Preview the Reading" (p. 5). On the facing page is a page from Don H. Hockenbury and Sandra Hockenbury, *Discovering Psychology,* Second Edition. The notes in the margin indicate what each feature is and what purpose it serves.

 PRACTICE 3   READING TEXTBOOKS

Using a textbook from another class, review a chapter for its special features. Then, on a separate piece of paper, write the title of the book, the class you are using it in, and a list of the special features it has.

You can use the following Critical Thinking guide when reading textbooks or any other readings assigned in college.

CRITICAL THINKING: READING IN COLLEGE

FOCUS
- Think carefully about any piece of writing you are assigned.

ASK
- Why am I being asked to read this? To understand course expectations? To understand certain concepts that I will be tested on? To show what I have learned (on a test or in a writing assignment)? To get background information?
- Given the purpose of my reading this, what parts of the text deserve special attention?
- How can I best use features like headings, boldface type, and summaries to make sure I understand the selection?

WRITE
- Answer any end-of-chapter or end-of-selection questions to reinforce and improve your understanding of key concepts. If you are asked to do other writing in response to the reading, follow your instructor's directions carefully and see the Critical Thinking box on page 20.

Subhead raises intriguing question answered in the text.

When Red + Blue + Green = White When light waves of different wavelengths are combined, the wavelengths are added together, producing the perception of a different color. Thus, when green light is combined with red light, yellow light is produced. When the wavelengths of red, green, and blue light are added together, we perceive the blended light as white.

Visual (with explanation) clarifies key concepts.

Definitions explain key terms for understanding text.

color
The perceptual experience of different wave-lengths of light, involving hue, saturation (purity), and brightness (intensity).

hue
The property of wavelengths of light known as color; different wavelengths correspond to our subjective experience of different colors.

saturation
The property of color that corresponds to the purity of the light wave.

brightness
The perceived intensity of a color, which corresponds to the amplitude of the light wave.

trichromatic theory of color vision
The theory that the sensation of color results because cones in the retina are especially sensitive to either red light (long wavelengths), green light (medium wave-lengths), or blue light (short wavelengths).

1st main heading sets up 1st topic: our experience of color

VISION   91

The Experience of Color
What Makes an Orange Orange?

To explain the nature of color, we must go back to the visual stimulus—light. Our experience of **color** involves three properties of the light wave. First, what we usually refer to as color is a property more accurately termed **hue.** Hue varies with the wavelength of light. Look again at Figure 3.2 on page 86. *Different wavelengths correspond to our subjective experience of different colors.* Wavelengths of about 400 nanometers are perceived as violet. Wavelengths of about 700 nanometers are perceived as red. In between are orange, yellow, green, and blue.

Second, the **saturation,** or *purity,* of the color corresponds to the purity of the light wave. Pure red, for example, produced by a single wavelength, is more *saturated* than pink, which is produced by a combination of wavelengths (red plus white light). In everyday language, saturation refers to the richness of a color. A highly saturated color is vivid and rich, whereas a less saturated color is faded and washed out.

The third property of color is **brightness,** or perceived intensity. Brightness corresponds to the amplitude of the light wave: the higher the amplitude, the greater the degree of brightness.

These three properties of color—hue, saturation, and brightness—are responsible for the amazing range of colors we experience. A person with normal color vision can discriminate from 120 to 150 color differences based on differences in hue, or wavelength, alone. When saturation and brightness are also factored in, we can potentially perceive millions of different colors (Bornstein & Marks, 1982).

Many people mistakenly believe that white light contains no color. White light actually contains all wavelengths, and thus all colors, of the visible part of the electromagnetic spectrum. A glass prism placed in sunlight creates a rainbow because it separates sunlight into all the colors of the visible light spectrum.

So we're back to the question: Why is an orange orange? Common sense tells us that the color of any object is an inseparable property of the object (unless we paint it, dye it, or spill spaghetti sauce on it). But, actually, *the color of an object is determined by the wavelength of light that the object reflects.* If your T-shirt is red, it's red because the cloth is *reflecting* only the wavelength of light that corresponds to the red portion of the spectrum. The T-shirt is *absorbing* the wavelengths that correspond to all other colors. An object appears white because it *reflects* all the wavelengths of visible light and absorbs none. An object appears black when it *absorbs* all the wavelengths of visible light and reflects none.

How We See Color

Color vision has interested scientists for hundreds of years. The first scientific theory of color vision, proposed by Hermann von Helmholtz (1821–1894) in the mid-1800s, was called the *trichromatic theory.* A rival theory, the *opponent-process theory,* was proposed in the late 1800s. Each theory was capable of explaining some aspects of color vision, but neither theory could explain all aspects of color vision. Technological advances in the last few decades have allowed researchers to gather direct physiological evidence to test both theories. The resulting evidence indicates that *both* theories of color vision are accurate. Each simply describes color vision at a different stage of visual processing (Hubel, 1995).

The Trichromatic Theory As you'll recall, only the cones are involved in color vision. According to the **trichromatic theory of color vision,** there are

Boldface emphasizes key words defined in text.

2nd main heading sets up 2nd topic: how we see color.

Subheading introduces a theory of color vision.

Excerpt from a chapter in a psychology textbook

Moving from Reading to Writing

Reading and writing skills are closely related: If you can read critically, you are in a good position to do the variety of writing assigned in college. (Remember that critical reading means understanding the main point and the support, thinking about how effective the support is, and considering your own response to the reading and how it relates to your own experiences.) In many of your courses, reading is used as a springboard to writing. Reading gives you not only interesting issues to write about but also examples of how to structure your writing—for instance, by stating a main point clearly and supporting it effectively.

Just as you will read many types of documents in college, you will write many types of assignments, such as essays, reports, summaries, reviews, exams, and research papers. Some types of writing will require skills that may be new to you. We will introduce those skills here so that you can draw on them when a writing assignment requires them.

Summary, Analysis, Synthesis, and Evaluation

College writing assignments often require you to demonstrate your deep understanding of subject matter, which you get through critical reading. For example, you may be asked to show some or all of the following about what you have read:

- Your basic understanding of its content (summarizing)
- Your ability to identify its points and parts (analyzing)
- Your ability to relate it to other information and experiences (synthesizing)
- Your ability to evaluate its effectiveness (evaluating)

The "Writing about Readings" assignments at the end of each chapter in Part Two, "Writing Different Kinds of Essays," will call on these skills, which are summarized in the following table and discussed in more detail later.

Read this textbook passage and the four sections that follow it. Each section covers one of the skills just described, defines the skill in more detail, and shows how it could be applied in writing about the passage.

On the surface, it seems simple: You eat because you're hungry. But it's not that simple. What, when, and how much you eat are influenced by diverse psychological, biological, social, and cultural factors.

Psychologically, eating can be related to emotional states, such as depression, anxiety, or stress. Interpersonally, eating is often used to

Key Skills for Writing about Reading

SKILL	DEFINITION	WORDING IN ASSIGNMENT OR TEST INDICATING THAT YOU MAY NEED TO USE THE SKILL
Summarizing	Putting the main points of a reading in your own words (and in a shorter form than the original)	*Draw on (evidence or examples from reading), summarize* *What evidence does the author provide for . . . ?* *How does the author back up his/her point that . . . ?*
Analyzing	Closely examining a reading or issue to understand its parts and their relationships; often used to get at why or how something happens, or what factors are involved	*Analyze, examine, explain (why, what, how), identify, take apart, trace*
Synthesizing	Bringing together information from several sources to make a new point	*Based on (evidence or examples from reading or your own experience), compare, draw on (evidence or examples from reading or your own experience), relate, synthesize*
Evaluating	Making an informed— and supported— judgment about a reading or issue	*Assess, evaluate, judge, weigh* *What is your opinion of . . . ?* *What is your view of . . . ?* *What is the significance of . . . ?*

build relationships, as when you have friends over for dinner or take a potential customer to lunch. In describing other people, we often use food-related adjectives, such as saying that someone has a "sweet" or "sour" personality. Without question, the themes of food and eating permeate many different dimensions of our lives.

> —From Don H. Hockenbury and Sandra Hockenbury, *Discovering Psychology*, Second Edition

Summary

■ For more on summarizing, see Chapter 19.

A **summary** is a condensed version of a piece of writing. It presents the main points and key support in a brief form and in your own words. Think of a summary as making a long story short.

> People eat for many reasons other than hunger. Eating is a big part of our lives, and eating behaviors are affected by psychological, biological, social, and cultural influences.

> [The example identifies the main point and lists the factors that the authors will use to support that main point.]

Analysis

An **analysis** breaks down the points a reading makes, and considers what they mean and how they relate to each other. For a writing assignment, you might choose one particular point to analyze. To examine that point, ask yourself questions about it, such as, "Do I agree with this?" "Is this a point the author can support with evidence?" "Have I seen examples of this?" or "Why do I agree or disagree?"

> The authors claim that eating can be related to emotional states, such as depression, anxiety, or stress. Although in this particular passage, they do not give examples of how emotional states influence people's eating behaviors, I believe that there is plenty of evidence to support their claim, and I would assume that they will provide this support later in the section or chapter. I have seen many examples of this influence among people I know, and I myself often eat in response to stress. For example, when I learned that I did not get the job I applied for, I went right into the kitchen, took out the chocolate fudge chip ice cream and ate the whole pint in about three minutes. I then went for the leftover Halloween candy and kept eating until I felt sick. The question I have, though, is *why* certain emotions affect eating behaviors.

> [The writer focuses on one of the points the authors make (the psychological influence on eating) and responds to it by detailing her own experience. She also reflects on questions the passage raises for her.]

Synthesis

A **synthesis** pulls together information from several sources to make a new point, beyond what an individual reading selection may provide. For example, in the analysis above, the writer raised the question of *why* certain emotions affect eating behaviors. She might then consult some other sources (print or online) and do further reading. In part, she is collecting evidence of *why,* but she may also be comparing what other experts have to say or have observed. And this reading may raise even more questions or areas of exploration for her. In the example below, the writer's synthesis builds on what she has discovered through analyzing. Note that the writer also summarizes readings; this is a common strategy in synthesizing.

NOTE: To save space, the following example does not include information about the sources the writer consulted. If the writing were to be handed in to the professor, sources would need to be cited in the text and then listed, with full publication information, at the end of the writing.

■ For more on citing and documenting sources, see Chapter 20.

> Drs. Hockenbury and Hockenbury write that emotional states, such as stress, influence eating behaviors. Because of evidence they provide and my own experience, I believe that this statement is true, and I have wondered *why* certain emotions affect eating. An article that quotes Dr. Rosemarie Kennaley provides one answer to my question. She writes that stress makes people crave sweets because it increases the level of the hormone cortisol. A researcher at the University of California, San Francisco, Elissa Epel, agrees and states further that stress eating is dangerous because of the type of fat it normally produces. The fat goes right to the belly and can put strain on the heart. Another article confirms that stress does affect eating because of cortisol and suggests both exercise and foods, such as apples, carrots, and cheese, that might be substituted for ice cream, cake, or cookies. This seems to be good advice that I can at least try when I get stress-produced cravings to eat.
>
> [The example brings in sources that provide additional information on the subject. The author uses this information to give a bigger picture of the original passage and what it means.]

Evaluation

An **evaluation** is your informed judgment about a reading or an issue. It considers the reading or issue independently and also in terms of what else you have learned about it. When you evaluate, you build on what you have discovered through summarizing, analyzing, and synthesizing.

> Drs. Hockenbury and Hockenbury make a valid claim when they write that emotional states influence eating behaviors. The emotional state produces chemical effects within the body, which in turn produce cravings for certain types of foods. Although in the excerpt the authors do not give examples, explain how or why, or suggest remedies, I assume that they do so in the actual full-length discussion. If they don't, their

claim is not adequately developed or supported. The Hockenburys' claim interested me and caused me to do additional reading on the subject that may be able to help me modify my own eating behaviors.

[The author evaluates the writers' claim and explains how it affected her.]

 PRACTICE 4   SUMMARIZING, ANALYZING, SYNTHESIZING, AND EVALUATING

According to your instructor's directions or your own preference, choose one of the following.

1. **Summary:** Summarize the plot of a movie or television program in one paragraph.

2. **Analysis:** Read a letter to the editor in the local paper. Whether you agree or disagree with the writer, write a paragraph analyzing the points he or she presents.

3. **Synthesis:** Read three letters to the editor on the same subject, either in a local paper or a magazine. In one paragraph, state your position on the subject according to your reading of the letters, and indicate what you think the general opinion is, drawing on evidence from the letters.

4. **Evaluation:** Consider your performance in a recent activity, such as a sport, an exam, a party, or a task at work, and write a paragraph evaluating how well you performed in the situation.

As you write in response to reading assignments, you may want to refer to the following Critical Thinking guide.

CRITICAL THINKING: WRITING ABOUT READINGS

FOCUS
• Carefully read the writing assignment.

ASK
• Does the assignment include any words that indicate the type of writing required (*summarize, analyze, describe, give examples of, compare,* and so on)?
• Is the writing supposed to be in response to the reading alone, or are you supposed to bring in other sources and points of view?

- Are you supposed to quote from the reading to support your point?
- Does the assignment ask you to evaluate the reading?

WRITE

- Apply your critical reading skills to the reading, and write a response to the reading that fulfills the requirements of the writing assignment.

Reading and Writing beyond College

Critical reading and writing are not limited to college classes: In many ways, they are even more important outside of college. Although no one will be grading you on how well you read real-world documents like job or credit-card applications (or write in response to them), your ability to take in and act on key information will make the difference between, for example, getting and not getting a job or saving and losing money.

The following are just some of the documents that you will be expected to read carefully and perhaps write responses to:

- Credit-card applications and statements
- Job applications
- Loan or refinance applications
- Forms for setting up a checking account
- Car or apartment leases
- Employment contracts (or other contracts)
- Life insurance forms
- Wills or living wills

Reading such documents carefully is crucial because they are financially or legally binding.

You might want to make notes on important documents, posing questions as they arise. If you need to keep a document free of marks, put your notes on a photocopy or on a separate sheet of paper. The following example shows some notes that one customer made on one of her first credit-card statements.

■ For experts' advice on reading credit-card agreements and other real-world documents, see Kathleen Squires's essay "Reading between the Lines," on page 638.

AnyBank Card

Statement
Nov. 10–Dec. 13, 2004

SEND PAYMENTS TO:
Box 54321
Anycity

Wow! This is a lot lower than my balance. But maybe I'll pay more interest this way?

NAME: Josephine Student
CREDIT LIMIT: $2,000

ACCOUNT #: 54-32-1
AVAILABLE CREDIT: $1,894.00

NEW BALANCE: $105.97

MINIMUM AMOUNT DUE: $20.00

Activity Since Last Statement

Two charges for the curtain rod I bought. Must be a mistake!

Trans	Posted	Description	Amount
	11/18	Payment – THANK YOU	−152.43
11/11	11/11	Campus Cafe	12.14
11/20	11/20	Bradley's Hardware	8.00
11/20	11/20	Bradley's Hardware	8.00
11/24	11/24	DiscKing Music	32.59
12/11	12/11	Howard's Books and Stationery	53.24

Total Standard Purchases: **$105.97**
Cash Advances: **$ 0.00**

NEXT PAYMENT DUE: January 3, 2005

Account Summary

I pay more if I pay late.

Previous Balance	152.43	New Balance	105.97
Purchases	105.97	Minimum Payment	20.00
Cash Advances	0.00	Amount Past Due	0.00
Payments	152.43	Amount Over Credit Line	0.00
Late Charges*	0.00	Finance Charges*	0.00

Finance Charge Information

	Purchases	Cash Advances
Periodic Rate	.04381%	.05477%
Annual Percentage Rate	15.990%	19.990%

I read the back and still don't understand these charges. Better ask customer service.

*See the reverse of this statement for an explanation of how finance charges and late charges are calculated.

Questions? Call Customer Service at 800-XXX-XXXX

PRACTICE 5   READING REAL-WORLD DOCUMENTS

Bring into class any document such as the ones listed previously. In a small group, highlight the parts of the document that contain important information that could easily be overlooked without critical reading. Then, share what you have found with the rest of the class.

Chapter Review

This chapter has five major headings that reflect the major topics covered:

1. **Why you read in college:** You will read in college to understand and fulfill course goals, to participate in class discussions based on the reading, to complete writing assignments based on reading, and to pass tests.

2. **How to read in college:** You must learn how to read critically and apply your critical reading skills to all documents, including course syllabi, tests, textbooks, essays, and short stories. The **four basics of critical reading** are:

   1. Preview the essay, article, or chapter.

   2. Find the main point and the support for that point.

   3. Take notes on paper or in the text.

   4. Review and respond to what you have read.

3. **Reading college textbooks:** Be aware of special features to help you find and understand key information. These features include headnotes, boldface type, headings, summaries and reviews, and checklists.

4. **Moving from reading to writing:** Several skills are important both for critical reading and for writing about the reading you have been assigned. These skills are **summarizing**, **analyzing**, **synthesizing**, and **evaluating**.

5. **Reading and writing beyond college:** Critical reading is important not just in college but also in everyday life, where it's key to understanding and acting on real-world documents such as credit-card applications and statements, job applications, loan applications, and leases.

2
Writing Basics

Audience, Purpose, and Process

Four elements are key to good writing. Keep them in mind throughout the writing process.

▪▪ FOUR BASICS OF GOOD WRITING

1. It considers the needs and knowledge of the audience.
2. It fulfills the writer's purpose.
3. It includes a clear, definite point.
4. It provides support that explains or proves the main point.

This chapter discusses audience and purpose first because they are key to effective writing; purpose determines a writer's **main point**, and audience determines how that point is made.

The chapter then discusses how to structure writing to meet the four basics. Finally, it outlines the writing process, previewing steps that will be covered in more detail in the next six chapters.

■ For a more on making a point, see Chapter 4. For more on supporting a point, see Chapter 5.

Understand Audience and Purpose

Audience

Your **audience** is the person or people who will read what you write. Whenever you write, always have at least one real person in mind as a reader. Think about what that person already knows and what he or she will need to know to understand your main idea. In most cases, assume that readers will know only what you write about your topic and main point.

Your writing may be very different for two different audiences. Read the following two examples, which describe the same situation but are written for different audiences. Notice both the tone and the content of each paragraph.

SITUATION: Janine Ronzo wakes up and realizes her alarm didn't ring, so she has overslept. She is now going to be late for an interview with Ms. Farina, a supervisor at her company who has a job opening that interests Janine. She leaves a quick note (A) for her roommate, Pat. When she gets to the interview a half hour late, she writes a note (B) for Ms. Farina, who has already left the office to attend a two-day meeting.

A.

AUDIENCE: Janine's roommate, Pat

Pat — overslept and am late for work. Cldn't clean up from last nite or feed Sparky. Sorry. J.

B.

AUDIENCE: Ms. Farina

Dear Ms. Farina:

I am very sorry that I missed our meeting today. Unfortunately, my usually reliable alarm chose not to go off this morning. When I awoke on my own, I immediately realized that it was later than usual and did everything I could to get here on time. However, I was a half hour late, and I missed our meeting.

Normally I am very prompt for work, a fact you can verify with my supervisor, Candy Silfer. I hope that we can reschedule our interview as I am very interested in discussing the position with you, and I believe I am a strong candidate. I look forward to hearing from you, and I apologize again for inconveniencing you today. I will set a foolproof alarm system before our next meeting.

Sincerely,
Janine Ronzo

■ PRACTICE 1 UNDERSTANDING AUDIENCE

Reread Janine's two notes and answer the following questions.

1. How does the note to Ms. Farina differ from the one to Pat? _____

   _____

2. How do the different audiences affect what the notes say (the content)

   and how they say it (the tone)? _____

   _____

   _____

3. Which note has more detail? _____ Why? _____

   _____

4. What three abbreviations in the note to Pat would have been spelled out

   had the note been to Ms. Farina? _____

Purpose

■ For more detail on typical college writing tasks, see Chapter 1, pages 16–21.

The **purpose** for a piece of writing is your reason for writing it. Often in college, your purpose for writing will be either to show something; to explain, analyze, or evaluate something; or to make a convincing argument.

■ PRACTICE 2 UNDERSTANDING PURPOSE

Reread Janine's two notes and answer the following questions.

1. What is Janine's purpose in the note to her roommate? _____

   _____

2. What is her purpose in the note to Ms. Farina? _____

   _____

   _____

Understand Paragraph and Essay Form

Throughout college and beyond, you will write paragraphs and essays. Each of these has a basic structure.

Paragraph Structure

A **paragraph** is a group of sentences that work together to make a point. A good paragraph has three necessary parts—the topic sentence, the body, and the concluding sentence. Each part serves a specific purpose.

PARAGRAPH PART	PURPOSE OF THE PARAGRAPH PART
1. The **topic sentence**	states the **main point**. The topic sentence is often either the first or last sentence of the paragraph.
2. The **body**	supports (shows, explains, or proves) the main point. It usually contains three to six **support sentences**, which present facts and details that develop the main point.
3. The **concluding sentence**	reminds readers of the main point and often makes an observation.

Read the paragraph that follows. The parts of the paragraph are labeled.

Asking your boss for a raise doesn't have to be painful if you plan the conversation well, using several simple but effective techniques. ⎤ *Topic sentence*

First, think about how you will introduce the subject when you talk with your boss. Then, make a list of reasons why you deserve the raise. Be prepared to give specific examples of your achievements. Also, consider the amount of the raise you will ask for. Always ask for more than you think you deserve. When your plan is ready, make an appointment to meet with your boss. ⎤ *Body made up of support sentences*

Your plan will allow you to be confident and will increase your chance of success. ⎤ *Concluding sentence*

Essay Structure

An **essay** is a piece of writing with more than one paragraph. A short essay may consist of four or five paragraphs, totaling three hundred to six hundred words. A long essay is six paragraphs or more, depending on what the essay needs to accomplish—persuading someone to do something, using research to make a point, or explaining a complex concept.

An essay has three necessary parts: an introduction, a body, and a conclusion.

ESSAY PART	PURPOSE OF THE ESSAY PART
1. The **introduction**	states the **main point**, or **thesis**, generally in a single strong statement. The introduction may be a single paragraph or multiple paragraphs.
2. The **body**	supports (shows, explains, or proves) the main point. It generally has at least three **support paragraphs**, each containing facts and details that develop the main point. Each support paragraph begins with a **topic sentence** that supports the thesis statement.
3. The **conclusion**	reminds readers of the main point. It may summarize and reinforce the support in the body paragraphs, or it may make an observation based on that support. Whether it is a single paragraph or more, the conclusion should relate back to the main point of the essay.

The parts of an essay correspond to the parts of a paragraph:

- The **thesis** of an essay is like the **topic sentence** of a paragraph.
- The **support paragraphs** in the body of an essay are like the **support sentences** of a paragraph.
- The **conclusion** of an essay is like the **concluding sentence** of a paragraph.

Read the following essay, in which the parts are underlined and labeled. It is on the same topic as the paragraph on page 27, but because it is an essay, it goes into greater detail.

Asking your boss for a raise doesn't have to be painful if you plan the conversation well, using several simple but effective techniques. These techniques will increase your chances of success and give you a blueprint for making the request professionally.

        Thesis statement

        Introductory paragraph

Topic sentence

First, think about how you will introduce the subject when you talk with your boss. You must ask for the raise; don't expect your employer to take the initiative. Before you confront your employer, stand in front of the mirror and rehearse, "I *deserve* a raise." Never say, "May I have a raise?" "Could I have a raise?" or "Is it time for my raise?" Always say, "I *deserve* a raise." You need to believe that before you can convince your employer.

        Support paragraph 1

Topic sentence

Then, make a list of the reasons why you deserve a raise. Write down exactly what you have done to deserve the raise. Use concrete, observable achievements that cannot be disputed, and be ready with specific examples. If a dollar value in savings to the company has resulted from your work, make sure you have documentation confirming this.

        Support paragraph 2

Topic sentence

Also, consider the amount of the raise you will ask for. Always ask for more than you think you deserve. The key word here is *more*. Rehearse this higher amount while standing in front of a mirror so that you won't hesitate or stutter when you ask your boss for the raise. Too many people ask for a modest raise, unaware that this simple request may have negative side effects. When a worker asks for an unusually small raise, the employer has a tendency to devalue the employee, in the same way that people may be skeptical about buying something that is priced too low.

        Body

        Support paragraph 3

Topic sentence

When your plan is ready, make an appointment to meet with your boss. If you give well-documented reasons why you are valuable to the company, your boss may see you in a new, more positive light. You may not get quite as much as you requested, but your boss is likely to act in some way on the new, positively revised image of you as an employee. Your plan will allow you to be confident and will increase your chance of success. — *Concluding sentence*

        Concluding paragraph

—Adapted from Perry W. Buffington, *Cheap Psychological Tricks: What to Do When Hard Work, Honesty, and Perseverance Fail,* 1996

RELATIONSHIP BETWEEN PARAGRAPHS AND ESSAYS

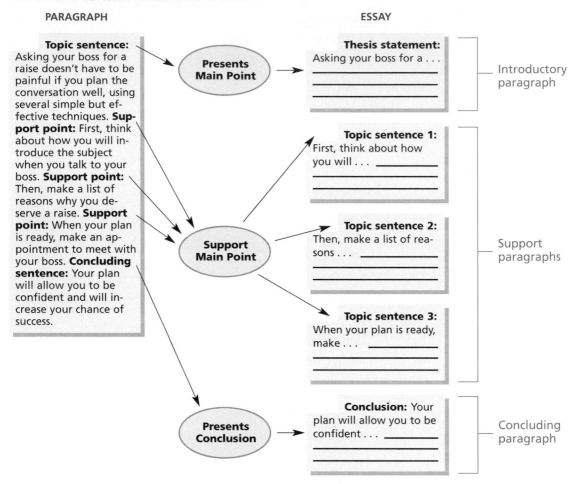

Understand the Writing Process

The **writing process** consists of five basic stages: generating ideas, planning, drafting, revising, and editing.

    Whenever you are first learning to do something—playing a sport, driving a car, riding a bicycle—the steps seem complicated. However, after you practice them, the individual steps seem to blend together and you just do them. The same thing will happen as you practice the steps in the writing process.

THE WRITING PROCESS

Generate Ideas

Consider: What is my purpose in writing? Given this purpose, what interests me? Who will read this? What do they need to know?

- Find and explore your topic (Chapter 3).
- Make your point (Chapter 4).
- Support your point (Chapter 5).

Plan

Consider: How can I organize my ideas effectively for my readers?

- Arrange your ideas and make an outline (Chapter 6).

Draft

Consider: How can I show my readers what I mean?

- Write a draft, including an introduction that will interest your readers, a strong conclusion, and a title (Chapter 7).

Revise

Consider: How can I make my draft clearer or more convincing to my readers?

- Look for ideas that don't fit (Chapter 8).
- Look for ideas that could use more detailed support (Chapter 8).
- Connect ideas with transitional words and sentences (Chapter 8).

Edit

Consider: What errors could confuse my readers and weaken my point?

- Find and correct errors in grammar (Chapters 21–32).
- Look for errors in word use (Chapters 33–34), spelling (Chapter 35), and punctuation and capitalization (Chapters 36–40).

The flowchart on page 31 shows the five basic stages of the writing process and the steps within each of those stages. The remaining chapters in Part One cover every stage except for editing, which is detailed later in the book. You will practice each stage, see how another student completes the stage, and write your own essay using the writing process.

3

Finding and Exploring Your Topic

Choosing Something to Write About

Understand What a Good Topic Is

A **topic** is who or what you are writing about. A **good topic** for an essay is one that interests you, that you know something about, and that you can get involved in.

Any topic that you choose to write about should pass the following test.

QUESTIONS FOR FINDING A GOOD TOPIC

- Does this topic interest me? If so, why do I care about it?
- Do I know something about it? Do I want to know more?
- Can I get involved with some part of it? Is it relevant to my life in some way?
- Is it specific enough for a short essay?

Choose one of the following topics, or one of your own, and focus on one aspect of it that you know about and are interested in. (For example, focus on one specific pet peeve you have, one personal goal, or one aspect of male/female relationships that interests you.)

A personal goal

A problem (personal/societal/professional)

A time I was really lucky/unlucky

A time I took a big risk

Male/female relationships

Something I'm really good at

Something I'm proud of

Something I'm really interested in (what I do in my spare time)

My family

Reality TV

A type of music

PRACTICE 1   FINDING A GOOD TOPIC

Ask the Questions for Finding a Good Topic (p. 33), about the topic you have chosen. If you answer "no" to any of the questions, look for another topic or modify the one you chose.

MY TOPIC: _____

Keeping in mind the general topic you have chosen, read the rest of this chapter and complete all of the practice activities. When you finish, you will have found a good topic to write about and explored ideas related to that topic.

Narrow Your Topic

To **narrow** a topic is to focus on the smaller parts of a general topic until you find a more limited topic or an angle that is interesting, familiar, and specific.

There are several ways to narrow the topic you have chosen.

1. Divide a general category into subcategories.

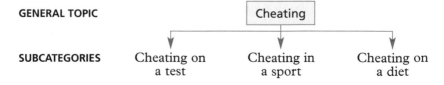

GENERAL TOPIC	Cheating	
SUBCATEGORIES	Cheating on a test	Cheating in a sport	Cheating on a diet

2. Think of specific examples.

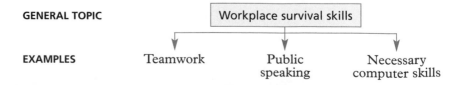

GENERAL TOPIC	Workplace survival skills	
EXAMPLES	Teamwork	Public speaking	Necessary computer skills

3. Consider events from the last week, month, or year.

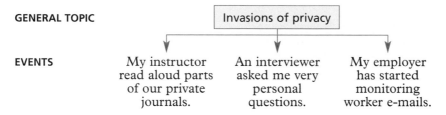

GENERAL TOPIC   Invasions of privacy

EVENTS   My instructor   An interviewer   My employer
              read aloud parts   asked me very   has started
              of our private   personal   monitoring
              journals.   questions.   worker e-mails.

A student, Roberta Fair, was assigned an essay on the general topic "A personal goal." First, she listed specific personal goals.

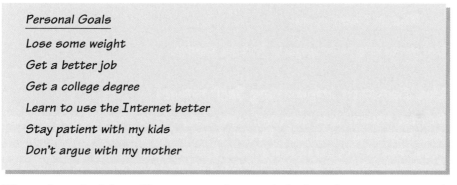

Personal Goals

Lose some weight

Get a better job

Get a college degree

Learn to use the Internet better

Stay patient with my kids

Don't argue with my mother

Then, she asked herself some questions to help her choose a narrowed topic.

QUESTIONS FOR CHOOSING A NARROWED TOPIC

- Which of the narrowed topics is the most important to me?
- Is it the right size for a short essay? Is it broad enough that I can make at least several major points about it? Is it narrow enough that I can tell the whole story in detail in a short essay?

Roberta then chose "Getting a college degree" as her narrowed topic.

TOPIC	NARROWED TOPIC
A personal goal	*Getting a college degree*

PRACTICE 2   NARROWING A TOPIC

Use one of the three methods on pages 34–35 to narrow your topic. Then, ask yourself the "Questions for Choosing a Narrowed Topic." Write your narrowed topic below.

NARROWED TOPIC: _____

Explore Your Topic

Explore a topic to get ideas you can use in your writing. **Prewriting techniques** are ways to come up with ideas at any point during the writing process: to find a topic, to get ideas for what you want to say about the topic, and to support your ideas.

QUESTIONS FOR EXPLORING A TOPIC

- What interests me about this topic?
- Why do I care about it?
- What do I know?
- What do I want to say?

Use prewriting techniques to find the answers.

Use Common Prewriting Techniques

You can explore your narrowed topic using one or more of several common prewriting techniques. Writers don't necessarily use all of these; instead, they choose the ones that work best for them after considering their assignment, their purpose for writing, and their narrowed topic.

- Freewrite
- List/brainstorm
- Question
- Discuss
- Cluster/map

You can also explore ideas by keeping a journal or using the Internet.

While exploring ideas, don't judge them. You can decide later whether they're good or not. At this point, your goal is to come up with as many ideas as possible, so don't say "Oh, that's stupid" or "I'm not sure about that." Just get your brain working by writing down all the possibilities.

The following sections detail techniques for exploring ideas and show how Roberta Fair used each one of them to get ideas about her topic, "Getting a college degree."

Freewrite

Freewriting is like having a conversation with yourself, on paper. To freewrite, just start writing everything you can think of about your topic. Write nonstop for at least five minutes. Don't go back and cross anything out, and don't worry about using correct grammar or spelling; just write.

> *I don't know, I don't think about goals more than just handling every day—I don't have time. The kids, my job, laundry, food, school, it's a lot. So I just get by day by day but I know that won't get me or my kids anywhere. I really do wish I could get a better job that was more interesting and I sure wish I could make more money and get my kids better stuff and live in a better place and not be worried all the time about money and our apartment and all that. I really do need to get that degree cause I know we'd have a better chance then. I know I need to finish college.*

List/Brainstorm

List all the ideas about your topic that you can think of. Write as fast as you can for five minutes without stopping.

> *So hard to find time to study*
>
> *Good in the long run*
>
> *Lots of advantages*
>
> *Better job*
>
> *Better place to live*
>
> *More money*
>
> *More opportunities*
>
> *A big achievement—no one in my family's ever gotten a degree*
>
> *But they don't give me support either*

Ask a Reporter's Questions

Ask yourself questions to start getting ideas. The following questions, which reporters use, give you different angles on a narrowed topic: Who? What? Where? When? Why? How?

> <u>*Who?*</u> *Me, a single mother and student*
>
> <u>*What?*</u> *Getting a college degree*
>
> <u>*Where?*</u> *Stetson Community College*
>
> <u>*When?*</u> *Taking classes off and on now, want a degree in next couple of years*
>
> <u>*Why?*</u> *Because I want more out of life for my kids and me*
>
> <u>*How?*</u> *Working like a dog to finish school*

Discuss

Many people find it helpful to discuss ideas with someone else before they write. As they talk, they get more ideas, and they get immediate feedback from the other person.

Team up with another person. If you both have writing assignments, first discuss one person's topic, then the other's. Ask questions about anything that seems unclear, and let the writer know what sounds interesting. Give thoughtful answers and keep an open mind. It is a good idea to take notes when your partner comments on your ideas.

> _Roberta:_ I guess my personal goal is getting a college degree.
>
> _Maria:_ Why?
>
> _Roberta:_ Well, I think it would help me.
>
> _Maria:_ How?
>
> _Roberta:_ You know, I have a lousy job, no money, the kids, stuff like that.
>
> _Maria:_ Yeah, so how will a college degree help?
>
> _Roberta:_ I know I could get a better job that paid more, so I wouldn't have to work so much. I could spend more time with the kids, and we could live in a better place, you know.
>
> _Maria:_ You sound pretty convinced. So what's the problem?
>
> _Roberta:_ Doing it. Time, money. But I know it's worth it for a while, just till I get the degree.

Cluster/Map

Clustering, also called mapping, is like listing except that you arrange your ideas visually. Using a blank sheet of paper, write your narrowed topic in the center and circle it. Then ask yourself some questions, such as "What about this topic is important to me?" or "What do I know about it?" Write your ideas around the narrowed topic, drawing lines from your topic to the ideas and circling them in turn. As you think of more ideas, add more lines and circles to connect them, as on the facing page.

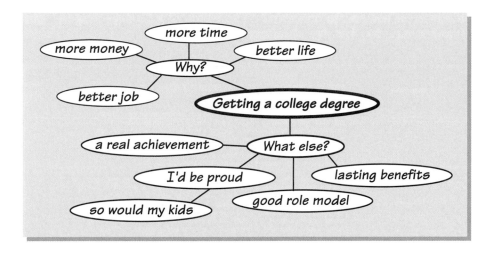

Use the Internet

Go to a search engine such as Google and type in key words related to your topic, being as specific as possible. The search will probably yield a lot of results that can give you more ideas about your topic. For example, Roberta entered *benefits of a college degree* into Google and found several useful links.

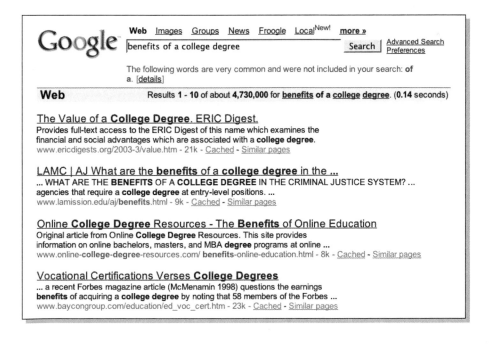

Roberta clicked on the link titled "The Value of a College Degree" and found some other benefits of college.

🔲 Privacy Policy

🔲 Resources for
Library Instruction

🔲 Information
Literacy Blog

THE ECONOMIC VALUE OF HIGHER EDUCATION

There is considerable support for the notion that the rate of return on investment in higher education is high enough to warrant the financial burden associated with pursuing a college degree. Though the earnings differential between college and high school graduates varies over time, college graduates, on average, earn more than high school graduates. According to the Census Bureau, over an adult's working life, high school graduates earn an average of $1.2 million; associate's degree holders earn about $1.6 million; and bachelor's degree holders earn about $2.1 million (Day and Newburger, 2002).

These sizeable differences in lifetime earnings put the costs of college study in realistic perspective. Most students today-- about 80 percent of all students--enroll either in public 4-year colleges or in public 2-year colleges. According to the U.S. Department of Education report, Think College Early, a full-time student at a public 4-year college pays an average of $8,655 for in-state tuition, room and board (U.S. Dept. of Education, 2002). A full-time student in a public 2-year college pays an average of $1,359 per year in tuition (U.S. Dept. of Education, 2002).

These statistics support the contention that, though the cost of higher education is significant, given the earnings disparity that exists between those who earn a bachelor's degree and those who do not, the individual rate of return on investment in higher education is sufficiently high to warrant the cost.

OTHER BENEFITS OF HIGHER EDUCATION

College graduates also enjoy benefits beyond increased income. A 1998 report published by the Institute for Higher Education Policy reviews the individual benefits that college graduates enjoy, including higher levels of saving, increased personal/professional mobility, improved quality of life for their offspring, better consumer decision making, and more hobbies and leisure activities (Institute for Higher Education Policy, 1998). According to a report published by the Carnegie Foundation, non-monetary individual benefits of higher education include the tendency for postsecondary students to become more open-minded, more cultured, more rational, more consistent and less authoritarian; these benefits

---

Keep a Journal

Another good way to explore ideas and topics for writing is to keep a journal. Set aside a few minutes a day, or decide on some other regular schedule to write in your journal. Your journal will be a great source of ideas when you need to find something to write about.

You can use a journal in many ways:

- To record and explore your personal thoughts and feelings
- To comment on things that happen either to you or in the neighborhood, at work, at your college, in the news, and so on
- To examine situations you don't understand (as you write, you may figure them out)

By the time Roberta had used all of the prewriting techniques, she had decided that her narrowed topic (getting a college degree) was a good one and had also generated some ideas to discuss in her essay.

ROBERTA'S JOURNAL ENTRY

> *I've been taking courses at the college for a couple of years but not really knowing whether I'd ever finish or not. It's so hard, and I'm so tired all the time that I sometimes think it would be easier (and cheaper!) to stop or to go one semester and not another, but then it's so easy to get out of the habit. I need to decide whether getting a degree is worth all of the effort it will take, and I'm starting to think it is. I don't want to live like this forever. I want a better life.*

 PRACTICE 3   PREWRITING

Choose *two* prewriting techniques, and use them to explore your narrowed topic. Keep your readers in mind as you explore your topic; find ideas that will be effective not only for your purpose but also for your readers' understanding.

You Know This

You have lots of experience understanding and stating main points.

- You explain to a friend why you are a vegetarian (what the point is).
- You understand the point of a movie.

4

Making a Point

Writing Your Thesis Statement

Understand What a Good Thesis Statement Is

The **thesis statement** of an essay states the main point you want to get across about your topic. It is your position on whatever you are writing about.

| Narrowed topic | + | Main point/position | = | Thesis statement |

Eating disorders are caused by both cultural and psychological factors.

A strong thesis statement has several basic features.

BASICS OF A GOOD THESIS STATEMENT

- It focuses on a single main point or position about the topic.
- It is neither too broad nor too narrow.
- It is specific.
- It is something that you can show, explain, or prove.
- It is a forceful statement written in confident, firm language.

WEAK THESIS STATEMENT   I think college is good, and there are lots of them.

There are several ways in which this statement does not follow the basics of a good thesis statement: It focuses on two points, not one; it is very broad; the word *good* is not specific; and the words *I think* are not forceful or confident.

GOOD THESIS STATEMENT	A college degree brings many concrete benefits such as better jobs, more career choices, and higher salaries.

This statement has all the basics of a good thesis statement. Check the list of basics yourself.

A good thesis statement is essential to most good essays. Early in your writing process, you may develop a *draft thesis* (or *working thesis*), a first-try version of the sentence that will state your main point. You can revise it into a final thesis statement later in the writing process.

Practice Developing a Good Thesis Statement

The explanations and practices in this section, which are organized according to the basics of a good thesis statement (p. 42), will help you write strong thesis statements for your own writing.

Write a Thesis That Focuses on a Single Main Point

Your thesis should focus on only one main point. If you try to address more than one main point in an essay, you will probably not be able to give adequate support for all the points. Also, you risk splitting your focus.

THESIS STATEMENT WITH TWO MAIN POINTS

In the next decade, many schools will have a drastic shortage of teachers, and teachers should have to take competency tests.

The two points are underlined. The writer would need to explain why there will be a shortage of teachers and also why teachers should take competency tests. These are both meaty points, and any writer would have trouble supporting them equally in a single essay.

REVISED

In the next decade, many schools will have a drastic shortage of teachers.

OR

Teachers should have to take competency tests.

THESIS STATEMENTS WITH TWO MAIN POINTS

<u>My sister showed great bravery during the war</u>, but <u>my family was very worried about her.</u>

<u>Summer internships offer excellent experience</u>, and <u>the job market is very tight now.</u>

REVISED

My sister showed great bravery during the war.

OR

While my sister was serving in the war, my family worried about her every single day.

Summer internships offer excellent experience.

OR

The job market for students is very tight right now, but there are several things you can do to help get a job.

Although a good thesis statement focuses on a single main point, it may include more than one idea if these ideas directly relate to the main point. For instance, the last thesis statement above includes two ideas: a tight job market and the "several things" (job-finding tactics) that can be done to get a job. However, the tight job market is the reason that job-finding tactics are necessary; the two points are closely related and essential to the thesis statement.

Write a Thesis That Is Neither Too Broad Nor Too Narrow

Your thesis should fit the size of the essay assignment. A thesis that is too broad is impossible to support fully in a short essay—there is just too much to cover well. In contrast, a thesis that is too narrow doesn't give you enough to write a whole essay on.

TOO BROAD   Family is an essential part of life.

[Both *family* and *life* are broad concepts, and the thesis would be impossible to explain in a short essay.]

REVISED   Time spent with my children is a welcome balance to time spent at work.

TOO BROAD   The Industrial Revolution was important in this country.

[The Industrial Revolution is too broad to cover in an essay.]

REVISED   Women played an important role in Lowell, Massachusetts, during the Industrial Revolution.

A thesis that is too narrow leaves the writer with little to show, explain, or prove. It can also make the reader think, "So what?"

TOO NARROW   My family members all have the same middle name.

[Once the writer says what the middle name is, there isn't much more to say, *unless* there's an interesting family story explaining why everyone has it.]

REVISED   An interesting event from long ago explains why my family members all have the same middle name.

TOO NARROW   Today I took my first guitar lesson.

REVISED   Learning to play the guitar is an important personal goal for me.

Write a Thesis That Is Specific

A strong thesis statement gives readers specific information so that they know exactly what the writer's main point is.

GENERAL   Writing is important for my job.

[Why is writing important, and for what kind of job?]

SPECIFIC   Although my primary job, as a nurse, is to care for others, I've found that I also need good writing skills.

[This thesis tells us that the job is nursing and suggests that the essay will discuss the types of writing a nurse does.]

One good way to be specific is to let your readers know what you will be discussing in your essay, to prepare them for what's to come.

MORE SPECIFIC   As a nurse, my ability to write clearly is essential in documents such as patient reports, status notes to nurses on other shifts, and e-mails to other hospital staff.

[This thesis tells the reader specific kinds of writing the essay will discuss.]

GENERAL   Next month is a big one for me.

SPECIFIC   Next month will bring several important events.

MORE SPECIFIC   Next month will bring several important events: My family is moving, I will be graduating, and I will be having a baby.

Write a Thesis That You Can Show, Explain, or Prove

If a thesis is so obvious that it doesn't need support, or if it states a known fact, you won't be able to say much about it.

OBVIOUS   Most teenagers drive.

Many people own pets.

Guns can kill people.

REVISED   The high accident rates among new teen drivers could be reduced with better and more extended driver training.

In many households, pets get all the respect and privileges of a family member.

Accidental handgun deaths could be prevented through three sensible measures.

FACT   A growing number of American children are overweight.

Our city has reported a 10 percent increase in racial-profiling cases since 2001.

Each year, more companies outsource jobs to foreign workers.

■ Note that the revised thesis statements in this chapter take a clear stand on issues and express a particular point of view. Starting with a topic that you care about can help. For more advice on choosing a topic, see Chapter 3.

REVISED   We must, as a nation, act to reduce obesity in our children.

Although racial profiling remains a serious problem, our city has taken some innovative steps to address it.

As more companies export jobs to foreign countries, we will see numerous negative effects.

Write a Thesis That Is Forceful and Confident

A strong thesis statement should be forceful and definite. Avoid writing a thesis statement that begins, "In this essay I will show . . . ." Don't say you will make a point. Just make it.

WEAK   In this essay, I will prove that high school dropouts have a difficult time in life.

FORCEFUL	High school dropouts can expect to face surprising hardships in life.

Also, avoid words and phrases—such as "maybe" and "I think"—that can indicate you lack confidence in your main point.

WEAK	I think you have to be careful when buying a used car.
FORCEFUL	Before buying a used car, get some basic information so that you don't pay more than you need to.
WEAK	Maybe it is time to evaluate our monthly spending.
FORCEFUL	We need to seriously review our monthly spending.

The practices that follow will help you write a good thesis statement. The first practice will help you develop a thesis statement from a narrowed topic. The rest of the practices focus on the basics of a good thesis statement (p. 42).

■ See Chapter 3 for advice on narrowing a topic.

PRACTICE 1   DEVELOP A THESIS STATEMENT FROM A NARROWED TOPIC

For each item, write a thesis statement from the narrowed topic.

EXAMPLE

GENERAL TOPIC	NARROWED TOPIC	THESIS
Foreign languages	Learning a foreign language	Learning a foreign language has many benefits.

GENERAL TOPIC	NARROWED TOPIC	THESIS
1. A memory	My first date	_____
2. Music	My favorite kind of music	_____
3. Friendship	My best friend	_____
4. Owning a car	Costs of owning a car	_____
5. Reality TV	(One show that you watch)	_____

■ For practice identifying thesis statements, visit Exercise Central at <bedfordstmartins.com/realessays>.

PRACTICE 2   WRITE THESIS STATEMENTS THAT FOCUS ON A SINGLE MAIN POINT

Rewrite the following thesis statements so that they focus on just one of the points made. You can add information to make the statements more specific.

> **EXAMPLE:** Juggling college and other responsibilities can be challenging, and rising college costs are putting higher education out of reach for many.

Juggling college and other responsibilities can be challenging.

1. Planning for college financial aid should begin long before a student's first year of college, and prospective students should also draw up a budget that includes all of their projected expenses.

   _____

2. My first job taught me the importance of cooperation, and I also learned how to manage my time effectively.

   _____

3. For several reasons, I'll never own my own business, but I do have what it takes to be a top athlete.

   _____

4. Organizations can reduce absenteeism by telling workers about several measures to prevent colds and flu, and they can increase morale by offering benefits such as discounts on gym memberships.

   _____

5. Given recent violent incidents, Riverside Mall needs to increase security, and the mall should also do a better job of plowing its parking lots in the winter.

   _____

 PRACTICE 3   WRITE THESIS STATEMENTS THAT ARE NOT TOO BROAD OR TOO NARROW

Read the following thesis statements and decide whether they are too broad, too narrow, or the right size for a short essay. For statements that are too broad, write "B" in the space to the left; for statements that are too narrow, write "N"; and for statements that are the right size, write "OK."

EXAMPLE: _N_ My dog will be ten years old next month.

_____ 1. Hinduism is a fascinating religion.

_____ 2. I am a vegetarian.

_____ 3. Being a vegetarian offers a wide range of food choices.

_____ 4. There are many vegetarians in this country.

_____ 5. Another gourmet coffee shop opened last week, the third one on a single block.

PRACTICE 4　WRITE THESIS STATEMENTS THAT ARE SPECIFIC

Rewrite each of the following thesis statements by adding at least two specific details.

EXAMPLE: **Electronic devices in high schools can be a huge problem.**

Cell phones that ring during a high school class disrupt students' concentration and learning.

1. I have a lot of useful skills.

_____

2. Tara's new puppy is adorable.

_____

3. I have always had trouble writing.

_____

4. Children have more allergies now than in the past.

_____

5. After I was robbed, I had many feelings.

_____

■ **PRACTICE 5   WRITE THESIS STATEMENTS THAT YOU CAN SHOW, EXPLAIN, OR PROVE**

Each of the following items is either obvious or a fact and therefore difficult to write about. Rewrite each sentence so that it would give you something to write in an essay.

> **EXAMPLE:** I have lived in this town for fourteen years. [Fact]
>
> In the fourteen years I have lived in this town, I've learned a lot about small towns.

1. Many teenagers experiment with drugs.

   _____

2. Every year my college tuition goes up.

   _____

3. I make $8.00 an hour.

   _____

4. I have just finished my first college course.

   _____

5. Sports stars make huge salaries.

   _____

■ **PRACTICE 6   WRITE FORCEFUL THESIS STATEMENTS**

Rewrite the weak thesis statements that follow to make them more forceful.

> **EXAMPLE:** In my opinion, my dog, Kayla, understands me better than any human being does.
>
> My dog, Kayla, understands me better than any human being does.

1. I will explain some examples of history repeating itself.

   _____

2. This college should provide better parking facilities, I think.

   _____

3. Given that I've improved my job performance and shown a lot of initiative, I'm pretty sure I'll get a raise this year.

   _____

4. It might be a good idea to warn young people about the possible dangers of Ecstasy.

   _____

5. In this paper, I'll describe three reasons why going to college has been a challenge for me.

   _____

PRACTICE 7   REVISING THESIS STATEMENTS

In the spaces provided below, revise each of the possible thesis statements that you wrote in Practice 1, improving them according to the basics of a good thesis statement (p. 42). Again, think of a statement that you would be interested in writing about. You may want to add more information to your thesis statements to make them more specific and forceful, but short, punchy thesis statements also can be very powerful.

   POSSIBLE THESIS: When the sun is shining, people's moods improve.

   REVISED THESIS: Bright sunshine dramatically improves people's
                    moods.

1. _____

2. _____

3. _____

4. _____

5. _____

Write Your Own Thesis Statement

Before selecting a writing assignment, read how a student, Derek Johnson, developed a thesis statement from his narrowed topic. Before writing his thesis, Derek did some freewriting about it.

GENERAL TOPIC	*Reality TV shows*
NARROWED TOPIC	*The Apprentice*

FREEWRITING: *Some people think reality TV is stupid, and some of it is, but there are also some good shows where you can learn a lot. Like The Apprentice. This show shows real business situations and you get to watch really smart people try to figure out how to do something in the business world so they will be chosen as Trump's apprentice. Trump is a very rich man and knows the business world, and working for him would be a great experience and probably have a good salary too. You actually learn stuff while watching TV and it's entertaining too. Other shows like Fear Factor are just dumb but some are excellent.*

Next, Derek decided on what point he wanted to make about *The Apprentice:*

POINT	*The Apprentice is really a good show.*

He then wrote a draft thesis statement:

DRAFT THESIS STATEMENT	*The Apprentice, a reality television show, is good because it can teach you a lot.*

Finally, Derek revised his thesis statement to make it more specific and forceful:

REVISED THESIS STATEMENT	*The Apprentice is an example of good reality television, where viewers can learn many useful lessons about the business world.*

As you write your essay, you will probably tinker with your thesis statement along the way, but the process that Derek followed should get you off to a good start.

■ **WRITING ASSIGNMENT**

Write a thesis statement using the narrowed topic and ideas you developed in Chapter 3 or one of the following topics (which will need to be narrowed).

Friendship	Fashion/style	A good cause
Drug use	Computer games	A waste of time
Good gifts	Stolen identity	A news item of interest
Exercise	Foreign customs	Lying

Before writing, read the following Critical Thinking box.

CRITICAL THINKING: WRITING A THESIS STATEMENT

FOCUS

- Read your narrowed topic.
- Decide what you think is important about it. You may want to use a prewriting technique.

ASK

- What is my position or my point about my topic?
- Why is it important to me?
- What do I want to show, explain, or prove?
- Can I think of additional ideas to support it?
- Is my position a single point?
- Is it a complete sentence?

WRITE

- Write a draft thesis statement and make sure that it follows the basics of a good thesis statement (p. 42).
- Revise your draft statement according to the basics of a good thesis statement and try to make it more specific and confident.

You Know This

You already know how to support a point you want to make.

- You explain to someone why you think a certain rule is unfair.
- You give reasons for important decisions you have made in life.

5

Supporting Your Point

Finding Details, Examples, and Facts

Understand What Support for a Thesis Is

Support consists of the evidence, examples, or facts that show, explain, or prove your main point, or thesis. **Primary support points** are the major support for your thesis. **Supporting details** (or secondary support points) are specifics that explain your primary support points.

Without support, you *state* the main point, but you don't *make* the main point. Consider the following statements:

> I didn't break the plates.
>
> I don't deserve an F on this paper.
>
> My telephone bill is wrong.

These statements may be true, but without support they are not convincing. Perhaps you have received the comment "You need to support (or develop) your ideas" on your papers; this chapter will show you how to do so.

Writers sometimes confuse repetition with support. Using the same idea several times in different words is not support; it is just repetition.

REPETITION, NOT SUPPORT	My telephone bill is wrong. The amount is incorrect. It shouldn't be this much. It is an error.
SUPPORT	My telephone bill is wrong. There are four duplicate charges for the same time and the same number. The per minute charge is not the one my plan offers. I did not call Antarctica at all, much less three times.

As you develop support for your thesis, make sure that each point has the following three basic features.

■ See Chapter 4 for advice on developing thesis statements.

BASICS OF GOOD SUPPORT

- **It relates to your main point, or thesis.** The purpose of support is to show, explain, or prove your main point, so the support you use must relate directly to that main point.

- **It considers your readers.** Aim your support at the people who will read your writing. Supply information that will convince or inform them.

- **It is detailed and specific.** Give readers enough detail, particularly through examples, so that they can see what you mean.

Practice Supporting a Thesis Statement

A short essay usually has between three and five primary points that support the thesis statement. Each primary support point becomes the topic sentence of its own paragraph. Each paragraph presents details that support that topic sentence.

The following sections detail the steps in supporting a thesis statement.

■ The diagram showing the relationship between paragraphs and essays on page 30 also shows how the thesis statement, topic sentences, and supporting details are organized.

Prewrite to Find Support

Reread your thesis and imagine your readers asking, "What do you mean?" To answer this question and generate support for your thesis, try using one or more of the prewriting techniques discussed in Chapter 3.

■ For more practice with support, visit Exercise Central at <**bedfordstmartins .com/realessays**>.

■ **PRACTICE 1   PREWRITE TO FIND SUPPORT**

Choose one of the following sentences or one of your own, and write for five minutes using one prewriting technique. You will need a good supply of ideas from which to choose support points for your thesis. Try to find at least a dozen different ideas.

SUGGESTED THESIS STATEMENTS

1. Everyone in my family _____.
2. Online dating services are wonderful for busy people.
3. Online dating services can be very disappointing.

4. Discrimination comes in many forms.

5. My parents still don't know about some things I did as a child (teenager).

NOTE: Imagine your reader asking, "What do you mean?"

Drop Unrelated Ideas

After prewriting, remind yourself of your main point. Then, review your rewriting carefully, and drop any ideas that are not directly related to your main point. If new ideas occur to you, write them down.

■   **PRACTICE 2   DROP UNRELATED IDEAS**

Each thesis statement below is followed by a list of possible support points. Cross out the unrelated ideas in each list. Be ready to explain your choices.

1. **THESIS STATEMENT:** Written communication must be worded precisely and formatted clearly.

   POSSIBLE SUPPORT POINTS

   use bulleted lists for important short points

   once I wrote a ridiculous memo to my boss but never sent it

   try to keep it to no more than a single page

   write the date

   get it done by the end of the day

   read it over before sending

   hate to put things in writing

   takes too much time

   make a copy

   getting forty e-mails in a day is too many

2. **THESIS STATEMENT:** Just this year, I experienced a day that was perfect in every way.

   POSSIBLE SUPPORT POINTS

   weather was beautiful

   on vacation

we'd had a great meal the night before

slept late

cold but inside fire was burning hot

new snow, all white

the year before we lost electricity

sky cloudless and bright blue

snow shimmering in the sunlight

perfect snow for skiing

no one else on the ski trail, very quiet

next Tuesday the ski resort would close for the season

3. **THESIS STATEMENT:** I know from experience that sometimes the customer is wrong.

   POSSIBLE SUPPORT POINTS

   work at supermarket

   customers often misread sale flyer

   they choose something like the item on sale but not it

   get mad and sometimes get nasty

   why do people bring screaming kids to the supermarket?

   they don't have any right to be rude but they are

   want to argue but I can't

   customers steal food like eating grapes that are sold by the pound

   sometimes they eat a whole box of cookies and bring up the empty box

   then the kids are always grabbing at the candy and whining, sometimes they just rip the candy open or put it in their mouths

   customers misread the signs like ones that say "save $1.50" and think the item is on sale for $1.50

   should get a different job

Select the Best Support Points

After dropping unrelated ideas, review the ones that remain and select the ones that will be clearest and most convincing to your readers. As noted earlier, short essays usually have three to five primary support points. They will become the topic sentences for your support paragraphs.

PRACTICE 3   SELECT THE BEST SUPPORT POINTS

For each item, circle the three points you would use to support the thesis statement. Be ready to explain your answers.

1. **THESIS STATEMENT:** A college degree should not be the only factor in hiring decisions.

   POSSIBLE SUPPORT POINTS

   job experience

   motivation and enthusiasm

   friends who work at the company

   appearance

   age

   reliability and honesty

   good transportation

   artistic talents

2. **THESIS STATEMENT:** People have a variety of learning styles.

   POSSIBLE SUPPORT POINTS

   learn by doing

   not interested in learning anything new

   learn by seeing

   don't bring their books to class

   disrupt the class

   learn by working with others

   get bored

bad learners

gifted students

3. **THESIS STATEMENT:** The beauty and grandeur of the cathedral astonished me.

   POSSIBLE SUPPORT POINTS

   four hundred feet high

   hundreds of tourists

   white, pink, and green marble gleaming in the sun

   junky gift shops in the circle around it

   interior very plain

   beautiful warm day

   built hundreds of years ago

   intricate carving on all sides

Add Supporting Details

Once you have chosen your primary support points, you will need to add details to explain or demonstrate each of those points. These supporting details can be examples, facts, or evidence. As the following example shows, a supporting detail is always more specific than a primary support point.

THESIS STATEMENT	I try to eat sensibly, but some foods are just too good to pass up.
PRIMARY SUPPORT POINT	Chocolate in any form is a major temptation for me.
SUPPORTING DETAIL	Peanut M&M's are especially tempting—I could eat a whole pound bag in one sitting.
SUPPORTING DETAIL	Canned chocolate frosting is great; I can eat it with a spoon right from the can.
SUPPORTING DETAIL	Big fat truffles with the creamy centers just melt on my tongue.
PRIMARY SUPPORT POINT	Freshly baked bread calls to me from the supermarket shelves.

SUPPORTING DETAIL   I can smell it as soon as I walk into the store.

SUPPORTING DETAIL   Sometimes it's still warm and soft, with steam on the wrapping.

SUPPORTING DETAIL   It reminds me of my grandmother making rolls for Thanksgiving dinners at her house in upstate New York.

PRIMARY SUPPORT POINT   I tell myself never to buy boxes of cheese crackers, but sometimes my hand doesn't listen to me.

SUPPORTING DETAIL   Cheddar's my favorite, with lots of salt and shaped in little bite-sized squares.

SUPPORTING DETAIL   Once I open the box, they'll be gone within a day, maybe even within a couple of hours, especially if I'm working at home.

SUPPORTING DETAIL   I start by eating one at a time, but I get into handfuls as I go along.

PRACTICE 4   ADD SUPPORTING DETAILS

For each primary support point, again imagine your readers asking, "What do you mean?" Add specific details to answer that question.

THESIS STATEMENT   I am an excellent baker.

PRIMARY SUPPORT POINT   My chocolate chip cookies are particularly good.

SUPPORTING DETAIL   I bake with the **extra-large double chocolate chips** that are **soft, gooey, and darkly sweet** when they are baked.

In the space indicated, write the points you chose in Practice 3, item 1 (p. 58), as the best support. Then, in the space to the right, add three details that would show, explain, or prove each primary support point.

THESIS STATEMENT: A college degree should not be the only factor in hiring decisions.

PRIMARY SUPPORT POINT	SUPPORTING DETAILS
_____	_____
	_____
	_____

PRIMARY SUPPORT POINT	SUPPORTING DETAILS
_____	_____
	_____
	_____

PRIMARY SUPPORT POINT	SUPPORTING DETAILS
_____	_____
	_____
	_____

Write Topic Sentences for Your Support Points

Your primary support points will form the topic sentences of the paragraphs that support your thesis statement. Each topic sentence should clearly relate to and support (show, explain, or prove) your thesis.

THESIS STATEMENT	Playing a team sport taught me more than how to play the game.
TOPIC SENTENCE (1st paragraph)	I learned the importance of regular, committed practice.
TOPIC SENTENCE (2nd paragraph)	I also realized that, in order to succeed, I had to work with other people.
TOPIC SENTENCE (3rd paragraph)	Most important, I learned to be responsible to others.

Your topic sentences must be clear and complete. Once you have developed topic sentences to support the thesis, you will need to back up your topic sentences with supporting details.

PRACTICE 5   WRITE TOPIC SENTENCES AND SUPPORTING DETAILS

Using the support points you generated in Practice 4, write topic sentences that support the thesis statement. Then, in the space under each topic sentence, list the details you selected. When you have completed this practice, you will have developed support for an essay.

THESIS STATEMENT: A college degree should not be the only factor in hiring decisions.

TOPIC SENTENCE (primary support point 1): _____

_____

    SUPPORTING DETAILS: _____

    _____

    _____

TOPIC SENTENCE (primary support point 2): _____

_____

    SUPPORTING DETAILS: _____

    _____

    _____

TOPIC SENTENCE (primary support point 3): _____

_____

    SUPPORTING DETAILS: _____

    _____

    _____

Write Your Own Support

Before selecting a writing assignment, read how a student, Carson Williams, developed support for his thesis.

THESIS STATEMENT: *Although my girlfriend and I are in love, we have some very different ideas about what a "good" relationship is.*

1. To generate ideas that might work as support, Carson used a prewriting technique: listing/brainstorming.

LISTING

She always wants to talk

Asks me how I feel, what I think, what I'm thinking about

Gets mad if I don't answer or thinks I'm mad about something

~~Talks during movies and annoys me~~

~~Puts makeup on in the car~~

Always wants to be affectionate, holding hands, kissing

Wants me to tell her I love her all the time

Wants to hear she's pretty

Gets jealous if I'm looking at another girl even though I'm not interested

~~Always asks me if she looks fat and gets mad whatever I say~~

~~Even when we're out she talks on her cell forever~~

Wants to talk about our "relationship" but I don't have anything to say, it's fine

~~Talks about her girlfriends and their relationships~~

Not wild about cars

~~Loves cats and tiny dogs~~

If I just don't feel like talking, she imagines I'm in a bad mood or mad

Hates TV sports

Wants me to go shopping with her

Doesn't like me going out with the guys

2. Next, Carson read his list and crossed out some things that seemed unrelated to his main point. (See the crossed-out items in the preceding list.)

3. He then reviewed the remaining ideas and noticed that they fell into three categories: differences in expectations about communication, differences about showing affection, and differences about how to spend time.

He grouped the ideas under these category labels and saw that the labels could serve as primary support points for his thesis. These support points could be turned into topic sentences of paragraphs backing his thesis, while the ideas under the labels could serve as supporting details for those topic sentences.

PRIMARY SUPPORT: *Differences in expectations about communication*

SUPPORTING DETAILS

She always wants to talk

Asks me how I feel, what I think, what I'm thinking about

Gets mad if I don't answer or thinks I'm mad about something

Wants to talk about our "relationship" but I don't have anything to say, it's fine

If I just don't feel like talking, she imagines I'm in a bad mood or mad

PRIMARY SUPPORT: *Differences about showing affection*

SUPPORTING DETAILS

Always wants to be affectionate, holding hands, kissing

Wants me to tell her I love her all the time

Wants to hear she's pretty

Gets jealous if I'm looking at another girl even though I'm not interested

PRIMARY SUPPORT: *Differences about how a couple in a "good" relationship should spend time*

SUPPORTING DETAILS

Not wild about cars

Hates TV sports

Wants me to go shopping with her

Doesn't like me going out with the guys

4. Finally, Carson wrote topic sentences for his primary support points.

TOPIC SENTENCES FOR PRIMARY SUPPORT

One big difference is in our expectations about communication.

Another difference is in how we show affection.

Another difference is in our views of how we think a couple in a "good" relationship should spend time.

WRITING ASSIGNMENT

Develop primary support points and supporting details for the thesis you wrote in Chapter 4 or for one of the following thesis statements.

> William Lowe Bryan said, "Education is one of the few things a person is willing to pay for and not get."
>
> Elderly people in this country are not shown any respect.
>
> Very few people know how to really listen.
>
> Some movies have made me cry from happiness.
>
> There is one book that really made me think and learn.

Before writing, read the following Critical Thinking box.

CRITICAL THINKING: SUPPORTING YOUR THESIS

FOCUS

- Reread your thesis.
- Think about the people who will read your writing.

ASK

- What support can I include that will show, explain, or prove what I mean?
- What do my readers need to know or understand in order to be convinced?
- What examples come to mind?
- What have I experienced myself?
- What details could I use to strengthen the support?

WRITE

- Use a prewriting technique to find as many support points as you can.
- Drop ideas that aren't directly related to your main thesis.
- Select the best primary support.
- Add supporting details.
- Write topic sentences for your primary support points.
- Make sure that all of your support points have the basics of good support (p. 55).

■ For examples of prewriting techniques, see pages 36–38.

You Know This

You have experi-
ence in planning.

- You make a list
of things you
need to do, with
the most impor-
tant things first.
- You keep track
of your appoint-
ments for the
day, arranged by
time.

6

Making a Plan

Arranging Your Ideas

Understand Ways of Ordering Ideas

In writing, **order** means the sequence in which you present your ideas: what comes first, second, third, and so on. Three common ways of order-ing your ideas are **chronological order** (by the sequence of time in which events happened), **spatial order** (by the physical arrangement of objects or features), and **order of importance** (by the significance of the ideas or reasons).

Chronological Order

Use **chronological order** (time order) to arrange points according to when they happened. Time order works well when you are telling the story of an event or explaining how an event happened. Usually, you go from what happened first to what happened last; in some cases, though, you can work back from what happened last to what happened first.

EXAMPLE USING CHRONOLOGICAL (TIME) ORDER

The cause of the fire that destroyed the apartment building was human carelessness. The couple in apartment 2F had planned a romantic din-ner to celebrate the woman's raise at work. They lit candles all over the apartment and then shared a bottle of wine and ate a delicious meal.

After dinner, they decided to go out to a club to continue the celebration. Unfortunately, they forgot to blow out all of the candles, and one of them was too close to a window curtain, which caught fire. First, the blaze burned slowly, but because the curtain was not flame retardant, the fire picked up force and spread quickly. It engulfed the apartment and then spread to other floors of the building. By the time another resident smelled smoke, the fire was uncontrollable. Before it was all over, the building was destroyed. Fortunately, rescuers were able to save everyone who was in the building. But all of the tenants lost their homes and most of their possessions. Human carelessness caused much human misery in this situation.

How does the writer use chronological order to arrange information?

_____

Spatial Order

Use **spatial order** to arrange ideas so that your readers see your topic as you do. Space order works well when you are writing about a physical object, a place, or a person's appearance. Using the sequence that will give your readers the best picture of what your topic looks like, you can move from top to bottom, bottom to top, near to far, far to near, left to right, right to left, back to front, or front to back.

EXAMPLE USING SPATIAL (SPACE) ORDER

I stood watching in horror while all-powerful flames devoured an entire building, including my apartment and everything I owned. The first few floors looked normal, except that firefighters were racing into the front entry. They wore the long slickers and the helmets that I'd seen on television. They focused only on the building and the fire. A couple of floors up, windows were breaking and gray, foul-smelling smoke was billowing out, as if to escape the building. I could see shadows of the firefighters moving in and out of the apartments. But my eyes were quickly drawn to the top two floors, where flames of orange and white darted out the windows and flickered in the background. A lone dog with brown and white spots barked furiously from the rooftop. Until you have actually witnessed a severe fire, you can't imagine how engulfing it is and how powerless you feel in its presence.

What type of spatial order does the writer use?

_____

Order of Importance

Use **order of importance** to arrange points according to their significance, interest, or surprise value. Usually, save the most important point for last. Then, you can build up to it as you explain or convince readers to accept your position on a topic.

EXAMPLE USING ORDER OF IMPORTANCE

Fires caused by human carelessness often have disastrous effects on many people's lives. In a recent incident, when an apartment building was completely destroyed by a fire, the owner and tenants had no homes to return to. They also lost all of their possessions: furniture, clothing, and treasured personal items that could never be replaced. Worse than that, however, was that the owner and many of the tenants had no insurance to help them find new housing and replace their possessions. Many had to depend completely on relatives, friends, and a fund that was started for them by neighbors. They would not soon have their own places to live in, nor could they buy enough clothing to replace what they had lost. The most disastrous effect of the fire was that a firefighter lost his life. The thirty-year-old man had a wife and three young children who were robbed of their loved one. Carelessness has no place around fire, which has the power to destroy.

What is this writer's most important point about the effects of fires?

Practice Ordering Your Ideas

As you arrange your ideas, consider using chronological order, spatial order, or order of importance.

PURPOSE	TYPE OF ORDER
To describe an experience as it happened	Chronological (time)
To help your reader see a person, place, or object as you see it	Spatial (space)
To persuade or convince someone of the significance of your points	Importance

■ **PRACTICE 1   USE CHRONOLOGICAL ORDER TO ARRANGE IDEAS**

Arrange the support for each of the thesis statements that follow according to chronological order. Indicate the sequence of ideas by writing a number in the blank at the left. (A number *1* indicates what would happen first, a number *2* indicates what would happen second, and so on.)

1. **THESIS:** Ordering out for pizza is the easiest way to get a good meal, fast.

   _____ Decide on what kind of toppings you want.

   _____ Call in the order.

   _____ Take out the menu for your favorite pizza shop.

   _____ Pay the delivery person.

   _____ Eat!

   _____ Wait for the buzzer and open the door.

2. **THESIS:** Taking the following steps will improve your chances of doing well on a test.

   _____ When you are ready to begin, read the instructions carefully.

   _____ Answer the easy questions first.

   _____ Review your answers.

   _____ Before beginning, preview the whole test, noting which parts are worth the most points.

   _____ Listen to the professor's instructions when you receive the test.

   _____ Allow enough time to answer the hardest, longest items that are worth the most points.

3. **THESIS:** Janeen's experience getting stuck in an elevator was frightening.

   _____ The elevator began to go up but jolted to a stop between floors.

   _____ First, the security person told her to press the release button, but nothing happened.

   _____ Janeen waited for a few minutes and then pressed the alarm button.

_____ Finally, the elevator repair people arrived and got the elevator going again.

_____ A security person answered through the speaker, and Janeen explained that the elevator had stopped.

_____ Again, nothing happened.

_____ Then, the security person tried to fix the problem internally.

PRACTICE 2   USE SPATIAL ORDER TO ARRANGE IDEAS

Arrange the support for each of the following thesis statements according to spatial order. Indicate the sequence of ideas by writing a number in the blank to the left. Then, indicate the type of spatial arrangement you are using on the line at the end of each item (top to bottom, bottom to top, near to far, far to near, left to right, right to left, back to front, front to back).

1. **THESIS:** Sal wanted to make sure that he looked professional.

   _____ didn't wear one of his baseball caps

   _____ shoes clean and polished

   _____ dress shirt that he had ironed and tucked in carefully

   _____ hair neatly combed and pulled back

   _____ pants belted and not too baggy

   TYPE OF SPATIAL ORDER: _____

   _____

2. **THESIS:** In the movie _Monster,_ Charlize Theron looked nothing like herself.

   _____ wrinkled T-shirts with tacky designs

   _____ hair that was long, wispy, and unstyled

   _____ teeth that stuck out

   _____ dark, penetrating eyes

   _____ loose jeans or poorly fitting skirt

TYPE OF SPATIAL ORDER: _____

_____

3. **THESIS:** Just outside of my hotel door was a tropical paradise.

_____ beyond the bar, a band playing island music

_____ first, a row of palm trees swaying in the breeze

_____ twenty steps to the rows of beach chairs lined up near the water

_____ a few steps beyond the trees, a small bar serving drinks and snacks

_____ as far as the eye could see, a sparkling greenish blue ocean with a gentle surf

TYPE OF SPATIAL ORDER: _____

PRACTICE 3   USE ORDER OF IMPORTANCE TO ARRANGE IDEAS

Arrange the support for each of the thesis statements that follow according to order of importance, starting with the *least* important. Indicate the sequence of ideas by writing the number in the blank at the left.

1. **THESIS:** Paying for a class and not getting the most from it is ridiculous.

_____ You're less likely to try it again.

_____ You lose the money you paid.

_____ Worst of all is that you have no one to blame but yourself.

_____ You don't get the credit or the information from the class.

_____ You're worse off than before because you've spent money.

2. **THESIS:** People who have a drinking problem should attend Alcoholics Anonymous meetings.

_____ They're more willing to try to change their behavior.

_____ They talk with others who haven't had a drink for a while.

_____ They realize that others have similar problems.

_____ They may save themselves from great tragedy or death.

_____ They can take positive steps to change their lives.

_____ They are assigned a mentor or partner who can help at any time and who understands.

3. **THESIS:** Voting is a right that every U.S. citizen should take advantage of.

_____ It makes you feel more a part of the community and country.

_____ It doesn't take much time.

_____ It's one of the many rights granted by the Constitution.

_____ Every vote really does count, as we saw in the 2000 presidential election between Al Gore and George W. Bush.

_____ Voting gives you a voice in deciding who will shape the government.

Practice Making a Plan

■ For a diagram of the relationship between paragraphs and essays, see page 30.

When you have decided how to order your ideas, make a written plan — an **outline** — starting with your thesis statement. Then state each of your primary support points as a topic sentence for one of the body paragraphs of the essay. Add supporting details to develop or explain the topic sentence. Your plan should also include a possible main point for the concluding paragraph. Although your outline serves as a good guide or blueprint, it can be modified as you draft your essay.

Many people find it useful to write complete sentences as they plan so that their outline is a more complete blueprint for the essay.

Also, there is no one right order for any essay. Use the order that will help you make your main point most effectively.

OUTLINE FOR A SHORT ESSAY: The example that follows uses "standard" or "formal" outline format, in which numbers and letters distinguish between primary support points and secondary supporting details. Some instructors require this format. If you are making an outline for yourself, you might choose to write a less formal outline, simply indenting secondary supporting details under the primary support rather than using numbers and letters.

> **Thesis statement** (part of introductory paragraph 1)
>> I.   **Topic sentence** for primary support point 1 (paragraph 2)
>>> A.   **Supporting detail** for support point 1
>>> B.   **Supporting detail** for support for support point 1 (and so on)

II. **Topic sentence** for primary support point 2 (paragraph 3)

   A. **Supporting detail** for support point 2

   B. **Supporting detail** for support for support point 2 (and so on)

III. **Topic sentence** for primary support point 3 (paragraph 4)

   A. **Supporting detail** for support point 3

   B. **Supporting detail** for support for support point 3 (and so on)

Concluding paragraph (paragraph 5)

> ■ For more advice on primary support and supporting details, see Chapter 5.

PRACTICE 4   OUTLINING PRIMARY SUPPORT POINTS AND SUPPORTING DETAILS

Arrange the primary support points and supporting details in the spaces provided, as illustrated in the example below.

THESIS STATEMENT: Being a good customer service representative in a retail store requires several important skills.

ORGANIZATION: Order of importance

PURPOSE AND AUDIENCE: To explain part of the job to someone who is interested in a job as a customer service representative

Filling out paperwork

Looking at person

Listening carefully

Making notes

Asking questions

Being pleasant and polite

Smiling, saying hello

Figuring out how to solve the problem

Calling the right people

I.   Being pleasant and polite ——— Primary support point

   A. Smiling, saying hello ⎤

                            Supporting details

   B. Looking at person ⎦

II. Listening carefully ——— Primary support point

   A. Making notes ⎤

                            Supporting details

   B. Asking questions ⎦

Primary support ————— III. Figuring out how to solve the problem
point
Supporting —————⌐   A. Calling the right people
details   ⌐   B. Filling out paperwork

1. **THESIS STATEMENT:** I didn't think I was college material.

   ORGANIZATION: Order of importance

   PURPOSE AND AUDIENCE: To explain to a college admissions officer why you took time off after high school before applying to college

   No one in my family had gone to college.
   I'd goofed off in high school.
   I didn't know anyone who could tell me what college was like.
   I've been out of high school for a while.
   My sister said college was a waste of time and money.
   I forgot what school was like.
   I didn't have good high school grades.
   I didn't care about school.
   I'm older than other students.

   I. _____

       A. _____

       B. _____

   II. _____

       A. _____

       B. _____

   III. _____

       A. _____

       B. _____

2. **THESIS STATEMENT:** Avoid being taken by telephone con artists.

   ORGANIZATION: Chronological order

PURPOSE AND AUDIENCE: To advise consumers on how to avoid getting scammed on the phone

Contact authorities after the call, if you're suspicious.

Can I call you back?

Personal information is private.

Your Social Security number can be misused.

Ask questions from the start.

It's good for authorities to track potential scams.

Your actions could protect other consumers.

Don't reveal personal information.

What is your address?

I. _____

    A. _____

    B. _____

II. _____

    A. _____

    B. _____

III. _____

    A. _____

    B. _____

PRACTICE 5   OUTLINING AN ESSAY

Outline the essay that follows. First, double-underline the thesis statement and the main point in the concluding paragraph. Underline each topic sentence, and put a check mark next to each supporting detail.

We all know people who seem to fall in love, over and over. They love

being in love. But others have different patterns. Some people seem to fall

in love once and stay there. Others avoid long-term commitment. Until now, we had no way to figure out why some people were steady lovers and others not. Some researchers now believe that the amount and type of certain hormones in a person's brain may determine a person's patterns of love.

Using mice as subjects, the researchers found that when two particular hormones (oxytocin and vasopressin) exist in the pleasure centers of the brain, they produce individuals with a pattern of long-lasting love. Male mice with these hormones in their pleasure centers were faithful to their partners. They stayed with their female mouse partners through pregnancy and the raising of offspring.

In contrast, when those same hormones existed outside of the pleasure center, the male mice sought constant sources of new love. They did not have steady partners and did not stick around when a female mouse became pregnant. The mice with hormones in this location were the ones who ran from commitment.

Unfortunately, the research did not deal with the most common love pattern: individuals involved in relationships that last for some time but not for life. In this pattern, people have a series of serious relationships that are often broken off when one person wants a formal commitment and the other doesn't. Perhaps this research will come next, as it is in these relationships where much of the pain of love exists.

Though these behaviors may be built into the brain, scientists are working on ways to modify the effects. They hope to find a balance so that love patterns can be modified. One humorous researcher suggested that before we select our mates, we should ask them to have a brain scan to determine whether they're likely to stay or go.

Write Your Own Plan

Before selecting a writing assignment, read how one student, Roberta Fair, generated an outline on the benefits of a college degree. You saw Roberta's prewriting on this subject in Chapter 3.

After reviewing her prewriting, Roberta saw that she could group her ideas about the benefits of college into three major points: She could get a better job, be a better parent to her children, and feel better about herself. She also used many of her prewriting ideas as supporting details for those three main points, and she added other ideas that occurred to her.

Roberta decided to organize her ideas by order of importance, building up to the most important point.

THESIS (part of paragraph 1): Getting a college degree will help me build a better life for me and my children.

I. **Primary support point 1** (paragraph 2): Could get a better job
   Supporting details:
   A. Get a less boring job
   B. Have more options for jobs
   C. Make more money and work one job, not two

II. **Primary support point 2** (paragraph 3): Be a better parent to my children
   Supporting details:
   A. Spend more time with them because I don't have to work two jobs
   B. Get them some things they want
   C. Live in a better place
   D. Be a good role model for them

III. **Primary support point 3** (paragraph 4): Feel better about myself
   Supporting details:
   A. Get respect from others
   B. Respect myself because I achieved an important goal
   C. Go on to achieve other goals

POSSIBLE POINT FOR CONCLUSION (paragraph 5): Won't be easy, but worth the time and effort involved

WRITING ASSIGNMENT

Develop a plan for your essay using the support you wrote in Chapter 5 or one of the following thesis statements.

Recently, I've been very worried about _____ because _____ .

I am looking forward to _____ because _____ .

My brother/sister has just joined the army, and I am _____ because _____ .

When I have a conflict, I usually _____ .

People think I'm a very strong person because _____ .

Before writing, read the following Critical Thinking box.

CRITICAL THINKING: MAKING A PLAN FOR YOUR ESSAY

FOCUS
- Reread your thesis statement and support points.

ASK
- What would be the best way to organize my support points? (Time? Space? Importance?)
- What point should come first? Next? After that? Last?
- What supporting details will show, explain, or prove each of my main points?
- Will this organization help me get my main point (my position) across? Will it help my readers follow my essay?

WRITE
- Write a plan that shows how you want to arrange your points.

7

Writing a Draft

Putting Your Ideas Together

Understand What a Draft Is

A **draft** is the first whole version of your ideas in writing. Do the best job you can in writing a draft, but remember that you will have a chance to make changes later. Think of your draft as a dress rehearsal for your final paper.

BASICS OF A GOOD DRAFT

- It has a thesis statement that presents the main point.
- It has primary support points that are stated in topic sentences that develop or explain the thesis statement.
- It has supporting details that develop or explain each topic sentence.
- It has an introduction that captures the readers' interest and lets them know what the essay is about.
- It has a conclusion that reinforces the main point and makes an observation.
- It follows standard essay form (introduction, body paragraphs, conclusion) and uses complete sentences.

■ For more on thesis statements, see Chapter 4. For more on support, see Chapter 5.

Practice Writing a Draft

The explanations and practices in this section will prepare you to write a good draft essay.

Draft the Body of the Essay

■ See Chapter 5 for advice on support and Chapter 6 for advice on planning. For a diagram showing the parts of an essay, see page 30, and for a complete draft of an essay, see page 91.

A good first step in drafting is to refer back to the plan for your essay. The plan should include your thesis statement, the primary support points for your thesis, and supporting details for your primary support points.

Referring to the plan, draft complete paragraphs that support your thesis. Each should contain a topic sentence that presents a primary support point as well as supporting details. At this point, you'll be drafting the body of your essay; you'll write the introduction and conclusion later. In general, essays have at least three body paragraphs.

If you are having trouble with a word or sentence as you draft, make a note to come back to it and then keep going.

 PRACTICE 1   WRITING TOPIC SENTENCES

Writing topic sentences for primary support points is a good way to start drafting the body of an essay. Below is an outline that appeared in Practice 4 of Chapter 6. Convert each of the primary support points into a topic sentence that supports the thesis. You can make up details if you'd like.

THESIS STATEMENT: Being a good customer service representative in a retail store requires several important skills.

I.   Being pleasant and polite [Primary support point 1]

    A. Smiling, saying hello [Supporting detail]

    B. Looking at person [Supporting detail]

TOPIC SENTENCE I: _____

II. Listening carefully [Primary support point 2]

    A. Making notes [Supporting detail]

    B. Asking questions [Supporting detail]

TOPIC SENTENCE II: _____

III. Figuring out how to solve the problem [Primary support point 3]

    A. Calling the right people [Supporting detail]

    B. Filling out paperwork [Supporting detail]

TOPIC SENTENCE III: _____

Write an Introduction

The introduction to your essay should capture your readers' interest and present the main point. Think of your introductory paragraph as a marketing challenge. Ask yourself: How can I get my readers to want to continue reading?

BASICS OF A GOOD INTRODUCTION

- It should catch readers' attention.
- It should present the essay's thesis statement (narrowed topic + main point).
- It should give readers an idea of what the essay will cover.

The thesis statement is often either the first or the last sentence in the introductory paragraph, though you may find essays in which the thesis statement is in the middle of the introductory paragraph.

Here are examples of common kinds of introductions that spark readers' interest.

Start with a Surprising Fact or Idea

Surprises capture people's attention. The more unexpected and surprising something is, the more likely people are to take notice of it and read on.

> I was saved from sin when I was going on thirteen. But not really saved. It happened like this. There was a big revival at my Auntie Reed's church. Every night for weeks there had been much preaching, singing, praying, and shouting, and some very hardened sinners had been brought to Christ, and the membership of the church had grown by leaps and bounds. Then just before the revival ended, they held a special meeting for children, "to bring the young lambs into the fold." My aunt spoke of it for days ahead. That night I was escorted to the front row and placed on the mourners' bench with all the other young sinners, who had not yet been brought to Jesus.
>
> —Langston Hughes, "Salvation" (See pp. 611–13 for the full essay.)

Open with a Quotation

A good short quotation can definitely get people interested. It must lead naturally into your main point, however, and not just be stuck there. If you start with a quotation, make sure that you tell the reader who the speaker or writer is (unless it is a general quote, like the proverb in the following excerpt).

> "Grow where you are planted" is an old proverb that is a metaphor for living. Although I had heard it before, it took me many years to understand and appreciate its meaning. If I had listened to that proverb earlier, I would have saved myself and others many painful experiences.
> —Teresa Fiori, "Appreciate What You Have"

Give an Example or Tell a Story

People like stories, so opening an essay with a brief story or illustration often draws them in.

> In December 1980, I made the hardest decision of my life. I told the police I suspected my younger brother of murder. Manny had come to live with my wife, Linda, and me in Sacramento that September after being released from a mental institution. He had been suffering from post-traumatic symptoms ever since he returned from Vietnam in 1969. During the 77-day siege at Khe Sanh, Manny picked up pieces of his fellow G.I.'s. Then he got wounded and medevacked out in a helicopter of dead bodies.
> —Bill Babbitt, "My Brother's Guilt Became My Own"

Offer a Strong Opinion

The stronger the opinion, the more likely it is that people will pay attention.

> Sex sells. This truth is a boon for marketing gurus and the pornography industry but a rather unfortunate situation for women. Every issue of *Playboy*, every lewd poster, and even the Victoria's Secret catalog transform real women into ornaments, valued exclusively for their outward appearance. These publications are responsible for defining what is sexy and reinforce the belief that aesthetic appeal is a woman's highest virtue.
> —Amy L. Beck, "Struggling for Perfection"
> (See pp. 682–85 for the full essay.)

Ask a Question

A question needs an answer. If you start your introduction with a question, you engage your readers by inviting them to answer it.

If you're a man, at some point a woman will ask you how she looks. "How do I look?" she'll ask.

You must be careful how you answer this question. The best technique is to form an honest yet sensitive opinion, then collapse on the floor with some kind of fatal seizure. Trust me, this is the easiest way out. Because you will never come up with the right answer.

—Dave Barry, "The Ugly Truth about Beauty"
(See pp. 671–74 for the full essay.)

PRACTICE 2   IDENTIFY TYPES OF INTRODUCTIONS

Read the following three paragraphs and identify the kind of introduction they use by writing the number in the space to the left of each.

1. surprising fact

2. quotation

3. example or story

4. strong opinion

5. question

_____   Several government studies have reported that the number of overweight children in the United States has doubled since the 1970s and that 13 to 15 percent of U.S. children are now overweight. The studies cite a number of causes for this increase; however, the biggest factor is simply overeating. The average serving at the leading fast-food restaurants has ballooned with the popularity of "supersize" meals. Many busy families now eat at these restaurants several times a week because the service is fast and the meals are a good value. But overindulging consumers—including children—are paying a severe price in terms of their health, for they face a higher risk of diabetes, heart disease, and other conditions.

_____   The U.S. people must stop wasting the world's resources. Although the United States accounts for less than 5 percent of the world's population, it uses 25 percent of the world's natural resources. One of the worst examples of waste is the amount of gas we consume. The popularity of sport utility vehicles (SUVs) has dramatically increased gas consumption. According to Northeast Environmental Watch, SUVs use 25 percent more gas per mile than the average car. We also waste vast supplies of water by using excessive amounts of water while we wash dishes, brush our teeth, take showers, water lawns, and do other chores. We must stop our excessive use of limited resources.

_____   What does the new business environment mean for college students—for your own education and career choices? A fast-changing business environment creates fast-growth careers at the same time that it turns other careers into dead ends. The conventional wisdom holds that the wisest course is to pick a field that is on the upswing. The conventional wisdom is right—to a degree. However, in a turbulent environment you cannot count on stability—especially in growth projections. Today's hot careers may soon be dead ends, replaced by tomorrow's hot careers. This means that success will come from considering first what you want to do and what you are good at, and then developing a set of all-purpose job skills that you can transfer to the next growth area.

—Kenneth H. Blanchard et al., *Exploring the World of Business*, 1996

PRACTICE 3   IDENTIFY STRONG INTRODUCTIONS

In a newspaper, a magazine, a catalog, an advertisement—anything written—find a strong introduction. Explain, in writing, why you think it is a strong introduction.

PRACTICE 4   MARKET YOUR MAIN POINT

As you know from watching and reading advertisements, a good writer can make just about anything sound interesting. For each of the following topics, write an introductory statement using the technique indicated. Make the statement punchy and intriguing enough to motivate your readers to stay with you as you explain or defend it. Even if you wouldn't choose to write about the topics given in this practice, try to make fascinating, provocative statements about them.

1. TOPIC: Mandatory drug testing in the workplace

   TECHNIQUE: Ask a question.

   _____

2. TOPIC: Teenage suicide

   TECHNIQUE: Present a surprising fact or idea (you can make one up for this exercise).

   _____

3. **TOPIC:** Free access to music on the Internet

   TECHNIQUE: Give a strong opinion.

   _____

4. **TOPIC:** The quality of television shows

   TECHNIQUE: Use a quotation (you can make up a good one for this exercise).

   _____

5. **TOPIC:** Blind dates

   TECHNIQUE: Give an example or tell a brief story (you can just sum it up).

   _____

■ **PRACTICE 5   ANALYZING WEAK INTRODUCTIONS**

Read the following three introductions. Then, indicate whether the introductions are weak (W) or okay (OK) by writing those letters in the space to the left of each passage. For any introduction that you mark as weak, use the spaces under it to explain why you think it is weak.

_____ In this essay I am going to write about my car. It is not new, but it is very important to me, and I drive it everywhere. It has a good sound system, and I can listen to music while I drive. Sometimes I open all the windows and turn the volume and bass way up so it sounds like the band is right there in my car. Also, it is pretty good on gas, getting 20 mph in city driving. Before I had a car, I had to take public transportation, which wasn't very reliable, so sometimes I was late for class or for work. It took all of the money I had saved, plus a loan, but my car was worth every penny. It has changed my life for the better.

   _____

   _____

_____ We have two good friends, quite dissimilar in most ways, who share one common characteristic—they have no sense of smell. Paul is an electrical engineer in his early thirties. Warren is a well-known professor of psychology some 20 years older. Although you might expect this condition to be extremely rare, the inability to smell, called "anosmia," is relatively common, occurring in about 1 in 500 people.

—Don H. Hockenbury and Sandra E. Hockenbury, *Discovering Psychology*, Second Edition, 2001

_____

_____

____ "If you can't change your fate, change your attitude" is a quote by the writer Amy Tan. I agree with this statement and have some experience with it. When I was thirteen, I was in an accident and lost vision in my left eye. For a long time I was really mad about it, but then I decided to accept it.

_____

_____

Write a Conclusion

Your conclusion should have energy and match the force of your thesis statement; it is your last chance to drive your main point home. Fading out with a weak conclusion is like slowing down at the end of a race: You lose ground. In writing, as in sports and other activities, you need to keep up the pace right to the very end. In fact, you should give yourself a last push at the end because people usually remember best what they see, hear, or read last. A good conclusion creates a sense of completion: It not only brings readers back to where they started but also shows them how far they have come.

BASICS OF A GOOD CONCLUSION

- It should refer to your thesis or main point.
- It should sum up the support points you have developed in the essay.
- It should make a further observation or point.

One of the best ways to end an essay is to refer directly to something in the introduction.

- If you asked a question, ask it again and answer it based on what you've said in your essay.
- If you started a story, finish it.
- If you used a quotation, use another one—by the same person or by another person on the same topic. Or, refer back to the quotation in the introduction.

- If you stated a surprising fact or idea, go back to it and comment on it, using what you have written in the body of the essay.

- Remind your reader of your original point, perhaps repeating key words that you used in your introduction.

Look again at three of the introductions you read earlier, each shown here with its conclusion.

OPEN WITH A QUOTATION

INTRODUCTION A: "Grow where you are planted" is an old proverb that is a metaphor for living. Although I had heard it before, it took me many years to understand and appreciate its meaning. If I had listened to that proverb earlier, I would have saved myself and others many painful experiences.

CONCLUSION A: Finally, I have learned to grow where I am planted, to appreciate the good things in my life rather than look for the bad and be angry. I have learned to take advantage of the many opportunities I have for personal and professional growth, right here and now. And I have vowed to help others around me grow also. My life is much richer now that I follow that old wisdom, and I will pass its lesson on to my children.

—Teresa Fiori, "Appreciate What You Have"

START WITH A STRONG OPINION OR POSITION

INTRODUCTION B: Sex sells. This truth is a boon for marketing gurus and the pornography industry but a rather unfortunate situation for women. Every issue of *Playboy,* every lewd poster, and even the Victoria's Secret catalog transform real women into ornaments, valued exclusively for their outward appearance. These publications are responsible for defining what is sexy and reinforce the belief that aesthetic appeal is a woman's highest virtue.

CONCLUSION B: Women are up against a long history of devaluation and oppression, and, unfortunately, the feminist movements have been only partially successful in purging those legacies. Sexually charged images of women in the media are not the only cause of this continuing problem, but they certainly play a central role.

—Amy L. Beck, "Struggling for Perfection"

ASK A QUESTION

INTRODUCTION C: If you're a man, at some point a woman will ask you how she looks. "How do I look?" she'll ask.

You must be careful how you answer this question. The best technique is to form an honest yet sensitive opinion, then collapse on the floor with some kind of fatal seizure. Trust me, this is the easiest way out. You will never come up with the right answer.

CONCLUSION C: To go back to my main point: If you're a man, and a woman asks you how she looks, you're in big trouble. Obviously, you can't say she looks bad. But you also can't say that she looks great, because she'll think you're lying, because she has spent countless hours, with the help of the multibillion-dollar beauty industry, obsessing about the differences between herself and Cindy Crawford. Also, she suspects that you're not qualified to judge anybody's appearance. This is because you have shaving cream in your hair.

—Dave Barry, "The Ugly Truth about Beauty"

PRACTICE 6   ANALYZE CONCLUSIONS

After reading the paired introductions and conclusions above, indicate the techniques used in each conclusion to refer back to its introduction.

A. Technique used to link introduction and conclusion: _____

_____

B. Technique used to link introduction and conclusion: _____

_____

C. Technique used to link introduction and conclusion: _____

_____

PRACTICE 7   IDENTIFY GOOD INTRODUCTIONS AND CONCLUSIONS

In a newspaper, magazine, or any other written material, find a piece of writing that has both a strong introduction and a strong conclusion. Answer the following questions about the introduction and conclusion.

1. What method of introduction is used? _____

2. What does the conclusion do? Does it restate the main idea? Sum up the points made in the piece? Make an observation? _____

_____

3. How are the introduction and the conclusion linked? _____

_____

PRACTICE 8   WRITE A CONCLUSION

Read the following introductory paragraphs, and then write a possible conclusion for each one. Your conclusions can be brief, but they should each include the basics of a good conclusion (p. 86) and consist of several sentences.

1. **INTRODUCTION:** When it comes to long-term love relationships, I very much believe Anton Chekhov's statement, "Any idiot can face a crisis; it's the day-to-day living that wears you out." When faced with a crisis, couples often pull together. A crisis is a slap in the face that reminds you of who and what is important in your life. It is the routine necessities of living that can erode a relationship as couples argue over who does the laundry, who does the cleaning, or cooking, or bill paying. The constant skirmishes over day-to-day living can do more serious damage over the long term than a crisis.

   CONCLUSION: _____

   _____

   _____

2. **INTRODUCTION:** Why do so many people feel that they must be available at all times and in all places? Until recently, the only way you could reach someone was by telephone or by mail. Now if you don't have a cell phone, an e-mail account, a beeper, and call waiting, people trying to reach you get annoyed. To me this is just a loss of privacy. I don't want to be available twenty-four hours a day.

   CONCLUSION: _____

   _____

   _____

Title Your Essay

Even if your title is the *last* part of the essay you write, it is the *first* thing that readers read. Use your title to get your readers' attention and to tell them what your essay is about. Use concrete, specific words.

BASICS OF A GOOD ESSAY TITLE

- It makes readers want to read the essay.
- It does not repeat the wording in your thesis statement.
- It may hint at the main point but does not necessarily state it outright.

One way to find a good title is to consider the type of essay you are writing. If you are writing an argument (as you will in Chapter 17), state your position in your title. If you are telling your readers how to do something (as you will in Chapter 12), try using the term *steps* or *how to* in the title. This way, your readers will know immediately both what you are writing about and how you will present it. For example, "Five Steps to Financial Independence" may be a more inviting and more accurate title for a process analysis essay than "Financial Independence."

■ PRACTICE 9   WRITE A TITLE

Read the following introductory paragraphs, and write a possible title for the essay each one begins. The first one is done as an example. Be prepared to explain why you worded each title as you did.

EXAMPLE

One of the hottest trends in youth marketing is age compression—the practice of taking products and marketing messages originally designed for older kids and targeting them to younger ones. Age compression includes offering teen products and genres, pitching gratuitous violence to the twelve-and-under crowd, cultivating brand preferences for items that were previously unbranded among younger kids, and developing creative alcohol and tobacco advertising that is not officially targeted to them but is widely seen and greatly loved by children. "By eight or nine they want 'N Sync," explained one tweening expert to me, in the days before that band was eclipsed by Justin Timberlake, Pink, and others.

POSSIBLE TITLE: *No Kidding: Marketers Target Younger and Younger*

Consumers

1. It is easy to take cheap shots at the owners of cellular phones. But before doing so, you should determine to which of the five following categories they belong.

POSSIBLE TITLE: _____

2. The other day I was thinking of writing an essay on being a cripple. I was thinking hard in one of the stalls of the women's room in my office build-

ing, as I was shoving my shirt into my jeans and tugging up my zipper. Preoccupied, I flushed, picked up my book bag, took my cane down from the hook, and unlatched the door. So many movements unbalanced me, and as I pulled the door open, I fell over backward, landing fully clothed on the toilet seat with my legs splayed in front of me: the old beetle-on-its-back routine. Saturday afternoon, the building deserted, I was free to laugh aloud as I wriggled back to my feet, my voice bouncing off the yellowish tiles from all directions. Had anyone been there with me, I'd have been still and faint and hot with chagrin. I decided that it was high time to write the essay.

POSSIBLE TITLE: _____

3. Is a girl called Gloria apt to be better-looking than one called Bertha? Are criminals more likely to be dark than blond? Can you tell a good deal about someone's personality from hearing his voice briefly over the phone? Can a person's nationality be pretty accurately guessed from his photograph? Does the fact that someone wears glasses imply that he is intelligent?

   The answer to all these questions is obviously, "No."

   Yet, from all the evidence at hand, most of us believe these things.

POSSIBLE TITLE: _____

Write Your Own Draft

Before selecting a writing assignment, read a sample draft by one student, Carson Williams. In Chapter 5, you saw how Carson developed support for this paper. Look back at his final list of primary support points and supporting details (p. 64) and notice what he has kept and what he has changed.

> ### Different but in Love
>
> Although my girlfriend, Carly, and I are in love, we have some very different ideas about what a "good" relationship is. She has very definite expectations, and I have none. Actually, we both have expectations, but hers demand more of me while mine require very little of her or of me. While you might think these levels of expectations would fit together perfectly (one expects a lot, the other very little), they often cause conflict and misunderstanding (mostly on her part).

Introduction with thesis (double-underlined)

Body
paragraphs
(with topic
sentences
underlined)

One big difference is in our expectations about communication. Carly always wants to talk. She asks me what I'm thinking about when I'm quiet. If I just don't feel like talking, she imagines I'm in a bad mood or mad about something. Or she gets mad. She wants to talk a lot about our relationship, and I don't have anything to say about it: It's fine. What else would I want to talk about? One question she asks a lot is how I "feel" about something. That question makes me never want to open my mouth again. I don't think much about how I feel, and I really don't want to have to talk about the subject. Carly wants to keep the communication up 24/7, or she thinks something is wrong. I like a little peace and quiet.

Another difference is how and where we show affection. Carly wants to be openly affectionate all the time, like holding hands wherever we are and kissing. While we're holding hands or kissing, she expects me to tell her I love her all the time. I don't understand why that is necessary: If I've already told her I love her, why does she need to hear it again and again? I haven't changed my mind. And sometimes I just want to walk without holding hands; that doesn't mean I don't love her. Carly expects that love should be reinforced every day, while I think once it's said, it's out there until something big changes.

A final difference is our expectations about how a couple in a "good" relationship should spend time. We're both busy people, with jobs and classes. When I have free time, I like to watch sports on television. Carly hates TV sports and wants to go out and do things. Mostly she wants to go shopping and talk about our future, like what she'd like for our house. I hate shopping and get bored. Or I get annoyed when she wants to try clothes on for me. I just have to sit there in the ladies' department doing nothing until she comes out. Then I'm supposed to be enthusiastic about whatever she has on. But she never believes what I say. She'll always ask, "Do you really like it, or are you lying?" "Are you sure?"

Conclusion

At times like these, I often think I'd rather go out with the guys, who just let me be who I am. But I really do love Carly, and I'm beginning to understand that even though she and I have different expectations, we can still be happy together if we learn to accept—and even appreciate—those differences.

WRITING ASSIGNMENT

Write a draft essay using the outline you developed in Chapter 6 or one of the following thesis statements.

These days, teenagers do not do much traditional dating.

Although cartoons are typically intended to entertain, they may also have important messages.

The most important skills a college student should have are _____.

My college professor does not understand that _____.

Living with roommates requires _____.

Before writing, read the following Critical Thinking box.

CRITICAL THINKING: WRITING A DRAFT ESSAY

FOCUS
- Reread your outline for the essay.

ASK
- Is my thesis clear?
- Are there topic sentences for each body paragraph?
- Do I have supporting details for each topic sentence?
- Is my support arranged in a logical order?
- What introductory technique will get my readers' attention and make my point stand out?
- How can I use the conclusion for one last chance to make my point?
- How can I link my conclusion to my introduction? What is the strongest or most interesting part of the introduction that I might refer back to in my conclusion?
- Will my title make readers want to read my essay?

WRITE
- Write a draft essay.

You Know This

You already revise in your everyday life.

• You get dressed and then change certain items because they don't look right together.

• You rework your job application letter and résumé each time you look for a better position.

8

Revising Your Draft

Improving Your Essay

Understand What Revision Is

Revising is looking for ways to make your ideas clearer, stronger, and more convincing. When revising, you might add, cut, move, or change whole sentences or paragraphs.

Editing is correcting problems with grammar, style, usage, and punctuation. While editing, you usually add, cut, or change words and phrases instead of whole sentences or paragraphs (as you might while revising).

Revising and editing are two different ways to improve a paper. Most writers find it difficult to do both at once. It is easier to look first at the ideas in your essay (revising) and then to look at the individual words and sentences (editing). Revising is covered in this chapter, and editing is covered in Chapters 21–40.

No one gets everything right in a draft—even professional writers need to revise. The tips below will help you with the revising process.

TIPS FOR REVISING

• Take a break from your draft—set it aside for a few hours or a whole day.

• Read your draft aloud and listen to what you have written.

• Imagine yourself as one of your readers.

• Get feedback from a friend, a classmate, or a colleague (see the next section of this chapter).

• Get help from a tutor at your college writing center or lab.

You may need to read what you have written several times before deciding what changes would improve it. Remember to consider your audience (the people who will read your essay) and your purpose (your reason for writing it).

■ For more on purpose and audience, see Chapter 2.

Understand What Peer Review Is

Peer review is the exchange of feedback on a piece of writing among fellow students, colleagues, or friends. Getting comments from a peer is a good way to begin revising your essay.

Other people can look at your work and see things that you might not—parts that are good as well as parts that need more explanation or evidence. The best reviewers are honest about what could be better but also sensitive to the writer's feelings. In addition, they are specific. Reviewers who say a paper is "great" without offering further comment do not help writers improve their work.

BASICS OF USEFUL FEEDBACK

- It is given in a positive way.
- It is specific.
- It offers suggestions.
- It may be given orally or in writing.

To get useful feedback, find a partner and exchange papers. Each partner should read the other's paper and jot down a few comments. The first time someone comments on what you have written, you may feel a little embarrassed, but you will feel better about the process once you see how your writing benefits from the comments.

The following box shows questions peer reviewers might consider as they read a draft.

> ## *Questions for Peer Reviewers*
>
> 1. What is the main point?
> 2. After reading the introductory paragraph, do you have an idea of what the essay will cover, and why?
> 3. How could the introduction be more interesting?
>
> *Questions continued on next page.*

4. Is there enough support for the main point? Where might the writer add support?

5. Are there confusing places where you have to reread something in order to understand it? How might the writer make the points, the organization, or the flow of ideas clearer or smoother?

6. How could the conclusion be more forceful?

7. What do you most like about the essay? Where could it be better? What would you do if it were your essay?

8. What other comments or suggestions do you have?

Practice Revising for Unity

Unity in writing means that all the points are related to your main point; they *unite* to support your main point.

Sometimes writers drift away from their main point, as the writer of the following paragraph did with the underlined sentences. The diagram after the paragraph shows where readers might get confused.

Just a few years ago, online dating services were viewed with great suspicion, but they now have millions of subscribers who say the services offer many advantages over searching for a partner on your own. With an online dating service, people set up their own dates and don't have to cruise the bars. Many people do not like the bar scene, which they describe as a "meat market." Online dating services also give users the opportunity to screen individuals and contact only those who interest them. That screening saves time and also helps people avoid many awkward first dates. Subscribers can exchange e-mails with prospective dates before arranging a meeting. But sometimes people lie. For example, my friend e-mailed with a guy who said he loved her, but she found out he was also e-mailing the same thing to her cousin! She cut it off right away! With people spending so much time working, it's hard to meet anyone outside of work, so online dating services expand the possibilities. The opportunity to "meet" many people without leaving your home and to screen out obvious duds is, for a growing number of people, the only way to play the dating game.

TOPIC SENTENCE: Just a few years ago, online dating services were viewed with great suspicion, but they now have millions of subscribers who say the services offer many advantages over searching for a partner on your own.

SUPPORT POINT 1: With an online dating service, people set up their own dates and don't have to cruise the bars.

SUPPORT POINT 2: Online dating services also give users the opportunity to screen individuals and contact only those who interest them.

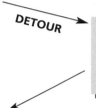

DETOUR

OFF MAIN POINT: But sometimes people lie. For example, my friend e-mailed with a guy who said he loved her, but she found out he was also e-mailing the same thing to her cousin! She cut it off right away!

SUPPORT POINT 3: With people spending so much time working, it's hard to meet anyone outside of work, so online dating services expand the possibilities.

CONCLUDING SENTENCE: The opportunity to "meet" many people without leaving your home and to screen out obvious duds is, for a growing number of people, the only way to play the dating game.

PRACTICE 1   EVALUATE UNITY

Read the following two paragraphs and underline any detours from the main point. In the lines provided at the end of paragraph 2, indicate which paragraph is more unified and explain why.

1. Identity theft is becoming very common in this country, but people can take several precautions to protect themselves. One way is to buy an inexpensive paper shredder and shred documents that contain your Social Security number or personal financial information. Shredded documents don't take up as much room in the trash, either. Another precaution is to avoid mailing change-of-address postcards. Thieves can intercept these

■ For more practice
in achieving unity
in writing, visit
Exercise Central at
<bedfordstmartins
.com/realessays>.

and use them to get mail sent to your old address. Half the time people never keep these cards, so they just waste the postage. It would be better to notify people of your address change by phone or e-mail. When I moved, I sent postcards that had a misprint, so they weren't good anyway. A third way is to avoid ever giving out your Social Security number, except when you are checking on your own accounts. Also, some states use a person's Social Security number as the driver's license number unless the person requests another number. Never use your Social Security number if you have another choice. Even these precautions don't guarantee that your identity won't be stolen, but they will help prevent what is a time-consuming and expensive problem to set right.

2. Many new markets have appeared to meet the needs of pet owners who treat their pets as if they were precious children. The most thriving market is clothing, especially items that allow owners and their dogs to dress alike. Designer pet and owner clothing is the fastest-growing segment of this market, and it includes cruisewear, formalwear, and jeweled loungewear. Another big market is made up of hotels all over the world that advertise themselves as pet-friendly. These hotels provide doggie or cat beds, on-site grooming, and pet care professionals. Many of these hotels don't even allow children, but they welcome pets. I recently saw an ad for the Bichon Frise Getaway Ranch, which has theme rooms that the owners can choose for their dogs to stay in while they are away. The rooms are uniquely decorated and provide special meals prepared and served to meet the needs of each "guest." Each guest also is treated to an individualized exercise program. These new markets don't cater to the conservative spender: They appeal to those pet owners who seem willing to spend any amount of money on luxuries for their pets. Live and let live, but it all seems mighty crazy to me.

MORE UNIFIED PARAGRAPH: _____

REASONS THAT THIS PARAGRAPH IS MORE UNIFIED THAN THE OTHER: _____

_____

_____

■ **PRACTICE 2   REVISE FOR UNITY**

Each of the following essays includes sentences that are off the main point. Underline those sentences. The main point in each essay is in boldface type.

1. Look for five off-the-point sentences.

Oprah Winfrey is one of the most influential people of our times, but that doesn't mean that life is easy for her. As a child in rural Mississippi, she was dirt-poor and sexually abused. Somehow, she managed to climb out of that existence and become successful. But because she is now a superstar, every aspect of her life is under the media spotlight, and she is frequently criticized for everything from her weight to her attempts to help people spiritually.

Oprah's roller-coaster weight profile is always news. Every supermarket tabloid, every week, seems to have some new information about Oprah and her weight. I can relate to how humiliating that must be. She looked like a balloon in a recent picture I saw, even fatter than my Aunt Greta.

Oprah is also criticized for her wealth, estimated to be at about $800 million. You never hear about the charitable work she does, only about how much money she has. She has a fabulous apartment overlooking Lake Michigan in Chicago. While many businesspeople are as wealthy as Oprah, few are criticized as often—or as publicly—as she is.

Even Oprah's book club and magazine, *O*, bring unwarranted negativity. "Who is she to recommend books?" say some, and "What does she know about publishing?" say others. I especially liked the book *She's Come Undone*. What could possibly be wrong with recommending books and championing literacy? Yet one high-profile author, Jonathan Franzen, said he did not want the Oprah book club logo on his novel *The Corrections* because he thought it would negatively affect his literary reputation. He's a real snob in my mind, and all my friends think so, too.

Oprah Winfrey, despite her wealth and fame, does not have an easy life. Her critics feel free to cut her down at every turn. Instead, why not celebrate her personal and professional achievements? She deserves respect, not ridicule.

2. Look for four off-the-point sentences.

A recent survey of the places students prefer to study revealed some strange results. We would expect the usual answers, such as the library, a bedroom, a desk, the kitchen, and the survey respondents did in fact name such areas. But some people prefer less traditional places.

One unusual place cited was a church. The respondent said it was a great spot to study when services weren't taking place because it was always quiet and not crowded. Some churches are locked during the day because of vandalism. Other churches have had big problems with theft.

Another unusual study area was the locker room during a football game. A problem is that the person would miss the game. Except for halftime, the large area was empty. The person who studied there claimed that there was a high energy level in the locker room that, combined with the quiet, helped him concentrate. I wonder what the smell was like, though.

The most surprising preference for a place to study was the bleachers by the pool of a gym. The light was good, said the student, she loved the smell of chlorine, and the sound of water was soothing.

The results may seem strange—a church, a locker room, and a pool—but they do share some characteristics: quiet, relative solitude, and no interruptions, other than half-time. Perhaps we should all think about new places that might help us study.

Practice Revising for Support and Detail

■ For more on primary support points and supporting details, see Chapter 5.

Support is the evidence, examples, or facts that show, explain, or prove your main point. **Primary support points** are the major ideas developed in the paragraphs that make up the body of your essay. **Secondary support points** (or supporting details) are the specifics that explain your primary support to your readers.

When you read your draft essay, imagine yourself as the reader and look carefully at the primary support points (topic sentences) and the supporting details you have developed. Do you provide enough information for your readers to understand the main point? Do you present enough evidence to convince your readers of that point? Look for places where you could add more support and detail.

Read the two paragraphs that follow and note the support and details that the writer added to the second one. Notice that she didn't simply add to the paragraph; she also deleted some words and rearranged others to make the story clearer to readers. The additions are underlined; the deletions are crossed out.

This morning I learned that my local police respond quickly and thoroughly to 911 calls. I meant to dial 411 for directory assistance, but by mistake I dialed 911. I hung up after only one ring because I realized what I'd done. A few seconds after I hung up, the phone rang, and it was the police dispatcher. She said that she'd received a 911 call from my number and was checking. I explained what happened, and she said she had to send a cruiser over anyway. Within a minute, the cruiser pulled in, and I explained what happened. I apologized and felt very stupid, but I thanked him. I am glad to know that if I ever need to call 911, the police will be there.

REVISED TO ADD SUPPORT AND DETAIL

This morning I tested the 911 emergency system and found that it worked perfectly. Unfortunately, the test was a mistake. ~~learned that my local police respond quickly and thoroughly to 911 calls~~. I meant to dial 411 for directory assistance, but without thinking ~~by mistake~~ I dialed 911. I frantically pushed the disconnect button ~~hung up~~ after only one ring because I realized my error. ~~what I'd done.~~ As I reached for the phone to dial 411, ~~A few seconds after I hung up,~~ it rang like an alarm. ~~the phone rang, and it was the police dispatcher~~. The police dispatcher crisply announced ~~She said~~ that she'd received a 911 call from my number and was checking. I laughed weakly and explained what happened, hoping she would see the humor or at least the innocent human error. Instead, the crispness of her voice became brittle as ~~and~~ she said she had to send a cruiser over anyway. I went to meet my fate. Within a minute, the cruiser pulled in, and a police officer swaggered toward me. I explained what had happened, apologized, and thanked him very humbly. I felt guilty of stupidity, at the very least. ~~and felt very stupid, but I thanked~~ We learn from our mistakes, and in this case I am glad to know that if I ever need to call 911, the police will be there.

PRACTICE 3   EVALUATE SUPPORT

In the two paragraphs that follow, the main points are in bold. Underline the primary support points and put a check mark by each supporting detail. Then, in the lines provided at the end of paragraph 2, indicate which paragraph provides better support and explain why.

1. **Women tend to learn the art of fly fishing more easily than men.** For one thing, they have more patience, which is key to successful fishing. It may take many hours of silent, solitary fishing to catch a single fish. Even long hours may net no fish, and men tend to be more eager for results. This can make them more careless. Women also tend to be more sensitive to subtle movements. This trait helps both in the casting motion and in the reeling in of a fish. Women are more likely to take breaks than men, who continue even when they are frustrated or tired. Women may also spend money on the appropriate attire for fishing, gear that is waterproof and warm. Finally, women are more receptive to fishing advice than are men. These feminine traits make a big difference in fly fishing.

2. **Because they are susceptible to certain safety problems, people over the age of seventy-five should be required by law to take a driving test every year.** Some people believe that such a law would represent age discrimination because many people are great drivers until they are in their nineties. But government statistics indicate that people over seventy-five have more accidents than younger drivers do. One common failing of older drivers is impaired peripheral vision. This makes it difficult for them to see cars on either side or at an intersection. Another common problem is a longer response time. Although older drivers may know to stop, it takes them much longer to move their foot from the gas pedal to the brake than it does younger drivers. This lengthened response

time is the most common cause of accidents among older drivers. The most dangerous failing among older drivers is a loss of memory. Consider this common scenario: The driver starts to back out of a parking space after checking to see that there's nothing behind him. He then notices that his sunglasses have fallen on the floor. He retrieves them and puts his foot back on the gas pedal without remembering that he needs to look again. Because he is still in reverse, the car moves quickly and hits the person or car now behind him. Although it may inconvenience older drivers to take annual driving tests, it will help save injuries and lives.

PARAGRAPH WITH BETTER SUPPORT: _____

REASONS THAT THIS PARAGRAPH'S SUPPORT IS BETTER: _____

_____

_____

_____

■ For more practice in revising for support, visit Exercise Central at <**bedfordstmartins.com /realessays**>.

■ PRACTICE 4   REVISE FOR SUPPORT

Read the following essay, and write in the space provided at least one additional support point or detail for each body paragraph and for the conclusion. Indicate where the added material should go in the paragraph by writing in a caret (∧).

If it's leather, I love it. Anything made of leather makes me want to spend some time admiring it. This appeal is not just limited to coats and jackets but includes furniture, bags, gloves, boots, and any other leather product I find. To me it's an all-around wonderful experience.

The smell of leather is intoxicating. It seems to hang in the air, inviting me to take a big whiff. I smell the leather, especially soft leather, and it is wonderful. I'd like to bury my nose in a soft leather jacket for hours.

_____

Leather also feels wonderful to the touch. It is smooth and silky. It feels soothing against my cheek and hands. When I'm wearing a leather jacket, I have to stop myself from running my hands up and down the sides and sleeves because it just feels so smooth and soft.

Finally, leather is comfortable, whatever form it comes in. A leather coat or jacket doesn't just look good—it's also very warm. Pull on a pair of leather gloves, and your hands won't be cold. And, best of all, sink into a soft, buttery leather easy chair. I guarantee it will relax you.

Just writing this essay about leather makes me want to put on a leather jacket and some soft leather slippers, and find a great leather chair to curl up in. It's my kind of heaven.

Practice Revising for Coherence

Coherence in writing means that all the support connects to form a whole. In other words, even when the support is arranged in a logical order, it still needs "glue" to connect the various points.

A piece of writing that lacks coherence sounds choppy, and it is hard for the reader to follow. Revising for coherence improves an essay by helping readers see how one point leads to another. The best way to improve coherence is to add transitions.

Transitions are words, phrases, and sentences that connect ideas so that writing moves smoothly from one point to another. Transitions can be used to connect sentences and ideas within a paragraph and also to connect one paragraph to another. In the box on page 105 are some, but not all, of the most common transitions and what they are used for.

The following essay shows how transitions link ideas within sentences and paragraphs and connect one paragraph to the next. It also shows another technique for achieving coherence: repeating key words and ideas related to the main point. The transitions and key words are underlined.

I thought I would never make it to work today. I had an important meeting, and it seemed as if everything was conspiring against me. The conspiracy started before I even woke up.

I had set my alarm clock, but it didn't go off, and therefore I didn't wake up on time. When I did wake up, I was already late, not just by a few

Continued on page 106.

Common Transitional Words and Phrases

INDICATE SPACE

above	below	near	to the right
across	beside	next to	to the side
at the bottom	beyond	opposite	under
at the top	farther	over	where
behind	inside	to the left	

INDICATE TIME

after	eventually	meanwhile	soon
as	finally	next	then
at last	first	now	when
before	last	second	while
during	later	since	

INDICATE IMPORTANCE

above all	in fact	more important	most
best	in particular	most important	worst
especially			

SIGNAL EXAMPLES

for example	for instance	for one thing	one reason

SIGNAL ADDITIONS

additionally	and	as well as	in addition
also	another	furthermore	moreover

SIGNAL CONTRAST

although	in contrast	nevertheless	still
but	instead	on the other hand	yet
however			

SIGNAL CAUSE OR CONSEQUENCE

as a result	finally	so	therefore
because			

minutes but by an hour and a half. To save time, I brushed my teeth while I showered. Also, I figured out what I was going to wear. Finally, I hopped out of the shower ready to get dressed. But the conspiracy continued.

The next act of the conspiracy concerned my only clean shirt, which was missing two buttons right in front. After finding a sweater that would go over it, I ran to the bus stop.

When I got to the stop, I discovered that the buses were running late. When one finally came, it was one of the old, slow ones, and it made stops about every ten feet. In addition, the heat was blasting, and I was sweating but couldn't take off my sweater because my shirt was gaping open. Now I was sweating, and perspiration was running down my scalp and neck. At least, I thought, I'll dry off by the time the bus gets to my work.

In fact, I did dry off a little, but the conspiracy didn't end there. When I finally got to work, the elevator was out of service, so I had to walk up ten flights of stairs. I was drenched, late, and inappropriately dressed. By the time I got to my desk, I knew that the hardest part of the day was behind me.

PRACTICE 5   ADD TRANSITIONAL WORDS

Read the following paragraphs. In each blank, add a transition that would smoothly connect the ideas. In each case, there is more than one right answer.

EXAMPLE: Today, many workers are members of labor unions that exist to protect worker rights. _However,_ until the 1930s, unions did not exist. In the 1930s, Congress passed laws that paved the way for unions. _After that,_ workers had the right to organize, bargain, and strike. _Today,_ unions are a powerful force in American politics.

1. The modern-day vending machine is based on an invention by a Greek scientist named Hero, who lived in the first century A.D. The machine that he invented required that the user insert a coin. _____ the coin

fell, it hit a lever. _____ out came the desired product: a cup of holy water.

2. _____ Jackie Robinson joined the Brooklyn Dodgers in 1947, he became the first African American to play major league baseball in the twentieth century. _____ he was the first, he was faced with what was called "breaking the color line" and received many death threats. _____ a few seasons of playing well, he spoke out against discrimination against African Americans. _____ his career, he played in six World Series and won the National League Most Valuable Player award in 1949.

3. Alcohol affects women more quickly than men. This is because women have more fat tissue, _____ men have more muscle tissue, which has more water than fat tissue. _____ men drink alcohol, it is diluted by the water in muscle. _____ when women drink, the alcohol becomes more concentrated in their bodies. _____ women get drunk much sooner than men do.

■ For more practice in achieving coherence in writing, visit Exercise Central at <bedfordstmartins .com/realessays>.

■ **PRACTICE 6   ADD TRANSITIONAL SENTENCES**

Read the following essay. Then, in the blanks, write a transitional sentence that would link each paragraph to the one following it. You may add your transitional sentence either at the end of a paragraph, at the beginning of the next paragraph, or in both places. There is no one correct answer.

Many teenagers today do not date in the traditional sense: one boy and one girl going on dates or going steady. Instead, they go out in groups. This gives many parents a sense that their sons and daughters are safe from premature sex and possible sexually transmitted diseases.

_____

_____

Although teenagers do not pair off romantically, they are getting plenty of sex, just not with people they care about. They care about their friends and don't want to risk ruining friendships, so they hook up with strangers they meet while out at night or online. "Hooking up" means having sex, and teens hook up only with people they have no other contact with, preferably from different schools or towns.

Teenagers often think that sex without emotional involvement will avoid heartbreak and breakups; however, many teens, both girls and boys, admit that it is difficult not to develop feelings for people that they have become physically intimate with. Often, one person begins to feel an attachment while the other doesn't, and a distancing occurs; that hurts. It's a breakup of a different sort.

Teenagers have always experimented with ways to do things differently than their parents did. This experimentation is important to teenagers' development and sometimes produces better ways of doing things. According to most teens, however, the hook-up isn't the answer to heartbreak: It's just another road to it. Perhaps teenagers are destined to experience some pain as they try to figure out what love means.

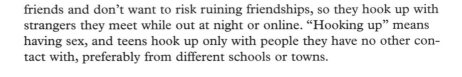 **PRACTICE 7   ADD TRANSITIONS**

The following essay has no transitions. Read it carefully and add transitions both within and between the paragraphs. There is no one correct answer.

Skydiving is the most thrilling activity I can ever imagine. I was scared, euphoric, and proud during my one skydive. I would encourage anyone to have the experience of a lifetime.

_____ I was scared as I looked down out of the plane, ready to jump. The ground was barely visible. My instructor gave the ready sign, assuring me that he would be guiding me all the way. I closed my eyes, and we jumped out of the plane together. It felt as if we were dropping very fast.

I opened my eyes and saw that, _____ we were. I panicked a little, fearing that the parachute wouldn't open or that my instructor would activate it too late, and we'd be killed.

I was ____ euphoric. My instructor opened the chute, and we just glided silently through the air. It was like flying. It was very peaceful and almost religious. I had never felt this way and knew that this was an important experience.

We landed, and I was proud of myself. It had taken a lot of courage to jump and to trust my life to another individual, my instructor. I had done it and done it well. I had benefited from the experience, mentally and spiritually. It was so thrilling and wonderful I probably won't do it again for fear that the second time would be an anticlimax. Do it!

Revise Your Own Essay

Before selecting a writing assignment, read how Derek Johnson, the student whose writing you saw in Chapter 4 as he developed a thesis, revised his draft essay. Look at the changes that Derek made in his revised essay. They are highlighted in bold.

DRAFT

The Apprentice is an example of good reality television, where viewers can learn many useful lessons about the business world, such as how to dress, what real-world business situations are like, and how to solve problems. Many people criticize reality TV for putting people into unrealistic situations. This criticism is true of programs like *Fear Factor* and *The Swan,* which are for entertainment only. But *The Apprentice* is both entertaining and educational.

Viewers of *The Apprentice* can learn how to dress for the business world. All of the candidates are very well dressed in a formal sense. They all wear suits at the beginning and are very neat.

Also, viewers can learn about real-world business situations. For example, people have to work together in teams. They have to elect a team leader and that person is responsible for the results of the team. And the winning team doesn't win because it is faster but because it uses better strategies. The team is creative. This is true of everything from running a lemonade stand to coming up with a marketing campaign for an airline.

Finally, viewers can learn about problem-solving in business. People on the show can't just say they have a problem and expect someone else to fix it. They have to figure out how to deal with the problem as a team. Like in the last episode, Bill was running a golf tournament and the sponsor's sign didn't show up. And Kwame was running a casino event starring Jessica Simpson, who got lost on the way to the event.

Some reality television is really useless, but *The Apprentice* gives viewers an opportunity to learn about business while they are being entertained. In fact, several business school programs have used *The Apprentice* episodes as case studies. I wish there were more of this kind of television.

REVISED (changes in bold)

Thesis (underlined) links to lessons described in later paragraphs. Introduction reorganized to build to main point.

Many people criticize reality TV for putting people into unrealistic situations. **Although** this criticism may be true of programs like *Fear Factor* and *The Swan*, which are for entertainment only, it does not apply to *The Apprentice*, which is entertaining and educational. *The Apprentice* is an example of good reality television, where viewers can learn many useful lessons about the business world, such as how to dress, what real-world business situations are like, and how to solve problems.

Links to thesis.

One good lesson viewers of *The Apprentice* can learn is how to dress for the business world. All of the candidates are very well dressed in a formal sense. **For example**, they all wear suits at the beginning, and they are very neat. **The women do not wear big jewelry or have messy hairstyles. Similarly, the men do not have long hair or visible piercings. Seeing how the** *Apprentice* **contestants dress made me realize that people can't wear everyday clothing at work. Before seeing** *The Apprentice,* **I didn't know that about business.**

Another lesson I learned from *The Apprentice* is that real-world business situations often require people to work together in teams. **First,** the group members have to elect a team leader who is responsible for the results of the team. **Then, they have to learn how to work well together. They learn to pool their ideas and listen to each other. Also, they learn to think critically together.** The winning team doesn't win because it is faster but because it uses better strategies. **In addition,** the team is creative. **Good teamwork is important in every situation,** from running a lemonade stand to coming up with a marketing campaign for an airline. **Before seeing *The Apprentice*, I didn't know how important teamwork was.**

— Links to thesis.

The most important lesson I learned was about problem-solving in business. People on the show can't just say they have a problem and expect someone else to fix it. They have to figure out how to deal with the problem as a team. **For example,** in the last episode, Bill was running a golf tournament and the sponsor's sign didn't show up. **Instead of panicking and yelling at other people, he organized a search and finally found the sign in a Dumpster.** And Kwame, **the other remaining contestant,** was running a casino event starring Jessica Simpson, who got lost on the way to the event. **Kwame stayed calm as usual and logically made a list of people to contact for information. Even though the problem seemed unsolvable and disaster inevitable, Kwame's strategy worked, and Jessica Simpson was found in time for the show. I know now that getting mad and panicking does not help solve a problem.**

— Links to thesis.

With all that I have learned from watching *The Apprentice*, I truly believe that it is a worthwhile and educational reality TV program. Some reality television is really useless, but *The Apprentice* gives viewers an opportunity to learn about business while they are being entertained. In fact, several business school programs have used *The Apprentice* episodes as case studies. I wish there were more of this kind of television.

— Links to thesis.

REVISING ASSIGNMENT

Revise an essay using the draft you developed in Chapter 7. Before revising, read the following Critical Thinking box.

CRITICAL THINKING: REVISING YOUR ESSAY

FOCUS
- After a break, reread your draft with a fresh perspective.

ASK
- What's my point or position? Does my thesis statement clearly state my main point?
- Does my essay have the following?
  —An introductory paragraph
  —Three or more body paragraphs
  —A topic sentence for each paragraph that supports the main point
  —A forceful concluding paragraph that reminds my readers of my main point and makes an observation
- Does my essay have unity?
  —Do all of the primary support points relate directly to my main point?
  —Do all the supporting details in each body paragraph relate to the paragraph's topic sentence?
  —Have I avoided drifting away from my main point?
- Do I have enough support?
  —Taken together, do the topic sentences of each paragraph give enough support or evidence for the main point?
  —Do individual paragraphs provide enough support for their topic sentences?
  —Would more detail strengthen my support?
- Is my essay coherent?
  —Have I used transitional words to link ideas?
  —Have I used transitional sentences to link paragraphs?

REVISE
- Revise your draft, making any improvements you can.

Part Two

Writing Different Kinds of Essays

9

Narration

Writing That Tells Stories

Understand What Narration Is

Narration is writing that tells a story of an event or experience.

▪▪ FOUR BASICS OF GOOD NARRATION

1. It reveals something of importance to you (**main point**).
2. It includes all of the major events of the story (**primary support**).
3. It uses details to bring the story to life for your audience (**supporting details**).
4. It presents the events in a clear order, usually according to when they happened.

In the following passage, each number corresponds to one of the four basics of good narration.

> **1** My guardian angel made sure I got to the interview that changed my life. **2** I went to bed early on the night before the most important job interview I have ever had. I felt that getting this job would be the best thing I would ever do, and I wanted it with all my heart. **3** I had laid my clothes out for the morning, and I had checked my alarm clock twice to make sure that I would wake up in plenty of time to get ready

4 Events in chronological order

and get to the interview on time. Everything was set, and I had no reason to worry.

2 At 2:00 a.m., I sat bolt upright in bed, absolutely certain that I was going to lose my electricity, the alarm wouldn't go off, and I would miss the interview. **3** It was a mild spring night, with no chance of high winds, snow, or lightning—the usual sources of power failure. Nevertheless, I knew I was going to lose power.

2 I was so certain that I called my mother right then and asked her to call me at 6:30 a.m. because I thought I was going to lose my electricity. **3** Groggily, she muttered, "Are you crazy? Why do you think you're going to lose power?" I couldn't really explain, and she thought I was just nervous about the interview. But she agreed to call me. Satisfied, I went back to sleep.

2 I was sound asleep when the phone rang hours later. **3** My mother said, "I am your wake-up call, you worrywart." When I looked at my clock, it was dead: I had indeed lost power. I told her and then asked what time it was. She assured me that it was only 6:35, and I had plenty of time. I had to go to her place to shower and get ready, **2** but I got to the interview on time, got the job, and, as I thought, changed the course of my life. **1** Since then, I've never doubted the existence of my guardian angel.

4 Events in chrono-logical order

Telling stories is one important way in which we communicate with one another. Whether they are serious or humorous, stories provide information and examples that can show, explain, or prove a point.

You can use narration in many practical situations. Consider the following examples:

COLLEGE	In a U.S. history course, you trace, in your own words, the specific sequence of events that led the United States to enter World War II.
WORK	A customer becomes angry with you and lodges a complaint with your boss. You recount—in writing—what happened.
EVERYDAY LIFE	Your wallet is stolen, and you file a written account with the police reporting exactly what happened.

■ For an example of an actual narration written for work, see page 123. The piece was written by the nurse who is profiled in the box on page 117.

Profile of Success

Patty Maloney
Clinical Nurse
Specialist

*(See Patty's
Narration at Work
on p. 123.)*

BACKGROUND: Patty says that she was always a terrible student who was shy and lacking in confidence. After high school, she took one course at a community college but quit because she didn't think she could do it.

After working as a typist, Patty got a job as a nursing assistant at Shriners Burn Center in Boston, working with children in the intensive care unit. This motivated her to become a licensed practical nurse (LPN).

As time went on, she wanted more responsibility, so she took courses that led, first, to a registered nurse (RN) degree and, finally, to a master's degree in nursing. In the various nursing degree programs she completed, Patty had to do lots of writing: long papers, summaries of articles, and analyses of diseases and of case studies.

EMPLOYER: All Children's Hospital, St. Petersburg, Florida

COLLEGES/DEGREES: Massachusetts Bay Community College, Labouré Junior College, Massachusetts College of Pharmacy (B.S.N.), Northeastern University (M.S.N.)

TYPES OF WRITING ON THE JOB: Observations of patients, notes about patients, memos to colleagues, instructions for junior staff, lots of e-mail

HOW PATTY USES NARRATION: Notes on patients are usually narratives. They need to be concise, precise, and clear, because both Patty and others will need to refer to them for patients' treatment.

TEAMWORK ON THE JOB: Most of nursing involves teamwork. Team members have regular conferences, write weekly summaries of patient care and patients' conditions, and write reports that they share with each other.

Main Point in Narration

Whenever you write a narration, you should have a **purpose** in mind, whether that is to explain what happened, to prove something, or simply to entertain someone. If you don't know the purpose of your narration, your readers won't know it either.

In addition to knowing your purpose, you should also be clear on your **main point**—what is important about the narration. Generally, college instructors will want your main point to indicate what is important to you about a story. Take another look at the passage under the Four Basics of Good Narration (p. 115). What if the main point had been stated as follows?

I lost electricity one night.

You might respond, "So what?" This statement doesn't indicate the importance of the event to the writer, and it doesn't promise a very interesting story. Now read the actual statement of the main point:

My guardian angel made sure I got to the interview that changed my life.

■ For more on topic sentences and thesis statements, see Chapter 4.

This statement emphasizes the event's importance to the writer. You need to express your main point clearly in topic sentences (for paragraphs) and in thesis statements (for essays). Topic sentences and thesis statements usually include your topic and your main point.

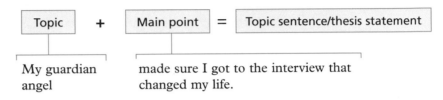

My guardian angel   made sure I got to the interview that
                         changed my life.

■ For online exercises on main point and support, visit Exercise Central at <**bedfordstmartins** .com/realessays>.

Although writers generally reveal the main point either at the beginning or at the end of their narration, we suggest that you both start off with your main point and remind readers of that main point at the end of your writing.

Support in Narration

The **support** for the main point of your narration is the presentation and explanation of the major events in the story, as well as details about those events. Your point of view determines how you present these events and details.

Point of View

In a narration, the events you include and the way you describe them create a story that is based on your point of view. For example, two people who witness or participate in the same series of events may give very different accounts, because they perceive what happened differently.

The stories that Gloria and Mason tell in the following two paragraphs reflect their different points of view regarding the same experience.

GLORIA'S STORY

This morning, Mason and I set out for what was supposed to be a great day at the beach, but Mason's stubborn behavior ruined everything. First, he took the longest route, so we hit traffic that we would have avoided by going the short route. Then, we got lost. When I suggested that we stop and ask for directions, Mason said he could get us there. After another hour of driving, we passed an intersection that we'd crossed earlier. I again suggested that we stop and ask for directions, but

Mason wasn't buying it. So we drove some more. Finally, we were about to run out of gas, so we pulled into a gas station. While Mason was filling the tank, I asked the attendant for directions. I swear, if we hadn't needed gas, we'd still be driving around looking for that beach!

MASON'S STORY

This morning, Gloria and I set out for what was supposed to be a great day at the beach, but Gloria wanted to pick a fight. First, she insisted I was going the wrong way, it was going to take us longer, and we'd hit more traffic. Then, she decided we were lost. I knew about where we were going and knew I could figure it out. Gloria kept on nagging me to stop and ask for directions. When we were almost there, I decided to get gas, and she had to ask the attendant for directions. I don't know what was going on with her, but she was really on my case.

When you write a narration, be careful to describe events in a way that will tell the story you want to tell.

Major Events and Details

The major events of a story are your primary support in narration, and they will usually become the topic sentences for the body paragraphs in your essay. Ask yourself what the major events are and what makes them important. To help your readers experience the events as you did, give supporting details that bring the experience to life.

■ For more on supporting a point, see Chapter 5.

For example, one student stated the main point of an event in the following thesis: *The theft of my wallet this morning showed me how easy it is to be deceived.*

The student then did some listing to come up with the major events and details about those events.

■ For more on listing, see page 37.

MAJOR EVENTS (primary support)	SUPPORTING DETAILS (secondary support)
Woman bumped into me	Light bump, but she dropped her folder of papers, and they scattered
I bent down to help her collect the papers	Wind was blowing, so I had to work fast
A man stopped and asked if he could help	I didn't get a good look at him because I was trying to get the papers, but he stood close to me and hung around for a minute just watching us. Then, he just left without saying anything.

Woman thanked me, and I said no problem	She had her head down and walked off fast
When I went to get coffee, I realized the wallet was gone	I broke into a sweat at the café and had that horrible panicked feeling
I realized that the man and woman were working together	Looking back on the details, it was clear how carefully they'd planned the scam

Organization in Narration

■ For more on chronological order, see page 66.

Because narration tells a story, it uses **chronological (time) order**. Start at the beginning of the story, and describe the events in the sequence in which they occurred.

Introduction (including thesis)

First major event

    Details about the first event

Second major event

    Details about the second event

Third major event

    Details about the third event

Conclusion

■ For more on transitions, see pages 104–06.

Time transitions (see the box that follows) are important in narration because they make the order of events clear to readers. Writers of narration use these common transitions not only within a paragraph to move from one detail about the event to the next but also between paragraphs to move from one major event to the next.

Common Time Transitions

after	eventually	meanwhile	soon
as	finally	next	then
at last	first	now	when
before	last	second	while
during	later	since	

Read and Analyze Narration

Before writing a narration essay, read the following examples of narration—one each from college, the workplace, and everyday life—and answer the questions that accompany them.

Narration in College

The following essay was written for a college writing course.

A Return to Education

Jordan Brown

For me, college has been an experience marked by anticipation, fear, and pride. I sometimes find myself still surprised that I am really here. The journey to get here has been a long one, but if I can put my fears behind me, I believe I will be able to accomplish something that I can really be proud of.

Finally being able to go to college is something that I have been anticipating for many years. Since I left high school and the California Bay Area behind, I have been on the go in one way or another. After graduation, I felt that I wasn't ready for the commitments or responsibilities of college. Instead, I enlisted in the army. The army provided me with the maturity and self-discipline that I desperately needed in my life; however, being in the army also provided me with very little time or money to go to college, so I put it off until "a later date."

After the army, I sought a higher-paying job, first becoming a truck driver. This job provided me with money but no time. Now I work for the railroad, and with my apprenticeship behind me, I have some free time for the first time in my life.

What I have been anticipating for years is finally here; I now have the time and money for college, but do I have the ability? It has been eleven years since I last sat in a classroom. This made me question myself: Can I do this? Will I succeed? Will I fail? Am I even capable of learning in a classroom environment? Although I had these questions, I knew that the only way to face my fears was to attack them head-on. I reminded myself that the only thing I could do is try.

When I first walked into Front Range Community College, I was nervous. I couldn't help but notice how young everyone looked. I got to my study skills class, sat down, and looked around. I felt out of place. Most of the people in the class looked as if they had just graduated from high school. However, when we did our introductions, I learned that one of the women sitting across the room had graduated from high school eleven years ago. I started to feel a little younger.

When I got to my philosophy class, I watched the other students come in and noticed that not everyone looked like a kid. This class looked very much like an American melting pot, with students of many ages and cultures. As we went around the room introducing ourselves, I felt very much more confident about my decision to try college. Many students were even older than I was. A woman sitting near me, who looked about my mom's age, said she was in college because all of her kids were in college now. She told us that she wanted a college education and a better job. An older gentleman across the room said that he was a business executive from Germany. His job had become boring, and he was looking for something more challenging. By the end of the introductions, I was convinced that this "college thing" might just work.

Since I have gone back to school, there has been a lot of pride surrounding me. My parents can't stop talking about me and how proud they are. My family and friends are excited for me and congratulate me on my decision. I am also proud of myself for making the tough decision to go back to school. I know that when I get my degree, I will have something to be truly proud of.

I still have fears and uncertainties. But I also have positive anticipation and hope. I know that I am on the right course. I know that as long as I have stamina and determination, nothing can stop me from achieving my dream of getting my degree in mechanical engineering.

1. Double-underline the **thesis statement**.

2. Underline each **topic sentence/major event**.

3. Put a check mark (✔) by the **supporting details**.

4. Circle the **time transitions**.

5. Does Jordan's essay have the **four basics of good narration**? Why or why not? _____

   ■ For a list of the four basics of good narration, see page 115.

6. When you started college, was your experience at all like Jordan's? Why or why not? If you were meeting a new student who felt as Jordan did, what would you say to him or her?

   ■ The final question after each reading in this section makes a good essay topic.

Narration at Work

As a neonatal clinical nurse specialist, Patty Maloney cares for at-risk infants. The following is a narrative that describes her experience with a patient, the patient's parents, and her staff. It was part of a seminar for nurses interested in becoming managers.

Patty Maloney
Clinical Nurse Specialist

(See Patty's Profile of Success on p. 117.)

In the neonatal intensive care unit, we work with high-risk infants. Because we are health care professionals, we must maintain objectivity and clinical distance, a tall order when patients are tiny humans just beginning life. As a clinical nurse specialist who manages other staff, I am responsible for helping others see the complete picture when they may be too involved with a patient to do so. Recently, my management skills were put to a painful test when a premature infant who weighed only 700 grams and who had been in critical condition since birth went into shock and experienced respiratory failure.

This crisis occurred late on Christmas Eve, creating a dilemma for hospital staff. Because of the holiday, the complete medical team wasn't on-site, but the physician and nurse who were caring for this child were unsure about how much longer the child would live. They were faced with a difficult question: Will maximum invasive medical therapy help this child?

The attending physician and nurse concluded that they had exhausted all treatment options. They then decided to call the family in to spend time with the infant and to discuss redirection of support (which means, in essence, acknowledging that most avenues have been exhausted). Redirection of support would avoid any treatment that would be both radical and unlikely to save the patient.

Before contacting the parents, however, the nurse sought my advice. She asked me if I felt there was anything more that she and the doctor could offer the infant. Based on the information I had received, I believed that further treatment was unlikely to change the child's condition. I offered that opinion.

The situation was particularly painful for the team: They did not want to unnecessarily prolong the inevitable death of the infant, so they were inclined to call the parents right away to discuss redirection of support. At this point, I realized that the caregivers' discomfort was preventing them from considering all aspects of the situation. It was my responsibility to fill in the whole picture.

I wanted to ease the pain of my colleagues, which I well understood, but I did not believe that calling the family on Christmas Eve was the best course of action. I explained that I fully appreciated why the team wanted to act quickly, but I also called upon my experience in working with bereaved families, which taught me that the most intense bereavement comes when a loved one dies on a holiday. In this particular case, I reasoned, the child was not going to die in the next few days, so the only reason to call the parents would be to ease the medical team's pain. Then, I suggested that we wait until after Christmas to meet with the parents, which would also mean that the rest of the medical team could be present and involved in the decision-making process. My colleagues agreed, and they planned a care conference for the day after Christmas.

Personally, I wanted to ease my colleagues' discomfort. Professionally, I couldn't do that. I had to give advice based on a range of circumstances that included my responsibilities to the patient, the patient's family, and my staff. Certainly I won't forget that Christmas Eve, but I know we made the right decisions.

1. Double-underline the **thesis statement**.

2. Underline each **topic sentence/major event**.

3. Put a check mark (✔) by the **supporting details**.

4. Circle the **time transitions**.

5. Double-underline the sentence in the concluding paragraph that relates back to the introduction.

6. Think of a time you were in a situation where you had to make a difficult decision. What did you do?

Narration in Everyday Life

This student essay was reprinted in an Allan Hancock College collection titled *Everchanging Winds.*

Showing Off
Larry Lane

Years ago, I learned a valuable lesson about not showing off and driving drunk.

When I was seventeen years old, I got a black 5.0 Mustang with gold rims and dark-tinted windows, and I worked hard to improve its performance. I souped up the engine by adding a performance cam, headers, and an 800 cfm four-barrel carburetor that made the engine roar like a lion when I stepped on the accelerator and growl at a low, rumbling pitch when idling. I beefed up the suspension with eleven-inch-wide low-pro tires and front and rear sway bars. These reduced the air flow under the car and made its center of gravity lower to the ground, making it hug the road on turns. I practiced driving on Suey Creek Road, the most narrow, winding, and curvy road in town. After a short time, I thought I was the best driver there ever was.

I took some friends out to Suey Creek Road and drove at high speeds. I slowed down to forty miles per hour going into turns and sped up to sixty going out of the turns. My passengers were screaming in terror and bracing for impact, holding on to anything they could to keep from being thrown around. They were holding on for dear life as I made each turn, up and down, left and right, like a roller coaster. I told them this was nothing, that I could push it even more by driving this road at night.

One of my friends challenged me to drive drunk that night, so later, after a few swigs, we started down the road again. Driving at night was more difficult because I had no landmarks to tell me what turns were ahead, and I had to react quickly to unexpected changes in the road. The alcohol impaired my reaction time, but in spite of this, I thought I was so good that I could drive the car anyway.

The first few turns were fine. Then, as I was going up a hill, my headlights aimed at the sky, I couldn't see what was at the bottom of the hill. When I drove down the hill with the car lights shining down, in a split second I saw the road had an immediate hard right turn. As fast as I could, I turned the steering wheel right, but the back tires caught gravel at the edge of the road. The car spun around like a top three times before it stopped two feet in front of a sidewall embankment.

We sat in dead silence. Then, I took my friends home, thinking about what I had done: I had almost lost the lives of my friends and me. I vowed never to drink and drive again, and I have kept that vow.

1. Double-underline the **thesis statement**.

2. Underline each **topic sentence/major event**.

3. Put a check mark (✔) by the **supporting details**.

4. Circle the **time transitions**, including transitional sentences.

5. Double-underline the sentence in the concluding paragraph that relates back to the introduction.

6. Think of a time you took a risk to show off for someone. What happened? What did you learn?

Write a Narration Essay

In this section, you will write your own narration essay based on one of the following assignments. Before you begin to write, review the four basics of good narration on page 115.

 ASSIGNMENT 1   WRITING ABOUT COLLEGE, WORK, AND EVERYDAY LIFE

Write a narration essay on *one* of the following topics or on a topic of your own choice.

COLLEGE

- Tell a story that shows something significant about one of your professors.
- Explain the most important or interesting event that has happened to you in college.
- Summarize an interesting story you learned in one of your other classes, such as psychology or history.

WORK

- Tell the story of something positive you did at work (some achievement).
- Explain what you learned from getting or doing your first job.
- Describe an incident that shows your boss as _____ (supportive/unsupportive, fair/unfair, clueless/sharp, realistic/unrealistic, honest/dishonest).

EVERYDAY LIFE

- Tell the story of your first love (or your most recent one), showing how it changed or influenced you.
- Recount the most embarrassing, rewarding, happy, or otherwise memorable moment in your life.
- Write about a time when you were proud or ashamed of your behavior.

 ASSIGNMENT 2   WRITING ABOUT AN IMAGE

Write a narration essay about what has happened (or is happening) in the picture on the next page. Be as creative as you like, but be sure to follow the four basics of good narration.

■ **ASSIGNMENT 3   WRITING TO SOLVE A PROBLEM**

THE PROBLEM: You order a computer from a mail-order company, but it doesn't work properly. You try every step from the online help guide, but nothing works. Then, after holding for a half hour on the customer-service line, you learn that you "might" get a refund after returning the computer and that the process would take as long as two months. You tell the phone rep that this policy is unacceptable. The rep, who suggests that others have complained about the company's refund practices, urges you to write an e-mail to the company's customer satisfaction service. He adds, "That's definitely gotten results in the past." You decide that's what you'll do.

THE ASSIGNMENT: Working on your own or with a small group, write a courteous but firm e-mail to the company, Computers Inc., describing your problems with the computer and with the company's refund practices. Ask for a replacement, give a desired deadline, and indicate the steps you are prepared to take if you don't get satisfaction.

■ Be sure to cite and document any sources you use in your papers. For advice, see Chapter 20.

RESOURCES: Review the chart on pages 726–27 for general advice about problem solving. You might also visit Web sites like Complaints.com (**<www.complaints.com>**) for ideas about how to phrase your complaint and what evidence to include. At Complaints.com, see especially the links "Browse Consumer Complaints — by Date" and "Complaint Posting Guidelines" (under "How It Works"). List any Web sites that you use.

■ ASSIGNMENT 4   **WRITING ABOUT READINGS**

In college, you will often be asked to write about assigned readings. This writing will range from simply reporting on what you have read to incorporating evidence from readings to support an argument or interpretation.

Read both "Showing Off" by Larry Lane (p. 126) and "The Dare" by Roger Hoffmann (p. 714) and think of a time when you were pressured to do something dangerous or otherwise risky. Then, in a brief paper that summarizes this experience, do one of the following:

■ For advice on summarizing, analyzing, synthesizing, and evaluating, see pages 16–20.

- Consider how the lessons from the experience were similar to or different from those of Lane and Hoffmann. Given what you've learned from Lane and Hoffmann, would you have done anything differently? Would you have advised them to do anything differently? Make sure to draw on evidence from both stories.

- Analyze what causes people to accept dares, drawing on your own experience and on the stories of Lane and Hoffmann.

- Persuade Larry Lane or Roger Hoffmann not to accept the dare. In your argument, draw on your own experiences and those of the writer (Lane or Hoffmann) you are *not* trying to persuade.

Follow the steps in the Writing Guide on the next page to help you prewrite, draft, revise, and edit your narration. Check off each step as you complete it.

WRITING GUIDE: NARRATION	
STEPS IN NARRATION	**HOW TO DO THE STEPS**
Focus.	❑ Think about who will read your narration and what point you want your readers to understand.
Prewrite to explore your topic. See Chapter 3 for more on prewriting.	❑ Determine your purpose for writing. ❑ Decide what story you want to tell. ❑ Use a prewriting technique to explore your thoughts about what happened; how it affected you or others; and what the story shows, explains, or proves.
Write a thesis statement. Topic + Main point = Thesis My father has become a complete stranger. See Chapter 4 for more on writing a thesis.	❑ Decide what is important to you about the story. Imagine a reader saying, "So what?" ❑ Specify the point you want your readers to understand. ❑ Write a thesis statement.
Support your thesis statement. The primary support points in narration are the major events of the story you want to tell. See Chapter 5 for more on supporting a thesis statement.	❑ List all of the major events in the story. ❑ Review your thesis and drop any events that do not help you explain, show, or prove your main point. Make your thesis more specific. ❑ Choose at least three major events that will help your readers understand your main point. ❑ Add supporting details about each event that will help your readers experience it as you did.
Make a plan. See Chapter 6 for more on planning.	❑ Arrange your major events according to when they occurred (chronological order). ❑ Write a plan or an outline for your narration that includes your main support points (the major events) and supporting details for each event.
Write a draft. See Chapter 7 for more on drafting.	❑ Write an introduction that gets your readers' interest and presents your thesis statement. See if you can use one of the introductory techniques in Chapter 7. ❑ Using your outline, write a topic sentence for each of the major events. ❑ Write body paragraphs that give specific details that bring the story to life. ❑ Write a concluding paragraph that reminds your readers of your main point and makes a final observation about the importance of the story. ❑ Title your essay.

continued

STEPS IN NARRATION	HOW TO DO THE STEPS
Revise your draft. See Chapter 8 for more on revising a draft.	❑ Ask another person to read and comment on your draft. ❑ Consider how you can make the point of the story clearer to your readers. ❑ Revise your thesis to make it more forceful. ❑ Make sure all of the events and details support your thesis. Add details that strengthen your support, and cut any details that aren't relevant. ❑ Reread your introduction and make changes if it is dull. ❑ Reread your conclusion to make sure that it is energetic and convincing, and that it reminds your readers of your main point. ❑ Add transitions (especially time transitions) to connect your ideas. ❑ Make at least five changes to your draft to improve unity, support, or coherence (see pp. 96–109). ❑ Check to make sure the draft follows the four basics of good narration.
Edit your draft. See Parts Four through Seven for more on editing.	❑ Use the spell checker and grammar checker on your computer, but also reread your essay carefully to catch any errors. ❑ Look for errors in grammar, spelling, or punctuation. Focus first on sentence fragments, run-ons, errors in subject-verb agreement, verb errors, and other areas where you know you often make mistakes. ❑ Ask yourself: Is this the best I can do?

10

Illustration

Writing That Shows Examples

Items confiscated at airport security

Understand What Illustration Is

Illustration is writing that uses examples to show, explain, or prove a point.

∷ FOUR BASICS OF GOOD ILLUSTRATION

1. It has a point to illustrate.

2. It gives specific examples to show, explain, or prove the point.

3. It gives details to support these examples.

4. It uses enough examples to get the writer's point across.

In the following paragraph, each number corresponds to one of the four basics of good illustration.

What's the strongest predictor of your health? **1** It may not be your income or age but rather your literacy. **2** People with low literacy skills have four times greater annual health costs than those with high skills. Why is literacy so important? **3** Most Americans read at an eighth- or ninth-grade level, and 20% read at just a fifth-grade level or below. However, most health-care materials are written above the tenth-grade level.

4 Enough examples given to back the writer's main point

133

4 Enough examples given to back the writer's main point

3 As many as half of all patients fail to take medications as directed, often because they don't understand the instructions. **2** Americans can improve their health literacy by asking their doctor or pharmacist **3** three questions: (1) "What is my main problem?" (2) "What do I need to do?" and (3) "Why is it important to do this?" If you're still confused, don't hesitate to ask your doctor, nurse, or pharmacist to go over the information again.

—"Literacy and Health," *Parade* magazine, January 18, 2004

■ For an example of an actual illustration written for work, see page 139. The piece was written by the student who is profiled in the box on page 135.

Whenever we explain something, we use examples to show what we mean. Here are some ways you might use illustration:

COLLEGE	In a criminal justice course, you discuss and give examples of the most common criminal violations.
WORK	Your written self-evaluation includes specific and measurable examples of how well (or poorly) you performed.
EVERYDAY LIFE	You take your car to a mechanic and give him or her examples that show how the car is not running properly.

Main Point in Illustration

Look at the opening sentences in the paragraph that follows the Four Basics of Good Illustration (p. 133).

What's the strongest predictor of your health? It may not be your income or age but rather your literacy.

In this case, the topic—the strongest predictor of your health—is in the opening sentence, which is followed by a surprising **main point:** that literacy might be a predictor of health. Because the point is surprising, the reader will be interested in reading on to find out how it could be true. The writer demonstrates the main point by giving examples.

Often, a thesis statement in illustration includes the topic and your main point.

■ For more on thesis statements, see Chapter 4.

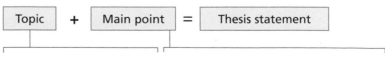

Topic	+	Main point	=	Thesis statement

Learning another language has many benefits, including some you might not expect.

Profile of Success

Rosa Fernández
Student, Wellesley
College, and Intern,
Casa Alianza

*(See Rosa's
Illustration at
Work on p. 139.)*

BACKGROUND: Rosa lived in the Dominican Republic until she was fourteen, when she and her twin sister joined their mother, who was living in the Bronx, New York. When she arrived in the United States, she didn't know English, so she went to a newcomers' school in New York City, where she was taught English as a second language. After a year at the newcomers' school, Rosa was ready to attend the Manhattan International High School, a small school for immigrant students. At Manhattan International, she had a very strong connection with her teacher and mentor, Elisabeth Levi. While at the school, Rosa served as a student representative on a committee designing a new school for Bronx students, called Discovery High School. To complete her college applications and essays, she used all the resources available to her: her mentor, writing center tutors, and an attorney she had met on the committee. Rosa was accepted at many colleges and is now a junior at Wellesley College in Massachusetts. She is majoring in Latin American Studies and Education.

EMPLOYER: Awarded a grant by Wellesley College to work at Casa Alianza (Covenant House), an agency in Costa Rica that helps people in need

TYPES OF WRITING ON THE JOB: Memos, press releases, English-Spanish translations, professional e-mails, grant proposals, a United Nations report on the state of children's rights in the Costa Rican media, and editing of the organization's book and updating of the list of children who have disappeared in Costa Rica

HOW ROSA USES ILLUSTRATION: Much of the writing Rosa did as an intern involved giving examples of what Casa Alianza found in its work with children. In her report about her experiences at this agency (see p. 139), Rosa gives examples of the kinds of work and writing she did.

TEAMWORK ON THE JOB: Teamwork was especially important in doing translations, both to prevent misunderstandings and to ensure that the material was well written in both Spanish and English.

Topic	+	Main point	=	Thesis statement

Holistic medicine is gaining support among doctors.

■ For online
exercises on main
point and support,
visit Exercise Central at
<bedfordstmartins
.com/realessays>.

Support in Illustration

In illustration, the examples show or prove your stated main point.

A student who had written the thesis *Homeschooling is beneficial to both the child and the parent* focused her prewriting on finding examples of benefits of homeschooling. Here are some examples from her brainstorming:

■ For more on brain-storming, see page 37. For more on support-ing a point, see Chapter 5.

individualized to child	*parent and child have control*
parent and child together	*more flexibility*
at child's own pace	*considers child's learning style*
one-on-one	*education is part of regular life*

An illustration essay usually uses several examples as **support points**. The writer of the prewriting on homeschooling selected "individualized to child" as one support point and asked herself, "What do I mean? How? In what ways?" to find supporting details.

She also chose "parent and child have control" as another major example that would support the thesis. She then asked herself, "How do they have more control?" and listed potential supporting details:

control over materials used (what books, what computer programs, what approach)

control over time of instruction (what hours of the day, based on child's natural rhythms, vacations — not tied to a school's calendar)

Organization in Illustration

■ For more on order of importance, see page 68.

Illustration typically uses **order of importance** to organize several examples, often saving the most vivid, convincing example for last. A typical plan for an illustration essay might look like this:

Introduction (including thesis)
First example
    Supporting details that explain the first example
Second example
    Supporting details that explain the second example
Third (and most important) example
    Supporting details that explain the third example
Conclusion (refers back to the main point and makes an observation)

Transitions are important in illustration because they signal to readers that you are moving from one example to another. Use transitions within a paragraph and also to move from one paragraph to another.

Common Transitions in Illustration

also	finally	for instance	in addition
another	for example	for one thing	one example . . . another example

---

Read and Analyze Illustration

Before writing an illustration essay, read the following examples of illustration—one each from college, the workplace, and everyday life—and answer the questions that accompany them.

Illustration in College

This essay was written by a student in a first-year writing course.

Jesse's Determination
Cecilia Guillen

In the novel *Jesse,* by Gary Soto, the title character will accomplish much in life because he is a hard worker, has good values, and is committed to getting an education.

For example, even though he is only seventeen, Jesse works in the fields with his brother on weekends and on vacations. One day while working, Jesse reports, "For nine hours, we chopped cotton, each earning sixteen dollars, enough to eat for the week" (Soto 10). On weekdays, he goes to college, where he studies hard. In addition, he collects aluminum cans he finds to get extra money.

Another reason Jesse will succeed in life is that he possesses good values. He believes in God, respects others, loves his family, and always tries to do the right thing. He has a conscience. For example, when he steals a small pine tree from the grove near his town's courthouse to make a project for his art class, Jesse regrets his action and hesitates to tell his brother about it. He explains, "I didn't want Abel to think that I went around stealing, but if I lied, then I would sin two times in one day" (Soto 145). He believes that wrong actions might interfere with his goals to succeed.

The most important reason that Jesse will accomplish his goals is that he is determined to get an education. He wants to be an artist and to travel in order to learn. Although he dropped out of high school, when he starts college he takes his classes very seriously and does extra work to change his grades from B's to A's. For example, he makes a bonsai for extra credit in his art class. In his music appreciation class, he attends a concert for extra credit.

Even though Jesse's life is not easy, he will achieve a better life for himself. His hard work, strong values, and determination assure his success in life.

Work Cited

Soto, Gary. *Jesse.* New York: Scholastic, 1994.

■ For coverage of citing and documenting sources, see Chapter 20.

1. Double-underline the **thesis statement**.

2. Underline the **topic sentences** that present the major examples supporting the thesis.

3. Put a check mark (✔) by the **supporting details** for the major examples.

4. Circle the **transitions** and **transitional sentences**.

5. How does Cecilia relate the **conclusion** back to the introduction?

   _____

   _____

6. What order of organization does Cecilia use? _____

7. Does Cecilia's essay have the **four basics of good illustration**? Why or why not? _____

■ For a list of the four basics of good illustration, see page 133.

8. Have you been assigned to write about a story or essay you have read? How might Cecilia's essay help you to do the assignment?

9. Think of someone you know who is like Jesse. How are they similar?

■ The final question after each reading in this section makes a good essay topic.

Illustration at Work

Crossing Frontiers: Scenes from a Summer with Casa Alianza

This past summer, I interned at Casa Alianza in San José, Costa Rica, an agency whose mission is "Help one child at a time." There, both my work and my writing took many forms as I labored to fulfill that mission.

I looked at the pictures and posters hanging on the walls at Casa Alianza: hungry, barefoot boys and girls sleeping on the streets or inhaling intoxicating shoe glue in garbage dumps, parks, and food markets. I thought, What can I do to help these children? Writing memos, translations, and press releases, editing articles, and researching topics for my coworkers became my day-to-day work, and the pictures became my source of inspiration and strength to keep going.

My work took a new direction when I was put in charge of editing a new publication by the organization. It was a book about the first murder case that attracted international attention to the violence faced by street children in Latin America. I soon became familiar with human rights violations against the most vulnerable and the legal proceedings of the Inter-American Court of Human Rights. I spent my days interpreting and defining legal terms, checking for typographical errors, and making sure

Rosa Fernández
Intern, Casa Alianza

(See Rosa's Profile of Success on p. 135.)

that the Spanish-English translations were accurate. My boss and I would stay until 7:00 p.m. rereading the book, talking about the cover and design, and choosing photographs for the book. I had to make decisions with serious consequences: Was our legal terminology correct? Should we use a photograph of smiling children, or would a disturbing picture of violence and poverty be more effective? I was often frustrated, trying to adjust to this position of so much decision-making responsibility.

I also had an opportunity to attend a hearing on a human rights case at the Inter-American Court of Human Rights. I sat in the first row, right next to the Guatemalan government's representatives, who during this case were stating their new political agenda: to protect human rights, pay for reparations, and ask for forgiveness from the victims of the country's civil war. I expected a more theoretical dialogue, a hearing about ideals and the principles of human rights. But the reality was different. I realized that the court was a medium to negotiate an agreement to pay reparations to the victims. I learned about the day-to-day proceedings of the court, the dynamics between the judges and the state, the legal language, and the history of the reconciliation process in Guatemala after thirty-six years of civil war. In addition, I saw that in order to make advances in the judicial system, it was necessary to find justice for victims of human rights in international courts such as this one; but the process, I saw, was imperfect and politically complicated.

The pivotal point of my summer came when I was asked to produce another type of writing: a report in Spanish for the United Nations. My objective was to determine whether or not the rights of children, guaranteed by the Convention of Human Rights and the Costa Rican Adolescent and Children's Code, were respected by the media in Costa Rica. I drew on the skills I had been developing through my courses at Wellesley. For the next six weeks, I gathered information from many sources, conducted phone interviews with journalists, carried out a sample study, and surveyed all the news on children over the past five years in Costa Rica. Additionally, I read hundreds of newspaper articles. The twenty-page report I wrote for the United Nations analyzed the information I had gathered and proposed alternative solutions.

From the start of the internship, I had dreamed of visiting the children's center in Nicaragua, but as a Dominican citizen, it was problematic for me to get the visas I needed to visit Nicaragua and return to Costa Rica. Why does it have to be so difficult? I thought. All I want is to meet the children I have been working for during these past two months.

I could not give up. I visited the immigration office in Costa Rica, the Nicaraguan embassy, talked to lawyers and Wellesley faculty, and wrote letters to immigration officers. Finally, I was able to get two visas: one to go to Nicaragua and the other to return to Costa Rica.

In Nicaragua, along with a Casa Alianza partner, I visited the markets, garbage dumps, and parks where small boys and girls lived as a result of wars, abuses at home, and lack of economic resources and educational opportunities. All were dirty and barefoot, sleepy, and drugged. They called me "teacher" and did not want to leave my side. Although I could not help every child, I could at least offer a smile and first-aid help. One hot morning, we rescued an eleven-year-old boy and took him to a children's center. On the bus ride, he told us he wanted to be a basketball player.

After a week, it was time to leave Nicaragua. I arrived at the Costa

Rican border, where on this barren piece of land, old women sold candy, barefoot children asked for money, and hundreds of Latin American families and tourists waited to cross. I tried to stay calm; although I had a visa to enter the country, I feared the immigration officer would not let me go. The moment came, and the immigration officer, after going over every page of my passport five times, stamped it and handed it back to me. I was able to breathe again.

Back in the office in Costa Rica, I felt impotent. I knew I could not save every child I saw in the streets of Nicaragua or the children in the hallway pictures. I realized that the most effective way for me to help Latin American children was to advocate for the protection of their human rights and to ask governments to finance programs to educate children, provide for basic needs, and eliminate poverty.

Is it effective to help one child at a time, as Casa Alianza's logo says? If the work of Casa Alianza is not complemented by public policies to develop communities, invest in education, and eradicate poverty, can the organization achieve its vision? Can the international community pressure Latin American governments to focus their national agendas on constructing a better place for children? How can we break through the apathy that prevents children's welfare from taking top priority on national and international agendas? My summer experience working in Costa Rica brought me new experiences and insights but also new questions, which stay with me as I return to my studies at Wellesley. I am, more than ever, determined to continue to search for ways to help build more equitable societies.

1. Double-underline the **thesis statement**.

2. Underline each **topic sentence**, and note which of them are examples of
   the author's main point. _____

   _____

3. Circle the **transitions** and **transitional sentences**.

4. Double-underline the sentence in the concluding paragraph that relates
   back to the introduction.

5. When have you been in, seen, or heard about a situation that was unfair?
   Give examples of how it was unfair.

Illustration in Everyday Life

The following letter was written by a town resident and father of a high
school student to the editor of the local newspaper. It shows how you
might use illustration in your everyday life to explain your point of view.

TO THE EDITOR:

   Last week, this paper reported in great detail the episode of drug dealing at the high school. An entire page was devoted to a description of what
happened, interviews with the principal and the arresting police officer,
and a disturbing picture of two handcuffed students being led out of school.
While I know that this is news, I wonder why this paper doesn't give equal
coverage to some of the many positive activities at the high school.

   Earlier this year, a group of high school students organized a fund-
raiser to help families who were left homeless after a fire. They worked
nights and weekends planning the event, a flea market. They solicited donations from residents and local businesses, and they baked items to sell.
They placed notices in the paper, the school newsletter, and buildings
around town. They worked the night before setting up, all the next day,
and the next night cleaning up. The paper reported the event in a single
paragraph on page 10.

Another example of positive behavior is the students' ongoing relationship with the senior center. Several times this year, students have organized events to entertain the seniors, including a performance by the jazz band, a humor night, and three dinners. In addition, the students organized a book drive for the senior center's library and collected hundreds of books and videos. Also, a group of students regularly visits the senior center to read to its residents. These activities weren't covered at all by this newspaper.

One last example of positive behavior is the tribute to a young teacher who suddenly passed away this year. The students put together a memorial for Ms. Sessions, with written stories and testimonials. For this event, they organized a class donation to a memorial scholarship fund and student speeches. They invited the teacher's family to the memorial, and the family was very moved.

Yes, we have problem students and, yes, they make sensational news. I don't suggest that this paper ignore the problems or gloss them over, but in the interest of balanced reporting, I ask that you give the good news equal time.

1. Double-underline the **thesis statement**.

2. Underline the **topic sentences** that present the major examples supporting the thesis.

3. Put a check mark (✔) by the **supporting details** for the major examples.

4. Circle the **transitions**.

5. What good works have students done in your community?

Write an Illustration Essay

In this section, you will write your own illustration essay based on one of the following assignments. Before you begin to write, review the four basics of good illustration on page 133.

 ASSIGNMENT 1   WRITING ABOUT COLLEGE, WORK, AND EVERYDAY LIFE

Write an illustration essay on *one* of the following topics or on a topic of your own choice.

COLLEGE

- Make a point about your college to a prospective student, and back it up with examples.
- Write about what you expect to get out of college.
- Write about something you learned in another course, and give examples to explain it to a friend who hasn't taken the course.

WORK

- Tell someone applying for a job like yours what his or her typical responsibilities might be.
- Explain to your supervisor your claim that there is too much work to be done in the time allotted.
- Demonstrate to an interviewer the following statement: "I am a very detail-oriented employee."

EVERYDAY LIFE

- Write a letter to your landlord about how your apartment's maintenance needs to be done more regularly.
- Write a letter to a friend in which you explain that your (mother, father, sibling, sweetheart) is the most (selfish, generous, irresponsible, capable) person you know.
- Name the most influential person in your life, and give examples of his or her characteristics.

 ASSIGNMENT 2   WRITING ABOUT AN IMAGE

Write an illustration essay that explains the caption of the cartoon on the next page, ". . . They all traded songs online! . . . ," and what the cartoon is demonstrating. Include examples from your own experience with music file sharing.

"THEY **ALL** DID IT! ... THEY ALL TRADED SONGS ONLINE! ..."

■ **ASSIGNMENT 3   WRITING TO SOLVE A PROBLEM**

THE PROBLEM: A good friend of yours is being sexually harassed at work by a supervisor who is not her boss. Although she has tried to let the person know that the advances are not welcome, the offending behaviors haven't stopped. Your friend is afraid that if she complains to her boss she will be fired. She asks your advice about what to do.

THE ASSIGNMENT: Working on your own or with a small group, give your friend some advice about how she could handle the problem. Try to give her several good resources to think about or use. Don't forget to include resources that her company might offer.

■ Be sure to cite and document any sources you use in your papers. For advice, see Chapter 20.

RESOURCES: Review the chart on pages 726–27 for tips about problem solving. Also, check some Web sites for ideas about dealing with sexual harassment. You can start by typing in *advice on sexual harassment* into a search engine. List any Web sites you use.

■ **ASSIGNMENT 4   WRITING ABOUT READINGS**

Reread both "Crossing Frontiers" by Rosa Fernández (p. 139) and "To the Editor" (p. 143). Then, read "On Compassion" by Barbara Lazear Ascher (p. 620). Write a short paper on one of the following:

• In an introductory paragraph, summarize Ascher's definition of compassion. Then, give two examples of compassion from both "Crossing Frontiers" and "On Compassion." In your concluding paragraph, give your own definition of compassion based on these readings and your own experience.

- In your opinion, are the characters in "On Compassion" acting compassionately or from some other motivation? Draw on examples from the essay to support your opinion.
- Using the letter to the editor as a model, write a letter that gives examples of how you or someone else has demonstrated compassion.

■ For advice on summarizing, analyzing, and synthesizing, see pages 16–19.

Follow the steps in the Writing Guide below to help you prewrite, draft, revise, and edit your illustration. Check off each step as you complete it.

WRITING GUIDE: ILLUSTRATION

STEPS IN ILLUSTRATION	HOW TO DO THE STEPS
Focus.	❏ Think about what you want to explain and who will read your illustration essay. Review the four basics of good illustration on page 133.
Prewrite to explore your topic. See Chapter 3 for more on prewriting.	❏ Use a prewriting technique to explore your topic and what is important about it to you. ❏ Narrow your ideas to a topic you can write about in a short essay, and generate examples that would demonstrate what you want to say about your topic.
Write a thesis statement. Topic + Main point = Thesis Homeschooling is beneficial to both the child and the parent. See Chapter 4 for more on writing a thesis statement.	❏ Decide what is important to you about your topic. ❏ Write a working thesis statement that presents your topic and what your point about that topic is.
Support your thesis statement. The major support points in illustration are the examples you give to demonstrate or prove your thesis. These examples will become the topic sentences for the body paragraphs.	❏ To come up with examples, assume someone has read your thesis and asked, "What do you mean?" or "Like what?" ❏ Use a prewriting technique to help you get ideas for examples. ❏ Choose at least three examples that will show your readers what you mean. ❏ Reread your prewriting to find supporting details. ❏ Find additional supporting details by asking yourself more questions: What do I mean? How? In what ways?

continued

STEPS IN ILLUSTRATION	HOW TO DO THE STEPS
See Chapter 5 for more on supporting a thesis statement.	❏ For each of your examples, add supporting details that will help your readers understand how the example demonstrates your main point.
Make a plan. See Chapter 6 for more on planning.	❏ Arrange your major support examples in order of importance, leading up to the one you think will have most impact on your readers. ❏ Make a plan or outline for your essay that includes your main support points (your examples) and supporting details for each example.
Write a draft. See Chapter 7 for more on drafting.	❏ Write an introduction that gets your readers' interest and presents your thesis statement. See if you can use one of the introductory techniques in Chapter 7. ❏ Using your outline, write a topic sentence for each of the major examples. ❏ Write body paragraphs that give specific details about each example. ❏ Write a concluding paragraph that reminds your readers of your main point and makes a final observation. ❏ Title your essay.
Revise your draft. See Chapter 8 for more on revising.	❏ Imagine that you are a reader, or ask someone else to read and comment on your draft. Look for the following: ___ Examples and details that don't really demonstrate your thesis. ___ Places where you would stop and think, "I don't get it," because there isn't enough concrete information. ___ Places where the examples need transitions to connect ideas and move a reader smoothly from one idea to the next. ❏ Reread your thesis statement. Revise it so that your point is more concrete and forceful. ❏ Reread your introduction and make changes if it is dull or weak. ❏ Reread your conclusion to make sure it is energetic and drives home your point. ❏ Make at least five changes to your draft to improve unity, support, or coherence (see pp. 96–109). ❏ Check to make sure the draft follows the four basics of good illustration.

STEPS IN ILLUSTRATION	HOW TO DO THE STEPS
Edit your draft. See Parts Four through Seven for more on editing.	❑ Use the spell checker and grammar checker on your computer, but also reread your essay carefully to catch any errors. ❑ Look for errors in grammar, spelling, or punctuation. Punctuation may be a special problem in illustration (see Chapters 36–39). ❑ Focus also on sentence fragments, run-ons, errors in subject-verb agreement, verb errors, and other areas where you know you often make mistakes. ❑ Ask yourself: Is this the best I can do?

11

Description

Writing That Creates Pictures in Words

Understand What Description Is

Description is writing that creates a clear and vivid impression of the topic. Description translates your experience of a person, place, or thing into words, often by appealing to the senses: sight, hearing, smell, taste, and touch.

▚ FOUR BASICS OF GOOD DESCRIPTION

1. It creates a main impression—an overall effect, feeling, or image—about the topic.
2. It uses specific examples to support the main impression.
3. It supports those examples with details that appeal to the senses: sight, hearing, smell, taste, and touch.
4. It brings a person, place, or physical object to life for the reader.

In the following paragraph, each number corresponds to one of the four basics of good description.

> 1 Nojoqui Falls, located near Solvang, California, is a very special place to me because it is so beautiful, and I have good memories of visiting the falls with my parents. As visitors approach the trail to the waterfalls, they see on the right a sign telling them how far they have to go.

2 The smell and sound of oak trees and pine trees at the start of the trail makes visitors feel they're up for the journey. **3** The sun hitting the trees makes the air fresh with a leafy aroma. Overhead, the wind blows through the leaves, making a soft noise. **2** Closer to the waterfall, the shade from the tall oak trees and short pine trees creates a shielding blanket. When the sun comes out, it fills the place with light, showing the vapor coming out of the trees and plants. To the left of the trail are rocks that are positioned perfectly for viewing the waterfall. **3** Water splashes as it hits the rocks. **2** To one side, a big rock with a sign describes how the waterfalls were formed. The waterfall itself is beautiful, like looking through a transparent, sparkling window of diamonds. **3** The water is so clear that objects on the other side are visible. It is like a never-ending stream of water that splashes onto the rocks.

4 All the details bring the falls to life.

—Liliana Ramirez, student

Being able to describe something or someone accurately and in detail is important not only in college but also in other settings. Describing something well involves using specific, concrete details. Here are some ways that you might use description:

COLLEGE	For a science lab report, you describe the physical and chemical properties of an element.
WORK	You write a letter to your office cleaning contractor describing the unacceptable conditions of the office.
EVERYDAY LIFE	You describe a jacket that you left at the movies to the lost-and-found department.

■ For an example of an actual description written for work, see page 157. The piece was written by the art director who is profiled in the box on page 152.

Main Point in Description

In descriptive writing, your **main point** conveys the way in which you want readers to see your topic. In other words, it conveys the main impression about your topic that you want to get across.

For example, if you are selling something, you will want to show it in the best possible light so that the reader will want to buy it. To do that, you might sum up the item's appeal in your main point (*Head-turning cherry red bike needs new home*) and then give several descriptive examples to back up that point. In college courses, you might describe something in the

Profile of Success

Daigo Fujiwara
Online Art Director

(See Daigo's Description at Work on p. 157.)

BACKGROUND: Daigo came to the United States from Japan as an exchange student when he was a senior in high school. After graduation, he wanted to attend college in the United States. However, his English-language test scores were low, so he took writing courses in English as a second language at Becker Junior College and then enrolled there.

EMPLOYER: *The Christian Science Monitor*

COLLEGE(S)/DEGREES: Becker Junior College (A.A.), Northeastern University (B.A.)

TYPES OF WRITING ON THE JOB: Summaries of articles for illustrators, memos to illustrators, follow-up letters to illustrators, notes about layout, directions for interns, forms describing necessary changes in artwork

HOW DAIGO USES DESCRIPTION: Daigo has to write detailed descriptions of what he needs for the newspaper's art program. These descriptions, called specifications, are written for freelance artists and photographers.

TEAMWORK ON THE JOB: Daigo works with editors at *The Christian Science Monitor* to develop a concept, to decide whether to use photographs or illustrations for each article, and to make individual selections.

service of showing your understanding of an issue or concept; for example, in a paper arguing that polling places need to be run more efficiently, you might describe the hectic scene at your local polling place on an election night.

Take another look at the paragraph on page 150. What if the topic sentence had been

I love Nojoqui Falls.

You wouldn't know why the writer likes the place. But the actual topic sentence conveys a main impression of the falls and lets you know why this place is important to the writer:

Nojoqui Falls, located near Solvang, California, is a very special place to me because it is so beautiful, and I have good memories of visiting the falls with my parents.

This statement provides a preview of what is to come, helping the audience read and understand the description.

The thesis statement in description typically includes the topic and the main impression about it that the writer wants to convey.

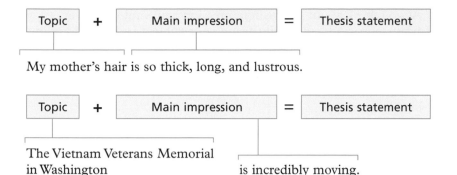

My mother's hair is so thick, long, and lustrous.

The Vietnam Veterans Memorial in Washington   is incredibly moving.

■ For online exercises on main point and support, visit Exercise Central at <bedfordstmartins.com/realessays>.

Support in Description

Good description uses specific, concrete details to present the sights, sounds, smells, tastes, and textures that contribute to vivid sensory images and a clear overall impression. These details constitute the **support** for a description. You can use prewriting techniques to generate or recall effective details that will help readers understand your experience.

SIGHT	SOUND	SMELL
Colors	Loud/soft	Sweet/sour
Shapes	Piercing/soothing	Sharp/mild
Sizes	Continuous/off-and-on	Good (like what?)
Patterns	Pleasant/unpleasant (how?)	Bad (rotten?)
Brightness	Does it sound like anything else?	New (like what?)
Does it look like anything else?	Does it sound like anything else?	Does it smell like anything else?

TASTE	TOUCH
Good (What does *good* taste like?)	Hard/soft
Bad (What does *bad* taste like?)	Liquid/solid
Bitter/sugary	Rough/smooth
Metallic	Dry/oily
Burning/spicy	Textures
Does it taste like anything else?	Does it feel like anything else?

As you think about the main impression you want to convey, ask your-self what sensory details might bring your subject to life. Add additional details to convey each sensation more accurately or vividly.

For example, one student wrote this thesis statement:

> When I take her coat from the closet, it's as if my grandmother is stand-ing beside me.

To support this main impression, the writer might include sensory de-tails about the smell of the coat (*sweet like Grandma's perfume, with a faint odor of mothballs and home-baked bread*); the feel of the fabric (*nubby and rough, with some smooth spots where the fabric has worn thin*); and the candy in the pocket (*single pieces of butterscotch that rustle in their wrappings and a round cylinder that is a roll of wintergreen Life Savers*).

Organization in Description

Description may use any of the orders of organization: **time**, **space**, or **importance**, depending on the purpose of the description. If you are de-scribing what someone or something looks like, you might use spatial order, the most common way to organize description.

You might also use order of importance. The student who is writing about her grandmother's coat might use order of importance, saving for last the sensory detail that most vividly brings her grandmother to life. Her plan for her description might be as follows:

Introduction (including thesis)
First major sensory detail (candy in the pocket)
    Supporting details
Second major sensory detail (feel of fabric)
    Supporting details
Most important sensory detail (smell of coat)
    Supporting details
    Why most important
Conclusion
    Reminds reader of the main impression (coat reminds me of grand-mother)
    Makes an observation (to others, it's just an old coat, but the feel and smell of it belong to my grandmother)

If you are writing a description in order to sell something, you might also use order of importance, saving the feature that would be most ap-pealing to potential buyers for last.

Add transitions to be certain that your readers can move smoothly from detail to detail.

Common Transitions in Description

TRANSITIONS TO SHOW ORDER OF IMPORTANCE	TRANSITIONS TO SHOW SPACE ORDER
the most	to the left/right
more	in front of/behind
even more	beyond
the strongest	above/underneath
the most intense	

Read and Analyze Description

Before writing a description essay, read the following examples of description — one each from college, the workplace, and everyday life — and answer the questions that accompany them.

Description in College

The following description essay was written by a student for a course assignment.

Photograph of My Father

Florence Bagley

This old black-and-white photograph of my father fills me with conflicting emotions. He died very young, and this photo is one of the few that my family has of him. The picture seems to show a strong, happy man, young and smiling, but to me it also reveals his weakness.

Looking at this picture of my father, I feel how much I have lost. In it, my father is sitting upright in a worn plaid easy chair. It was "his" chair, and when he was at work I'd curl up in it and smell his aftershave lotion and cigarette smoke. His pitch-black hair is so dark that it blends into the background of the photo. His eyes, though indistinct in this photo, were a deep, dark brown. Although the photo is faded around my father's face, I still can make out his strong jaw and the cleft in his chin. In the photo my father is wearing a clean white T-shirt that reveals his thick, muscular arms. Resting in the crook of his left arm is my younger brother, who was about one year old at the time. Both of them are smiling.

However, when I study the photo, my eyes are drawn to the can of beer that sits on the table next to him. Against my will, I begin to feel resentful. I have so many wonderful memories of my father. Whether he was carrying me on his shoulders, picking me up from school, or teaching me to draw, he always made time for me. All of these memories fade when I see that beer. From what I remember, he always made time for that beer as well. The smell of beer was always on him, the cool, sweating can always within reach.

In this photo, my father appears to be a strong man; however, looks are deceiving. My father died at the age of thirty-seven because he was an alcoholic. I was eleven when he died, and I really did not understand that his drinking was the reason for his death. I just knew that he left me without a father and the possibility of more memories. He should have been strong enough to stop drinking.

In spite of the resentment I may feel about his leaving me, this photo holds many loving memories as well. It is of my father—the strong, wonderful man and the alcoholic—and it is the most precious thing I own. Although I would much rather have him here, I stay connected to him when I look at it.

1. Double-underline the **thesis statement**.

2. Underline each **topic sentence**.

3. Put a check mark (✔) by the **supporting details** that back Florence's topic sentences.

4. Circle the **transitions**.

5. Does Florence's essay have the **four basics of good description**? Why or why not? _____

■ For a list of the four basics of good description, see page 150.

6. What descriptive details does Florence use to show her conflicted feelings about her father? _____

7. What other kind of sensory details might Florence have used to make her father more alive to you? _____

■ The final question after each reading in this section makes a good essay topic.

8. Who among your relatives or friends do you remember vividly? What, if any, photographs do you have of that person?

Description at Work

The following is an example of the kind of description that Daigo writes in his job as an online art director.

Daigo Fujiwara
Online Art Director

(See Daigo's Profile of Success on p. 152.)

July 2, 2004

To: Chris Hruska, Photo Researcher

Fr: Daigo Fujiwara, Art Director

Re: Coverage of Democratic National Convention

As we discussed earlier today, we want to recreate both the excitement and complexity of the Democratic National Convention for an online photo slide show presentation. For the photographic piece of the presentation, capture candid shots that span the range of activities. For example, photos of speeches should graphically reveal the speakers' emotions, gestures, and expressions. Get close-ups as well as shots from a more distant vantage point. Photos of the audience should show the crowd listening and responding, particularly responding as a group with a sense of powerful energy and enthusiasm. Show the diversity of people: ages, genders, races, differences in clothing, etc. The overall climate and environment are filled with both tension and excitement, and the photos need to capture those qualities graphically. Capitalize on the vivid colors and visual displays.

Other issues that need to be revealed in the photographs are the high level of security, showing restrictions outside of the center, including snarled traffic and armed security forces. At least some of these photos should contrast very obviously with the inside photos, showing shadows and darker images. Also, get the protesters in the midst of a demonstration, with close-ups of expressions and longer-range photos showing the size of the protest group. Because there is some controversy regarding the cordoned-off area to which the protesters are confined, examine that area closely.

The convention is a huge event, and your images need to capture the magnitude of its scope — the crowds, the highs and lows, the power of the assembly.

1. Does Daigo's memo have a **thesis statement**? _____ If so, double-underline it.

2. What does Daigo want the photo researcher to understand? _____

   _____

3. Underline the three **supporting details** that you felt were the strongest.

4. Circle five words or phrases that stood out to you and helped you understand what Daigo wanted.

5. What big event have you attended or witnessed that you could write about?

Description in Everyday Life

The following is a description of an item for sale on an online auction site. To place an item for sale, the seller has to include a written description.

This poster, "Tournée du Chat Noir," is one of the most popular posters ever created. It is from a series of French paintings and pictures a large, elegant black cat with six curved whiskers and stunning, slanted yellow eyes. Behind the cat's head is a red design or logo that looks almost as if it is a halo for the cat. The background is yellow, and to the right of the cat are the words "Tournée du Chat Noir" with the first letters of each word written in black and the rest of each word in red. The cat is perched on a red platform that contains the words "de Rodolphe Salis," though it is hard to read the second word because the cat's luxurious tail curls through it. The colors are very strong, and the poster creates a sense of whimsy combined with both contemporary and classical design. This poster is brand new and still in its original box. You won't find a better one!

1. What is the **main impression** the writer creates? _____

   _____

2. Underline some of the **specific details** that catch your attention.

3. If you were interested in purchasing this poster, what other details would you want to know about it? _____

   _____

4. Can you visualize this poster? If not, what else could the seller have told you? _____

   _____

5. If you wanted to sell one of your possessions online, how would you make it stand out so that prospective buyers would choose your item?

Write a Description Essay

In this section, you will write your own description essay based on one of the following assignments. Before you begin to write, review the four basics of good description on page 150.

ASSIGNMENT 1   WRITING ABOUT COLLEGE, WORK, AND EVERYDAY LIFE

Write a description essay on *one* of the following topics or on a topic of your own choice.

COLLEGE

- Describe your favorite place on campus so that a reader understands why you like to be there.
- Describe what you imagine a character looked like in something you have read.
- Describe an event or setting that you learned about in one of your courses.

WORK

- Describe an area of your workplace that is not worker-friendly.
- Describe a product or service that your company produces.
- Describe a specific area at work that you see every day but haven't really noticed. Look at it with new eyes.

EVERYDAY LIFE

- Describe a favorite photograph.
- Describe a favorite food without naming it. Include how it looks, smells, and tastes.
- Describe a local landmark, and have others in the class identify it after reading your description.

ASSIGNMENT 2   WRITING ABOUT AN IMAGE

Write a descriptive essay about the messy space on page 161 or about a messy space in your own home or workplace. Be sure to use plenty of details.

ASSIGNMENT 3   WRITING TO SOLVE A PROBLEM

THE PROBLEM: A wealthy alumna has given your college money for a new student lounge. The president has selected a group of students (including you) to advise him on the lounge and has asked that the group be as specific as possible in its recommendations.

THE ASSIGNMENT: Working on your own or, preferably, in a small group, write a description of an ideal student lounge to send to the president. Make sure to think about the various purposes the lounge should serve, where it should be located, what it should have in it, and what it should look like.

RESOURCES: Review the chart on pages 726–27 for advice about problem solving. Also, search the Web using the words *student lounges* or *design, student lounges.* You might also go to the library and look for design or architecture books and magazines that have pictures of different kinds of rooms. List any Web sites or publications that you consult.

 **ASSIGNMENT 4   WRITING ABOUT READINGS**

Read both Rubén Martínez's "Mexico to Mecca: The Flores Family" (p. 625) and the first seven paragraphs of Robb Walsh's "The Inkblot Test" (p. 675). The descriptions in these essays create very different impressions because of the images the writers use. First, write a sentence about each reading that characterizes the main impression that the writers create. Then, underline some details from each that helped create that impression. Reread your underlinings and write a short essay on *one* of the following:

- Analyze how each reading creates its main impression. In the introduction, you might state the main impression conveyed by each essay. Then, in the body paragraphs, discuss ways in which the essays get their main impressions across, drawing on examples from each piece.

- Write a response to Robb Walsh, the author of "The Inkblot Test," describing to him your favorite place to eat. In your introduction, refer to the diner he describes and the impression he has created. Then, tell him the name of your chosen restaurant and your main impression of it. In the body paragraphs, use some of the same sorts of images he does.

- Write to the Flores family, describing where you live and, perhaps, why it is a better place to live than the places described in Martínez's essay. In your introduction, state where you live and the main impression you have about it. In the body paragraphs, use strong images that will give the Flores family a detailed picture of the place.

Follow the steps in the Writing Guide below to help you prewrite, draft, revise, and edit your description. Check off each step as you complete it.

WRITING GUIDE: DESCRIPTION	
STEPS IN DESCRIPTION	**HOW TO DO THE STEPS**
Focus.	❑ Think about what you want to describe and the overall impression you want to give your readers. Review the four basics of good description on page 150.
Prewrite to explore your topic. See Chapter 3 for more on prewriting.	❑ Write some ideas about impressions you have when you think about your topic. ❑ Use a prewriting technique to explore these impressions, generating details that appeal to the five senses.
Write a thesis statement. The thesis statement in description includes the topic and the main impression about it that you want to convey to your reader. Topic + Main impression = Thesis My grandmother's coat evokes her image. See Chapter 4 for more on writing a thesis statement.	❑ Review your prewriting and decide what main impression you want to create. ❑ Write a thesis statement that includes your topic and main impression.

STEPS IN DESCRIPTION	HOW TO DO THE STEPS
Support your thesis statement. The major support points in description are the sensory details that, together, create the main impression. See Chapter 5 for more on supporting a thesis statement.	❑ Review your thesis statement and prewriting, and make other notes. ❑ Try to find strong sensory details that will support your main impression and make the topic come alive for your readers. ❑ Choose at least three major sensory details that will help to convey your main impression. ❑ Add specific supporting details that bring to life the major sensory details. Try to appeal to the senses: sight, sound, smell, touch, and taste.
Make a plan. See Chapter 6 for more on planning.	❑ Write a plan or an outline for your description that includes your main support points (the major sensory details) and supporting details. ❑ Organize your support using either spatial order or order of importance.
Write a draft. See Chapter 7 for more on drafting.	❑ Write an introduction that gets your readers' interest and presents your thesis statement. See if you can use one of the introductory techniques in Chapter 7. ❑ Using your outline, write a topic sentence for each of the major supporting details. ❑ Write body paragraphs that give additional details for each of the major support points. ❑ Write a concluding paragraph that reminds readers of your main point and makes a final observation about what you are describing. ❑ Title your essay.
Revise your draft. See Chapter 8 for more on revising a draft.	❑ Ask another person to read and comment on your draft. ❑ Consider how you can make your descriptions more vivid for readers. To get ideas, refer back to the categories under "Support in Description" on page 153 (sight, sound, smell, taste, and touch). ❑ Revise your thesis to make it more forceful and vivid. ❑ Make sure all of the images and details support your thesis. Add details that make your topic more alive for your readers, and cut any details that aren't relevant. ❑ Reread your introduction and make changes if it is dull. ❑ Reread your conclusion to make sure that it is energetic and convincing, and that it reminds your readers of your main impression.

continued

STEPS IN DESCRIPTION	HOW TO DO THE STEPS
(Revision, continued)	❑ Add transitions (space or importance) to connect your ideas. ❑ Make at least five changes to your draft to improve unity, support, or coherence (see pp. 96–109). ❑ Check to make sure the draft follows the four basics of good description.
Edit your draft. See Parts Four through Seven for more on editing.	❑ Use the spell checker and grammar checker on your computer, but also reread your essay carefully to catch any errors. ❑ Look for errors in grammar, spelling, or punctuation. Run-on sentences and the proper use of adjectives and adverbs can be a particular problem in description, so focus first on those. Then, read for fragments, errors in subject-verb agreement, verb errors, and other areas where you know you often make mistakes. ❑ Ask yourself: Is this the best I can do?

12

Process Analysis

Writing That Explains How Things Happen

Understand What Process Analysis Is

Process analysis either explains how to do something (so your readers can do it) or explains how something works (so your readers can understand it). Both types of process analysis present the steps involved in the process.

▪▪ FOUR BASICS OF GOOD PROCESS ANALYSIS

1. It helps readers either perform the steps themselves or understand how something works.
2. It presents the essential steps in the process.
3. It explains the steps in detail.
4. It arranges the steps in a logical order (usually in chronological order).

In the following paragraph, each number corresponds to one of the four basics of good process analysis.

1 The Web site MapQuest.com can get you from where you are to where you want to go in several easy steps. **2** First, type in the Web address (www.mapquest.com) and wait for the home page to appear. Then, click on the link titled "Directions." You will be prompted to type in your starting address and the address of your destination. **3** It's

4 Steps arranged in a logical order

165

4 Steps arranged in a logical order

important to supply complete information, including the street address, city, and state (or zip). **2** Next, click on "Get Directions." This screen will present you with written directions and a map showing the route to take. **3** The written directions guide you step-by-step and include the mileage for each step. The map allows you to zoom in and out to get a better view. Although sometimes I have found errors in them, MapQuest directions are usually correct and take me exactly where I want to go.

Whenever you give someone directions about how to do something or explain how something works, you are using process analysis. Here are some ways you might use process analysis:

<table>
<tr><td>COLLEGE</td><td>In an information management course, you write an essay explaining the process for implementing a new data management system.</td></tr>
<tr><td>WORK</td><td>The office has a new security system, and you are asked to write a memo explaining to employees how to access their work areas during and after normal business hours.</td></tr>
<tr><td>EVERYDAY LIFE</td><td>You write directions telling your child how to operate the microwave oven.</td></tr>
</table>

■ For an example of an actual process analysis written for work, see page 172. The piece was written by the human re-sources director who is profiled in the box on page 167.

Main Point in Process Analysis

Your **purpose** in process analysis is to clearly explain the process so that readers can either do the process themselves or understand how it works. Your **main point** lets your readers know what you think about that process—for example, whether it's easy or complicated. The topic sentence of the paragraph on page 165 does just that:

> The Web site MapQuest.com can get you from where you are to where you want to go in several easy steps.

A thesis statement for a process analysis usually identifies the process and the point you want to make about it. The thesis should also suggest what you want your readers to know or learn about the process.

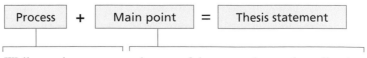

Process + Main point = Thesis statement

Wallpapering a room takes careful preparation and application.

Maureen Letendre

Director of Human Resources and Organizational Development

(See Maureen's Process Analysis at Work on p. 172.)

BACKGROUND: After graduating from the commercial studies program at her high school, Maureen worked as a clerk. She then got a job at Digital Equipment Corporation's clerical placement group, where she was given many promotions because of her hard work and commitment. In each position, she found a mentor to help her. Maureen is now human resources director for a construction and mill company.

EMPLOYER: Woodmeister Corporation

COLLEGE(S)/DEGREES: Framingham State College (B.A.)

TYPES OF WRITING ON THE JOB: Personnel-related reports and memos, employee development plans, explanations to managers of how to implement new plans, and summaries of meetings, among other things. Maureen also publishes a company newsletter, for which she writes many articles. She is particularly careful writing e-mail messages because, although they seem informal and casual, the e-mails often become part of a permanent record.

HOW MAUREEN USES PROCESS ANALYSIS: Maureen uses process analysis when she writes to managers and employees to explain how to implement a new program or policy or to explain how a new plan works.

TEAMWORK ON THE JOB: Woodmeister must coordinate work done on the same project by the millwork group and the construction team.

In process analysis, it helps readers to know from the start what the process and the purpose are, so be sure to include your thesis statement in your introduction.

■ For online exercises on main point and support, visit Exercise Central at <bedfordstmartins.com/realessays>.

Support in Process Analysis

A clear process analysis presents all the essential steps in the process; these steps constitute the **major support**. Each step is explained by supporting details. For example, the writer of the thesis *Learning how to use the advanced functions on my computer is frustrating* might identify several essential steps and the details to explain each step.

ESSENTIAL STEPS

- **Step 1:** Using the Help feature or a tutorial

  SUPPORTING DETAILS

  Trying to find useful help

  Trying a few options

  Following those options

  Finding that none work

- **Step 2:** Consulting a reference book such as *Word 2003 for Dummies*

  SUPPORTING DETAILS

  Trying to find the function in the table of contents or index

  First finding advice that isn't really what you need

  Finding the right explanation

  Deciding that you don't want to use the function

- **Step 3:** Trying to undo automatic functions

  SUPPORTING DETAILS

  Reading about the Undo function and trying it once, trying it again

  Finally calling a friend

  Etc.

Sometimes you will write about a process that you are very familiar with but that your readers are not. Make sure to include all of the essential steps in the process, particularly if you want your readers to be able to do something on the basis of your instructions. Read the following process analysis example. What essential step is missing?

> Please do the laundry before I get home. The clothes are in the baskets next to the machine. One of the baskets has all dark clothes. Put these in the washing machine, with the heaviest, biggest items on the bottom. You can fill the machine to the top, but don't mash the clothes down. If you put in too many clothes, the machine will stall. As you load the machine, check to make sure that there aren't any white things mixed in by mistake. After all of the clothes are in, set the level on Extra High. Then, turn the knob on the left to Warm Wash, Cool Rinse. Press the Start button. After about half an hour, the laundry should be done, and you can transfer it to the dryer.

MISSING STEP: _____

Organization in Process Analysis

Because process analysis explains how to do something or how something works, it usually uses **chronological (time) order**. Start with the first step, and then explain each step in order as it should occur. The plan for a process analysis often looks like this:

Introduction (including thesis)

First step

    Details about the first step

Second step

    Details about the second step

Third step

    Details about the third step

Conclusion

Add transitional words and sentences to your essay to help readers follow each step in the process.

Common Transitions in Process Analysis

after	eventually	meanwhile	soon
as	finally	next	then
at last	first	now	when
before	last	second	while
during	later	since	

Read and Analyze Process Analysis

Before writing your own process analysis, read the following examples of process analysis—one each from college, the workplace, and everyday life—and answer the questions that accompany them.

Process Analysis in College

Taking Notes

David DePalma

I have this recurring nightmare. It's the morning of my midterm exam in history, and I've overslept. I rush out of the house with my hair still wet, run every red light on the way to school, and park in a handicapped space, chancing a ticket, to get to class. Even so, I'm twenty minutes late, and my teacher glares at me as she hands me a test that looks about one hundred pages long. "Good luck," she says, smirking. *I'll be okay,* I think. *This test is open notes.* I pull out my notebook and flip it open. But all of the pages are blank. I didn't take notes, I realize! I don't remember anything that the teacher talked about! Fortunately, I wake up and all is well; my notebooks are filled with my bad penmanship. Taking good notes is essential to succeed in college, but not all students know how to take notes effectively.

First of all, don't try to write down everything the teacher says. It's impossible to do, and you'll just get behind and miss important information. You need to filter information as you listen, which means paying close attention. For example, if your economics teacher is lecturing on supply and demand and begins telling the class about the movie he saw last night, chances are good that that information won't be on the test. If you listen actively, you can get a sense of what kinds of information will be important to remember, such as dates or statistics. Also, develop some kind of shorthand. Use abbreviations or symbols for words you use often, such as "w/" for *with* and "dept" for *department* and "info" for *information.* This will save some time, but be sure to use a code that you will remember how to decode later.

Second, pay attention to signals that the teacher gives you, and organize your notes as you go. Often, for example, a teacher will say, "This is a key idea" or "This was a turning point." Words such as *important, essential, key, central,* and *primary* are clues that the information should be written down. Also, if the teacher enumerates items in a list (*first, second, third*) or writes something on the board, it's a dead giveaway that you need to include it in your notes. In addition, it helps to organize your notes as you go. If the teacher changes to a new subject, skip a line and write an asterisk in the left margin so that you can easily see the division. Then, indent and keep related notes in the same area. Underline ideas that you have trouble with so that you can come back to them easily. It sometimes helps to leave a little blank space, too, so that you can add to your notes after class.

Finally, once you have taken notes, review them often. Begin by looking them over right after class to see if you can read your own handwriting and abbreviations, and add anything that you think will help when you come back to them later. In one experiment, students who reviewed their notes right after a lecture remembered one-and-a-half times more than students who didn't review. Also, it is important that you review your notes frequently. Don't wait until the night before a test; studies have shown that we forget 80 percent of what we read or hear after just two weeks! To master the material, you need repeated exposure to it. If you wait for two weeks to look at your notes, there's a good chance the ideas will look like Greek to you.

Following this advice won't guarantee you all A's, but it will help you become a better, more organized student. Taking good notes is an important, essential, key skill for doing well in college and anywhere else where you want to remember the material.

1. Double-underline the **thesis statement**.

2. Underline the **topic sentences** that present each major step of the process.

3. Put a check mark (✔) by the **supporting details** that David gives to help the reader understand each step of the process.

4. Circle the **transitions** (words, phrases, and sentences) that David uses to guide readers from one step to the next.

5. Double-underline the sentence in the last paragraph that links the concluding paragraph to the thesis statement.

■ For a list of the four basics of good process analysis, see page 165.

6. Does David's essay have the **four basics of good process analysis**? Why or why not? _____

_____

■ The final question after each reading in this section makes a good essay topic.

7. David writes about a process that is important for success in college. What other important process in college could you write about?

Maureen Letendre

Director of Human Resources and Organizational Development

(See Maureen's Profile of Success on p. 167.)

Process Analysis at Work

Maureen wrote the following piece on communication for her company's newsletter. Because two separate divisions of the company are trying to merge successfully into one, Maureen wants to help employees develop good communication skills.

Did You Say What I Think You Said?
The Challenge of Effective Communications

Maureen Letendre

Why is it that when we speak not everyone hears what we intend, and how can we improve our communications? We can start by learning what the different levels of communication are and move, then, to the process of effective communication.

According to Christine Mockler Casper, author of *From Now On with Passion: A Guide to Emotional Intelligence* (87), there are basically four levels of communication.

- The first and most basic level is the **superficial level**. It happens naturally, for instance, when you pass someone and say, "Hi, how are you?" It's unlikely that you are really interested in that person's current health; it's merely a greeting.

- The next level is the **factual level**. These conversations include observations such as "Worcester Polytechnic Institute (WPI) offers a degree program in construction management." This is a fact, but it hasn't told you anything about the person who stated it.

- When individuals begin to relate what they are thinking, they enter into the next level: the **thought level**. An example of this type of communication would be "WPI offers a degree program in construction management. For a while now, I've been thinking about getting my degree, and construction has always interested me. I think I'll get more information on WPI's program." Now the listener is beginning to learn something about the person speaking.

- The most critical level of communication is the **feeling level**. This is where you hear things that help you to understand what a person is feeling. In our example, it would go something like this: "WPI offers a degree program in construction management. I'm thinking about applying for that program. I've been working for a company called Woodmeister Corp., and I really feel good about working there. I never realized how satisfied I would feel by helping people to achieve their goal of building their own home."

  Now the listener is learning more. Why is that important? Because the more you learn about the speaker's intent, the quicker you will understand what it means to you and how it impacts what you need to do with the information.

High-performing organizations communicate at the thought and feeling levels. The goal is to use all levels well, and that involves understanding the process of effective communication.

THE PROCESS OF EFFECTIVE COMMUNICATION

- Think about how to make the information clear to the person or people to whom you are speaking, considering who they are and what your purpose is in speaking with them. In other words, don't use the same words or speech in all contexts, for all people.
- Let people know what your subject is right from the start.
- Be attentive and maintain focus. Maintain good eye contact and lean into the conversation.
- Listen using all your senses, not just your hearing. Pay attention to tone and inflection. It's not always what is said but how it's

delivered. Be aware of body language (posture, facial expression, eye movement)—both yours and that of the other person.

- Be sure your thoughts and expressions are clear; if you are in doubt, ask.
- Summarize key points you have made or key points you have understood.
- If follow-up is needed, make that clear and set a time frame.

Stay tuned for more information in next month's newsletter, which will address, more specifically, how some of these communication issues affect us in our day-to-day dealings with each other at Woodmeister, present some possible solutions, and offer a model that will help us to think about what happens when we communicate.

Work Cited

Casper, Christine Mockler. *From Now On with Passion: A Guide to Emotional Intelligence.* Fort Bragg: Cypress House, 2001.

1. What is the **purpose** of Maureen's memo? _____

   _____

2. Double-underline the **thesis statement**.

3. Put a check mark (✔) next to where the steps of good communication start.

4. Why does Maureen provide details about the next newsletter? _____

   _____

   _____

5. Think of someone who is a particularly good (or bad) communicator. What parts of the process does that person use (or omit)?

Process Analysis in Everyday Life

The following process analysis provides practical advice on how to do something—in this case, do well at a job fair.

How to Succeed at the Job Fair

The job market is tight. You want to make the most of this great opportunity to meet with recruiters who are actively hiring for entry-level jobs. There are several good strategies for succeeding at a job fair and getting you off to a good start with your job search.

Even before the job fair you need to prepare. Recruiters will ask you lots of questions, and you want to be able to answer them quickly and intelligently. After all, you are there to market yourself as the best candidate for the job.

First, know about the industry and occupation that you want to go into. Be able to answer questions about it. Go online and get some information about the companies who you want to see at the job fair. You want the interviewer to know that you've thought about and done some research on your career choice.

Next, you will be meeting a lot of people, and you might practice a good icebreaker to start off the interview. Prepare a short, one-minute introduction that starts with your name. Then, give a brief overview of your background, and finish with your career goals. Practice your introduction aloud to yourself before the fair so that you sound relaxed and confident. Smile, and don't rush.

Finally, before the fair, make sure that you develop a good, current résumé that is factual and error-free and contains a telephone number where you can be reached directly. Make sure you bring at least twenty copies printed on good paper.

On the day of the fair, dress professionally. Men should wear either a suit or a good pair of slacks, a button-down shirt, and a tie. Women can wear a suit or a plain skirt (knee-length), hosiery (bare legs won't work), and a conservative blouse with minimal jewelry.

When you actually meet the recruiter, make direct eye contact and shake hands firmly. Listen to all questions and think about your answers before speaking. Finally, make sure you thank the interviewer for taking the time to talk with you.

Before you leave, always ask the recruiter for a business card. You will need it in order to complete the final step in the job fair process: writing a thank you letter. In the letter, thank the recruiter for his or her time, remind him of your qualifications, and provide contact information.

Following this process will help you have a successful job fair experience and will give you experience that you can apply to other interviews. With a little preparation, you will do well and better your chances of breaking into this tight job market. Good luck!

> —Adapted from an article in a *Boston Globe* advertising supplement,
> "Boston Career Connections," April 1, 2004

1. Double-underline the **thesis statement**.

2. Underline the **topic sentences** that present each of the major steps.

3. Put a check mark () by the **supporting details** about each step.

4. How is the essay organized? _____

5. Did you learn anything new by reading this essay? If so, what? If not, how have you prepared for and participated in job fairs?

Write a Process Analysis Essay

In this section, you will write your own process analysis essay based on one of the following assignments. Before you begin to write, review the four basics of good process analysis on page 165.

▌ ASSIGNMENT 1   WRITING ABOUT COLLEGE, WORK, AND EVERYDAY LIFE

Write a process analysis essay on *one* of the following topics or on a topic of your own choice.

COLLEGE

- How to apply for financial aid
- How to study for a test
- How (a process in your major field of study) works

WORK

- How to do one of your major tasks at work
- How to get a job at your place of work
- How to get fired/how to get promoted

EVERYDAY LIFE

- How to calm down or get to sleep
- How to do (something you do well)
- How to break up with someone

ASSIGNMENT 2   WRITING ABOUT AN IMAGE

The person whose hands appear in this photograph is obviously in the middle of something. What is the "something," and what is the process? You can either look up the "something" online to get the steps of the process, or you can write about some other process familiar to you.

ASSIGNMENT 3   WRITING TO SOLVE A PROBLEM

THE PROBLEM: Your friend is in an awful situation. Because of her great grades in high school, she was accepted at an excellent and expensive private university and received a lot of money in student aid. Even so, she began falling behind with tuition payments and had to drop out. At this point, her full loan payment came due. She wanted to transfer to a public university where the tuition was much lower and the salary from her part-time job would go further. However, when she requested that a transcript be sent by the private university to the public one, she was told her records would not be sent until she had paid the charges on her loan. She very much wants to continue her studies but doesn't know how to manage this financially.

THE ASSIGNMENT: Working on your own or in a small group, research the options your friend has, and write some steps she could take to resolve her problem and be able to continue her education.

RESOURCES: Review the chart on pages 726–27 for advice on problem solving. Additionally, the Internet has many sites that offer advice on repayment of student loans. A good one to start with is at <**www.credit.about .com/cs/loansstudent/a/012800.htm**>. Or try typing *student loan repayment* into a search engine. List any Web sites that you use.

ASSIGNMENT 4   WRITING ABOUT READINGS

Review three readings: David DePalma's "Taking Notes" (p. 169), Maureen Letendre's "Did You Say What I Think You Said?" (p. 172) and the section on critical reading in Chapter 1 (pp. 4–13). Then, write a short paper titled "Reading, Note Taking, and Communicating: Different Activities, Similar Processes." In your paper, summarize the process that each reading presents, and then prove that the processes are, in fact, similar. Draw examples from each of the readings. Your audience for this paper is a student who doesn't understand how to do any of the activities effectively and who has no idea how the three are related. Writing this paper will help your audience, but it will also help you understand these skills that are so essential for success in college and beyond.

Follow the steps in the Writing Guide on the next page to help you prewrite, draft, revise, and edit your process analysis. Check off each step as you complete it.

WRITING GUIDE: PROCESS ANALYSIS	
STEPS IN PROCESS ANALYSIS	**HOW TO DO THE STEPS**
Focus.	❏ Think about the process you want to explain to your readers, the steps involved in the process, and the main point you want to make. Review the four basics of good process analysis on page 165.
Prewrite to explore your topic. See Chapter 3 for more on prewriting.	❏ Choose a process you know about and understand. ❏ Use a prewriting technique to jot down some ideas about the steps in the process and about how to explain the process to readers who aren't familiar with it.
Write a thesis statement. The thesis statement in a process analysis usually identifies the process and the main point you want to make about that process. Process + Main point = Thesis Learning how to use the advanced functions on my computer is frustrating. See Chapter 4 for more on writing a thesis statement.	❏ Decide on the main point you want to make about the process. ❏ Decide what you want your readers to know or learn about this process. ❏ Once you know your main point, write a thesis statement that contains both the process (your topic) and your main point about that process.
Support your thesis statement. The major support points in a process analysis are the essential steps involved in explaining how to do the process or showing how the process works. See Chapter 5 for more on supporting a thesis statement.	❏ List all the essential steps in the process. ❏ Review your thesis statement, and drop any steps that are not essential. ❏ Choose the steps that are necessary for readers to perform this activity or to understand how it works. ❏ Add details that describe the steps and that would help your readers do this activity correctly. ❏ Imagine that you are not already familiar with the process, and ask yourself whether you could do it or understand how it works after reading the essay.
Make a plan. See Chapter 6 for more on planning.	❏ Arrange the steps in the process in chronological order. ❏ Make a plan for your process analysis that includes your major support points (the steps in the process) and supporting details.
Write a draft. See Chapter 7 for more on drafting.	❏ Write an introduction that gets your readers' interest and presents your thesis statement. See if you can use one of the introductory techniques in Chapter 7.

continued

STEPS IN PROCESS ANALYSIS	HOW TO DO THE STEPS
(Drafting, continued)	❏ Write topic sentences for the essential steps in the process, supported by explanations of those steps. ❏ Add time transitions to move readers smoothly from one step to another. ❏ Write a concluding paragraph that has energy, refers back to your point about the process, and makes a final observation or recommendation. ❏ Title your essay.
Revise your draft. See Chapter 8 for more on revising a draft.	❏ Ask another person to read and comment on your draft. ❏ Revise your thesis to make it more energetic. ❏ Reread the body of your essay to make sure you haven't left out any essential steps. Try to imagine that you have no idea of how to perform the process or how the process works. Add any details that would make the steps clearer, and cut details that aren't relevant. ❏ Reread your introduction and make changes if it is dull or weak. ❏ Reread your conclusion to make sure that it is energetic, convincing, and reminds your readers of your main impression. ❏ Add time transitions to connect your ideas. ❏ Make at least five changes to your draft to improve unity, support, or coherence (see pp. 96–109). ❏ Check to make sure the draft follows the four basics of good process analysis.
Edit your draft. See Parts Four through Seven for more on editing.	❏ Use the spell checker and grammar checker on your computer, but also reread your essay carefully to catch any errors. ❏ Look for errors in grammar, spelling, or punctuation. Fragments and run-on sentences can be a particular problem in process analysis, so focus first on those. Then, read for errors in subject-verb agreement, verb errors, and other areas where you know you often make mistakes. ❏ Ask yourself: Is this the best I can do?

13

Classification

Writing That Puts Things into Groups

Understand What Classification Is

Classification is writing that organizes, or sorts, people or items into categories.

The **organizing principle** for a classification is *how* you sort the people or items, not the categories themselves. The organizing principle is directly related to the **purpose** of your classification. For example, you might sort clean laundry (your purpose) using one of the following organizing principles (how you achieve your purpose): by ownership (yours, your roommate's, and so on) or by where it goes (the bedroom, the bathroom).

▶ FOUR BASICS OF GOOD CLASSIFICATION

1. It makes sense of a group of people or items by organizing them into meaningful categories.
2. It has a purpose for sorting the people or items.
3. It uses a single organizing principle.
4. It gives detailed examples or explanations of the people or items that fit into each category.

In the following paragraph, each number corresponds to one of the four basics of good classification.

When a person **2** decides to purchase an **3** Apple computer, there are three types to consider. **1** The first type is Apple's most popular computer, the iMac. **4** This computer is specifically designed for the

181

user who primarily wants access to the Internet. Apple made the iMac very easy to set up and use; in fact, it takes less than ten minutes to unpack the equipment and get started using the Internet. Also, the iMac has a very distinctive look. The translucent plastic that houses the computer is available in a wide range of colors. **1** For the person who wants a more powerful computer, the Power Mac G5 is the best choice. **4** This model is available in four different speeds; the speed the user should choose depends on the type of work he or she wants to perform. For example, the typical user might choose the entry-level G5 for basic functions, while a professional graphic artist might prefer the high-end model for its speed in using desktop publishing programs. **1** The third type of Apple computer is the iBook. **4** This is Apple's laptop computer. The iBook is ideal for traveling business professionals, or it may be a good choice for college students. What sets the iBook apart from the iMac and G5 is that it runs on batteries, or it can be plugged into an outlet using an adapter. The iBook costs a little more than the iMac, but for those who want portability, it is well worth the extra money. Each of these models is unique, but their ease of use makes them a wise choice for anyone interested in purchasing a computer.

—Joe Neat, Student

Whenever you organize or sort things to make sense of them, you are classifying them. Here are some ways that you might use classification:

■ For an example of an actual classification written for work, see page 188. The piece was written by the consultant who is profiled in the box on page 183.

COLLEGE	In a nursing course, you discuss three types of antibiotics used to treat infections.
WORK	For a report on inventory at a software store, you list the types of software carried and report how many of each type you have in stock.
EVERYDAY LIFE	You look at the types of payment plans that are available with your car loan.

Main Point in Classification

The **main point** in classification uses a single **organizing principle** to sort items in a way that serves the writer's purpose. The categories must be useful—helping to achieve the purpose of the classification. Imagine the following situation, in which a classification system isn't logical or useful.

Profile of Success

Giovanni Bohorquez

Technical Consultant

(See Giovanni's Classification at Work on p. 188.)

BACKGROUND: At the age of eleven, Giovanni left Colombia and came to the United States to live with his father in New Jersey. His father was poor, so Giovanni worked several jobs and was earning significant wages by the age of twelve. After high school, Giovanni went to a community college and then transferred to the University of California–Los Angeles (UCLA), where he finished his bachelor's degree. He then went to work for Ernst & Young, a financial consulting company, and is now pursuing a master's degree in business administration (M.B.A.) at UCLA's Anderson School while continuing to work.

EMPLOYER: Hewlett-Packard Consulting

COLLEGE(S)/DEGREES: El Camino College (A.A.), UCLA (B.S.)

TYPES OF WRITING ON THE JOB: Proposals, project plan reports, contracts, sales letters, documentation of business processes, change order reports, e-mail

HOW GIOVANNI USES CLASSIFICATION: Giovanni writes many analyses and reports for his clients. He recently completed a detailed analysis of the types of emerging technologies.

TEAMWORK ON THE JOB: Giovanni's analytical work often involves both Hewlett-Packard Consulting employees and employees from the client's company. Teamwork is essential in compiling all of the technical information necessary to generate a thorough analysis.

You go into your video store to find that it has been rearranged. The signs indicating the location of different types of videos—comedy, action, drama—are gone. You don't know how the videos are now classified, so you don't know where to look for what you want.

When you ask the clerk at the desk how to find a video, she says, "The videos over on this side are arranged by length of the film, starting with the shortest. The videos on the other side are arranged alphabetically by the leading actor's last name."

This new arrangement is confusing for three reasons:

- It doesn't serve the purpose of helping customers find videos.
- It doesn't sort things into useful categories. (Who's likely to select a video based on its length?)
- It doesn't have a single organizing principle. (Even if you know the length of the video and the actor's last name, you still don't know on which side of the store to start looking.)

The following diagram shows how videos at most stores are classified to serve a purpose, using a single organizing principle.

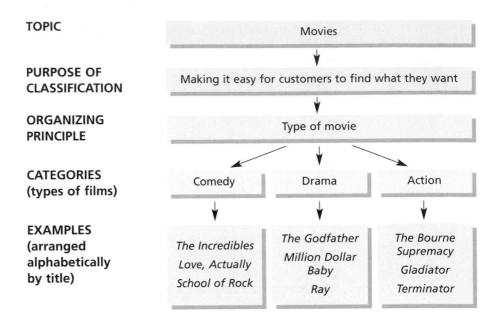

The following examples show how thesis statements for classification express the organizing principle and purpose.

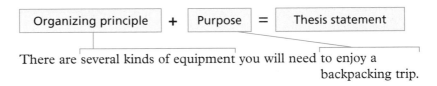

In addition to the purpose and organizing principle, a thesis statement in a classification may also include the categories that will be explained.

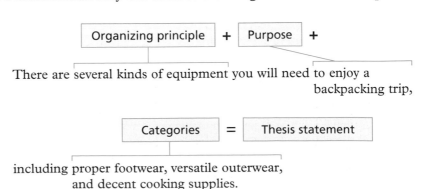

■ For online exercises on main point and support, visit Exercise Central at <bedfordstmartins .com/realessays>.

Support in Classification

The **primary support** consists of the categories that serve the purpose of the classification. The **supporting details** are examples or explanations of what is in each category.

The **categories** in classification are the "piles" into which the writer sorts a topic (the items to be classified). These categories will become the topic sentences for the body paragraphs of the essay.

TOPIC	College costs
THESIS STATEMENT	Tuition is only one of the many costs of going to college.
ORGANIZING PRINCIPLE	Types of costs other than tuition
PURPOSE	To show the different kinds of costs and their significance
CATEGORIES/ PRIMARY SUPPORT	Fees, costs of course materials, transportation expenses

The **examples** are the various items that fall within each category. These are important because readers may not be familiar with your categories.

CATEGORY: Fees

> **EXAMPLES/SUPPORTING DETAILS:** General student fee assessed to each student, lab fees, computer fees

CATEGORY: Costs of course materials

> **EXAMPLES/SUPPORTING DETAILS:** Costs of books, lab manuals, software

CATEGORY: Transportation expenses

> **EXAMPLES/SUPPORTING DETAILS:** Costs of gas, parking, bus fare

Organization in Classification

Classification can be organized in different ways depending on its purpose. For example, read the thesis statements and purposes that follow:

THESIS STATEMENT	The high costs of college make higher education impossible for many students.
PURPOSE	To show how the kinds of costs are too expensive

How might this classification be organized? _____

THESIS STATEMENT	My daughter has every kind of mess imaginable in her room, making it clear that she needs a lesson in taking care of her space and her things.
PURPOSE	To prove the need for the lesson by describing the messes

How might this classification be organized? _____

THESIS STATEMENT	During my teenage years, I adopted three distinct styles.
PURPOSE	To show how a person's style changed

How might this classification be organized? _____

As you write your essay, the following transitions may be helpful in leading from one category to the next or from one example to another.

Common Transitions in Classification

another	first, second, third, and so on
another kind	for example
for instance	

Read and Analyze Classification

Before writing a classification essay, read the following examples—one each from college, the workplace, and everyday life—and answer the questions that accompany them.

Classification in College

The following student essay was written for an English composition class.

Blood Type and Personality
Danny Fitzgerald

In Japan, the question "What's your blood type?" is as common as "What's your sign?" in the United States. Some Japanese researchers claim that people's personalities can be classified by their blood types. You may be skeptical about this method of classification, but don't judge its validity before you read the descriptions the researchers have put together. Do you see yourself?

If you have blood type O, you are a leader. When you see something you want, you strive to achieve your goal. You are passionate, loyal, and self-confident, and you are often a trendsetter. Your enthusiasm for projects and goals spreads to others, who happily follow your lead. When you want something, you may be ruthless about getting it or blind to how your actions affect others.

Another blood type, A, is typically associated with a social, people person. You like people and work well with them. You are sensitive, patient, compassionate, and affectionate. You are a good peacekeeper because you want everyone to be happy. In a team situation, you resolve conflicts and keep things on a smooth course. Sometimes type A's are stubborn and find it difficult to relax. They may find it uncomfortable to do things alone.

People with type B blood are usually individualists who like to do things on their own. You may be creative and adaptable, and you usually say exactly what you mean. Although you can adapt to situations, you may choose not to do so because of your strong independent streak. You may prefer working on your own to being part of a team.

The final blood type is AB, and if you have this blood type, you are a natural entertainer. You draw people to you because of your charm and easygoing nature. AB's are usually calm and controlled, tactful and fair. On the downside, though, they may take too long to make decisions. And they may procrastinate, putting off tasks until the last minute.

Classifying people's personalities by blood type seems very unusual until you examine what researchers have found. Most people find the descriptions fairly accurate. When you think about it, classification by blood type isn't any more far-fetched than classification by horoscope sign. What will they think of next? Classification by hair color?

1. Double-underline the **thesis statement**.

2. What is Danny's single organizing principle? _____

3. What **introduction techniques** does Danny use to get the reader's attention? _____

4. Underline the **topic sentences** that present the categories.

5. Put a check mark (✔) by the supporting details.

■ For a list of the four basics of good classification, see page 181.

6. Does Danny's essay have the **four basics of good classification**? Why or why not? _____

7. What other methods are used to classify people by personality?

**Giovanni
Bohorquez**

Technical Consultant

*(See Giovanni's
Profile of Success
on p. 183.)*

Classification at Work

The following essay was part of Giovanni's application to the Anderson School, the graduate business school at UCLA. Notice how Giovanni presents the types of key skills he has learned.

One day I would like to manage a high-tech product, so over the last ten years I have learned the types of skills that product managers must have: production management, system design, and entrepreneurism.

I learned the first type of skill—production management—when I worked as a plant controller for three years with control over production of modem components and responsibility for more than one hundred employees. As a plant controller, I managed the raw materials, created production schedules, and oversaw inventory.

I learned the second type of skill—system design—by designing and implementing Enterprise Resource Planning (ERP) systems, which are integrated information-sharing software programs that serve the needs of all departments within a single company. Companies such as ConAgra, SUN, and Genentech are currently benefiting from systems that I have designed.

The third type of skill—entrepreneurism—I learned by consulting with start-up and middle-market projects. Although entrepreneurial environments need to cultivate creativity and vision, they also need to recognize and meet the realities of a business environment. Many good entrepreneurial ventures fail because, though they have a wealth of good ideas, they do not understand accounting, production, and the need for good systems. As a consultant, I have been able to help entrepreneurs recognize business necessities.

With these types of key skills, I am closer to being able to attain my goal of managing a product. I have worked steadily and purposefully to acquire these types of skills, and now I am ready to learn the other skills that will allow me to successfully manage a product. It is for this reason that I am applying to the Anderson School, where I believe I can develop the expertise I need to become a well-rounded, responsible member of the business community.

1. What is Giovanni's **purpose** for writing? _____

_____

2. Double-underline the **thesis statement**.

3. What is Giovanni's organizing principle? _____

4. Underline the **topic sentences** that present the categories.

5. What observation does the concluding paragraph make? _____

_____

_____

6. If you were writing an application essay about the skills you have, what skills would you include?

■ The final question after each reading in this section makes a good essay topic.

Classification in Everyday Life

The following essay was written by a student who considers herself an expert in yard sale bargain hunting.

Yard Sale Treasures
Susan Robinson

When I started attending yard sales several years ago, I bought a lot of items that were inexpensive but turned out to be low-quality junk. Now I search only for the treasures that I know are real deals. As part of my education as a bargain hunter, I have learned to look for three kinds of items.

The first kind of yard sale treasure is children's items. You can find lots of nearly new equipment, furniture, toys, and clothing at yard sales.

Often, there's nothing wrong with the merchandise; owners just want to sell items that take up room in the house or the basement once their children have outgrown them. Last year, one of my friends found a nearly new name-brand baby stroller at a yard sale and paid $15 for it. Others have found good cribs, swings, and baby clothing that has never been worn—all at bargain prices.

Another treasure I've come to respect is costume jewelry. People tend to collect tons of inexpensive jewelry over the years, and jewelry doesn't wear out. In the $1 box at a recent yard sale, I bought a "pearl" necklace and matching earrings for $2. They weren't real pearls, but they looked so real that no one but an expert would know the difference. In the same box, my friend found a "ruby" ring that looked authentic, with a small, well-shaped stone and an antique-like setting.

A third kind of treasure is kitchenware of all sorts, especially sets of plates, sets of glasses, serving pieces, and vases. When you are setting up an apartment, there is no better place than a yard sale to find dishes and glasses. Maybe a set of dishes that originally had twelve pieces is down to ten, but who really needs twelve of the same dish?

When people have yard sales, they put out all kinds of things, and shoppers should beware of junk. Instead, look for the things that you know are good values, and avoid the odd knickknacks or old Christmas decorations or worn-down shoes. You can get great bargains at yard sales if you choose carefully. A word of caution to the buyer of junk: You will soon have to have your own yard sale.

1. Double-underline the **thesis statement**.

2. What is Susan's **organizing principle**? _____

3. What three **categories** does Susan use? _____

_____

4. Underline the **topic sentences** that present the categories.

5. Circle the **transitions**.

6. What kinds of items have you seen at a yard sale or a flea market? What kinds of items have you bought?

Write a Classification Essay

In this section, you will write your own classification essay based on *one* of the following assignments. Before you begin to write, review the four basics of good classification on page 181.

 ASSIGNMENT 1   WRITING ABOUT COLLEGE, WORK, AND EVERYDAY LIFE

Write a classification essay on *one* of the following topics or on a topic of your own choice.

COLLEGE

- Types of degree programs
- Types of students
- Skim a textbook from another class to find a topic that is broken into categories to help readers understand it. Then, in your own words, summarize the classification of the topic.

WORK

- Types of work spaces
- Types of customers or clients
- Types of skills needed for a particular job. (It would be useful to research what skills are needed for the kind of job *you* want to get.)

EVERYDAY LIFE

- Types of drivers
- Types of restaurants in your town
- Types of cell phones

ASSIGNMENT 2   WRITING ABOUT AN IMAGE

Write an essay that describes how the merchandise in this store is classified. Be sure to use at least three categories, and give examples of items in
each category.

ASSIGNMENT 3   WRITING TO SOLVE A PROBLEM

THE PROBLEM: When you were a freshman in college, you received a flood of credit-card offers, and you signed up for three credit cards. You have charged most of your expenses rather than paying cash, and over time you have run up a big debt, partly from the charges themselves and partly from the interest that has mounted every month. Now you have finally acknowledged that you are seriously in debt and don't know how to get out of it.

THE ASSIGNMENT: Working on your own or in a small group, first classify your monthly expenses. Then, divide them into "necessary expenses" and "unnecessary expenses." Once you have done this, write an essay that classifies your expenses. Finally, cite some options you will pursue to pay down your debt.

RESOURCES: Review the chart on pages 726–27 for advice on problem solving. Also, check Web sites for advice about paying down debt without getting into even bigger trouble. You might start by typing in the words *advice on how to pay off credit cards* into a search engine. List any Web sites that you use.

 ASSIGNMENT 4   WRITING ABOUT READINGS

Read both Scott Russell Sanders's "The Men We Carry in Our Minds" (p. 645) and Amy Tan's "Mother Tongue" (p. 652). Then, write a short paper based on one of the following assignments:

• Both Sanders and Tan describe people who have influenced their lives and their ways of seeing themselves and the world. Write an essay classifying important people in your life by the ways in which they have influenced you. Begin by summarizing the influences described by Tan and Sanders.

• Tan refers to the "different Englishes" she uses. Analyze Tan's use of this term and try to come up with your own definition of it. Then, classify the "different Englishes" we typically use depending on whom we are speaking with (parents, spouses, children, friends, and so on). Be sure to present your definition of "different Englishes," and draw on examples from Tan's essay.

Follow the steps in the Writing Guide on the next page to help you prewrite, draft, revise, and edit your classification essay. Check off each step as you complete it.

WRITING GUIDE: CLASSIFICATION	
STEPS IN CLASSIFICATION	**HOW TO DO THE STEPS**
Focus.	❑ Think about what you want to classify (sort) for your readers and what **purpose** your classification will serve. Review the four basics of good classification on page 181.
Prewrite to explore your topic. See Chapter 3 for more on prewriting (including clustering).	❑ Select the topic or group that you want to classify. ❑ Decide on the purpose of the classification. ❑ Use a prewriting technique to generate useful categories for sorting your topic. Clustering works well for classification.
Write a thesis statement. Topic + Organizing principle = Thesis Three professions top the list of hot jobs in 2005. Topic + Organizing principle Three professions top the list of hot jobs in 2005: + Categories = Thesis health care, finance, and home services. See Chapter 4 for more on writing a thesis statement.	❑ Identify the organizing principle you will use to sort your topic into categories. ❑ Write a thesis statement that follows one of the suggested formats in the column to the left.
Support your thesis statement. The primary support in classification consists of the categories into which you sort your topic. See Chapter 5 for more on supporting a thesis statement.	❑ Remind yourself of your purpose and organizing principle. ❑ Choose categories that will serve the purpose of your classification. ❑ Give detailed examples of what fits into each category.
Make a plan. See Chapter 6 for more on planning.	❑ Decide how the categories you have chosen should be arranged. Their arrangement should serve the purpose of your classification (see p. 185). ❑ Make a written plan that includes your primary support points (the categories) and supporting examples for the categories.

STEPS IN CLASSIFICATION	HOW TO DO THE STEPS
Write a draft. See Chapter 7 for more on drafting.	❑ Write an introduction that includes your thesis statement. See if you can use one of the introductory techniques in Chapter 7. ❑ Write topic sentences for each of the categories. ❑ Write body paragraphs that give detailed examples of what is in each category. ❑ Write a concluding paragraph that makes an observation about the way you have classified the topic and why (your purpose). ❑ Title your essay.
Revise your draft. See Chapter 8 for more on revising a draft.	❑ Ask another person to read and comment on your draft. ❑ Make sure that you have just one organizing principle. ❑ Review the categories you have chosen to make sure they serve the purpose of your classification. ❑ Review the examples you give for each category. Delete any that don't really fit, and add any that you think would give the readers a better idea of what is in the category. ❑ Add transitions to connect your ideas. ❑ Reread your thesis statement. Revise it so that your point is more concrete and forceful. ❑ Reread your introduction and make changes if it is dull or weak. ❑ Reread your conclusion to make sure it is energetic and drives home your point. ❑ Make at least five changes to your draft to improve unity, support, or coherence (see pp. 96–109). ❑ Check to make sure the draft follows the four basics of good classification.
Edit your draft. See Parts Four through Seven for more on editing.	❑ Use the spell checker and grammar checker on your computer, but also reread your essay carefully to catch any errors. ❑ Look for errors in grammar, spelling, and punctuation. Focus first on sentence fragments, run-ons, errors in subject-verb agreement, verb errors, and other areas where you often make mistakes. ❑ Ask yourself: Is this the best I can do?

14

Definition

Writing That Tells What Something Means

Understand What Definition Is

Definition is writing that explains what a term or concept means.

■■ FOUR BASICS OF GOOD DEFINITION

1. It tells readers what term is being defined.
2. It presents a clear basic definition.
3. It uses examples to show what the writer means.
4. It gives details about the examples that readers will understand.

In the following paragraph, each number corresponds to one of the four basics of good definition.

1 Internet addiction is **2** chronic, compulsive use of the Internet that interferes with the addicts' lives or their relationships with others. **3** For example, addicts may spend so much time online that they are unable to perform as expected at home, work, or school. **4** These addicts may spend hours surfing the Web, playing games, or e-mailing friends and family. **3** In other cases, the Internet addiction can cause financial problems, or worse. **4** For example, online shoppers who go to extremes can find themselves in debt and, as a result, damage their credit, not to mention personal relationships. **3** Still other Internet addictions involve potentially dangerous or illegal activities. **4** These activities can include meeting people online, gambling, viewing pornography, and engaging in cybersex. However, for Internet addicts, the problem usually isn't *how* they use the Internet; the problem is that they cannot stop using it, even if they want to.

The 5th Wave   By Rich Tennant

"It happened around the time we subscribed to an online service."

Many situations require you to explain the meaning of a term, particularly how you are using it.

COLLEGE	On a U.S. history exam, you define the term *carpetbagger*.
WORK	You describe a coworker as "dangerous" to a human resources staffer, and the staffer asks what you mean exactly.
EVERYDAY LIFE	You explain the term *fair* to your child in the context of games or sports.

■ For an example of an actual definition written for work, see page 204. The piece was written by the business owner who is profiled in the box that follows.

Profile of Success

Gary Knoblock

Business Owner

(See Gary's Definition at Work on p. 204.)

BACKGROUND: Gary grew up in New Orleans, where, after high school, he tried college for a year but was told by a professor that he wasn't college material and should try manual labor. Gary left college and moved to Fort Worth, Texas, where he became a police officer. During his ten years with the force, he attended a junior college at night, earning an associate's degree. He also had numerous promotions at work and became a member of the force's SWAT team. In 1999, Gary decided to start his own business. He moved to Mississippi and started a sign company, Lightning Quick (LQ) Signs. Since then, the company has grown steadily into a successful business.

EMPLOYER: Self

COLLEGE(S)/DEGREES: Tarrant County Junior College (A.A.)

TYPES OF WRITING ON THE JOB: Proposals to get jobs, advertising copy, follow-up reports and letters, loan applications, correspondence with clients and prospective clients, precise and descriptive specifications for government jobs

HOW GARY USES DEFINITION: Gary often needs to define terms for clients. In addition, his letter about the company that he uses in sales situations defines how LQ Signs is customer-oriented.

TEAMWORK ON THE JOB: Teamwork saved Gary's life a number of times when he was a police officer and SWAT team member. He brings the value of teamwork to his own small business. He and his employees work as a team to prioritize and schedule activities, assign responsibilities, prepare job sites, secure any necessary permits, and plan graphics.

Main Point in Definition

In definition essays, your **main point** typically defines your topic. The main point is directly related to your **purpose**: to get your readers to understand a term or concept as you do in the context in which you are using it. Although writers do not always define a term or concept in a thesis statement, it helps readers if they do.

A thesis statement in definition can follow a variety of different patterns, two of which include the term and its basic definition.

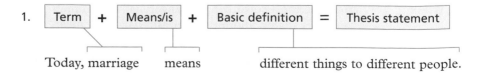

1. | Term | + | Means/is | + | Basic definition | = | Thesis statement |

Today, marriage   means   different things to different people.

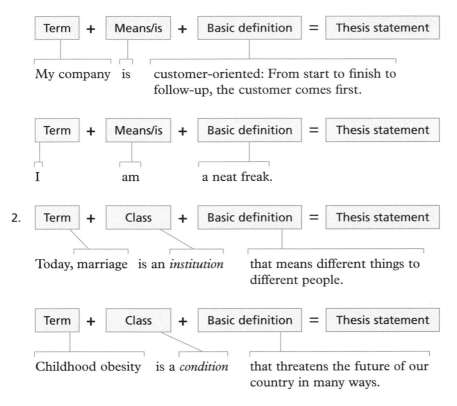

My company is customer-oriented: From start to finish to follow-up, the customer comes first.

I am a neat freak.

2. Today, marriage is an *institution* that means different things to different people.

Childhood obesity is a *condition* that threatens the future of our country in many ways.

■ For online exercises on main point and support, visit Exercise Central at <bedfordstmartins.com/realessays>.

Your thesis statement might not follow either of these patterns, but it should tell your readers what you mean by your use of a term.

In essays based on the following thesis statements, readers would expect the italicized terms and concepts to be defined through examples that show the writer's meaning.

What does *marriage* mean today?

I am a *neat freak*.

The concept of *equal pay for equal work* is a joke.

Many people do not understand what *affirmative action* really means.

Support in Definition

If a friend says, "Summer in New York City is awful," you don't know what she means by *awful*. Is it the weather? The people? The transportation? Until your friend explains what she means, you won't know whether or not you would think New York City in the summer is awful.

Support in definition explains what terms or concepts mean by providing specific examples. Read the two thesis statements that follow and the lists of examples that could be used as support.

THESIS   Today, marriage means different things to different people.

SUPPORT   A union of one man and one woman

A union of two people of either sex

A union that is supported by state law

A union that is supported by the Constitution

A union that is supported by both the law and the church

THESIS   I am a neat freak.

SUPPORT   I clean compulsively.

I'm constantly buying new cleaning products.

My cleaning habits have attracted the notice of friends and family.

In both of these examples, the writer would then go on to develop the examples with details.

THESIS   I am a neat freak.

SUPPORT   I clean compulsively.

DETAILS: I clean in the morning and at night, can't let a spot on the counter go for a second, fret when I can't clean as much as I'd like to.

SUPPORT   I'm constantly buying new cleaning products.

DETAILS: Every week, I buy new products, have a closet full of them, always think there's something better around the corner.

SUPPORT   My cleaning habits have attracted the notice of friends and family.

DETAILS: Kids used to appreciate the clean house, now they complain that I'm compulsive; friends tease me, but I wonder if they think I go too far.

Organization in Definition

The examples in a definition essay are often organized by **importance,** or the impact you think the examples will have on your readers. Save the most important example for last.

The plan for a definition essay might look like this:

Introduction (including thesis)

First example of your meaning

> Specific details that show how that example demonstrates your definition

Second example of your meaning

> Specific details that show how that example demonstrates your definition

Third example of your meaning

> Specific details that show how that example demonstrates your definition

Conclusion

As you write, add transitions to connect one example to the next.

Common Transitions in Definition

another	for example
another kind	for instance
first, second, third, and so on	

Read and Analyze Definition

Before writing a definition essay, read the following examples—one each from college, the workplace, and everyday life—and answer the questions that accompany them.

Definition in College

The following student essay was written for this assignment in an introductory psychology course:

> Define a term from Part One of the textbook, and give examples of that term in a well-organized essay that demonstrates your understanding of the term.

Two Intelligences

Emma Brennan

Until this semester, I thought that intelligence was just being smart academically. Over the course of the semester, I learned that while intelligence means "acquired or applied knowledge," there are different types of intelligence, two of which I will discuss here.

The first type, crystallized intelligence, is the knowledge an individual has built up and stored in memory. This intelligence includes information, skills, and experiences that a person can draw on to operate in this world. The basic math skills that we learn and use in a variety of ways—to add a tip to a restaurant bill, to add the prices of items we want to purchase, to calculate whether we have enough gas to get home—are examples of crystallized intelligence. Another is the ability to read. Once we know how to read, we don't have to relearn that skill every time we need to do it. We also store information such as what dates are holidays or important events in history, what substances are poisonous, and what our Social Security number is. We have learned how to handle situations such as being hurt (emotionally or physically), being in danger, and being hungry. We walk around with a whole universe of facts, information, skills, and strategies that we can call up at any time. These things are just with us, part of our past experiences.

Fluid intelligence, on the other hand, is the ability to deal with new problems and situations. Fluid intelligence, although it may draw upon information and experience that are part of crystallized intelligence, is an individual's ability to meet completely new challenges and contexts and learn how to work within them. For example, if at work you have a problem that you've never experienced before, the amount of fluid intelligence you have will determine whether you try to solve the problem or just give up. If you have a new computer program and something goes wrong, for example, fluid intelligence would prompt you to try to figure out a solution and move forward. If your fluid intelligence is not highly developed, you will likely either call the help line or sit there frustrated.

Both types of intelligence are important because one, crystallized intelligence, allows us to incorporate the sum of what we have learned into our supply of skills and behaviors, while the other, fluid intelligence, allows us to continue to learn and rise to new challenges. Although an individual may have natural abilities (and natural weaknesses) in a variety of areas, it is the preservation and balance of these two basic types of intelligence that allow him or her to be successful in the world.

1. What is Emma's **purpose** in this essay? _____

_____

2. Double-underline the **thesis statement**.

3. Underline the **topic sentences**.

4. Circle the **transitions**.

5. In your own words, define crystallized intelligence and fluid intelligence.

_____

6. Does Emma's essay have the **four basics of good definition**? Why or why not? _____

■ For a list of the four basics of good definition, see page 196.

7. Based on your own experiences, how do you define intelligence?

■ The final question after each reading in this section makes a good essay topic.

Gary Knoblock

Business Owner

(See Gary's Profile of Success on p. 198.)

Definition at Work

Gary Knoblock uses this essay to get contracts for his sign company, for advertising copy, and for his company's mission statement.

The fundamental principle of Lightning Quick (LQ) Signs is customer orientation. While most companies claim that they are customer-oriented, most have no idea what that really means. I tell my employees that I would like to have a customer giggle at the completion of the job, delighting in the product and service we have delivered, his every expectation met and exceeded. For all of us at LQ Signs, *customer-oriented* means that from start to finish to follow-up, the customer comes first.

Our customer orientation begins before the job begins. Before doing anything, we interview the customer to learn what his or her needs are and to determine the most cost-effective route to meet those needs. No job for us is "standard." Each is unique.

Our customer orientation means that we produce high-quality products quickly. We keep signs simple, because our customers want their prospective customers to be able to read the sign in a glance. We use the most current digital printing processes to produce sharp, readable signs quickly. Because we have previously determined, with the customer, the most cost-effective method of producing the signs, the high quality and rapid return do not come at extra cost.

Our customer orientation means that our products are thoroughly checked for flaws and installed at the customer's convenience. Our signs leave our workshop in perfect condition, as the customer has ordered. Our well-trained team of installers works with the customer to determine the installation schedule.

Finally, our customer orientation means that the job is not complete when the sign is in place. We follow up every sale to make sure that the product is in top shape and that the customer is pleased.

LQ Signs is truly customer-oriented, from start to finish to follow-up. Our customers are our partners.

1. What is Gary's **purpose**? _____

_____

2. Double-underline the **thesis statement**.

3. Underline the **topic sentences**.

4. Were you familiar with the term that Gary defined? Restate the meaning

of *customer-oriented* in your own words. _____

_____

5. If you were writing a definition of *customer-oriented,* how would you define it?

Definition in Everyday Life

This piece won an essay contest for college journalists sponsored by *Newsweek* and MTVU, MTV's college channel. It was published in *Newsweek* on July 12, 2004, before George W. Bush defeated Senator John Kerry in that year's presidential race.

I Cannot Be Charted

Traci E. Carpenter

I am the youth vote. And I'm tired of being preached at, studied, and wooed. I want to be educated, listened to, and, most of all, respected. Everyone has a theory as to why I don't vote, but no one really asks me. So I'll explain.

I am neither lazy nor apathetic. I'm confused and frustrated. I am told to care about issues like Social Security and health care, when chances are high that I won't even find a job after I graduate from college. I juggle low-wage, part-time jobs or a full-time class schedule, and I'm not necessarily available on November 2, 2004.

I cannot be accurately represented by percentages and statistics. I cannot be graphed and charted. I am not a Democrat, Republican, or other. I'm a mixed bag of experiences and influences, and no one can pre-dict how I will vote when I do vote.

I am not ignorant. I know what's going on in the world—even if I hear it mostly from *The Daily Show with Jon Stewart*. And yes, at times I do care more about the latest episode of *The Sopranos* than the headline news. That's because I live the headline news. I know about poverty and crime. I live it every day.

I am not disengaged; I'm worn out. Sometimes I feel that no matter how I vote, there will still be war, crime, and poverty. And I have other things on my mind. I am worried about skin cancer, drunken drivers, eating disorders, what I'm going to be when I grow up, how I'm going to get there, and what I'm going to do Friday night.

I don't know the difference between President George W. Bush and Senator John Kerry because they don't take time out from kissing babies and the behinds of corporate executives to tell me. Anyway, sex scandals, wars based on false pretenses, and broken promises have left me cynical about all politicians.

Howard Dean tried to change my mind about the political process. He made me a part of his campaign, rather than a target. He recognized the power I hold, rather than ignoring my potential.

I am active on campuses across the country, but this part of me is recognized only as a minority—a few bright stars in an otherwise dark night.

I am not a dark knight. I will not ride in on my horse come November and steal the election for one candidate or another. I don't know if I will even really vote at all. But I do know that I am 48 million strong. And if someone would just reach out to me—not just during election years, but every day—I would show them overwhelming support at the polls.

I am the youth vote.

1. Double-underline the **thesis statement**.

2. Do you understand the term *youth vote* as Carpenter defines it? Why or why not? _____

_____

3. In your own words, what is Carpenter's definition of the youth vote?

_____

4. Are the examples she gives detailed enough for you? _____

_____

5. Would you characterize yourself as part of the youth vote? Why or why not?

Write a Definition Essay

In this section, you will write your own definition essay based on one of the following assignments. Before you begin to write, review the four basics of good definition on page 196.

 ASSIGNMENT 1   WRITING ABOUT COLLEGE, WORK, AND EVERYDAY LIFE

Write a definition essay on *one* of the following topics or on a topic of your own choice.

COLLEGE

- A term or concept from another course you have taken
- A good/inspiring/motivating teacher
- Cheating

WORK

- Any term you use at work
- McJobs
- A model employee

EVERYDAY LIFE

- An attitude or behavior (such as assertiveness, generosity, negativity, optimism, and so on)
- Morality
- Road rage

 ASSIGNMENT 2   WRITING ABOUT AN IMAGE

What point is the woman in the following picture trying to make? How might she define *patriotism*? Write a definition essay presenting your definition of patriotism.

ASSIGNMENT 3   **WRITING TO SOLVE A PROBLEM**

THE PROBLEM: Your company is putting together a new employee handbook. To make the handbook both realistic and relevant, the company has decided that the contents will come directly from the employees. Your department has been assigned the section on communication.

THE ASSIGNMENT: Working on your own or with a small group, write a short piece defining *good communication skills,* giving detailed examples of how those skills should be applied in your company.

RESOURCES: Review the chart on pages 726–27 for advice on problem solving. You might also

- Set up an informational interview with a human resources worker to find out about your subject.

- Type *definition of good communication skills* into a search engine. List any Web sites you use.

- Read Maureen Letendre's essay "Did You Say What I Think You Said?" (Chapter 12, p. 172).

ASSIGNMENT 4   WRITING ABOUT READINGS

In "I Cannot Be Charted" (p. 205), Traci E. Carpenter declares, "I am the youth vote." Likewise, in "On Being a Cripple" (p. 660), Nancy Mairs uses definition to describe one aspect of life. Read both of these essays and write a short paper on one of the following:

- "I am _____" or "On Being _____." To write this paper, you will need to choose an element of yourself to define and describe. As you plan your paper, think about how Carpenter and Mairs have used examples to explain their definition of themselves.

- Respond to Carpenter's essay by writing your own piece, titled "I Am Also the Youth Vote." In your paper, refer to her essay and point out how your definition and hers differ or are the same.

- Do you agree with Mairs's definition of herself as a "cripple"? Analyze why she says she is a cripple, as opposed to "differently abled" or some other, less critical term. Write a paper that casts Mairs in a different light, such as "I am a survivor" or as an example of the first line of the "Serenity Prayer," in which one asks for "the serenity to accept the things I cannot change." Summarize points from Mairs's essay as needed.

Follow the steps in the Writing Guide below to help you prewrite, draft, revise, and edit your definition essay. Check off each step as you complete it.

WRITING GUIDE: DEFINITION	
STEPS IN DEFINITION	**HOW TO DO THE STEPS**
Focus.	❑ Think about what the term you are defining means to you and what it is likely to mean to your readers. Review the four basics of good definition on page 196.
Prewrite to explore your topic. See Chapter 3 for more on prewriting (including clustering).	❑ Make a list of some topics you would be interested in defining—for example, a type of person, a belief that is important to you, or a term that you think is often misused. ❑ Choose one of the topics and prewrite to come up with ideas about what you are defining. (Clustering works well for definition.) What does it mean to you? Decide on the meaning that you will develop in your essay.

continued

STEPS IN DEFINITION	HOW TO DO THE STEPS
Write a thesis statement. A thesis statement in definition can follow one of these patterns: Term + Means/is + Binge drinking is a Basic definition = Thesis killer. Term + Class + Yoga is an exercise that Basic definition = Thesis helps people find serenity. *Or,* write a thesis statement that names the term and indicates what your essay will say: I am a geek and proud of it. See Chapter 4 for more on the thesis.	❑ Review your prewriting about what your topic means to you. ❑ Write a working thesis statement that either includes both the term and how you are defining it or the term and some idea of what your essay will explain. ❑ Think about your readers and revise your thesis statement to make it either clearer to them or more likely to interest them in your essay.
Support your thesis statement. Support in definition explains what terms or concepts mean by providing specific examples. See Chapter 5 for more on supporting a thesis statement.	❑ Prewrite to find examples that explain how you are defining your topic. ❑ Review the examples and get rid of any that don't show your meaning of the term. Choose at least three good examples. ❑ With your readers in mind, add specific details to the examples that show your readers what you mean by your definition. Think about what kinds of examples and details will make sense to them.
Make a plan. See Chapter 6 for more on planning.	❑ Choose an order for your support points. A definition essay generally uses order of importance, building up to the example that will have the most impact on readers. ❑ Make a written plan that includes the major support points (examples) and supporting details.

STEPS IN DEFINITION	HOW TO DO THE STEPS
Write a draft. See Chapter 7 for more on drafting.	❑ Write an introduction that includes your thesis statement. See if you can use one of the introductory techniques in Chapter 7. ❑ Write topic sentences for each of the examples. ❑ Write body paragraphs that give detailed explanations of each example. ❑ Write a concluding paragraph that makes an observation about the term based on the examples you have given. ❑ Title your essay.
Revise your draft. See Chapter 8 for more on revising a draft.	❑ Ask another person to read and comment on your draft. ❑ See if your thesis statement and introduction could be clearer or more interesting to your readers. ❑ Reread the body of your essay to make sure the examples explain your definition and the details explain the examples. Add other examples and details that would help explain what you mean by the term. ❑ Reread your conclusion to make sure it reinforces your definition. ❑ Add transitions to connect your ideas. ❑ Make at least five changes to your draft to improve unity, support, or coherence (see pp. 96–109). ❑ Check to make sure the draft follows the four basics of good definition.
Edit your draft. See Parts Four through Seven for more on editing.	❑ Use the spell checker and grammar checker on your computer, but also reread your essay carefully to catch any errors. ❑ Look for errors in grammar, spelling, and punctuation. Run-ons and punctuation errors are common in definition, so check for those first. Then, focus on sentence fragments, errors in subject-verb agreement, verb errors, and other areas where you often make mistakes. ❑ Ask yourself: Is this the best I can do?

★ Annual Cost of Your Caffeine Fix

15

Comparison and Contrast

Writing That Shows Similarities and Differences

Understand What Comparison and Contrast Are

Comparison is writing that shows the similarities among subjects—people, ideas, situations, or items; **contrast** shows the differences. In conversation, we often use the word *compare* to mean either compare or contrast, but as you work through this chapter, the terms will be separated.

■■ **FOUR BASICS OF GOOD COMPARISON**
■■ **AND CONTRAST**

1. It uses subjects that have enough in common to be usefully compared and contrasted.

2. It serves a purpose—either to help readers make a decision or to understand the subjects.

3. It presents several important, parallel points of comparison and contrast.

4. It is organized either point-by-point or whole-to-whole (see pp. 216–17).

In the following paragraph, which contrasts the subjects, each number corresponds to one of the four basics of good comparison and contrast.

1 My current boyfriend and my ex-boyfriend treat me in extremely different ways. **3** One difference is that my current boyfriend opens the door when I get in the car as well as when I get out. In contrast, my ex-boyfriend never opened the door of the car, or any other door. **3** My current boyfriend likes to tell me that he loves me. For example, we went to the beach, and he screamed that he loved me to the four winds so everyone could hear. My ex, on the other hand, always had a ready excuse for why he couldn't say that he loved me, ever. His parents weren't loving, so he didn't know how to express his feelings about me. However, he wanted me to tell him I loved him all the time. **3** Another difference between the two is that my boyfriend treats me well. When we go out to a restaurant, he pulls out the chair for me, and he pays for the meal. My ex just never seemed to have money to pay for dinner or anything else. He would say it was because he forgot to bring his wallet, and I would have to pay for the food. **3** To me, the most important difference between the two guys is that my current boyfriend is honest. He never lies to me about anything, and he makes me feel confident about our relationship. In contrast, I never could tell if my ex was lying or telling the truth because he often lied about his family and other things, and I never knew what to believe. **1** To sum it all up, my current boyfriend is a gentleman, and my ex was a pig.

—Liliana Ramirez, student

2 Helps readers understand how two boyfriends treated writer

4 Uses point-by-point organization (see p. 216).

Many situations require you to understand similarities and differences. Here are some examples of how you might use comparison and contrast.

COLLEGE	In a business course, you compare and contrast practices in e-commerce and traditional commerce.
WORK	You compare and contrast two health insurance options offered by your company in order to select the one that is best for you.
EVERYDAY LIFE	Before choosing a telephone plan, you compare and contrast the rates, services, and options each offers.

■ For an example of an actual comparison/contrast written for work, see page 220. The piece was written by the financial consultant who is profiled in the box on page 214.

Profile of Success

Salvador Torres
Financial Consultant

(See Salvador's Comparison and Contrast at Work on p. 220.)

BACKGROUND: Salvador is the son of farmworkers who moved to California from rural Mexico. His parents always insisted he should try to do better for himself. A high school teacher and counselor encouraged Salvador academically and introduced him to several people who, like Salvador, had started with poor grades and English skills but had attended college and were successful professionals. Salvador later worked with the Puenté Project, a program for Hispanic students who are at risk of not completing college. He is now a mentor who helps others like him to stay—and succeed—in college.

EMPLOYER: Public Financial Management, Inc.

COLLEGE(S)/DEGREES: Gavilan College (A.A.), Stanford University (B.A.), Princeton University (M.P.A.)

TYPES OF WRITING ON THE JOB: Memos to clients on a variety of financial topics, financial reports and analyses, e-mail

HOW SALVADOR USES COMPARISON/CONTRAST: Because Salvador is a financial consultant, he has to compare and contrast investment options for clients.

TEAMWORK ON THE JOB: On every project, a consultant works with various other advisers—experts in investment banking, law, insurance, and credit. All of these individuals must pool their knowledge to advise a client who has hired Public Financial Management, Inc.

Main Point in Comparison and Contrast

A comparison/contrast essay shows readers how two or more subjects are alike or different. The **purpose** of a comparison/contrast may be to have readers understand the subjects or to help them make a decision. For example, you might compare and contrast two characters in a book to show that you understand them. Or you might compare and contrast kinds of dogs to help a potential owner choose among them.

In comparison and contrast, your **main point** expresses similarities or differences in your subjects. For example, in the paragraph on page 213, Liliana Ramirez contrasts her two boyfriends' treatment of her. Her purpose is to help readers understand how different the two are, and her thesis states that difference as her main point.

Typically, thesis statements in comparison/contrast present the central subjects and indicate whether the writer will show similarities, differences, or both.

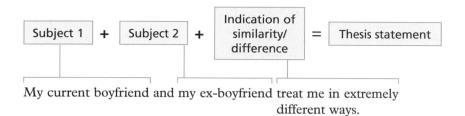

My current boyfriend and my ex-boyfriend treat me in extremely
different ways.

To determine your main point, decide whether you want to show similarities, differences, or both. To make this decision, you need to think
about what your purpose is—what you want your readers to understand—
and what will be meaningful to those readers.

Liliana knew that she wanted to show how her current boyfriend is
much better than her ex, so she focused on differences (contrasts) between
them—specifically, the differences in how each one treated her.

■ For online exercises
on main point and
support, visit
Exercise Central at
<bedfordstmartins
.com/realessays>.

Support in Comparison and Contrast

Once you have decided what you want to show about the subjects you are
comparing or contrasting, you need to find **supporting points** of comparison or points of contrast—parallel or matched points that will show
how the subjects are similar or different. **Supporting details** then explain
these points for each subject.

For example, one student, Daniel, wrote the following thesis, which
indicates that his essay will focus on the differences between the ages of
twenty and forty:

The ages of twenty and forty are both enjoyable, but they represent
very different stages in life.

To support this thesis, Daniel needs to find several points of contrast
between twenty and forty. He generates this list:

DIFFERENCES BETWEEN TWENTY AND FORTY

appearance

place in life

perspective

Then, for each point of comparison, Daniel lists some details that explain the differences:

	AGE TWENTY	AGE FORTY
APPEARANCE	smooth skin	some wrinkles
	trendy haircut	classic hairstyle
	rounded features	well-defined features
PLACE IN LIFE	just starting out	established
	single, no children	married with children
	living at home	own home
PERSPECTIVE	self-centered	more thoughtful
	choices to make	many choices made
	uncertainty	wisdom

Organization in Comparison and Contrast

After you have developed points of comparison or contrast and support-ing details for each of those points, you need to decide how to present them in your essay.

Comparison/contrast can be organized in two basic ways: A **point-by-point** organization first presents one point of comparison or contrast be-tween the two subjects and then moves to the next point of comparison or contrast. A **whole-to-whole** organization first presents all the points of comparison or contrast for one subject and then all the points for the sec-ond. To decide which organization to use, consider which of the two will best serve your purpose of explaining similarities or differences to your readers. Once you choose an organization, stick with it throughout the essay.

The two organizations look like this:

POINT-BY-POINT	**WHOLE-TO-WHOLE**
Introductory paragraph	Introductory paragraph
Topic sentence, point 1	Topic sentence, subject 1
subject 1	point 1
subject 2	point 2
Topic sentence, point 2	point 3
subject 1	Topic sentence, subject 2
subject 2	point 1
Topic sentence, point 3	point 2
subject 1	point 3
subject 2	Concluding paragraph
Concluding paragraph	

Although the whole-to-whole organization looks as if it might be shorter, the organization has little effect on the length. Select the organization that will be clearest and easiest for readers to follow. Arrange the points and details in a sequence that suits what you have to say—chronological (time) order, spatial order, or order of importance. As you write your essay, add transitions to lead from point to point and subject to subject.

Common Transitions in Comparison and Contrast

COMPARISON	CONTRAST
one similarity	one difference
another similarity	another difference
similarly	in contrast
like	now/then
both	unlike
	while

Read and Analyze Comparison and Contrast

Before writing a comparison/contrast essay, read the following examples—one each from college, the workplace, and everyday life—and answer the questions that accompany them.

Comparison and Contrast in College

The following is an excerpt from a college textbook.

When the Regulation of Eating Behavior Fails: Anorexia and Bulimia

Two life-threatening eating disorders are common, especially among females, and while they may have similar psychological causes, the behaviors themselves are quite different. Both of these disorders lie at the opposite end of the spectrum from obesity.

Anorexia nervosa is a potentially life-threatening psychological disorder that involves near self-starvation. This psychological disorder has three key symptoms: The individual refuses to maintain a minimally normal body weight, is extremely afraid of gaining weight or becoming fat, and has a distorted perception of the size of his or her body. Approximately 90 percent of cases of anorexia nervosa occur in adolescent or young adult females (American Psychiatric Association, 1994).

It is rare for a person with anorexia to lose her appetite completely. Rather, she places herself on a very restricted diet that may be limited to just a few foods. Weight loss is also often accomplished by excessive exercise, fasting, self-induced vomiting, or the misuse of laxatives. By reducing total food intake, individuals with anorexia drop 15 percent or more below their optimal body weight. Depression, social withdrawal, insomnia, and failure to menstruate frequently accompany the disorder.

A hallmark of anorexia is distorted self-perception. Despite her emaciated appearance, the person with anorexia looks in the mirror and sees herself as still overweight. Or she expresses displeasure with certain parts of her body, such as her abdomen or thighs, that are "too fat." Weight loss is viewed with pride and regarded as an act of extraordinary self-discipline. Approximately 10 percent of people with anorexia nervosa die from starvation, suicide, or physical complications of extreme weight loss (American Psychiatric Association, 1994).

In contrast, people with **bulimia nervosa** are within their normal weight range and may even be slightly overweight. People with bulimia engage in binge eating and then purge themselves of the excessive food consumption by self-induced vomiting. Less often, they may use laxatives or enemas to purge themselves of the food.

People suffering from bulimia usually conceal their eating problems from others. Episodes of binge eating typically occur in secrecy. A binge usually includes the consumption of high-caloric, sweet foods that can be swallowed quickly, such as ice cream, cake, and candy. Once they begin eating, people with bulimia often feel as though they cannot control their food intake. Sometimes consuming as much as 50,000 calories at one time, they eat until they are uncomfortably, even painfully, full (American Psychiatric Association, 1994; Johnson, Stuckey, Lewis, & Schwartz, 1982).

Diverse cultural, psychological, social, and genetic factors seem to be involved in both anorexia nervosa and bulimia nervosa (North, Gowers, & Byram, 1995; Steinhausen, 1994). There is strong cultural pressure, especially for young Western women, to achieve the thinness ideal. The higher incidence of eating disorders among women may be related to their greater dissatisfaction with their appearance. Women are much more likely to have a poor body image than are men of the same age (Feingold & Mazzella, 1998).

—From Don H. Hockenbury and Sandra Hockenbury, *Discovering Psychology,* Second Edition, 2001

References

American Psychiatric Association. (1994). *Diagnostic and statistical manual of mental disorders* (4th ed.). Washington, D.C.: American Psychiatric Association.

Feingold, A., & Mazzella, R. (1998). Gender differences in body image are increasing. *Psychological Science, 9,* 190–195.

Johnson, C. L., Stuckey, M. K., Lewis, L. D., & Schwartz, D. M. (1982). Bulimia: A descriptive survey of 316 cases. *International Journal of Eating Disorders, 2,* 3–16.

North, C., Gowers, S., & Byram, V. (1995). Family functioning in adolescent anorexia nervosa. *British Journal of Psychiatry, 151,* 82–88.

Steinhausen, H. C. (1994). Anorexia and bulimia nervosa. In M. Rutter, E. Taylor, & L. Hersov (Eds.), *Child and adolescent psychiatry: Modern approaches.* Boston: Blackwell Scientific Publications.

NOTE: The National Association of Eating Disorders reports that 10 million females and 1 million males suffer from anorexia or bulimia.

1. Double-underline the **thesis statement**.

2. Underline each **topic sentence**.

3. Does this piece of writing use point-by-point or whole-to-whole organization? _____

4. Circle the **transition** that signals a move from one subject to the other.

5. What are two main points of contrast in this piece? _____

   _____

   _____

■ For a list of the four basics of good comparison and contrast, see page 212.

6. Does this excerpt follow the **four basics of good comparison and contrast**? Why or why not? _____

7. In what other ways might you characterize the behavior of someone who is anorexic or bulimic?

Comparison and Contrast at Work

The following memo is similar to those that Salvador prepares for clients. Although it is not in essay form, it is an example of how comparison/contrast is used in the workplace.

Salvador Torres
Financial Consultant

(See Salvador's Profile of Success on p. 214.)

TO: Investment Client

Based on our discussion of your investment needs, I would recommend that you invest in Stock Mutual Funds rather than Bond Mutual Funds. Your three expressed preferences were (1) to hold on to the stock for more than ten years, (2) that the funds you invest in be professionally managed, and (3) that you want a high potential for gain and are not overly concerned with risk and the daily fluctuations of funds. You have no need for present annual income from your investments. We determined, after reviewing numerous options, that either Bond Mutual Funds or Stock Mutual Funds would meet your criteria.

There are several similarities between Bond Mutual Funds and Stock Mutual Funds. One is that they both offer investment horizons greater than ten years. Another is that both are professionally managed. A third is that either fund may pay annual income. Based on these factors, either fund fulfills your investment needs.

However, there are differences worth noting. One is that Stock Mutual Funds have higher potential gains over a ten-year period, though they have more risk and fluctuation in the shorter term. Additionally, though both funds may pay annual incomes, the Bond Mutual Fund is more likely to do so, at the expense of greater long-term appreciation.

Both funds meet some of your criteria, but the Stock Mutual Funds are more tailored to your expressed preferences than the Bond Mutual Funds. The Stock Mutual Funds are likely to have a greater return on investment over a ten-year period. Since this is a high priority for you, I suggest that you invest in Stock Mutual Funds. I can monitor this investment and inform you of its status at any time.

If you have questions or need further clarification, please do not hesitate to ask. I look forward to meeting with you again to determine the precise funds in which to invest. Thank you.

1. Who is the audience for this memo? _____

2. What is the purpose of the memo? _____

   _____

3. Double-underline the **thesis statement**.

4. Underline each **topic sentence**.

5. Does the writer use point-by-point or whole-to-whole organization?

   _____

6. Think of two similar products you're interested in. How would you compare or contrast them?

■ The final question after each reading in this section makes a good essay topic.

Comparison and Contrast in Everyday Life

The following comparison and contrast was done by Karron Tempesta to help her decide which of two job offers to accept. When comparing things in order to make a decision, it is often helpful to list the points of comparison next to each other so that the differences are easy to see. First, look at Karron's list, which is like prewriting, and then read the essay she wrote, which is more casual than a formal essay.

COMPANY A	COMPANY B
• higher salary	• lower salary, but a good bonus plan
• big company	• small company
• farther away but on bus line	• near home
• more jobs at the company because it's big	• fewer jobs because it's small, but maybe more chance to do more and be rewarded
• nice people	• nice people
• entry-level job	• more responsibilities and challenge
• good benefit plan	• okay benefit plan

The job offers I received from Company A and Company B are both good, but they differ on a number of points. I'm writing this because sometimes I think better when I can see things in print, and this is an important decision that I want to think about seriously.

The first difference is the location of the companies. Company A is way across town. It's on a bus line, and that's good, but it would still take me anywhere from thirty to forty-five minutes to get there. It makes for a longer day. Company B, on the other hand, is very close by. I could ride my bicycle and be there in ten minutes. I'd also save the bus fare. But what about when it's raining or really hot?

Another difference is in the salaries. The actual salary at Company A is higher than that at Company B. However, Company B is experiencing rapid growth, and it has a good bonus plan. Although I can't count on it,

I have the opportunity with Company B to make more than at Company A. But then again, maybe I wouldn't get a good bonus.

Probably the most important difference is the size of the two companies: Company A is big, and Company B is small. Size is probably the reason that Company A has a better benefit plan—there are more people to enroll, so it gets a good rate. In contrast, Company B has fewer people and probably pays a higher rate as a result.

Size also affects the type of job and where it will lead. At Company A, the job is an entry-level position with clearly defined responsibilities that aren't that interesting. But the company has lots of jobs, so I'd have more opportunities once I was there. At Company B, the job has more responsibility, and I'd learn more and be more interested. Because it's small, people are more likely to let me try new things—and to notice when I've done well. So there are good opportunities there, too.

So there are the differences. Which of these differences are most important to me, and where will I be the happiest? The location isn't really very important. I need money, so a higher salary is attractive, but I like the idea of being rewarded with a bonus if I do well. I might make more at Company B that way, and it's good motivation. Also, I like smaller companies better; I just felt better there, and I like that I get to do more on the job and be noticed. The benefits aren't as good at Company B, but I think, overall, Company B is best. I'll go with it.

1. What is Karron's purpose for this comparison? _____

_____

2. Double-underline the **thesis statement**.

3. Underline each **topic sentence**.

4. Circle the **transitions**.

5. Does Karron use point-by-point or whole-to-whole organization?

_____

6. What order of organization (chronological, spatial, or importance) does Karron use? _____

7. What other points of contrast might have Karron have considered? What else might you consider when thinking about what is important in a job?

Write a Comparison and Contrast Essay

In this section, you will write your own comparison/contrast essay based on *one* of the following assignments. Before you begin to write, review the four basics of good comparison and contrast on page 212.

 ASSIGNMENT 1   WRITING ABOUT COLLEGE, WORK, AND EVERYDAY LIFE

Write a comparison/contrast essay on *one* of the following topics or on a topic of your own choice.

COLLEGE

- Two professors
- Two courses you are taking or have taken
- Being an older, returning student versus coming right from high school

WORK

- Two jobs you have had
- Two companies you have worked for
- A job and a career

EVERYDAY LIFE

- Two places you have lived
- Good customer service and bad customer service
- Two of your friends or relatives

ASSIGNMENT 2   **WRITING ABOUT AN IMAGE**

Write an essay comparing or contrasting the women shown in the photograph. Or, if you prefer, write about two photographs of yourself or someone else taken at different ages. Be as detailed as possible, particularly if you are writing about photographs other than the one in the book.

ASSIGNMENT 3   **WRITING TO SOLVE A PROBLEM**

THE PROBLEM: Your college has mandated that all students have laptop computers. Many laptop computers are available, and though you are tempted to buy the cheapest one you can find, you decide you should compare a few before buying. You consult *Consumer Reports'* ratings in the chart on page 226.

THE ASSIGNMENT: Working either on your own or with a small group, write a comparison or contrast essay on the three "budget laptops" listed in the chart. Focus on three of the features that are important to you. In your concluding paragraph, indicate which of the three models you will purchase and why.

Ratings laptop computers

1 Compaq

- **Availability** Most models at stores and online at least through January 2005.

Legend: ● Excellent ◓ Very good ○ Good ◒ Fair ● Poor

Within types, in performance order. Blue key numbers indicate Quick Picks; see box above.

The following table reproduces the numeric and text data from the ratings chart. Test-result, warranty, and overall-score columns are shown as rating symbols in the image.

Key number	Brand & model	Price	Battery (hr.)	Hard drive (GB)	Carry weight (lb.)	Travel weight (lb.)	Memory-card slot	FireWire port	DVD writer
	BUDGET LAPTOP COMPUTERS *Good performance in a reasonably lightweight package (15-inch display).*								
1	**Compaq** Presario 2100Z 2500+ Athlon XP-M ⒹR3000Z	$924	3½	40	6.8	8.2	N	N	N
2	**Dell** Inspiron 1150 2.6 GHz Celeron	1,027	4¼	30	8.0	10.2	N	N	N
3	**IBM** ThinkPad G40 2.4 GHz Pentium 4	1,440	3¾	40	8.4	10.4	N	N	N
	WORKHORSE LAPTOP COMPUTERS *Better performance but higher cost (15-inch display).*								
4	**Compaq** Presario x1000 1.7 GHz Pentium M 735	1,652	4¼	80	6.8	8.6	Y	Y	Y
5	**HP** Pavilion zt3000 1.7 GHz Pentium M 735	1,500	3¾	60	6.8	8.5	Y	Y	Y
6	**Sony** Vaio VGN-A130 1.7 GHz Pentium M 735	1,870	3½	40	6.6	8.4	Y	Y	Y
7	**Gateway** 450X 1.7 GHz Pentium M 735	1,843	3	40	6.1	8.0	N	Y	Y
8	**Dell** Inspiron 5150 2.8 GHz Mobile Pentium 4 Ⓓ5160	1,526	3½	60	8.0	10.8	N	Y	Y
9	**Toshiba** Satellite A55-S326 1.6 GHz Pentium M 725	1,550	3½	60	5.8	7.4	N	Y	Y
	SLIM AND LIGHT LAPTOP COMPUTERS *Meant for traveling; expensive (12-inch display).*								
10	**Sony** Vaio PCG-V505 1.4 GHz Pentium M	1,750	4¼	40	4.4	5.9	Y	Y	N
11	**Toshiba** Portege M205-S810 1.5 GHz Pentium M	2,400	4	60	4.5	6.0	Y	N	N
12	**IBM** ThinkPad X31 1.4 GHz Pentium M	1,994	4¼	40	3.6	4.9	Y	Y	N
	MACINTOSH LAPTOP COMPUTERS *The Apple version of workhorse and budget hardware.*								
13	**Apple** PowerBook 15" 1 GHz PowerPC G4	2,300	2¼	60	5.7	7.0	N	Y	Y
14	**Apple** iBook 14" Combo 933 MHz PowerPC G4	1,300	3½	40	6.0	7.2	N	Y	N

Ⓓ *Discontinued, but similar model is available. Price is for similar model.*

Guide to the Ratings

Overall score includes most of the same factors used in rating desktop computers. **Battery** life numbers are for our continuous-use test. **Features** include: **carry weight** is the weight with battery and any removable drives; **travel weight** adds the power adapter and one spare battery. **Price** is approximate retail. The Compaq budget laptop has 192 MB of RAM, the other budget models have 256 MB. All the other laptops have 512 MB. All models have either 2 or 3 USB ports and a PC-card slot (except the iBook).

RESOURCES: Review the chart on pages 726–27 for general advice about problem solving. In addition to consulting the *Consumer Reports* ratings, you might want to type "best laptop computers" into a search engine to see if Web sources give the same assessments as *Consumer Reports*. List any Web sites you use.

ASSIGNMENT 4   WRITING ABOUT READINGS

Read "The Ugly Truth about Beauty" by Dave Barry on page 671. Next, review the "When the Regulation of Eating Behavior Fails: Anorexia and Bulimia" by Don H. Hockenbury and Sandra Hockenbury on page 217 and Assignment 2 on page 225. Then, write a brief paper on *one* of the following:

- Although their tones are very different, both Barry and the Hockenburys make a similar point about women's images of themselves. Explain that point, bringing in references from the two readings and the photograph. In your concluding paragraph, indicate which of the three sources makes the point most effectively to you, and why.

- Analyze what makes people subject to advertising images or unrealistic expectations of themselves. To do this, draw on the three sources and on experiences you or people you know have had.

- Persuade a friend who has a negative self-image that this image isn't accurate and that holding on to it could be damaging.

- Look for an ad on television, in a magazine, or online that encourages people to have unrealistic expectations about their appearance, and relate what you find to one or two of the sources here.

Follow the steps in the Writing Guide below to help you prewrite, draft, revise, and edit your comparison/contrast essay. Check off each step as you complete it.

WRITING GUIDE: COMPARISON AND CONTRAST	
STEPS IN COMPARISON AND CONTRAST	**HOW TO DO THE STEPS**
Focus.	❏ Think about what you want to compare or contrast and the main point you want to make about your subjects. Review the four basics of good comparison and contrast on page 212.
Prewrite to explore your topic. See Chapter 3 for more on prewriting.	❏ Decide on your purpose for the comparison or contrast: to help readers understand the two subjects or to help them make a decision. ❏ Make a side-by-side list of possible parallel points of comparison or contrast between your two subjects.
Write a thesis statement. A thesis statement in comparison/contrast usually presents the central subjects and indicates whether the writer will show similarities, differences, or both.	❏ Write a thesis statement that includes your subjects and indicates whether you will discuss similarities or differences.

continued

STEPS IN COMPARISON AND CONTRAST	HOW TO DO THE STEPS
Subject 1/Subject 2 + The ages of twenty and forty are both enjoyable, but Indication of similarity/ difference = Thesis they represent very different stages in life. The job offers I received from Subject 1 + Subject 2 + Company A and Company B are both good, but Indication of similarity/ difference = Thesis they differ on a number of points. See Chapter 4 for more on writing a thesis statement.	
Support your thesis statement. The major support for comparison/contrast consists of points of comparison or points of contrast. See Chapter 5 for more on supporting a thesis statement.	❑ Review the list of possible points of comparison or contrast from your prewriting. ❑ Select from your list the points of comparison or contrast that your readers will understand and that will serve your purpose. ❑ Add supporting details and examples to explain the points of comparison.
Make a plan. See Chapter 6 for more on planning.	❑ Decide whether you will use a point-by-point or whole-to-whole organization. ❑ Make a plan or outline that follows the point-by-point or whole-to-whole structure and that organizes support points most effectively (using time order, space order, or order of importance).

STEPS IN COMPARISON AND CONTRAST	HOW TO DO THE STEPS
Write a draft. See Chapter 7 for more on drafting.	❑ Write an introduction that includes your thesis statement. See if you can use one of the introductory techniques in Chapter 7. ❑ Write topic sentences either for each of the subjects or for each point of comparison or contrast. ❑ Write body paragraphs that give detailed examples to support your topic sentence. ❑ Write a concluding paragraph that makes an observation about the subjects based on the points you have made in your essay. ❑ Title your essay.
Revise your draft. See Chapter 8 for more on revising a draft.	❑ Ask another person to read and comment on your draft. ❑ See if your thesis statement could be clearer or more interesting to your readers. ❑ Reread the body of your essay to make sure the points of comparison or contrast are parallel and support your thesis. Add other examples and details that would further show the similarities or differences between your subjects. ❑ Add transitions to connect your ideas. ❑ Reread your introduction and make changes if it is dull or weak. ❑ Reread your conclusion to make sure it reinforces your main point. ❑ Make at least five changes to your draft to improve unity, support, or coherence (see pp. 96–109). ❑ Check to make sure the draft follows the four basics of good comparison and contrast.
Edit your draft. See Parts Four through Seven for more on editing.	❑ Use the spell checker and grammar checker on your computer, but also reread your essay carefully to catch any errors. ❑ Look for errors in grammar, spelling, and punctuation. In comparison/contrast, some students write fragments and/or run-ons and make errors in subject-verb agreement. Focus first on these errors, and then edit for verb errors and other areas where you often make mistakes. ❑ Ask yourself: Is this the best I can do?

16

Cause and Effect

Writing That Explains Reasons or Results

Understand What Cause and Effect Are

A **cause** is what makes an event happen. An **effect** is what happens as a result of an event.

▪▪ FOUR BASICS OF GOOD CAUSE AND EFFECT

1. The main point reflects the writer's purpose: to explain causes, effects, or both.
2. If the purpose is to explain causes, it presents concrete causes.
3. If the purpose is to explain effects, it presents actual effects.
4. It gives readers clear and detailed examples or explanations of the causes and/or effects.

In the following paragraph, each number corresponds to one of the four basics of good cause and effect.

> **1** Little doubt remains that global warming is a threat to our world, but not everyone understands why it is happening and what the effects really are. Many experts believe that this warming trend is largely the result of **2** greenhouse gases, including **4** carbon dioxide emissions, mainly from cars, and pollutants from industrial processes. **2** Deforestation is another significant cause. To date, the United States

230

has refused to ratify the worldwide Kyoto Protocol, an agreement that would limit emissions of the gases that cause global warming. Ironically, if current warming trends continue, the United States is most at risk for **1** negative consequences, although the entire world will be affected. Scientists predict that **3** sea levels will rise dangerously and **4** flood coastal areas. There will also be a **3** greater incidence of droughts and changes in precipitation patterns, **4** such as the rapid sequence of hurricanes in the fall of 2004. In addition, and possibly most destructive, is the **3** threat to plant and animal life and, consequently, to public health.

Analyzing causes and effects goes beyond asking "What happened?" to also ask "Why?" and "How?"

SITUATION: On a hot summer day, you leave a video you need to return on the front seat of your car while you are at work. When you come out of work, you find the video has melted.

The **cause** of the video melting was **leaving it all day in a hot car**. The **effect** of leaving the video in a hot car all day was that **it melted**.

Jim Rice of Quinsigamond Community College helps his students visualize the cause/effect relationship by suggesting that they think of three linked rings:

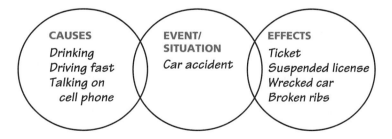

Many situations require you to determine causes or effects.

COLLEGE	In an information technology course, you must discuss the effects of a virus on a local-area computer network.
WORK	You analyze the likely effects of laying off 15 percent of your department's employees.
EVERYDAY LIFE	You try to figure out what is causing your computer to freeze.

■ For an example of an actual cause/effect written for work, see page 237. The piece was written by the attorney/consultant who is profiled in the box on page 232.

Profile of Success

Jolanda Jones

Attorney and
Consultant

*(See Jolanda's
Cause/Effect at
Work on p. 237.)*

BACKGROUND: Jolanda grew up in a housing project in Houston, Texas, where she lost several relatives to street violence. A good student, she became a three-time NCAA heptathlon champion, two-time Academic All-American, and a 1989 U.S. heptathlon champion. She participated in the 1996 U.S. Olympic Team trials and won the high jump, beating Jackie Joyner-Kersee, an elite track and field athlete and gold medalist. Jolanda went to college and to law school, and then went on to practice law. In 2000, she received the NAACP's Award for Legal Excellence for dedication to community service. She still practices law, and she has her own consulting business.

EMPLOYER: Self

COLLEGE(S)/DEGREES: University of Houston, Central Campus (B.A.), University of Houston–Bates School of Law (J.D.L.)

TYPES OF WRITING ON THE JOB: Legal briefs, proposals, letters, evaluations, e-mails, Web site content, speeches

HOW JOLANDA USES CAUSE/EFFECT: As part of her consulting business, Jolanda speaks to inner-city youth. When she addresses students, she emphasizes the importance of understanding that for every action they take, there is a consequence that they should consider.

TEAMWORK ON THE JOB: In her legal practice, Jolanda and her clients must work together as a team to win cases. As a consultant to schools, she works with administrators, teachers, parents, and students to achieve common goals.

Main Point in Cause and Effect

The **main point** in a cause/effect essay should reflect your **purpose**. For example, if you are writing about why a certain event in history happened, your main point would be to explain the causes. If you are writing about what happened as a result of that event, your main point would be to explain the effects.

Sometimes a thesis statement for a cause/effect essay will include both the topic and an indication of whether the essay will be about what caused the topic, what resulted from the topic, or both. The topic sentence in the paragraph on page 230 follows this pattern, as does the example on page 233.

Topic

Little doubt remains that global warming is a threat to our world, but not everyone understands why it is happening and what the effects are.

Indicates causes   Indicates effects

The main point of the essay is to explain the causes and effects of global warming.

Topic/cause   Effect

Drunk driving causes thousands of deaths every year.

The main point of the essay is to discuss the effects of drunk driving—thousands of deaths. The body of the essay will probably give examples of how drunk driving causes those deaths.

Or the writer may not directly indicate causes or effects in the thesis statement, as in the following example:

> Until local police departments enforce restraining orders, women and children will continue to be the victims of violence.

Although the writer does not specifically indicate a cause or effect, the main point of the essay is clear: to discuss how unenforced restraining orders have resulted in violence. The body of the essay will likely give examples of such situations.

As you begin to write cause/effect essays, it may be helpful for you to include in your thesis statement both the topic and an indicator of cause, effect, or both.

■ For online exercises on main point and support, visit Exercise Central at <**bedfordstmartins .com/realessays**>.

Support in Cause and Effect

In a cause/effect essay, **support** consists of explanations of causes or effects, and it demonstrates the main point stated in your thesis. Take, for example, this thesis statement:

> Irresponsible behavior caused my car accident.

The writer supported this thesis by presenting the causes with details that explain them.

CAUSE   Driving too fast   **CAUSE**   Talking on my cell phone

    DETAILS: DETAILS:

    Rainy and slippery   Not paying close attention

    Going too fast to control car   Hit a curve while laughing

    Couldn't stop   Didn't react fast enough

CAUSE   Drinking

    DETAILS:

    Not focused

    Slowed reaction time

When you are writing about causes, be careful that you don't say something caused an event or situation just because it happened beforehand. For example, many of us have had the experience of getting sick after a meal and assuming that the food caused the sickness, only to find out that we'd been coming down with the flu even before the meal.

When you are writing about effects, do not confuse something that happened after something else with the effect. To return to the previous example, just as the meal didn't cause the illness, the illness was not the effect of the meal.

Organization in Cause and Effect

Cause/effect essays are often organized by **order of importance**, saving the most important or intense cause or effect for last in order to create a strong impression on readers. The plan for a cause/effect essay generally looks like this:

Introduction (including thesis)
First cause or effect
      Explanation of cause or effect
Second cause or effect
      Explanation of cause or effect
Most important cause or effect
      Explanation of cause or effect
Conclusion

As you write your essay, add transitions to show how each cause or effect relates to your main point. Here are some common transitions that are used in cause/effect writing.

Common Transitions in Cause and Effect

one cause, reason, effect, result	as a result
also	because
another	thus
first, second, third, and so on	

Read and Analyze Cause and Effect

Before writing your own cause/effect essay, read the following examples—one each from college, the workplace, and everyday life—and answer the questions that accompany them.

Cause and Effect in College

The following is an excerpt from a college textbook.

What Makes Marriages Work?

From a developmental perspective, marriage is a useful institution: Children generally thrive when two parents are directly committed to their well-being, and adults thrive if one other person satisfies their need for intimacy and for generativity. Yet, clearly, not all marriages accomplish these goals. Why do some marriages work well, while others do not?

Generativity means a desire to nurture children.

One developmental factor that influences the success of a marriage is the maturity of the partners. In general, the younger the bride and groom, the less likely their marriage is to succeed (Amato, Johnson, Booth, & Rogers, 2003). That may be because, as Erikson pointed out, intimacy is hard to establish until identity is secure. Thus, in a series of studies, college students who were less advanced on Erikson's identity and intimacy stages tended to define love in terms of passion, not intimacy or commitment—butterflies and excitement, not openness, trust, and loyalty (Aron & Westbay, 1996).

A second influence on marital success is the degree of similarity between husband and wife. Anthropologists distinguish between **homogamy**, or marriage within the same tribe or ethnic group, and **heterogamy**, or marriage outside the group. Traditionally, homogamy meant marriage between people of the same cohort, religion, socioeconomic status, ethnicity, and education. For contemporary marriages, homogamy and heterogamy refer to similarity [and difference, respectively] in interests, attitudes, and goals (Cramer, 1998).

One study of 168 young couples found that **social homogamy**, defined as similarity in leisure interests and role preferences, is particularly important to marital success (Houts, Robins, & Huston, 1996). For instance, if both spouses enjoyed (or hated) picnicking, dancing, swimming, going to the movies, listening to music, eating out, or entertaining friends, the partners tended to be more "in love" and more committed to the relationship. Similarly, if the two agreed on who should make meals, pay bills, shop for groceries, and so on, then ambivalence and conflict were reduced.

A third factor affecting the success of a marriage is **marital equity**, the extent to which the two partners perceive a rough equality in the partnership. In many modern marriages, the equity that is sought is in shared contributions. Both partners expect equality and sensitivity to their needs regarding dependence, sexual desire, shared confidences, and so on, and happier marriages are those in which both partners are adept at emotional perception and expression (Fitness, 2001). What matters most is the perception of fairness, not absolute equality.

> —From Kathleen Stassen Berger, *The Developing Person Through the Life Span,* Sixth Edition, 2005

References

Amato, P. R., Johnson, D. R., Booth, A., & Rogers, S. J. (2003). Continuity and change in marital quality between 1980 and 2000. *Journal of Marriage and Family, 65,* 1–22.

Aron, A., & Westbay, L. (1996). Dimensions of the prototype of love. *Journal of Personality and Social Relationships, 70,* 535–51.

Cramer, D. (1998). *Close relationships: The study of love and friendship.* New York: Oxford University Press.

Fitness, J. (2001). Intimate relationships. In J. Ciarrochi, J. R. Forgas, & J. D. Mayer (Eds.), *Emotional intelligence in everyday life: A scientific inquiry* (pp. 98–112). Philadelphia: Psychology Press.

Houts, R. M., Robins, E., & Huston, T. L. (1996). Compatibility and the development of premarital relationships. *Journal of Marriage and the Family, 58,* 7–20.

1. Double-underline the **<u>thesis statement</u>** (the sentence indicating whether the piece will discuss causes or effects).

2. Put a check mark (✔) by each cause.

3. Why do you think certain words are in bold type? _____

    _____

    _____

4. Circle the **transitions**.

5. Does the piece have the **four basics of good cause and effect**? Why or why not? _____

    _____

6. What do you think are the most important factors for a marriage or other committed relationship?

■ For a list of the four basics of good cause and effect, see page 230.

■ The final question after each reading in this section makes a good essay topic.

Cause and Effect at Work

The following is a talk that Jolanda Jones gives to students.

Some of the worst life situations I've seen were caused simply by people failing to consider the effects of their actions. Each of you in this room must learn for yourselves that every single decision you make has consequences. It is important that you think about the decisions you make **before** you make them because if you don't, then you will end up somewhere you didn't plan for.

My best decisions are the ones I make when I think my grandmother might find out about them. If I would be proud for her to know the

Jolanda Jones
Attorney and Consultant

(See Jolanda's Profile of Success on p. 232.)

decision I've made, then it's probably a good decision. If I have to sneak or would be ashamed for her to know my decision, then it is probably a bad decision. In any case, here are some examples of the thought process in good decision making. They show what happens when you don't consider consequences.

Some of you girls might be getting pressured by your boyfriends to have sex. What should you think about? Well, you're probably wondering what he'll say if you don't sleep with him. Will he break up with you or call you "prude"? Well, don't let him define you. What if you get pregnant? What if you get a sexually transmitted disease? What if you get AIDS? What if you break up after you have sex with him? Will he tell everyone how good you were in bed? Will everyone know your business?

Single parenthood is hard. I know from personal experience. I had graduated from college, was working as a minority recruiter and admissions counselor, and was training for the Olympics. I also planned to go to law school at Stanford. Then, I got pregnant without planning for it. All of a sudden, I was expecting a child with a man who was both abusive and unsupportive. I was not married. I was disappointed in myself. I was ashamed of the shame I brought on my grandmother. I was a coward. I fled the United States and hid my pregnancy in Spain. I absolutely love my son, but I gave up my Olympic aspirations and Stanford Law School.

Some of you might be thinking about using drugs. Think long and hard. I have crackheads in my family whose lives have been destroyed. Some are homeless. Some are dying of AIDS. My aunt was murdered in a drug house. My brother was murdered buying marijuana. I have an alcoholic cousin who does not take care of her children, and she is on welfare. People who do drugs come to love drugs more than they love anyone or anything else. Then, the drugs control you. You lose control of your life.

What about crime, just little stuff, like shoplifting that little pair of earrings at the neighborhood Target? When I was sixteen, I'd worked to earn money to buy stuff I wanted. I wanted a pair of jeans. Instead, my mother took my check for herself. I still thought I was entitled to the jeans, so I went to Target and took a pair. I got caught. I was arrested, handcuffed, put in the back of a patrol car, and detained. I ducked my head down in the back of the patrol car. I just knew the whole world was looking at me. I was humiliated. I should have thought about the consequences. It wasn't right to steal from Target even if my mother took my check. You best believe I've thought about that ever since that date because I've never shoplifted again. I even told my son about it. I don't want him to make the same mistake that I did.

You have choices in life, and it's up to you to make the decisions that will most positively benefit your life. We are all capable of thinking through stuff and making the right decision. The question is: Are you going to do it or are you going to just take the easy road through life? My grandmother said, "If you make a bad decision, learn from it and move on; that way it's not your fault. If, however, you make the same mistake twice, you're stupid and it is your fault." I don't know about you, but I'm not stupid.

I've made good and bad decisions in my life. Thankfully, I've made more good ones than bad. I hope to continue to make good decisions by considering consequences and learning from my mistakes. I hope that's your philosophy too.

1. What grade level of students do you think Jolanda is addressing? _____

   _____

2. What is Jolanda's **purpose**? _____

   _____

3. Double-underline the **thesis statement** (the sentence indicating whether the piece will discuss causes or effects).

4. Underline each **topic sentence**.

5. Use ring diagrams (p. 240) to show one of the situations Jolanda presents, along with the causes or effects.

6. Double-underline the sentence in the concluding paragraph that restates Jolanda's main point.

7. Write about a time when you didn't consider the negative consequences of an action.

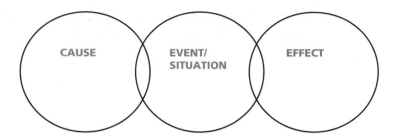

Cause and Effect in Everyday Life

The following example of cause/effect writing appeared in a popular magazine.

New Thoughts about Aromatherapy

People have been using fragrance to cure what ails them for thousands of years. Yet until recently, scientists have viewed aromatherapy as hocus-pocus. Now, however, researchers are finding that some scents do have real effects.

In a recent study, the pungent aroma of peppermint helped college athletes perform better with less effort, or at least it made them feel like superstars. In fact, according to measurements such as heart rate and blood pressure, the athletes got just as much benefit from the scent of jasmine and a stinky chemical called dimethyl sulfite. But in sports, believing you have a mental edge can translate into the real thing, and that's what matters, right?

Some scents can produce a calming effect. When you're anxious, sniff something that you associate with a more relaxed time in your life, suggests Will A. Wiener, Ph.D., a psychologist and director of the Institute for Performance Enhancement in Manhattan. This strategy has helped one of Wiener's clients, a professional basketball player who gets petrified at the free-throw line. Just before he shoots a basket, the player buries his nose in a handkerchief scented with a loved one's favorite cologne. The smell allows him to block out the jeering crowd and concentrate.

Researchers in Miami found that adults who sniffed lavender before and after tackling simple math problems worked faster, felt more relaxed, and made fewer mistakes. The fragrant herb can also improve your nights: In a small study, a British doctor found that lavender helped elderly insomniacs fall asleep sooner—and sleep longer—than sedatives did.

Although aromatherapy is not new, it has only recently been recognized by scientists and physicians as legitimate. In pharmacies and supermarkets throughout the country—in everything from shampoo to candles—aromatherapy is touted as having significant positive effects. Since the fragrances are natural, even if they don't produce significant results, it may well be worth giving them a try.

—Gabrielle Glaser, Health, July/August 2001

1. Double-underline the **thesis statement** (the sentence indicating whether the piece will discuss causes or effects).

2. Underline each **topic sentence**.

3. Put a check mark (✔) next to the effects of aromas.

4. What smells do you associate with a relaxed time in your life?

Write a Cause and Effect Essay

In this section, you will write your own cause/effect essay based on *one* of the following assignments. Before you begin to write, review the four basics of good cause and effect on page 230.

 ASSIGNMENT 1   WRITING ABOUT COLLEGE, WORK, AND EVERYDAY LIFE

Write a cause/effect essay on *one* of the following topics or on a topic of your own choice.

COLLEGE

• Immediate effects of being in college, or the desired long-term effects of going to college

- Causes of a legitimate absence that resulted in your missing a test (directed to your professor)
- From another course you are taking, the causes or effects of something that was discussed in the course or the textbook

WORK

- Causes of low employee morale
- Causes, effects, or both of a situation at work
- Effects of juggling work, school, and family

EVERYDAY LIFE

- Causes of an argument with a friend or a member of your family
- Effects of moving to a new place
- Effects of sleep deprivation (look for articles or Web sites)

ASSIGNMENT 2   WRITING ABOUT AN IMAGE

This photograph was taken at a summer camp for overweight youth. Write a cause/effect essay about either the causes or effects of childhood obesity.

ASSIGNMENT 3   WRITING TO SOLVE A PROBLEM

THE PROBLEM: Your child has been diagnosed with attention-deficit/hyper-activity disorder (ADHD), and the doctor has recommended that he take the drug Ritalin. The doctor assures you that Ritalin is very commonly prescribed for children with ADHD, but you are uncomfortable giving your child a drug that you know little about.

THE ASSIGNMENT: Working on your own or with a small group, write a paper that discusses the effects of Ritalin on children with ADHD. In your con-clusion, indicate whether you will put your child on Ritalin or not, based on what you now know.

RESOURCES: Review the chart on pages 726–27 for general advice on prob-lem solving. Also, type *effects of Ritalin on children with ADHD* into a search engine and view some of the Web sites on the subject. Make sure that the Web sites you consult are sponsored by medical organizations rather than drug companies. List any Web sites you use.

 ASSIGNMENT 4   WRITING ABOUT READINGS

Society's standards of who and what are good or bad are reflected in televi-sion, magazines, music, and virtually every other type of media. Media im-ages affect us all, whether or not we are aware of it, and several of the readings in this book deal with how people can be harmed by them. Choose one of the reading pairs below and write an essay on the topic that follows it.

1. Amy L. Beck's "Struggling for Perfection" on page 682 and "When the Regulation of Eating Behavior Fails: Anorexia and Bulimia" on page 217.

   • Discuss the issue that Beck raises and how the piece on anorexia and bulimia supports her point. Refer to both readings, and bring in your own experiences with media portrayals as well, including how you or people you know have been affected.

2. Amy L. Beck's "Struggling for Perfection" on page 682 and Tiffany Shale's "Lasting Lessons in *The Bluest Eye*" on page 285.

   • Discuss how both Pecola Breedlove and women today are affected by standards of beauty. What do they hope to gain? Refer specifically to each of the selections in your response. How have you been affected by society's standards of physical perfection?

3. Amy L. Beck's "Struggling for Perfection" on page 682 and Dave Barry's "The Ugly Truth about Beauty" on page 671.

   • Discuss the authors' different approaches to a similar topic. Analyze the differences, and discuss which piece is more effective to you and why.

4. Amy L. Beck's "Struggling for Perfection" on page 682 and Brent Staples's "Just Walk on By: Black Men and Public Space" on page 687.

   • How have the two different groups the authors portray been negatively affected by portrayals in the media? Bring in references from each reading along with your experiences of how the media can cause people to have incorrect, and sometimes dangerous, perceptions of themselves and others.

Follow the steps in the Writing Guide below to help you prewrite, draft, revise, and edit your comparison/contrast essay. Check off each step as you complete it.

WRITING GUIDE: CAUSE AND EFFECT

STEPS IN CAUSE AND EFFECT	HOW TO DO THE STEPS
Focus.	❑ Think about an event or situation that matters to you and whether you want to describe its causes, its effects, or both. Review the four basics of good cause and effect on page 230.
Prewrite to explore your topic. See Chapter 3 for more on prewriting.	❑ State what your purpose for writing is: to explain the causes, effects, or both. ❑ Use the ring diagram or clustering to get ideas about the causes or effects of your topic.
Write a thesis statement. The thesis statement in a cause/effect essay often includes the topic and an indicator of whether you will be discussing causes, effects, or both. Topic · Indicates effect A camping trip resulted in greater understanding among my family members. See Chapter 4 for more on writing a thesis statement.	❑ Write a thesis statement that includes your topic and an indicator of cause, effect, or both.

STEPS IN CAUSE AND EFFECT	HOW TO DO THE STEPS
Support your thesis statement. The major support for a cause/effect essay consists of the explanations of the causes or effects. See Chapter for 5 more on supporting a thesis statement.	❑ List the most important causes or effects of the event or situation mentioned in your thesis. ❑ For each cause or effect, give an example and details about how it caused or resulted from the event or situation. ❑ Add other causes or effects that you think of and delete any that are weak or won't make sense to your readers.
Make a plan. See Chapter 6 for more on planning.	❑ Make a plan or outline that presents your causes or effects according to order of importance or some other logical order.
Write a draft. See Chapter 7 for more on drafting.	❑ Write an introduction that includes your thesis statement. See if you can use one of the introductory techniques in Chapter 7. ❑ Write topic sentences for each paragraph, and give detailed examples or explanations of the cause or effect that you are presenting in that paragraph. ❑ Write a concluding paragraph that makes an observation about the topic and its causes or effects, based on the points you have made in your essay. ❑ Title your essay.
Revise your draft. See Chapter 8 for more on revising a draft.	❑ Ask another person to read and comment on your draft. ❑ See if your thesis statement and introduction could be clearer or more interesting to your readers. ❑ Reread the body of your essay to make sure the causes or effects really have caused the topic or resulted from it. ❑ Reread your conclusion to make sure it reinforces your main point. ❑ Add transitions to connect your ideas. ❑ Make at least five changes to your draft to improve unity, support, or coherence (see pp. 96–109). ❑ Check to make sure the draft follows the four basics of good cause and effect.
Edit your draft. See Parts Four through Seven for more on editing.	❑ Use the spell checker and grammar checker on your computer, but also reread your essay carefully to catch any errors. ❑ Look for errors in grammar, spelling, and punctuation. Focus first on fragments, run-ons, subject-verb agreement, verb problems, and other areas where you often make mistakes. ❑ Ask yourself: Is this the best I can do?

Whenever you try to convince some-one to do or avoid doing something, you use argument.

- You persuade a friend to lend you some money.
- You understand the argument being made in a public-service ad.

In the United States 5,000 children die each year from unintentional gun injuries. 300 of them are younger than 10.

17

Argument

Writing That Persuades

Understand What Argument Is

■ **IDEA JOURNAL**
Write about a time that you got some-thing you wanted by giving someone good reasons and making a good case.

Argument is writing that takes a position on an issue and offers reasons and supporting evidence to convince someone else to accept, or at least consider, that position. Argument is also used to persuade someone to take an action (or not to take an action).

⊞ FOUR BASICS OF GOOD ARGUMENT

1. It takes a strong and definite position on an issue or advises a par-ticular action.
2. It gives good reasons and supporting evidence to defend the posi-tion or recommended action.
3. It considers opposing views.
4. It has enthusiasm and energy from start to finish.

In the following paragraph, each number corresponds to one of the four basics of good argument.

4 Writing is enthusiastic and energetic

1 The drinking age should be lowered from twenty-one to eighteen. **2** The government gives eighteen-year-olds the right to vote. If they are adult enough to vote for the people and policies that run this country, they should be mature enough to have a drink. **2** The U.S. penal system also regards eighteen-year-olds as adults. If an eighteen-year-old commits a crime and goes to trial, he or she is tried and sentenced as an adult, not as a minor. That means that if the crime is murder, an eighteen-year-old could receive the death penalty. Eighteen-year-olds are not given special treatment. Most important is the fact that at eighteen, individuals can enlist in the armed forces and go to war. The government considers them old enough to die for their country but not old enough to have a drink? This makes no sense. **3** Opponents to lowering the drinking age justify their position by saying that if the age is lowered, teenagers will start drinking even earlier. However, there is no evidence to show that legal age is a major influence on teenage drinking. Other factors involved, such as peer pressure and the availability of fake IDs, have more impact on whether teenagers drink. While the government does need to address the issue of teenage drinking, forbidding eighteen-year-olds to drink while granting them other, more important rights and responsibilities at the same age is neither consistent nor reasonable.

Putting together a good argument is one of the most useful skills you can learn. Knowing how to argue well will equip you to defend effectively what you believe and to convince others to agree with you. We present an argument to persuade someone to give us a job, not to give us a parking ticket, to buy something we're selling, or to give us more time to finish a task. And we argue when something important is at stake, like keeping a job or protecting our rights. To argue effectively, we need to do more than just say what we want or believe; we need to give solid reasons and evidence.

Argument is the method you use to persuade people to see things your way, or at least to understand your position. Argument helps you to take action in problem situations rather than to stand by, silent and frustrated. Although knowing how to argue won't eliminate all such situations, it will help you to defend your position.

Many situations require good argument skills.

COLLEGE	An exit essay from a writing course contains the following instruction: "Develop a well-balanced argument on the subject of free speech on the Internet."
WORK	You present reasons why you should get a raise.
EVERYDAY LIFE	You convince a large company that it has made a mistake on your bill.

■ For an example of an actual argument written for work, see page 257. The piece was written by the college admissions officer who is profiled in the box on page 248.

Profile of Success

Wayne Whitaker

Assistant Director of Admissions

(See Wayne's Argument at Work on p. 257.)

BACKGROUND: Wayne grew up in New York City's South Bronx and Brooklyn. School was difficult for him, and most of his classes were in the vocational/technical program. At the end of his senior year, Wayne told his guidance counselor that he wanted to go to college. Although his grades weren't good, he was admitted to Bloomsburg University through a special admissions program, ACT 101. Wayne, now a recruiter for the school he attended, helps others also gain admission to Bloomsburg University.

EMPLOYER: Bloomsburg University

COLLEGE(S)/DEGREES: Bloomsburg University (B.A. and M.S.)

TYPES OF WRITING ON THE JOB: Letters to students telling them about Bloomsburg and encouraging them to apply, federal and state grant proposals for recruitment programs, reports to administration and granting agencies, frequent e-mails, presentations to prospective students

HOW WAYNE USES ARGUMENT: It is part of Wayne's job to convince students to apply to and attend Bloomsburg. He does this through persuasive letters, presentations, and personal conversations.

TEAMWORK ON THE JOB: As a recruiter, Wayne works with high school guidance counselors, colleagues, the athletic department, and other offices. To ensure successful campus visits, he works with everyone from maintenance and cafeteria staff to faculty and administration.

Main Point in Argument

Your **main point** in an argument is the position you take on the issue you are writing about. When you are free to choose an issue, choose something you care about strongly. But even when you are assigned an issue, find something about it that you feel strongly about and take a definite position. You should approach your argument feeling committed to and enthusiastic about your position.

Take a few minutes to think about the issue, talk it over with a partner, or jot down ideas related to it. On the next page are some tips to get you started.

Once you have decided on your position and have built up some heat for it, write a thesis statement that includes the issue and your position on it.

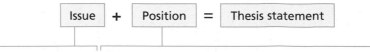

| Issue | + | Position | = | Thesis statement |

The drinking age should be lowered from twenty-one to eighteen.

Tips for Building Energy and Enthusiasm

- Imagine yourself arguing your position with someone who holds the opposite position.
- Imagine that your whole grade rests on persuading your teacher of your position.
- Imagine how this issue could affect you or your family personally.
- Imagine that you are representing a large group of people who very much care about the issue and whose lives will be forever changed by it. It's up to you to win their case.

The current minimum wage is not enough to live on.

The most important thing about a marriage is that two people love and respect each other, not what sex they are.

Sometimes the thesis combines the issue and the position, as in the following statements:

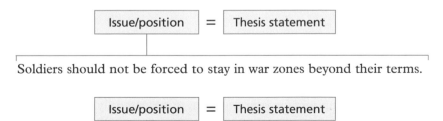

Soldiers should not be forced to stay in war zones beyond their terms.

All eighteen-year-olds should be drafted into the military.

Try to make the thesis statement for any argument as specific as possible to help guide your writing and your readers.

VAGUE	Our health care system is disgraceful.
MORE SPECIFIC	Two key reforms would make health care more afford-able for all. [The paper would detail the two reforms.]

Many thesis statements for arguments use words such as the following be-cause they clearly express a position:

could (not)   ought (not)

must (not)   requires

must have   should (not)

needs   would

■ **PRACTICE 1   WRITING A STATEMENT OF YOUR POSITION**

Write your position on the following issues.

Banning junk food and sugary drinks from elementary and high schools

_____

Mandatory drug testing as a requirement for employment

_____

Free college courses for prisoners

_____

Now, take one of the position statements that you just wrote and put more energy into it.

_____

Support in Argument

However strongly you may feel about an issue, if you don't provide solid **support** for your position, you will not convince anyone to see it your way. As you develop support for your position, think carefully about your read-ers and what kind of information will be most convincing to them.

■ For online exercises on main point and support, visit Exer-cise Central at <**bedfordstmartins** .com/realessays>.

Reasons and Evidence

The major support for your position consists of the **reasons** that you give for that position. These reasons must be backed up with **evidence**, such as facts, examples, and expert opinions. The success of your argument depends on the quality of the reasons and evidence that you present to support your position.

Facts are statements or observations that can be proved true. **Statistics**—numerical facts based on research—can be persuasive evidence to back up your position. **Examples** are specific experiences or information that support your position. **Expert opinion** is the opinion of someone who is considered an expert in the area you are writing about. *Note:* The fact that a person's opinion appears on a Web site does not necessarily mean that he or she has any expertise. When in doubt about a source's authority, consult your instructor or a research librarian.

■ For more on finding sources, using quotations, and citing sources, see Chapter 20.

POSITION	It pays to stay in college.
REASON	College graduates earn more than high school graduates.
EVIDENCE/ FACT	College graduates earn 68 percent more than high school graduates and 320 percent more than high school dropouts.
REASON	Students learn up-to-date skills that they will need to find a job.
EVIDENCE/ EXAMPLE	Understanding how to use technology in your field may make the difference between getting a job and coming in second.
REASON	An increasing number of jobs require college degrees.
EVIDENCE/ EXPERT OPINION	John Sterling, president of one of the largest recruiting agencies, said recently, "Ten years ago, a college degree was perceived as an advantage. Today, the college degree is the basic ticket of entry for the majority of jobs." [*Note:* When you use expert opinion, you need to identify the source of the quote.]

As you choose reasons and evidence to support your position, consider your readers. Are they likely to agree with you, to be uncommitted, or to be hostile? Choose the support that is most likely to convince them, drawing on outside sources (such as the library or Internet) as needed.

Opposing Positions

Part of supporting your position is acknowledging the opposing position and presenting some evidence against it. If, for example, you are arguing in favor of lowering the drinking age to eighteen, you should not ignore the position that it should be kept at age twenty-one. If you don't say anything about the other position, you are leaving your argument unprotected. To defend your own position, show some weakness in the opposing position.

The writer of the paragraph on page 246 might consider the opposing position as follows:

POSITION   The drinking age should be lowered from twenty-one to eighteen.

OPPOSING POSITION   The drinking age should not be lowered because people begin drinking before the legal age. If the age were lowered to eighteen, more sixteen-year-olds would drink.

ACKNOWLEDGING THE OPPOSING POSITION: Laws should not be based on the extent to which they are likely to be abused or broken. Enforcement (or lack of enforcement) should not influence the law itself.

The writer expanded his response to the opposing position in this way:

There is no evidence to show that legal age is a major influence on teenage drinking. Other factors involved, such as peer pressure and the availability of fake IDs, have more impact on whether teenagers drink.

PRACTICE 2   ACKNOWLEDGING AND ADDRESSING THE OPPOSING VIEW

For each of the following positions, in the spaces indicated, state the opposing position and at least one point someone holding the opposing view might make against your position.

ISSUE: The "Three Strikes and You're Out" rule in some high schools that requires students to be expelled after three serious offenses

POSITION: Against it

OPPOSITION POSITION: _____

POINT THAT SOMEONE HOLDING THE OPPOSITION POSITION WOULD MAKE:

_____

ISSUE: Mandatory retirement at age sixty-seven

POSITION: In favor of it

OPPOSING POSITION: _____

POINT THAT SOMEONE HOLDING THE OPPOSING POSITION WOULD MAKE:

_____

Tips for Supporting Your Position by Addressing the Opposing Position

- Visualize someone who holds the opposing position and what that person would say to defend it.
- In part of the body of your essay, acknowledge the opposing position. Do so politely; if you try to ridicule the opposing view, you will alienate people and immediately weaken your argument.
- Poke some holes in the opposing position by addressing it head-on and showing what's wrong, or misguided, about the position. Again, do this politely; don't make your opposition look foolish.
- Return to the reasons and the evidence that support your position.

ISSUE: Stricter gun control laws

POSITION: Against it

OPPOSING POSITION: _____

POINT THAT SOMEONE HOLDING THE OPPOSING POSITION WOULD MAKE:

_____

In a short essay, you may not be able to address all the points of the opposing view, but you should know what they are and address at least the most important ones. As you gather support for your position, keep the opposing position in mind and follow the tips given in the box.

Organization in Argument

Argument most often uses **order of importance** to organize reasons for the writer's position on the issue. Consider what you think your readers will find your most convincing reason. Arrange your reasons and evidence so that they build the strongest case for your position, and save the most convincing reason for last. Do not forget to acknowledge and address the opposing position somewhere in your argument. The plan for an argument often looks like this:

Introduction (including thesis statement)
First reason
    Evidence to back up reason

Second reason

    Evidence to back up reason

Most important reason

    Evidence to back up reason

Conclusion

    Reminds readers of your position on the issue and makes a final pitch for that position

    May also make a further recommendation or issue a warning about what will happen if your position is ignored or defeated

As you write your argument, use transitions to connect your reasons to your thesis and your evidence to your reasons. Here are some transitions often used for argument.

Common Transitions in Argument

TRANSITIONS FROM ONE POINT TO ANOTHER	TRANSITIONS TO ADD EMPHASIS
also	above all
another fact to consider	best of all
another reason	especially
another thing	in fact
consider that	in particular
for example	more important
in addition	most important
in the first place	remember
	the last point to consider
	worst of all

Read and Analyze Argument

Before writing your own argument essay, read the following examples — one each from college, the workplace, and everyday life — and answer the questions that accompany them.

Argument in College

The following student essays take opposing views in response to the question "Should public schools celebrate religious holidays?" The essays originally appeared in *The New York Times Upfront*.

Yes

Vidhya Murugesan

From kindergarten through high school, I have been fortunate enough to be exposed to a wide array of cultures. This often included participating in the religious holidays celebrated by my classmates: everything from Easter egg hunts to menorah lightings. Though creationism in science classes and schoolwide prayer have no place in public schools, coming in contact with holy celebrations from around the world can promote a culture consciousness that is irreplaceable. As long as several religious holidays are given equal standing in classrooms, and administrators take care not to advocate any particular religion or induce devotion or worship of any kind, there is no reason for a church-versus-state conflict.

In most cases, culture and religious holidays are inextricably linked. Students should never be required to check their culture at the door. By forbidding them to participate in religious festivities, schools would succeed only in depriving students of experiences, traditions, and backgrounds other than their own.

Living in a multicultural society like the United States is an advantage that most people around the world do not have. Why should we scoff at the opportunities that are available to us because of that diversity? Taking the steps to understand other cultures, such as participating in religious holidays, is instrumental in fostering true tolerance, and political correctness should not get in the way of letting students experience that.

No

Katie Smith

Although I am quite religious, I feel there is no need to openly celebrate religion in school. By celebrating religious holidays, the school system is breaking apart a diverse body of students and making them unequal.

As with anything else, there will always be the student in the class who doesn't celebrate Christmas or Hanukkah or Kwanzaa. How will those students feel when the class is cutting out construction-paper Christmas trees? Or making menorahs? Or, even worse, how will the other kids react to their different beliefs? Although it may not be right, it is human nature that many people pick on others for not believing what they do. By openly celebrating holidays in school, teachers are setting up these vulnerable children who may not fall into the majority religious beliefs.

Not only does celebrating religious holidays in school cause disruptions in school, but it can also cause disruptions at home. Some parents may not want their children exposed to certain religions. This practice may not be looked highly upon, but it is any parent's right to make these decisions. If they do not want their child, especially a young child, learning about certain religions, then that exposure should not occur in our schools.

The Constitution specifically separates church and state for good reason. It protects the people and maintains equality. If we begin to break apart the Constitution by making exceptions for special holidays, what right might we lose next?

1. Double-underline the **thesis statement** in each essay.

2. Underline the **topic sentences** in each essay.

3. What kinds of **support** (facts, examples, expert opinion) does each student use? _____

4. Regardless of your own position, which student's argument is the most convincing? _____

■ For a list of the four basics of good argument, see page 246.

5. Which of the four basics of good argument does each student omit?

_____

■ The final question after each reading in this section makes a good essay topic.

6. Which position do you agree with and why?

Argument at Work

When you write an argument at work, the issue may not be one you feel passionately about. However, you still use the four basics of good argument. When you work with others and your success depends partly on what they do, hardly a day will go by when you don't use argument strategies to convince someone of something.

The following letter to a student is similar to ones that Wayne Whitaker writes when he is trying to persuade a student to apply to Bloomsburg University. One measure of Wayne's success at his job is how many students enroll for each new class, so it is important that he persuade people to apply. Note how Wayne uses what he knows about his audience, the student Ms. Petrona, to present reasons that will be important to her.

Wayne Whitaker

Assistant Director of Admissions

(See Wayne's Profile of Success on p. 248.)

Dear Ms. Petrona:

I'm glad that we had an opportunity to talk during your recent visit to Bloomsburg University. Based on our conversation, I am convinced that Bloomsburg is the ideal college for you. I hope to convince you of that, too.

Bloomsburg University will offer you unparalleled support that will help you adjust to and succeed in college. We discussed the fact that you feel a little intimidated by the whole idea of college. Well, Ms. Petrona, you certainly aren't alone in that feeling, and I can assure you that we have the resources you need to set you on the strong course. Our ACT 101 summer program will ensure that you have the basic skills you need for your first-year courses. Your ACT 101 counselor will be your mentor and adviser throughout college, a wise and savvy guide who is there to help you with any issue. As one of our ACT 101 graduates, Roberta Connoni, said, "I wouldn't have made it in college without ACT 101. The people there gave me the information and confidence I needed to believe I could get a college degree."

Bloomsburg University also has a very strong business program that should be attractive to you since you are interested in majoring in business. Our courses are small, so you receive individual attention. Many of our faculty members are also working professionals who have real-life experience to bring to the classroom. And the university has strong relationships with local and state businesses. Last year, 85 percent of our business majors had received job offers prior to graduation.

Bloomsburg University is a community, not just an institution. Our rural location helps us focus on our shared purpose: to learn and develop as citizens. We are a community of learners rather than some buildings set among other city buildings. This setting reinforces our mission and joins us all in the mission of learning.

Ms. Petrona, you will thrive here. Based on your background and the needs you cited, Bloomsburg is a perfect match. We are eager to welcome you to our community and will look forward to helping you achieve your best.

1. What is Wayne's **purpose**? _____

2. Double-underline Wayne's **thesis statement**.

3. Put a check mark (✔) by the reasons he gives Ms. Petrona.

4. Underline the sentence in which he addresses Ms. Petrona's possible opposing position.

5. If you were a potential applicant to Bloomsburg University, would Wayne's argument convince you to apply? Why or why not?

Argument in Everyday Life

The following is the body of a letter that one Philadelphia-area resident wrote to the chair of the school committee in her town.

I am painfully aware that violence in schools is a clear and present danger, in our town as everywhere. I realize that schools must take precautions to ensure the safety of their students. However, recent events in our schools make me wonder whether we have overreacted to the threat of violence and have lost our common sense. With the enactment of new rules, we must make sure that common sense still prevails as the judge of what is punishable behavior.

Common sense dictates that there are legitimate exceptions to every rule. Many items are banned from school for good reason: guns, knives, and so on. The penalty for having any contraband item is immediate suspension. These rules make sense. But what of the young woman, a diabetic, at the high school who was suspended for having a needle? It was part of her medical kit—she gives herself daily injections of insulin. Does it make sense to suspend her without consideration of the circumstances?

Common sense also dictates that a student should not be punished for fulfilling an assignment. What about the student whose teacher made an assignment to write an imaginative short story, a horror story, with details that made it lifelike and truly scary? When the student wrote a powerful short story about a student who stalks and then murders an English teacher, the student was suspended because of the threat to the teacher. Maybe the student didn't use the best judgment, but was there a punishable act?

In both of the above cases, the students were eventually reinstated, but not without a good deal of trauma and embarrassment for everyone involved. What message does that send to our students? I believe that common sense is a key element to good judgment, something I want my children to learn. What are they learning when common sense goes out the window? As adults, we need to apply common sense, particularly in the schools, our institutions of learning.

1. What is the writer's **purpose**? _____

   _____

2. What does the letter suggest about the writer's **audience**? _____

   _____

3. What is the writer's position on the issue? _____

   _____

4. Double-underline the **thesis statement**.

5. Underline each **topic sentence**.

6. Does the writer offer convincing evidence? Why or why not?

7. What behaviors should or should not be punished in schools?

Write an Argument Essay

In this section you will write your own argument essay based on *one* of the following assignments. Before you begin to write, review the four basics of good argument on page 246.

 ASSIGNMENT 1 WRITING ABOUT COLLEGE, WORK, AND EVERYDAY LIFE

Write an argument essay on *one* of the following topics or on a topic of your own choice. Select an issue that you care about so that you can argue powerfully.

COLLEGE

- Persuade one of your teachers to raise the grade on your last assignment (in a course you are currently taking).
- Defend the following statement: "A college degree means something."
- Present your instructor with reasons why you should be able to make up a test that you missed.
- For a political science course, write an essay agreeing or disagreeing with the statement "Marriage is a lifelong union between a man and a woman."

WORK

- Argue against a company policy that you believe is unfair.
- Argue that you should get a promotion.
- Argue that an employer should/should not have the right to intervene in office romances.
- Argue that employers should/should not outsource jobs to foreign countries.

EVERYDAY LIFE

- Argue against a rent increase.
- Argue for or against McDonald's being sued by obese people who have eaten there regularly.
- Take a stand on a local issue or policy that you believe is unfair.

ASSIGNMENT 2   **WRITING ABOUT AN IMAGE**

The people in the photograph are protesting proposed reductions in federal rent subsidies for low-income people. In cities with high rental costs,
the reductions will force many people out of their homes.

Choose a proposed change that threatens your personal security and
present an argument against it.

 ASSIGNMENT 3   **WRITING TO SOLVE A PROBLEM**

THE PROBLEM: An alumnus has given your college a large donation that is
intended to improve the quality of student life. The president has set up a
committee to determine several possible uses for the money, and you are
one of the students on that committee.

THE ASSIGNMENT: Working either on your own or with a small group, first
decide on three possible uses of the money that would improve the quality of student life. Then, choose one of them and write a letter to the president arguing for this use of the donation. Be sure to include solid reasons
for your choice.

RESOURCES: To help you decide which of the three possible uses you will
argue for, you might type into a search engine key words related to areas
in need of improvement at your college (for example, *[your college] computer center*). List any Web sites that you use.

ASSIGNMENT 4   WRITING ABOUT READINGS

On pages 693–706 are pro and con arguments on two issues (reinstating the draft and same-sex marriage). Take a position on one of these issues, reading the relevant essays to inform your position. Then, using the Internet or the library, find another piece that supports your stance. Write an argument essay based on *one* of the following assignments:

- Defend your position on the issue, citing the source you have found and the essay in this book that shares your view. Be sure to answer the opposing arguments from the essay that counters your view. To complete this assignment, you will need to summarize the positions that each essay presents.

- Write a response to the author who takes the opposing view. Use both the other two essays and your own thoughts to support your position.

- Write a letter to your senator expressing your position on gay marriage or reinstating the draft. Support your position by drawing on the two pieces that share your view.

- Referring to the four basics of good argument (p. 246), analyze one of the arguments presented on pages 693–706. Consider how well the writer supports his or her position with reasons and evidence. Try to suggest at least two ways in which the argument could have been improved.

 ASSIGNMENT 5   ARGUMENT WRITING TESTS

Many states and colleges require students to take a timed writing test. Often the test calls for an argument essay on an assigned issue, and students must argue for or against the issue, as directed. Many people believe that a good writer should be able to argue either side of an issue regardless of his or her personal feelings. Choose one of the following questions, come up with evidence to support both sides of the issue, and write an essay defending one side or another. *Note:* Part of the requirement of the essay is to be able to support each side, so you will need to turn in the support you develop for each side of the position.

- Should students be penalized for poor attendance?
- Should the government make it more difficult for couples to divorce?
- Should personal e-mail messages written on a company's computer be company property or personal property?

Follow the steps in the Writing Guide on the next page to help you prewrite, draft, revise, and edit your argument. Check off each step as you complete it.

WRITING GUIDE: ARGUMENT	
STEPS IN ARGUMENT	**HOW TO DO THE STEPS**
Focus.	❑ Before and as you write, think about your position on an issue and how you can persuade readers to see things your way. Review the four basics of good argument on page 246.
Prewrite to explore your topic. See Chapter 3 for more on prewriting (including freewriting).	❑ Use a prewriting technique to explore an issue that you care about and your position on it. Freewriting is a good technique for many people. ❑ Consider why the issue is important to you and how it affects you. ❑ Think about what reasons you have for your position. ❑ Take a few minutes to build some energy about the issue.
Write a thesis statement. The thesis statement of an argument essay usually includes the issue and the writer's position on that issue. Issue + Position = Thesis The minimum wage should be raised. See Chapter 4 for more on writing a thesis statement.	❑ Consider your readers and what their opinions might be. ❑ Write a thesis that includes the issue and your position.
Support your thesis statement. The major support for an argument consists of the reasons for the writer's position. These reasons must be backed by evidence, such as facts, examples, and expert opinions. See Chapter 5 for more on supporting a thesis statement.	❑ Think about your readers and what will convince them of your position. ❑ Use a prewriting technique to come up with good reasons for your position. ❑ Choose the most persuasive reasons, selecting at least three. (Drop reasons or evidence that are weak or not directly related to your position on the issue.) ❑ Back your reasons with facts, good examples, or expert opinions. (Consider whether you will need to use outside sources.) ❑ Consider and address opposing positions.
Make a plan. See Chapter 6 for more on planning.	❑ Write a plan or outline, arranging your reasons according to order of importance and saving the most important reason for last.

continued

STEPS IN ARGUMENT	HOW TO DO THE STEPS
Write a draft. See Chapter 7 for more on drafting.	❏ Write an introduction that gets your readers' interest and presents your thesis. See if you can use one of the introductory techniques in Chapter 7. ❏ Using your outline, write a topic sentence for each of your reasons. ❏ Write body paragraphs with supporting evidence for each of your reasons. ❏ Write a concluding paragraph that makes a final case for your position based on the reasons you have presented. ❏ Title your essay.
Revise your draft. See Chapter 8 for more on revising a draft.	❏ Ask another person to read and comment on your draft. ❏ Cut any reasons that don't directly support your point or that seem weak. ❏ Add reasons and evidence that might help convince readers of your position. ❏ Add transitions to move readers smoothly from one reason to another. ❏ Rewrite your thesis statement to make it more concrete and forceful. ❏ Reread your introduction to make sure that it states your position with confidence and hooks your readers. ❏ Reread your conclusion to make sure it reminds readers of your position and makes a final pitch for it. ❏ Make sure that the essay as a whole is energetic and drives home your point. ❏ Make at least five changes to your draft to improve its unity, support, or coherence (see pp. 96–109). ❏ Check to make sure the draft follows the four basics of good argument.
Edit your draft. See Parts Four through Seven for more on editing.	❏ Use the spell checker and grammar checker on your computer, but also reread your essay carefully to catch any errors. ❏ Look for errors in grammar, spelling, or punctuation. Focus first on sentence fragments, run-ons, errors in subject-verb agreement, verb errors, and other areas where you often make mistakes. ❏ Ask yourself: Is this the best I can do?

Part Three

Special College Writing Projects

18

Writing under Pressure

Tests, Essay Exams, and Timed Writing

Studying for Tests

Everyone gets nervous about taking tests. The trick is to turn that nervousness into positive energy by learning test-taking strategies. This chapter will give you tips on studying for tests as well as specific advice about essay exams and other timed writing assignments.

Here are five reliable tips to help you study for any exam:

TIPS FOR STUDYING

- Ask about the test.
- Study with a partner or group.
- Predict what will be on the exam.
- Use study aids.
- Review actively.

Ask about the Test

Ask your instructor about an upcoming test. Just make sure you ask reasonable questions.

ASK	NOT
• What part of the course or text will it cover?	• What's on the test?

ASK	NOT
• Will the format be multiple choice, short answer, or essay?	• You're not going to give us an essay question, are you?
• Will we be allowed to use notes or books?	• We can just look up the answers, right?
• What percentage of my course grade will this count for?	• Is this test important?
• Can you recommend what to review?	• Do I need to read the book? Is the stuff you said in class important?
• Will we have the whole period to complete the test?	• How long is it?
• I know I have to miss class that day (give your reason). Can I arrange to take the test at another time?	• Is there a makeup test?

Write down your instructor's answers to your questions. Don't rely on your memory; you will be busy enough remembering the material for the exam without having to remember what your instructor said.

Study with a Partner or a Group

Forming a study group is well worth the time and effort it takes. Setting a time to study with others guarantees that you'll study, and pooling ideas improves everyone's ability to predict what will be on the test. Do some preparation before group meetings so that you make the most of the study time. The following are some tips on how study group members can prepare for a meeting:

- Each person can take responsibility for a particular section of the material, preparing a list of five to ten questions that might be on the test. Questions and possible responses can then be discussed in the group.
- Each person can copy his or her notes on a particular chapter, section, or topic and distribute them to the members of the group.
- Each person can come up with a list of the five most important things he or she learned about the material to be covered on the test.
- Each person can make a list of things he or she doesn't understand.

Predict What Will Be on the Exam

Whether you are studying with other people or by yourself, make a list of what you think will be on the exam. Look over your notes, assignments, and any previous tests or quizzes. Try writing questions for that material, and then try answering your own questions.

If you are confused about any material, ask about it either in class, after class, or during your instructor's office hours. Your instructor will probably welcome questions by e-mail as well. Do not go into an exam knowing that you don't understand a major concept.

PRACTICE 1   PREDICTING THE CONTENT OF A TEST

Imagine that you are having a quiz in this class next week. With a partner or in a small group, identify three topics that might be on that quiz, and write one question for each.

TOPIC: Process for solving a problem

QUESTION: List the steps involved in the problem-solving process.

TOPIC: _____

QUESTION: _____

TOPIC: _____

QUESTION: _____

TOPIC: _____

QUESTION: _____

Use Study Aids

Use one or more of the following study aids—or any other that is available to you—to ensure your success:

• Reread your notes, looking especially for anything you've underlined or marked in some other way.

• If you are being tested on material from your textbook, reread chapter reviews, summaries, or boxes containing key concepts.

- Review handouts from your instructor.
- Consider other available ways to review material—audiotapes, videos, computer exercises, study guides, the course or textbook Web site, and so on.

Review Actively

■ For more on active, critical reading, see Chapter 1, pages 4–15.

The following are some suggestions for reviewing material actively:

- To review material from a book, take notes. Improve your memory by writing information in your own words.
- To review handouts, use a colored pen or highlighter to mark the most important ideas, most useful facts, and other key information.
- Say important material aloud. Many people learn well by hearing something in addition to seeing it.
- To review notes, rewrite them in other words or in another format. For example, if you've written an outline, transform it into a chart or diagram that shows the relationships among ideas (see, for example, the clustering diagram on p. 39).

Doubling Your Chances of Passing Exams

Some students fail exams or get low grades because they don't understand the material. Others know the material but still score low because they don't have any useful strategies for taking exams.

STRATEGIES FOR TAKING EXAMS

- Be prepared.
- Manage your nerves.
- Understand the directions.
- Survey the whole exam before starting.
- Develop a plan.

Be Prepared

If you have followed the advice in the first part of this chapter, you've already done the most important preparation. But don't arrive at the exam and discover that you've left something essential at home. Take some time the night before to think about what you need. Make a list of what to bring (pen? books? calculator? notebook? textbook? computer disk? watch?), and assemble everything so that it's ready to go.

Manage Your Nerves

Get as much rest as possible the night before the exam, and allow extra time to get to class. Arrive early enough to settle in. Sit up straight, take a deep breath, and remind yourself that you know the material. You're pre-pared; you're ready; you will pass. When your instructor starts to talk, look up and listen.

Understand the Directions

Misunderstanding or ignoring directions is a major reason students do poorly on exams, so please pay attention to the advice here. First, listen to the **spoken directions** your instructor gives. It's tempting to start flipping through the exam as soon as you get it rather than listening to what your instructor is saying. Resist the temptation. Your instructor may be giving you key advice or information that's not written elsewhere, and you may miss it if you're not paying attention.

Second, when you begin the test, carefully read the **written direc-tions** for each part. Sometimes, students answer all of the questions in a section only to find out afterward that the directions said to answer only one or two. If you don't understand any part of the directions, be sure to ask your instructor for clarification.

Survey the Whole Exam before Starting

Look over the whole exam before doing anything. See how many parts the exam has, and make sure to look on both sides of all pages. Note the kinds of questions and how many points each question or part is worth. Often, the toughest questions (and the ones worth the most points) are at the end, so you will want to leave enough time to answer those.

Develop a Plan

First, **budget your time**. After surveying the whole test, write down how much time you will allow for each part. You might even find it helpful to calculate what time you want to start each section: Part 1 at 9:40, Part 2 at 9:55, and so on. Make sure you leave enough time for the parts with the highest point values, such as essay questions: They can take longer than you think they will. As you plan your time, keep in mind how much time you *really* have for the exam: A "two-hour" exam may be only one hour and fifty minutes once your instructor has finished giving directions. Remember also to leave a few minutes to check your work.

Second, **decide on an order**: where you should start, what you should do second, third, and so on. Start with the questions you can answer quickly and easily, but stay within your time budget on them.

Finally, **monitor your time** during the exam. If you find you're really stuck on a question and you're going way over your time budget, move on. If you have time at the end of the exam period, you can always go back to it.

Answering an Essay Question or a Timed Writing Assignment

An **essay question** is an examination item that asks you to write one or several paragraphs explaining and illustrating your answer. A **timed writing** is an assignment that requires writing one or several paragraphs in response to a question or prompt within a set amount of time.

Essay questions on an exam are usually worth more points than short-answer or multiple-choice questions, so they deserve special attention. Apply the following strategies to both essay questions and timed writings.

> **STRATEGIES FOR ANSWERING AN ESSAY QUESTION**
> **OR TIMED WRITING ASSIGNMENT**
>
> • Read the question carefully.
> • Write a thesis statement.
> • Make an outline.
> • Write your answer.
> • Reread and revise your answer.

Read the Question Carefully

Read an essay question or writing assignment carefully so that you know exactly what it calls for you to do. Look for three kinds of key words:

• Words that tell you *what subject* to write on.
• Words that tell you *how to write about it.*
• Words that tell you *how many parts* your answer should have.

Tells how many parts the answer should have

Discuss two major causes of personal bankruptcy in this country.

Tells how to write the response   Tells what subject to write about

Define and give examples of the phenomenon of global warming.

Tells how to write the response   Tells what subject to write about

Once you understand the type of answer expected, you can both follow the directions and draw on your experience writing similar essays.

Common Key Words in Essay Exam Questions

■ For additional terms that may come up on tests and assignments (and definitions of these terms), see the chart on page 17 of Chapter 1.

KEY WORD	WHAT IT MEANS
Analyze	Break into parts (classify) and discuss
Define	State the meaning and give examples
Describe the **stages** of	List and explain steps in a process
Discuss the **causes** of	List and explain the causes
Discuss the **concept** of	Define and give examples
Discuss the **differences between**	Contrast and give examples
Discuss the **effects/results** of	List and explain the effects
Discuss the **meaning** of	Define and give examples
Discuss the **similarities between**	Compare and give examples
Discuss the **stages/steps** of	Explain a process
Evaluate	Make a supported judgment
Explain the **term**	Define and give examples
Follow/trace the **development** of	Give the history; narrate the story
Follow/trace the **process** of	Explain the sequence of steps or stages in the process
Identify	Define and give examples
Should . . . ?	Argue for or against
Summarize	Give a brief overview

■ **PRACTICE 2   IDENTIFYING KEY WORDS**

Read the following essay questions, and then circle the key words that tell what subject to write about, how to write about it, and how many parts to write. In the space below each item, explain what the question is asking the writer to do.

EXAMPLE: (Define) and (illustrate)(dependency.)

Give the meaning of the term dependency and give examples of it.

1. Identify three causes of the second war in Iraq.

2. Trace the stages of grieving.

3. Discuss the problem of the current energy crisis.

4. Should drivers be banned from using handheld cell phones while driving? Why or why not?

Write a Thesis Statement

■ For more on writing a thesis statement, see Chapter 4.

Your response should include a thesis statement that is simple and clear. In the thesis statement, you may want to preview what you plan to cover in your answer, because sometimes an instructor will give partial credit for information contained in the thesis even if you run out of time to explain fully.

The best way to stay on track in an essay exam is to write a thesis statement that contains the key words from the essay question and restates the question as a main idea. It also helps to reread your thesis statement several times as you write your exam response.

The following are possible thesis statements for the four essay questions from Practice 2. Because the answers would depend on material covered in a course or on particular student opinions, we have used blanks instead of specific answers.

Three major causes underlie the second Iraq war: _____,
_____, and _____.

People normally move through _____ stages of grieving:
_____, _____, _____, (and however
many there are).

The current energy crisis is a problem because it _____,
_____, and _____.

Drivers should be banned from using handheld cell phones while
driving because of _____ and _____ (or however
many reasons).

PRACTICE 3 WRITING THESIS STATEMENTS

Write possible thesis statements in response to the following sample essay
exam questions. Even if you do not know the answer to the question, write
a thesis statement that responds to the question and lets the reader know
what you will cover (as in the possible answers above).

ESSAY EXAM QUESTION: Discuss the concept of First Amendment (free
speech) protection as it relates to pornography on the Internet.

POSSIBLE THESIS STATEMENT: The protection of First Amendment rights is
often cited as a reason not to ban pornography on the Internet.

1. Discuss the causes of the decline of the traditional "nuclear family"
   (two married parents and their children living under the same roof,
   without others).

   _____

2. Explain the effects of binge drinking.

   _____

3. Trace the development of the Industrial Revolution in Lowell,
   Massachusetts.

   _____

4. Describe the atmospheric conditions that precede a thunderstorm.

   _____

5. Discuss three advantages or three disadvantages of reliance on e-mail.

   _____

Make an Outline

■ For more on outlining, see Chapter 6.

Make a short, informal outline to map out your answer to an essay question or writing prompt. Include any important names, dates, or facts that occur to you. This outline will help you stick to your main points and remember essential details as you write.

Write Your Answer

■ For more on the parts of an essay, see pages 28–30 and Chapters 6 and 7.

Your answer to an essay question should always be in essay form, with an introductory paragraph, several support points, and a concluding paragraph.

Here is an essay written by Brenda White of Quinsigamond Community College, in response to the essay prompt "Discuss your role model."

Introduction states thesis and previews support points.

My role model is my best friend, Tanya, a single mother. Although young, unmarried parents are often looked down upon in our society, Tanya has overcome many obstacles and is doing an excellent job raising her son. I admire her patience, independence, and willingness to work hard. With these qualities, she defies the stereotype of the teen parent.

Support point 1

Tanya could have made the choice to terminate her pregnancy, but she decided not to because she knew that she had the patience to raise a child, even under difficult circumstances. She has incredible patience with her son, Quentin. For example, when he's crying—even for a long time—she'll just rock him until he sleeps. Tanya also has patience with her friends. She understands that they have other things to do and can't always be counted on to watch Quentin. Tanya never gets mad if we can't help her out. She is also patient with her mother, who is very critical. Tanya's steady patience has gotten her through many difficult situations.

Support point 2

Independence is another trait that makes Tanya a good role model. She is raising her son without the help of her parents and mostly without Quentin's father. Tanya does not rely on others to care for her son or make decisions about his care; she does what needs to be done. She is also financially independent. She spends the money she earns wisely, only on things that are necessary. She pays her own tuition, rent, and, of course, the expenses of bringing up Quentin. Tanya has earned her independence and is wise about the actions she takes.

Support point 3

Tanya is a very hard worker, pushing herself to the maximum. She works two jobs so she can provide for her growing son. Tanya also maintains an A average in her college courses. She has always gone beyond the normal, everyday achievements. For example, she graduated from high school on the honor roll while living on her own and supporting her son. She works hard and sticks to her belief that education is valuable. Tanya has gone beyond the traditional definition of hardworking.

In some people's eyes, Tanya is just a single, teenage mother, a burden on society. But to me, Tanya is a wonderful role model. She has accomplished a lot in her young life. She has also gained control of her life and her surroundings by being patient, independent, and hardworking. Tanya is a single, teenage parent, but she is also a worthy role model.

Conclusion sums up and strengthens response to essay prompt.

Reread and Revise Your Answer

After you have finished writing your answer to an essay question, reread it carefully. Then, revise your response to make it clearer, more precise, and more detailed.

Teachers sometimes use a *scoring rubric,* which consists of the criteria— or standards—they use to judge the quality of an essay. Although scoring rubrics vary from one teacher to the next, most rubrics used to evaluate writing include some basic elements:

- Fulfills the assignment. (Has the writer followed the assignment and answered the question? Does the essay stay focused on the topic?)
- Contains a thesis statement. (Does the essay clearly state the topic and the writer's main point about it?)
- Contains accurate information. (Does the essay include correct answers or reliable information?)
- Provides adequate support for the thesis. (Is the thesis backed by major support points, which are in turn supported by examples and details?)
- Uses correct language and expression. (Is the essay free of major errors in grammar, mechanics, and usage?)

Scoring rubrics often have points or percentages attached to each element. A typical scoring rubric might look like this:

ELEMENT	TOTAL POINTS POSSIBLE	STUDENT SCORE
Adherence to assignment	20	18
Thesis statement	15	15
Accurate information	30	25
Development of ideas	25	20
Language and expression	10	10
TOTAL POSSIBLE POINTS	**100**	**88**

If your teacher provides you with a rubric, use it to set priorities as you review and revise your essay. Otherwise, consider the elements in the sample rubric as you revise your essay exam.

■ For more on revising, see Chapter 8.

When you are writing by hand (rather than using a computer), revise your essay by neatly crossing out mistakes and adding extra words or sentences between the lines or in the margin, like this:

Groups of people living together have expectations about how

the group should function and how to keep order within the group.

~~Societies need to have rules and laws.~~ This semester, we learned about

social deviance, which is any behavior that does not conform to

expectations of the group and which violates the group's sense of

                          , those who break society's rules,

order. For example, criminals ^ are social deviants. Rather than

thinking that we can or should eliminate deviant behavior altogether,

I agree with sociologist Emile Durkheim that deviance is

~~necessary.~~ a necessary element of any healthy social group.

WRITING ASSIGNMENTS

Choose one of the following topics and write an essay on it, using the strategies for answering an essay question or timed writing assignment beginning on page 272. To practice with timed writing, give yourself a fifty-minute time limit.

1. Write an essay agreeing or disagreeing with one of the following statements:

   Schoolchildren have too many vacations.

   Most students cheat.

   People should be required to retire at age sixty-seven.

   People should live together before they get married.

   There are no valuable lessons to be learned from studying history.

2. Define *responsibility.*

3. Propose a solution to a major problem in your town or city.

4. Discuss a person who has had great influence on you.

5. Discuss an event that changed your life.

19

Writing Summaries and Reports

Important College Writing Tasks

Writing a Summary

A **summary** is a condensed version of a piece of writing, a conversation, or an event. It presents main ideas and key support points, stripping down the information to its essential elements.

⬛ FOUR BASICS OF A GOOD SUMMARY

1. It includes a thesis statement that identifies what is being summarized and its main idea.
2. It concisely identifies the key support points or events.
3. It includes any final observations or recommendations made in the original.
4. It is written in your own words and is objective in tone, presenting information without opinions.

Because a summary must be stated in your own words, you need to understand what you are summarizing. If you are summarizing a piece of writing, read it carefully to make sure you understand the main idea and key points. Then, try to write the first draft of the summary without looking at the original. When you're done, check the summary for accuracy against the original. *Note:* Even though summaries do not use the original source's exact words (unless quotations are included), you still must cite and document the source.

■ For more on citing and documenting sources, see Chapter 20. For more on summarizing, see Chapters 1 and 20.

The following paragraph summarizes the reading on page 9. Read the original piece and then the summary. The numbers in the paragraph correspond to the four basics of a good summary.

Source and relevant page number are cited.

4 Summary is in the writer's own words

Exact words from original are in quotation marks.

1 In their book *Discovering Psychology,* Don H. Hockenbury and Sandra Hockenbury explain that the way we see color is determined by properties of light waves: hue, saturation, and brightness (91). **2** Hue is actually color, and the way we see color is determined by the wavelength of the light. Different wavelengths result in our seeing different colors. Saturation is how pure the light wave is. The more saturation, the deeper the color: Red is more saturated than pink, for example. Brightness is how intense the color looks and is caused by the strength of the light wave. **3** Although most of us think that the color of an item is built into that item—like our jeans are blue—the color is actually determined by the "wavelength of light that the object reflects" (91). The jeans reflect the wavelength of the blue on the spectrum of color, and dark blue jeans have a higher saturation and brightness than light blue jeans.

There are many uses for summarizing.

COLLEGE	You answer exam questions that ask you to summarize information.
WORK	You write a memo that summarizes the issues discussed and decisions made at a meeting.
EVERYDAY LIFE	You summarize for a partner your conversation with a plumber who was at your home to fix a pipe.

Follow the steps in the Writing Guide on the next page to help you with the summary assignments that follow it. Also, review the four basics of a good summary on page 279. Check off each step in the guide as you complete it.

Although this guide is geared to summaries of texts, you can also use it when summarizing films, events, and other nontext sources. First, note the key stages or details of the film, event, or whatever you are summarizing. Next, work through this guide, beginning with the "Review" step.

WRITING GUIDE: SUMMARY	
STEPS IN SUMMARIZING	**HOW TO DO THE STEPS**
Focus.	❏ As you read, think about how you will summarize the piece.
Read the selection you want to summarize. See Chapter 1 for advice on reading.	❏ Highlight key points or put a check mark (✔) next to them. ❏ Note the title and headings, words in **boldface** or *italics,* and boxed information or diagrams.
Review your highlighting and make notes. See Chapter 1 for advice on taking notes while reading.	❏ Note the author's main idea and the major events or support. ❏ Jot down the details about the major events or support that will explain them to your readers. ❏ Decide whether to quote specific parts of the original, and note any page references.
Make an outline. See Chapter 6 for more on outlining.	❏ Arrange the major events and details in a logical order.
Draft the summary. See Chapter 7 for more on drafting.	❏ As you write, refer to the original, but use your own words. ❏ Include a thesis statement that expresses the author's main idea, and present a condensed version of the support for the thesis.
Revise the draft. See Chapter 8 for more on revising.	❏ Read your draft. ❏ Make sure it includes the author's main idea and key points. ❏ Add transitions to help your reader move smoothly from one key point to another. ❏ Make sure you have given enough examples that readers who haven't read the piece can understand the main idea. ❏ Make sure you have cited the source of the piece, and if you have quoted from it, be sure to include the page reference (if it's a print work) and quotation marks. For more on using quotations, see page 310. ❏ Make sure the summary (apart from direct quotations) is in your own words. ❏ Check to make sure it follows the four basics of a good summary.
Edit your work. See Parts Four through Seven for editing advice.	❏ Check for errors in grammar, spelling, and punctuation. ❏ Ask yourself: Is this the best I can do?

■ SUMMARY ASSIGNMENT

Read the article that follows and, using the Writing Guide, write a summary of it.

Survey Finds Many Firms Monitor Staff

Your employer could be watching you. Such are the findings of a new study released last week by the American Management Association (AMA) in New York. The survey of 1,626 large and midsize companies found that nearly 80 percent of major U.S. firms routinely check their employees' e-mail, Internet, or telephone connections, and some regularly videotape them at work.

■ This article uses direct quotations from personal interviews conducted by the writer.

"It's not just a matter of corporate curiosity," said Eric R. Greenberg, director of management studies at the American Management Association. "Personal e-mail can clog a company's telecommunications system, and sexually explicit or other inappropriate material downloaded from the Internet can lead to claims of a hostile work environment."

Researchers have found that companies are more likely to conduct random checks versus 24-hour surveillance of messages, phone conversations, or Internet usage. Even so, the AMA advises that employees use discretion at work.

According to the survey, 63 percent of U.S. companies check employees' Internet connections, up 54 percent since last year. Forty-seven percent read workers' e-mail, up from 38 percent in the year 2000. Forty percent have installed firewalls to prevent employees from using the Internet inappropriately, up from 29 percent last year.

When asked whether they had fired workers because of inappropriate use of electronic equipment, 27 percent of the employers said they had dismissed staff for misuse of office e-mail or Internet connections. Sixty-five percent of the companies had disciplined offenders. Ellen Bayer, the AMA's practice leader on human rights issues, said the findings indicate that privacy in the modern-day workplace is "largely illusory."

"In this era of open space cubicles, shared desk space, networked computers, and teleworkers, it is hard to realistically hold onto the belief in private space," said Bayer. She added that some employees do not understand that their employers have a legal right to monitor equipment that workers use on the job.

> "In this era of open space cubicles, shared desk space, networked computers, and teleworkers, it is hard to realistically hold onto the belief in private space," said Bayer.

Employers also reported other forms of surveillance, such as monitoring telephone numbers called (43 percent), logged computer time (19 percent), and video surveillance for security purposes (38 percent).

"In previous years, the growth in monitoring went hand in hand with increases in the share of employees gaining access to e-mail and the Internet," added AMA's Greenberg. "This year, the average share of employees with office connections barely grew at all, while monitoring of those activities rose by nearly 10 percent. It is important to note, however, that 90 percent of the companies engaging in any of these practices inform their employees that they are doing so."

But companies don't have to inform employees of any monitoring practice. In fact, most U.S. courts have ruled in favor of employers who routinely monitor telephones, computers, or other electronic equipment used on the job. It is best not to misuse company media: Your employer may be watching you.

— Staff reporter, "Survey Finds Many Firms Monitor Staff,"
Boston Sunday Globe, April 29, 2001

MORE SUMMARY ASSIGNMENTS

1. Summarize the cover story of a recent issue of a magazine (print or online).

2. Summarize the plot of a movie you have seen recently.

3. Summarize an article from today's newspaper.

4. Summarize an essay or article, either from this book (see Part Eight) or from another book you use in a course.

5. Summarize Giovanni Bohorquez's classification essay from Chapter 13 (p. 188).

■ For online exercises on summarizing, visit Exercise Central at <bedfordstmartins.com/realessays>.

Writing a Report

A **report** usually begins with a summary that condenses a piece of writing, a conversation, or an event, and then it moves to some type of analysis. Recall that a summary is objective: You present a brief version without stating your opinions. In contrast, a report summarizes key points and also includes reactions to, opinions about, or recommendations based on the original piece.

▪▪ FOUR BASICS OF A GOOD REPORT

1. It identifies the title and author of the original piece in the first sentence or paragraph.

2. It summarizes the original piece, including the main idea and key support points or events.

3. It moves to the writer's reactions to the piece. This part of the report may relate the piece to the writer's own experiences, giving specific examples to support the responses.

4. It has a conclusion that evaluates the original piece on a variety of possible aspects: originality, realism, accuracy, intensity, interest, and so on. The conclusion usually gives a thumbs-up or thumbs-down for readers.

NOTE: Reports often use specific passages or quotations for support in both the summary and the response sections.

In college classes, you may be assigned to write a book report. A student, Tiffany Shale, wrote the report that follows on Toni Morrison's best-selling novel *The Bluest Eye*. The numbers in it correspond to the four basics of a good report.

Before reading Tiffany's report, read her comments about her process for completing the assignment.

I knew I had to write a report on this book, so I read it in a different way than I would have otherwise. I kept a highlighter beside me when I read and turned down the pages where I highlighted things that I thought might be important. The passages I highlighted really did help me write the report. If you note what's important as you read, you don't have to go back at the end and look for quotes to use, and the key ideas are easy to find.

Here's what I did to write the report:

1.   I typed some of the highlights (or what was important about them) and their page numbers onto the computer.

2.   Separately, I wrote a short outline describing what happened in the book.

3.   Using the outline, I wrote the summary part, and then I went back and put some of the highlighted stuff into the summary.

4.   I wrote down some of my reactions to the book, including ones I'd jotted down while reading. Then, I picked the ones I wanted to write about. Next, I wrote the section that gave details about

my reactions and went back to the highlights again and used any I could to support my reactions.

5.   Then, I reread my draft and made changes.

When I started the book, I thought it was stupid and didn't like it at all. But I knew I had to read it, and by the end I thought it was good. I don't think boys would like it, though. I felt bad for Pecola and what the world had done to her. Writing the report was hard, but when I finished, I really felt like I had understood the book, and I felt smart, like I was doing real college work.

Lasting Lessons in *The Bluest Eye*

1 In her first novel, *The Bluest Eye,* Toni Morrison writes about a time when racial and social prejudices were very strong. White people were more highly valued by society, and many African Americans learned to hate the characteristics that made them black. In *The Bluest Eye,* a young girl is destroyed by a society she longs to be part of.

2 The tragic story of Pecola Breedlove is a flashback to 1941, told by two narrators. One is Claudia, a young girl whose family took in Pecola after her father burned down the family's house. Claudia's narrative opens each of the four parts of the book, which are arranged by seasons, starting with "Autumn" and ending with "Summer." In "Autumn," Pecola is staying with Claudia's family. In one scene, Frieda, Claudia's sister, and Pecola are admiring the image of Shirley Temple on a mug. Claudia doesn't like Shirley and talks about dolls she receives every Christmas. She says, "I destroyed white baby dolls. But the dismembering of dolls was not the true horror. The truly horrifying thing was the transference of the same impulses to little white girls" (22). Eventually, she learns to stop hating the white baby dolls and loves Shirley Temple. At the end of Claudia's autumn narrative, Pecola has started to menstruate. Frieda tells her that now she can have a baby, when someone loves her. Pecola asks, "How do you do that? I mean, get somebody to love you?" (31).

The omniscient narrator takes over, telling how Pecola's parents have a history of fighting violently. During the fights, Pecola wants to

■ Note that the present tense is used to describe the actions in a literary work.

— Thesis statement

— Topic sentence

— Specific example

Direct quotation with page reference (see throughout)

— Specific example

— Topic sentence

Specific example —

disappear and wonders why everyone either ignores or hates her. Every night, she prays for blue eyes because she believes that if she had blue eyes, like Shirley Temple or like white girls, people would love her.

Topic sentence —

As the story continues, the reader learns more about the dismal history of Pecola's parents, who have learned to hate themselves and each other. They neglect Pecola, reinforcing her view that no one loves her and intensifying her wish for blue eyes, the feature that she believes

Specific example —

would transform her life. In one very ugly scene, Pecola's father rapes her, and her mother beats her when learning what happened. Pecola becomes pregnant, and Claudia and Frieda pray that her baby will be born healthy. But the baby dies.

Topic sentence —

Abandoned and miserable, Pecola visits a sham mystic, begging him to give her blue eyes. To get rid of a dog he hates, the mystic gives

Specific example —

Pecola a poisoned piece of meat to feed the dog and tells her that if there is a sign, she will have blue eyes. The dog dies, and Pecola takes it as a sign. But she is sickened by the dog's death.

Topic sentence —

In the final chapters of the book, Pecola is having a conversation with an imagined friend. She has gone mad. But she believes that she has blue eyes and that people stare at her in envy. She fears, however, that perhaps someone else has bluer eyes, but her friend assures her she

Specific example —

has "the bluest eyes." Morrison writes, "A little black girl yearns for the blue eyes of a little white girl, and the horror at the heart of her yearning is exceeded only by the evil of fulfillment" (204). Pecola gets her wish only by being destroyed.

Topic sentence —

3 When I first started reading *The Bluest Eye,* I didn't like it, but now I realize that it is a fine book written by a talented author. One part of Morrison's writing that impressed me was her use of symbols, like flower seeds and blue eyes. Claudia's first narrative begins, "Quiet as it's kept, there were no marigolds in the fall of 1941" (6). Claudia and Frieda plant marigold seeds and believe that if they grow, Pecola's baby will live. But

Specific example/ support —

they die, and so does the baby. In the last paragraph of the book, Claudia says, "I even think now that the land of the entire country was hostile to marigolds that year" (206). The marigold seeds are like Pecola, and just as the soil was hostile to them, society was hostile to Pecola, and they both died. The author often refers to blue eyes. They symbolize black women's wish to look white at a time when society's racism considered white features to be the ideal of beauty.

— Specific support

I learned about history from the book. I knew people were prejudiced before, but I didn't know that many African Americans tried to be like whites. I didn't know that their attempts showed a self-hatred caused by racism, or that they hated those who were poorer and "blacker" than they were. In "Winter," Claudia writes about Maureen Peal, a new girl in school whom everyone loves. She is very light-skinned and dresses like white girls. In one scene, Maureen, Claudia, and Frieda come upon a group of boys who have surrounded Pecola and are making fun of her. Maureen breaks it up with just a look, after Claudia and Frieda have tried without luck. The boys hate Pecola because she is beneath them. As Morrison states, "It was their contempt for their own blackness that gave the first insult its teeth. . . . their exquisitely earned self-hatred was . . . sucked up into a fiery cone of scorn that had burned for all ages . . . and consumed whatever was in its path" (65). This book taught me about an important time that I didn't know about.

— Topic sentence

— Specific support

What I most liked about *The Bluest Eye* is that I related to the story about people wanting to fit in, even if it means not being true to themselves. At first, Claudia doesn't love Shirley Temple, but she learns to love her and to dislike herself. Pecola just wants to be loved and thinks that if only she had blue eyes, she would be, but trying to be someone she isn't destroys her. I think many young people do things just to fit in because of pressure from their friends or other people's ideas of what is good. Morrison's book focuses on African Americans, but her lesson about not trying to be someone else applies to everyone.

— Topic sentence

— Specific support

4 I think *The Bluest Eye* is an important book that is very well written. I would recommend that everyone read it because it has some important lessons not only about history but also about our lives today. I would like to read other books that Morrison has written.

— Conclusion

Works Cited

Morrison, Toni. *The Bluest Eye.* New York: Penguin, 1970.

— Works Cited entry with publication information

■ In reports, writers typically analyze and evaluate. For more on these and other typical college writing skills, see pages 16–20.

Although many reports, like this one, begin with a summary and move on to an analysis, some writers weave the summary and analysis together. Look at newspaper or magazine reviews of books, films, and other works to see different ways that reports are constructed.

Many occasions call for your being able to report on things:

COLLEGE   An instructor in a business class assigns you to write a report based on a campus event, such as a presentation on marketing trends by a local professional.

WORK   Your manager asks you to review software from different suppliers who want your company's business. Your review must recommend which supplier to use.

EVERYDAY LIFE   You informally review a new restaurant or health club for your friends.

Follow the steps in the Writing Guide on the next page to help you with the report assignments below. Also, review the four basics of a good report (p. 284). Check off each step in the guide as you complete it.

Although this guide is geared to reports about texts, you can also use it when writing about films, events, and other nontext sources. First, note the key parts of the film, event, or whatever you are reporting on, and then jot down your reactions. Next, work through this guide, beginning with the "Review" step.

■ REPORT ASSIGNMENTS

1. Read an essay that your instructor assigns from Part Eight of this book and write a report on it.

2. Write a review of a book that you have read for either this class or another one.

3. Write a review of a movie or live performance that you either very much liked or very much disliked.

4. Write a report that includes a summary of and reaction to a recent or proposed change in your town or on your campus.

5. Write a report of a class that you have taken recently.

WRITING GUIDE: REPORT

STEPS IN WRITING REPORTS	HOW TO DO THE STEPS
Focus.	❑ Read with the idea in mind that you will be writing a report on the piece.
Read the piece you are to report on. See Chapter 1 for advice on reading.	❑ As you read, highlight key points or put a check mark (✓) next to them. ❑ Note the title and any headings, words in **boldface** or *italics,* and boxed information or diagrams.
Review your highlighting and make notes. See Chapter 1 for advice on taking notes while reading.	❑ Jot down the author's main idea and key points for the summary part of the report. ❑ Think about your reactions to the piece: What do *you* want to say about it? What did you learn? How does it relate to your experience? Would you recommend it to others? Why or why not? ❑ Write down your reactions and support for them. ❑ Note any sentences in the text that you may use in the report, including page numbers (if you are reporting on a print work).
Make an outline. See Chapter 6 for more on outlining.	❑ Organize your report, starting with the summary and explanation of major events and moving to your reactions to the piece. Or you can interweave the summary and analysis if that organization is more logical for your subject.
Draft the report. See Chapter 7 for more on drafting.	❑ Write the summary, referring to the original but using your own words. ❑ Write the reaction part of the report, evaluating the piece as well as relating it to your own experience. ❑ Use material from the original to explain or support your ideas. ❑ If you quote directly from the original, make sure to use quotation marks and page numbers (if you're reporting on a print source). For more on using quotations, see page 310. ❑ Write an introduction that includes a thesis statement with your stance on the piece. ❑ Write a concluding paragraph that restates your opinion of the piece and makes a recommendation. ❑ Title your report.
Revise the draft. See Chapter 8 for more on revising.	❑ Read your draft. ❑ Make sure it includes the author's main idea and key points.

continued

STEPS IN WRITING REPORTS	HOW TO DO THE STEPS
(Revision, continued)	❑ Consider your reactions and add details, either from your own experience or from the original piece. ❑ Add transitions to help your reader move smoothly from one key point to another. ❑ Make sure you have given enough examples so that readers who haven't read the piece can understand the main idea. ❑ Check to make sure it follows the four basics of a good report.
Edit your work. See Parts Four through Seven for editing advice.	❑ Check for errors in grammar, spelling, and punctuation. ❑ Ask yourself: Is this the best I can do?

20

Writing the Research Essay

Using Outside Sources

This chapter will guide you through the process of writing a research essay. Throughout the chapter, we show how one student, Messelina Hernandez, worked through key steps in the process. Messelina's completed research essay on mandatory school uniforms appears on pages 321–24.

■ Tammy S. Sugarman, a librarian at Georgia State University, provided many useful suggestions for this chapter.

STEPS TO WRITING A GOOD RESEARCH ESSAY

1. Make a schedule.
2. Choose a topic.
3. Find sources.
4. Evaluate sources.
5. Avoid plagiarism by taking careful notes.
6. Write a thesis statement.
7. Make an outline.
8. Write your essay.
9. Cite and document your sources correctly.
10. Revise and edit your essay.

Make a Schedule

After you receive your assignment, make a schedule that divides your research assignment into small, manageable tasks. There is no way that you can do every step the day (or even a few days) before the assignment is due, so give yourself a reasonable amount of time to begin the assignment, and do each of the steps. Your instructor may suggest how much time to allow; take his or her advice. Once you have made your schedule, keep it handy and refer to it often.

You can use the following schedule as a model for making your own:

SAMPLE RESEARCH ESSAY SCHEDULE

Assignment: _____
(Write out what your instructor has assigned.)

Length: _____

Draft due date: _____

Final due date: _____

My general topic: _____

My narrowed topic: _____

STEP	DO BY
Choose a topic.	_____
Find and evaluate sources.	_____
Take notes, keeping publication information for each source.	_____
Write a working thesis statement by answering a research question.	_____
Review all notes; choose the best support for your working thesis.	_____
Make an outline that includes your thesis and support.	_____
Write a draft, including a title.	_____
Review the draft; get feedback; add more support if needed.	_____
Revise the draft.	_____
Prepare a list of Works Cited using correct documentation form.	_____
Edit the revised draft.	_____
Submit the final copy.	_____

Choose a Topic

Your instructor may assign a topic or want you to think of your own topic for a research paper assignment. If you are free to choose your own topic, find a subject that you are personally interested in or curious about. If you need help, try asking yourself some of the following questions.

1. What is going on in my own life that I want to know more about?
2. What have I heard about lately that I'd like to know more about?
3. What am I interested in doing in the future, either personally or professionally, that I could investigate?
4. What famous person—living or deceased—most interests me?
5. What do I daydream about? What frightens me? What do I see as a threat to me or my family? What inspires or encourages me?
6. Is there something I do in my spare time (sports, music, computer games) that I'd like to know more about?

POSSIBLE TOPICS FOR A RESEARCH ESSAY

Abortion/pro life

Assisted suicide

Causes of stress

Childhood obesity

Corporal punishment for children

Date rape

Dieting/eating disorders

Ethics: business/political/personal

Executive salaries

The family in America

Gay/lesbian marriage/adoption

Homeschooling

Hunger in America

Identity theft

An illness

Internet games

Limiting cell phone use

Mandatory drug testing

Mandatory school uniforms

Marijuana for medical purposes

Medical insurance

The military draft

The minimum wage

Music downloading

Online dating services

Outsourcing jobs to foreign countries

Patients' rights

Pets and mental health

Presidential campaigns

Reality television programs

Rights of children of illegal immigrants

Road rage

(continued)

POSSIBLE TOPICS FOR A RESEARCH ESSAY

Sexual harassment	Violence in the media
Standardized testing/placement testing	Women in military combat
	Working parents

When you have a general topic, jot down some answers to these questions:

1. Why is this topic important to me or of interest to me? How does it affect me? What do I hope to gain by exploring it?

2. What do I know about the topic? What do I want to find out?

■ For more on narrowing a topic, see Chapter 3.

Although a research essay may be longer than some of the other writing you have done, the topic still needs to be narrow enough to write about in the assigned length. It would be impossible, for example, to write a good five-page essay on the general topic "Crime." A more specific topic—something like "Neighborhood watch programs as crime deterrents"—is more manageable.

Before writing a working thesis statement, you need to learn more about your topic. It helps to come up with a **guiding research question** about your narrowed topic. This question—often a variation of "What do I want to find out?"—will help to guide and focus your research.

MESSELINA HERNANDEZ'S GUIDING RESEARCH QUESTION

Messelina chose school uniforms as her topic. She used the following research question to guide her research: *What are the effects of school uniforms?*

Find Sources

With both libraries and the Internet available to you, finding information is not a problem. Knowing how to find good, reliable sources of information, however, can be a challenge. Using the following strategies will help you.

Consult a Reference Librarian

The Internet does not reduce the need for reference librarians, who are essential resources in helping to find appropriate information in both print and electronic forms. In fact, with all of the information available to you, librarians are a more important resource than ever, saving you time and possible frustration in your search for relevant material.

If your library allows, schedule an appointment with the librarian. Before your appointment, jot down some questions to ask, such as those on the following list. Begin your conversation by telling the librarian your re-search topic.

QUESTIONS FOR THE LIBRARIAN

- How do I use an online catalog or a card catalog? What information will the library's catalog give me?
- Can I access the library catalog and article databases from home or other locations?
- What other reference tools would you recommend as a good starting place for research on my topic?
- Once I identify a source that might be useful, how do I find it?
- Can you recommend an Internet search engine that will help me find information on my topic? Can you also recommend some useful key words?
- How can I tell whether a Web site is reliable?
- I've already found some articles related to my topic. Can you suggest some other places to look for sources?

Use the Online Catalog or Card Catalog

Most libraries now list their holdings online rather than in a card catalog, but both systems give the same information: titles, authors, subjects, publication data, and call numbers. If you are working with a librarian, he or she may offer step-by-step instructions for using the online catalog. If you are working on your own, the online catalog help is usually easy to find (generally on the screen or in a Help menu) and easy to follow. Catalogs allow you to search by author, title, subject, or key word. If you are just beginning your research, you will probably use the keyword search because you may not know specific authors or titles.

■ For more on conducting keyword searches, see page 298.

Messelina Hernandez, whose research essay on mandatory school uniforms appears on pages 321–24, searched her library's online catalog using the key words *mandatory school uniforms*. Here is a book she found:

Author:	Hudson, David L., 1969-
Title:	Rights of Students
Published:	Philadelphia: Chelsea House Publishers, c2004
Location:	Briggs Nonfiction
Call #:	344.73/BRI
Status:	Available

continued

Description:	120 p.; 23 cm./Part of "Point-Counterpoint" series
Contents:	Discusses constitutional rights in schools. Includes point/counterpoint discussion of mandatory school uniforms.
ISBN:	0-7910-7920-1
OCLC #:	ocm53376048

A call number is a book's library identification number. Knowing the call number will help you to locate a source in the library. Once you do locate the source, browse the shelves around it. Since a library's holdings are organized by subject, you may find other sources related to your topic nearby.

If the book is available only at another library, you can ask a librarian to have the book sent to your library.

Look at Your Library's Web Site

Many libraries have Web sites that can help researchers find useful information. The library's home page may have links to electronic research sources that it subscribes to and that are free to library users. It will also list the library's hours and resources, and it may offer research tips and other valuable information. It is a good idea to bookmark this site for future use.

Use Other Reference Materials

The reference section of the library has many resources that will help you find information on your topic. Here is a sampling of common reference sources. Most are available online or on CD-ROM.

Periodical Indexes and Databases

Magazines, journals, and newspapers are called *periodicals*. Periodical indexes help you locate information published in these sources. Online periodical indexes are called *periodical databases* and often include the full text of magazine, journal, or newspaper articles. If your topic is a current one, such as Messelina Hernandez's on mandatory school uniforms, you may find more information in periodicals than in books. Following are some of the most popular periodical indexes and databases:

- InfoTrac
- LexisNexis

- NewsBank
- *New York Times Index*
- ProQuest
- *Readers' Guide to Periodical Literature*

Specialized Indexes

Specialized indexes—in book form, online, or on CD-ROM—direct you to resources in various broad subject areas. A few of the many indexes are the following:

- *America: History and Life*
- *Biological Abstracts*
- Educational Resources Information Center (ERIC)
- *MLA International Bibliography of Books and Articles on the Modern Languages and Literatures*
- PsychLIT

Encyclopedias

Encyclopedias can give you an overview of a subject, although most instructors will want you to use more specialized sources such as those listed previously. You might also consult the bibliography of other useful sources that conclude most encyclopedia entries. Some encyclopedias, like the *Encyclopaedia Britannica,* are available in print, online, and on CD-ROM.

In addition to general encyclopedias, your library may have specialized encyclopedias that give more detailed information on your topic. For instance, you might consult the *Encyclopedia of Psychology* for a research paper in a psychology course.

Statistical Sources

Statistical data, or facts and figures, that are directly related to your thesis can provide sound support. As one example, the *Statistical Abstract of the United States* (published annually by the U.S. Census Bureau) can help you locate useful statistics related to social issues, population trends, economics, and other topics.

■ Visit <**www.census .gov**>, the official Web site of the U.S. Census Bureau, for current state and national statistical data related to population, economics, and geography.

Use the Internet

The Internet, a vast global computer network, now provides access to all kinds of information. The biggest part of the Internet is called the World Wide Web, which allows users to jump from site to site using hyperlinks.

If you are new to using the Web, this section will offer some basics. You might also want to work with a librarian, a writing-center tutor, or a knowledgeable friend to help you navigate the Web. To get started, you can go to some sites that categorize information on the Web, such as the Internet Public Library (<**www.ipl.org**>) or the Librarian's Index to the Internet (<**www.lii.org**>).

NOTE: Some Internet sites charge fees for information (such as archived newspaper or magazine articles). Before using any of these, check to see if the sources are available free through your library's database.

Uniform Resource Locator (URL)

Every Web site has an address, called a uniform resource locator (URL). You may already be familiar with some frequently advertised URLs, such as <**www.amazon.com**> (the Internet address for bookseller Amazon.com) or the URL for your college's Web site. If you know the URL of a Web site that you think would be helpful to your research, enter it into the address field of your Web browser. (Web browsers, like Microsoft Internet Explorer and Netscape Navigator, are software programs that allow a computer to read Web pages.)

Search Engines and Searching with Key Words

If you do not know the URL of a particular site you want to visit, or if you want to look at multiple Web sites related to your topic, you will need to use a search engine. Of the following commonly used search engines, Google is the most popular.

- AltaVista <**www.altavista.com**>
- Ask Jeeves <**www.askjeeves.com**>
- Excite <**www.excite.com**>
- Google <**www.google.com**>
- HotBot <**www.hotbot.com**>
- Lycos <**www.lycos.com**>
- Yahoo <**www.yahoo.com**>

To use a search engine, type in key words from your subject. Because the Web is so large (Google searches more than four billion pages), adding more specific key words or phrases and using an advanced-search option may narrow down the number of entries (called *hits*) you have to sift through to find relevant information. Also, search engines typically have a Help feature that offers guidance in using the engine, selecting key words, and refining your search.

Google search using phrase in quotes

*Refined Google search (phrase in quotes plus additional term—*mandatory*)*

When Messelina Hernandez entered *school uniforms* as a search term in Google, her search netted more than 709,000 hits. (She put quotation marks around *school uniforms* to tell Google she wanted items related to this phrase only, not to *school* and *uniforms* separately, which would have returned many more results not related to her research topic.) She immediately saw some irrelevant entries, such as those related to purchasing school uniforms.

Messelina then refined her search by adding the word *mandatory* to the phrase *school uniforms*. This strategy reduced the number of hits to 19,900 and produced results more relevant to Messelina's research question.

Messelina's search helped her refine her research question:

> **MESSELINA HERNANDEZ'S REFINED RESEARCH QUESTION:** *What are the effects of mandatory school uniforms?*

Adding additional search terms can narrow a search even more.

When you discover a Web site that you might want to return to, save the URL so that you don't have to remember it each time you want to go to the site. Different browsers have different ways of saving URLs; choose "Bookmarks" in Netscape or Firefox, or choose "Favorites" in Microsoft Internet Explorer.

Online Research Sites

Online research sites constitute another valuable source of information on how to do research. For example, at **<www.bedfordstmartins.com/researchroom>**, the publisher of this book hosts the Bedford Research Room which includes guided tutorials on research processes; advice on finding, evaluating, and documenting sources; tips on avoiding plagiarism; and more. Other useful sites include:

THE BEDFORD
research room Mike Palmquist

Welcome to the Bedford Research Room, formerly the English Research Room. Mike Palmquist has revised the site so that it's more useful for writing in all disciplines. In addition to research manuals and tutorials, Mike's made available the collection of research activity worksheets and checklists that he created to accompany *The Bedford Researcher*. With these tools, students can better engage the research process and instructors have a ready to use library of helpful tools for inclusion in their courses.

Research Resources

● **Manuals on Research Tools**   ● **Links to Research Resources**

● **Guided Tutorials on Research**   ● **Research Activities and Checklists**
    Processes

Other Research Resources

● **St. Martin's Tutorial on Avoiding**   ● **Evaluating Online Sources: A**
    Plagiarism   **Tutorial by Roger Munger**

● **Diana Hacker's Research and**   ● **Diana Hacker's Research Exercises**
    Documentation Online
                                                                     ● **St. Martin's Handbook Guide to**
● **Plagiarism Handouts**   **Citing Sources**

● **St. Martin's Handbook Writer's**
    Almanac

- Citing Electronic Sources (from the Internet Public Library) at **<www.ipl .org/div/farq/netciteFARQ.html>**. This site contains links to various sources that explain how to document information found online.

- Evaluating Web sites (from the Ohio State University) at **<http://gateway**

.lib.ohio-state.edu/tutor/les1/>. This site gives tips on finding useful Internet sources.

- OWL (Purdue University's Online Writing Lab) at **<http://owl .english.purdue.edu>**. This site offers a variety of materials and resources for writers, including research information.

Interview People

Personal interviews can be excellent sources of information. Before interviewing anyone, however, plan carefully. First, consider what kind of person to interview. Do you want information from an expert on the subject or from someone directly affected by the issue? How would the experience or comments of each person help support your points? The person should be knowledgeable about the subject and have firsthand experience. When you have decided whom to interview, schedule an appointment.

Next, to get ready for the interview, prepare a list of five to ten questions. Ask more open-ended questions (What is your position on regulating cell-phone use by drivers?) than questions that require only a simple yes-or-no response (Do you favor regulating cell-phone use by drivers?). Leave space for notes about the person's responses and for additional questions that may occur to you during the interview. Include in your research notes the person's full name and qualifications and the date of the interview.

As you conduct the interview, listen carefully and write down any important ideas. If you plan to use any of the interviewee's exact words, put them in quotation marks in your notes. Doing so will help you remember if your notes are the exact words of the person you interviewed, your own interpretation of something he or she said, or a thought you had during the interview. For more on using direct quotes, see pages 308 and 310 of this chapter and Chapter 38.

NOTE: Recording what a person says without being granted permission is unethical and, in some states, against the law. If you plan to record an interview, get your subject's permission first.

Evaluate Sources

Evaluating sources means judging them to determine how reliable and appropriate for your topic they are. Reliable sources present accurate, up-to-date information written by authors with appropriate credentials for the subject matter. Reliable sources support claims with evidence and use objective, reasonable language. Research materials found in a college library (books, journals, and newspapers, for example) are generally considered reliable sources.

Don't assume that an Internet source is reliable just because it exists online; anyone can create a Web site and put whatever he or she wants on it. If you are searching the Web for information about the psychological benefits of weight loss, for example, you may find a range of sources — reliable ones such as an article published by the *Journal of the American Medical Association* or a report by faculty at Johns Hopkins University and questionable ones such as an individual's personal weight-loss story or an advertisement for a miraculous weight-loss product. Whether you are doing research for a college course, a work assignment, or personal use, make sure that the sources you draw on are reliable and appropriate for your purpose.

When you're viewing a Web site, try to determine its purpose. A Web site set up solely to provide information may be more reliable than an online product advertisement. A keyword search for attention-deficit/hyperactivity disorder (ADHD), for example, would point a researcher to thousands of sites; the two shown below are just samples. Which do you think contains more reliable information?

❶ Site sponsored by the makers of the ADHD drug Concerta and designed to promote the product.

❷ Links offer ADHD-related information and "success stories" supportive of the drug's use.

❸ No specific publication date or date of last update given.

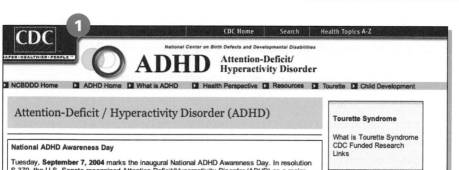

CDC Home | Search | Health Topics A-Z

National Center on Birth Defects and Developmental Disabilities

ADHD Attention-Deficit/ Hyperactivity Disorder

SAFER·HEALTHIER·PEOPLE™

► NCBDDD Home ► ADHD Home ► What is ADHD ► Health Perspective ► Resources ► Tourette ► Child Development

Attention-Deficit / Hyperactivity Disorder (ADHD)

National ADHD Awareness Day

Tuesday, **September 7, 2004** marks the inaugural National ADHD Awareness Day. In resolution S.370, the U.S. Senate recognized Attention-Deficit/Hyperactivity Disorder (ADHD) as a major public health concern and encouraged the federal government to raise public awareness about ADHD and to improve access to mental health services for children and adults with the illness. National ADHD Awareness Day highlights the significance of this disorder to many American children, families, and adults. For the actual Senate Resolution 370.

Attention-Deficit/Hyperactivity Disorder (ADHD) is one of the most common childhood behavioral disorders and can persist through adolescence and into adulthood. The causes are currently unknown.

Announcing
The
National
Resource Center
on AD/HD

May 20, 2003 marked the official opening of the Children and Adults with Attention-Deficit/Hyperactivity Disorder's (CHADD) National Resource Center (NRC) on AD/HD, the country's first and only national clearinghouse dedicated to the evidence-based science and treatment of AD/HD. The clearinghouse is a collaboration between the CDC and CHADD, an advocacy organization serving individuals with AD/HD...

National Resource Center website, http://www.help4adhd.org has a toll-free number (800-233-4050).The Website answers many of your questions about AD/HD and directs you to other reliable sources online. New material is regularly being added. If you don't find the answers you are looking for, you can click on Ask a question about AD/HD, found on every page of this site. Your question will be directed to one of the knowledgeable Health Information Specialist for a response.

What is AD/HD?

According to the 2000 American Psychiatric Association's Diagnostic and Statistical Manual, Text Revision, of Mental Disorders-IV (DSM-IV-TR), ADHD is a Disruptive Behavior Disorder characterized by on-going inattention and/or hyperactivity-impulsivity occurring in several settings and more frequently and severely than is typical for individuals in the same stage of development. Symptoms begin before age 7 years and can cause serious difficulties in home, school or work life. ADHD can be managed through behavioral or medical interventions, or a combination of the two.

The National Center on Birth Defects and Developmental Disabilities has developed a research agenda in ADHD for CDC and/or other public agencies (click here for research agenda).

[ADHD References]

[Return to Top]

This page was last updated September 02, 2004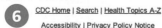

Sidebar

Tourette Syndrome

What is Tourette Syndrome
CDC Funded Research
Links

Report

Report of the Surgeon General's Conference on Children's Mental Health: A National Action Agenda

Search Health Topics

Birth Defects
Developmental Disabilities
Human Development
Disability and Health
Hereditary Blood Disorders

Publications Search

Search by Author
Search by Keyword
Search by Title
Search by Year

Contact Us

Thank you for visiting the CDC-NCBDDD Web site. In order to contact the National Center on Birth Defects and Developmental Disabilities, please click here

---

ADHD Home | What is ADHD? | Symptoms of ADHD | Peer Relationships | ADHD and Risk of Injuries | Public Health Perspective | Conference | Publications | ADHD References | Internet Links | CDC Funded Research | Contact Us

CDC Home | Search | Health Topics A-Z

Accessibility | Privacy Policy Notice

Centers for Disease Control and Prevention
National Center on Birth Defects and Developmental Disabilities

We promote the health of babies, children, and adults, and enhances the potential for full, productive living. Our work includes identifying the causes of birth defects and developmental disabilities, helping children to develop and reach their full potential, and promoting health and well-being among people of all ages with disabilities.

Margin annotations

1 Site sponsored by the Centers for Disease Control, a U.S. government agency dedicated to protecting the health of American citizens by providing information

2 Objective presentation of information

3 Links to current information

4 Clear contact information

5 Date of last update, showing that information is current

6 Links to related information, including "ADHD references," with full information on the sources cited

■ For more informa-
tion on evaluating
online sources,
visit <www
.bedfordstmartins
.com/researchroom>.

Here are some questions you can ask to evaluate a source. If you answer "no" to any of these questions, think twice about using the source.

QUESTIONS FOR EVALUATING A PRINT OR ELECTRONIC SOURCE

• Is the source up-to-date?
• Is the source reliable? Is it from a reputable publisher or Web site? (For
  Web sites, consider the URL extension; see the box below.)
• Is the information appropriate for your research topic?
• Is the author qualified to write reliably about the subject? If there is no
  biographical information, try an online search using the author's name.
• Who sponsored the publication or Web site? Be aware of the sponsor's
  motives (for example, to market a product) and how they might affect
  the type of information presented.
• Does the information seem fair and objective? If there is a bias, does the
  author state his or her position up front?
• Does the author provide adequate support for key points, and does he
  or she cite the sources of this support?

Guide to URL Extensions

EXTENSION	TYPE OF SITE	HOW RELIABLE?
.com	A commercial, or business, organization	Varies. Consider whether you have heard of the organization, and be sure to read its home page or "About us" link carefully.
.edu	An educational institution	Reliable, but may include many varied course materials.
.gov	A government agency	Generally reliable.
.net	A commercial or business organization, or a personal site	Varies. This extension indicates just the provider, not anything about the source. Go to the source's home page to find out what you can about the author or the sponsor.
.org	A nonprofit organization	Generally reliable, although each volunteer or professional group promotes its own view or interests.

Avoid Plagiarism

Plagiarism is passing off someone else's ideas and information as your own. Turning in a paper written by someone else, whether it is from the Internet or written by a friend or family member who gives you permission, is deliberate plagiarism. Sometimes, however, students plagiarize by mistake because they have taken notes that do not distinguish a source's ideas from their own or that do not fully record source information, including publication data. As you find information for your research essay, do not rely on your memory to recall details about your sources; take good notes from the start.

NOTE: This section's advice on recording source information, and on citing and documenting sources, reflects Modern Language Association (MLA) style, the preferred style for the humanities.

Keep a Running Bibliography

A **bibliography** is a complete list, alphabetized by author, of the outside sources you consult. A **list of works cited** is a complete list, alphabetized by author, of the outside sources that you actually use in your essay. Most instructors require a list of works cited at the end of a research essay. Some may require a bibliography as well.

You can keep information for your bibliography and list of works cited on notecards or on your computer. Whatever method you use, be sure to record complete publication information for each source at the time you consult it; this will save you from having to look up this information again when you are preparing your list of works cited.

The following is a list of information to record for each source. For Messelina Hernandez's list of works cited, see page 324.

BOOKS	ARTICLES	WEB SITES
Author name(s)	Author name(s)	Author name(s) (if any)
Title and subtitle	Title of article and page number(s)	Title of page or site
Year of publication	Title of magazine, journal, or newspaper	Date of publication or latest update (if available)
Publisher and location of publisher	Year, month, day of publication (2006, January 4)	Name of sponsoring organization
		Date on which you accessed the source
		The URL (online address) in angle brackets (</>)

You will probably integrate source material by summary, paraphrase, and direct quotation. As you take notes, record which method you are using so that you don't accidentally plagiarize.

The information on page 308 explains each method, describes its typical use, and shows how a single source was summarized, paraphrased, and quoted to support a thesis. Note how the writer cites the source in each case; full publication information for the source is provided in an entry on the list of works cited. Note also how the writer clearly connects the source information to the thesis.

Below and also on pages 310–11 is more advice and examples for summarizing, paraphrasing, and quoting.

Indirect Quotation: Summary

■ For more on writing summaries, see Chapter 19.

A summary puts the main point of a piece of writing in your own words. Be careful if you choose to summarize, for it is easy to think you are using your own words when you are actually mixing your own and the author's or speaker's. When you summarize, follow these guidelines:

- Don't look at the source while you are writing the summary.
- Check your summary against the original source to make sure you have not used the author's words or copied the author's sentence structure.
- Make sure to introduce the outside source—for example, "In their article 'Effects of Student Uniforms on Attendance, Behavior Problems, Substance Abuse, and Academic Achievement,' David L. Brunsma and Kerry A. Rockquemore state . . .'"
- Include in parentheses the page number(s), if available, of the entire section you have summarized. (You will need to provide full publication information later, in a list of works cited.)

SUMMARY OF AN ARTICLE

Identifying information —

Using the National Educational Longitudinal Study of 1988, David L. Brunsma and Kerry A. Rockquemore set out to test the claims of behavioral and academic benefits stemming from mandatory school uniforms. They report their findings in their article "Effects of Student Uniforms on Attendance, Behavior Problems, Substance Abuse, and Academic Achievement," which indicates that there are no direct positive effects on substance abuse, behavior, or attendance. In fact, they claim that uniforms may have a negative effect on academic achievement (53–62).

Parenthetical reference

Indirect Quotation: Paraphrase

Paraphrasing is restating another's ideas in your own words. These guidelines can help:

- Don't look at the source while you are writing the paraphrase.
- Check your paraphrase against the original source to make sure you have not used the author's words or copied the author's sentence structure.
- Make sure to introduce the outside source—for example, "Marie Winn says that . . ."
- Include in parentheses the page number(s), if available, of the entire section you have paraphrased. (You will need to provide full publication information later, in a list of works cited.)

Read the examples that follow to see acceptable and unacceptable paraphrases.

ORIGINAL SOURCE

   Not unlike drugs or alcohol, the television experience allows the participant to blot out the real world and enter into a pleasurable and passive mental state. To be sure, other experiences, notably reading, also provide a temporary respite from reality. But it's much easier to stop reading and return to reality than to stop watching television. The entry into another world offered by reading includes an easily accessible return ticket. The entry via television does not. In this way television viewing, for those vulnerable to addiction, is more like drinking or taking drugs—once you start, it's hard to stop.

                              —from Marie Winn, *The Plug-In Drug*

UNACCEPTABLE PARAPHRASE, TOO CLOSE TO ORIGINAL

   Marie Winn says that like drugs or alcohol, television allows people to blot out reality and escape into the passive world of television. Reading also provides a break from the real world, but it's easier to put down a book than to turn off the television. Therefore, in people susceptible to addiction, television viewing is more like drinking or taking drugs than reading: It's much harder to stop once you've started.

An explanation of why this paraphrase is unacceptable is on page 310.

Student Thesis: Although labor unions may have declined in power in recent decades, some worker groups have recently launched high-profile challenges to what they say are unfair labor practices.

Indirect Quotation: Summary: A condensed form of a piece of writing that presents only the main points in your own words.

- **TYPICAL USE:** To briefly note major evidence from a source that supports your thesis (or a topic sentence backing that thesis).

- **WHAT TO FOCUS ON IN YOUR SOURCE:** Focus on the major points that support your thesis—in this case unfair labor practices. See the aqua highlighting in the facing article.

- **EXAMPLE:** The student's own thoughts—in other words, the "glue" connecting the source information to the thesis—are in blue.

  One of the most prominent targets of lawsuits charging unfair labor practices has been the retailer Wal-Mart, which has been the subject of more than thirty lawsuits charging the company with not paying workers all of the overtime due to them (Cullen 44). Wal-Mart has also been charged with sex discrimination and been criticized for fighting unions, paying less than a living wage, and offering unaffordable health care, among other criticisms.

Indirect Quotation: Paraphrase: A restatement of someone else's ideas in your own words. A paraphrase preserves more ideas from a particular article or passage than does a summary.

- **TYPICAL USE:** In contrast to a summary, a paraphrase tends to focus more on particular details that illuminate a specific angle of an issue—for example, why Wal-Mart may have a discriminatory culture.

- **WHAT TO FOCUS ON IN YOUR SOURCE:** Focus on details that provide specific reasons, examples, and other evidence. The example below focuses on the yellow paragraph of the facing article.

- **EXAMPLE:** Again, paraphrases need "glue" to connect the source information to the thesis. These connecting thoughts are in blue.

  Experts point to a variety of possible causes when explaining unfair labor practices. At Wal-Mart, according to author Ellen Rosen,

such practices may be the result of a "conservative, Southern culture" that began with Sam Walton, the company's founder (Cullen 44). Such an environment can foster discriminatory behavior, like the "chauvinistic" comment a male worker directed toward colleague Deborah Zambrana when she asked for his assistance in sorting lingerie. Rather than being punished for his behavior, he was promoted.

Direct Quotation: The reproduction of a source's exact words, which are placed in quotation marks (" ").

- **TYPICAL USE:** Quotations tend to be used only when the original author's or speaker's words are especially striking, memorable, or expressive.

- **WHAT TO FOCUS ON IN YOUR SOURCE:** Look for striking quotations that clearly support your point, but avoid overquoting. See the green section of the facing article.

- **EXAMPLE:** Again, note the words (in blue) that connect the quotation to the writer's larger point.

  In the case of Wal-Mart, the recent lawsuits have shed important light on the problem of labor discrimination. "The point is that more people are aware," according to former employee Gretchen Adams, quoted in *Time* (Cullen 44). "They're finally seeing what's behind that smiley face."

Works Cited Entry: Regardless of whether you summarize, paraphrase, or quote, you'll need to provide full publication information at the end of your paper for all sources you cite in the body of your paper. Here's the MLA style for the facing article's entry on a list of works cited:

Author   Title

Cullen, Lisa Takeuchi. "Wal-Mart's Gender Gap: What a Landmark Lawsuit Aims to Prove about How the No. 1 Retailer Pays Its Female Workers." *Time* 5 July 2004: 44.

Date   Page number   Publication

BUSINESS

Wal-Mart's Gender Gap

What a landmark lawsuit aims to prove about how the No. 1 retailer pays its female workers

Author

By **LISA TAKEUCHI CULLEN**/WILSON

GRETCHEN ADAMS HAS MORE THAN A few bones to pick with Wal-Mart, but she figures its treatment of women is a good place to start. The mother of four took an hourly job at a Wal-Mart in Stillwater, Okla., in 1993 and was quickly promoted to head the deli department. Soon she was managing 60 workers and flying around the country to train hundreds more. When she learned that a man she had trained was earning $3,500 more than she was, "they told me it was a fluke." But as other male colleagues leapfrogged past, her salary never rose above $60,000 and she never landed the promised job of store manager. When she complained, "they told me where to go," says Adams, 57. She quit at the end of 2001.

Adams may yet have the last laugh. The retail giant—the nation's biggest private employer—has weathered a yearlong maelstrom of bad press about its employment practices. More than 30 lawsuits have accused it of cheating workers out of overtime pay. In a case in Oregon, the company was found to have forced employees to punch out and then return to work off the clock. A federal investigation discovered that in dozens of stores Wal-Mart used contractors that hired illegal immigrants. Now a federal judge in San Francisco has ruled that a sex-discrimination lawsuit filed in 2001 by six women can proceed as a class action on behalf of all Wal-Mart's current and former female employees. With up to 1.6 million plaintiffs, it will be the largest private civil rights case in U.S. history.

In many ways, Wal-Mart's problems stem from the conservative, Southern culture fostered by founder Sam Walton, according to Ellen Rosen, who is writing a book about the role of women at retail companies, including Wal-Mart. The old-fashioned values were one of the things that attracted Deborah Zambrana, 37, an 11-year employee of the store in Wilson, N.C. Then a note she wrote requesting help sorting lingerie came back scrawled with a chauvinist comment. When a male colleague admitted to the deed, "instead of being reprimanded," says Zambrana, who

NO SMILES: Zambrana was not amused when a man was rewarded for bad behavior

like Adams is not one of the lead plaintiffs, "he was promoted to assistant manager."

Wal-Mart, known for its smiley-face icon, is confronting other complaints too. It has successfully fought to keep out unions—so far. The average wage for hourly workers barely exceeds the federal poverty level for those with families, and the company's health-care plan is so expensive that only half its workers choose to be covered. Workers have charged that they were locked inside stores at night and that managers secretly "shaved" their time sheets to meet budgets.

Wal-Mart has tried to downplay the complaints, suggesting they are a natural outgrowth of success. With an organization of this size and status, "anyone who says something is not going to go bump in the night is not being realistic," said human-resources head Coleman Peterson in an interview before he retired last month.

The company denies that it mistreats workers and plans to appeal the class-action ruling on the sex-discrimination suit. "The company does not condone discrimination of any kind," says spokeswoman Sarah Clark, adding that female employees are fairly promoted and paid. Some Wal-Mart employees agree. Says Brenda Dobbins, 50, an hourly worker in Wilson: "I've had all sorts of opportunities here, and I've always been treated fairly." Yet changes to some of its employment practices suggest that Wal-Mart is responding to the criticism. In June the company adjusted pay for many jobs; later this year its electronic job-posting system will notify workers of desirable openings. It created a department to promote diversity. CEO H. Lee Scott Jr. has warned that executives will see their bonuses reduced if they fail to meet diversity goals.

Even a whopping settlement is unlikely to hobble Wal-Mart, which rang up $9 billion in profits for the latest fiscal year. Nonetheless, its bottom line is likely to be redrawn by the suits. The sex-discrimination case alone could result in a multibillion-dollar settlement, says plaintiffs' attorney Joseph Sellers. Wal-Mart's reputation as a harsh employer, along with concerns about unfair competition, has spurred communities in Chicago, Dallas and Inglewood, Calif., to block construction of new stores. The outcome of the cases, thanks to the retailer's prominence, could affect how companies all over the world treat their workers. "The point is that more people are aware," says ex-employee Adams, who now works to unionize Wal-Mart stores. "They're finally seeing what's behind that smiley face." And these days, it's not a lot of smiles. ∎

WOMEN VS. WAL-MART

Plaintiffs claim that 2001 payroll stats show these discriminatory patterns:

In 2001 female workers in hourly jobs took home **$1,100 less** than men, while women managers earned **$14,500 less** than their male counterparts

65% of Wal-Mart's hourly employees were female, but two-thirds of the company's managers were men

On average, it took men **2.86 years** to get promoted to assistant manager. It took women **4.38 years**, despite better performance ratings

Source: Richard Drogin—Drogin, Kakigi & Associates

The paraphrase at the bottom of page 307 is unacceptable for several reasons:

- The first sentence uses the same structure and some of the same words as the first sentence of the original.
- The paraphrase too closely follows the wording of the original.
- The writer hasn't included the page numbers of the source.
- The writer has obviously written the paraphrase while looking at the original source rather than expressing the ideas in his or her own words.

ACCEPTABLE PARAPHRASE

Identifying phrase ———————— Marie Winn says that although television and reading both offer a break from reality, television watching is harder to stop and can therefore be considered "addictive," in a way that reading cannot (32).

Parenthetical reference

The acceptable paraphrase presents Winn's basic ideas, but in the writer's own words and structures. It also includes a parenthetical reference. The writer carefully read Winn's paragraph but then wrote the paraphrase without looking at the original. Then, the writer checked the original again to make sure she hadn't missed any ideas or repeated words or sentence structures.

Direct Quotation

Use these guidelines when you write direct quotations:

- Record the exact words of the source.
- Include the name of the writer or speaker. If there is more than one writer or speaker, record all names.
- Enclose the writer's or speaker's words in quotation marks.
- For print sources, include the page number, if available, on which the quote appeared in the original source. The page number should go in parentheses after the end quotation mark but *before* the period. If the person quoted is not the author of the book or the article, give the author's name in parentheses along with the page number. If there are two or three authors, give all names.
- If a direct quotation is more than four typed lines or forty words, indent the whole quotation and do not use quotation marks. Place the page number, in parentheses, *after* the final punctuation.

DIRECT QUOTATION   Quotation marks

Identifying phrase ———— According to Dr. Min Xiao, "The psychological benefits of a well-lit workspace are significant" (28).———— Parenthetical reference

According to Dr. Min Xiao,

> The psychological benefits of a well-lit workspace are significant.
> Obviously, workers can see what they are doing better and don't
> have to squint or lean over their work to see it. Moreover, the light
> can provide a sense of well-being, simulating daylight. This is partic-
> ularly important when workers are in cubicles in the middle of a
> floor with no natural light. (28)

■ For online exercises
on summarizing, para-
phrasing, and quoting,
visit Exercise Central at
<bedfordstmartins
.com/realessays>.

Write a Thesis Statement

After you have taken notes on the sources you gathered, you should be
ready to write a thesis statement, which states the main idea of your research essay. You can start by turning your guiding research question into
a statement that answers the question, as Messelina does below. Note how
she revises her thesis to make it more forceful and concrete.

■ For more on writing
a thesis statement, see
Chapter 4.

> **MESSELINA HERNANDEZ'S GUIDING RESEARCH QUESTION:** *What are the
> effects of mandatory school uniforms?*
>
> **THESIS STATEMENT:** *Mandatory school uniforms have positive effects on
> students.*
>
> **REVISED THESIS STATEMENT:** *Mandatory school uniforms have extraordi-
> nary benefits to students and school systems, including improvements
> in student self-esteem, attendance and academic performance, and
> safety.*

As you write and revise your essay, your thesis statement may change, but
having a good working one helps you focus your writing and see where you
might need to do additional research.

Make an Outline

The notes you have taken need to be organized into an outline that supports your thesis. First, write down your thesis statement. Then, review
your notes to decide what your major support points will be. Write these
under your thesis statement and order them with a letter or number.
Under the major support points, which will become the topic sentences
for the support paragraphs, write supporting details.

■ For more on outlin-
ing, see Chapter 6.

Many students, like Messelina, find it helpful to use complete sentences in their outlines so that when they write a draft it will be easy to remember what they wanted to say. They can change the sentences as they write and revise their drafts and also add further details.

MESSELINA HERNANDEZ'S OUTLINE

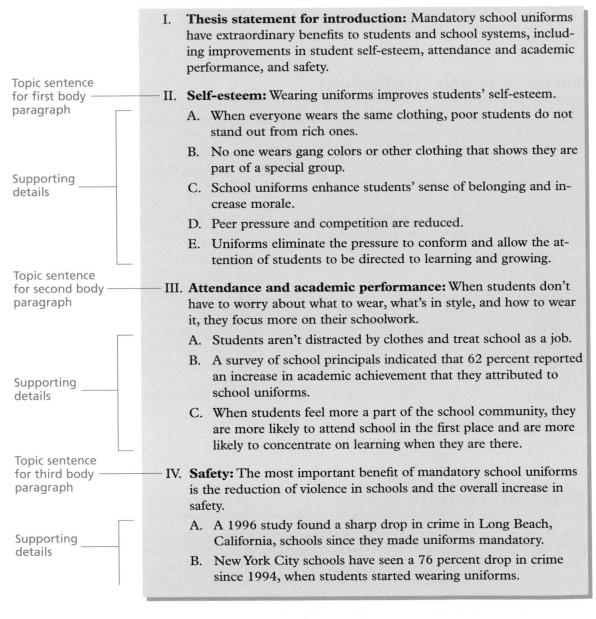

Topic sentence for first body paragraph

Supporting details

Topic sentence for second body paragraph

Supporting details

Topic sentence for third body paragraph

Supporting details

I. **Thesis statement for introduction:** Mandatory school uniforms have extraordinary benefits to students and school systems, including improvements in student self-esteem, attendance and academic performance, and safety.

II. **Self-esteem:** Wearing uniforms improves students' self-esteem.
   A. When everyone wears the same clothing, poor students do not stand out from rich ones.
   B. No one wears gang colors or other clothing that shows they are part of a special group.
   C. School uniforms enhance students' sense of belonging and increase morale.
   D. Peer pressure and competition are reduced.
   E. Uniforms eliminate the pressure to conform and allow the attention of students to be directed to learning and growing.

III. **Attendance and academic performance:** When students don't have to worry about what to wear, what's in style, and how to wear it, they focus more on their schoolwork.
   A. Students aren't distracted by clothes and treat school as a job.
   B. A survey of school principals indicated that 62 percent reported an increase in academic achievement that they attributed to school uniforms.
   C. When students feel more a part of the school community, they are more likely to attend school in the first place and are more likely to concentrate on learning when they are there.

IV. **Safety:** The most important benefit of mandatory school uniforms is the reduction of violence in schools and the overall increase in safety.
   A. A 1996 study found a sharp drop in crime in Long Beach, California, schools since they made uniforms mandatory.
   B. New York City schools have seen a 76 percent drop in crime since 1994, when students started wearing uniforms.

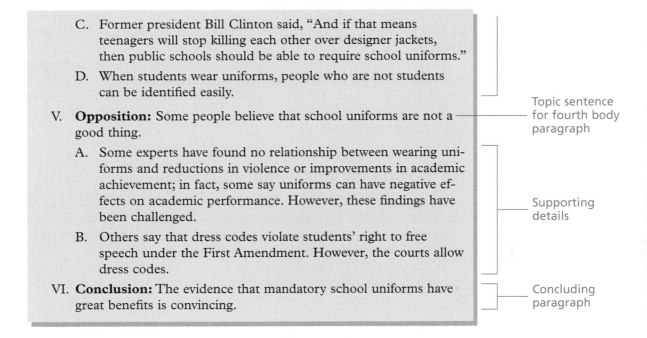

C. Former president Bill Clinton said, "And if that means teenagers will stop killing each other over designer jackets, then public schools should be able to require school uniforms."

D. When students wear uniforms, people who are not students can be identified easily.

V. **Opposition:** Some people believe that school uniforms are not a good thing.

A. Some experts have found no relationship between wearing uniforms and reductions in violence or improvements in academic achievement; in fact, some say uniforms can have negative effects on academic performance. However, these findings have been challenged.

B. Others say that dress codes violate students' right to free speech under the First Amendment. However, the courts allow dress codes.

VI. **Conclusion:** The evidence that mandatory school uniforms have great benefits is convincing.

Topic sentence for fourth body paragraph

Supporting details

Concluding paragraph

Write Your Essay

Using your outline, write a draft of your research essay. (For more information on writing a draft, see Chapter 7.)

Your **introduction** should include your thesis statement and a preview of the support you will provide in the body of the essay. If you are taking a stand on an issue, the introduction should let your readers know what your position is. The **body** of the essay will present your major support points for your thesis backed by supporting details from your research. The **conclusion** will remind readers of your main point and make a further observation based on the information you have presented.

For Messelina Hernandez's completed research paper, see pages 321–24.

Cite and Document Your Sources

As discussed on page 305, you need to document, or give credit to, your sources at the end of your research essay in a **list of works cited**; your instructor may also require a bibliography. In addition, you need to include in-text citations of sources as you use them in the essay.

No one can remember the specifics of correct citation and documentation, so be sure to refer to this section or the reference that your instructor

■ For more information on documenting sources, visit <**www .bedfordstmartins .com/researchroom**>.

prefers. Be sure to include all of the correct information, and pay attention to where punctuation marks such as commas, periods, and quotation marks should go.

There are several different systems of documentation. Most English professors prefer the Modern Language Association (MLA) system, which is used in this chapter. However, when you are writing a research paper in another course, you may be required to use another system. When in doubt, always ask your instructor.

Use In-Text Citations within Your Essay

In-text citations like the ones shown in this section are used for books and periodicals. For Web sites and other electronic sources, you typically will not be able to include page numbers, although you can note any screen or paragraph numbers used in place of page numbers.

When you refer to the author(s) in an introductory phrase, write just the relevant page number(s), if available, in parentheses at the end of the quotation.

> **DIRECT QUOTATION:** In her book *Born to Buy*, Juliet B. Schor notes, "The world of children's marketing is filled with variants of the us-versus-them message" (53).

> **INDIRECT QUOTATION:** In her book *Born to Buy*, Juliet B. Schor notes that marketing aimed at youth often sets children against adults (53).

When you do not refer to the author(s) in an introductory phrase, write the author's name followed by the page number(s), if available, at the end of the quotation. If an author is not named, use the title of the source.

> **DIRECT QUOTATION:** "The world of children's marketing is filled with variants of the us-versus-them message" (Schor 53).

> **INDIRECT QUOTATION:** Marketing aimed at youth often sets children against adults (Schor 53).

Use a List of Works Cited at the End of Your Essay

Books

BOOK BY ONE AUTHOR

Publisher's city

Publisher's name, shortened

Shipler, David K. The Working Poor: Invisible in America. New York: Knopf, 2004.

Author   Title   Publication date

WHAT TO LOOK FOR IN A BOOK

Title page (Publication city and date are sometimes on the copyright page.)

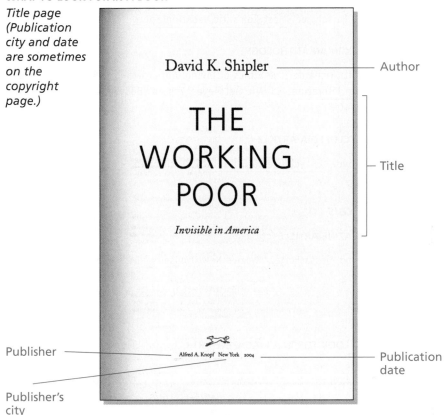

David K. Shipler ——— Author

THE WORKING POOR

Invisible in America

⌐ Title

Publisher ———

Alfred A. Knopf New York 2004 ——— Publication date

Publisher's city

TWO OR MORE ENTRIES BY THE SAME AUTHOR

---. Arab and Jew: Wounded Spirits in a Promised Land. New York: Penguin, 2002.

Use three hyphens instead of repeating "Shipler, David K."

BOOK BY TWO OR THREE AUTHORS

Piccioto, Richard, and Daniel Paisner. Last Man Down: A New York City Fire Chief and the Collapse of the World Trade Center. New York: Berkley, 2002.

Quigley, Sharon, Gloria Florez, and Thomas McCann. You Can Clean Almost Anything. New York: Sutton, 1999.

BOOK WITH FOUR OR MORE AUTHORS

Roark, James L., et al. The American Promise: A History of the United States. 3rd ed. Boston: Bedford/St. Martin's, 2005.

NOTE: *et al.* means "and others."

BOOK WITH AN EDITOR

Tate, Parson, ed. Most Romantic Vacation Spots. Cheyenne: Chandler, 2000.

WORK IN AN ANTHOLOGY

Wright, Richard. "The Ethics of Living Jim Crow." The Bedford Introduction to Literature. Ed. Michael Meyer. 7th ed. Boston: Bedford/St. Martin's, 2005. 540-42.

ENCYCLOPEDIA ARTICLE

"Kosovo." Encyclopaedia Britannica. 16th ed. 1999.

Periodicals

MAGAZINE ARTICLE   Author   Title of article   Title of periodical   Date

Netting, Jessa Forte. "Brazil's New Dinosaur." Discover. Mar. 2005: 13.

Page number (Include page range for longer articles.)

WHAT TO LOOK FOR IN A MAGAZINE ARTICLE

Title of article

Brazil's New Dinosaur

During his daily walk seven years ago, retired refrigerator repairman Tolentino Marafiga spotted some unusual bones poking out of a road construction site in southern Brazil. It was a major find, paleontologists say: a new dinosaur species, one of the most primitive ever found.

The reptile walked on Earth 200 million to 225 million years ago, in the late Triassic, when dinosaurs were rare and new. Eight feet long and only 155 pounds, the lithe forest dweller was a delicate ancestor of the sauropods, the largest land animals that ever lived.

Like the most famous sauropod giant, *Brontosaurus,* the new dinosaur fed on plants, says Artemio Leal of Brazil's National Museum in Rio de Janeiro and lead author of the paper describing the find. A biped, it probably moved through conifer forests in a herd, shearing off bits of ferns and palmlike cycads with its serrated, spatulate teeth, suggests Leal.

The biggest surprise is that *Unaysaurus tolentinoi,* named for its discoverer, was a close cousin of dinosaurs found in what is now Germany. This bolsters the prevailing concept that all the world's continents were once jammed together as a single giant landmass called Pangaea.

Also intriguing is the dinosaur's well-preserved skull, with depressions and protrusions not seen before. The novel features helped paleontologists determine that the dinosaur was a new species but raised other questions in the process, says Alexander Kellner, the paper's coauthor. "Sometimes paleontologists observe anatomic differences but cannot explain what their purposes were."

—*Jessa Forte Netting*

DISCOVER MARCH 2005   **13**

Author

Page number

Date

Title of periodical

NEWSPAPER ARTICLE

Fox, Maggie. "Scientists Report Experiment Creating Immune Cells."
    Boston Globe 1 May 2002: A20.

EDITORIAL IN A MAGAZINE OR NEWSPAPER (author's name given)

Udall, Don. "When Someone Is Alive but Not Living." Editorial. Newsweek 14
    June 1999: 12.

EDITORIAL IN A MAGAZINE OR NEWSPAPER (author's name not given)

"The Fall of a Telecom Gunslinger." Editorial. New York Times 1 May 2002: A22.

LETTER TO THE EDITOR IN A MAGAZINE OR NEWSPAPER (author's name given)

Vos, Peter. Letter. Atlantic Nov. 2004: 24.

Electronic Sources

Electronic sources include Web sites; databases or subscription services such
as ERIC, InfoTrac, LexisNexis, and ProQuest; and electronic communications such as e-mail. Because electronic sources change often, always note
the date you accessed or read the source as well as the date on which the
source was posted or updated online, if this information is available.

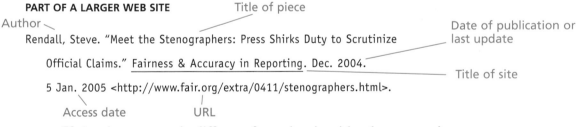

NOTE: If the site sponsor is different from the site title, the sponsor's
name should appear before the access date.

WHAT TO LOOK FOR IN A WEB SITE

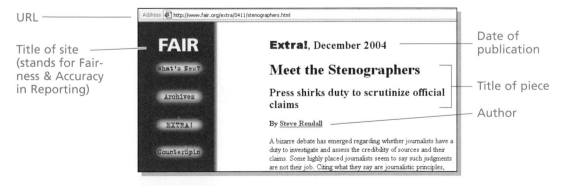

ARTICLE FROM A DATABASE

Author — Rivero, Lisa. "Secrets of Successful Homeschooling." Understanding our Gifted

Article title | Publication title

Volume and issue numbers — Date — Database title

15.4 (2003): 8-11. ERIC. CSA Illumina. Boston Public Lib., Boston, MA.

Inclusive pages — Name of provider — Name and location of library

Access date — 3 Jan. 2005. <http://md2.csa.com>.

Main URL

WHAT TO LOOK FOR IN A DATABASE

Main URL | Name of provider

http://md2.csa.com/ids70/view_record.php?id=1&recnum=7&SID=9635c9721847ffc4e9ef3e90b0952ab2&mark_id=cache%3A0&mark_low=0&mark_high=10

CSA ILLUMINA

Logout | Quick Search | Advanced Search | Search Tools | 0 Marked Records | Search History | Alerts

Record View | Return to Results | Help & Support

8 of 63
< Previous | Next >   ☐ Mark This Record | Update Marked List | Save, Print, Email

Database ERIC — Database title

Title **Secrets of Successful *Homeschooling*.** — Article title

Author Rivero, Lisa — Author

Source Understanding Our Gifted; v15 n4 p8-11 Sum 2003 — Issue number / Date

Publication title — ISSN 1040-1350 — Volume number — Inclusive pages

Descriptors ☐ Elementary Secondary Education ☐ *Gifted ☐ *Home Schooling ☐ *Parent Student Relationship
☐ *Parents as Teachers ☐ *Persistence ☐ Student Needs ☐ Teaching Methods

New Search Using Marked Terms: ○ Use **AND** to narrow ⊙ Use **OR** to broaden [Go]

Abstract This article offers the following advice for parents of gifted students who wish to home school: have patience with the children and with yourself; practice the arts of home schooling and parenting; and persist in the face of complexity. Parents are urged to be flexible in accommodating changing learning style preferences. (Contains 2 references.) (CR)

ARTICLE IN AN ONLINE PERIODICAL

Author — Weine, Stevan M. "Survivor Families and Their Strengths: Learning from Bosnians

Article title

after Genocide. " Other Voices: The (e)Journal of Cultural Criticism. 2.1

Name of online periodical

Publication date — (2000). 1 May 2002 <http://www.othervoices.org/2.1/weine/bosnia.html>.

Volume number

Access date | URL

E-MAIL OR ONLINE POSTING

Eisenhauer, Karen. "Learning Styles." E-mail to Susan Anker. 24 Apr. 2005.

Collins, Terence. "Effective Grammar Activities." Online posting. 14 Dec. 2001.
    CBW Listserv. 3 May 2002 <cbw-l@tc.umn.edu>.

■ For online exercises on documenting sources in MLA style, visit Exercise Central at **<bedfordstmartins .com/realessays>**.

Other Sources

PERSONAL INTERVIEW

Okayo, Margaret. Personal interview. 16 Apr. 2005.

SPEECH

Glenn, Cheryl. "Toward an Understanding of Silence and Silencing." Conf. on Coll.
    Composition and Communication Convention. Minneapolis Convention Center,
    Minneapolis. 13 Apr. 2000.

FILM, VIDEO, OR DVD

Million Dollar Baby. Dir. Clint Eastwood. Perf. Clint Eastwood, Hilary Swank, and
    Morgan Freeman. Warner Brothers, 2004.

TELEVISION OR RADIO PROGRAM

"Third-Day Story." West Wing. NBC. WCMH, Columbus. 3 Nov. 2004.

RECORDING

Keys, Alicia. "A Woman's Worth." Songs in A Minor. J-Records, 2001.

Revise and Edit Your Essay

After a break, reread your draft with fresh eyes and an open mind. Then, ask yourself these questions:

- Does my introduction state my thesis?
- Does each of the body paragraphs contain a topic sentence that directly supports my thesis? Do the supporting details in each paragraph relate to and explain the topic sentence?
- Do I provide a conclusion that reminds readers of my main point and makes a further observation?

- Have I included enough support for the thesis that readers are likely to see my topic the way I do? Is there anything else I could add to make my point?

- Are there transitions to help readers move from one idea to the next?

- Have I integrated source material smoothly into the essay? Do I need to smooth out anything that seems to be just dumped in?

- Have I reread the essay carefully, looking for errors in grammar, spelling, and punctuation?

- Have I cited and documented my sources?

- Are all of my citations and Works Cited entries in correct form (MLA or whatever style the instructor specifies)?

- Is this the best I can do?

For more on revising, see Chapter 8. When checking for grammar, spelling, and punctuation errors, consult Parts Four through Seven of this book. Look first at Chapter 21 beginning on page 327.

Sample Student Research Essay

The student essay that follows is annotated to show both typical features of research essays, such as references to sources, and elements of good writing, such as the thesis statement and topic sentences. The paper also shows formatting, such as margins, spacing between lines, and placement of the title. Your instructor may specify different or additional formatting in class or in your syllabus.

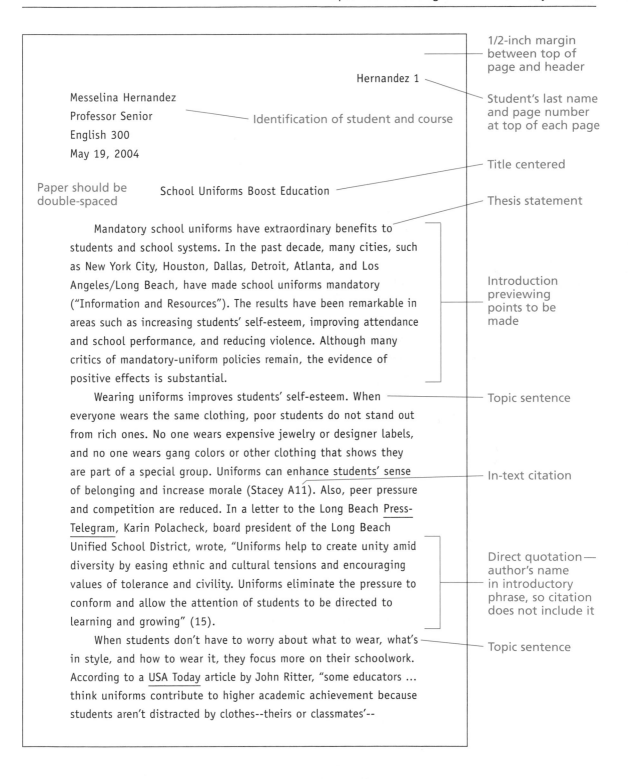

Hernandez 1

Messelina Hernandez
Professor Senior   — Identification of student and course
English 300
May 19, 2004

Paper should be   School Uniforms Boost Education
double-spaced

   Mandatory school uniforms have extraordinary benefits to
students and school systems. In the past decade, many cities, such
as New York City, Houston, Dallas, Detroit, Atlanta, and Los
Angeles/Long Beach, have made school uniforms mandatory
("Information and Resources"). The results have been remarkable in
areas such as increasing students' self-esteem, improving attendance
and school performance, and reducing violence. Although many
critics of mandatory-uniform policies remain, the evidence of
positive effects is substantial.

   Wearing uniforms improves students' self-esteem. When
everyone wears the same clothing, poor students do not stand out
from rich ones. No one wears expensive jewelry or designer labels,
and no one wears gang colors or other clothing that shows they
are part of a special group. Uniforms can enhance students' sense
of belonging and increase morale (Stacey A11). Also, peer pressure
and competition are reduced. In a letter to the Long Beach Press-
Telegram, Karin Polacheck, board president of the Long Beach
Unified School District, wrote, "Uniforms help to create unity amid
diversity by easing ethnic and cultural tensions and encouraging
values of tolerance and civility. Uniforms eliminate the pressure to
conform and allow the attention of students to be directed to
learning and growing" (15).

   When students don't have to worry about what to wear, what's
in style, and how to wear it, they focus more on their schoolwork.
According to a USA Today article by John Ritter, "some educators ...
think uniforms contribute to higher academic achievement because
students aren't distracted by clothes--theirs or classmates'--

Annotations in right margin:

1/2-inch margin between top of page and header

Student's last name and page number at top of each page

Title centered

Thesis statement

Introduction previewing points to be made

Topic sentence

In-text citation

Direct quotation— author's name in introductory phrase, so citation does not include it

Topic sentence

Hernandez 2

and they treat school as their job" (1A). Uniforms also improve
students' test scores and attendance. A survey of school principals
indicated that 62 percent reported an increase in academic
achievement that they attributed to school uniforms ("Information
and Resources"). When students feel more a part of the school
community, they are more likely to attend school in the first place
and are more likely to concentrate on learning when they are
there. If wearing school uniforms can help promote learning in any
way, the controversy that mandatory uniforms may cause is well
worth it.

> *Indirect quotation, paraphrase*

        The most important benefit of mandatory school uniforms is
the reduction of violence in schools and the overall increase in
safety. For example, in 1994, when the Long Beach, California,
school district became the first large urban system to adopt school
uniforms, it drew extensive national attention and generated a
good deal of controversy; however, the results were overwhelmingly
positive. In a 1996 study of data from the Long Beach schools, the
U.S. Department of Education found a 36 percent decline in overall
crime in elementary and middle schools, a 50 percent decrease in
weapons offenses, a 34 percent drop in assaults, and a 19 percent
decline in vandalism ("School Uniformity" 40). Similarly, New York
City schools have seen a 76 percent drop in crime since 1994,
when students started wearing uniforms (Fanning). In a 1996 State
of the Union Address, former president Bill Clinton drew more
national attention to the issue when he said, "And if that means
teenagers will stop killing each other over designer jackets, then
public schools should be able to require school uniforms." Since
then, many more schools have made school uniforms mandatory.

> *Topic sentence*

        When students wear uniforms, people who are not students
can be identified easily. In my cousin's school in Detroit, many
times kids who have dropped out come to the school and start
violence. If they could be spotted around the school, they could
be kicked out before they caused any trouble.

Hernandez 3

Students need to feel safe in their schools, or they won't come, and they can't concentrate when they do. When two students at Columbine High School in Colorado murdered teachers and fellow students with bombs and guns, survivors recalled that the two were part of a group of students--a "trenchcoat mafia"--who dressed distinctively to set themselves off from other students, particularly student athletes. Maybe if all students had worn uniforms, the alienation that the two student killers felt would not have been so strong. Maybe people would not have died.

Some people believe that school uniforms are not a good thing. For instance, in a 1998 study, David L. Brunsma and Kerry A. Rockquemore found no relationship between wearing uniforms and reductions in violence or improvements in academic achievement; in fact, they reported that uniforms could be correlated with reduced academic performance (53-62).

However, their data analysis has since been challenged (Bodine 69). Other experts say that dress codes violate students' right to free speech under the First Amendment and their liberty interest under the due process clause of the Fourteenth Amendment (Hudson 87, West 22). The courts have ruled, however, that schools may regulate what students wear. Others claim that most of the evidence of benefits of wearing school uniforms is not scientific but is just feelings that principals and parents have. I would direct those opponents to many other studies that have found that there are direct benefits, starting with a bibliography that the National Association of Elementary School Principals provides on its Web site (<www.naesp.org>).

The evidence that mandatory school uniforms have great benefits is convincing. If such a small change in policy can make any improvements in students' self-esteem and academic performance, the change should be at least tried. And if that change can in any way make our schools safer, why would anyone question the rightness of a school uniform? It is worth a try.

Acknowledgment of opposing view

Indirect quotation, summary

Summary

Conclusion reminding readers of main point (includes personal observation based on evidence presented)

■ Note that in Works
Cited entries, all lines
after the first one are
indented. Also, titles
of books, periodicals,
and Web sites are un-
derlined, and page
ranges are included
when available. URLs
are included for Web-
based sources.

Hernandez 4

Works Cited

Bodine, Ann. "School Uniforms, Academic Achievement, and Uses
of Research." Journal of Educational Research 97.2 (2003):
67-72.

Brunsma, David L., and Kerry A. Rockquemore. "Effects of Student
Uniforms on Attendance, Behavior Problems, Substance Abuse,
and Academic Achievement." Journal of Educational Research
92.1 (1998): 53-62.

Clinton, William Jefferson. State of the Union Address. Washington.
23 Jan. 1996.

Fanning, Karen. "To Wear or Not to Wear?" Scholastic News 11 May
1998. ProQuest Direct. Allan Hancock Coll. Lib., Santa Maria.
27 Apr. 2004 <http://www.umi.com/proquest>.

Hudson, David L., Jr. Rights of Students. Philadelphia: Chelsea
House, 2004.

Source without
author ———————— "Information and Resources: Public School Uniforms." National
Association of Elementary School Principals. 10 May 2004
<http://www.naesp.org>.

Polacheck, Karin. Letter. Press-Telegram. Jan. 1996: 15.

Ritter, John. "Uniforms Changing Culture of the Nation's
Classrooms." USA Today 15 Oct. 1998: 1A.

Source without
author ———————— "School Uniformity Yields High Marks." DSN Retailing Today 3 May
2004: 39-40.

Stacey, Julie. "Our View: Morale Is Up, Crime Is Down, and Kids
Can Concentrate on Learning Instead of Self-Protection." USA
Today 22 Aug. 1995: A11.

West, Charles K., et al. "Attitudes of Parents about School
Uniforms." Journal of Family and Consumer Sciences Mar.
1999. ProQuest Direct. Allan Hancock Coll. Lib., Santa Maria.
5 Apr. 2004 <http://www.umi.com/proquest/>.

Part Four

The Four Most Serious Errors

21

The Basic Sentence

An Overview

The Four Most Serious Errors

This book puts special emphasis on the four grammar errors that people most often notice. These four errors may make your meaning harder to understand, but even if they don't, they give a bad impression of you.

1. Fragments (see Chapter 22).
2. Run-ons (see Chapter 23).
3. Problems with subject-verb agreement (see Chapter 24).
4. Problems with verb form and tense (see Chapter 25).

If you can edit your writing to correct the four most serious errors, your sentences will be clearer and your grades will improve. Learning how to correct these errors will make a big difference in your writing.

This chapter will review the basic elements of the sentence; the next four chapters cover the four most serious errors.

The Basic Sentence

A **sentence** is the basic unit of written communication. A complete sentence written in standard English must have three elements:

- A **subject**
- A **verb**
- A **complete thought**

ESL NOTE: The basic pattern of an English sentence is subject-verb-object.

S   V   O

Maya threw the ball.

The English language's conventions for ordering words and forming negatives may differ from the conventions of your first language. For more details, see Chapter 32.

To edit your writing, you need a clear understanding of what a sentence *is* and what a sentence *is not*. You can find out if a group of words is a complete sentence by checking to see if it has a subject, a verb, and a complete thought.

Subjects

■ For a list of pronoun types, see page 428.

The **subject** of a sentence is the person, place, or thing that the sentence is about. The subject of the sentence can be a noun (a word that names the person, place, or thing) or a pronoun (a word that replaces the noun, such as *I, you, she,* or *they*).

■ In this section on subjects, only the subject is underlined.

ESL NOTE: English sentences always have a subject.

INCORRECT   Is hot outside.

CORRECT   It is hot outside

If you write sentences without any subject, see page 510.

To find the subject, ask yourself, "Who or what is the sentence about?"

PERSON AS SUBJECT   Vivian works for the police department.

[*Who* is the sentence about? *Vivian*]

THING AS SUBJECT   The tickets cost $65 apiece.

[*What* is the sentence about? The *tickets*]

ESL NOTE: The two sentences above use the word *the* before the noun (*the police department, the tickets*). *The, a,* and *an* are called *articles.* If you have trouble deciding which article to use with which nouns, or if you often forget to use an article, see page 503.

A **compound subject** consists of two (or more) subjects joined by *and, or,* or *nor.*

TWO SUBJECTS	<u>Marty</u> and <u>Kim</u> have a new baby girl.
SEVERAL SUBJECTS	The <u>jacket</u>, <u>pants</u>, and <u>sweater</u> match perfectly.
SEVERAL SUBJECTS	<u>Kim</u>, <u>Juan</u>, or <u>Melba</u> will bring dessert.

A **prepositional phrase** is a word group that begins with a preposition and ends with a noun or pronoun. A **preposition** is a word that connects a noun, pronoun, or verb with some other information about it.

The subject of a sentence is *never* in a prepositional phrase.

> **ESL NOTE:** If you have trouble deciding which prepositions to use, see page 330.

Preposition

The <u>check</u> is in the mail.

Prepositional phrase

The subject of the sentence is *check.* The subject can't be the word *mail,* which is in the prepositional phrase *in the mail.*

Preposition

<u>One</u> of my best friends is a circus clown.

Prepositional phrase

Although the word *friends* may seem to be the subject of the sentence, it isn't. *One* is the subject. The word *friends* can't be the subject because it is in the prepositional phrase *of my best friends.*

When you are looking for the subject of a sentence in your writing, it may help to cross out any prepositional phrases, as in the following sentences.

The <u>rules</u> ~~about smoking~~ are posted everywhere.

The <u>sound</u> ~~of lightning striking a tree~~ is like gunfire.

<u>Many</u> ~~of the students~~ work part-time.

Common Prepositions

about	beneath	like	to
above	beside	near	toward
across	between	next to	under
after	by	of	until
against	down	off	up
along	during	on	upon
among	except	out	with
around	for	outside	within
at	from	over	without
before	in	past	
behind	inside	since	
below	into	through	

■ **PRACTICE 1   IDENTIFYING SUBJECTS AND PREPOSITIONAL PHRASES**

In each of the following sentences, cross out any prepositional phrases and underline the subject of the sentence.

> **EXAMPLE:** ~~For several months~~, <u>Ronald</u> has been raising a guide dog ~~for the blind.~~

1. Many other people around the country are raising guide dog puppies.

2. However, Ronald's situation is unusual because he is in prison.

3. Ronald is participating in a program called Puppies Behind Bars.

4. The dog he is raising, a black Labrador puppy named Cooper, lives with Ronald twenty-four hours a day.

5. Whenever Ronald's cell is locked, Cooper stays in the cell with him.

6. In the cell, Ronald plays with the dog, rolling on the floor with him and talking to him in a high voice.

7. Ronald teaches Cooper manners and obedience before the start of Cooper's formal guide dog training.

8. In return, Ronald gains a sense of responsibility.

9. When he finishes his formal training, Cooper will be matched with a blind person.

10. Ronald believes that he and Cooper are contributing an important service to society.

■ For more practice, visit Exercise Central at <**bedfordstmartins.com/realessays**>.

Verbs

Every sentence has a **main verb**, the word or words that tell what the subject does or that link the subject to another word that describes it. Verbs do not always immediately follow the subject: Other words may come between the subject and the verb.

There are three kinds of verbs: action verbs, linking verbs, and helping verbs.

■ In this section on verbs, the subject is underlined <u>once</u>, and the verb is underlined <u>twice</u>.

ESL NOTE: Be careful with -*ing* and *to* forms of verbs (*reading, to read*).

INCORRECT   Terence loves to be reading.

CORRECT   Terence loves reading. *or* Terence loves to read.

If you make errors like this, see page 511.

Action Verbs

An **action verb** tells what action the subject performs.

To find the main action verb in a sentence, ask yourself, "What action does the subject perform?"

ACTION VERBS

The baby cried all night.

The building collapsed around midnight.

After work, we often go to Tallie's.

My aunt and uncle train service dogs.

Linking Verbs

A **linking verb** connects (links) the subject to a word or group of words that describe the subject. Linking verbs show no action. The most common linking verb is *be,* along with all its forms (*am, is, are,* and so on). Other linking verbs, such as *seem* and *become,* can usually be replaced by the corresponding form of *be,* and the sentence will still make sense.

To find linking verbs, ask yourself, "What word joins the subject and the words that describe the subject?"

LINKING VERBS

The dinner is delicious.

I felt great this morning.

This lasagna tastes just like my mother's.

The doctor looks extremely tired.

Some words can be either action verbs or linking verbs, depending on how they are used in a particular sentence.

ACTION VERB   The dog smelled Jake's shoes.

LINKING VERB   The dog smelled terrible.

Common Linking Verbs

FORMS OF *BE*	FORMS OF *BECOME* AND *SEEM*	FORMS OF SENSE VERBS
am	become, becomes	appear, appears
are	became	appeared
is	seem, seems	feel, feels, felt
was	seemed	look, looks
were		looked
		smell, smells
		smelled
		taste, tastes, tasted

ESL NOTE: The verb *be* cannot be left out of sentences in English.

INCORRECT   Tonya well now.

CORRECT   Tonya **is** well now.

Helping Verbs

A **helping verb** joins with the main verb in the sentence to form the **complete verb**. The helping verb is often a form of the verb *be, have,* or *do.* A sentence may have more than one helping verb along with the main verb.

| Helping verb | + | Main verb | = | Complete verb |

HELPING VERBS + MAIN VERBS

Sunil <u>was talking</u> on his cell phone.

[The helping verb is *was,* and the main verb is *talking.* The complete verb is *was talking.*]

Charisse <u>is taking</u> three courses this semester.

Tomas <u>has missed</u> the last four meetings.

My <u>brother</u> <u>might have passed</u> the test.

Common Helping Verbs

FORMS OF *BE*	FORMS OF *HAVE*	FORMS OF *DO*	OTHER
am	have	do	can
are	has	does	could
been	had	did	may
being			might
is			must
was			should
were			will
			would

ESL NOTE: The verb *be* cannot be left out of sentences in English.

INCORRECT   Greg <u>studying</u> tonight.

CORRECT   Greg **is** <u>studying</u> tonight.

PRACTICE 2   IDENTIFYING THE VERB (ACTION, LINKING, OR HELPING + MAIN)

In the following sentences, underline each subject and double-underline each verb. Then, identify each verb as an action verb, a linking verb, or a helping verb + a main verb.

> **EXAMPLE:** At first, <u>Miguel</u> <u><u>did not want</u></u> to attend his high school
>
> reunion. *helping verb + main verb*

1. Miguel's family moved to Ohio from Guatemala ten years ago.

2. He was the new kid at his high school that fall.

3. Miguel was learning English at that time.

4. The football players teased small, quiet boys like him.

5. After graduation, he was delighted to leave that part of his life behind.

6. Recently, the planning committee sent Miguel an invitation to his high school reunion.

7. His original plan had been to throw the invitation in the trash.

8. Instead, he is going to the reunion to satisfy his curiosity.

9. His family is proud of Miguel's college degree and his new career as a graphic artist.

10. Perhaps some of the other students at the reunion will finally get to know the real Miguel.

Complete Thoughts

A **complete thought** is an idea, expressed in a sentence, that makes sense by itself, without other sentences. An incomplete thought leaves readers wondering what's going on.

INCOMPLETE THOUGHT	as I was leaving [*What's going on?*]
COMPLETE THOUGHT	The phone rang as I was leaving.
INCOMPLETE THOUGHT	the people selling the car [*What's going on?*]
COMPLETE THOUGHT	The people selling the car placed the ad.

To identify a complete thought, ask yourself, "Do I know what's going on, or do I have to ask a question to understand?"

INCOMPLETE THOUGHT   in the apartment next door

[Do I know what's going on, or do I have to ask a question to understand? *You would have to ask a question, so this is not a complete thought.*]

COMPLETE THOUGHT   Carlos lives in the apartment next door.

PRACTICE 3   IDENTIFYING COMPLETE THOUGHTS

Some of the following items contain complete thoughts, and others do not. In the space to the left of each item, write either "C" for complete thought or "I" for incomplete thought. If you write "I," add words to make a sentence.

I cleaned the bathroom because

EXAMPLE: __I__ ~~Because~~ my mother asked me to do it.
              ^

____ 1. Smiling broadly as the cameras flashed all around him.

____ 2. Nobody spoke.

____ 3. The man who lives in the big brick house on Valley Street.

____ 4. Her shoes were tight.

____ 5. It's raining.

____ 6. After the last customer had gone home.

____ 7. Which explains why she missed class last week.

_____ 8. Although you could have gotten away with cheating.

_____ 9. Leave them alone.

_____ 10. On the five o'clock train.

22

Fragments

Incomplete Sentences

Understand What Fragments Are

A **sentence** is a group of words that has a subject and a verb and expresses a complete thought, independent of other sentences. A **fragment** is a group of words that is missing a subject or a verb or that does not express a complete thought.

SENTENCE	I'm going to a concert on Friday at Memorial Arena.
FRAGMENT	I'm going to a concert on Friday. *At Memorial Arena.*
	[*At Memorial Arena* does not have a subject or a verb.]

In the Real World, Why Is It Important to Correct Fragments?

A fragment is one of the grammatical errors that people notice most, as the following example shows.

SITUATION: In response to an ad for a job at a consulting firm, James sends the following cover letter, along with his résumé.

Dear Ms. Letendre:

I am interested in the computer technician position I saw. In the *Lowell Sun.* I have held two similar positions that I have described. In my

Maureen Letendre

Director of Human Resources and Organizational Development

(See Maureen's Profile of Success on p. 167.)

attached résumé. I believe I have the skills you are looking for. I would like an opportunity to meet with you. To discuss possible employment opportunities.

Thank you for your consideration.

Sincerely,

James Cosentini

RESPONSE: Maureen Letendre, the human resources director profiled in Chapter 12, had the following response to James's letter.

This letter and résumé go right into the "reject" pile.

Find and Correct Fragments

To find fragments in your own writing, look for five trouble spots that often signal fragments. When you find these trouble spots, read the sentence carefully to make sure it has a subject, has a verb, and expresses a complete thought.

FRAGMENT TROUBLE SPOTS

- A word group that **starts with a preposition**, such as *in, at,* or *with* (for a list, see p. 330).

FRAGMENT	I found that lost sock. *In the sleeve of my shirt.*
CORRECTED	I found that lost sock in the sleeve of my shirt.

- A word group that **starts with a dependent word**, such as *although, because, who,* or *that.*

FRAGMENT	*Because I woke up late.* I missed my first class.
CORRECTED	Because I woke up late, I missed my first class.

- A word group that **starts with an -*ing* verb form**, such as *running, studying,* or *looking.*

FRAGMENT	*Running the fastest.* Aurora won the event.
CORRECTED	Running the fastest, Aurora won the event.

- A word group that **starts with *to* and a verb**, such as *to pass, to help,* or *to understand.*

FRAGMENT	Donna signed up for the walk. *To raise money for tsunami victims.*
CORRECTED	Donna signed up for the walk to raise money for tsunami victims.

- A word group that **starts with an example or explanation**.

FRAGMENT	Some really old people are incredibly sharp. *Like my grandfather.*
CORRECTED	Some really old people are incredibly sharp, like my grandfather.

When you find a fragment, you can usually correct it in one of two ways.

WAYS TO CORRECT FRAGMENTS

- Add what is missing (a subject, a verb, or both).
- Attach the fragment to the sentence before or after it.

■ **PRACTICE 1 FINDING AND CORRECTING FRAGMENTS**

Underline the three fragments in James Cosentini's letter on pages 337–38.

Fragments That Start with Prepositions

Whenever a preposition starts what you think is a sentence, check for a subject, a verb, and a complete thought. If any one of those is missing, you have a fragment.

■ For a list of common prepositions, see page 330.

FRAGMENT	The plane crashed into the house. *With a deafening roar.*

[*With a deafening roar* is a prepositional phrase starting with the preposition *with* and ending with the noun *roar.* The phrase has neither a subject nor a verb. It is a fragment.]

FRAGMENT	Take the second left and head west. *Toward the highway.*

[*Toward the highway* is a prepositional phrase starting with the preposition *toward* and ending with the noun *highway.* The phrase has neither a subject nor a verb. It is a fragment.]

Remember, the subject of a sentence is *never* in a prepositional phrase (see p. 329).

Correct a fragment that starts with a preposition by connecting the fragment to the sentence either before or after it. If you connect a fragment to the sentence after it, put a comma after the fragment to join it to the sentence.

FRAGMENT   The plane crashed into the house. *From a height of eight hundred feet.*

CORRECTED   The plane crashed into the house. *f* From a height of eight hundred feet.

CORRECTED   From a height of eight hundred feet, the plane crashed into the house.

PRACTICE 2   CORRECTING FRAGMENTS THAT START WITH PREPOSITIONS

In the following items, circle any preposition that appears at the beginning of a word group. Then, correct any fragment by connecting it to the previous or the next sentence.

EXAMPLE: (To) many people. *, c* Computer hackers are the same as terrorists.

1. With their technical talents. Hackers try to break into computer systems.

2. Hackers follow their own ways of thinking. Outside the established rules.

3. Some hackers offer excuses for meddling. With computer systems.

4. They say that security has improved. Since the start of hacking.

5. Sometimes, hackers are kids looking for something different. From the routines of school, chores, and ordinary play.

6. Hacking is just a game. For most of these kids.

7. Upon catching a hacker doing something illegal. The government may try to send him or her to jail.

8. After their computer-hacking days. Some former hackers go on to start successful companies.

9. For example, one former hacker founded a computer security company that got many contracts. With the U.S. government and several large companies.

10. Nevertheless, most people agree that the world would be a better place. Without computer hacking.

■ For more practice with correcting fragments, visit Exercise Central at <bedfordstmartins.com/realessays>.

Fragments That Start with Dependent Words

A **dependent word** is the first word in a dependent clause. Some dependent words are **subordinating conjunctions** (*after, before, since,* and so on); others are **relative pronouns** (*who, which, that*). A dependent clause does not express a complete thought even though it has a subject and a verb. Whenever a dependent word starts what you think is a sentence, look for a subject, a verb, and a complete thought.

FRAGMENT   I didn't fill out an application. *Because the apartment was already rented.*

[*Because* is a dependent word introducing the dependent clause *because the apartment was already rented.* The clause has a subject, *apartment,* and a verb, *rented,* but it does not express a complete thought. Because what?]

FRAGMENT   The server remembered the two sets of twins. *Who came into the restaurant last week.*

[*Who* is a dependent word introducing the dependent clause *who came into the restaurant last week.* The clause has a subject, *who,* and a verb, *came,* but does not express a complete thought. What about the who?]

Common Dependent Words

after	if	what(ever)
although	since	when(ever)
as	so that	where
because	that	whether
before	though	which(ever)
even though	unless	while
how	until	who/whose

When a word group starts with *who, whose,* or *which,* it is not a complete sentence unless it is a question.

FRAGMENT	John is the friend I told you about. *Whose brother is an astronaut.*
QUESTION	Whose brother is an astronaut?

Correct a fragment that starts with a dependent word by connecting it to the sentence before or after it. If the dependent clause is connected to the sentence before it, you usually do not need to put a comma in front of it. If the dependent clause is joined to the sentence after it, put a comma after the dependent clause.

FRAGMENT	Chris looked for a job for a whole year. *Before he found the right one.*
CORRECTED	Chris looked for a job for a whole year. Before he found the right one.
CORRECTED	Before he found the right one, Chris looked for a job for a whole year.
FRAGMENT	My boss docked my pay for the half hour I was late. *Even though I worked through my lunch hour.*
CORRECTED	My boss docked my pay for the half hour I was late. Even though I worked through my lunch hour.

■ PRACTICE 3   CORRECTING FRAGMENTS THAT START WITH DEPENDENT WORDS

In the following items, circle any dependent word that appears at the beginning of a word group. Then, correct any fragment by connecting it to the previous or the next sentence.

EXAMPLE: (Although) astronauts have traveled in space for decades now. There are still many unanswered questions about the safety of space travel.

1. Because we are considering a future human mission to Mars. These questions are more important now than ever before.

2. One problem is that there can be a serious loss of bone tissue. When an astronaut spends more than a few months in space.

3. After enough bone tissue is lost. Bones become dangerously thin and fragile.

4. So that astronauts can maintain their bone tissue at a healthy level. They might be advised to exercise in space.

5. Another solution may be the use of the drugs. That people on Earth use to help maintain bone mass.

6. Even though physical problems are serious for astronauts. They can also have other difficulties.

7. One astronaut said that he felt isolated. Unless he could speak with his family more than once a week.

8. Fatigue is also an issue; for example, an accident resulted from an error by a Russian cosmonaut. Who was exhausted after four months in space.

9. Although all of these problems are serious. Most scientists believe they can be addressed.

10. Until space travel is safer. Some experts advocate sending robots into space instead of humans.

Fragments That Start with *-ing* Verb Forms

An ***-ing* verb form** (also called a **gerund**) is the form of a verb that ends in *-ing: walking, writing, swimming.* Unless it has a helping verb (*was walking, was writing, was swimming*), it can't be a complete verb in a sentence. Sometimes an *-ing* verb form is used as a subject at the beginning of a complete sentence.

-ING FORM USED AS A SUBJECT

Swimming is a wonderful form of exercise.

[In this sentence, *swimming* is the subject and *is* is the verb.]

Running strains the knees.

[In this sentence, *running* is the subject, not the verb; *strains* is the verb.]

-ING FORM USED WITH A HELPING VERB AS A VERB

I *am working* every day this summer.

[In this sentence, *am* is the helping verb; *am working* is the complete verb.]

Tom *was running* when he saw the accident.

[In this sentence, *was* is the helping verb; *was running* is the complete verb.]

ESL NOTE: English uses both *-ing* verb forms (*Kara loves* **singing**) and *infinitives* (*to* before the verb) (*Kara loves* **to sing**). If these forms confuse you, pay special attention to this section and see also page 511.

Whenever a word group begins with a word in *-ing* form, look carefully to see if the word group contains a subject and a verb and if it expresses a complete thought.

FRAGMENT   Snoring so loudly I couldn't sleep.

[If *snoring* is the main verb, what is the subject? There isn't one. Is there a helping verb used with *snoring*? No. It is a fragment.]

FRAGMENT   *Hoping to make up for lost time.* I took a back road to school.

[If *hoping* is the main verb, what is the subject? There isn't one. Is there a helping verb used with *hoping*? No. It is a fragment.]

Correct a fragment that starts with an *-ing* verb form either by adding whatever sentence elements are missing (usually a subject and a helping verb) or by connecting the fragment to the sentence before or after it. Usually, you will need to put a comma before or after the fragment to join it to the complete sentence.

-*ING* FRAGMENT   The audience applauded for ten minutes. *Whistling and cheering wildly.*

CORRECTED   The audience applauded for ten minutes. , w Whistling and cheering wildly.

CORRECTED	The audience applauded for ten minutes. ~~Whistling~~ *They were whistling* and cheering wildly.
-ING FRAGMENT	*Working two jobs and going to school.* I am tired all the time.
CORRECTED	Working two jobs and going to school, I am tired all the time.
CORRECTED	~~Working~~ *I am working* two jobs and going to school. I am tired all the time.

■ **PRACTICE 4   CORRECTING FRAGMENTS THAT START WITH *-ING* VERB FORMS**

In the following items, circle any *-ing* verb that appears at the beginning of a word group. Then, correct any fragment either by adding the missing sentence elements or by connecting it to the sentence before or after it.

EXAMPLE: (Quilting) with a group of other women, My grandmother found a social life and a creative outlet.

1. My grandmother spent her entire life. Living on a farm in eastern Wyoming.

2. Growing up during World War II. She learned from her mother how to sew her own clothes.

3. She was a natural seamstress. Creating shirts and dresses more beautiful than anything available in a store.

4. Joining a quilting circle at the age of twenty. My grandmother learned how to make quilts.

5. The quilting circle made quilts for special occasions. Using scraps of cloth left over from other sewing projects.

6. Laying the scraps out in an interesting pattern. The women then chose a traditional design for the stitching that joined the top and bottom parts of the quilt.

7. Celebrating the birth of her first child, my father. The quilting circle gave my grandmother a baby quilt that is now a treasured heirloom.

8. She told me that the quilt was made of memories. Incorporating fabric from her wedding dress, her maternity outfits, and all of the baby clothes she had stitched.

9. Looking at each bit of cloth in that quilt. My grandmother could still describe, years later, the garment she had made it from.

10. Trying to ensure that those memories would survive. I asked her to write down everything she recalled about my father's baby quilt.

Fragments That Start with *to* and a Verb

An **infinitive** is the word *to* plus a verb: *to hire, to eat, to study.* These phrases are all called *infinitive forms.* Although they contain verbs, infinitive forms function as nouns, adjectives, or adverbs.

If a word group begins with *to* and a verb, it must have another verb or it is not a complete sentence.

FRAGMENT   I will go to the store later. *To buy a card.*

[The first word group is a sentence, with *I* as the subject and *will go* as the verb. There is no subject in the word group *to buy a card,* and there is no verb outside of the infinitive.]

FRAGMENT   Last week, a couple in New York fulfilled their wedding fantasy. *To get married on the top of the Empire State Building.*

[The first word group is a sentence, with *couple* as the subject, and *fulfilled* as the verb. In the second word group, there is no subject or verb outside of the infinitive.]

Correct a fragment that starts with *to* and a verb by connecting it to the sentence before or after it or by adding the missing sentence elements (a subject and a verb).

FRAGMENT   Geri climbed up on the roof. *To watch the fireworks.*

CORRECTED   Geri climbed up on the roof, to watch the fireworks.

CORRECTED   Geri climbed up on the roof. She wanted to watch the fireworks.

FRAGMENT   *To save on her monthly gas bills.* Tammy sold her SUV and got a Honda Civic Hybrid.

CORRECTED   To save on her monthly gas bills, Tammy sold her SUV and got a Honda Civic Hybrid.

CORRECTED   *Tammy wanted to*   *She*
              ~~To~~ save on her monthly gas bills. ~~Tammy~~ sold her SUV and got a Honda Civic Hybrid.

ESL NOTE: Do not confuse the infinitive (*to* before the verb) with *that.*

INCORRECT   My brother wants *that* his girlfriend cook.

CORRECT   My brother wants his girlfriend *to cook.*

PRACTICE 5   FINDING AND CORRECTING FRAGMENTS THAT START WITH *TO* AND A VERB

In the following items, circle any examples of *to* and a verb that begin a word group. Then, correct each fragment either by adding the missing sentence elements or by connecting it to the previous or the next sentence.

EXAMPLE: In the 1940s, when Joe Gold was in his teens, he decided,
          t
          (To become) a member of the Muscle Beach Weightlifting
          Club.

1. To lift weights. Bodybuilders then met at the Muscle Beach of Santa Monica in Los Angeles.

2. When Joe Gold thought of opening a gym in 1965, he knew exactly where. To locate it.

3. Muscle Beach had become known as Venice by then, but bodybuilders still went there. To lift railroad ties and buckets filled with concrete.

4. Gold invented several new workout machines. To give the bodybuilders more useful exercise.

5. To get the best possible workout. Arnold Schwarzenegger regularly went to Gold's Gym in Venice.

6. Schwarzenegger won the title of Mr. Universe and later successfully ran in an election. To become governor of California.

7. To have a realistic setting for the 1977 movie *Pumping Iron.* The filmmaker selected Gold's Gym.

8. *Pumping Iron,* featuring Schwarzenegger and other weight lifters, helped. To make Gold's Gym famous.

9. In the early 1970s, however, Joe Gold made a decision. To sell his original business along with the name *Gold's Gym* to another company.

10. Later, Gold went on. To create World Gym, which now has more than three hundred locations around the world.

Fragments That Start with Examples or Explanations

As you edit your writing, pay special attention to groups of words that are examples or explanations of information you presented in the previous sentences. These word groups may be fragments.

FRAGMENT   Shoppers find many ways to save money on food bills. *For example, using double coupons.*

[The second word group has no subject and no verb. The word *using* is an *-ing* verb form that needs either to be the subject of a sentence or to have a helping verb with it.]

FRAGMENT   Parking on this campus is a real nightmare. *Especially between 8:00 and 8:30 a.m.*

[The second word group has no subject and no verb.]

Finding fragments that start with examples or explanations can be difficult, because there is no single kind of word to look for. The following are a few starting words that may signal an example or explanation, but fragments that are examples or explanations do not always start with these words:

| especially | for example | like | such as |

When a group of words that you think is a sentence gives an example or explanation of information in the previous sentence, stop to see if it has a subject and a verb and if it expresses a complete thought. If it is missing any of these elements, it is a fragment.

FRAGMENT   The Web has many job search sites. *Such as Monster.com.*

[Does the second word group have a subject? No. A verb? No. It is a fragment.]

FRAGMENT   I wish I had something to eat from Chipotle's right now. *A giant burrito, for example.*

[Does the second word group have a subject? Yes, *burrito*. A verb? No. It is a fragment.]

FRAGMENT   I had to push seven different voice-mail buttons before I spoke to a real person. *Not a helpful one, though.*

[Does the second word group have a subject? Yes, *one*. A verb? No. It is a fragment.]

To correct a fragment that starts with an example or an explanation, connect it either to the previous sentence or to the next one. Sometimes, you can add the missing sentence elements (a subject, a verb, or both) instead. When you connect the fragment to a sentence, you may need to reword or to change some punctuation. For example, fragments that are examples and fragments that are negatives are often set off by commas.

FRAGMENT   The Web has many job search sites. *Such as Monster.com.*

CORRECTED   The Web has many job search sites, such as Monster.com.

FRAGMENT   I had to push seven different voice-mail buttons before I spoke to a real person. *Not a helpful one, though.*

CORRECTED   I had to push seven different voice-mail buttons before I spoke to a real person, though not a helpful one.

CORRECTED   I had to push seven different voice-mail buttons before I spoke to a real person. He was not a helpful one, though.

PRACTICE 6   CORRECTING FRAGMENTS THAT ARE EXAMPLES OR EXPLANATIONS

In the following items, circle any word groups that are examples or explanations. Then, correct each fragment either by connecting it to the previous sentence or by adding the missing sentence elements.

EXAMPLE: Some studies estimate that the number of teenage girls suffering dating abuse is very high. Perhaps as many as one out of three girls, *experiences some type of abuse from her boyfriend.*

1. Many parents believe that they would know if their daughters were being abused. Either physically or emotionally.

2. Most parents would certainly be concerned to see signs of violence on their children. Such as bruises or scratches.

3. A young man can be abusive without laying a finger on his girlfriend. A guy who monitors her actions and keeps her from spending time with other friends.

4. Abusive boyfriends often want to control their partners. Make sure that their girlfriends dress a certain way, for example.

5. Around her parents, a teenager's boyfriend may act like a perfect gentleman. Polite, attentive, and kind to the young woman.

6. When the couple is alone, however, he may be giving her verbal abuse. Like telling her that she is fat, stupid, and ugly.

7. A young woman with an abusive boyfriend may develop psychological problems that will be difficult to treat. Such as low self-esteem.

8. Parents should look for signs that their daughter needs help. Like slipping grades, loss of interest in her friends, and unwillingness to confide in parents.

9. Friends who think that a young woman is involved in an abusive relationship should try to be supportive of her. Not turn away even if she refuses to leave her boyfriend.

10. Young women need to know that help is available. From parents, guidance counselors, women's support services, and even the police, if necessary.

Edit Paragraphs and Your Own Writing

As you edit the following paragraphs and your own writing, use the Critical Thinking guide that follows. You may also want to refer to the chart on page 354.

CRITICAL THINKING: EDITING FOR FRAGMENTS

FOCUS
- Whenever you see one of the five trouble spots in your writing, stop to check for a possible fragment.

ASK
- Does the word group have a subject?
- Does it have a verb?
- Does it express a complete thought?

EDIT
- If your answer to any of these questions is "no," you have a fragment that you must correct.

Find and correct any fragments in the following paragraphs.

■ **EDITING REVIEW 1**

(1) Genetically modified foods are being marketed. (2) As the foods of the future. (3) For the past decade, gene technology has been advancing dramatically. (4) Inserting a gene from one species into the DNA of another species is easily possible. (5) A gene from a fish may be found. (6) To make tomatoes more resistant to disease. (7) Of course, genetic modification may have unintended effects. (8) As in the case of genetically modified corn. (9) Which may harm monarch butterfly caterpillars. (10) Arguing that the long-term effects of genetic modification may not be known for years to come. (11) Some scientists urge caution before marketing genetically modified foods.

■ EDITING REVIEW 2

(1) The year 2001 brought more bad news. (2) For beef eaters and for British cattle farmers struggling to overcome the bad publicity brought on by mad cow disease. (3) Cattle in England and Scotland suffered an epidemic of an extremely contagious illness. (4) Hoof-and-mouth disease. (5) Many people were frightened of eating British beef even though hoof-and-mouth disease does not harm humans. (6) To contain the outbreak. (7) Hiking trails were closed. (8) Because the disease could travel on the shoes or clothing of people walking from one region to another. (9) Before the epidemic was contained, thousands of infected cattle were slaughtered. (10) In the end, many farmers wondered how they would be able to survive. (11) After losing so many of their livestock.

■ EDITING REVIEW 3

(1) The term *organic* means different things. (2) To different people. (3) Organic foods are supposed to be grown without pesticides. (4) A method that reduces a farm's impact on the environment. (5) But is organic food a healthier choice for the person eating it? (6) Most people who buy organic food think so. (7) They pay premium prices for organic products because they think the food is good for their own well-being. (8) Not just that of the environment. (9) Surprisingly, however, some foods labeled organic today are highly processed. (10) The label merely means that the ingredients meet a certain government standard. (11) While guaranteeing nothing about the nutritional content or health benefits of the food.

■ EDITING REVIEW 4

(1) For several years. (2) The U.S. Department of Agriculture has permitted the irradiation of certain foods sold in American supermarkets.

(3) Irradiating produce kills bacteria on the food. (4) Increasing its shelf life. (5) Without irradiation, a strawberry may last only a day or two after being purchased. (6) An irradiated strawberry, in contrast, can last a week or more. (7) Because the bacteria that would cause it to spoil are killed by radiation. (8) While some consumers worry about buying irradiated food. (9) Others dismiss these concerns as the effect of too many science-fiction movies. (10) In stores where irradiated fruits and vegetables are sold under banners announcing the radiation treatment. (11) The owners report a booming market.

EDITING REVIEW 5

(1) Bacteria that resist antibiotics could be a real health threat in the next century. (2) Doctors have begun to explain to their patients. (3) That antibiotics are useful only for certain kinds of infections and that patients must finish every course of antibiotics they start. (4) Antibiotic use in agriculture, however, has continued. (5) To increase. (6) The government does not even keep records. (7) Of antibiotic use in farm animals. (8) Many cattle, pigs, and chickens get antibiotics for economic reasons. (9) Such as to keep them healthy and to make them grow faster. (10) Many scientists fear that antibiotic residue in the meat Americans eat may contribute to antibiotic resistance. (11) If so, agricultural antibiotics could eventually endanger human health.

PRACTICE 7   EDITING YOUR OWN WRITING FOR FRAGMENTS

As a final practice, edit fragments in a piece of your own writing—a paper you are working on for this class, a paper you've already finished, a paper for another course, or a recent piece of writing from your work or everyday life. Use the Critical Thinking guide on page 351 and the chart on page 354 to help you.

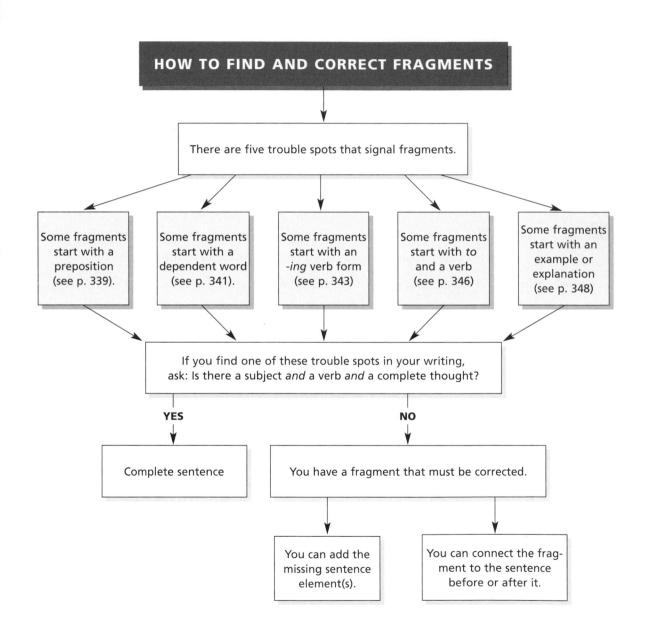

HOW TO FIND AND CORRECT FRAGMENTS

There are five trouble spots that signal fragments.

Some fragments start with a preposition (see p. 339).	Some fragments start with a dependent word (see p. 341).	Some fragments start with an *-ing* verb form (see p. 343)	Some fragments start with *to* and a verb (see p. 346)	Some fragments start with an example or explanation (see p. 348)

If you find one of these trouble spots in your writing, ask: Is there a subject *and* a verb *and* a complete thought?

YES

Complete sentence

NO

You have a fragment that must be corrected.

You can add the missing sentence element(s).

You can connect the fragment to the sentence before or after it.

23

Run-Ons

Two Sentences Joined Incorrectly

Understand What Run-Ons Are

A sentence is also called an **independent clause**, a group of words with a subject and a verb that expresses a complete thought. Sometimes, two independent clauses can be joined in one sentence.

SENTENCES WITH TWO INDEPENDENT CLAUSES

Independent clause   Independent clause

The fog was very thick, so the airport closed.

    Independent clause   Independent clause

Passengers were delayed for hours, and many were angry.

■ In the examples throughout this section, the subject is underlined once, and the verb is underlined twice.

A **run-on** is two sentences (each containing a subject and a verb and expressing a complete thought) that are joined incorrectly and written as one sentence. There are two kinds of run-ons: **fused sentences** and **comma splices**.

A **fused sentence** is two complete sentences joined without any punctuation.

    Independent clause   Independent clause

FUSED SENTENCE   Anger is a dangerous emotion it has many bad effects.

↑
No punctuation

A **comma splice** is two complete sentences joined by only a comma instead of a comma and one of the following words: *and, but, for, nor, or, so, yet.*

COMMA SPLICE   Anger is a dangerous emotion, it has many bad effects.

Comma

Patty Maloney

Clinical Nurse
Specialist

*(See Patty's Profile
of Success on
p. 117.)*

In the Real World, Why Is It Important to Correct Run-Ons?

Run-ons are errors that many people, including instructors and employers, will notice, as the following example shows.

SITUATION: Marion is new to her position as a licensed practical nurse at a large hospital. Each day, she updates patients' records and writes brief summaries of their progress for other nurses. The following is a report that Marion wrote in her first week on the job.

> Trudari Kami is a premature infant she was born with a birth weight of 1.7 pounds her lungs were not fully developed and she was not able to breathe on her own. As of 2:15 a.m. on Thursday, April 6, she remains in stable condition her condition is still critical though she is being carefully monitored.

RESPONSE: Patty Maloney, the clinical nurse specialist profiled in Chapter 9, had the following response to Marion's report.

> I had to meet with Marion, who is obviously not sure how to communicate clearly in medical documents. I explained to her that what she had written was very difficult to understand, and I worked with her on editing the report so that the next person would understand what Marion was trying to say. I had to do this because the reports must be clear; otherwise, the next person might not be sure how to treat the baby.

Find and Correct Run-Ons

To find run-ons, focus on each sentence in your writing one at a time. Until you get used to finding run-ons, this step will take time, but after a while you will not make the error as often.

Read the following paragraph. Does it include any run-ons? _____

If so, how many? _____

The concert to benefit AIDS research included fabulous musicians and songs. One of the guitarists had six different guitars they were all acoustic. One had a shiny engraved silver shield on it, it flashed in the lights. The riffs the group played were fantastic. All of the songs were original, and many had to do with the loss of loved ones. At the end of some songs, the audience was hushed, too moved with emotion to begin the applause right away. When the concert was over, the listeners, many of them in tears, gave the performers a standing ovation.

PRACTICE 1   FINDING RUN-ONS

Find and underline the four run-ons in Marion's report on page 356.

When you find a run-on in your writing, you can correct it in one of four ways.

WAYS TO CORRECT A RUN-ON

- Add a period.
- Add a semicolon.
- Add a comma and a coordinating conjunction.
- Add a dependent word.

Add a Period

You can correct a run-on by adding a period to make two separate sentences.

FUSED SENTENCES (corrected)

I tried to call about my bill. I got four useless recorded messages.

I finally hung up. My question remained unanswered.

COMMA SPLICES (corrected)

My sister found a guy she likes in a chat room. She is going to meet him.

I warned her that she should choose a public place. Applebee's at lunch would be good.

Add a Semicolon

A second way to correct a run-on is to join the two independent clauses into one sentence by adding a semicolon (;). Use a semicolon only when the two independent clauses express closely related ideas that make sense in a single combined sentence.

Independent clause   Independent clause

FUSED SENTENCES (corrected)

My father had a heart attack he is in the hospital.

My mother called 911 the ambulance was there in four minutes.

COMMA SPLICES (corrected)

The emergency room wasn't like the one on the show *ER*, the doctors and nurses were rude.

He was in the emergency room for over three hours, there wasn't a bed for him.

A semicolon is sometimes used before a transition from one independent clause to another, and the transition word is followed by a comma.

TRANSITION BETWEEN SENTENCES

Transition

I tried to visit my father; however, I couldn't get a ride.

Semicolon   Comma

■ **PRACTICE 2   CORRECTING A RUN-ON BY ADDING A PERIOD OR A SEMICOLON**

For each of the following run-ons, indicate in the space to the left whether it is a fused sentence (FS) or a comma splice (CS). Then, correct the run-on by adding a period or a semicolon.

EXAMPLE: __CS__ A cellular phone in the car can be a lifesaver in an

emergency, a cell phone may also contribute to

an accident.

_____ 1. The invention of cell phones made telephoning from a car possible people could telephone for help if they were stranded on the highway.

_____ 2. Almost as soon as cell phones became common, people began to use them in traffic, some drivers were undoubtedly distracted by their telephones, creating a danger.

_____ 3. Some communities in the United States have banned drivers from talking on handheld cell phones, a driver must stop the car to place a call legally in those areas.

_____ 4. Cell-phone makers have come up with hands-free phones even in places with cell-phone restrictions, these phones can be used by the driver of a moving car.

_____ 5. No one debates that drivers can be distracted by cell phones some people wonder, however, whether the problem is really the fact that a driver is holding the phone.

_____ 6. If lawmakers simply want to make sure that drivers have their hands free, they should ban eating while driving as well, they could also stop people from shaving or putting on makeup behind the wheel.

_____ 7. Some people worry that drivers are distracted not by holding the telephone but by having a conversation a tense discussion with the boss or good news from a relative can take the driver's attention from traffic.

_____ 8. Cell-phone supporters argue that the same kinds of distractions can come from elsewhere in the car, music and talk radio, for example, can suddenly make a driver lose concentration.

■ For more practice correcting run-ons, visit Exercise Central at <**bedfordstmartins .com/realessays**>.

_____ 9. There are differences, however, between talking on a cell phone and listening to music in the car, the telephone requires interaction from the driver, but the radio calls for passive listening.

_____ 10. Drivers who love making calls on the road will resist cell-phone restrictions many other people will feel safer in communities that do not allow driving while telephoning.

Add a Comma and a Coordinating Conjunction

A third way to correct a run-on is to add a comma and a **coordinating conjunction**: a link that joins independent clauses to form one sentence. Some people remember the seven coordinating conjunctions (*and, but, for, nor, or, so, yet*) by using the memory device of *fanboys*, for **f**or, **a**nd, **n**or, **b**ut, **o**r, **y**et, **s**o.

To correct a fused sentence, add both a comma and a coordinating conjunction. A comma splice already has a comma, so just add a coordinating conjunction that makes sense in the sentence.

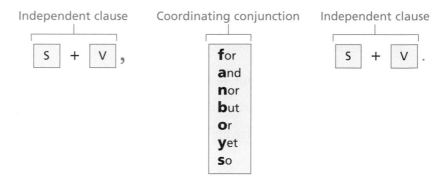

Independent clause	Coordinating conjunction	Independent clause
S + V ,	for and nor but or yet so	S + V .

FUSED SENTENCES (corrected)

We warned Tim to wear a seat belt ^, *but* he never did.

He got into an accident ^, *and* he went through the windshield.

COMMA SPLICES (corrected)

He was unbelievably lucky, *for* he got just scrapes and bruises.

He's back driving again, *but* ^ he always buckles his seatbelt before starting the car.

ESL NOTE: **Coordinating** conjunctions need to connect two independent clauses. They are not used to join a dependent and an independent clause.

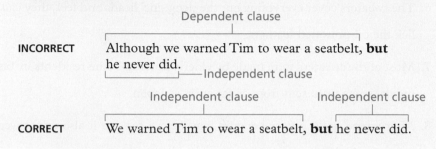

INCORRECT   Dependent clause

Although we warned Tim to wear a seatbelt, **but** he never did.

Independent clause

CORRECT   Independent clause   Independent clause

We warned Tim to wear a seatbelt, **but** he never did.

■ **PRACTICE 3   CORRECTING A RUN-ON BY ADDING A COMMA AND A COORDINATING CONJUNCTION**

Correct each of the following run-ons. First, underline the subjects and double-underline the verbs to find the separate sentences. Then, add a comma (unless the run-on already includes one) and a coordinating conjunction.

EXAMPLE: Tasmania, an island off the coast of Australia, is the

home of many unusual kinds of wildlife, *but* it also has been

the site of several oil spills.

1. Fairy penguins, a small breed of penguin, live in Tasmania these birds have often been the victims of oil spills.

2. The birds clean their feathers with their beaks they swallow the oil on their feathers.

3. Unfortunately, the penguins' attempts to clean off their feathers can be fatal crude oil is poisonous to penguins.

4. Wildlife conservationists in Tasmania expected future spills, they created a plan to save the penguins.

5. One of the conservationists created a pattern for a sweater for the penguins volunteers from around the world knitted these unusual sweaters.

6. The sweaters cover everything but the penguins' heads and feet, they can't lick the oil-poisoned feathers.

7. Most of the sweaters were made by elderly nursing-home residents in Tasmania, some were sent from as far away as Japan.

8. After future spills, a fairy penguin may wear a sweater it also might wear a tiny football jersey.

9. Some creative knitters made tuxedo-patterned sweaters a few of these penguin suits even have bow ties.

10. The penguins have a variety of protective outfits they don't like any of the garments.

Add a Dependent Word

The fourth way to correct a run-on is to make one of the complete sentences a dependent clause by adding a dependent word (a **subordinating conjunction** or a **relative pronoun**), such as *after, because, before, even though, if, though, unless,* or *when.* Choose the dependent word that best expresses the relationship between the two clauses.

Use a dependent word when the clause it begins is less important than or explains the other clause.

FUSED SENTENCES (corrected)

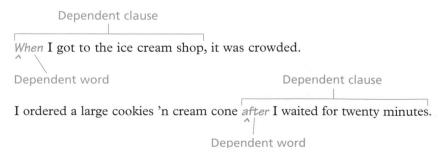

COMMA SPLICES (corrected)

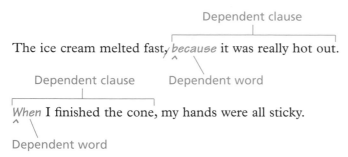

Dependent clause

The ice cream melted fast, *because* it was really hot out.

Dependent clause   Dependent word

When I finished the cone, my hands were all sticky.

Dependent word

When the dependent clause starts off the sentence, you need to add a comma after it, as in the first and fourth sentences in the preceding examples. When the dependent clause is after the independent clause, there is no comma, as in the second and third examples.

Common Dependent Words

after	if	what(ever)
although	since	when(ever)
as	so that	where
because	that	whether
before	though	which(ever)
even though	unless	while
how	until	who/whose

PRACTICE 4   CORRECTING A RUN-ON BY MAKING A DEPENDENT CLAUSE

Correct each of the following run-ons. First, underline the subjects and double-underline the verbs to find the separate sentences. Then, make one of the clauses dependent by adding a dependent word. Add a comma after the dependent clause if it comes first in the sentence.

EXAMPLE: Everyone knows where a compass points, ~~it points~~
which is
toward the north.

1. This phenomenon is something we take for granted, it may be changing.

2. A change in magnetism is possible the earth's magnetic field is getting weaker.

3. Such a change happened before in the earth's history, magnetic materials pointed south instead of north for long periods.

4. A complete reversal could take thousands of years, some effects of the weaker magnetic field are already apparent.

5. The change in magnetism has affected some satellites, the satellites have been damaged.

6. Animals may also be affected some of them use the earth's magnetic field to sense where they are located.

7. Bees, pigeons, salmon, turtles, whales, newts, and even bacteria need the magnetic field to navigate, they will adjust to the magnetic change.

8. However, it could take five thousand to seven thousand years compasses would point south instead of north.

9. The processes affecting magnetism may unfold much more slowly, the magnetic change may not occur for millions of years.

10. The dinosaurs roamed the earth for about thirty-five million years, the earth's magnetic field did not change during all this time.

A Word That Can Cause Run-Ons: *Then*

Many run-ons are caused by the word *then*. You can use *then* to join two sentences, but if you add it without the correct punctuation and/or joining word, the resulting sentence will be a run-on. Often, writers mistakenly use just a comma before *then*, but that makes a comma splice. To correct a run-on caused by the word *then*, you can use any of the four methods presented in this chapter.

COMMA SPLICE	I grabbed the remote, then I ate my pizza.
CORRECTED	I grabbed the remote, then I ate my pizza. [period added]
CORRECTED	I grabbed the remote, then I ate my pizza. [semicolon added]
CORRECTED	I grabbed the remote, then I ate my pizza. [coordinating conjunction *and* added]
CORRECTED	I grabbed the remote, ~~then~~ I ate my pizza. [dependent word *before* added to make a dependent clause]

Edit Paragraphs and Your Own Writing

As you edit the following paragraphs and your own writing, use the Critical Thinking guide that follows. You may also want to refer to the chart on page 368.

CRITICAL THINKING: EDITING FOR RUN-ONS

FOCUS
- Read each sentence aloud, and listen carefully as you read.

ASK
- Am I pausing in the middle of the sentence?
- If so, are there two subjects and two verbs?
- If so, are there two complete sentences in this sentence?
- If there are two sentences (independent clauses), are they separated by punctuation? If the answer is "no," the sentence is a **fused sentence**.
- If there is punctuation between the two independent clauses, is it a comma only, with no coordinating conjunction? If the answer is "yes," the sentence is a **comma splice**.

EDIT
- If the sentence is a run-on, correct it using one of the four methods for editing run-ons.

Find and correct any run-ons in the following paragraphs. Use whichever of the four methods of correcting run-ons that seems best to you.

■ **EDITING REVIEW 1**

(1) Your memory can play tricks on you. (2) It's often easy to forget things you want desperately to remember them. (3) You have probably had the experience of forgetting an acquaintance's name the name comes to your mind only when it's too late. (4) You have also probably been unable to find your keys once in a while, you put them down somewhere without thinking. (5) At other times, however, you may find it difficult to forget some things, you wish you could never think of them again. (6) If you have an annoying song in your mind, you may spend hours wishing desperately to forget it. (7) Sometimes, you may find yourself forced to relive your most embarrassing moment over and over again in your mind your memory won't let you leave that part of your past behind. (8) Some scholars believe that these annoying habits of memory evolved for a reason, it's hard to imagine, though, any good reason for developing the ability to forget where you left your keys.

■ **EDITING REVIEW 2**

(1) Most scientists now agree that human beings are changing the climate industrial activities release gases into the air that trap heat in the earth's atmosphere. (2) The number one problem gas is carbon dioxide, factories and gasoline engines release tons of it into the air. (3) In international discussions of global warming, industrial countries like the United States have argued that planting forests might reduce the amount of carbon dioxide in the air. (4) Trees absorb carbon dioxide, then they release oxygen. (5) A recent study tested trees in North Carolina it exposed them to high levels of carbon dioxide. (6) At first, the trees grew rapidly,

after a while, their growth returned to normal. (7) Dead trees did not release their accumulated carbon into the soil instead, the carbon went back into the air as carbon dioxide. (8) The study will continue for years, this is not the last word on the subject. (9) However, perhaps reducing carbon dioxide in the atmosphere will be difficult the United States may yet have to come up with a way to reduce the amount of the gas getting into the air in the first place.

PRACTICE 5   EDITING YOUR OWN WRITING FOR RUN-ONS

As a final practice, edit run-ons in a piece of your own writing—a paper you are working on for this class, a paper you've already finished, a paper for another course, or a recent piece of writing from your work or everyday life. Use the Critical Thinking guide on page 365 and the chart on page 368 to help you.

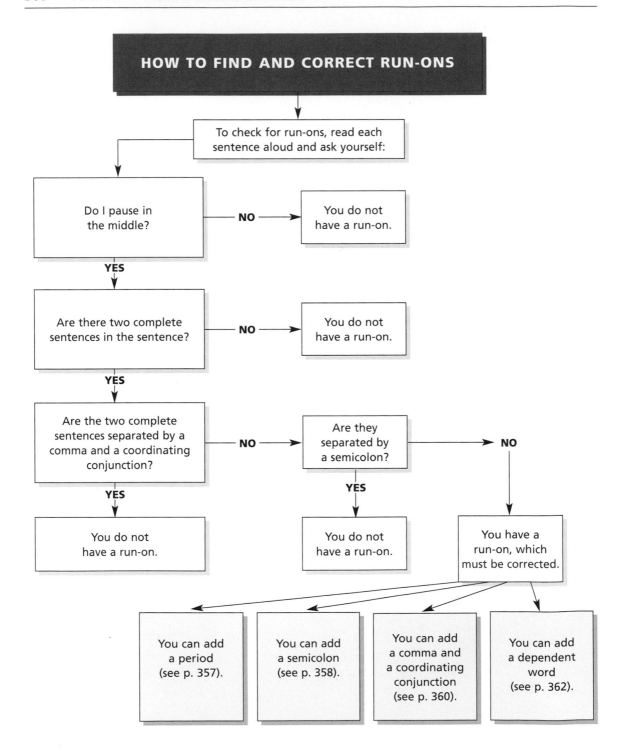

24

Problems with Subject-Verb Agreement

When Subjects and Verbs Don't Match

Understand What Subject-Verb Agreement Is

In any sentence, **the subject and the verb must match—or agree— in number.** If the subject is singular (one person, place, or thing), then the verb must also be singular. If the subject is plural (more than one), the verb must also be plural.

■ In the examples throughout this chapter, the <u>subject</u> is underlined once, and the <u>verb</u> is underlined twice.

SINGULAR   The <u>phone</u> <u><u>rings</u></u> constantly at work.

[The subject, *phone*, is singular—just one phone—so the verb must take the singular form: *rings.*]

PLURAL   The <u>phones</u> <u><u>ring</u></u> constantly at work.

[The subject, *phones*, is plural—more than one phone—so the verb must take the plural form: *ring.*]

Regular verbs, verbs that follow standard English patterns, have two forms in the present tense: one that does not add an ending and one that ends in *-s*. First-person (*I, we*) subjects, second-person (*you*) subjects, and plural subjects (more than one person, place, or thing) have verbs with no *-s* ending. Third-person singular subjects (*he, she, it,* and singular nouns) always have a verb that ends in *-s*. The chart that follows shows the differences.

■ For more on regular verbs and how they differ from irregular verbs, see Chapter 25.

Regular Verbs, Present Tense

	SINGULAR FORM	PLURAL FORM
First person	I walk.	We walk.
Second person	You walk.	You walk.
Third person	He/she/it walks.	They walk.
	Percy walks.	Percy and Don walk.
	The dog walks.	The dogs walk.

Daigo Fujiwara
Online Art Director

(See Daigo's Profile of Success on p. 152.)

In the Real World, Why Is It Important to Correct Subject-Verb Agreement Problems?

Like fragments and run-ons, subject-verb agreement errors are significant problems that can make a bad impression with instructors, employers, and others.

SITUATION: Daigo Fujiwara, the online art director profiled in Chapter 11, communicates frequently with freelance artists and designers. The following e-mail message from one designer caught his attention.

> The assignment we discussed, which is very exciting, have lots of great possibilities. Several of the concepts in your memo is challenging, and I look forward to the work. My portfolio have several examples that I will send you by the end of the week. Everything in the shots meet your description.

RESPONSE: I had to reread this message a few times to make sure I understood. These kinds of mistakes make me stop, so it takes longer for me to process the message. On the one hand, I sympathize with the person because I also had to learn to write correct English. On the other hand, when my writing was really bad, I reread anything I wrote very carefully to make sure that it was right, and I think this person should have taken the time to do that.

Find and Correct Errors in Subject-Verb Agreement

To find problems with subject-verb agreement in your own writing, read carefully and look for the following trouble spots.

SUBJECT-VERB AGREEMENT TROUBLE SPOTS

• The verb is a form of *be, have,* or *do.*

INCORRECT	You is correct.
CORRECT	You are correct.

• Words or phrases come between the subject and the verb.

INCORRECT	The people who shop at the mini-mart pays more.
CORRECT	The people who shop at the mini-mart pay more.

• The sentence has a compound subject.

INCORRECT	Either my husband or my son drive my mother home.
CORRECT	Either my husband or my son drives my mother home.

• The subject is an indefinite pronoun.

INCORRECT	Everyone know the time.
CORRECT	Everyone knows the time.

• The verb comes before the subject.

INCORRECT	Where is the men now?
CORRECT	Where are the men now?

PRACTICE 1   FINDING SUBJECT-VERB AGREEMENT PROBLEMS

Find and underline the four subject-verb agreement problems in the e-mail sent to Daigo Fujiwara on page 370.

The Verb Is a Form of *Be, Have,* or *Do*

The verbs *be, have,* and *do* do not follow the regular patterns for forming singular and plural forms; they are **irregular verbs**.

These verbs cause problems for people who use only one form of the verb in casual conversation: *You is the richest* (incorrect). *He is the richest* (correct). In college and at work, use the correct form of the verbs *be, have,* and *do* as shown in the charts on page 372.

are
You is the craziest person I've ever known.

has
Johnson have the best car in the lot.

does
Valery do the bill paying on the first of every month.

Forms of the Verb Be

PRESENT TENSE	SINGULAR	PLURAL
First person	I am	we are
Second person	you are	you are
Third person	she/he/it is	they are
	the student/Joe is	the students are
PAST TENSE		
First person	I was	we were
Second person	you were	you were
Third person	she/he/it was	they were
	the student/Joe was	the students were

Forms of the Verb Have, *Present Tense*

	SINGULAR	PLURAL
First person	I have	we have
Second person	you have	you have
Third person	she/he/it has	they have
	the student/Joe has	the students have

Forms of the Verb Do, *Present Tense*

	SINGULAR	PLURAL
First person	I do	we do
Second person	you do	you do
Third person	she/he/it does	they do
	the student/Joe does	the students do

PRACTICE 2   CHOOSING THE CORRECT FORM OF *BE, HAVE,* OR *DO*

In each sentence, underline the subject of the verb *be, have,* or *do,* and circle the correct form of the verb.

EXAMPLE: A <u>sport</u> (has)/ have) an important role in many children's lives.

1. I (was / were) involved in Little League during fifth and sixth grades.

2. My parents (was / were) happy to cheer at most of the games.

3. Now I (has / have) a Little Leaguer of my own, my daughter Tina.

4. She (am / is / are) not a natural athlete.

5. Still, the games (am / is / are) usually a lot of fun for her.

6. She (does / do) not see too many parents who can't control their temper.

7. Once in a while, though, incidents (does / do) happen because of angry parents.

8. The local Little League organization (has / have) very strict rules about parents' interference.

9. Children (does / do) not need to see parents cursing at the opposing team or threatening the coaches.

10. Sports teams (am / is / are) supposed to be a way to learn about good sportsmanship, not an opportunity for parents to be terrible role models.

■ For more practice with subject-verb agreement, visit Exercise Central at <bedfordstmartins .com/realessays>.

PRACTICE 3   USING THE CORRECT FORM OF *BE, HAVE,* OR *DO*

In each sentence, underline the subject and fill in the correct form of the verb (*be, have,* or *do*) indicated in parentheses.

EXAMPLE: Our <u>professor</u> ___*has*___ (*have*) forty papers to grade this weekend.

1. Most students _____ (*be*) used to the idea that computers sometimes grade tests.

2. You _____ (*have*) probably taken standardized tests and filled in small ovals with a pencil.

3. A computer _____ (*do*) not have to be sophisticated to read the results of such tests.

4. Surprisingly, a new software program _____ (*be*) designed to grade student essays.

5. The program _____ (*have*) the ability to sort words in an essay and compare the essay to others in its database.

6. The software _____ (*do*) not check grammar or spelling.

7. Teachers _____ (*be*) still needed to supplement the computer grade, according to the software manufacturer.

8. If a computer grades your essay, you _____ (*have*) to write about one of five hundred specified topics.

9. A computer _____ (*do*) check the organization, clarity, and style of your writing.

10. Some teachers _____ (*be*) excited about their new computerized assistant, but I _____ (*do*) not like the idea of a computer grading my essays.

Words Come between the Subject and the Verb

When the subject and the verb aren't right next to each other, it can be difficult to make sure that they agree. Most often, what comes between the subject and the verb is either a prepositional phrase or a dependent clause.

Prepositional Phrase between the Subject and the Verb

A **prepositional phrase** starts with a preposition and ends with a noun or pronoun: The line *for the movie* went *around the corner*.

■ For a list of common prepositions, see page 330.

  Remember, the subject of a sentence is never in a prepositional phrase. When you are looking for the subject, you can cross out any prepositional phrases. This strategy should help you find the real subject and decide whether it agrees with the verb.

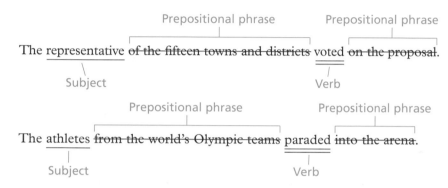

PRACTICE 4   MAKING SUBJECTS AND VERBS AGREE WHEN THEY ARE SEPARATED BY A PREPOSITIONAL PHRASE

In each of the following sentences, first cross out the prepositional phrase between the subject and the verb, and then circle the correct form of the verb. Remember, the subject of a sentence is never in a prepositional phrase.

  EXAMPLE: Twenty-eight million people ~~in the United States~~ (am / is /

    (are)) deaf or hard of hearing.

1. Most parents with hearing loss (has / have) children who can hear.

2. Many of these children (learns / learn) sign language as a first language.

3. Communication with words (comes / come) later.

4. Few people in the hearing world (understands / understand) the lives of deaf people completely.

5. Many deaf people in this country (feels / feel) closer to deaf people from other parts of the world than to hearing Americans.

6. The hearing children of deaf parents (comes / come) closer to under-standing deaf culture than most hearing people.

7. A hearing child in a deaf household (resembles / resemble) a child of im-migrant parents in many ways.

8. Adapting to two different cultures (makes / make) fitting in difficult for some young people.

9. Sometimes, ties to the hearing world and the deaf world (pulls / pull) in opposite directions.

10. Bridges between cultures (am / is / are) more easily built by people who understand both sides.

Dependent Clause between the Subject and the Verb

A **dependent clause** has a subject and a verb, but it does not express a complete thought. When a dependent clause comes between the subject and the verb, it usually starts with the word *who, whose, whom, that,* or *which.*

The subject of a sentence is never in the dependent clause. When you are looking for the subject, you can cross out any dependent clauses.

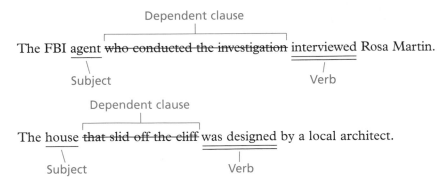

PRACTICE 5   MAKING SUBJECTS AND VERBS AGREE WHEN THEY ARE SEPARATED BY A DEPENDENT CLAUSE

In each of the following sentences, cross out any dependent clauses. Then, correct any problems with subject-verb agreement. If a sentence has no problem, write "OK" next to it.

is
EXAMPLE: A person ~~who lies in job applications are~~ likely to get caught.

1. A résumé, which is a job applicant's first contact with many prospective employers, contain details about past work experience and education.

2. Many people who write résumés are tempted to exaggerate.

3. Perhaps an applicant who held a previous job for two months claim to have spent a year there.

4. A job title that sounds impressive look good on a résumé, whether or not it is accurate.

5. Often, a person who never received a college degree wants to add it to a résumé anyway.

6. A person who is considering untrue résumé additions need to think twice.

7. Employers who like a résumé checks the information provided by the applicant.

8. A résumé that contains false information goes in the reject pile.

9. In addition, many people who invent material on a résumé forgets the inventions when they face a prospective employer in an interview.

10. Even a company that does not check all of the information on résumés pays attention when interviewees seem to forget some of their qualifications.

The Sentence Has a Compound Subject

A **compound subject** consists of two (or more) subjects connected by *and, or,* or *nor* (as in *neither/nor* expressions). If two subjects are joined by *and,* they combine to become a plural subject, and the verb must take a plural form as well.

Subject   *and*   Subject   Plural form of verb

The director *and* the producer decide how the film will be made.

If two subjects are connected by *or* or *nor,* they are considered separate, and the verb should agree with the subject closest to it.

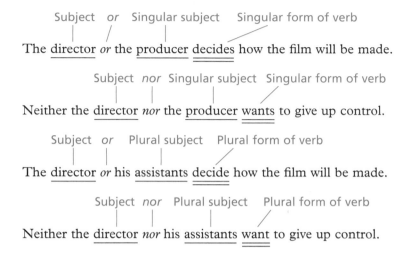

Subject   *or*   Singular subject   Singular form of verb

The director *or* the producer decides how the film will be made.

Subject *nor* Singular subject Singular form of verb

Neither the director *nor* the producer wants to give up control.

Subject   *or*   Plural subject   Plural form of verb

The director *or* his assistants decide how the film will be made.

Subject *nor*   Plural subject   Plural form of verb

Neither the director *nor* his assistants want to give up control.

PRACTICE 6   CHOOSING THE CORRECT VERB IN A SENTENCE WITH A COMPOUND SUBJECT

In each of the following sentences, underline the word (*and, or,* or *nor*) that joins the parts of the compound subject. Then, circle the correct form of the verb.

> EXAMPLE: A child <u>and</u> an adult (has /(have)) different nutritional needs.

1. Fruits and vegetables (does / do) not make up enough of most Americans' diets.

2. The U.S. government and other organizations concerned with health and nutrition (recommends / recommend) that people eat at least five servings of fruits and vegetables a day.

3. Whole-grain cereal or bread (is / are) another important part of a healthy diet.

4. Neither vitamins nor fiber (is / are) found in many popular snack foods.

5. Potato chips and candy (contains / contain) few useful nutrients.

6. Neither fat nor sugar (helps / help) build a healthy body.

7. However, in small amounts, fat and sugar (contributes / contribute) beneficially by making food taste good.

8. Motivated dieters and certain health fanatics (eats / eat) nutritious food that tastes terrible.

9. Neither dieters nor health fanatics (is / are) likely to keep eating the unappetizing food for a lifetime.

10. Choosing nutritious food and preparing it well (allows / allow) a person to feel healthy and satisfied.

The Subject Is an Indefinite Pronoun

Indefinite pronouns, which refer to unspecified people or objects, are often singular, although there are exceptions.

Indefinite Pronouns

ALWAYS SINGULAR

anybody	everyone	nothing
anyone	everything	one (of)
anything	much	somebody
each (of)	neither (of)	someone
either (of)	nobody	something
everybody	no one	

MAY BE SINGULAR OR PLURAL

all	none
any	some

When you find an indefinite pronoun in your writing, use this table to help you determine the correct verb form, singular or plural. If the pronoun may be singular or plural, you'll need to check whether the word it refers to is singular or plural to determine what verb form to use.

Everyone <u>loves</u> vacations.

[*Everyone* is always singular, so it takes the singular verb *loves.*]

<u>Some</u> of the wreckage <u>was recovered</u> after the crash.

[In this case, *some* is singular, referring to *wreckage,* so it takes the singular verb *was recovered.*]

<u>Some</u> of the workers <u>were delayed</u> by the storm.

[In this case, *some* is plural, referring to *workers,* so it takes the plural verb *were delayed.*]

Often, an indefinite pronoun is followed by a prepositional phrase or a dependent clause; remember that the subject of a sentence is never found in either of these. To choose the correct verb, you can cross out the prepositional phrase or dependent clause to focus on the indefinite pronoun.

<u>All</u> ~~of my first day on the job~~ <u>was devoted</u> to filling out forms.

<u>Some</u> ~~who are longtime residents~~ <u>recommend</u> a rent strike.

PRACTICE 7   CHOOSING THE CORRECT VERB WHEN THE SUBJECT IS AN INDEFINITE PRONOUN

In each of the following sentences, underline the subject and cross out any prepositional phrases or dependent clauses that come between the subject and the verb. Then, circle the correct verb.

> **EXAMPLE:** <u>One</u> ~~of the best things about the Internet~~ (**is**)/ are) the
>
> way people can use it to get information from around the
>
> world.

1. Anyone who wants to take college courses (needs / need) access to a college campus.

2. Today, nobody with a computer and Internet access (lives / live) too far from a college to get a degree.

3. Some of the hundreds of accredited colleges in the United States (offers / offer) online degree programs.

4. Everything that students need to pass the course (is / are) available online.

5. Everyone who takes online courses (has / have) to participate in e-mail discussions and write papers.

6. No one in an online class (gets / get) to sit silently in the back of the room.

7. Someone who learns best by listening (is / are) probably not a good candidate for an online college course.

8. Many students learn well by reading, and many others by working independently; either of these types (has / have) a good chance to pass an online course.

9. Anybody who is considering an online class (needs / need) to work well without supervision.

10. Some of the people in online college classes (expects / expect) to earn a degree without ever visiting the campus.

The Verb Comes before the Subject

In most sentences, the subject comes before the verb. Two kinds of sentences reverse that order: questions and sentences that begin with *here* or *there*. In these two types of sentences, you need to check carefully for errors in subject-verb agreement.

Questions

In questions, the verb or part of the verb comes before the subject. To find the subject and verb, you can turn the question around as if you were going to answer it.

> Where is the nearest gas station? The nearest gas station is . . .
>
> Are the keys in the car? The keys are in the car.

Sentences That Begin with Here or There

When a sentence begins with *here* or *there,* the subject always follows the verb. Turn the sentence around to find the subject and verb.

Here <u>are</u> the hot dog <u>rolls</u>. The hot dog <u>rolls</u> <u>are</u> here.

There <u>is</u> a <u>fly</u> in my soup. A <u>fly</u> <u>is</u> in my soup.

ESL NOTE: *There is* and *there are* are common in English. If you have trouble using these expressions, see page 502.

■ **PRACTICE 8   CORRECTING A SENTENCE WHEN THE VERB COMES BEFORE THE SUBJECT**

Correct any problems with subject-verb agreement in the following sentences. If a sentence is already correct, write "OK" next to it.

EXAMPLE: There ~~is~~ ^are^ several openings for bilingual applicants.

1. Where is the corporation's main offices located?

2. There is branch offices in Paris, Singapore, and Tokyo.

3. How well do the average employee abroad speak English?

4. What do the company manufacture?

5. How many languages are the manual written in?

6. Does the company employ college graduates as translators?

7. There is some machines that can do translation.

8. Does learning a second language give an applicant a special advantage?

9. There is never a disadvantage in knowing another language.

10. Here is the names of several qualified people.

Edit Paragraphs and Your Own Writing

As you edit the following paragraphs and your own writing, use the Critical Thinking guide that follows. You may also want to refer to the chart on page 386.

CRITICAL THINKING: EDITING FOR SUBJECT-VERB AGREEMENT

FOCUS

- Whenever you see one of the five trouble spots in your writing (listed on p. 371), stop to check that the subject and the verb agree.

ASK

- Where is the subject in this sentence? Where is the verb?
- Do the subject and verb agree in number? (Are they both singular or both plural?)

EDIT

- If you answer "no" to the agreement question, you need to correct the sentence.

Find and correct any problems with subject-verb agreement that you find in the following paragraphs.

EDITING REVIEW 1

(1) School systems around the country is embracing educational standards. (2) The idea of standards sound reasonable. (3) Does anyone want to argue that students should not have to meet certain requirements to graduate? (4) A national standard for all American students have many supporters, too. (5) If the requirements for graduation in Oregon and Tennessee is the same, everyone with a high school diploma gets a similar education. (6) There is a catch, of course. (7) Not everyone with a professional or personal interest in school quality is able to agree on these requirements. (8) Mathematics and writing is important, but so is music and physical education. (9) How is parents, teachers, and administrators ever going to find standards that everyone accepts?

EDITING REVIEW 2

(1) Agreeing on school standards are only part of the battle over education. (2) How is students going to prove that they have met the standards

before graduation? (3) The answer, in many cases, are testing. (4) School tests that are required by state law is becoming more and more common. (5) These tests are standardized, so all of the students taking an eighth-grade test in a particular state is given the same test. (6) Both the individual student and his or her school district is evaluated by the scores. (7) The parents of a student learns not only what their child's score is but also how the school compares with others around the state. (8) Then, children who need extra help is supposed to receive it, and schools with very low scores year after year becomes eligible for additional resources.

■ EDITING REVIEW 3

(1) In reality, standardized tests for schools have many problems. (2) Most school districts that have a testing program uses tests that can be scored by a computer. (3) Computers cannot read, so the tests that they grade usually offers multiple-choice questions. (4) A multiple-choice test in science or mathematics do not allow students to demonstrate critical thinking. (5) How does students show their writing ability on such a test? (6) There is tricks to answering multiple-choice questions that many students learn. (7) Frequently, a high score on such a test says more about the student's test-taking ability than about his or her knowledge of a subject. (8) Nevertheless, the quick results and low cost of a computer-graded multiple-choice test means that this imperfect testing system is used in many school systems.

■ EDITING REVIEW 4

(1) Another problem with standardized tests are that test material can begin to change the curriculum. (2) Everyone who teaches want his or her students to get high scores on the tests. (3) For one thing, a teacher of un-

derperforming students are likely to be criticized for not preparing them better. (4) One result of teachers' fears are that they spend most of the class time preparing students for the test. (5) In some cases, the phenomenon of "teaching to the test" become school policy. (6) A creative teacher or one who has been teaching for years are no longer trusted to engage students with a subject. (7) School officials, who also want high scores for their districts, encourage teachers to focus on material that the test will cover. (8) Other material, which may be fascinating to students, are ignored because the test does not require it.

▓ EDITING REVIEW 5

(1) Many parents who send their children to public school fears that the schools are not teaching the students adequately. (2) As these fears increase, the number of states that require tests rise as well. (3) But there has been some teachers and parents willing to resist standardized testing. (4) A few parents has kept their children home on test days. (5) In rare cases, teachers who oppose testing has refused to administer standardized tests to their students. (6) In the places that require students to pass tests in order to graduate, rebellion against tests have serious consequences for the student. (7) Elsewhere, however, a parent or student has the option to refuse. (8) People who believe that standardized testing is not the answer is still trying to change this growing national trend.

▓ PRACTICE 9   EDITING YOUR OWN WRITING FOR SUBJECT-VERB AGREEMENT

As a final practice, edit for subject-verb agreement in a piece of your own writing—a paper you are working on for this class, a paper you've already finished, a paper for another course, or a recent piece of writing from your work or everyday life. Use the Critical Thinking guide on page 383 and the chart on page 386 to help you.

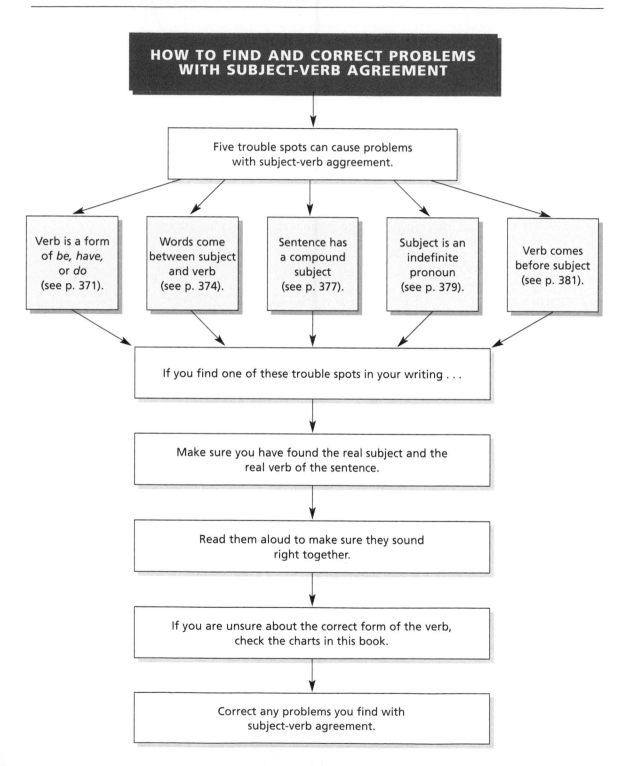

HOW TO FIND AND CORRECT PROBLEMS WITH SUBJECT-VERB AGREEMENT

Five trouble spots can cause problems with subject-verb aggreement.

Verb is a form of *be, have,* or *do* (see p. 371).

Words come between subject and verb (see p. 374).

Sentence has a compound subject (see p. 377).

Subject is an indefinite pronoun (see p. 379).

Verb comes before subject (see p. 381).

If you find one of these trouble spots in your writing . . .

Make sure you have found the real subject and the real verb of the sentence.

Read them aloud to make sure they sound right together.

If you are unsure about the correct form of the verb, check the charts in this book.

Correct any problems you find with subject-verb agreement.

25

Verb Problems

*Avoiding Mistakes in Verb Form
and Verb Tense*

Understand What Verb Form and Verb Tense Are

Verb forms are the different ways a verb can be spelled and pronounced. For example, here are three different forms of the same verb:

talk   talks   talked

Verb tense tells *when* the action of a sentence occurs: in the present, in the past, or in the future. Verbs change their form and use the helping verbs *have* or *be* to indicate different tenses.

To choose the correct form and tense, consider whether the subject is singular or plural *and* when the action occurs.

<table>
<tr><td>PRESENT TENSE</td><td>Teresa and I talk every day. [Plural subject]</td></tr>
<tr><td>PRESENT TENSE</td><td>She also talks to her mother every morning. [Singular subject]</td></tr>
<tr><td>PAST TENSE</td><td>Yesterday, they talked for two hours. [Plural subject]</td></tr>
<tr><td>FUTURE TENSE</td><td>Tomorrow, they will talk again. [Plural subject]</td></tr>
</table>

Regular verbs follow a few standard patterns in the present and past tenses, and their past-tense and past-participle forms end in *-ed* or *-d*.

■ For more on subject-verb agreement and singular versus plural verb forms, see Chapter 24.

387

ESL NOTE: Using the correct form and tense of verbs is very important in English, and the rules differ from some other languages, so pay close attention to this chapter.

Irregular verbs change spelling in the past-tense and past-participle forms. (For more on irregular verbs, see pp. 401–09.)

❡ In the examples throughout this chapter, the subject is underlined once, and the verb is underlined twice.

	REGULAR VERB: *WALK*	**IRREGULAR VERB:** *EAT*
Past tense	walked [I walked.]	ate [I ate.]
Past participle	walked [I have/had walked.]	eaten [I have/had eaten.]

In the Real World, Why Is It Important to Use Correct Verbs?

Errors in verb form and verb tense can create a negative impression of the writer, as the following example shows.

SITUATION: A college student submits an essay to a contest in hopes that the piece will be published in the school's literary magazine and that she will win the $100 prize. Here is the beginning of the student's essay:

I likes writing because it is fun to express myself. I always enjoys sharing writing with my friends. They appreciates my creativity.

RESPONSE: One of the judges, a professional journalist, said this to his fellow judges: "I read exactly two lines, not even enough to really get an idea of what the essay was about. Clearly, the person is a poor writer, and I just couldn't bear the idea of having to read the whole piece: It wasn't worth my time."

Use Correct Verbs

Verbs have several tenses to express past, present, and future time. This section will explain what those tenses are and how to use them correctly when you write.

Regular Verbs

To avoid mistakes with regular verbs, understand the basic patterns for forming the present, past, and future tenses.

Present Tense

The **simple present tense** is used for actions that are happening at the same time that you are writing about them and about actions that are on-going. There are two forms for the simple present tense of regular verbs: **-s ending** or **no added ending**. Use the *-s* ending when the subject is *she, he,* or *it,* or the name of one person or thing. Do not add any ending for other subjects.

Simple Present Tense

	SINGULAR	PLURAL
First person	I laugh.	We laugh.
Second person	You laugh.	You laugh.
Third person	She/he/it laughs.	They laugh.
	The baby laughs.	The babies laugh.

PRACTICE 1   FINDING PRESENT-TENSE ERRORS

Find and underline the three present-tense verb errors in the student essay excerpt on page 388.

PRACTICE 2   USING THE SIMPLE PRESENT TENSE

In each of the following sentences, first underline the subject and then circle the correct verb form.

  EXAMPLE: Do you (play / plays) golf?

1. Golfers (decide / decides) to either ride a golf cart or walk as they play.

2. Now golfers who walk do not (need / needs) to carry their heavy bags of golf clubs.

■ For more practice
with verbs, visit
Exercise Central at
<bedfordstmartins
.com/realessays>.

3. Some (use / uses) a RoboKaddy to carry their golf bags.

4. This three-wheeled machine (carry / carries) a golf bag.

5. As the golfer (walk / walks), the RoboKaddy follows with the golf bag.

6. The golfer (operate / operates) the RoboKaddy by remote control.

7. The RoboKaddy (stop / stops) instantly because it has electronic brakes.

8. Some golfers who walk (enjoy / enjoys) the luxury of a motorized golf-bag carrier.

9. Other golfers (want / wants) a human to carry their golf bags.

10. Human carriers sometimes (provide / provides) useful advice on which club to use.

Two other present-tense forms to be aware of are the present progressive tense and the present perfect tense. The **present progressive tense** is used to describe actions that are in progress. It is formed as follows:

Present-tense form of *be* (helping verb)	+	Main verb with *-ing* ending

Present Progressive Tense

	SINGULAR	PLURAL
First person	I am laugh**ing**.	We are laugh**ing**.
Second person	You are laugh**ing**.	You are laugh**ing**.
Third person	She/he/it is laugh**ing**.	They are laugh**ing**.
	The baby is laugh**ing**.	The babies are laugh**ing**.

ESL NOTE: Some languages, such as Russian, do not use the progressive tense. If your first language does not use the progressive tense, pay special attention to this section.

■ **PRACTICE 3   USING THE PRESENT PROGRESSIVE TENSE**

In each of the following sentences, underline the helping verb (a form of *be*), and fill in the correct form of the verb in parentheses.

>   **EXAMPLE:** My grandmother is ___*looking*___ (*look*) into our family
>   history.

1. She is _____ (*start*) with my grandfather's side of the family, the Mancinis.

2. To learn more about the Mancinis, she is _____ (*contact*) several of my grandfather's relatives to get birth documents and other information.

3. Also, she is _____ (*gather*) information about the Mancinis through genealogy sites on the Internet.

4. She is _____ (*learn*) a lot about my grandfather's ancestors; for instance, they were peasants who fled Italy around 1910 because of difficult living conditions.

5. My sister and I are _____ (*help*) our grandmother by looking at online records from Ellis Island.

6. Also, we are _____ (*think*) of taking a course in genealogical research at a local college.

7. Even our mother is _____ (*pitch*) in.

8. For example, she is _____ (*call*) older Mancinis to get family stories.

9. She is constantly _____ (*share*) the stories with my sister and me; for instance, she learned that our great-grandfather helped to organize a coal-miner strike soon after coming to America.

10. "These stories are _____ (*remind*) me of some modern Mancinis," she said. "We like to stir things up."

The **present perfect tense** is used for an action begun in the past that is ongoing into the present or that was completed at some unspecified time in the past. It is formed as follows:

■ *Be* and *have* are irregular verbs. For more details on irregular verbs, see pages 401–09.

Present-tense form of *have* (helping verb)	+	Past participle

Present Perfect Tense

	SINGULAR	PLURAL
First person	I have laughed.	We have laughed.
Second person	You have laughed.	You have laughed.
Third person	She/he/it has laughed.	They have laughed.
	The baby has laughed.	The babies have laughed.

■ **PRACTICE 4   USING THE PRESENT PERFECT TENSE**

In each of the following sentences, underline the helping verb (a form of *have*), and fill in the correct form of the verb in parentheses.

> **EXAMPLE:** My father has ___*served*___ (*serve*) in the army for twenty years.

1. My father's military career has _____ (*force*) our family to move many times.

2. We have _____ (*live*) in seven towns that I remember.

3. I have _____ (*attend*) three different high schools.

4. None of the towns has ever really _____ (*seem*) like home.

5. I have never _____ (*object*) to my family's traveling life.

6. None of us has ever _____ (*expect*) to stay in one place for long.

7. My closest friends have all _____ (*travel*) a lot, too.

8. One of them has _____ (*visit*) Egypt, Australia, Turkey, Pakistan, and seventeen other countries.

9. She has always _____ (*like*) the idea of becoming a travel agent.

10. But she has _____ (*decide*) to accept a position with a large international corporation that will allow her to travel.

Past Tense

The **simple past tense** is used for actions that have already happened. An **-ed ending** is needed for all regular verbs in the past tense.

	SIMPLE PRESENT	SIMPLE PAST
First person	I rush to work.	I rush**ed** to work.
Second person	You lock the door.	You lock**ed** the door.
Third person	Rufus seem**s** strange.	Rufus seem**ed** strange.

PRACTICE 5   USING THE SIMPLE PAST TENSE

In each of the following sentences, fill in the correct past-tense form of the verb in parentheses.

EXAMPLE: After the Revolutionary War __ended__ (*end*), American

politicians __turned__ (*turn*) their anger against each other.

(1) In general, politicians after the war _____ (*decide*) to support either Alexander Hamilton, who favored a strong central government, or Thomas Jefferson, who advocated states' rights. (2) Rival politicians were _____ (*concern*) about the direction of the new democracy, so they _____ (*attack*) each other with great passion. (3) Few people _____ (*care*) about facts or honesty in their attacks. (4) Some politicians eagerly _____ (*challenge*) President George Washington and _____ (*call*) him a would-be king. (5) Hamilton _____ (*engage*) in personal attacks that were especially nasty. (6) In return, Hamilton's enemies _____ (*accuse*) him of planning to bring back the British monarchy.

(7) In six different instances, Hamilton _____ (*participate*) in fierce arguments that _____ (*stop*) just short of causing a duel.

(8) He _____ (*fail*) to avoid a duel in his long dispute with Vice President Aaron Burr. (9) For years, Hamilton _____ (*charge*) Burr with being corrupt and dishonest. (10) When they _____ (*duel*) in 1804, each _____ (*fire*) a shot from a pistol. (11) Burr was not hit, but Hamilton was seriously wounded, and he _____ (*die*) the next day.

SIMPLE PAST TENSE   My car stalled.

■ Be careful not to confuse the simple past tense with the present perfect tense (see p. 392).

[The car stalled at some point in the past but does not stall now, in the present.]

PRESENT PERFECT TENSE   My car has stalled often.

[The car began to stall in the past but may continue to do so into the present.]

PRACTICE 6   USING THE SIMPLE PAST TENSE AND PRESENT PERFECT TENSE

In each of the following sentences, circle the correct verb form.

EXAMPLE: Within the last twenty years, racial profiling (became/ (has become)) a significant source of disagreement between law enforcement agencies and some communities of color.

1. Numerous charges of racial profiling (increased/have increased) the tension between local police and members of various ethnic groups.

2. Law enforcement agencies (used/have used) profiling for a long time.

3. With this practice, they (attempted/have attempted) to identify people who might be participating in criminal activity by their behavior and the conditions of a particular situation.

4. Once these "profiled" individuals (were singled out/have been singled out), the police questioned or searched them for drugs, guns, or other illegal material.

5. In 1998, an investigation of the New Jersey State Police (raised/has raised) the public's awareness of this issue.

6. The extensive publicity from this investigation (defined / has defined) racial profiling as the separating out of members of racial or ethnic groups for minor traffic or criminal offenses.

7. Investigators reviewing past law-enforcement activity concluded that the New Jersey State Police (violated / have violated) civil rights on numerous occasions.

8. Since this case was made public, other police departments (initiated / have initiated) investigations into their own possible profiling activities.

9. Similarly, communities (started / have started) to demand that the police be more accountable in their relationships with members of minority racial or ethnic groups.

10. The issue of profiling (endured / has endured) in the public mind and continues to be controversial.

Two other past-tense forms are the past progressive tense and the past perfect tense. The **past progressive tense** is used to describe actions that were ongoing in the past. It is formed as follows:

Past-tense form of *be* (helping verb)	+	Main verb with *-ing* ending

Past Progressive Tense

	SINGULAR	PLURAL
First person	I was laugh**ing**.	We were laugh**ing**.
Second person	You were laugh**ing**.	You were laugh**ing**.
Third person	She/he/it was laugh**ing**.	They were laugh**ing**.
	The baby was laugh**ing**.	The babies were laugh**ing**.

◾ PRACTICE 7   USING THE PAST PROGRESSIVE TENSE

In each of the following sentences, underline the helping verb (a form of *be*), and fill in the correct form(s) of the verb in parentheses.

> **EXAMPLE:** When your father and I met, I was not <u>looking</u> (*look*) for romance.

1. I was _____ (*study*) full-time and _____ (*work*) as a waitress on evenings and weekends.

2. Also, I was _____ (*garden*) for friends to make some extra cash.

3. When I first saw your father, he was _____ (*walk*) past the restaurant where I worked.

4. He was _____ (*read*) a book and not _____ (*pay*) attention to where he was going.

5. I happened to notice that he was _____ (*head*) right for a huge pothole in the sidewalk.

6. Before I knew it, I was _____ (*run*) for the door, but I didn't make it in time.

7. When I got to the sidewalk, he'd already fallen, but I saw that he was _____ (*laugh*).

8. I asked him if he was OK, and he said, "I'm so embarrassed. Did you see what I was _____ (*do*)?"

9. "Yes," I said. By now, I was _____ (*smile*), too.

10. We were _____ (*talk*) for a long time when one of us—I can't remember who—asked if we could meet again. The rest is history.

The **past perfect tense** is used for an action that was begun in the past but was completed before some other past action took place. It is formed as follows:

| Past-tense form of *have* (helping verb) | + | Past participle |

■ *Be* and *have* are irregular verbs. For more details on irregular verbs, see pages 401–09.

Past tense of *have*   Past participle

PAST PERFECT TENSE   My head had ached for a week before I called a doctor.

[Both of the actions (*head ached* and *I called*) happened in the past, but the ache happened before the calling.]

Be careful not to confuse the simple past tense with the past perfect tense.

SIMPLE PAST TENSE   My car stalled.

[One action (the car's stalling) occurred in the past.]

PAST PERFECT TENSE   By the time Jill arrived, my car had stalled.

[Two actions (Jill's arrival and the car's stalling) occurred in the past, but the car stalled before Jill's arrival.]

PRACTICE 8   USING THE PAST PERFECT TENSE

In each of the following sentences, circle the correct verb form. *Note:* Some of the verbs are irregular. For a chart showing forms of these verbs, see pages 403–06.

EXAMPLE: **By the time I reached home, rolling blackouts (darkened/ (had darkened)) the city.**

1. The temperature was unseasonably hot when I (got / had gotten) out of bed that morning.

2. By noon, the air conditioners at the office (were running / had been running) at high power for three hours.

3. My boss told me that she (heard / had heard) that energy use that day was skyrocketing.

4. I (asked / had asked) how we could conserve energy.

5. I mentioned that I (just learned / had just learned) that some household and office machines use power even when they are turned off.

6. My boss (read / had read) the same information, so we unplugged computers in the office that were not in use.

7. We also (raised / had raised) the office temperature from sixty-eight degrees to seventy-two, and then we turned off some of the lights.

8. By late afternoon, we (did / had done) everything we could think of to save energy, but it was not enough.

9. We knew that the city (warned / had warned) residents that rolling blackouts were possible.

10. However, when the office (suddenly darkened / had suddenly darkened), everyone was stunned.

Future Tense

The **simple future tense** is used for actions that will happen in the future. It is formed with the helping verb *will*.

Simple Future Tense		
	SINGULAR	**PLURAL**
First person	I will graduate in May.	We will graduate in May.
Second person	You will graduate in May.	You will graduate in May.
Third person	She/he/it will graduate in May.	They will graduate in May.
	My son will graduate in May.	My sons will graduate in May.

Two other future tense forms to be familiar with are the future progressive tense and the future perfect tense. The **future progressive tense** is used to describe actions in the future that are continuing. It is formed as follows:

Will	+	*Be*	+	Main verb with *-ing* ending

Future Progressive Tense

	SINGULAR	**PLURAL**
First person	I will be working Friday.	We will be working Friday.
Second person	You will be working Friday.	You will be working Friday.
Third person	She/he/it will be working Friday.	They will be working Friday.
	The boss will be working Friday.	The bosses will be working Friday.

The **future perfect tense** is used to describe actions that will be completed in the future before another action in the future. It is formed as follows:

$$\boxed{\textit{Will have}} \ + \ \boxed{\text{Past participle}}$$

Future Perfect Tense

	SINGULAR	**PLURAL**
First person	I will have finished by 10:00.	We will have finished by 10:00.
Second person	You will have finished by 10:00.	You will have finished by 10:00.
Third person	She/he/it will have finished by 10:00.	They will have finished by 10:00.
	The painter will have finished by 10:00.	The painters will have finished by 10:00.

PRACTICE 9   USING THE FUTURE TENSE

In each of the following sentences, circle the correct verb form. *Note:* Some of the verbs are irregular. For a chart showing forms of these verbs, see pages 403–06.

EXAMPLE: I ((will finish)/ will be finishing / will have finished) my carpentry class next month.

1. Afterward, my friend Sara and I (will begin / will be beginning / will have begun) restoring an old carriage house behind her home.

2. Sara is an expert carpenter, so I (will learn / will be learning / will have learned) a lot from working with her.

3. The project (will involve / will be involving / will have involved) reshingling the carriage house, patching the walls and ceilings, and refinishing the floors.

4. By the end of spring, we (will complete / will be completing / will have completed) the reshingling — or at least that's the goal.

5. It doesn't bother me that I (will work / will be working / will have worked) every weekend, and many weeknights, on the project.

6. I (will hone / will be honing / will have honed) my carpentry skills, and I will be returning a favor to Sara, who used to babysit for me.

7. Next week, Sara and I (will discuss / will be discussing / will have discussed) the general plan for the renovation.

8. Soon after, we (will gather / will be gathering / will have gathered) materials for the project.

9. We probably (will need / will be needing / will have needed) more supplies eventually, but we can't anticipate all of our needs now.

10. If all goes as planned, we (will finish / will be finishing / will have finished) the project by summer's end.

Irregular Verbs

Unlike regular verbs, which have past-tense and past-participle forms that end in *-ed* or *-d,* **irregular verbs** change spelling in the past-tense and past-participle forms.

Present-Tense Irregular Verbs

Only a few verbs are irregular in the present tense. The ones most commonly used are the verbs *be* and *have.*

	BE		HAVE	
	SINGULAR	PLURAL	SINGULAR	PLURAL
First person	I am	we are	I have	we have
Second person	you are	you are	you have	you have
Third person	he/she/it is	they are	he/she/it has	they have
	the dog is	the dogs are	the dog has	the dogs have
	Chris is	Chris and Dan are	Chris has	Chris and Dan have

> **PRACTICE 10 USING *BE* AND *HAVE* IN THE PRESENT TENSE**

In each of the following sentences, fill in the correct form of the verb indicated in parentheses.

EXAMPLE: Disc golf ___is___ (*be*) played with Frisbees.

1. I _____ (*be*) a fanatical disc golfer.

2. The game _____ (*have*) eighteen holes, like regular golf, but uses a Frisbee instead of a ball.

3. A disc golf course _____ (*have*) fairways and holes.

4. A tee _____ (*be*) at the beginning of each fairway.

5. Players _____ (*be*) eager to get the Frisbee from the tee into a metal basket in the fewest possible throws.

6. Some disc golfers _____ (*have*) special Frisbees for teeing off and putting.

7. My brother, who also plays disc golf, _____ (*have*) thirty different Frisbees for the game.

8. His wife _____ (*be*) surprisingly patient with his enthusiasm for the sport.

9. "You _____ (*be*) in the middle of a second adolescence," she tells him.

10. However, she, too, _____ (*have*) formidable Frisbee technique.

Past-Tense Irregular Verbs

As discussed earlier, the past-tense and past-participle forms of irregular verbs do not follow a standard pattern. For example, they do not use the *-ed* ending for past tense, although the past participle uses a helping verb, just as regular verbs do.

PRESENT TENSE	PAST TENSE	PAST PARTICIPLE
Tony makes hats.	Tony made hats.	Tony has/had made hats.
You write well.	You wrote well.	You have/had written well.
I ride a bike.	I rode a bike.	I have/had ridden a bike.

The verb *be* is tricky because it has two different forms for the past tense: *was* and *were*.

The Verb Be, *Past Tense*

	SINGULAR	PLURAL
First person	I was	we were
Second person	you were	you were
Third person	she/he/it was	they were
	the car was	the cars were
	Jolanda was	Jolanda and Ti were

■ PRACTICE 11   **USING PAST-TENSE FORMS OF THE VERB** *BE*

In the paragraph that follows, fill in each blank with the correct past-tense form of the verb *be*.

EXAMPLE: Your father and I ___*were*___ struggling to make ends meet.

(1) Before you _____ born, your father and I _____ very worried. (2) He _____ still in school at the time. (3) I _____ a part-time waitress, so we _____ not exactly rich in those days. (4) Having a baby _____ a big step for us. (5) My mother _____ thrilled that she would be a grandmother, but she _____ not even in the same state. (6) Your other grandparents _____ no longer living. (7) I _____ terrified that we would not be able to take good care of you. (8) But when you _____ born, your father's friends and my coworkers _____ an amazing support system. (9) They _____ all as much in love with you as we _____. (10) You _____ the most beautiful thing that any of us had ever seen.

As you write and edit, consult the following chart to make sure that you use the correct form of irregular verbs.

Irregular Verb Forms		
PRESENT TENSE	**PAST TENSE**	**PAST PARTICIPLE** (with helping verb)
am/are/is	was/were	been
become	became	become
begin	began	begun
bite	bit	bitten
blow	blew	blown
break	broke	broken
bring	brought	brought
build	built	built

continued

PRESENT TENSE	PAST TENSE	PAST PARTICIPLE (with helping verb)
buy	bought	bought
catch	caught	caught
choose	chose	chosen
come	came	come
cost	cost	cost
do	did	done
draw	drew	drawn
drink	drank	drunk
drive	drove	driven
eat	ate	eaten
fall	fell	fallen
feed	fed	fed
feel	felt	felt
fight	fought	fought
find	found	found
forget	forgot	forgotten
freeze	froze	frozen
get	got	gotten
give	gave	given
go	went	gone
grow	grew	grown
have/has	had	had
hide	hid	hidden
hit	hit	hit
hold	held	held
hurt	hurt	hurt
keep	kept	kept
know	knew	known
lay	laid	laid
leave	left	left
let	let	let
lie	lay	lain

PRESENT TENSE	PAST TENSE	PAST PARTICIPLE (with helping verb)
light	lit	lit
lose	lost	lost
make	made	made
mean	meant	meant
meet	met	met
pay	paid	paid
put	put	put
quit	quit	quit
read	read	read
ride	rode	ridden
run	ran	run
say	said	said
see	saw	seen
sell	sold	sold
send	sent	sent
set (to place)	set	set
shake	shook	shaken
show	showed	shown
shut	shut	shut
sing	sang	sung
sink	sank	sunk
sit (to be seated)	sat	sat
sleep	slept	slept
speak	spoke	spoken
spend	spent	spent
stand	stood	stood
steal	stole	stolen
stick	stuck	stuck
sting	stung	stung
strike	struck	struck, stricken
swim	swam	swum
take	took	taken

continued

PRESENT TENSE	PAST TENSE	PAST PARTICIPLE (with helping verb)
teach	taught	taught
tear	tore	torn
tell	told	told
think	thought	thought
throw	threw	thrown
understand	understood	understood
wake	woke	woken
wear	wore	worn
win	won	won
write	wrote	written

PRACTICE 12   USING PAST-TENSE IRREGULAR VERBS

In each of the following sentences, fill in the correct past-tense form of the irregular verb in parentheses. If you do not know the answer, find the word in the chart of irregular verb forms on pages 403–06.

   EXAMPLE: The *Titanic* _____*set*_____ (*set*) out from England in 1912.

1. The White Star Line _____ (*build*) the *Titanic,* which was the biggest moving object in the world at that time.

2. The huge ship _____ (*hold*) over 2,200 passengers on its maiden voyage.

3. The newspapers _____ (*write*) that twenty lifeboats, which could hold 1,178 people altogether, hung from the upper deck of the *Titanic.*

4. The shipbuilders _____ (*feel*) that the giant liner was the safest ship in the world and that more lifeboats were simply unnecessary.

5. On April 14, 1912, during its first trip across the Atlantic, the *Titanic* _____ (*strike*) an iceberg.

6. The sharp ice _____ (*tear*) a gaping hole in the bottom of the ship.

7. Icy ocean water _____ (*begin*) to pour into the hold, dragging the
   Titanic down in the water.

8. Few passengers _____ (*understand*) the danger at first.

9. Half-empty lifeboats _____ (*leave*) the sinking ship while other passengers _____ (*stand*) on deck, refusing to depart.

10. Hundreds of people _____ (*freeze*) to death in the ocean before the
    nearest ship _____ (*come*) to rescue the *Titanic*'s 705 survivors.

■ PRACTICE 13   USING PAST-TENSE IRREGULAR VERBS

In the following paragraph, replace any incorrect present-tense verb forms
with the correct past-tense form of the verb. If you do not know the
answer, look up the verbs in the chart of irregular verb forms on pages
403–06.

EXAMPLE: Dewayne faced a judge and jury of his fellow high school
          hit
          students after he ~~hits~~ a boy in the classroom.
                            ^

(1) Two years ago, my high school sets up a student court to give students a voice in disciplining rule breakers. (2) Before the court opened
its doors, adults teach students about decision making and about court-
room procedures. (3) Some of us served as members of juries, and others
become advocates or even judges. (4) I sit on a jury twice when I was a
junior. (5) Then, last spring, my friend Dewayne appeared before the student court after he loses his temper and strikes a fellow student. (6) I agreed
to be his advocate because I think he truly regretted his behavior. (7) I tell
the jury that he knew his violent reaction was a mistake. (8) The jury
sends Dewayne for counseling to learn to manage his anger and made
him write an apology to the other student. (9) After hearing the verdict,

Dewayne shakes hands with all the jurors and thanked them for their fairness. (10) The experience makes me eager to learn more about America's system of justice.

■ **PRACTICE 14   USING PAST-PARTICIPLE FORMS FOR IRREGULAR VERBS**

In each of the following sentences, underline the helping verb (a form of *have*) and fill in the correct past-participle form of the verb in parentheses. If you do not know the correct form, find the word in the chart on pages 403–06.

> **EXAMPLE:** Hector <u>has</u>   ___*found*___   (*find*) that a dot-com career has ups and downs.

1. By the time Hector graduated from college in 1998, he had _____ (*take*) dozens of hours of computer courses.

2. He had _____ (*choose*) a career in programming.

3. Before getting his diploma, Hector had _____ (*begin*) to work for an Internet service provider.

4. By the end of the summer, a rival online service had _____ (*steal*) Hector away from his employer.

5. His new bosses had _____ (*be*) in business for only a few months.

6. After a year, the company still never had _____ (*make*) a profit.

7. However, hundreds of investors had _____ (*buy*) shares of the company's stock.

8. By early 2000, the stock's price had _____ (*grow*) to more than fifty times its original worth.

9. Hector often wishes that he had _____ (*sell*) his shares then and retired a rich man.

10. Instead, the company went bankrupt, and Hector has _____ (*go*) to

work for an old-fashioned but secure banking firm.

Passive Voice

A sentence that is written in the **passive voice** has a subject that performs no action. Instead, the subject is acted upon. To create the passive voice, combine a form of the verb *be* with a past participle.

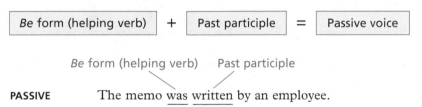

| *Be* form (helping verb) | + | Past participle | = | Passive voice |

Be form (helping verb)   Past participle

PASSIVE   The memo was written by an employee.

[The subject, *memo,* did not write itself. An employee wrote the memo, but the subject in the sentence, *memo,* performs no action.]

In sentences that use the **active voice**, the subject performs the action.

ACTIVE   An employee wrote the memo.

Use the passive voice when no one person performed the action, when you don't know who performed the action, or when you want to emphasize the receiver of the action. Use active voice whenever possible, and use passive voice sparingly.

PASSIVE   The dog was hit by a passing car.

[If the writer wants to focus on the dog as the receiver of the action, the passive voice is acceptable.]

ACTIVE   A passing car hit the dog.

ESL NOTE: Other languages, such as Russian and Korean, form the passive voice differently. If your first language is not English, pay particular attention to this section.

◼ **PRACTICE 15   CHANGING FROM PASSIVE VOICE TO ACTIVE VOICE**

Rewrite the following sentences in the active voice.

Officers control the
EXAMPLE: ~~The~~ *Queen Mary 2,* the world's largest cruise ship, ~~can be~~
‸
~~controlled~~ with a joystick.

1. The *Queen Mary 2* is equipped with a grand lobby and an old-style three-story restaurant.

2. Its bridge, however, is filled with advanced consoles, screens, and joysticks.

3. The effects of the wind, waves, and ocean currents can be automatically corrected by the ship's computer systems.

4. During the ship's first docking in New York, the joystick was not touched by the captain.

5. He said the joystick would probably be used more by him in the future.

Consistency of Verb Tense

Consistency of verb tense means that all the actions in a sentence that happen (or happened) at the same time are expressed in the same tense. If all of the actions happen in the present, use the present tense for all verbs in the sentence. If all of the actions happened in the past, use the past tense for all verbs in the sentence.

	Past tense Present tense
INCONSISTENT TENSE	The bell chimed just as I am running up the stairs.
	Present tense Present tense
CONSISTENT PRESENT TENSE	The bell chimes just as I am running up the stairs.
	Past tense Past tense
CONSISTENT PAST TENSE	The bell chimed just as I was running up the stairs.

■ **PRACTICE 16   USING CONSISTENT TENSE**

In each of the following items, double-underline the verbs in the sentence, and correct any unnecessary shifts in verb tense by writing the correct form of any incorrect verb in the blank space provided.

EXAMPLE: ___*use*___ People either <u>ride</u> bicycles for leisurely jour-

neys or they <u>used</u> bikes for serious exercise.

1. _____ Those who want a good workout needed different kinds of equipment than those interested in an easy ride.

2. _____ For example, serious cyclists who had bikes with wide padded seats face the chance of injuries.

3. _____ A wide seat makes the rider shift from side to side, and it caused painful rubbing.

4. _____ In addition, the seat should have been high enough so that the rider cannot put his or her feet on the ground.

5. _____ Serious riders wore special shoes that snap onto the pedals to allow pushing up as well as pushing down.

6. _____ Serious money is also a factor, because custom bicycles were expensive.

7. _____ Once an experienced cyclist chose the proper bicycle, he or she knows how to ride it properly.

8. _____ For instance, knowledgeable riders move around as they ride so that they exercised different muscle groups.

9. _____ The smart rider also kept his or her knees slightly bent, which eases the strain on the knees.

10. _____ Of course, those who just wished to have a fun ride through the park ignore all of this advice.

Edit Paragraphs and Your Own Writing

As you edit the following paragraphs and your own writing, use the Critical Thinking guide that follows. You may also want to refer to the chart on page 415.

CRITICAL THINKING: EDITING FOR VERB PROBLEMS

FOCUS
- Read all of your sentences carefully, looking for verb problems.

ASK
- Is my sentence about the present? About the past? About something that happened before something else?
- Is each verb a regular verb or an irregular verb?
- Have I used the tense that tells the reader when the action happened?
- Have I used the correct form of the verb?
- If the verbs in the sentence are not all in the same tense, is it because the actions actually happened at different times?

EDIT
- Edit to correct any problems with verb form or verb tense.

Find and correct any problems with verb form or tense in the following paragraphs.

◼ EDITING REVIEW 1

(1) Since 1835, trapeze artists consider the triple somersault the most dangerous maneuver. (2) That year, a performer tried to do a triple somersault on a trapeze for the first time and dies in the attempt. (3) Only one person has managed to do the trick successfully in the next sixty-three years. (4) That man, a trapeze artist named Armor, did a triple somersault in 1860 and is afraid to try it again. (5) According to circus legend, the second person to survive the triple, Ernie Clarke, once done a quadruple

somersault in private. (6) Ernie Lane, the third person to complete a triple somersault, was later killed by the maneuver when his catcher missed. (7) Circus historians now believed that Alfredo Codona, a performer in the 1920s and 1930s, was the greatest master of the triple somersault. (8) He has went down in history as the King of Trapeze.

EDITING REVIEW 2

(1) Many people go through life without even knowing that there is a record for peeling an apple or hopping on a pogo stick. (2) However, some people are very aware of such records, and ordinary folks around the world have did some peculiar things to qualify for the *Guinness Book of World Records*. (3) For example, a New Jersey disc jockey, Glen Jones, recently setted a new record for the longest continuous radio broadcast. (4) In the spring of 2001, he has stayed on the air for one hundred hours with only a few fifteen-minute breaks. (5) Another world record, for hopping up steps on a bicycle, is hold by Javier Zapata of Colombia. (6) He climbed 943 steps without letting his feet touch the ground, breaking a record that he has previously set. (7) Ashrita Furman of New York also be a record breaker. (8) She balanced a milk bottle on her head and then walks almost eighty-one miles around a track. (9) These strange endurance contests may not make Jones, Zapata, and Furman famous, but their names had entered the record book.

EDITING REVIEW 3

(1) The Olympic Games first let women compete in swimming events in 1912, and with that, the swimsuit revolution begun. (2) In 1913, the first mass-produced women's swimsuit hit the market. (3) Before that

year, women have only been able to wade at the beach in bathing costumes with long, baggy legs. (4) The 1913 suits, designed by Carl Jantzen, was ribbed one-piece outfits that allowed actual swimming. (5) An engineer, Louis Réard, comed up with the next major development in swimwear in 1946 while working in the lingerie business. (6) He has called it the "bikini," after a Pacific island used for testing the atomic bomb. (7) In the 1950s, few Americans had dared to wear bikinis, which was considered scandalous. (8) Two-piece swimsuits catch on in the 1960s and 1970s. (9) The bikini losted some popularity in the last decades of the twentieth century, but it has made a triumphant return in the new millennium.

 PRACTICE 17   EDITING YOUR OWN WRITING FOR CORRECT VERB TENSE AND FORM

As a final practice, edit for verb problems in a piece of your own writing — a paper you are working on for this class, a paper you've already finished, a paper for another course, or a recent piece of writing from your work or everyday life. Use the Critical Thinking guide on page 412 and the chart on page 415 to help you.

USING THE CORRECT TENSE

Present Tense: For Current and Ongoing Actions

		How to Form
Simple present	I paint houses.	Verb + *-s* or no ending (see p. 389)
Present progressive	I am painting houses.	Present tense of *be* + main verb with *-ing* ending (see p. 390)
Present perfect	I have painted houses every summer.	Present tense of *have* + past participle (see p. 392)

Past Tense: For Past Actions

		How to Form
Simple past	They lived in Argentina.	For regular verbs: *-ed* ending (see p. 393) For irregular verbs, see the chart on pages 403–06.
Past progressive	They were living in Argentina.	Past tense of *be* + main verb with *-ing* ending (see p. 395)
Past perfect	They had lived in Argentina before moving here.	Past tense of *have* + past participle (see p. 397)

Future Tense: For Future Actions

		How to Form
Simple future	We will move soon.	*Will* + main verb (see p. 398)
Future progressive	We will be moving soon.	*Will* + *be* + main verb with *ing* ending (see p. 398)
Future perfect	We will have moved by next month.	*Will have* + past participle (see p. 399)

Part Five
Other Grammar Concerns

26

Pronouns

Using Substitutes for Nouns

Understand What Pronouns Are

Pronouns replace nouns (or other pronouns) in a sentence so that you do not have to repeat the nouns.

>   *her*
> Tessa let me borrow ~~Tessa's~~ jacket.
>
>   *He*
> You have met Carl. ~~Carl~~ is my cousin.

The noun (or pronoun) that a pronoun replaces is called the **antecedent**. The word *antecedent* means "something that comes before." In most cases, a pronoun refers to a specific antecedent nearby.

> I filled out the (health form.) It was complicated.
>
>   Antecedent   Pronoun replacing antecedent

■ PRACTICE 1   IDENTIFYING PRONOUNS

In each of the following sentences, circle the pronoun, underline the antecedent (the noun to which the pronoun refers), and draw an arrow from the pronoun to the antecedent.

> **EXAMPLE:** My <u>uncle</u> is a hardworking entrepreneur who knew (he)
>
> could succeed with a business loan.

419

■ For more practice
with pronouns, visit
Exercise Central at
<bedfordstmartins
.com/realessays>.

1. Many poor people don't feel as if they can depend on big banks.

2. A bank in an underdeveloped area, however, needs to find customers wherever it can.

3. Microlending has become a popular banking trend. It has helped people in impoverished neighborhoods all over the world.

4. Microlending has succeeded because it involves lending very small amounts of money.

5. For many poor owners of a small business, microlending helps them to get a jump start.

6. For example, street vendors sell small quantities and earn small profits, so they may never save up enough to expand.

7. Yet a woman selling tacos from a cart may have enough experience to manage her own business successfully.

8. If the taco vendor gets a microloan, she may be able to open a storefront restaurant and earn larger profits.

9. After receiving a small loan, a young entrepreneur can make his or her business more successful.

10. According to my uncle, getting a microloan allowed him to pursue a childhood dream.

Practice Using Pronouns Correctly

Check for Pronoun Agreement

A pronoun must agree with (match) the noun or pronoun it refers to in number: It must be singular (one) or plural (more than one). If it is singular, it must also match its noun or pronoun in gender (*he, she,* or *it*).

CONSISTENT   Sherry talked to *her* aunt.

[*Her* agrees with *Sherry* because both are singular and feminine.]

CONSISTENT   The Romanos sold *their* restaurant.

[*Their* agrees with *Romanos* because both are plural.]

Watch out for singular nouns that are not specific. If a noun is singular, the pronoun must be singular as well.

INCONSISTENT   Any athlete can tell you about *their* commitment to practice.

[*Athlete* is singular, but the pronoun *their* is plural.]

CONSISTENT   Any athlete can tell you about *his* or *her* commitment to practice.

[*Athlete* is singular, and so are the pronouns *his* and *her.*]

As an alternative to using the phrase *his or her,* make the subject plural if you can. (For more on this, see the note below.)

CONSISTENT   All athletes can tell you about *their* commitment to practice.

Two types of words often cause errors in pronoun agreement: indefinite pronouns and collective nouns.

Indefinite Pronouns

An **indefinite pronoun** does not refer to a specific person, place, or thing; it is general. Indefinite pronouns often take singular verbs. Whenever a pronoun refers to an indefinite person, place, or thing, check for agreement.

Someone forgot ~~their~~ *his* coat.

Everybody practiced ~~their~~ *his or her* lines.

NOTE: Although it is grammatically correct, using a masculine pronoun (*he, his,* or *him*) alone to refer to a singular indefinite pronoun such as *everyone* is now considered sexist. Here are two ways to avoid this problem:

1. Use *his or her.*

Someone forgot his or her coat.

Indefinite Pronouns

ALWAYS SINGULAR

anybody	everyone	nothing
anyone	everything	one (of)
anything	much	somebody
each (of)	neither (of)	someone
either (of)	nobody	something
everybody	no one	

MAY BE SINGULAR OR PLURAL

all	none
any	some

2. Change the sentence so that the pronoun refers to a plural noun or pronoun.

The children forgot their coats.

■   **PRACTICE 2   USING INDEFINITE PRONOUNS**

Circle the correct pronoun or group of words in parentheses.

(1) Everyone who has battled an addiction to alcohol has (his or her / their) own view of the best ways to stop drinking. (2) Millions of former problem drinkers have quit, and many have made (his or her / their) way through recovery programs. (3) Few begin the road to recovery without attending (his or her / their) first Alcoholics Anonymous (AA) meeting. (4) With its famous twelve-step program, AA has helped countless alcoholics, but someone who is not religious may find that (he or she / they) has difficulty with one of the twelve steps. (5) No one can complete the whole AA recovery program without turning (himself or herself / themselves) over to a "higher power." (6) In addition, everybody who joins AA is asked to admit that (he or she is / they are) powerless over alcohol.

(7) Many object that (he or she needs / they need) to feel empowered rather than powerless in order to recover. (8) Anyone who does not feel that (he or she / they) can believe in a higher power might participate instead in a group like Secular Organizations for Sobriety. (9) Some can take responsibility for (his or her / their) drinking and stop more easily with groups such as Smart Recovery. (10) Different approaches work for different people, but former problem drinkers offer this sober advice to others with alcohol problems: Anyone can quit drinking if (he or she wants / they want) to stop badly enough.

Collective Nouns

A **collective noun** names a group that acts as a single unit.

Common Collective Nouns

audience	company	group
class	crowd	jury
college	family	society
committee	government	team

Collective nouns are usually singular, so when you use a pronoun to refer to a collective noun, it too must usually be singular.

its
The class had ~~their~~ final exam at 8:00 a.m.

its
The group turned in ~~their~~ report.

If the people in a group are acting as individuals, however, the noun is plural and should be used with a plural pronoun.

The audience took *their* seats.

The drenched crowd huddled under *their* umbrellas.

◼ PRACTICE 3   USING COLLECTIVE NOUNS AND PRONOUNS

Fill in the correct pronoun (*their* or *its*) in each of the following sentences.

> **EXAMPLE:** The basketball team was playing all of __*its*__ games in a damp, dark gymnasium.

1. The downtown branch of the university needed to overhaul several buildings on _____ campus.

2. The theater department wanted to enlarge the auditorium used for _____ productions.

3. In the present theater, the audience had to wait in _____ seats until the performance was over and then exit through the stage door.

4. A sorority also needed more space to house _____ members.

5. In addition, the football team could not go to any out-of-town games because _____ bus had broken down.

6. The science teachers had to hold _____ office hours in the student cafeteria.

7. The university president appointed a commission to study renovations and agreed to abide by _____ findings.

8. The graduating class agreed to step up _____ fund-raising campaign.

9. One wealthy family donated _____ slightly used luxury car to a fund-raising auction.

10. A record homecoming crowd shouted _____ approval as the renovation plans were announced.

Make Pronoun Reference Clear

If the reader isn't sure what a pronoun refers to, the sentence may be confusing.

Avoid Ambiguous or Vague Pronoun References

In an **ambiguous pronoun reference**, the pronoun could refer to more than one noun.

AMBIGUOUS   Michelle told Carla that she should get a better hourly wage.

[Did Michelle tell Carla that Michelle herself should get a better hourly wage? Or did Michelle tell Carla that Carla should get a better hourly wage?]

EDITED   Michelle told Carla that she wanted a better hourly wage.

AMBIGUOUS   I threw my bag on the table and it broke.

[Was it the bag or the table that broke?]

EDITED   My bag broke when I threw it on the table.

In a **vague pronoun reference**, the pronoun does not refer clearly to any particular person or thing. To correct a vague pronoun reference, substitute a more specific noun for the pronoun.

VAGUE   After an accident at the intersection, they installed a traffic light.

[Who installed the traffic light?]

EDITED   After an accident at the intersection, the highway department installed a traffic light.

VAGUE   When I heard it, I laughed.

[Heard what?]

EDITED   When I heard the message, I laughed.

PRACTICE 4   **AVOIDING AMBIGUOUS OR VAGUE PRONOUN REFERENCES**

Edit each of the following sentences to eliminate any ambiguous or vague pronoun references. Some sentences may be revised correctly in more than one way.

EXAMPLE: In a recent study, ~~they~~ found that people do not always
                                        scientists

see objects that are in unexpected places.

1. In a psychology study, volunteers watched a video of two basketball teams, and they had to count the number of passes.

2. As the volunteers focused on the players, some of them did not notice a person in a gorilla suit walking onto the basketball court.

3. Later, when the volunteers met with the researchers, many of them asked, "What gorilla?"

4. By the end of the study, the researchers had learned that if it was unexpected, many people simply could not see it.

5. The way the human brain processes visual information may keep people from using it wisely.

6. For example, if a car crosses into the lane facing oncoming traffic, it may not register in the mind of a driver who expects a routine trip.

7. A stop sign appearing at an intersection cannot prevent an accident if drivers do not see it.

8. Before the psychology study, they thought that drivers who missed signs of danger were simply not paying attention.

9. However, the study indicates that drivers make mistakes because they may not see them ahead.

10. Traffic safety regulations cannot make people's brains and eyes work differently, but they can make them wear seat belts.

Avoid Repetitious Pronoun References

In a **repetitious pronoun reference**, the pronoun repeats a reference to a noun rather than replacing the noun. Remove the repetitious pronoun.

The police officer ~~he~~ told me I had not stopped at the sign.

The sign~~, it~~ was hidden by a tree.

> **ESL NOTE:** In some languages, like Spanish, it is correct to repeat the noun with a pronoun. In formal English, however, a pronoun is used to replace a noun, not to repeat it.

PRACTICE 5   AVOIDING REPETITIOUS PRONOUN REFERENCES

Correct any repetitious pronoun references in the following sentences.

> EXAMPLE: The science of robotics ~~it~~ already has practical applications.

1. Robots they have been part of many science-fiction classics, from *The Jetsons* to *Star Wars*.

2. Is there any child who he hasn't wished for a robot friend, a robot tutor, or a robot maid?

3. In some industries, robots they are already part of the workforce.

4. Robots they make sushi for some Japanese fast-food restaurant chains.

5. Additionally, a factory might use robots to handle substances that they are dangerous for humans to touch.

6. But business it is not the only area in which the robot population is increasing.

7. Some children who they wanted a robot friend have already gotten their wish.

8. Toy manufacturers have created a robot dog that it can respond to human commands.

9. The robot dog it was first on many holiday and birthday gift lists for children in the past few years.

10. Also, some house-cleaning robots they are on the market; for example, one vacuums floors.

Use the Right Type of Pronoun

There are three basic types of pronouns: **subject** pronouns, **object** pronouns, and **possessive** pronouns. Note the pronouns in the following sentences.

The linebacker tackled him, and he went down hard.

Possessive
|
His shoulder was injured.

Pronoun Types

	SUBJECT	OBJECT	POSSESSIVE
First person *(singular/plural)*	I/we	me/us	my, mine/ our, ours
Second person *(singular/plural)*	you/you	you/you	your, yours/ your, yours
Third person *(singular)*	he, she, it	him, her, it	his, her, hers, its
Third person *(plural)*	they who/who	them whom/whom	their, theirs its, whose

ESL NOTE: Notice that pronouns have gender (*he/she, him/her, his/ her/hers*). The pronoun must agree with the gender of the noun it refers to.

INCORRECT   Carolyn went to see *his* boyfriend.

CORRECT   Carolyn went to see *her* boyfriend.

Also, notice that English has different forms for subject and object pronouns, as shown in the preceding chart.

Subject Pronouns

■ For more on sub-jects, see Chapter 21.

Subject pronouns serve as the subject of a verb.

She took my parking space.

I honked my horn.

ESL NOTE: Some languages omit subject pronouns, but English sentences always have a stated or written subject.

INCORRECT   Hates cleaning.

CORRECT   *He* hates cleaning.

Object Pronouns

Object pronouns either receive the action of a verb (the object of the verb) or are part of a prepositional phrase (the object of the preposition).

OBJECT OF THE VERB	Carolyn asked *me* to drive.
	Carolyn gave *me* the keys.
OBJECT OF THE PREPOSITION	Carolyn gave the keys to *me*.

Possessive Pronouns

Possessive pronouns show ownership. Note that you never need an apostrophe with a possessive pronoun.

Giselle is *my* best friend.

That jacket is *hers*.

Certain kinds of sentences can make choosing the right type of pronoun a little more difficult: ones that have compound subjects or objects; ones that make a comparison; and ones where you have to choose between *who* or *whom*.

Pronouns Used with Compound Subjects and Objects

A **compound subject** has more than one subject joined by a conjunction such as *and* or *or*. A **compound object** has more than one object joined by a conjunction.

COMPOUND SUBJECT	Tim and *I* work together.
COMPOUND OBJECT	Kayla baked the cookies for Jim and *me*.

■ When you are writing about yourself and someone else, always put yourself after everyone else: *my friends and I*, not *I and my friends*.

To decide what type of pronoun to use in a compound construction, try leaving out the other part of the compound and the conjunction. Then, say the sentence aloud to yourself.

~~Jerome and~~ (me /(I)) like chili dogs.

[Think: *I* like chili dogs.]

The package was for ~~Karen and~~ (she /(her)).

[Think: The package was for *her*.]

If a pronoun is part of a compound object in a prepositional phrase, use an object pronoun.

I will keep that information just between you and (I /(me)).

[*Between you and me* is a prepositional phrase, so an object pronoun, *me*, is required.]

■ Many people make the mistake of writing *between you and I.* The correct pronoun with *between* is the object *me.* If *between me* sounds odd to you, try thinking *between us.*

■ **PRACTICE 6   EDITING PRONOUNS IN COMPOUND CONSTRUCTIONS**

Edit each sentence using the proper type of pronoun. If a sentence is already correct, write "C" next to it.

                                       she   *I*

EXAMPLE: Megan and I love soda, and ~~her~~ and ~~me~~ regularly have

     two cans a day each.

1. However, a TV program on dental health started making she and I rethink our soda-drinking habit.

2. Her and me paid close attention as we watched a dentist, Dr. Jenine Summers, and her assistant, Ian, conduct an experiment.

3. Dr. Summers asked Ian to place a tooth in a bottle of soda, and her and him observed what happened to the tooth.

4. Megan and me watched as time-elapse photography showed how the tooth changed from day to day.

5. The result of the experiment surprised her and I.

6. At the end of the experiment, Dr. Summers and Ian looked in the bottle of soda for the tooth, and she and he showed that it had disappeared.

7. Them and us said "Wow" at the same time.

8. Dr. Summers explained how acids in the soda broke down the tooth; her comments about soda's sugar content were equally shocking to Megan and me.

9. Megan and me learned that each can of soda we drink contains about ten teaspoons of sugar, which creates even more tooth-dissolving acid and contributes to weight gain.

10. Therefore, us and some other friends have decided to ban soda from our refrigerators.

Pronouns Used in Comparisons

Using the wrong type of pronoun in comparisons can give a sentence an unintended meaning. Editing sentences that contain comparisons can be tricky, because comparisons often imply words that aren't actually included in the sentence.

To find comparisons, look for the words *than* or *as*. To decide whether to use a subject or object pronoun in a comparison, try adding the implied words and saying the sentence aloud.

Bill likes Chinese food more than *I*.

[This sentence means Bill likes Chinese food more than I like it. The implied word after *I* is *do*.]

Bill likes Chinese food more than *me*.

[This sentence means Bill likes Chinese food more than he likes me. The implied words after *than* are *he likes*.]

The professor knows more than (us /(we)).

[Think: The professor knows more than *we know*.]

Jen likes other professors more than (he /(him)).

[Think: Jen likes other professors more than *she likes him*.]

■ **PRACTICE 7   EDITING PRONOUNS IN COMPARISONS**

Edit each sentence using the correct pronoun type. If a sentence is correct, put a "C" next to it.

EXAMPLE: Gardening was a competitive sport for my mother, and I

                            she

take it almost as seriously as ~~her~~.

1. My mother and father had a garden in their backyard, but she spent much more time there than him.

2. My father always said that my mother had a greener thumb than he.

3. The garden was filled with tomatoes because my mother loved no other vegetable as much as they.

4. No one I have ever known has had as many tomato recipes as her.

5. She won many blue ribbons at the county fair with her garden produce, and nothing in our house was displayed more proudly than they.

6. My brother, who is two years older than me, began helping her when he was a little boy.

7. He made sure that each plant was free of slugs, for few other garden pests are as destructive as them.

8. To this day, he is a better gardener than me.

9. I spend just as much time as him working in the garden, however.

10. Every summer, we compare notes to see if I have grown as many tomatoes as him.

Choosing between Who and Whom

Who is always a subject; use it if the pronoun performs an action. *Whom* is always an object; use it if the pronoun does not perform any action.

WHO = SUBJECT   Janis is the friend *who* introduced me to Billy.

WHOM = OBJECT   Billy is the man *whom* I met last night.

In most cases, for sentences where the pronoun is followed by a verb, use *who*. When the pronoun is followed by a noun or pronoun, use *whom*.

The person (who / whom) spoke was boring.

[The pronoun is followed by the verb *spoke*. Use *who*.]

The person (who / (whom)) I met was boring.

[The pronoun is followed by another pronoun: *I*. Use *whom*.]

■ *Whoever* is a subject pronoun; *whomever* is an object pronoun.

■ **PRACTICE 8 CHOOSING BETWEEN *WHO* AND *WHOM***

In each sentence, circle the correct word, *who* or *whom*.

> **EXAMPLE:** Chester Himes was the writer ((who) / whom) created the
>
> characters Coffin Ed Johnson and Grave Digger Jones.

1. Chester Himes, (who / whom) readers know best as a detective novelist,
   wrote several novels in the 1940s and 1950s analyzing race relations in the
   United States.

2. Himes, (who / whom) was the youngest son of a middle-class family, spent
   many years living in Los Angeles.

3. Like many African American writers (who / whom) he knew, Himes
   moved to Paris in the 1950s.

4. One of his novels about two African American detectives (who / whom)
   work in Harlem, *Cotton Comes to Harlem,* was made into a successful movie.

5. Himes, (who / whom) died in Spain in 1984, actually knew other parts of
   the United States and of Europe much better than he knew Harlem.

Make Pronouns Consistent

Pronouns have to be consistent in **person**, which is the point of view a
writer uses. Pronouns may be in first person (*I, we*); second person (*you*);
or third person (*he, she, it,* or *they*). (See the chart on page 428.)

> **INCONSISTENT PERSON** *I* wanted to use the copy machine, but the atten-
> dant said *you* had to have an access code.

[The sentence starts in the first person (*I*) but shifts to the second person (*you*).]

> **CONSISTENT PERSON** *I* wanted to use the copy machine, but the atten-
> dant said *I* had to have an access code.

[The sentence stays with the first person, *I*.]

INCONSISTENT PERSON	After *a caller* presses 1, *you* get a recording.

[The sentence starts with the third person (*a caller*) but shifts to the second person (*you*).]

CONSISTENT PERSON	After *a caller* presses 1, *he or she* gets a recording.

CONSISTENT PERSON, PLURAL	After *callers* press 1, *they* get a recording.

[In these last two examples, the sentence stays with the third person.]

PRACTICE 9   MAKING PRONOUNS CONSISTENT IN PERSON

In the following items, correct the shifts in person. There may be more than one way to correct some sentences.

EXAMPLE: **I have a younger brother with an allergy to peanuts, so**
                           I
~~you~~ have to be very careful with his food.
                 ^

1. Experts agree that the percentage of people with allergies to foods is rising, but we don't know why.

2. Someone who has a mild allergic reaction the first time you eat a food may develop more severe allergies from future contacts with the food.

3. If a person has a severe allergy to a food and unknowingly eats even a small amount of that food, you could die.

4. However, if people with allergies are protected from any contact with the food for several years, his or her allergies may disappear or become milder.

5. When a child has severe allergies, their parents can be extremely cautious.

6. My little brother is severely allergic to peanuts, so you are not allowed to eat anything containing peanuts while he is nearby.

7. He carries an adrenaline pen that can save your life if you go into shock from a food allergy.

8. I love peanut butter, but you can't eat a peanut butter sandwich in my house.

9. My mother will not take my brother to any public place where you can even smell peanuts.

10. Some people think that her precautions are extreme, but she knows that you can't be too careful when your child's life is at stake.

Edit Paragraphs and Your Own Writing

Edit the following paragraphs for pronoun errors, referring to the chart on page 438 as you need to.

■ EDITING REVIEW 1

(1) More and more people are using videoconferencing, and you can see why. (2) Anyone whom has a video camera hooked up to a home computer can connect, via networking technology, to someone else with a similar setup. (3) A person simply sits in front of the camera and talks; a person or group of people on the other end is able to see and hear them. (4) It has been wonderful for both businesses and families.

(5) In the new global economy, a company often has their offices all over the world. (6) Once, a businessperson might have had to travel a great deal to keep in touch with their clients, suppliers, and fellow employees around the globe. (7) Today, much it can be done with videoconferencing. (8) Anyone can attend a meeting and see their clients face to face while remaining on a different continent. (9) The technology has improved so that you can transmit high-quality images and sound, and the cost of videoconferencing continues to drop. (10) And of course, a videoconferencing

businessperson with competitors who travel the world will save much more money than them on airfare and accommodations.

(11) Businesses are not the only ones to benefit from videoconferencing technology. (12) A family today may find that it often must spend time apart. (13) A parent traveling for business may not see their spouse or children for days at a time. (14) People move across the country from where you grew up, leaving parents and siblings behind. (15) Parents they sometimes divorce, and sometimes one starts a new job far away from the children. (16) Today, however, someone who cannot be present to kiss their children goodnight or wish their sister a happy birthday can see family members across the miles through videoconferencing. (17) Divorced parents who judges have allowed to move to another state have actually been required by law to buy videoconferencing technology to keep in touch with their children.

(18) Most people do not believe that videoconferencing can replace being physically present with family members and clients, but it costs less than regular visits while offering more intimacy than a telephone call. (19) They say that the eyes are the windows of the soul, and videoconferencing helps people look into those windows and stay connected.

■ EDITING REVIEW 2

(1) Some people travel the world without ever leaving his or her house by reading books about exotic locations. (2) A person who is afraid to fly can nevertheless immerse themselves in a far-off place. (3) Someone whom does not speak a word of any foreign language can pretend to fit in like a native while reading travel literature. (4) At the end of a good travel

book, you can feel as if you know a place you've never visited—even if you never want to go there. (5) Armchair travel is, in fact, less dangerous and more comfortable than much actual tourism. (6) Unfamiliar customs and food that might make a traveler feel out of place often seem very amusing when it is described in a good book. (7) And many people who read avidly about a traveler getting food poisoning in a strange place or sitting on a plane that nearly crashes say to themselves, "I am glad that happened to him rather than I!" (8) Armchair travel books often turn up on best-seller lists. (9) A growing audience can't seem to get their fill of such books.

PRACTICE 10   EDITING YOUR OWN WRITING FOR PRONOUN USE

As a final practice, edit for pronoun use in a piece of your own writing— a paper you are working on for this course, a paper you've already finished, a paper for another course, or a recent piece of writing from your work or everyday life. You may want to use the chart on page 438 as you edit.

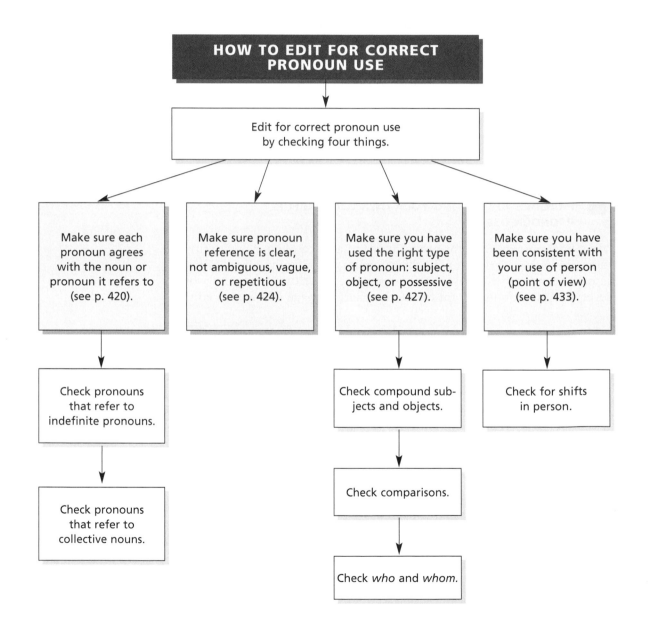

HOW TO EDIT FOR CORRECT PRONOUN USE

Edit for correct pronoun use by checking four things.

Make sure each pronoun agrees with the noun or pronoun it refers to (see p. 420).

Make sure pronoun reference is clear, not ambiguous, vague, or repetitious (see p. 424).

Make sure you have used the right type of pronoun: subject, object, or possessive (see p. 427).

Make sure you have been consistent with your use of person (point of view) (see p. 433).

Check pronouns that refer to indefinite pronouns.

Check pronouns that refer to collective nouns.

Check compound subjects and objects.

Check comparisons.

Check *who* and *whom*.

Check for shifts in person.

27
Adjectives and Adverbs

Describing Which One? *or* How?

Understand What Adjectives and Adverbs Are

Adjectives describe nouns (words that name people, places, or things) and pronouns (words that replace nouns). They add information about what kind, which one, or how many.

City traffic was *terrible* last night.

The highway was *congested* for *three* miles.

Two huge old tractor trailers had collided.

ESL NOTE: In English, adjectives do not indicate whether the word they modify is singular or plural, unless the adjective is a number.

INCORRECT   The three babies are *adorables.*

[The adjective *three* is fine because it is a number, but the adjective *adorables* should not end in *-s*.]

CORRECT   The three babies are *adorable.*

Adverbs describe verbs (words that tell what happens in a sentence), adjectives, or other adverbs. They add information about how, how much, when, where, why, or to what extent. Adverbs often end with *-ly*.

MODIFYING VERB	Dave drives *aggressively.*
MODIFYING ADJECTIVE	The *extremely* old woman swims every day.
MODIFYING ANOTHER ADVERB	Dave drives *very* aggressively.

Note that both adjectives and adverbs can come before or after the words they modify and that you can use more than one adjective or adverb to modify a word.

> **ESL NOTE:** For more on how to order adjectives in a sentence, see page 517.

Practice Using Adjectives and Adverbs Correctly

Choosing between Adjective and Adverb Forms

Many adverbs are formed by adding *-ly* to the end of an adjective.

ADJECTIVE	ADVERB
The *new* student introduced himself.	The couple is *newly* married.
That is an *honest* answer.	Please answer *honestly.*

To decide whether to use an adjective form or an adverb form, find the word you want to describe. If that word is a noun or a pronoun, use the adjective form. If it is a verb, an adjective, or another adverb, use the adverb form.

■ PRACTICE 1 CHOOSING BETWEEN ADJECTIVE AND ADVERB FORMS

In each sentence, underline the word or phrase in the sentence that is being described, and then circle the correct word in parentheses.

EXAMPLE: Teenagers who want a summer job (usual /(usually)) can find work.

1. Even in a slowing economy, many summer jobs for unskilled workers are (easy / easily) to find.

2. Of course, teenage workers without much experience should not have (extreme / extremely) rigid requirements for a summer job.

3. Fast-food restaurants (frequent / frequently) employ teenagers.

4. The wages at a fast-food restaurant will not be (high / highly) for a starting position, however.

5. In addition, the work may not be very (interesting / interestingly).

6. However, teenagers can learn (valuable / valuably) lessons from going to almost any job.

7. Arriving on time and behaving (responsible / responsibly) will impress any supervisor.

8. Working (close / closely) with other employees also may teach a teenage worker to get along with people who are not friends or family.

9. Earning money can make a high school student feel more (financial / financially) independent.

10. Saving for college tuition is one way in which a teenager can use money from a summer job (wise / wisely).

■ For more practice with adjectives and adverbs, visit Exercise Central at **<bedfordstmartins .com/realessays>**.

Using Adjectives and Adverbs in Comparisons

To compare two persons, places, or things, use the **comparative** form of adjectives or adverbs.

> Sheehan drives *faster* than I do.
>
> Francis is *more gullible* than Destina is.

To compare three or more persons, places, or things, use the **superlative** form of adjectives or adverbs.

Sheehan drives the *fastest* of all our friends.

Francis is the *most gullible* of the children.

Comparatives and superlatives can be formed either by adding an ending to an adjective or adverb or by adding a word. If an adjective or adverb is short (one syllable), add *-er* to form the comparative and *-est* to form the superlative. Also use this pattern for adjectives that end in *-y* (but change the *-y* to *-i* before adding *-er* or *-est*). If an adjective or adverb has more than one syllable, add the word *more* to make the comparative and the word *most* to make the superlative.

Comparative and Superlative Forms

ADJECTIVE OR ADVERB	COMPARATIVE	SUPERLATIVE
ADVERBS AND ADJECTIVES OF ONE SYLLABLE		
tall	taller	tallest
fast	faster	fastest
ADJECTIVES ENDING IN -Y		
happy	happier	happiest
silly	sillier	silliest
ADVERBS AND ADJECTIVES OF MORE THAN ONE SYLLABLE		
graceful	more graceful	most graceful
gracefully	more gracefully	most gracefully
intelligent	more intelligent	most intelligent
intelligently	more intelligently	most intelligently

■ For more on changing a final *-y* to *-i* when adding endings, and on other spelling changes involving endings, see Chapter 35.

Use either an ending (*-er* or *-est*) or an extra word (*more* or *most*) to form a comparative or superlative — not both at once.

One of the ~~most~~ easiest ways to beat stress is to exercise regularly.

It is ~~more~~ harder to study late at night than during the day.

ESL NOTE: Some languages, such as Spanish, always use words meaning *more* or *most* in comparisons, even when there is already the equivalent of an *-er* or *-est* ending on an adjective or adverb. If you do that in your writing, pay special attention to this section and the practices.

■ **PRACTICE 2 USING COMPARATIVES AND SUPERLATIVES**

In the space provided in each sentence, write the correct form of the adjective or adverb in parentheses. You may need to add *more* or *most* to some adjectives and adverbs.

EXAMPLE: One of the ___*most loved*___ (*loved*) treats is chocolate.

1. Some people think that Americans are the _____ (*big*) consumers of chocolate in the world.

2. Actually, the people who eat the _____ (*great*) amount of chocolate are the British.

3. In fact, the British are nearly 40 percent _____ (*fond*) of chocolate than Americans are.

4. British chocolate makers are concerned because they expected British people's chocolate consumption to grow _____ (*robustly*) than it has in recent years.

5. However, a small company that makes chocolate with organically grown ingredients has experienced some of the _____ (*healthy*) sales of all chocolate manufacturers in recent years.

6. Even though this organic chocolate is _____ (*expensive*) than regular chocolate, people are willing to pay the price.

7. People have come to expect that organic foods will carry a _____ (*high*) price than conventional foods.

8. Another type of chocolate is also enjoying _____ (*strong*) sales in Britain than regular chocolate.

9. This chocolate does not contain the vegetable solids found in most British chocolate; therefore, it is considered by some chocolate lovers to be _____ (*pure*).

10. This "real" chocolate is expensive, but its sales are expected to continue

to grow _____ (*fast*) than sales of other premium chocolates.

Using *Good, Well, Bad,* and *Badly*

Four common adjectives and adverbs have irregular forms: *good, well, bad,* and *badly*.

Forms of Good, Well, Bad, *and* Badly		
	COMPARATIVE	**SUPERLATIVE**
ADJECTIVE		
good	better	best
bad	worse	worst
ADVERB		
well	better	best
badly	worse	worst

People often get confused about whether to use *good* or *well*. *Good* is an adjective, so use it to describe a noun or pronoun. *Well* is an adverb, so use it to describe a verb or an adjective.

ADJECTIVE	She is a *good* friend.
ADVERB	He works *well* with his colleagues.

Well can also be an adjective to describe someone's health:

I am not feeling *well* today.

■ PRACTICE 3   USING *GOOD* AND *WELL*

Complete each sentence by circling the correct word in parentheses. Underline the word that *good* or *well* modifies.

EXAMPLE: A ((good) / well) <u>storyteller</u> can hold an audience's

attention.

1. Mark Twain's ability to tell an amusing story is (good / well) known.

2. Twain's famous story "The Notorious Jumping Frog of Calaveras County" is a (good / well) example of traditional American tale-telling.

3. The story is narrated by an Easterner whose proper speech contrasts (good / well) with the country dialect of Simon Wheeler, a storyteller he meets.

4. Wheeler may not be (good / well) educated, but he is a master of the tall tale.

5. The narrator claims that Wheeler has told him a "monotonous" story, but the tale is apparently (good / well) enough for the narrator to repeat.

6. The frog in the story is famous for being a (good / well) jumper.

7. Wheeler explains that the frog's owner lives (good / well) by gambling on the frog's jumping ability.

8. The frog's owner, Jim Smiley, makes the mistake of leaving the frog with a man whom Smiley does not know (good / well).

9. The stranger makes the frog swallow heavy shot so that he can no longer jump (good / well).

10. In Twain's story, Simon Wheeler has such a (good / well) time telling stories that the narrator has to escape from him at the end.

PRACTICE 4 USING COMPARATIVE AND SUPERLATIVE FORMS OF *GOOD* AND *BAD*

Complete each sentence by circling the correct comparative or superlative form of *good* or *bad* in parentheses.

EXAMPLE: The (better /(best)) way my family found to learn about another culture was to allow an exchange student to live in our home.

1. Simone, a French high school student, spent last summer getting to know the United States (better / best) by living with my family.

2. She had studied English since the age of five, and her understanding of grammar was (better / best) than mine.

3. She told me that she had the (worse / worst) accent of any student in her English classes, but I liked the way she spoke.

4. Her accent was certainly no (worse / worst) than mine would be if I tried to speak French.

5. My (worse / worst) fear was that she would find our lives boring.

6. However, the exchange program's administrator explained that the (better / best) way for Simone to learn about our country was for us to do ordinary things.

7. For me, the (better / best) part of Simone's visit was the chance to see my world through fresh eyes.

8. I felt (better / best) about my summer job, trips to the supermarket, and afternoon swims at the pool because Simone found all of these things exotic and fascinating.

9. Simone even liked summer reruns on television; she claimed that French television was much (worse / worst).

10. The (worse / worst) part of the visit was having to say goodbye to Simone at the end of the summer.

Edit Paragraphs and Your Own Writing

Edit the following paragraphs for adjective and adverb errors, referring to the chart on page 449 as you need to.

EDITING REVIEW 1

(1) For an average European in the Middle Ages, wearing stripes was not simple a fashion mistake. (2) According to Michel Pastoureau, a scholar of the medieval period, wearing stripes was one of the worse things a European Christian could do in the thirteenth and fourteenth centuries. (3) Stripes might be taken as a sign that the wearer was more sillier than other people; jesters, for example, often wore them. (4) Prostitutes also wore striped clothes, so stripes might be seen as an indication that the person was sinfuller than others. (5) Wearing stripes was dangerousest for clergymen. (6) At least one clergyman in fourteenth-century France was executed because he had been foolishly enough to wear striped clothes. (7) Carmelite monks who wore striped cloaks were frequent attacked, and several popes insisted that the monks change to a more simple costume. (8) People in medieval Europe certainly took their clothing serious. (9) The only reason some people don't wear stripes today is that they are afraid of looking fat.

EDITING REVIEW 2

(1) Many people no longer find it embarrassingly to admit that they have seen a psychotherapist. (2) Some patients argue that it is gooder to seek mental help than to suffer silently. (3) Others seem to feel that needing a therapist is a sign that their lives are interestinger than other people's. (4) At any rate, the stigma that some people once attached to psychotherapy is disappearing quick. (5) Therapists have lately become visibler in popular culture, and this visibility may result in even wider acceptance of psychotherapy. (6) For example, when a mobster on the cable television show *The Sopranos* asks a therapist to treat his panic attacks,

viewers see that the most tough of men is still able to discuss his relationships and feelings with a mental health specialist. (7) If Tony Soprano can do it, what ordinary person is going to feel badly about seeking help for ordinary problems?

(8) However, people considering seeing a therapist are not the only ones who love to watch Tony Soprano trying to work through his problems. (9) Indeed, *The Sopranos,* which is one of the bigger hits ever on cable television, includes many psychologists in its audience. (10) One online magazine regular publishes a therapist's analysis of each episode. (11) Other therapists chat online about whether or not the psychologist on the television show is practicing psychology. (12) The audiences of psychological professionals seem to agree that therapy is portrayed accurater on the show than in many popular films. (13) As they point out, at least the therapist is not in love with her patient, unlike several psychiatrists in recently movies. (14) Although Mr. Soprano, like many actual therapy patients, does things that are not good for his mental health, his therapist thinks that he is functioning best now than before. (15) Perhaps someday he will honest discuss his criminal day job with her—and if he does, even the therapists tuning in might have trouble figuring out the bestest possible response.

■ PRACTICE 5   EDITING YOUR OWN WRITING FOR CORRECT ADJECTIVES AND ADVERBS

As a final practice, edit a piece of your own writing for correct use of adjectives and adverbs. It can be a paper you are working on for this course, a paper you've already finished, a paper for another course, or a recent piece of writing from your work or everyday life. You may want to use the chart on page 449 as you edit.

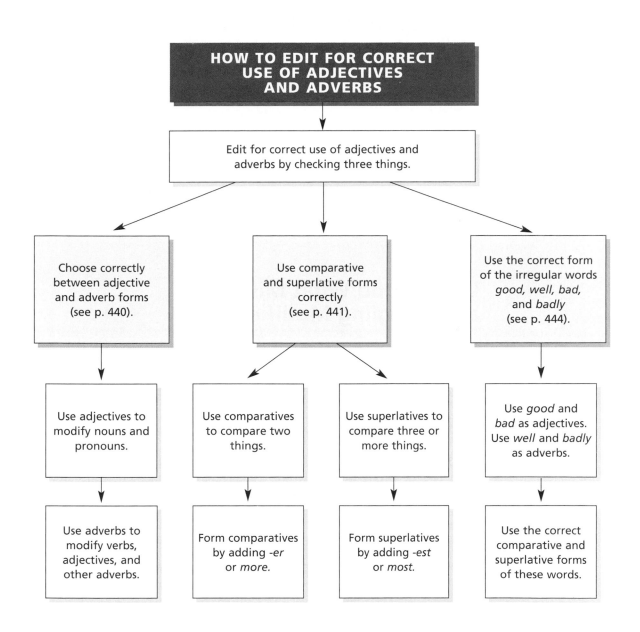

HOW TO EDIT FOR CORRECT USE OF ADJECTIVES AND ADVERBS

Edit for correct use of adjectives and adverbs by checking three things.

Choose correctly between adjective and adverb forms (see p. 440).

Use comparative and superlative forms correctly (see p. 441).

Use the correct form of the irregular words *good, well, bad,* and *badly* (see p. 444).

Use adjectives to modify nouns and pronouns.

Use comparatives to compare two things.

Use superlatives to compare three or more things.

Use *good* and *bad* as adjectives. Use *well* and *badly* as adverbs.

Use adverbs to modify verbs, adjectives, and other adverbs.

Form comparatives by adding *-er* or *more.*

Form superlatives by adding *-est* or *most.*

Use the correct comparative and superlative forms of these words.

28

Misplaced and Dangling Modifiers

Avoiding Confusing Descriptions

Understand What Misplaced and Dangling Modifiers Are

Modifiers are words or word groups that describe other words in a sentence. Unless the modifier is near the words it modifies, the sentence can be misleading or unintentionally funny.

Misplaced Modifiers

A **misplaced modifier**, because it is not correctly placed in the sentence, describes the wrong word or words. To correct a misplaced modifier, move the modifier as close as possible to the word or words it modifies. The safest choice is often to put the modifier directly before the sentence element it modifies.

MISPLACED   Rudy saw my dog *driving his car on the highway.*

[Was my dog driving a car? No, Rudy was, so the modifier must come right before or right after his name.]

CORRECT   *Driving his car on the highway,* Rudy saw my dog.

MISPLACED   Claudia could not see the stop sign *without sunglasses.*

[Did the sign need sunglasses? No, Claudia did.]

CORRECT   *Without sunglasses,* Claudia could not see the stop sign.

Four constructions in particular often lead to misplaced modifiers:

Modifiers such as *only, almost, hardly, nearly,* and *just*

ordered only
I ~~only ordered~~ half a pound.

collected nearly
Griffin ~~nearly collected~~ one hundred cans.

Modifiers that start with *-ing* verbs

Using cash,
Timothy bought the car ~~using cash.~~

Wearing an oven mitt,
Elena took out the hot pizza ~~wearing an oven mitt.~~

Modifiers that are prepositional phrases

to the house for his sister.
Jim was carrying the bags ~~for his sister to the house.~~

for ice cream in her glove compartment.
Julie found money ~~in her glove compartment for ice cream.~~

Modifiers that are clauses starting with *who, whose, that,* or *which*

that was missing
I finally found the sock stuck to a T-shirt ~~that was missing.~~

who call people during dinner
Telemarketers are sure to be annoying ~~who call people during dinner.~~

Dangling Modifiers

A **dangling modifier** "dangles" because the word or words it is supposed to modify are not in the sentence. Dangling modifiers usually appear at the beginning of a sentence and may seem to modify the noun or pronoun that immediately follow—but they merely dangle.

Correct dangling modifiers either by adding the word being modified right after the opening modifier or by adding the word being modified to the opening modifier. Note that to correct a dangling modifier, you might have to reword the sentence.

DANGLING	*Talking on the telephone,* the dinner burned.

[Was the dinner talking on the telephone? No.]

CORRECT	*While Sharon was talking on the telephone,* the dinner burned.
	The dinner burned *while Sharon was talking on the telephone.*
DANGLING	*While waiting in line,* the alarms went off.

[Were the alarms waiting in line? No.]

CORRECT	*While waiting in line,* I heard the alarms go off.
	While I was waiting in line, the alarms went off.

Even if readers can guess what you are trying to say, misplaced and dangling modifiers are awkward. Be sure to look for and correct any misplaced and dangling modifiers in your writing.

Practice Correcting Misplaced and Dangling Modifiers

 PRACTICE 1   CORRECTING MISPLACED MODIFIERS

Find and correct any misplaced modifiers in the following sentences. If a sentence is correct, write a "C" next to it.

EXAMPLE: Many nurses are being trained to perform therapeutic touch. ~~who work in U.S. hospitals.~~ *who work in U.S. hospitals*

1. Are there energy fields that can be touched by trained professionals in a human body?

2. People claim to be able to feel and move invisible energy fields who practice therapeutic touch.

3. According to believers in therapeutic touch, an energy field can cause pain and illness that is out of alignment.

■ For more practice with correcting misplaced and dangling modifiers, visit Exercise Central at <bedfordstmartins .com/realessays>.

4. A practitioner treating a patient does not touch the sick person.

5. After a session of therapeutic touch, many patients just report that they felt better without knowing why.

6. Emily Rosa, the twelve-year-old daughter of a nurse, made news when her experiment appeared in an important medical journal to test practitioners of therapeutic touch.

7. In her experiment, practitioners were supposed to use the invisible energy field to determine when her hands were near theirs who could not see Emily.

8. Even though guessing should have allowed a 50 percent accuracy rating, the practitioners Emily tested were correct only 44 percent of the time.

9. Anyone who can demonstrate the ability to detect a human energy field can claim a million-dollar prize in a similar experiment.

10. The prize has not been awarded yet, which is offered by a foundation that investigates supernatural claims.

■ **PRACTICE 2   CORRECTING DANGLING MODIFIERS**

Find and correct any dangling modifiers in the following sentences. If a sentence is correct, write "C" next to it. It may be necessary to add new words or ideas to some sentences.

EXAMPLE: Selling a used car, a resale *the owner will get a better price for* ~~will bring a better price~~ than a trade-in.

1. Trading in a used car, a buyer will offer a better price if the car is clean.

2. Hiring a professional detailer, a used car can be given a more polished appearance.

3. Looking like new, the owner can get the best price for a trade-in or a resale.

4. With essential repairs completed, a used car should be in good working order to be sold.

5. Approved as safe and drivable by a reputable mechanic, minor mechanical problems may not have to be fixed.

6. Winning points for honesty, prospective buyers should know about a used car's minor problems.

7. Deducted from the asking price, the owner can be fair with a buyer.

8. No matter how expensive, decorative lighting and other details usually do not add to the value of a car.

9. With higher than usual mileage, the owner may have to reduce the asking price.

10. Advertising in a local newspaper, a used car is likely to reach its target market.

Edit Paragraphs and Your Own Writing

Edit the following paragraphs for misplaced and dangling modifiers, referring to the chart on page 457 as you need to.

■ EDITING REVIEW 1

(1) When ordering items online, shipping and handling costs can make or break a business. (2) By charging too much, customers may abandon their order. (3) A customer may never return to the site who feels that shipping and handling charges are too high. (4) Most people have shipped packages, so they know how much shipping costs at least occasionally.

(5) Going too far in the other direction, some online customers get free shipping and handling. (6) The sites lose money that offer free shipping and may have to either close down for good or start charging shipping fees. (7) Most shipping companies charge by weight. (8) Buying from the sites that use these shippers, the online sites must either charge a flat fee, which may be too much or too little, or make the customer wait until the order is complete to find out the shipping fee. (9) Neither option is perfect, so a business must choose the least unattractive solution that wants to keep expanding its online customer base.

EDITING REVIEW 2

MEMO

To: All staff

From: Sara Hollister

Re: Dress code

(1) After encouraging employees to wear casual clothing on Fridays, the casual dress code was soon in force all week long. (2) With some uncertainty about what was appropriate casual wear, a memo was circulated last year with guidelines for dress. (3) Wearing khakis and polo shirts, suits and ties became very rare in the halls of Wilson and Hollister. (4) Some younger staff members almost never wore anything but jeans. (5) Arriving in the office in a Hawaiian shirt, some employees hardly recognized Mr. Wilson without his trademark pinstriped suit. (6) Believing that informality improved productivity and morale, the casual dress code was well liked.

(7) The company must recommend for several reasons changes in the dress policy now. (8) The human resources department feels that the relaxed attitude toward dress may have contributed to the recent increases

in absenteeism and lateness at Wilson and Hollister. (9) Other problems have also surfaced. (10) Clients have sometimes expressed surprise who have dropped in unexpectedly. (11) Hoping to keep their respect and their business, the clients appear to feel more comfortable with employees in suits. (12) Finally, fearing an increase in sexual harassment, sleeveless shirts, shorts, miniskirts, and halter tops will no longer be permitted. (13) Human resources almost recommends a complete change in the casual-dress policy. (14) While continuing to wear casual clothing on Friday, business attire Monday through Thursday, is effective immediately. (15) As an employee who prefers casual clothing, this news is rather sad, but the decision is for the best. (16) Certain that you will understand the necessity for these changes, your cooperation is appreciated.

 PRACTICE 3   EDITING YOUR OWN WRITING FOR MISPLACED AND DANGLING MODIFIERS

As a final practice, edit a piece of your own writing for misplaced and dangling modifiers. It can be a paper you are working on for this course, a paper you've already finished, a paper for another course, or a recent piece of writing from your work or everyday life. You may want to use the chart on page 457 as you edit.

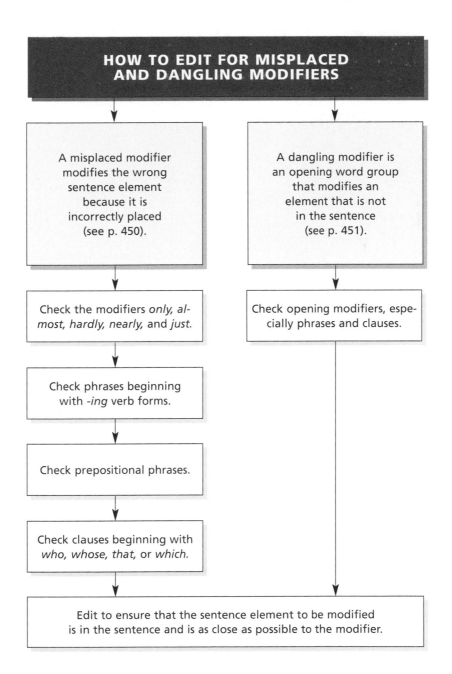

HOW TO EDIT FOR MISPLACED AND DANGLING MODIFIERS

A misplaced modifier modifies the wrong sentence element because it is incorrectly placed (see p. 450).

A dangling modifier is an opening word group that modifies an element that is not in the sentence (see p. 451).

Check the modifiers *only, almost, hardly, nearly,* and *just.*

Check opening modifiers, especially phrases and clauses.

Check phrases beginning with *-ing* verb forms.

Check prepositional phrases.

Check clauses beginning with *who, whose, that,* or *which.*

Edit to ensure that the sentence element to be modified is in the sentence and is as close as possible to the modifier.

29

Coordination and Subordination

Joining Ideas

Understand Coordination and Subordination

Coordination is used to join two sentences when the ideas in them are equally important.

TWO SENTENCES	The internship at the magazine is very prestigious. Many interns have gone on to get good jobs.
JOINED THROUGH COORDINATION	The internship at the magazine is very prestigious, *and* many interns have gone on to get good jobs.

Subordination is used to join two sentences when one idea is less important than the other. Adding a dependent word (such as *although, because, if,* or *that*) to one sentence shows that it is subordinate to, or less important than, the other.

TWO SENTENCES	The internship was advertised last week. The magazine received many calls about it.
JOINED THROUGH SUBORDINATION	*When* the internship was advertised last week, the magazine received many calls about it.

[The word *when* makes the first sentence dependent, or subordinate, and puts more emphasis on the second part, the idea that the magazine received many calls.]

If all of your sentences are short, they will seem choppy and hard to read. To vary the rhythm and flow of your writing and to clarify the relationship between ideas, use coordination or subordination to join sentences with related ideas.

Practice Using Coordination and Subordination

Using Coordinating Conjunctions

A **conjunction** is a word that joins words, phrases, or clauses. **Coordinating conjunctions** (*and, but, for, nor, or, so,* and *yet*) join ideas of equal importance. You can remember them by keeping the word *fanboys* in mind: **f**or, **a**nd, **n**or, **b**ut, **o**r, **y**et, **s**o. Choose the conjunction that makes the most sense, and make sure to put a comma before it when joining two independent clauses.

Equal idea	Coordinating conjunction , **f**or , **a**nd , **n**or , **b**ut , **o**r , **y**et , **s**o	Equal idea

My friend is coming   , and   I'm excited to see her.

[*And* simply joins two ideas.]

We were best friends   , but   I haven't seen her for years.

[*But* indicates a contrast.]

I'm a little nervous   , for   we may not have anything in common anymore.

[*For* indicates a reason or cause.]

We haven't talked much   , nor   have we written.

[*Nor* indicates a negative.]

Maybe we will pick up our friendship	, or [*Or* indicates alternatives.]	we may be like strangers.
We are meeting tonight	, so [*So* indicates a result.]	we will know soon.
It's hard to keep old friends	, yet [*Yet* indicates a reason.]	they are very important.

■ PRACTICE 1 JOINING IDEAS WITH COORDINATING CONJUNCTIONS

In each of the following sentences, fill in the blank with an appropriate co-ordinating conjunction. There may be more than one correct answer for some sentences.

EXAMPLE: **Millions of people get motion sickness while traveling,**

_____*and*_____ **it can turn an enjoyable experience into a night-**

mare.

1. Nearly 60 percent of children get carsick or airsick, _____ many also get sick on amusement park rides.

2. Some amusement park operators are aware of this, _____ a major theme park recently handed out "stomach distress" bags to customers for one of its rides.

3. Most people have experienced motion sickness at one time or another, _____ there are ways of easing or even avoiding its effects.

4. Motion sickness happens when a person's eyes and ears sense that he or she is moving one way, _____ his or her brain detects movement in an-other way.

5. When in a car, you want to see the car's movement while you are feeling it, _____ sit in the front seat and watch the road.

6. On a ship, you need to find a level point to focus on, _____ you should keep your eyes on the horizon.

■ For more practice with coordination and subordination, visit Exercise Central at <bedfordstmartins .com/realessays>.

7. When you are flying, choose a window seat, _____ look outside to watch and sense the plane's movement.

8. You can get some prescription medications to prevent motion sickness, _____ you can even buy some effective medications without a prescription.

9. Taking ginger may be an even better way to prevent motion sickness, _____ you can simply buy ginger tea or raw ginger at a supermarket.

10. If you use a medication, be sure to take it one hour before you travel, _____ there may not be enough time for it to take effect.

■ **PRACTICE 2   COMBINING SENTENCES WITH COORDINATING CONJUNCTIONS**

Combine each pair of sentences into a single sentence by using a comma and a coordinating conjunction. In some cases, there may be more than one correct answer.

> **EXAMPLE:** Americans have recently experienced unpleasant shocks
> at the gas station. ~~People~~ *, but people* in the United States still pay lower gas
> prices than much of the world.

1. Gasoline prices are lower in the United States than in many other industrialized countries. Most Americans do not find this news comforting.

2. People in the United States are used to low gas prices. Many drivers feel cheated when prices increase.

3. European drivers pay more than five dollars a gallon for gasoline. Gas prices in Asia have been triple those in the United States.

4. Canadians also pay higher gas prices than Americans pay. The taxes on gasoline are higher in Canada than they are in this country.

5. Few people would argue that gasoline prices in the United States are too low. The reason for these relatively cheap prices is that gasoline is not heavily taxed.

6. In many countries, taxes on gasoline support social services. The money may also pay for research on reducing air pollution.

7. Gasoline taxes can help to pay for roads. They can raise money for research into fuel efficiency.

8. However, taxes on gasoline are very unpopular with most drivers. Politicians are not eager to vote for gasoline taxes.

9. Many Americans do not want to pay gas taxes of even two or three cents per gallon. Most also do not want to spend tax money on mass transit systems.

10. Gasoline prices will probably never be as high in the United States as they are in Asia. A few Americans are not sure that this is a good thing.

Using Semicolons

A **semicolon** is a punctuation mark that can join two sentences through coordination. When you use a semicolon, make sure that the ideas in the two sentences are not only equally important but also closely related.

EQUAL IDEA	;	EQUAL IDEA
My computer crashed	;	I lost all of my files.
I had just finished my research paper	;	I will have to redo the whole thing.

A semicolon alone does not tell readers much about the relationship between the two ideas. Use a **conjunctive adverb** after the semicolon to give more information about the relationship. Put a comma after the conjunctive adverb.

The following are some of the most common conjunctive adverbs, along with a few examples of how they are used.

Equal idea	; afterward, ; also, ; as a result, ; besides, ; consequently, ; frequently, ; however, ; in addition, ; in fact, ; instead, ; still, ; then, ; therefore,	Equal idea

My computer crashed	; as a result,	I lost all my files.
I should have made backup files	; however,	I did not.
The information is lost	; therefore,	I will have to try to rebuild the files.

PRACTICE 3   JOINING IDEAS WITH SEMICOLONS

Join each pair of sentences by using a semicolon alone.

> **EXAMPLE:** In the wake of recent corporate scandals, many businesses are using new techniques to identify job candidates who may be problematic. ~~Graphology~~ *; graphology* is one such technique.

1. Graphology involves identifying personality features on the basis of a person's handwriting. These features include honesty, responsibility, and loyalty.

2. Graphology is now used widely in France, Germany, and England. Many American graphologists say their business has also grown significantly in recent years.

3. An owner of a jewelry business says that an increase in employee theft made him use a graphology consultant. He says that handwriting analysis helped to identify the thieves.

4. Many scientists and doctors, however, believe that graphology is not reliable or scientific at all. They state that there is no evidence that graphology can uncover a person's true character.

5. Nevertheless, even some job seekers are beginning to use graphology to help them find work. One says he submitted his handwriting analysis report along with his résumé and got the job he wanted.

PRACTICE 4   COMBINING SENTENCES WITH SEMICOLONS AND CONNECTING WORDS (CONJUNCTIVE ADVERBS)

Combine each pair of sentences by using a semicolon and a connecting word followed by a comma. Choose a conjunctive adverb that makes sense for the relationship between the two ideas. In some cases, there may be more than one correct answer.

EXAMPLE: Most people do not own a gas mask. *; however, after* ~~After~~ 9/11, some may feel more comfortable having one available.

1. Two inventors believed that Americans would welcome the opportunity to have a gas mask. They invented one that is part of a baseball cap.

2. Professional gas masks are costly, heavy, and hard to use. Most consumers would not find them appealing.

3. The new baseball-cap gas mask is small and lightweight. It can fit in the corner of a drawer, in a coat pocket, or in a briefcase.

4. This mask can easily fit children as well as adults. It may sell for as little as twenty dollars.

5. The wearer slips a thin sheet of transparent plastic attached to the hat over his or her head. The plastic sheet can be tied shut at the back of the neck.

6. Air from the outside is pulled in by a tiny fan. The air is forced through a filter of activated carbon in the hat's brim.

7. The inventors say that the plastic sheet allows the wearer to see clearly. It does not make the wearer feel too closed in.

8. The mask is not intended for long-term use. It is meant to be worn for about fifteen to thirty minutes.

9. The goal is to allow the wearer to get out of the contaminated area quickly. The wearer can simply slip on the mask and then move into fresh air.

10. The inventors are now looking for a company to make the new gas mask. Consumers will be able to obtain the gas masks from the manufacturer.

Using Subordinating Conjunctions

A **conjunction** is a word that joins words, phrases, or clauses. **Subordinating conjunctions** are dependent words that join two sentences when one is more important than the other. The sentence with the subordinating conjunction in front of it becomes a subordinate or dependent clause; because of the subordinating conjunction, it no longer expresses a complete thought and cannot stand by itself as a sentence.

Choose the conjunction that makes the most sense with the two sentences. Here are some of the most common subordinating conjunctions.

Main idea	after since although so that as unless as if until because when before where even though while if	Subordinate idea

| I decided to go to work | although | I had a terrible cold. |
| I hate to miss a day | unless | I absolutely can't get there. |

When a subordinate idea ends a sentence (as in the preceding examples), it usually does not need to be preceded by a comma unless it is showing a contrast. When a subordinate idea begins a sentence, use a comma to separate it from the rest of the sentence.

Subordinating conjunction	Subordinate idea	**,**	Main idea
Although	I had a terrible cold	**,**	I decided to go to work.
Unless	I absolutely can't get there	**,**	I hate to miss a day.

■ **PRACTICE 5   JOINING IDEAS THROUGH SUBORDINATION**

In the following sentences, fill in the blank with an appropriate subordinating conjunction. In some cases, there may be more than one correct answer.

> **EXAMPLE:** Smokey Bear spent most of his life in the National Zoo in
>
> Washington, D.C., ___*where*___ he received so much mail
>
> that he had his own zip code.

1. Smokey Bear began reminding people that "Only you can prevent forest fires" in 1944 _____ government officials during World War II were concerned about preserving valuable resources like trees.

2. However, Smokey Bear existed only as a cartoon _____ a tragedy occurred six years later.

3. _____ a fire destroyed part of Lincoln National Forest near Capitan, New Mexico, in 1950, forest rangers found a badly burned bear cub clinging to a tree.

4. The "real" Smokey Bear became a celebrity _____ the public heard his story.

5. After his death, Smokey Bear's body was returned to New Mexico _____ he could be buried near his former home.

6. The character of Smokey Bear has been used continuously in U.S. and Canadian fire safety campaigns _____ it first appeared more than fifty years ago.

7. Smokey has also appeared in public service announcements in Mexico, _____ he is known as Simon.

8. Recently, Smokey's famous line was changed to "Only you can prevent wildfires" _____ research indicated that most adults did not believe they could cause a wildfire.

9. However, humans can easily set fires _____ they discard cigarettes carelessly, burn trash on windy days, or even park a car with a catalytic converter in a dry field.

10. _____ the Smokey Bear campaign heads into its seventh decade, Smokey is as recognizable to most Americans as Mickey Mouse and Santa Claus.

◼ PRACTICE 6   COMBINING SENTENCES THROUGH SUBORDINATION

Combine each pair of sentences into a single sentence by using an appropriate subordinating conjunction either at the beginning or between the two sentences.

    EXAMPLE: **Children like to assert themselves.** *when they* **They are between one and four years old.**

1. Toddlers do not get to make many decisions. They want to have some power over their own lives.

2. Young children often become frustrated. Parents do not let them have their own way.

3. Parents want to avoid power struggles with their toddlers. The parents should learn to pick their battles.

4. Experts recommend letting even young children make some choices. The children will feel that they have some control.

5. Parents should not let a child do anything dangerous. The child may want to.

6. Toddlers can be difficult to handle. Most parents worry more about power struggles with their teenagers.

7. Adolescents need to establish their independence from their parents. They also want their parents to set some limits.

8. Teenagers can be skilled at arguments. Parents should learn not to argue about or renegotiate rules that the household has established.

9. Food, sleep, clothes, and grooming are often battlefields for children and parents. Parents remember their own rebellious phases and try to understand what their children are feeling.

10. Parents and children can work through power struggles. They have respect for each other.

Edit Paragraphs and Your Own Writing

Join the underlined sentences by using either coordination or subordination, referring to the chart on page 470 as you need to. Be sure to punctuate correctly.

EDITING REVIEW 1

(1) Lyme disease is carried by deer ticks. (2) The disease appears most frequently in the northeastern United States. (3) Hikers, gardeners, and other lovers of the outdoors in that area often become victims of the illness. (4) People venture into tall grass or brush against other foliage. (5) They should inspect any exposed skin carefully for the minuscule ticks. (6) Researchers now know that the disease is more widespread than was once thought. (7) Limiting exposed skin by wearing socks, long pants, and long sleeves gives ticks fewer chances to attach themselves. (8) So does

washing exposed skin within about ninety minutes of being outdoors. (9) These simple precautions can prevent most cases of potentially dangerous Lyme disease.

◼ EDITING REVIEW 2

(1) Al-Qurain is a community in the small Middle Eastern country of Kuwait. (2) Thirty years ago, Kuwait City officials began to use an abandoned quarry in al-Qurain as a garbage dump. (3) None of them thought the area would ever be populated. (4) Fifteen years ago, the government began to build subsidized housing in al-Qurain. (5) The dump was supposed to be closed. (6) Kuwaitis continued to use the al-Qurain landfill. (7) People soon lived all around the foul-smelling garbage pit. (8) Residents of the area were teased and insulted for living in the neighborhood. (9) Al-Qurain now houses sixty thousand people.

(10) For years, the dump sickened people around it. (11) Sometimes the garbage caught fire and sent fumes into the homes nearby. (12) Finally, the Kuwaiti Environmental Protection Agency decided to try to help. (13) The agency gets little government funding. (14) It needed to rely on donations for the cleanup effort. (15) Soon, a mountain of garbage had been removed. (16) The leveled site was covered with pebbles from the desert. (17) Engineers found a way to siphon methane gas from the seventy-five-foot-deep garbage pit. (18) Kuwait is famous for oil production. (19) A methane-powered generator may soon provide electricity for al-Qurain residents. (20) The air in the neighborhood now ranks among the country's cleanest. (21) For many environmentalists and residents of this neighborhood, the cleanup of al-Qurain is almost a miracle.

■ **PRACTICE 7   EDITING YOUR OWN WRITING FOR COORDINATION AND SUBORDINATION**

As a final practice, edit a piece of your own writing for coordination and subordination. It can be a paper you are working on for this course, a paper you've already finished, a paper for another course, or a recent piece of writing from your work or everyday life. You may want to use the following chart as you edit.

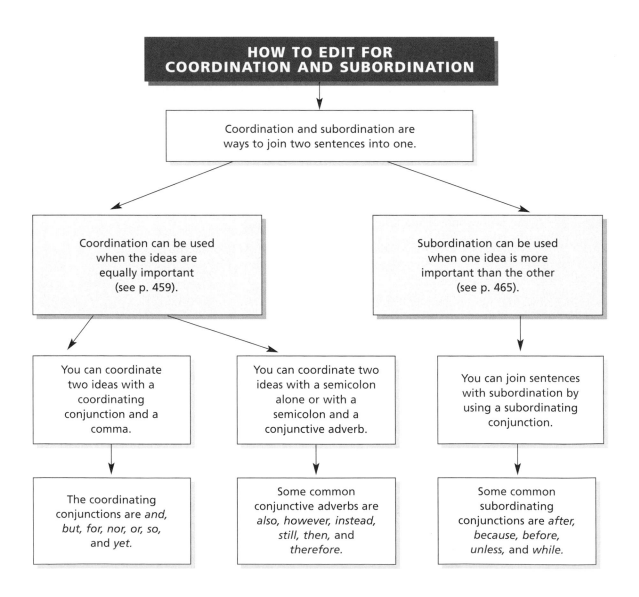

HOW TO EDIT FOR COORDINATION AND SUBORDINATION

Coordination and subordination are ways to join two sentences into one.

Coordination can be used when the ideas are equally important (see p. 459).

Subordination can be used when one idea is more important than the other (see p. 465).

You can coordinate two ideas with a coordinating conjunction and a comma.

You can coordinate two ideas with a semicolon alone or with a semicolon and a conjunctive adverb.

You can join sentences with subordination by using a subordinating conjunction.

The coordinating conjunctions are *and*, *but*, *for*, *nor*, *or*, *so*, and *yet*.

Some common conjunctive adverbs are *also*, *however*, *instead*, *still*, *then*, and *therefore*.

Some common subordinating conjunctions are *after*, *because*, *before*, *unless*, and *while*.

30

Parallelism

Balancing Ideas

Understand What Parallelism Is

Parallelism in writing means that similar parts in a sentence are balanced by having the same structure. Put nouns with nouns, verbs with verbs, and phrases with phrases.

> **NOT PARALLEL**   I like <u>math</u> more than <u>studying English</u>.
>
> [*Math* is a noun, but *studying English* is a phrase.]
>
> **PARALLEL**   I like <u>math</u> more than <u>English</u>.
>
> **NOT PARALLEL**   On vacation, we <u>swam</u>, <u>snorkled</u>, and <u>were eating</u> at great restaurants.
>
> [Verbs must be in the same tense to be parallel.]
>
> **PARALLEL**   On vacation, we <u>swam</u>, <u>snorkled</u>, and <u>ate</u> at great restaurants.
>
> **NOT PARALLEL**   Last night we went <u>to a movie</u> and <u>dancing at a club</u>.
>
> [*To a movie* and *dancing at a club* are both phrases, but they have different forms. *To a movie* should be paired with another prepositional phrase: *to a dance club*.]
>
> **PARALLEL**   Last night we went <u>to a movie</u> and <u>to a dance club</u>.

Practice Writing Parallel Sentences

Parallelism in Pairs and Lists

When two or more items in a series are joined by the word *and* or *or,* use a similar form for each item.

NOT PARALLEL	The fund-raiser included a bake sale and also holding an auction.
PARALLEL	The fund-raiser included a bake sale and an auction.
NOT PARALLEL	Students got items for the auction from local businesses, from their own families, and ran an advertisement in the newspaper.
PARALLEL	Students got items for the auction from local businesses, from their own families, and from their advertisement in the newspaper.

PRACTICE 1   MAKING PAIRS AND LISTS PARALLEL

In each sentence, underline the parts of the sentence that should be parallel. Then, edit the sentence to make it parallel.

EXAMPLE: Sometimes even a well-maintained car can break down
  run out of gas.
  or you might forget to fill up the gas tank.

1. When your car breaks down on the road, you should follow simple rules to remain safe and so that assistance will come quickly.

2. When contacting a garage for help, you should give your location accurately by identifying the street or highway, the nearest cross street or exit, and which landmarks or stores are nearby.

3. All of the cars in a parking lot look similar, so a mechanic may have trouble finding your car unless you open the hood, put on emergency flashers, or you could tie a handkerchief to the antenna.

4. If you decide to read a book or a nap sounds good while you wait for the mechanic, you may not see the tow truck.

5. A mechanic who sees no obviously broken-down car and he or she has other calls to deal with may simply go on to the next customer.

6. Leaving a cell phone number or if you provide the number of a nearby business will allow the mechanic to call you back.

7. Most pay phones nowadays do not receive incoming calls, so the garage may not be able to call you back on a pay phone to let you know about problems or if there are delays.

8. The garage will not be able to reach you on your cell phone if you make a lot of calls or it is time for a long talk with your best friend.

9. Sitting in a car or if you stand behind it can be very dangerous when a breakdown occurs on the side of the highway.

10. Relying on common sense, patience, and remembering basic safety guidelines will help you get through your car's breakdown.

■ For more practice with parallelism, visit Exercise Central at <bedfordstmartins .com/realessays>.

Parallelism in Comparisons

In comparisons, the items being compared should have parallel structures. Comparisons often use the words *than* or *as.* When you edit for parallelism, make sure that the items on either side of the comparison word are parallel.

NOT PARALLEL	Driving downtown is as fast as the bus.
PARALLEL	Driving downtown is as fast as taking the bus.

NOT PARALLEL	Running is more tiring than walks.
PARALLEL	Running is more tiring than walking. *Or,*
	A run is more tiring than a walk.

To make the parts of a sentence parallel, you may need to add or drop a word or two.

NOT PARALLEL	A multiple-choice test is easier than answering an essay question.
PARALLEL, WORD ADDED	*Taking* a multiple-choice test is easier than answering an essay question.

<table>
<tr><td>NOT PARALLEL</td><td>The cost of a train ticket is less than <u>to pay the cost</u> of a plane ticket.</td></tr>
<tr><td>PARALLEL, WORDS DROPPED</td><td>The cost of a train ticket is less than <u>the cost</u> of a plane ticket.</td></tr>
</table>

▪ PRACTICE 2   MAKING COMPARISONS PARALLEL

In each sentence, underline the parts of the sentence that should be parallel. Then, edit the sentence to make it parallel.

EXAMPLE: <u>New appliances</u> are usually much more energy-efficient than ~~running~~ <u>old ones.</u>

1. For many people, getting the household electric bill is more worrisome than to pay the rent each month.

2. The amount of the rent bill usually changes much less from month to month than what an energy company charges.

3. Saving money appeals to many consumers more than to use less electricity.

4. Compact fluorescent lightbulbs use less energy than continuing to use regular incandescent bulbs.

5. In most households, running the refrigerator uses more energy than the use of all other appliances.

6. Many people worry that buying a new refrigerator is more expensive than if they simply keep the old one.

7. However, an energy-efficient new refrigerator uses much less electricity than running an inefficient older model.

8. Some new refrigerators use only as much energy as keeping a 75-watt light bulb burning.

9. Householders might spend less money to buy an efficient new refrigerator than it would take to run the old one for another five years.

10. Researching information about energy efficiency can save consumers as much money as when they remember to turn off lights and air conditioners.

Parallelism with Certain Paired Words

When a sentence uses certain paired words, called **correlative conjunctions**, the items joined by these words must be parallel. Correlative conjunctions, shown below, link two equal elements and show the relationship between them.

both . . . and   neither . . . nor   rather . . . than
either . . . or   not only . . . but also

NOT PARALLEL   Brianna dislikes *both* fruit *and* eating vegetables.

PARALLEL   Brianna dislikes *both* fruit *and* vegetables.

NOT PARALLEL   She would *rather* eat popcorn every night *than* to cook.

PARALLEL   She would *rather* eat popcorn every night *than* cook.

▦ PRACTICE 3   MAKING SENTENCES WITH PAIRED WORDS PARALLEL

In each sentence, circle the paired words and underline the parts of the sentence that should be parallel. Then, edit the sentence to make it parallel. You may need to change the second part of the correlative conjunction.

EXAMPLE: A recent survey of young women reported that a majority of them would (rather) lose twenty pounds permanently (than) to live to be ninety.

1. People in the United States are both pressed for time and have gotten used to convenient but fattening foods.

2. Many Americans are neither willing to exercise regularly nor do they have to do anything physical during a normal day.

3. Being overweight can be unhealthy, but many Americans would rather look thinner than to stay the same size and get in better shape.

4. In fact, some Americans are not only out of shape but are dangerously obsessed with being thin.

5. The idea that thinner is better affects both overweight people and it even influences people of normal weight.

6. In their quest to lose weight, many Americans have tried either fad diets or have taken prescription drugs.

7. Dozens of healthy, average-sized Americans in the past ten years have died from either surgical procedures to remove fat or they have died from dangerous diet drugs.

8. A thin person is neither guaranteed to be attractive nor is he or she necessarily healthy.

9. Some people who are larger than average are not only in good health but also can be physically fit.

10. Americans who would rather pay for risky drugs and surgery than eating moderately and exercising may have hazardous priorities.

■   **PRACTICE 4   COMPLETING SENTENCES WITH PAIRED WORDS**

The following items contain only the first part of a correlative conjunction. Complete the correlative conjunction and add more information to form a whole sentence. Make sure that the structures on both sides of the correlative conjunction are parallel.

    EXAMPLE: **I am both enthusiastic about your company** _and eager_

        to work for you   .

1. I could bring to this job not only youthful enthusiasm _____

_____.

2. I am willing to work either in your Chicago office _____

_____.

3. My current job neither encourages creativity _____.

4. I would rather work in a difficult job _____.

5. In college I learned a lot both from my classes _____.

Edit Paragraphs and Your Own Writing

Edit the following paragraphs for parallelism, referring to the chart on page 479 as you need to.

■ EDITING REVIEW 1

(1) Some employees who want to advance their careers would rather transfer within their company than looking for a new job elsewhere. (2) In-house job changes are possible, but employees should be sure that they both meet the criteria of the job and to avoid making their present boss angry. (3) Because businesses invest money in each person they hire, many companies would rather hire from within and not bring an outsider into a position. (4) By hiring an employee from another department, a company neither needs to make an investment in a new employee but may also prevent the current employee from leaving. (5) Transfers usually go more smoothly now than in the past; however, an in-house job move can still require diplomacy and being honest. (6) Experts caution employees who are considering an in-house transfer to tell their current manager the truth and that they should discuss their wish to transfer with the potential new manager. (7) Employees should neither threaten to quit if they do not get the new job nor is it a good idea to spread the word around the department that they are anxious to leave their present job. (8) Employees' goals for in-house transfers should be career advancement and making sure that they create no bad feelings with the move.

EDITING REVIEW 2

(1) Black motorists frequently arouse police suspicion either when driving in neighborhoods that are mainly white or when they are driving an expensive car. (2) A higher percentage of African Americans than among people who are white are pulled over by the police. (3) Many African Americans feel insulted, endangered, and react with anger when they are stopped seemingly randomly. (4) African Americans are liable to be singled out by police who suspect they are criminals not only while in a car but African Americans also report being wrongly stopped on foot. (5) Racial profiling is illegal yet a fairly common phenomenon. (6) According to a 2001 poll, among black women the figure is 25 percent, and 52 percent of black men have been singled out by police. (7) Victims of racial profiling have done nothing wrong, yet they are made to feel that others are either afraid or do not trust them. (8) Law-abiding African Americans should neither expect such treatment nor should they put up with it from public officials who are supposed to protect citizens. (9) Police departments around the country must make their employees aware that automatically stopping, asking them questions, and searching African Americans will not be tolerated. (10) Treating all citizens fairly is a more important American value than that there is a high arrest rate for the police.

**PRACTICE 5   EDITING YOUR OWN WRITING
FOR PARALLELISM**

As a final practice, edit a piece of your own writing for parallelism. It can be a paper you are working on for this course, a paper you've already finished, a paper for another course, or a recent piece of writing from your work or everyday life. You may want to use the chart on page 479 as you edit.

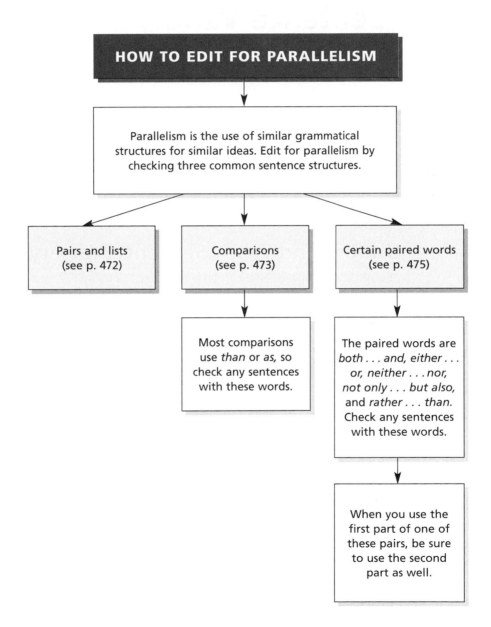

HOW TO EDIT FOR PARALLELISM

Parallelism is the use of similar grammatical structures for similar ideas. Edit for parallelism by checking three common sentence structures.

Pairs and lists
(see p. 472)

Comparisons
(see p. 473)

Certain paired words
(see p. 475)

Most comparisons use *than* or *as,* so check any sentences with these words.

The paired words are *both . . . and, either . . . or, neither . . . nor, not only . . . but also,* and *rather . . . than.* Check any sentences with these words.

When you use the first part of one of these pairs, be sure to use the second part as well.

31

Sentence Variety

Putting Rhythm in Your Writing

Understand What Sentence Variety Is

Having **sentence variety** in your writing means using assorted sentence patterns, lengths, and rhythms. Sometimes writers use too many short, simple sentences, thinking that short is always easier to understand than long. In fact, that is not true, as the following examples show.

WITH SHORT, SIMPLE SENTENCES

Age discrimination can exist even in unpaid jobs. The newspaper today reported that a magazine has been accused of age discrimination. The magazine is the *Atlantic Monthly*. A woman was told she was too old to be an unpaid intern. The woman was forty-one. The position was for a senior in college. The woman was a senior. She had raised three children before going to college. She is suing the magazine. The next day, another woman, age fifty-one, reported that the same thing had happened to her a year earlier. She had filed a discrimination suit. The suit was brought to court by the Council on Age Discrimination. The magazine never showed up. The court never took any follow-up action against the magazine. Apparently, the matter was not of great importance to either the magazine or the justice system.

WITH SENTENCE VARIETY

Age discrimination can exist even in unpaid jobs. The newspaper today reported that a forty-one-year-old woman has accused a magazine, the *Atlantic Monthly,* of age discrimination. This woman, who raised three children before going to college and is now in her senior year, was told she was too old to be an unpaid intern, even though the position was for a college senior. She is suing the magazine. The next day, another woman, age fifty-one, reported that the same thing had happened to her a year earlier, and she, too, had filed an age discrimination suit. The suit was brought to court by the Council on Age Discrimination, but the magazine didn't appear for the court date, and the court never took any follow-up action. Apparently, the matter was not of great importance to either the magazine or the justice system.

Sentence variety is what gives your writing good rhythm and flow.

Practice Creating Sentence Variety

To create sentence variety, write sentences of different types and lengths. Because many writers tend to write short sentences that start with the subject, this chapter will focus on techniques for starting with something other than the subject and for writing a variety of longer sentences.

Remember that the goal is to use variety to achieve a good rhythm. Do not simply change all your sentences from one pattern to another, or you still won't have variety.

■ For two additional techniques used to achieve sentence variety, coordination and subordination, see Chapter 29.

Start Some Sentences with Adverbs

Adverbs are words that describe verbs, adjectives, or other adverbs; they often end with *-ly.* As long as the meaning is clear, you can place an adverb at the beginning of a sentence instead of in the middle. An adverb at the beginning is usually followed by a comma. You may not need a comma after an adverb that indicates time, such as *often* or *always,* but you should always use a comma if the reader pauses slightly after the adverb.

ADVERB IN MIDDLE	Stories about haunted houses *frequently* surface at Halloween.
ADVERB AT BEGINNING	*Frequently,* stories about haunted houses surface at Halloween.
ADVERB IN MIDDLE	These tales *often* reveal the life stories of former inhabitants.
ADVERB AT BEGINNING	*Often* these tales reveal the life stories of former inhabitants.

■ For more about adverbs, see Chapter 27.

■ **PRACTICE 1**   **STARTING SENTENCES WITH AN ADVERB**

■ For more practice
with sentence variety,
visit Exercise Central
at <**bedfordstmartins
.com/realessays**>.

Edit each sentence so that it begins with an adverb.

          Frequently, hurricanes
   EXAMPLE: ~~Hurricanes frequently~~ strike barrier islands.
          ^

1. Harsh weather takes a toll annually on sandy beaches.

2. That island house once stood on solid ground.

3. The ocean eventually washed the ground out from under it.

4. The house was finally condemned as unsafe.

5. It is now going to be demolished.

■ **PRACTICE 2**   **STARTING SENTENCES WITH AN ADVERB**

This practice continues the story from the previous exercise. In each sentence, fill in the blank with an adverb that makes sense, adding a comma when necessary. There may be several good choices for each item.

   EXAMPLE: _Fortunately,_ no one was living in the house at the time.

1. _____ a row of houses stood on the east side of the channel.

2. _____ a hurricane washed away most of the land nearby.

3. _____ most of the houses vanished.

4. _____ the house stood alone on a sandy peninsula.

5. _____ maps of the island were redrawn.

■ **PRACTICE 3**   **WRITING SENTENCES THAT START
WITH AN ADVERB**

Write three more sentences that start with an adverb, using commas as necessary. Choose from the following adverbs: *often, sadly, amazingly, luckily, lovingly, gently, frequently, stupidly, quietly.*

   EXAMPLE: _Luckily, I remembered to save my file on a disk._

1. _____

2. _____

3. _____

Join Ideas Using an *-ing* Verb Form

One way to combine sentences is to turn one of them into a phrase using an *-ing* **verb form** (such as *walking* or *racing*). The *-ing* verb form indicates that the two parts of the sentence are happening at the same time. The more important idea (the one you want to emphasize) should be in the main clause, not in the phrase you make by adding the *-ing* verb form.

| TWO SENTENCES | Jonah did well in the high jump. He came in second. |
| JOINED WITH *-ING* VERB FORM | Jonah did well in the high jump, coming in second. |

To combine sentences this way, add *-ing* to the verb in one of the sentences and delete the subject. You now have a phrase that can be added to the beginning or the end of the other sentence, depending on what makes sense.

                 , breaking
He also won the long jump. ~~He broke~~ the record.

If you add the phrase to the end of a sentence, you will usually need to put a comma before it unless the phrase is essential to the meaning of the sentence, as in the following example.

                         using
The thief broke into the apartment. ~~The thief used~~ a crowbar.

If you add a phrase starting with an *-ing* verb form to the beginning of a sentence, put a comma after it. Also, be sure that the word being modified follows immediately after the phrase. Otherwise, you will create a dangling modifier.

TWO SENTENCES	I dropped my bag. My groceries spilled.
DANGLING MODIFIER	Dropping my bag, my groceries spilled.
EDITED	Dropping my bag, I spilled my groceries.

■   **PRACTICE 4   JOINING IDEAS USING AN *-ING* VERB FORM**

Combine each pair of sentences into a single sentence by using an *-ing* verb form. Add or delete words if necessary.

                        Wanting
    EXAMPLE: ~~My son Sean wanted~~ the guests at his fourth birthday
                                                    , my son Sean
    party to stay away from his toys. ~~He~~ hit the other children.

1. Children pay attention to role models. Some children—maybe even Sean—learn aggression from people at home, at school, or on television.

2. I react to some frustrating situations with fury. I forget that Sean watches and learns from me.

3. His favorite television characters do not model good behavior, either. They act violently under stress.

4. I wanted expert advice on anger management. I feared that Sean would not learn to control his temper.

5. I punished my son for his angry outbursts. I used to take away his toys and privileges.

6. An expert told me that angry children need positive lessons in how to cope. She said that punishing Sean for losing his temper was ineffective.

7. I taught my son concrete ways to react to his anger. I gave him something to focus on before lashing out.

8. I did not try to reason with my son when he was furious. I saved the lessons for his calm moods.

9. Sean counts to ten when he gets angry. He now gives himself time to cool off.

10. Preschoolers can learn ways to handle their anger. They can modify their reactions before they understand why they should.

■ PRACTICE 5   **JOINING IDEAS USING AN *-ING* VERB FORM**

Fill in the blank in each sentence with an appropriate *-ing* verb form. There are many possible ways to complete each sentence.

> EXAMPLE: *Owning*   the rights to the character Spider-Man,
>
> Marvel Enterprises has been making big money lately.

1. _____ from losses of tens of millions of dollars a year, Marvel now turns a profit of more than $150 million a year, thanks to Spider-Man.

2. Marvel dominates the comic-book market, _____ sixty comic books a month.

3. _____ 83 percent of its profits from licensing its characters for films and related merchandise, Marvel makes only 15 percent of its profits from comic-book sales.

4. Marvel keeps tight control of the characters it licenses to filmmakers, _____ no costume changes or added superpowers without Marvel's approval.

5. _____ any film studio from having Spider-Man kill anyone, for example, Marvel maintains the character as it believes he should be.

■ PRACTICE 6   **JOINING IDEAS USING AN *-ING* VERB FORM**

Write two sets of sentences, and join each set using an *-ing* verb form.

> EXAMPLE: a.   *Teresa signed on to eBay.com.*
>
>   b.   *She used her password.*
>
> COMBINED: *Using her password, Teresa signed on to eBay.com.*
>
>   *Teresa signed on to eBay.com using her password.*

1. a. _____

   b. _____

   COMBINED: _____

   _____

2. a. _____

   b. _____

   COMBINED: _____

   _____

Join Ideas Using an *-ed* Verb Form

Another way to combine sentences is to turn one of them into a phrase using an ***-ed* verb form** (such as *waited* or *walked*). You can join sentences this way if one of them has a form of *be* as a helping verb along with the *-ed* verb form.

■ For more on helping verbs, see Chapters 21 and 25.

TWO SENTENCES	Leonardo da Vinci was a man of many talents. He was noted most often for his painting.
JOINED WITH *-ED* VERB FORM	Noted most often for his painting, Leonardo da Vinci was a man of many talents.

To combine sentences this way, drop the subject and the helping verb from a sentence that has an *-ed* verb form. You now have a modifying phrase that can be added to the beginning or the end of the other sentence, depending on what makes the most sense.

Interested   *Leonardo*
~~Leonardo was interested~~ in many areas, ~~He~~ investigated problems of

geology, botany, mechanics, and hydraulics.

If you add a phrase that begins with an *-ed* verb form to the beginning of a sentence, put a comma after it. Also, be sure the word that the phrase modifies follows immediately, or you will create a dangling modifier. Sometimes, you will need to change the word that the phrase modifies from a pronoun to a noun, as in the previous example.

■ For more on finding and correcting dangling modifiers, see Chapter 28.

PRACTICE 7   JOINING IDEAS USING AN -*ED* VERB FORM

Combine each pair of sentences into a single sentence by using an -*ed* verb form.

> _Hatched_
> **EXAMPLE:** ~~Alligators are hatched~~ from eggs when they are only a
>   ^
> few inches long, ~~Alligators~~ can reach a length of ten feet or more
>   _, alligators_
>   ^
> as adults.

1. An alligator was spotted in a pond in Central Park in New York City. Many New Yorkers refused to believe in the existence of the alligator.

2. Alligators were released by their owners for growing too large to be pets. These alligators were sometimes said to be living in New York City sewers.

3. Rumors were believed by some gullible people. The rumors about giant sewer alligators were untrue.

4. The story of the alligator in Central Park was denied by city officials. The story sounded like another wild rumor.

5. Central Park alligator sightings were reported by several New Yorkers. The sightings were confirmed when a television news crew filmed a reptile in the pond.

6. A professional alligator wrestler was hired to catch the reptile. He came to New York from Florida.

7. The pond in Central Park was surrounded by news cameras and curious onlookers. It was brightly lit just before 11:00 p.m. on the day the alligator wrestler arrived.

8. The creature was captured in just a few minutes by the alligator wrestler's wife. The so-called alligator turned out to be a spectacled caiman, a species native to Central and South America.

9. Some New Yorkers were surprised to find that the caiman was only two feet long. They may have felt a bit foolish for expecting to see a giant alligator in the park.

10. The caiman was removed from Central Park. It soon found a home in a warmer climate.

■ PRACTICE 8   JOINING IDEAS USING AN *-ED* VERB FORM

Fill in the blank in each sentence with an appropriate *-ed* verb form. There are several possible ways to complete each sentence.

> **EXAMPLE:**   *Decorated*   in unusual colors and textures, fingernails are sometimes as stylish as clothing.

1. _____ to perform manicures, nail stylists are setting up shop all over the United States.

2. Style-conscious women today are seldom satisfied with old-fashioned fingernails _____ with a simple solid color.

3. _____ as an art form, manicures have become a new fashion trend.

4. Some expensive manicures turn fingernails into exotic little sculptures _____ to last only a few days.

5. _____ to create fingernail designs to match the latest fashions, a manicurist with an artistic touch can make a good living today.

■ PRACTICE 9   JOINING IDEAS USING AN *-ED* VERB FORM

Write two sets of sentences and join them using an *-ed* verb form.

> **EXAMPLE:**   a.   *Lee is training for the Boston Marathon.*
>
> b.   *It is believed to have the most difficult hill to run.*

COMBINED: *Lee is training for the Boston Marathon, believed to*

have the most difficult hill to run.

1. a. _____

   b. _____

COMBINED: _____

_____

2. a. _____

   b. _____

COMBINED: _____

_____

Join Ideas Using an Appositive

An **appositive** is a phrase that renames a noun. Appositives, which are nouns or noun phrases, can be used to combine two sentences into one.

TWO SENTENCES	Elvis Presley continues to be popular many years after his death. He is "the King."
JOINED WITH AN APPOSITIVE	Elvis Presley, "the King," continues to be popular many years after his death.

[The phrase *"the King"* renames the noun *Elvis Presley.*]

To combine two sentences this way, turn the sentence that renames the noun into a phrase by dropping its subject and verb. The appositive phrase can appear anywhere in the sentence, but it should be placed before or after the noun it renames. Use a comma or commas to set off the appositive.

, Graceland,

Millions of people visit Elvis's home each year. ~~It is called Graceland.~~

■   **PRACTICE 10   JOINING IDEAS USING AN APPOSITIVE**

Combine each pair of sentences into a single sentence by using an appositive. Be sure to use a comma or commas to set off the appositive.

EXAMPLE: William Shakespeare *, one of the greatest writers in the English language,* was famous and financially comfortable during his lifetime. ~~Shakespeare was one of the greatest writers in the English language.~~

1. Shakespeare grew up in Stratford, England. He was the son of a former town leader.

2. Shakespeare attended the local grammar school until his father could no longer afford it. His father was a poor manager of money.

3. In 1582, Shakespeare, just eighteen, married twenty-six-year-old Anne Hathaway. She was a farmer's daughter.

4. Three years later, he left for London. London was the center of England's theater world.

5. Young Shakespeare was once a simple country boy. He soon became involved in acting, writing, and managing for one of London's theater companies.

6. By 1592, he was famous enough to be criticized in writing by one of the leading playwrights of the time. This playwright was Robert Greene.

7. Greene's publisher soon printed a public apology for the criticism. This was proof that Shakespeare had won the respect of some influential figures.

8. Shakespeare is said to have performed for Queen Elizabeth I. She was a theater fan and supporter.

9. Eventually, Shakespeare returned to Stratford and purchased a large home where he lived until his death in 1616. The house was called New Place.

10. Shakespeare remains highly popular today, and more than 250 movies have been made of his plays or about his life. His life is a rich enough source of drama for any movie producer.

■ **PRACTICE 11   JOINING IDEAS USING AN APPOSITIVE**

Fill in the blank in each sentence with an appropriate appositive. There are many possible ways to complete each sentence.

> **EXAMPLE:** My sister Clara, _____*a busy mother of three*_____, loves to watch soap operas.

1. Clara's favorite show, _____, comes on at three o'clock in the afternoon.

2. Clara, _____, rarely has the time to sit down in front of the television for the broadcast.

3. Instead, she programs her VCR, _____, and tapes the show for later.

4. Clara's husband, _____, used to tease her for watching the soaps.

5. But while he was recovering from the flu recently, he found her stack of tapes, _____, and Clara insists that he watched every show of the previous season.

Join Ideas Using an Adjective Clause

An **adjective clause** is a group of words with a subject and a verb that describes a noun. Adjective clauses often begin with the word *who, which,* or *that* and can be used to combine two sentences into one.

TWO SENTENCES	Lorene owns an art and framing store. She is a good friend of mine.
JOINED WITH AN ADJECTIVE CLAUSE	Lorene, who is a good friend of mine, owns an art and framing store.

■ Use *who* to refer to a person, *which* to refer to places or things (but not to people), and *that* for people, places, or things. When referring to a person, *who* is preferable to *that*.

To join sentences this way, use *who, which,* or *that* to replace the subject of a sentence that describes a noun that is in the other sentence. Once you have made this change, you have an adjective clause that you can move so that it follows the noun it describes. The sentence with the idea you want to emphasize should become the main clause. The less important idea should be in the adjective clause.

TWO SENTENCES   Rosalind is director of human services for the town of Marlborough. Marlborough is her hometown.

[The more important idea here is that Rosalind is director of human services. The less important idea is that the town is her hometown.]

JOINED WITH AN   Rosalind is director of human services for the town
ADJECTIVE CLAUSE   of Marlborough, which is her hometown.

NOTE: If an adjective clause can be taken out of a sentence without completely changing the meaning of the sentence, put commas around the clause.

Lorene, who is a good friend of mine, owns an art and framing store.

[The phrase *who is a good friend of mine* adds information about Lorene, but it is not essential; the sentence *Lorene owns an art and framing store* means almost the same thing as the sentence in the example.]

If an adjective clause is essential to the meaning of a sentence, do not put commas around it.

The meat was recalled for possible salmonella poisoning. I ate it yesterday.

The meat that I ate yesterday was recalled for possible salmonella poisoning.

[The clause *that I ate yesterday* is an essential piece of information. The sentence *The meat was recalled for possible salmonella poisoning* changes significantly with the adjective clause *that I ate yesterday.*]

■ **PRACTICE 12   JOINING IDEAS USING AN ADJECTIVE CLAUSE**

Combine each pair of sentences into a single sentence by using an adjective clause beginning with *who, which,* or *that.*

           Allergies that

EXAMPLE: ~~Some allergies~~ cause sneezing, itching, and watery eyes.

~~They~~ can make people very uncomfortable.

1. Cats produce a protein. It keeps their skin soft.

2. This protein makes some people itch and sneeze. The protein is the reason for most allergic reactions to cats.

3. Some cat lovers are allergic to cats. They can control their allergies with medication.

4. Allergic cat lovers may get another option from a new company. The company wants to create a genetically engineered cat.

5. Scientists have successfully cloned mice. Some mice have been genetically engineered for scientific study.

6. Researchers may soon have the technology to clone cats. Cats could be genetically engineered to remove the allergen.

7. Many people have allergic reactions to cats. According to cat experts, more than 10 percent of those people are allergic to something other than the skin-softening protein.

8. A single gene produces a cat's skin-softening protein. Scientists are not sure whether the gene is necessary for the cat's good health.

9. However, owning a genetically engineered cat would allow an allergic person to avoid taking allergy medications. The medications can sometimes cause dangerous side effects.

10. Cloning and genetic engineering raise ethical questions. These are difficult to answer.

PRACTICE 13   JOINING IDEAS USING AN ADJECTIVE CLAUSE

Fill in the blank in each of the following sentences with an appropriate adjective clause. Add commas, if necessary. There are many possible ways to complete each sentence.

EXAMPLE: Interactive television ____ , *which has started to become*

_____*available to consumers,*_____ is a potential threat

to viewers' privacy.

1. Many Web sites _____

try to make a profit by selling information about visitors to the site.

2. Consumers _____ must

provide information to retail Web sites before being allowed to complete

a purchase.

3. Consumer privacy _____

is suffering further with interactive television.

4. A viewer _____ may

not realize that the broadcaster is collecting information about him or her.

5. The sale of personal information _____

_____ can bring huge profits.

Edit Paragraphs and Your Own Writing

Create sentence variety in the following paragraphs by joining at least two
sentences in each of the paragraphs. Try to use several of the techniques
discussed in this chapter. There are many possible ways to edit each paragraph. You may want to refer to the chart on page 496.

■ EDITING REVIEW

(1) Lotteries were illegal until recently in most U.S. states. (2) They

have now been legalized in most parts of this country. (3) The lotteries

are run by state governments in many places. (4) Lotteries allow the gov-

ernments to raise money without raising taxes. (5) The money can help

fund education and other projects. (6) These projects are necessary and

expensive. (7) Many citizens consider lotteries an ideal way to raise funds. (8) These people reason that no one is forced to buy a lottery ticket. (9) However, lotteries have a dark side that should be discussed more often.

(10) Many experts on gambling worry about the increasing numbers of state lotteries. (11) Lotteries are difficult for many people to resist. (12) The games offer prizes of millions of dollars. (13) They make people fantasize about easy wealth. (14) Lottery tickets cost very little. (15) They are sold in grocery stores and shops in every neighborhood. (16) Unfortunately, the people least able to afford lottery tickets spend the most money on them. (17) They are convinced that they will strike it rich someday. (18) In many impoverished areas, large numbers of people regularly buy several lottery tickets each week. (19) They hope to escape boring, low-paying jobs.

(20) Nor are the poor the only victims of lottery fever. (21) Many people are addicted to gambling. (22) They do not consider the nearly impossible odds of winning a lottery jackpot. (23) They are hooked by occasional small payoffs of two or three dollars. (24) Addicted gamblers will keep buying tickets until they have no money left.

(25) Lotteries promise a big payoff for a little investment. (26) They bring vast amounts of money into state treasuries. (27) Many people believe that lotteries save everyone money. (28) But lottery supporters seldom think about the victims of lotteries. (29) When taxes fund state programs, wealthier people must contribute more than poorer people. (30) But gambling addicts and people desperate to escape poverty pay more heavily than anyone else into state lottery funds. (31) Governments should not rely on the poor and addicted to come up with money to run essential state programs.

PRACTICE 14 EDITING YOUR OWN WRITING FOR SENTENCE VARIETY

As a final practice, edit a piece of your own writing for sentence variety. It can be a paper you are working on for this course, a paper you've already finished, a paper for another course, or a recent piece of writing from your work or everyday life. You may want to use the following chart as you edit.

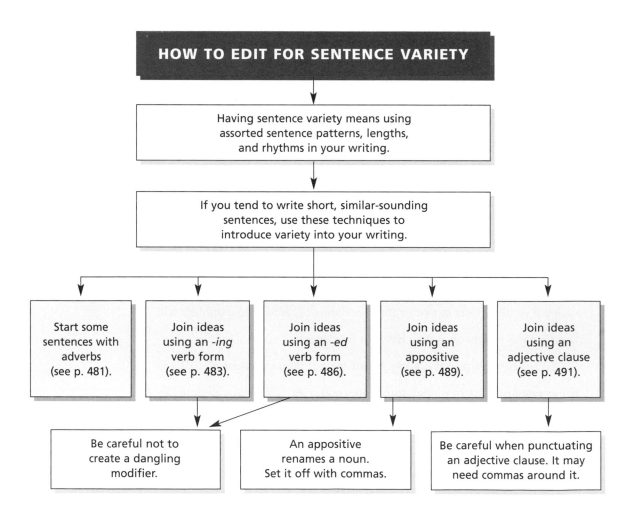

HOW TO EDIT FOR SENTENCE VARIETY

Having sentence variety means using assorted sentence patterns, lengths, and rhythms in your writing.

If you tend to write short, similar-sounding sentences, use these techniques to introduce variety into your writing.

Start some sentences with adverbs (see p. 481).

Join ideas using an *-ing* verb form (see p. 483).

Join ideas using an *-ed* verb form (see p. 486).

Join ideas using an appositive (see p. 489).

Join ideas using an adjective clause (see p. 491).

Be careful not to create a dangling modifier.

An appositive renames a noun. Set it off with commas.

Be careful when punctuating an adjective clause. It may need commas around it.

32

ESL Concerns

Grammar Trouble Spots for Multilingual Students

Academic, or formal, English is the English you will be expected to use in college and in most work situations, especially in writing. If your first language is not English, or if you grew up in a home with non–English speakers, some conventions of formal English may be challenging to you. This chapter focuses on those areas, moving from sentence patterns to individual words. With practice, you'll grow more comfortable with all of the conventions.

NOTE: In this chapter, we use the word *English* to refer to formal English.

Sentences

Word Order

The most basic sentence in English consists of a subject and a verb **(S-V)** that express a complete idea.

$$\overset{\text{S}}{\text{The pitcher}} \overset{\text{V}}{\text{threw.}}$$

Other English sentence patterns build on that structure. One of the most common patterns is subject-verb-object **(S-V-O)**. The object in the **S-V-O** pattern can be a either direct object **(DO)**, which takes the action of the verb directly, or an indirect object **(IO)**, which doesn't take the action. Rather, the action is performed for or to the person.

```
      S      V      DO
      |      |       |
The pitcher threw the ball.
```

```
      S      V    IO     DO
      |      |     |      |
The pitcher threw me the ball.
```

or

```
      S      V     DO    IO
      |      |      |      |
The pitcher threw the ball to me.
```

```
   S     V      DO
   |     |       |
John sent the letter.
```

```
   S     V   IO     DO
   |     |    |       |
John sent Beth the letter.
```

or

```
   S     V      DO     IO
   |     |       |       |
John sent the letter to Beth.
```

Note that the **S-V-O** pattern differs from the sentence patterns in some other languages. For example, in some languages (like Arabic) the pattern may be **S-O-V**; other languages don't have as strictly defined a word order (Spanish, Italian, and Russian, for example).

Another common sentence pattern is subject-verb-prepositional phrase. In standard English, the prepositional phrase typically follows the subject and verb.

■ For more on preposi-
tions, see pages 514–17.
For more on the parts
of sentences, see Chap-
ter 21.

```
   S     V    Prepositional phrase
   |     |    ┌──────────┴──────────┐
Lilah went to the movies.
```

PRACTICE 1   USING CORRECT WORD ORDER

Read each of the sentences that follow. If the sentence is correct, write "C" in the blank to the left of it. If it is incorrect, write "I" and rewrite the sentence using correct word order.

EXAMPLE: *I*   The ball to me Sara threw.

REVISION: _____ *Sara threw the ball to me.* _____

_____ 1. Sports Sara likes a lot.

REVISION: _____

■ For more practice with ESL grammar issues, visit Exercise Central at <bedfordstmartins.com/realessays>.

_____ 2. To baseball camp she went this spring.

REVISION: _____

_____ 3. At the camp, she met many other good players.

REVISION: _____

_____ 4. At the end of camp, she gave to the other players her address.

REVISION: _____

_____

_____ 5. With them she will try to stay in touch.

REVISION: _____

Negatives

To form a negative statement, use one of these words.

never	nobody	no one	nowhere
no	none	not	

SENTENCE	The store sells cigarettes.
NEGATIVE	The store ~~no~~ ^no^ sells cigarettes.
SENTENCE	Jonah talks too much.
NEGATIVE	Jonah ~~not~~ ^never^ talks too much.
SENTENCE	Johnetta will call.
NEGATIVE	Johnetta ~~no~~ ^not^ will call.

Notice in the last two sentences that the verb is *will call* (the helping verb *will* and the verb *call*). When using *not* to form a negative statement, *not* comes after the helping verb.

INCORRECT	My sister *no* is coming with us.
CORRECT	My sister is *not* coming with us.

[*Not* must come after the helping verb *is.*]

■ For more on helping verbs and their forms, see Chapter 21.

The helping verb cannot be omitted in expressions using *not.*

INCORRECT	The store *not sell* cigarettes.
CORRECT	The store *does not sell* cigarettes.

[*Does,* a form of the helping verb *do,* must come before *not.*]

CORRECT	The store *is not selling* cigarettes.

[*Is,* a form of *be,* must come before *not.*]

Common Helping Verbs

FORMS OF *BE*	FORMS OF *HAVE*	FORMS OF *DO*	OTHER VERBS
am	have	do	can
are	has	does	could
been	had	did	may
being			might
is			must
was			should
were			will

Double negatives are not standard in English.

Johnetta will ~~not~~ call no one.

                                   anybody.
Johnetta will not call ~~no one.~~

Questions

To turn a statement into a question, move the helping verb so that it comes before the subject. Add a question mark **(?)** to the end of the question.

STATEMENT	Danh *can work* late.
QUESTION	*Can* Danh *work* late?

If the only verb in the statement is a form of *be,* it should be moved before the subject.

STATEMENT	Phuong *is* smart.
QUESTION	*Is* Phuong smart?

If there is no helping verb or form of *be* in the statement, add a form of *do* and put it before the subject. Be sure to end the question with a question mark (**?**).

STATEMENT	Norah sings in the choir.
QUESTION	*Does* Norah sing in the choir?
STATEMENT	Amy visited the elderly woman.
QUESTION	*Did* Amy visit the elderly woman?

[Notice that the verb *visited* changed to *visit* once the helping verb *did* was added.]

■ For more on questions, see Chapter 24.

■ PRACTICE 2 CORRECTING PROBLEMS WITH NEGATIVES AND QUESTIONS

In the spaces provided, rewrite the following sentences to correct improperly formed negatives and questions.

EXAMPLE: Asking questions like "~~You do~~ smoke or drink?" is part of
every good doctor's job.
                              Do you

1. Sometimes, doctors will ask questions that seem odd, like "You do wear a seat belt?"

2. They no are being nosy; they just want a picture of your overall health.

3. For example, if you not wear a seat belt, you are more likely to be injured in a car accident.

4. Doctors not concerned with just your physical health.

5. They may also ask you questions like "You can think of a recent time when you have been depressed?"

6. If you show signs of depression, doctors no will ignore it; they might refer you to a mental-health specialist.

7. Not nobody feels happy all the time, but serious depression should be treated.

8. Of course, doctors will ask you the expected questions, such as "You do eat a balanced diet?" and "You can touch your toes?"

9. Don't be embarrassed if your answers not what you think the doctor will want to hear.

10. Finally, good doctors will always respect your privacy; they will not tell no one about the information you share with them.

There Is and *There Are*

English sentences often include *there is* or *there are* to indicate the existence of something.

> *There is* a man at the door.
>
> [You could also say, *A man is at the door.*]
>
> *There are* many men in the class.
>
> [You could also say, *Many men are in the class.*]

When a sentence includes the words *there is* or *there are,* the verb (*is, are*) comes before the noun it goes with. The verb must agree with the noun in number. For example, the first sentence above uses the singular verb *is* to agree with the singular noun *man,* and the second sentence uses the plural verb *are* to agree with the plural noun *men.*

The *there is/there are* structure does not exist in some other languages, such as Japanese and some forms of Spanish, and speakers of those languages sometimes leave out these words when writing in English.

INCORRECT	My mother said much work to do.
	Much work to do.

CORRECT	My mother said *there is* much work to do.

> *There is* much work to do.
>
> [*Is* is the verb that goes with the noun *work.*]

INCORRECT	I told the guard too many people in the room.
	Are too many people in the room.

CORRECT   I told the guard *there are* too many people in the room.

                There are too many people in the room.

                [*Are* is the verb that goes with the noun *people*.]

In questions, the word order in *there is* and *there are* is inverted.

STATEMENTS   *There is* plenty to eat.

                There are some things to do.

QUESTIONS   *Is there* plenty to eat?

                Are there some things to do?

■ PRACTICE 3   USING *THERE IS* AND *THERE ARE*

In each of the following sentences, fill in the blank with *there is* or *there are*. Remember that these words are inverted in questions.

     EXAMPLE: Although my parents are busy constantly, they say

       <u>there is</u> always more that can be done.

1. Every morning, _____ flowers to water and weeds to pull.

2. Later in the day, _____ more chores, like mowing the lawn or cleaning out the garage.

3. I always ask, "_____ anything I can do?"

4. They are too polite to say that _____ work that they need help with.

5. If _____ more productive parents in the world, I'd be surprised.

Articles

Articles indicate that a noun is coming up. English uses only three articles: *a, an,* and *the*. The same articles are used for both masculine and feminine nouns.

Using Definite and Indefinite Articles

The is a **definite article**, used before a specific person, place, or thing. *A* and *an* are **indefinite articles**, used with a person, place, or thing whose specific identity is not known; they are nonspecific.

DEFINITE ARTICLE   *The* man knocked on *the* door.

[This sentence suggests that the man and the door are already known to the writer and reader: A specific man and a specific door are meant.]

INDEFINITE ARTICLE   *A* man knocked on *a* door.

[The sentence suggests that a man unknown to the writer and reader knocked on a door.]

DEFINITE ARTICLE   *The* hostess showed us to our seats.

INDEFINITE ARTICLE   *A* hostess showed us to our seats.

When the word following the article begins with a vowel (*a, e, i, o, u*), use *an* instead of *a*.

An energetic hostess showed us to our seats.

PRACTICE 4   **CHOOSING BETWEEN DEFINITE AND INDEFINITE ARTICLES**

In each of the following sentences, circle the correct article in parentheses.

EXAMPLE: When we arrived at the Weary Traveler Hotel, we saw

((a)/ an / the) mysterious stranger in the lobby.

1. We had never been to (a / an / the) hotel before, and we didn't know what to expect.

2. (A / An / The) stranger certainly was a surprise, though.

3. He wore (a / an / the) dark coat, dark glasses, and (a / an / the) angora scarf that covered most of his face.

4. We approached (a / an / the) man slowly, uncertain of how he might react.

5. Just then, (a / an / the) black cat with white paws darted from a corner and ran across (a / an / the) floor in front of the man.

6. All of a sudden, he pulled (a / an / the) scarf from his face and cried, "Mittens! Where have you been?"

7. Mittens, apparently, was (a / an / the) cat's name.

8. He caught (a / an / the) cat and held it close, enjoying (a / an / the) soft purring sounds it made.

9. Then, he approached us, introduced himself as (a / an / the) owner of the hotel, and explained that he was just about to go out.

10. He gave us such (a / an / the) warm welcome that we laughed at our initial reaction to him.

Using Articles with Count and Noncount Nouns

To use the correct article, you need to know what count and noncount nouns are. **Count nouns** name things that can be counted. **Noncount nouns** name things that cannot be counted.

COUNT NOUN   I sold ten of the *CDs* at the yard sale.

NONCOUNT NOUN   I sold lots of *music* at the yard sale.

[A *CD* can be counted; *music* cannot.]

Here are some more examples of count and noncount nouns. This is just a brief list; all nouns in English are either count or noncount. Usually, the plural form of count nouns ends in -*s*.

COUNT	NONCOUNT		
apple/apples	beauty	honey	rain
tree/trees	flour	information	rice
chair/chairs	furniture	jewelry	salt
dollar/dollars	grass	mail	sand
letter/letters	grief	milk	spaghetti
smile/smiles	happiness	money	sunlight
	health	postage	thunder
	homework	poverty	wealth

Count nouns can be made plural. Generally, noncount nouns cannot be plural; they are usually singular.

COUNT/SINGLE   I got a *ticket* for the concert.

COUNT/PLURAL   I got two *tickets* for the concert.

NONCOUNT   The Internet has all kinds of *information*.

[You would not say, *The Internet has all kinds of informations.*]

Using A and An

A and *an,* as indefinite articles, are used with count nouns whose identity is unknown or unspecified (*A car pulled into the driveway*). *A* and *an* are also used with countable quantities of noncount nouns (*a bag of flour, a cup of rice*). The word *some* can also be used with indefinite amounts (*some rice, some furniture*).

When the word following the article begins with a vowel (*a, e, i, o, u*), use *an* instead of *a.*

Dom has *an i*dea for *a* vacation.

I need *a* card for *an u*ncle.

Gabriella got *an i*Pod as *a* gift.

Using The

The, as a definite article, is used with both count and noncount nouns whose identity is known or specified.

Please put *the* exam on my desk.

The flowers are beautiful.

Be sure to wipe off *the* sand from your feet.

Using No Article

No article is necessary when you are speaking of a category of noun in general. Again, you can use *some* when referring to indefinite amounts of something.

Friends are important.

Buddy loves *bones.*

Money isn't everything.

Dominick brought *some dessert.*

Use the chart that follows to determine when to use *a, an, the,* or no article.

Articles with Count and Noncount Nouns

COUNT NOUNS	ARTICLE USED
SINGULAR	
Identity known	*the*
	I want to read *the book* on taxes that you recommended.
	[The sentence refers to one particular book: the one that was recommended.]
	I can't stay in *the sun* very long.
	[There is only one sun.]
Identity not known	*a* or *an*
	I want to read *a book* on taxes.
	[It could be any book on taxes.]
PLURAL	
Identity known	*the*
	I enjoyed *the books* we read.
	[The sentence refers to a particular group of books: the ones we read.]
Identity not known or a general category	**no article** or *some*
	I usually enjoy *books*.
	[The sentence refers to books in general.]
	She found *some books*.
	[I don't know which books she found.]

NONCOUNT NOUNS	ARTICLE USED
SINGULAR	
Identity known	*the*
	I put away *the food* we bought.
	[The sentence refers to particular food: the food we bought.]
Identity not known or a general category	**no article** or *some*
	There is *food* all over the kitchen.
	[The reader doesn't know what food the sentence refers to.]
	Give *some food* to the neighbors.
	[The sentence refers to an indefinite quantity of food.]

PRACTICE 5   USING THE CORRECT ARTICLE WITH COUNT AND NONCOUNT NOUNS

Circle the correct article (or choose "no article") for each of the following sentences.

EXAMPLE: Just about everyone has used (a / an / the /(no article)) spices at one time or another, but not many people are aware of the long and interesting history of these additives.

1. Scientists believe that as long ago as 50,000 B.C., people were using spices to improve (a / an / the / no article) taste of food.

2. This first use might have been (a / an / the / no article) accident, occurring when someone wrapped meat in leaves before roasting it, to keep ash off of the flesh.

3. (A / An / The / no article) cook discovered that the leaves transferred a pleasant flavor to the meat.

4. In addition to flavoring foods, (a / an / the / no article) spices also became valued for their medicinal and deodorizing properties.

5. Eventually, spices became so prized—and expensive—that only (a / an / the / no article) richest people could afford them.

6. In fact, (a / an / the / no article) peppercorns were sometimes used as money in medieval times.

7. (A / An / The / no article) high cost of spices was partly the result of duties charged at major trading points in Asia and Europe.

8. Fortunately, we can now get just about any spice we want in the grocery store, at (a / an / the / no article) reasonable price.

9. Although (a / an / the / no article) spices are now used largely for flavoring, consumers have shown renewed interest in their medicinal properties.

10. Researchers have started to look into whether (a / an / the / no article) health benefits claimed for certain spices have any basis in fact.

PRACTICE 6   EDITING NOUNS AND ARTICLES

Edit the following paragraph, adding and changing articles and nouns as necessary.

EXAMPLE: Restaurant work is not an easy way to earn ~~the~~ money.

(1) I am waitress at the restaurant four days a week. (2) My shift is at lunchtimes, and it is usually very busy then. (3) There is a university close by, so the many college students eat at my restaurant because it serves cheap foods. (4) I am college student too; however, some of my student customers do not treat me as a equal. (5) They seem to think that it is okay to be rude to person serving them. (6) Many of them do not tip me well even though I am very good waitress and take good cares of my customers. (7) I do not make high salaries, so I need the tips from my customers to make good living. (8) I understand that college students are often pinching penny. (9) However, I think that peoples who cannot afford to leave tip should not eat in a restaurant.

Subjects

The **subject** of a sentence is the person, place, or thing the sentence is about. It is a noun, a pronoun (a word that substitutes for a noun), or a word or phrase that functions like a noun. Be sure to include a subject in every sentence and every dependent clause.

■ For more on dependent clauses, see pages 341–42.

Include a Subject for Each Verb

Some languages—Spanish, Italian, and Chinese, for example—can omit the subject of a verb because the verb form indicates the subject. In English, however, each sentence must have a subject.

It is
~~Is~~ hot outside.
^

Geraldo has
~~Has~~ a new car.
^

We enjoy
~~Enjoy~~ the beach.
^

Avoid Repeating the Subject

Do not use a pronoun to repeat the subject.

My father ~~he~~ did not graduate from high school.

The orange tree ~~it~~ died from the frost.

My sisters ~~they~~ went to the movies.

■ For more on sub-
jects and pronouns,
see Chapter 26.

 PRACTICE 7   EDITING FOR OMITTED AND REPEATED SUBJECTS

Edit the following paragraph, deleting repeated subjects and adding subjects as needed.

EXAMPLE: Gardening ~~it~~ isn't hard if you know some basics.

(1) The first thing to do ~~it~~ is to put the right plants in the right places. (2) Plants that need a lot of light ~~they~~ will not do well in the shade. (3) Also, is a good idea to test the soil before planting to make sure the plants will have enough of the right nutrients. (4) Inexpensive and easy-to-use home soil tests are available. (5) Come with charts that help amateur gardeners interpret the results. (6) After the test, can add any important nutrients that are missing. (7) Adding compost ~~it~~ is an especially good way to enrich the soil. (8) Throughout the growing season, keeping on top of the weeding ~~it~~ will help your plants stay healthy.

Verbs

Verbs tell what action the subject in a sentence performs or link the subject to a word that describes it.

■ For more on verbs, see Chapters 21, 24, and 25.

Using Gerunds or Infinitives after Verbs

A **gerund** is a verb form that ends in -*ing* and acts as a noun. An **infinitive** is a verb form that is preceded by the word *to*. Gerunds and infinitives cannot be the main verbs in sentences; each sentence must have another word that is the main verb.

■ For advice on verbs with prepositions, see page 514. For more on the position of verbs in questions, see page 500. For other problems with verbs, see Chapter 25.

GERUND   I like *running*.

[*Like* is the main verb, and *running* is a gerund.]

INFINITIVE   I like *to run*.

[*Like* is the main verb, and *to run* is an infinitive.]

How do you decide whether to use a gerund or an infinitive? The decision often depends on the main verb in a sentence. Some verbs can be followed by either a gerund or an infinitive.

■ To improve your ability to write and speak standard English, read magazines and your local newspaper, and listen to television and radio news programs. Also, read magazines and newspaper articles aloud; it will help your pronunciation.

Verbs That Are Followed by Either a Gerund or an Infinitive

begin	forget	like	remember	stop
continue	hate	love	start	try

Sometimes, using an infinitive or gerund after one of the verbs listed in the preceding box results in the same meaning.

GERUND   I love *listening* to Ray Charles and Norah Jones.

INFINITIVE   I love *to listen* to Ray Charles and Norah Jones.

Other times, however, the meaning changes depending on whether you use an infinitive or a gerund.

Mario stopped to smoke.

[This sentence means that Mario stopped what he was doing and smoked a cigarette.]

Mario stopped smoking.

[This sentence means that Mario no longer smokes cigarettes.]

Verbs That Are Followed by an Infinitive

agree	decide	need	refuse
ask	expect	offer	want
beg	fail	plan	
choose	hope	pretend	
claim	manage	promise	

Aunt Sally wants *to help.*

Cal hopes *to become* a millionaire.

Verbs That Are Followed by a Gerund

admit	discuss	keep	risk
avoid	enjoy	miss	suggest
consider	finish	practice	
deny	imagine	quit	

The politician risked *losing* her supporters.

Sophia often considers *quitting* her job.

Using the Progressive Tense

The **progressive tense** consists of a form of *be* followed by a verb with an *-ing* ending. It is used to indicate a continuing activity. Use the present progressive tense to indicate that an action is in progress now.

Lottie is ~~to be~~ learning to paint.

Our instructor is posting grades today.

The patient is ~~being~~ recovering rapidly.

Not all verbs can form the progressive tense. Certain verbs that indicate sensing or a state of being are not generally used this way.

> ## *Verbs That Usually Cannot Form the Progressive Tense*
>
> | | | | |
> |---|---|---|---|
> | appear | have | need | want |
> | believe | hear | see | weigh |
> | belong | know | seem | |
> | cost | like | taste | |
> | hate | mean | understand | |

■ For more on the progressive tense, see Chapter 25.

appears
The dog ~~is appearing~~ angry.
^

costs
That bag ~~is costing~~ too much.
^

■ PRACTICE 8   EDITING VERBS

Edit the following paragraph to make sure that the verbs are used correctly.

(1) Marlene and Agnetha wanted seeing a certain movie after they saw the advertisement for it in the newspaper. (2) David Manning, the reviewer who was quoted in the ad, was liking the film a lot. (3) The two women did not want to miss to see the film at their neighborhood theater, so they arranged their schedules carefully. (4) They managed attending the first show on Saturday afternoon. (5) After they were seeing the movie, they were very angry that they had wasted their time and money. (6) They were not understanding how the reviewer could have enjoyed to watch such a stupid film. (7) Then, Marlene read in a different newspaper that the movie studio had admitted to invent David Manning. (8) Every well-known film critic was hating the movie. (9) Therefore, the studio executives had decided publishing advertisements that contained a made-up quotation saying that the film was wonderful. (10) Marlene and

Agnetha were so disgusted by this deception that they planned to write to the head of the movie studio and ask getting their money back.

Prepositions

■ For more on prepositions, see Chapter 21. For a list of prepositions, see page 330.

A **preposition** is a word (such as *of, above, between, about*) that connects a noun, pronoun, or verb with other information about it. The correct preposition to use is often determined by idiom or common practice rather than by the preposition's actual meaning.

An **idiom** is any combination of words that is always used the same way, even though there is no logical or grammatical explanation for it. The best way to learn English idioms is to listen and read as much as possible and then to practice writing and speaking the correct forms.

Prepositions with Adjectives

Certain prepositions often follow certain adjectives. Here are some common examples:

afraid of	full of	responsible for
ashamed of	happy about	scared of
aware of	interested in	sorry about/sorry for
confused by	proud of	tired of
excited about	reminded of	

Tanya is excited *about* ~~of~~ going to Mexico.

However, she is afraid *of* ~~by~~ taking time off.

Prepositions with Verbs

Many verbs in English consist of a verb plus a preposition (or an adverb). The meaning of these combinations is not usually the literal meaning the verb and the preposition would each have on its own. Often, the meaning of the verb changes completely depending on which preposition is used with it.

You must *take out* the trash. [*take out* = bring to a different location]

You must *take in* the exciting sights of New York City. [*take in* = observe]

Here are a few common examples:

call off (cancel)	They *called off* the pool party.
call on (choose)	The teacher always *calls on* me.
drop in (visit)	*Drop in* when you are in the area.
fight against (combat)	He tried to *fight against* the proposal.
fight for (defend)	We need to *fight for* our rights.
fill in (refill)	Please *fill in* the holes in the ground.
fill out (complete)	Please *fill out* this application form.
fill up (make something full)	Don't *fill up* with junk food.
find out (discover)	Did you *find out* what happened?
give up (forfeit)	Don't *give up* your place in line.
go over (review)	He wants to *go over* our speeches.
grow up (mature)	All children *grow up*.
hand in (submit)	You may *hand in* your homework now.
lock up (secure)	Don't forget to *lock up* before you go to bed.
look up (check)	I *looked up* the word in the dictionary.
pick out (choose)	Sandy *picked out* a puppy.
pick up (take or collect)	When do you *pick up* the keys?
put off (postpone)	I often *put off* doing dishes.
sign up (register for)	Cressia *signed up* for three classes.

■ **PRACTICE 9   EDITING PREPOSITIONS**

Edit the following sentences to make sure that the correct prepositions are used.

EXAMPLE: Several U.S. presidents have said that they were sorry ~~of~~ ^for^

the mistreatment of Japanese Americans during World

War II.

1. During World War II, more than 120,000 Japanese Americans were locked

down in internment camps.

2. Many young Japanese Americans still chose to sign away for the U.S. military.

3. These soldiers often had to fight for prejudice as well as the enemy.

4. About eight hundred Japanese American soldiers gave in their lives during the fighting.

5. After the war, many Japanese Americans who had been interned were ashamed for their experience.

6. More than fifty years after the war, some Americans of Japanese descent became interested on creating a memorial to the Japanese Americans of the war years.

7. They wanted to make other Americans aware on the sacrifices of Japanese Americans during World War II.

8. A city full with memorials to the country's past, Washington, D.C., was chosen to be the site of the National Japanese American Memorial, unveiled in 2000.

9. For the center of the memorial park, the designers picked on a sculpture by a Japanese American artist, Nina Akamu, featuring two cranes tangled in barbed wire.

10. Visitors to the park are now reminded on Japanese Americans' struggle for acceptance in the United States.

PRACTICE 10   EDITING PREPOSITIONS

Edit the following paragraph to make sure that the correct prepositions are used.

(1) Students who are anxious on mathematics take fewer math classes and perform worse in them than students who do not have math anxiety.

(2) Scientists used to believe that students were afraid about math because they were not good at it, but that belief was incorrect. (3) It turns up that worry prevents students from understanding mathematics as well as they could. (4) Fear interferes in the working memory that is necessary for math, making students less able to think about math problems. (5) Starting on about the age of twelve, students with math anxiety become less able to compensate for the loss of working memory. (6) The good news is that effective treatment is available for math anxiety. (7) Students who once thought they would never be able to understand math may someday find up that they can conquer their anxiety and cope with numbers.

Adjectives

Adjectives describe nouns and pronouns. Many sentences have several adjectives that modify the same word.

■ For more on adjectives, see Chapter 27.

> The happy old brown dog slept on the sidewalk.
>
> They saw a very old rusty Ford truck in a ditch.

When you use more than one adjective to modify the same word, you should use the conventional order for adjectives in standard English. The list that follows indicates this order.

1. Judgment or overall opinion: *awful, friendly, intelligent, strange, terrible.*
2. Size: *big, huge, tiny, small, large, short, tall.*
3. Shape: *round, square, fat, thin, circular.*
4. Age: *old, young, new, youthful.*
5. Color: *blue, green, yellow, red.*
6. Nationality or location: *Greek, Italian, California, southern.*
7. Material: *paper, glass, plastic, wooden.*

EXAMPLE, ORDER OF ADJECTIVES

The (1) friendly (4) old (5) black terrier was chasing the squirrel.

I lost a (2) small (3) round (6) Italian (7) leather purse on the subway.

■ **PRACTICE 11   EDITING ADJECTIVES**

For each item, write a sentence using the noun listed and the adjectives in
parentheses. Be sure to put the adjectives in the correct order: judgment or
overall opinion, size, shape, age, color, nationality or location, and material.

> EXAMPLE: program (television, silly, black-and-white, old)
>
> *We watched a silly old black-and-white television program*
>
> *last night.*

1. handkerchief (faded, lace)

   _____

   _____

2. creature (green, frightening, Martian)

   _____

   _____

3. stairway (marble, massive, new)

   _____

   _____

4. classroom (cold, downstairs, little)

   _____

   _____

5. tomatoes (red, New Jersey, delicious)

   _____

   _____

Part Six
Word Use

33
Word Choice

Avoiding Language Pitfalls

Understand the Importance of Choosing Words Carefully

In conversation, much of your meaning is conveyed by your facial expression, your tone of voice, and your gestures. In writing, you have only the words on the page to make your point, so you must choose them carefully. If you use vague or inappropriate words, your readers may not understand you. Carefully chosen, precise words tell your readers exactly what you mean.

Two resources will help you find the best words for your meaning: a dictionary and a thesaurus.

Dictionary

You need a dictionary. For a very small investment, you can get a complete resource for all kinds of useful information about words: spelling, division of words into syllables, pronunciation, parts of speech, other forms of words, definitions, and examples of use.

The following is a part of a dictionary entry:

Spelling and end-of-line division

Pronunciation

Parts of speech

Other forms ——————

Definition ——————

Example ——————

con • crete (kon′ krēt, kong′- krēt, kon krēt′, kong- kret′), *adj., n., v.*
-cret • ed, -cret • ing, *adj.* **1.** constituting an actual thing or instance;
real; perceptible; substantial: *concrete proof.* **2.** pertaining to or concerned
with realities or actual instances rather than abstractions; particular as
opposed to general: *concrete proposals.* **3.** referring to an actual substance
or thing, as opposed to an abstract quality: The words *cat, water,* and
teacher are concrete, whereas the words *truth, excellence,* and *adulthood*
are abstract. . . .

—*Random House Webster's College Dictionary*

Thesaurus

■ To look up words
in both the dictionary
and the thesaurus on
the Web, visit Merriam-
Webster Online at
<**www.m-w.com**>.

A thesaurus gives *synonyms* (words that have the same meaning) for the
words you look up. Like dictionaries, thesauruses come in inexpensive and
even electronic editions. Use a thesaurus when you can't find the right
word for what you mean. Be careful, however, to choose a word that has
the precise meaning you intend. If you are not sure how a word should be
used, look it up in the dictionary.

> **Concrete,** *adj.* 1. Particular, specific, single, certain, special, unique,
> sole, peculiar, individual, separate, isolated, distinct, exact, precise,
> direct, strict, minute; definite, plain, evident, obvious; pointed, empha-
> sized; restrictive, limiting, limited, well-defined, clear-cut, fixed, finite;
> determining, conclusive, decided.
>
> —J. I. Rodale, *The Synonym Finder*

Practice Avoiding Four Common Word-Choice Problems

Four common problems with word choice can make it difficult for readers to understand your point. You can avoid them by using specific words
that fit your meaning and make your writing clearer.

Vague and Abstract Words

Your words need to create a clear picture for your readers. **Vague and abstract words** are too general to make an impression. Here are some common vague and abstract words.

Vague and Abstract Words			
a lot	dumb	nice	school
awful	good	OK (okay)	small
bad	great	old	thing
beautiful	happy	person	very
big	house	pretty	whatever
car	job	sad	young

When you see one of these words or another general word in your writing, try to replace it with a concrete or more specific word. A **concrete word** names something that can be seen, heard, felt, tasted, or smelled. A **specific word** names a particular individual or quality. Compare these two sentences:

VAGUE AND ABSTRACT   It was a beautiful day.

CONCRETE AND SPECIFIC   The sky was a bright, cloudless blue; the sun was shimmering; and the temperature was a perfect 78 degrees.

The first version is too general to be interesting. The second version creates a clear, strong image.

Some words are so vague that it is best to avoid them altogether.

VAGUE AND ABSTRACT   It's like *whatever*.

[This sentence is neither concrete nor specific.]

PRACTICE 1 AVOIDING VAGUE AND ABSTRACT WORDS

In the following sentences, underline any words that are vague or abstract. Then, edit each sentence by replacing any vague or abstract words with concrete, specific ones. You may invent any details you like.

■ For more practice with word choice, visit Exercise Central at <bedfordstmartins .com/realessays>.

EXAMPLE: My ~~relatives are weird.~~   *cousin Jonathan collects teeth, and my aunt Farielle has the world's loudest laugh.*

1. My little sister is a good girl.

2. Both of my parents work a lot, so I babysit pretty often.

3. My sister and I have fun.

4. Our relatives visit very frequently.

5. My grandmother is the nicest person I know.

6. She likes to cook things that remind her of home.

7. One of my uncles is a little crazy.

8. He does dumb things to get my attention.

9. He treats me as if I were very young.

10. I guess he is just happy to see me.

Slang

Slang is informal and casual language shared by a particular group. Slang should be used only in informal and casual situations. Avoid it when you write, especially for college classes or at work. Use language that is appropriate for your audience and purpose.

SLANG	EDITED
I prefer to *chill* at home.	I prefer to relax at home.
I *dumped* Destina.	I told Destina that I did not want to continue our relationship.
You have to give Jill her *props* for that speech.	Jill deserves recognition for that speech.

PRACTICE 2   AVOIDING SLANG

In the following sentences, underline any slang words. Then, edit the sentences by replacing the slang with language appropriate for a formal audience and purpose. Imagine that you are writing to a supervisor at work.

EXAMPLE: The company's offer of paid paternity leave to full-time

employees is ~~way cool.~~ *generous*

1. I wanted to express my appreciation for the fab new benefits package.

2. If I didn't have insurance through the company, the premiums would really put the hurt on my paycheck.

3. Now that my wife and I are starting a family, insurance is a biggie.

4. I am planning to take two weeks of paternity leave in October when our rug rat arrives.

5. Without the company paying for this leave, I would no way be able to afford the time off.

6. Doing the quality-time thing is very important to me.

7. I know that adjusting to fatherhood will not be cake.

8. We are both mad grateful that the company is rewarding its employees in this way.

9. If I can do anything to make my absence easier on my coworkers, please give me a shout.

10. This new company policy really is all that, and my family and I thank you.

Wordy Language

Sometimes people think that using more words, or using big words, will make them sound smart and important. But using too many words in a piece of writing can obscure or weaken the point.

Wordy language includes phrases that contain too many words, unnecessarily modify a statement, or use slightly different words without adding any new ideas. It also includes overblown language: unnecessarily complicated words and phrases, often used to make the writer or writing sound important.

WORDY   We have no openings *at this point in time.*

EDITED   We have no openings now.

[The phrase *at this point in time* uses five words to express what could be said in one word: *now.*]

WORDY   *In the opinion of this writer,* tuition is too high.

EDITED   Tuition is too high.

[The qualifying phrase *in the opinion of this writer* is not necessary and weakens the statement.]

WORDY   In our advertising, we will *utilize* the *superlative photographic images* of ArtSense.

EDITED   Our advertising will use ArtSense photographs.

[The words *utilize* and *superlative photographic images* are overblown.]

Common Wordy Expressions

WORDY	EDITED
As a result of	Because
Due to the fact that	Because
In spite of the fact that	Although
It is my opinion that	I think (or just make the point)
In the event that	If
The fact of the matter is that	(Just state the point.)
A great number of	Many
At that time	Then
In this day and age	Now
At this point in time	Now
In this paper I will show that	(Just make the point; don't announce it.)

 PRACTICE 3   AVOIDING WORDY LANGUAGE

In the following sentences, underline the wordy language. Then, edit each sentence to make it more concise.

All
EXAMPLE: ~~The fact of the matter is that all~~ drivers get angry sometimes, but nobody has ever heard of a car getting angry.

1. At this point in time, that may be changing, thanks to four Japanese inventors.

2. They are the people who have recently patented a car that can look angry
and appear to cry, laugh, or wink.

3. The patent application describes a car with an antenna that wags, headlights that become dimmer and then grow brighter in an expressive fashion, and ornaments that look like eyebrows, eyelids, and tears.

4. The car would seem to be "sleeping" at the point in time in which its
headlights, or eyes, are closed, and the antenna is limp.

5. In order to have the vehicle express anger, the car's hood would glow red
as the eyebrows light up.

6. The operator of the motor vehicle would be able to make the car "wink"
by dimming one headlight and vibrating the antenna.

7. In the event that the driver wants the car to "cry," he or she could make
the hood dark blue, shade the headlights, and show a blinking "tear" light.

8. The inventors believe that orange is the best color to show happiness and
that red is the best color for anger, in spite of the fact that others may disagree.

9. The inventors say that their ideas could be applied not just to cars but
could also be taken advantage of for motorcycles, ships, or aircraft.

10. Critics of the expressive car have put forward the opinion that it might be
too distracting to other drivers.

Clichés

Clichés are phrases used so often that people no longer pay attention to them. To get your point across and to get your readers' attention, replace clichés with fresh language that precisely expresses your meaning.

CLICHÉS	EDITED
Passing the state police exam is no *walk in the park*.	Passing the state police exam requires careful preparation.
I was *sweating bullets* until the grades were posted.	I was anxious until the grades were posted.

COMMON CLICHÉS

as big as a house	last but not least
as hard as a rock	no way on earth
as light as a feather	110 percent
the best/worst of times	playing with fire
better late than never	spoiled brat
break the ice	spoiled rotten
climb the corporate ladder	starting from scratch
crystal clear	sweating blood/bullets
a drop in the bucket	work like a dog
easier said than done	worked his/her way up
hell on earth	

◼ PRACTICE 4   AVOIDING CLICHÉS

In the following sentences, underline the clichés. Then, edit each sentence by replacing the clichés with fresh, precise language.

EXAMPLE: Keeping children safe is ~~easier said than done.~~
                                   a challenging task.

1. People with young children need eyes in the back of their heads.

2. Children can put themselves in danger faster than lightning.

3. Parents of a toddler should have their heads examined if they do not lock cabinets containing household chemicals.

4. Toddlers grow by leaps and bounds, and new levels of childproofing must be done as children learn to climb gates and open doors.

5. Parents sometimes recognize dangers in the nick of time and stop their children from injuring themselves.

6. When their children play at another child's house, some parents may worry that the other parents will not keep an eagle eye on their youngsters.

7. Parents have mortal fears of their young children running into traffic to chase a ball.

8. A swimming pool can be a deathtrap unless it is surrounded by a high fence with a locked gate.

9. Children must be taught that if they find a gun in someone's home, they should keep their hands to themselves and they should leave the area immediately.

10. Someday, young children will be old enough to be independent, but their independence can also drive parents out of their minds with worry.

Edit Paragraphs and Your Own Writing

Edit the following paragraphs for vague and abstract language, slang, wordiness, or clichés, referring to the chart on page 531 as you need to.

■ EDITING REVIEW

(1) Being the big kahuna at a major American corporation almost always pays extremely well. (2) CEOs earn millions of dollars each and every year, and most also get stock options. (3) Even if the company goes off the rails and the CEO gets fired, he (and it is almost always a guy

thing) often gets a severance package that is worth additional millions. (4) A CEO's salary in the United States is usually several hundred times larger than the average that is paid for a company worker's wages. (5) This ratio is pretty big compared with the ratios in other industrialized countries. (6) In Japan, for example, a CEO's salary maxes out at about ten times that of a worker. (7) Are American CEOs really that great? (8) Are they, in actual fact, worth what they are paid?

(9) The fact of the matter is that highly paid CEOs can rarely do what corporate directors hope. (10) They may have earned sky-high profits at a previous corporation, but every business is different. (11) There is no guarantee that these men will be able to keep up the good work. (12) If a company promoted a worker from within, he or she probably would not only know the biz inside and out but also work for fewer bucks than a hired gun from outside. (13) Then, the corporation would be ahead of the game to the tune of a few million dollars. (14) Why, then, are corporations willing to pay a lot of money to recruit expensive outsiders as CEOs?

(15) The problem with promoting a CEO from within the company is the fact that few companies want to take risks. (16) For a decade or more, hiring a CEO has meant finding the CEO of another company and paying him enough to get him to jump ship. (17) Company directors think that their stockholders have the expectation that the company will bring in a highly paid outsider. (18) The directors are freaked out by the idea that an insider might fail and disappoint stockholders. (19) Of course, most CEOs brought in from elsewhere also end up in the dumpster, but the corporate boards can at least reassure themselves that their choice has a track record when he arrives. (20) Corporations claim to want leaders who can think outside the box. (21) However, there are few corporate

boards of directors who are willing to look anywhere other than conventional places for their next leaders. (22) This conventional thinking will eventually be lousy for business; perhaps only then will the trend toward hiring expensive CEOs change.

PRACTICE 5   EDITING YOUR OWN WRITING FOR WORD CHOICE

As a final practice, edit a piece of your own writing for word choice. It can be a paper you are working on for this course, a paper you've already finished, a paper for another course, or a recent piece of writing from your work or everyday life. You may want to use the following chart as you edit.

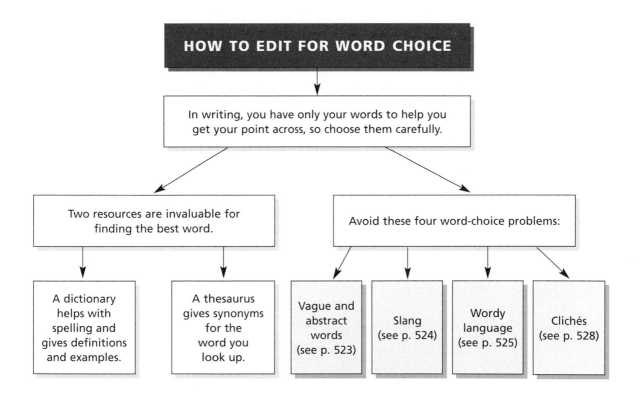

HOW TO EDIT FOR WORD CHOICE

In writing, you have only your words to help you get your point across, so choose them carefully.

Two resources are invaluable for finding the best word.

A dictionary helps with spelling and gives definitions and examples.

A thesaurus gives synonyms for the word you look up.

Avoid these four word-choice problems:

Vague and abstract words (see p. 523)

Slang (see p. 524)

Wordy language (see p. 525)

Clichés (see p. 528)

34

Commonly Confused Words

Avoiding Mistakes with Sound-Alikes

Understand Why Certain Words Are Commonly Confused

■ To understand this chapter, you need to know what nouns, verbs, adjectives, and adverbs are. For a review, see Chapters 21, 25, and 27.

Certain words in English are confusing because they sound alike and may have similar meanings. In writing, words that sound alike may be spelled differently, and readers rely on the spelling to understand what you mean. Edit your writing carefully to make sure that you have used the correct words.

STRATEGIES FOR EDITING SOUND-ALIKES

1. Proofread carefully, using the techniques discussed on page 547.

2. Use a dictionary to look up any words you are unsure of.

3. Focus on finding and correcting mistakes you make with the twenty-seven sets of commonly confused words covered in this chapter.

4. Develop a personal list of sound-alikes that confuse you. Before you turn in any piece of writing, consult your personal list to make sure you have used the correct words.

Practice Using Commonly Confused Words Correctly

Study the different meanings and spellings of these twenty-seven sets of commonly confused words. Complete the sentence after each set of words, filling in each blank with the correct word.

A /An /And

a: used before a word that begins with a consonant sound

A bat was living behind the shutter.

an: used before a word that begins with a vowel sound

An elderly lady sat beside me.

and: used to join two words

My sister *and* I went to the amuscment park.

A friend *and* I got lost in *an* old maze.

Most classrooms have _____ worn-out chair _____ _____ old desk for the teacher.

Accept/Except

accept: to agree to receive or admit (verb)

I plan to *accept* the offer.

except: but, other than (conjunction)

The whole family was there *except* my brother.

I *accept* all your requests *except* the one to borrow my car.

Do not _____ anything from people at airports _____ from family members.

Advice /Advise

advice: opinion (noun)

I would like your *advice* on this decision.

advise: to give an opinion (verb)

My boyfriend *advises* me about car repairs.

Please *advise* me what to do; your *advice* is always helpful.

_____ me of your plans, particularly if you don't follow my _____ .

Affect / Effect

affect: to have an impact on, to change something (verb)

>   The whole region was *affected* by the drought.

effect: a result (noun)

>   The lack of water will have a tremendous *effect* on many businesses.

The sunny weather has had a positive *effect* on people's moods, but it will negatively *affect* the economy.

Since this year's drought will _____ the cost of food, we'll be feeling

its _____ personally.

Are / Our

are: a form of the verb *be*

>   The flowers *are* ready to bloom.

our: a pronoun showing ownership

>   I am proud of *our* garden.

Gardens *are* rare in *our* neighborhood.

_____ bulbs _____ arriving this week.

By / Buy

by: next to or before

>   I'll be standing *by* the door.
>   We have to be at the restaurant *by* eight o'clock.

buy: to purchase (verb)

>   I would like to *buy* a new car.

By the time I'm ready to leave the dollar store, I have found too much I want to *buy*.

I have decided to _____ the model _____ the showroom entrance.

Conscience / Conscious

■ Remember that one of the words is *con-science;* the other is not.

conscience: a personal sense of right and wrong (noun)

>   My *conscience* keeps me from doing bad things.

conscious: awake, aware (adjective)

The patient is now *conscious*.

Shelly was *conscious* of Sam's feelings.

Danny made a *conscious* decision to listen to his *conscience*.

The burglar was _____ that someone else was in the house and

for a moment felt a twinge of _____.

■ Some commonly confused words—such as *conscience* and *conscious*, *loose* and *lose*, and *of* and *have*— sound similar but not exactly alike. To avoid confusing these words, practice pronouncing them correctly.

Fine/Find

fine: of high quality (adjective); feeling well (adverb); a penalty for breaking a law (noun)

She works in the *fine* jewelry department.

After taking some aspirin, Shana felt *fine*.

The *fine* for exceeding the speed limit is $100.

find: to locate, discover (verb)

Can you help me *find* the key?

You will *find* a *fine* leather jacket in the coat department.

A _____ partner is hard to _____.

Its/It's

its: a pronoun showing ownership

The bird went back to *its* nest.

it's: a contraction of the words *it is*

It's important for you to be on time.

It's amazing to see a butterfly come out of *its* cocoon.

_____ good news for us that the bus changed _____ route.

■ If you are not sure whether to use *its* or *it's* in a sentence, try substituting *it is*. If the sentence doesn't make sense with *it is*, use *its*.

Knew/New/Know/No

knew: understood; recognized (past tense of the verb *know*)

I *knew* we took the wrong turn.

new: unused, recent (adjective)

Jane has a *new* boyfriend.

know: to understand, to have knowledge of (verb)

I *know* him from work.

no: used to form a negative

There are *no* other classes at that time.

I *knew* that Jason would need *new* shoes.

The _____ employee already _____ some of the other employees.

There is *no* way to *know* what will happen.

Do you _____ what _____ means?

Loose/Lose

loose: baggy, not fixed in place (adjective)

That button is *loose*.

lose: to misplace, to forfeit possession of (verb)

I don't want to *lose* my job.

If the muffler is *loose,* you might *lose* it.

You will _____ that bracelet if it's too _____.

Mind/Mine

mind: to object to (verb); the thinking or feeling part of one's brain (noun)

I don't *mind* loud music.

Sometimes I think I am losing my *mind*.

mine: belonging to me (pronoun); a source of ore and minerals (noun)

That parking space is *mine*.

That store is a gold *mine*.

Keep in *mind* that the sweater is *mine*.

Your _____ is a lot sharper than _____.

Of/Have

of: coming from; caused by; part of a group; made from (preposition)

The president *of* the company pleaded guilty to embezzlement.

have: to possess (verb; also used as a helping verb)

> Do you *have* a schedule?

> Jeannie should *have* been here by now.

■ Do not use *of* after *would, should, could,* and *might.* Use *have* after those words.

I would *have* helped if you had told me you were out *of* change.

Joe might _____ been part _____ the band.

Passed/Past

passed: went by or went ahead (past tense of the verb *pass*)

> Tim *passed* us a minute ago.

past: time that has gone by (noun); gone by, over, just beyond (preposition)

> The school is just *past* the traffic light.

This *past* school year, I *passed* all of my exams.

If you go _____ the church, you have _____ the right turn.

Peace/Piece

peace: no disagreement; calm

> The sleeping infant is at *peace*.

piece: a part of something larger

> May I have a *piece* of paper?

We will have no *peace* until we give the dog a *piece* of that bread.

Selling his _____ of land will give Uncle Joe _____ of mind.

Principal/Principle

principal: main or chief (adjective); head of a school or a leader of an organization (noun)

> Making sales calls is your *principal* responsibility.

> Darla is a *principal* of the company.

> Mr. Tucker is the *principal* of the Sawyer School.

principle: a standard of beliefs or behaviors (noun)

> The issue is really a matter of *principle*.

The *principle* at stake is the *principal* issue of the court case.

The _____ problem with many criminals is that they do not have

good _____.

Quiet/Quite/Quit

quiet: soft in sound; not noisy (adjective)
> The library was very *quiet.*

quite: completely, very (adverb)
> I have had *quite* enough to eat after that half-pounder and fries.

quit: to stop (verb)
> Will you please *quit* bothering me?

It is not *quite* time to *quit* yet.

The machine _____ running, and the office was _____.

Right/Write

right: correct; in a direction opposite from left (adjective)
> Are you sure this is the *right* way?
> Take a *right* after the bridge.

write: to put words on paper (verb)
> I will *write* soon.

Please be sure to *write* the *right* address.

_____ your name in the _____ column.

Set/Sit

set: a collection of something (noun); to place an object somewhere (verb)
> Junior has a great train *set.*
> Please *set* the package on the table.

sit: to rest with one's rear end supported by a chair or other surface
> You can *sit* right over there.

Set your coat down before you *sit.*

Let's _____ and look over my _____ of travel photos.

Suppose/Supposed

suppose: to imagine or assume to be true

Suppose you could go anywhere in the world.

I *suppose* you want some dinner.

supposed: past tense of *suppose;* intended

The clerk *supposed* the man was over twenty-one.

The meeting was *supposed* to be over by noon.

You are *supposed* to call when you are going to be late, but I *suppose* that's too much to expect.

I was _____ to take the ten o'clock train, but I _____ the eleven o'clock is okay.

Than/Then

than: a word used to compare two or more things or persons

Joanne makes more money *than* I do.

then: at a certain time

I will look forward to seeing you *then.*

I weigh a lot more *than* I used to back *then.*

If you want to lose weight, _____ you will have to eat less _____ you do now.

Their/There/They're

their: a pronoun showing ownership

Their new apartment has two bedrooms.

there: a word indicating location or existence

Your desk is over *there.*

There is more work than I can handle.

they're: a contraction of the words *they are*

They're going to Hawaii.

Their windows are open, and *there* is a breeze, so *they're* not hot.

_____ going to be away, so my friend will be staying _____ and taking care of _____ cat.

■ If you aren't sure whether to use *their* or *they're*, substitute *they are.* If the sentence doesn't make sense, use *their.*

Though/Through/Threw

though: however; nevertheless; in spite of (conjunction)

I'll be there, *though* I might be a little late.

through: finished with (adjective); from one side to the other (preposition)

Jenna is *through* with school in May.

Go *through* the first set of doors.

threw: hurled, tossed (past tense of the verb *throw*)

She *threw* away the garbage.

Jimmy *threw* the ball, and it went *through* the window, *though* he had not aimed it there.

_____ she loved him, she _____ him out because she couldn't

go _____ any more pain.

To/Too/Two

to: a word indicating a direction or movement (preposition); part of the infinitive form of a verb

I am going *to* the food store.

Do you want *to* see a movie?

too: also; more than enough; very (adverb)

Toni was sick *too.*

The car was going *too* fast.

two: the number between one and three

There are *two* tables.

They went *to* a restaurant and ordered *too* much food for *two* people.

The _____ friends started _____ dance, but it was _____ crowded

to move.

Use/Used

use: to employ or put into service (verb)

I *use* this grill all the time.

used: past tense of the verb *use. Used to* can indicate a past fact or state, or it can mean "familiar with."

I *used* the grill last night to cook chicken.

I *used* to do yoga.

I am *used* to juggling school and work.

Paolo *used* to be a farmer, so he knows how to *use* all the equipment.

When you last _____ the oven, what did you _____ it for?

Who's/Whose

who's: a contraction of the words *who is* or *who has*

Who's hungry?

Who's been here the longest?

whose: a pronoun showing ownership

Whose bag is this?

The person *whose* name is first on the list is the one *who's* going next.

_____ the man _____ shoes are on the table?

■ If you aren't sure whether to use *whose* or *who's*, substitute *who is*. If the sentence doesn't make sense, use *whose*.

Your/You're

your: a pronoun showing ownership

I like *your* shirt.

you're: a contraction of the words *you are*

You're going to run out of gas.

You're about to get paint all over *your* hands.

_____ teacher says _____ always late to class.

■ If you aren't sure of whether to use *your* or *you're*, substitute *you are*. If the sentence doesn't make sense, use *your*.

■ **PRACTICE 1   USING THE RIGHT WORD**

In each of the following items, circle the correct word in parentheses.

EXAMPLE: (You're /(Your)) résumé is a critical computer file.

1. I tell all my friends to back up important data on (their / there) computers.

2. Unfortunately, I sometimes forget to take my own (advice / advise).

3. My computer had a serious crash, and now I cannot (find / fine) the most recent copy of my résumé.

4. I should (have / of) made a hard copy and a backup on a disk, but I didn't.

5. Today I have (a / an / and) interview for a job I really want, and I can't locate any résumés (accept / except) one from 2003.

6. (Loosing / Losing) a résumé is not the end of the world, but it will be (quiet / quite) a job reconstructing it.

7. It took me hours to (right / write) and proofread my most recent résumé.

8. This morning, I quickly (set / sit) down some information to give to the interviewer, but this version is sloppier (than / then) the résumé I (use / used) to have.

9. (Though / Through) I believe that I am well qualified for this job, I'm afraid that this résumé may have a bad (affect / effect) on my chances of being hired.

10. An interviewer (who's / whose) task is to hire the best person must pay attention (to / too / two) small details.

■ For more practice with commonly confused words, visit Exercise Central at <bedfordstmartins .com/realessays>.

Edit Paragraphs and Your Own Writing

Edit the following paragraphs for commonly confused words.

■ EDITING REVIEW 1

(1) Most people no that Americans love to drive there cars. (2) However, many people may not be conscience of how much the government does to support our car culture. (3) For instance, the United States would never of had so many good highways without federal and state assistance for road construction and maintenance. (4) New highways are usually

paid for mainly buy tax money. (5) It is rare for a new road too be paid for with tolls, which would come exclusively from the people driving on it. (6) Americans also expect they're roads to be well maintained, and they may right to their representatives to complain about potholes and aging road surfaces. (7) The government is even responsible for keeping gas prices lower here then in most other industrialized nations.

(8) Few people mine that the government assists drivers in these ways. (9) Some would argue that its a government's job to help pay for transportation. (10) However, other forms of transportation in this country are often past over when Congress hands out funds. (11) Amtrak, the U.S. railroad, may soon loose virtually all government funds, even though many government officials are skeptical of it's ability to keep operating without government assistance. (12) Accept for a few places like New York and San Francisco, most U.S. cities do not have good mass transit systems. (13) Americans who's travels have taken them to certain parts of the world praise the national train systems and city transit systems they find there. (14) As traffic gets worse in our nation's urban and suburban areas, some people fine it odd that the United States does not invest more in transportation that would allow people to leave there cars at home.

EDITING REVIEW 2

(1) Hoping to keep are nation's blood supply safe, the U.S. government has placed restrictions on donating blood. (2) Anyone whose spent more than five years in Europe or more than three months in England since 1980 is not allowed to give blood. (3) Officials hope that asking about time in Europe will help them fine people who might of been exposed to mad cow disease. (4) Men are also asked whether they have had

sexual relations with other men in the passed ten years. (5) If they have, their asked not to give blood. (6) This is suppose to protect the blood supply from the AIDS virus. (7) Of course, they're are some problems with these restrictions. (8) First, know one knows how much exposure to infected meat can give a person mad cow disease, and know one is sure how long the disease can hide in a human body. (9) Second, many gay men our not infected with HIV, and many women, who are not asked about sexual activity, are infected. (10) Restricting certain groups of people from giving blood may not do anything to protect the blood supply, but it will certainly effect the amount of blood available. (11) Is it better to allow the blood supply to become dangerously low then to allow people who's blood might carry a disease to donate blood?

■ PRACTICE 2 EDITING YOUR OWN WRITING FOR COMMONLY CONFUSED WORDS

As a final practice, edit a piece of your own writing for commonly confused words. It can be a paper you are working on for this course, a paper you've already finished, a paper for another course, or a recent piece of writing from your work or everyday life. Add any misused words you find to your personal list of confusing words.

35

Spelling

Using the Right Letters

Spelling errors are the fifth most serious writing error identified by teachers in the United States. Because spell checkers cannot find every mistake, it is important to proofread your writing for spelling errors.

Understand the Importance of Spelling Correctly

Unfortunately, spelling errors are easy for readers to spot, and they make a bad impression. Fortunately, practice greatly improves spelling.

Read the following paragraph, the body of a follow-up letter one student wrote to a prospective employer after an interview:

> Thank you for the oportunity to meet about the summer internship at Margate Associates. I hope you will find that my coursework in graphic design and my excellant communication skills make me a promiseing candidate for the position. I look forward to hearing from you soon. I am happy to provide you with referances if you need them.

PRACTICE 1   FINDING SPELLING ERRORS

■ For more spelling
practice, visit Exer-
cise Central at
**<bedfordstmartins
.com/realessays>**.

Underline the four spelling errors in the preceding paragraph. In the space
provided, write the correct spelling of each word.

_____

If you are serious about improving your spelling, you need to have a
dictionary and a spelling list (a list of words you often misspell)—and you
need to use them.

A **dictionary** contains the correct spellings of words, along with information on how they are pronounced, what they mean, and where they
came from. When proofreading your papers, use a current dictionary either in print or online. The following are two popular online dictionaries:

- Merriam-Webster Online at **<www.m-w.com>**. This dictionary has a
  wildcard search feature. If you are fairly sure how the beginning of a
  word is spelled, you can enter those letters and then an asterisk (*) and
  get a list of the words that begin with the letters. From the list, you can
  choose the word you want.

- Your Dictionary at **<www.yourdictionary.com>**. This site features
  specialty dictionaries for business, computers, law, medicine, and other
  fields.

■ For a sample dic-
tionary entry, see
page 522.

If you have trouble finding words in a regular dictionary, get a spelling
dictionary, which is designed to help you find a word even if you have no
idea how to spell it. Checking a dictionary is the single most important
thing you can do to improve your spelling.

Keeping a **spelling list** will help you edit your papers and learn how
to write the words correctly. From this list of words you often misspell,
identify your personal spelling "demons"—the five to ten words that you
misspell most frequently. Write these words, spelled correctly, on an index
card, and keep the card somewhere handy so that you can consult it whenever you write.

Practice Spelling Correctly

Don't try to correct your grammar, improve your message, and check your
spelling at the same time. Instead, do separate proofreading passes for
each editing task. Remember to check the dictionary whenever you are unsure about the spelling of a word and to add all the spelling mistakes you
find to your personal spelling list.

Most word-processing programs have a **spell checker** that finds and
highlights a word that may be misspelled and suggests other spellings. Use

this feature after you have completed a piece of writing but before you print it out.

However, no spell checker can catch every mistake. A spell checker ignores anything it recognizes as a word, so it will not help you find words that are misused or misspellings that are also words. For example, a spell checker would not highlight any of the problems in the following phrases:

Just to it.	(Correct: Just do it.)
The strap is lose.	(Correct: The strap is loose)
my writing coarse	(Correct: my writing course)

Use some of the following **proofreading techniques** to focus on the spelling of one word at a time. Different techniques work for different people, so try them all and then decide which ones work for you.

- Put a piece of paper or a ruler under the line you are reading.
- Cut a "window" in an index card that is about the size of a long word (such as *misunderstanding*), and place it over your writing to focus on one word or phrase at a time.
- Proofread your paper backward, one word at a time.
- If you are using a computer, print out a version of your paper that looks noticeably different: Make the words larger, make the margins larger, triple-space the lines, or do all of these. Read this version carefully.
- Read your paper aloud. This strategy will help you if you tend to leave words out.
- Exchange papers with a partner for proofreading. Your only task as you proofread your partner's paper should be to identify possible misspellings. The writer of the paper should be responsible for checking the words you have identified and correcting any that are actually misspelled.

After you proofread each word in your paper, look at your personal spelling list and your list of demon words one more time. If you used any of these words in your paper, go back and check their spelling again. You may be surprised to find that you missed seeing the same old spelling mistakes. Most word-processing programs allow you to search for specific words using Find or Search commands from the Edit menu.

PRACTICE 2   FINDING AND CORRECTING SPELLING MISTAKES

Take the last paper you wrote—or one that you are working on now—and find and correct any spelling errors using the tools discussed previously: a dictionary, your personal spelling list, proofreading techniques, and a spell checker. How many spelling mistakes did you find? Were you surprised? How was the experience different from what you normally do to edit for spelling?

Five Steps to Better Spelling

Learning to find and correct spelling mistakes that you have already made is only half the battle. You also need to become a better speller so that you do not make so many mistakes in the first place. Here are five ways to do so.

Step 1. Master Ten Troublemakers

The ten words on the following list were identified by writing teachers as the words most commonly misspelled. Because there are only ten, you should be able to memorize them.

INCORRECT	CORRECT
alot	a lot
arguement	argument
definate, defenite	definite
develope	develop
lite	light
necesary, nesesary	necessary
recieve	receive
seperate	separate
surprize, suprise	surprise
untill	until

Step 2. Master Your Personal Spelling Demons

Once you know what your personal spelling demons are, you can master them. Try some of the following techniques.

- Create a memory aid—an explanation or saying that will remind you of the correct spelling. For example, "*surprise* is no *prize*" may remind you to spell *surprise* with an *s,* not a *z.*
- Break the word into parts, and try to master each part. You can break it into syllables (*Feb ru ar y*) or separate the prefixes and endings (*dis appoint ment*).
- Write the word correctly ten times.
- Write a paragraph in which you use the word at least three times.
- Say the letters of the word out loud. See if there's a rhythm or a rhyme you can memorize.

- Say the whole word out loud, emphasizing each letter and syllable even if that's not the way you normally say it. For example, say *prob a bly* instead of *prob ly*. Try to pronounce the word this way in your head each time you spell it.
- Ask a partner to give you a spelling test.

Step 3. Master Commonly Confused Words

Refer back to Chapter 34, which covers twenty-seven sets of words that are commonly confused because they sound alike, such as *write/right* and *its/it's*. If you can master these commonly confused words, you will avoid many spelling mistakes.

Step 4. Learn Six Spelling Rules

If you can remember the rules, you can avoid or correct many of the spelling errors in your writing.

Before the six rules, here is a quick review of vowels and consonants.

Vowels: a e i o u

Consonants: b c d f g h j k l m n p q r s t v w x y z

Consonants are all the letters that are not vowels. The letter *y* can be either a vowel or a consonant. It is a vowel when it sounds like the *y* in *fly* or *hungry*. It is a consonant when it sounds like the *y* in *yellow*.

Rule 1.   *I* before *e*
Except after *c*.
Or when sounded like *a*
As in *neighbor* or *weigh*.

Many people repeat this rhyme to themselves as they decide whether a word is spelled with an *ie* or an *ei*.

piece (*i* before *e*)

receive (except after *c*)

eight (sounds like *a*)

EXCEPTIONS: either, neither, foreign, height, seize, society, their, weird

Rule 2.   Drop the final *e* when adding an ending that begins with a vowel.

hop**e** + ing = hoping

imagin**e** + ation = imagination

Keep the final *e* when adding an ending that begins with a consonant.

> achieve + ment = achievement
>
> definite + ly = definitely

> **EXCEPTIONS:** argument, awful, simply, truly (and others)

Rule 3.   When adding an ending to a word that ends in *y*, change the *y* to *i* when a consonant comes before the *y*.

> lonely + est = loneliest
>
> happy + er = happier
>
> apology + ize = apologize
>
> likely + hood = likelihood

Do not change the *y* when a vowel comes before the *y*.

> boy + ish = boyish
>
> pay + ment = payment
>
> survey + or = surveyor
>
> buy + er = buyer

> **EXCEPTIONS:** 1. When adding *-ing* to a word ending in *y*, always keep the *y*, even if a consonant comes before it: study + ing = studying.
>
> 2. Other exceptions include *daily, dryer, said,* and *paid.*

Rule 4.   When adding an ending that starts with a vowel to a one-syllable word, follow these rules.

Double the final consonant only if the word ends with a consonant-vowel-consonant.

> strap + ed = strapped
>
> occur + ence = occurrence
>
> prefer + ed = preferred
>
> commit + ed = committed

Do not double the final consonant if the word ends with some other combination.

VOWEL-VOWEL-CONSONANT	VOWEL-CONSONANT-CONSONANT
cl**ean** + est = cleanest	sl**ick** + er = slicker
p**oor** + er = poorer	te**ach** + er = teacher
cl**ear** + ed = cleared	l**ast** + ed = lasted

Rule 5.   When adding an ending that starts with a vowel to a word of two or more syllables, follow these rules.

Double the final consonant only if the word ends with a consonant-vowel-consonant and the stress is on the last syllable.

ad**mit** + ing = admitting

con**trol** + er = controller

ad**mit** + ed = admitted

Do not double the final consonant in other cases.

problem + atic = problematic

understand + ing = understanding

offer + ed = offered

Rule 6.   Add -*s* to most words, including words that end in *o* preceded by a vowel.

MOST WORDS	WORDS THAT END IN VOWEL PLUS *O*
book + s = book**s**	vid**eo** + s = videos
college + s = college**s**	ster**eo** + s = stereos
jump + s = jump**s**	rad**io** + s = radios

Add -*es* to words that end in *s*, *sh*, *ch*, or *x* and *o* preceded by a consonant.

WORDS THAT END IN *S*, *SH*, *CH*, OR *X*	WORDS THAT END IN CONSONANT PLUS *O*
clas**s** + es = class**es**	pota**to** + es = potatoes
pu**sh** + es = push**es**	he**ro** + es = heroes
ben**ch** + es = bench**es**	**go** + es = goes
fa**x** + es = fax**es**	

EXCEPTIONS: pianos, solos (and others)

Step 5: Consult a Spelling List

The following is a list of the one hundred most commonly misspelled words. Consult this as you proofread your writing.

One Hundred Commonly Misspelled Words

absence	convenient	height	receive
achieve	cruelty	humorous	recognize
across	daughter	illegal	recommend
aisle	definite	immediately	restaurant
a lot	describe	independent	rhythm
already	dictionary	interest	roommate
analyze	different	jewelry	schedule
answer	disappoint	judgment	scissors
appetite	dollar	knowledge	secretary
argument	eighth	license	separate
athlete	embarrass	lightning	sincerely
awful	environment	loneliness	sophomore
basically	especially	marriage	succeed
beautiful	exaggerate	meant	successful
beginning	excellent	muscle	surprise
believe	exercise	necessary	truly
business	fascinate	ninety	until
calendar	February	noticeable	usually
career	finally	occasion	vacuum
category	foreign	occurrence	valuable
chief	friend	perform	vegetable
column	government	physically	weight
coming	grief	prejudice	weird
commitment	guidance	probably	writing
conscious	harass	psychology	written

Edit Paragraphs and Your Own Writing

Find and correct any spelling mistakes in the following paragraphs.

EDITING REVIEW 1

(1) Anyone intrested in wierd events should visit New York City on October 31, when the bigest Halloween parade in the country takes place. (2) Everyone in the city, it seems, marchs in the parade, yet they're are still an estimated two million people watching from the sidewalks. (3) The parade had its beginings in Greenwich Village, and original parade-goers walked though the small, winding streets of that old New York nieghborhood. (4) Buy now, the parade has goten so large that it has to go down one of the city's broad avenues. (5) The Halloween parade suprises alot of people who see it for the first time. (6) The merryment begins early in the evening, as costumed paraders line up. (7) Your likely to see a huge group of freinds dressed as one hunderd and one dalmatians or perhaps some comicaly exaggerated versions of goverment officials. (8) Every kind of costume is permited in the parade, and some people attend skimpyly dressed, aparently without embarassment, in spite of the October chill. (9) For a fascinateing look at how strangly people can behave on Halloween, the New York City Halloween parade is the place to bee.

EDITING REVIEW 2

(1) During the summer months, people love to head to the beachs. (2) Accept for those who have recently seen *Jaws*, most people don't consider going to the ocean a dangerous activity. (3) Usualy, people can swim safly at the beach, but its always wise to be cautious. (4) Shark attacks are very rare—worldwide their are usually only fifty to seventy per year—

but a majority of them happen in the waters around the United States. (5) Shiney jewelery can attract sharks because it resembles fish scales, and swimers in the early morning or late evening are more likely to encounter sharks who are hopeing to grab a byte to eat. (6) Of course, people are much more apt to meet up with jellyfish than with sharks, but even a jellyfish sting can leave a beachgoer acheing for hours. (7) Finaly, everyone ought to be aware that waist sometimes gets into seawater, specially near urban areas. (8) Testing is suppose to be done periodicaly, and any beach with unsafe water should be closed; anyone who doesn't trust government testing can by a kit and do the job at home. (9) People who think to much about the dangers of going in the ocean may feel safer lying peacfully in the sand. (10) That's probly fine—as long as they wear plenty of sonscreen.

PRACTICE 3   EDITING YOUR OWN WRITING FOR SPELLING

As a final practice, edit a piece of your own writing for spelling, using the techniques described in this chapter. It can be a paper you are working on for this course, a paper you've already finished, a paper for another course, or a recent piece of writing from work or everyday life.

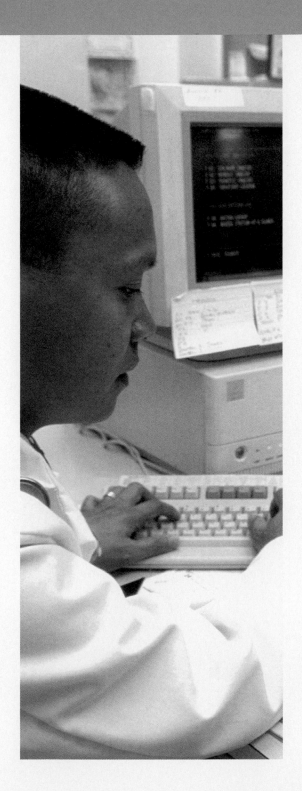

Part Seven

Punctuation and Capitalization

36

Commas

,

Understand What Commas Do

Commas (,) are punctuation marks that separate words and word groups to help readers understand a sentence. Read aloud the following three sentences. How does the use of commas change the meaning?

NO COMMA   After you call Jim I'll leave for the restaurant.

ONE COMMA   After you call Jim, I'll leave for the restaurant.

TWO COMMAS After you call, Jim, I'll leave for the restaurant.

Commas signal particular meanings to your readers, so it is important that you understand when and how to use them.

Practice Using Commas Correctly

Commas between Items in a Series

Use commas to separate three or more items in a series. This includes the last item in the series, which usually has *and* before it.

When you go to the store, please pick up *milk, bread, orange juice,* and *bananas.*

Last semester I took *math, reading,* and *composition.*

Students may take the course as a *regular classroom course,* as an *online course,* or as a *distance learning course.*

NOTE: Some magazines, newspapers, literary pieces, and business publications do not use a comma before the final item. In college writing, it is always best to include it.

■ PRACTICE 1   USING COMMAS IN SERIES

Edit the following sentences by underlining the items in the series and adding commas where they are needed. If a sentence is already correct, put a "C" next to it.

> **EXAMPLE:** The money we <u>touch</u>,<u>carry in our wallets</u>,and <u>give to other people</u> may be covered with germs.

1. Money has been called "the root of all evil" and "filthy lucre."

2. Apparently, money actually is dirty tainted and germ-covered.

3. A recent study of sixty-eight dollar bills found five carrying germs that could infect healthy people fifty-nine harboring bacteria that could sicken people with depressed immune systems and only four that were free of dangerous infectious agents.

4. The bills were selected randomly taken to a laboratory and tested for germs.

5. Of course, this study involved a very small localized and not necessarily representative sample of bills.

6. My mother, a highly trained, experienced, and conscientious nurse, always told me to wash my hands after handling money.

7. Once, when I was attempting to open my purse accept a receipt from a cashier and hold my change at the same time, I stuck some dollar bills in my mouth for a moment.

8. My mother was astonished concerned and a little angry as she snapped at me to get the money out of my mouth.

9. Although the study of the sixty-eight dollar bills did not reveal whether germs can survive for long periods on money transfer from bills to people or otherwise contribute to human illness, reading about it made me realize that my mother had been right to be worried.

10. I wonder what would happen if researchers tested random bathroom doors bus seats or any other public and frequently touched objects.

■ For more practice using commas, visit Exercise Central at <bedfordstmartins.com/realessays>.

Commas in Compound Sentences

A **compound sentence** contains two independent clauses (sentences) joined by one of these words: *and, but, for, nor, or, so, yet.* Use a comma before the joining word to separate the two clauses.

■ The words *and, but, for, nor, or, so,* and *yet* are called coordinating conjunctions. See Chapter 29 for more details.

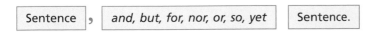

| Sentence | **,** | *and, but, for, nor, or, so, yet* | Sentence. |

Tom missed class yesterday**,** *and* he called to ask me what he missed.

I would have been happy to help him**,** *but* I was absent too.

I told him I wasn't there**,** *so* he said he would e-mail the professor.

NOTE: A comma is not needed if the word *and, but, for, nor, or, so,* or *yet* joins two sentence elements that are not independent clauses.

PRACTICE 2   USING COMMAS IN COMPOUND SENTENCES

Edit the following compound sentences by adding commas where they are needed. If a sentence is already correct, put a "C" next to it.

EXAMPLE: The population of the United States is getting older, but
the number of people trained to care for the elderly is
declining.

1. Working in a nursing home is a difficult job for elderly patients can seldom do much for themselves.

2. The labor is sometimes physically difficult but it can also be mentally draining.

3. Few trained nurses and nurse's aides want nursing-home jobs for the pay is also usually lower than that offered by hospitals.

4. Nursing-home workers have high turnover rates and the facilities are constantly in need of new personnel.

5. More workers will be needed as the baby boomers become elderly yet there is already a shortage of people willing to do the tough and often unpleasant work.

6. A director sometimes must hire undertrained workers or the nursing home will face a severe staff shortage.

7. Workers without education and training may have difficulty understanding a doctor's orders, so the patients' care may suffer.

8. Home health aides and hospice workers are also in short supply and the need for such workers is growing every day.

9. Solving these problems will be difficult for long-term care for the elderly is already very expensive.

10. People caring for elderly patients must get better pay or no one will be available to do the work in a few years.

Commas after Introductory Word Groups

Use a comma after an introductory word or word group. An introductory word group can be a word, a phrase, or a clause. The comma lets your readers know when the main part of the sentence is starting.

| Introductory word or word group | , | Main part of sentence. |

INTRODUCTORY WORD   *Happily,* I turned in my final paper.

INTRODUCTORY PHRASE   *According to the paper,* the crime rate went down.

INTRODUCTORY CLAUSE   *As you know,* the store is going out of business.

> ### PRACTICE 3   USING COMMAS AFTER INTRODUCTORY WORD GROUPS

In each item, underline any introductory word or word group. Then, add commas after introductory word groups where they are needed.

EXAMPLE: Every year, more than two hundred motorists die in collisions with animals.

1. Along roadsides all across the country drivers see the bodies of animals hit by cars.

2. Usually the victims are common species of wildlife, such as deer and raccoons.

3. Of course hitting a deer is not only disturbing but also potentially harmful or fatal to the occupants of a car.

4. However the deer population has not suffered much of a decline from traffic accidents.

5. On the other hand drivers in wilderness areas may accidentally kill endangered species.

6. For instance wildlife experts believe that 65 percent of the population of endangered Florida panthers has been killed on highways in the past twenty years.

7. Maintaining the world's largest network of roads the U.S. Forest Service tries to balance the needs of humans and wildlife.

8. To get access to wilderness areas humans, many of whom strongly favor protecting the environment, need roads.

9. Unfortunately wilderness roads may isolate populations of animals that will not cross them and kill animals that make the attempt.

10. Although expensive underpasses and overpasses have been successful in some areas at reducing human collisions with animals.

Commas around Appositives and Interrupters

■ For more on appositives, see pages 489–91.

An **appositive,** a phrase that renames a noun, comes directly before or after the noun.

> Dick, *my neighbor,* is being sued by a builder.

> Apartment prices are high at Riverview, *the new complex.*

■ An interrupter that appears at the beginning of a sentence can be treated the same as an introductory word group.

An **interrupter** is an aside or transition that interrupts the flow of a sentence and does not affect its meaning.

> Campus parking fees, *you should know,* are going up by 30 percent.

> A six-month sticker will now be $45, *if you can believe it.*

Putting commas around appositives and interrupters tells readers that these elements give extra information but are not essential to the meaning of a sentence. If an appositive or interrupter is in the middle of a sentence, set it off with a pair of commas, one before and one after. If an appositive or interrupter comes at the beginning or end of a sentence, separate it from the rest of the sentence with one comma.

> *Incidentally,* your raise has been approved.

> Your raise, *incidentally,* has been approved.

> Your raise has been approved, *incidentally.*

NOTE: Sometimes, an appositive is essential to the meaning of a sentence. When a sentence would not have the same meaning without the appositive, the appositive should not be set off with commas.

The actor *John Travolta* has never won an Academy Award.

[The sentence *The actor has never won an Academy Award* does not have the same meaning.]

The lawyer *Clarence Darrow* was one of history's greatest speakers.

[The sentence *The lawyer was one of history's greatest speakers* does not have the same meaning.]

PRACTICE 4 USING COMMAS TO SET OFF APPOSITIVES AND INTERRUPTERS

Underline any appositives or interrupters in the following sentences. Then, use commas to set them off.

EXAMPLE: The reason for the delay, a mechanical problem with the airplane, was not mentioned.

1. Road rage as most people have heard occurs when an angry driver overreacts.

2. Another phenomenon air rage involves out-of-control and often intoxicated passengers on an airplane.

3. One famous air rage incident a confrontation between a drunken businessman and a flight attendant ended with the passenger tied to his seat for the rest of the flight.

4. Ground rage like air rage is a term used for incidents between airline passengers and airline employees.

5. Ground rage as the name suggests occurs in the terminal, not in the air.

6. Gate agents the people who check tickets and allow passengers to board the plane are frequent victims of ground rage.

7. Oversold seats a common occurrence in air travel can mean that some passengers are forced to miss a flight.

8. Passengers many of whom are on a tight schedule or have a connecting flight to catch find delayed flights infuriating as well.

9. Some delayed or bumped passengers take out their anger on the gate agent a convenient target.

10. Although some airline employees may not be helpful or friendly, their attitudes do not excuse passengers who commit assault a serious crime.

Commas around Adjective Clauses

An **adjective clause** is a group of words that often begins with *who, which,* or *that;* has a subject and verb; and describes the noun right before it in a sentence. Whether or not an adjective clause should be set off from the rest of the sentence by commas depends on its meaning in the sentence.

If an adjective clause can be taken out of a sentence without completely changing the meaning, put commas around the clause.

> The mayor**,** *who was recently elected***,** has no political experience.

> SuperShop**,** *which is the largest supermarket in town***,** was recently bought by Big Boy Markets.

> I have an appointment with Dr. Kling**,** *who is the specialist.*

If an adjective clause is essential to the meaning of a sentence, do not put commas around it. You can tell whether a clause is essential by taking it out and seeing if the meaning of the sentence changes significantly, as it would if you took the clauses out of the following examples:

> The hair salon *that I liked* recently closed.

> Salesclerks *who sell liquor to minors* are breaking the law.

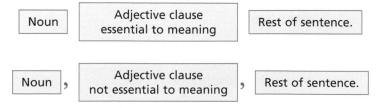

■ For more on adjective clauses, see pages 491–94.

Use *who* to refer to a person; *which* to refer to places or things (but not to people); and *that* for people, places, or things. When referring to a person, *who* is preferable to *that.*

**PRACTICE 5 USING COMMAS TO SET OFF
ADJECTIVE CLAUSES**

Edit the following sentences by putting any needed commas around adjective clauses. Remember that if an adjective clause is essential to the meaning of the sentence, you should not use commas. If a sentence is already correct, put a "C" next to it.

EXAMPLE: Stephen King‚who understands how to frighten his readers‚has depicted evil clowns in his work.

1. The only thing that terrifies Maria is a person dressed as a clown.

2. The fear of clowns which is called *coulrophobia* is fairly common among children.

3. Some young children who develop this fear are not prepared adequately before seeing a clown for the first time.

4. Clowns who usually wear heavy makeup and brightly colored wigs do not look like ordinary people.

5. Clowns also make sudden and surprising movements that frighten many youngsters.

6. Most children who fear clowns will get over their phobia as they grow up.

7. Such people who may never love clowns will still be able to tolerate having them around.

8. Many adults have read books and seen movies that show clowns as evil killers.

9. Few adults admit to having coulrophobia which is most effectively treated when the sufferer confronts the fear.

10. Unlike some other phobias which can trap people in their homes or make them unable to work coulrophobia has little effect on most sufferers, who are not likely to meet clowns frequently in everyday life.

Other Uses for Commas

Commas with Quotation Marks

■ For more on quotation marks, see Chapter 38.

Quotation marks are used to show that you are using a direct quotation, repeating exactly what someone said or wrote. Generally, use commas to set off the words inside quotation marks from the rest of the sentence.

"Excuse me," said the old woman in back of me.

"Did you know," she asked, "that you just cut in front of me?"

I exclaimed, "Oh, no. I'm so sorry!"

Notice that a comma never comes directly *after* a quotation mark.

Commas in Addresses

Use commas to separate the elements of an address included in a sentence. However, do not use a comma before a zip code.

My address is 4498 Main Street, Bolton, Massachusetts 01740.

If a sentence continues after the address, put a comma after the address. Also, use a comma after individual elements used to name a geographical location such as a city and state.

The house was moved from Cripple Creek, Colorado, to the lot on Forest Street.

Commas in Dates

Separate the day from the year with a comma. If you give only the month and year, do not separate them with a comma.

She wrote the letter on April 1, 2005.

The next session is in January 2010.

If a sentence continues after a date that includes the day, put a comma after the date.

He waited until April 15, 2005, to file his 2004 tax return.

Commas with Names

Put commas around the name of someone you are addressing by name.

> Don, I want you to come look at this.
>
> Unfortunately, Marie, you need to finish the report by next week.

Commas with *Yes or* No

Put a comma after the word *yes* or *no* in response to a question.

> No, that isn't what I meant.

PRACTICE 6   USING COMMAS

Edit the following sentences by adding commas where they are needed. If a sentence is already correct, put a "C" next to it.

> EXAMPLE: The new regulations of telemarketing went into effect on
>
> April 1, 2001.

1. My sister asked "James do you get a lot of telemarketing calls?"

2. "Yes I do" I replied "and they always come at dinnertime."

3. She told me that new laws that could help me protect my privacy had taken effect in April 2001.

4. I wrote to the governor's office in Albany New York for information about the telemarketing registry.

5. My address which is 21 Highland Road Binghamton New York has now been added to the state registry.

6. For a while I still got occasional calls that began with an unfamiliar voice saying "James I have an exciting offer for you."

7. I simply replied "No I have news for you."

8. I pointed out that on August 11 2001 I had added my name and address to a list of people who do not want to receive calls about exciting offers.

9. "As you probably know" I told my unwanted callers "it is illegal for you to contact me in this way."

10. The marketing calls had stopped completely by November 1.

Edit Paragraphs and Your Own Writing

Edit the following paragraphs by adding commas where they are needed.

EDITING REVIEW 1

(1) Everyone who uses cleaning products at home has probably seen warning labels on those products for most household cleaners contain harsh chemicals. (2) The warnings which are required by law are so common that many users probably ignore them. (3) However all cleaning products should be used with care and some of them can seriously injure children or anyone else who misuses them. (4) Drain cleaners toilet bowl cleaners and chlorine bleach can all cause serious damage to skin eyes and other sensitive tissue. (5) Glass cleaners can react with bleach to produce toxic fumes. (6) Alternative cleansers nontoxic products that can be made from items in an average kitchen are cheaper than brand-name cleaning products and usually work just as well. (7) For most cleaning jobs a solution of vinegar and water or baking soda and water is effective. (8) A plunger can often fix a clogged drain as well as a drain cleaner can and club soda cleans windows nicely. (9) As for air fresheners one expert advises "Open your windows." (10) Economy efficiency and safety are three excellent reasons for choosing homemade cleansers.

EDITING REVIEW 2

(1) A few days ago I received an e-mail that told a terrifying story. (2) At a large discount store in Austin Texas a four-year-old girl had disappeared and her mother had asked for the store employees' help in finding the child. (3) Thinking quickly the employees locked all of the doors posted an employee at every exit and systematically searched the store. (4) The child who was found in a bathroom was safe but half of her head had been shaved. (5) In addition someone had changed her clothes so it seemed obvious that an abductor had been trying to slip her out of the store unnoticed. (6) The e-mail message which came from a distant acquaintance ended by advising me "Don't let your children out of your sight!"

(7) Later that day I was talking to my neighbor and I happened to mention the message. (8) She too had seen it and the story had shocked her. (9) Something about the story made me suspicious however so I decided to do some Internet research. (10) I found a site that discussed urban legends Internet hoaxes and chain letters. (11) On the site I discovered an exact copy of the e-mail I had received. (12) I also learned that my neighbor and I were not the first people to fall for this hoax for Ann Landers had even printed a version of it several years earlier. (13) When she learned that she had been fooled she printed a retraction a column explaining that the story was fictional. (14) A reader wrote to her and said "Reminding people to be cautious is one thing. Scaring the pants off of them is another."

(15) After doing the research I felt better about the scary e-mail story but I felt sad that we are so distrustful of one another. (16) Such stories can make us fear that potential abductors are everywhere. (17) Thirty

years ago most parents were not usually afraid to let children walk to school alone or play outside but today's parents rarely let children out of their sight until the kids are in their teens. (18) The difference is not in the number of abductions of children a very small number that has remained nearly constant over the decades. (19) No the difference is that people now hear about these unusual and terrifying instances over and over. (20) Eventually they reach the conclusion that these stories must be true and they are convinced that such dreadful things must happen frequently. (21) The e-mail I had received was contributing I decided to this climate of irrational fear. (22) "Ann Landers's reader was right" I said to myself. (23) "We should teach our children caution but we can harm them and ourselves by making them believe that evil strangers are lurking around every corner."

PRACTICE 7   EDITING YOUR OWN WRITING FOR COMMAS

As a final practice, edit a piece of your own writing for commas. It can be a paper you are working on for this course, a paper you've already finished, a paper for another course, or a recent piece of writing from your work or everyday life.

37

Apostrophes

Understand What Apostrophes Do

An **apostrophe** (') is a punctuation mark that either shows ownership (*Susan's*) or indicates that a letter has been intentionally left out to form a contraction (*I'm, that's, they're*). Although an apostrophe looks like a comma (,), it is not used for the same purpose, and it is written higher on the line than commas are.

> ■ To understand this chapter, you need to know what nouns and pronouns are. For a review, see Chapters 21, 26, and 32.

apostrophe'   comma,

Practice Using Apostrophes Correctly

Apostrophes to Show Ownership

- **Add -'s to a singular noun to show ownership even if the noun already ends in -s.**

  Darcy's car is being repaired.

  Joan got all the information she needed from the hotel's Web site.

  Chris's house is only a mile away.

- **If a noun is plural and ends in -*s*, just add an apostrophe to show ownership. If it is plural but does not end in -*s*, add -'*s*.**

  The actors' outfits were dazzling. [More than one actor]

  Seven boys' coats were left at the school.

  The children's toys were all broken.

- **The placement of an apostrophe makes a difference in meaning.**

  My neighbor's twelve cats are howling. [One neighbor who has twelve cats]

  My neighbors' twelve cats are howling. [Two or more neighbors who together have twelve cats]

- **Do not use an apostrophe to form the plural of a noun.**

  Use the stair's or the elevator.

  All of the plant's in the garden are blooming.

- **Do not use an apostrophe with a possessive pronoun. These pronouns already show ownership (possession).**

  Do you want to take my car or your's?

  That basket is our's.

Possessive Pronouns

my	his	its	their
mine	her	our	theirs
your	hers	ours	whose
yours			

Its *or* It's

The single most common error with apostrophes and pronouns is confusing *its* (a possessive pronoun) with *it's* (a contraction meaning "it is"). Whenever you write *it's*, test to see if it's correct by reading it aloud as *it is*.

■ **PRACTICE 1   USING APOSTROPHES TO SHOW OWNERSHIP**

Edit the following sentences by adding -'s or an apostrophe alone to show ownership and by crossing out any incorrect use of an apostrophe or -'s.

EXAMPLE: ~~Fever's~~ *Fevers* are an important part of the human ~~bodys~~ *body's* system of defense against infection.

1. A thermometers indicator mark at 98.6 degrees is supposed to show a persons normal body temperature.

2. However, normal body temperature can range from 97 degrees to 100.4 degrees, so most doctors view of a temperature lower than 100.5 is that its not a fever at all.

3. Fever's help the body combat virus's and stimulate the immune system.

4. Unless a persons temperature is raised by an outside source, the bodys regulatory system will not usually let a fever go higher than 106 degrees.

5. A fevers appearance is not necessarily a reason to take fever-reducing medication's, which can lower a bodys temperature without doing anything to fight the infection.

6. Taking fever-reducing drug's can actually make an illness take longer to run it's course.

7. Many doctors' do not recommend using any drugs to treat a fever if its lower than 102 degrees.

8. Parents should be aware that childrens fevers can go even higher than their's.

9. Some parents fears of fever are so intense that they suffer from "fever phobia" and overreact to their childrens' symptoms.

■ For more practice with apostrophe usage, visit Exercise Central at <bedfordstmartins .com/realessays>.

10. Fever phobia can cause parent's to give their child extra medicine, but overdoses of ibuprofen and other fever reducers can impair the livers' ability to work properly and can therefore complicate the childs sickness.

Apostrophes in Contractions

A **contraction** is formed by joining two words and leaving out one or more of the letters. When writing a contraction, put an apostrophe where the letter or letters have been left out, not between the two words.

NOTE: In academic writing, contractions are rarely used.

Carol's studying to be a nurse. = *Carol is* studying to be a nurse.

I'll go when you come back. = *I will* go when you come back.

Be sure to put the apostrophe in the right place.

Don does'n't work here anymore.

■ Do not use contractions in formal papers or reports for college or work.

Common Contractions

aren't = are not	she'll = she will
can't = cannot	she's = she is, she has
couldn't = could not	there's = there is
didn't = did not	they'd = they would, they had
don't = do not	they'll = they will
he'd = he would, he had	they're = they are
he'll = he will	they've = they have
he's = he is, he has	who'd = who would, who had
I'd = I would, I had	who'll = who will
I'll = I will	who's = who is, who has
I'm = I am	won't = will not
I've = I have	wouldn't = would not
isn't = is not	you'd = you would, you had
it's = it is, it has	you'll = you will
let's = let us	you're = you are
she'd = she would, she had	you've = you have

■ **PRACTICE 2   USING APOSTROPHES IN CONTRACTIONS**

Read each sentence carefully, looking for any words that have missing letters. Edit these words by adding apostrophes where needed. Or, if apostrophes are misplaced, cross out and correct the error.

EXAMPLE: ~~Its~~ *It's* sadly true that some athletes will use performance-enhancing drugs if they can get away with it.

1. Those who do often say theyre using these drugs because their competitors are probably using them too.

2. Performance-enhancing drugs help some athletes win competitions, but for other athletes, these drugs arent enough to ensure victory.

3. Most athletes taking steroids and other substances say they would'nt use these drugs if they could be certain that their opponents are'nt using them.

4. Wholl be the one to put a stop to this drug use?

5. If sports organizations do'nt eliminate drug use, we all know whos the loser.

6. Youre the loser, Im the loser, and all athletes are the losers.

7. When even one athlete gets away with using drugs, we ca'nt trust that any athletic competition has been won fairly.

8. Youve got to take a stand, Ive got to take a stand, and anyone who believes in fairness has got to take a stand.

9. Lets eliminate performance-enhancing drugs now.

10. If we all are'nt ready to unite against drug use in sports, we might as well change the word *athlete* to *actor*.

Apostrophes with Letters, Numbers, and Time

- **Use -'s to make letters and numbers plural. The apostrophe prevents confusion or misreading.**

  Mississippi has four i's.

  In women's shoes, size 8's are more common than size 10's.

- **Use an apostrophe or -'s in certain expressions in which time nouns are treated as if they possess something.**

  I get two weeks' vacation next year.

  Last year's prices were very good.

███   **PRACTICE 3   USING APOSTROPHES WITH LETTERS, NUMBERS, AND TIME**

Edit the following sentences by adding apostrophes where needed and fixing incorrectly used apostrophes.

>   *weeks'*
>
> **EXAMPLE:** I just updated my blog by entering the last three ~~week's~~
>
> worth of entries.

1. Next months schedule is less busy, so I think I'll be able to keep my blog current then.

2. Arthur's blog details an entire winters worth of concerns about his social life.

3. His blog is a little hard to read because he always leaves out certain letters, such as as, es, and os.

4. Katie's blog also gets confusing when she puts all of her 4s and 8s in Roman numerals.

5. When Manny's computer was stolen, he lost notes for his blog and two year's work on his novel.

Edit Paragraphs and Your Own Writing

Edit the following paragraphs by adding apostrophes where needed and crossing out incorrectly used apostrophes. If a sentence is already correct, put a "C" after it.

■ EDITING REVIEW 1

(1) Some of the first discussion's of global warming focused attention on one of the gases that contributes to the greenhouse effect: methane. (2) Like other greenhouse gases, methane helps to keep the earths' heat trapped in our atmosphere, and the temperature of the earth goes up as a result. (3) Humans are'nt the only producers of methane; its also a by-product of cow's digestion of their food. (4) For a while, many Americans knowledge of global warming didnt go much further than cow jokes. (5) As scientists' have become more convinced that global warming is real and a potential threat to human's, our knowledge of the causes of the greenhouse effect has expanded. (6) Cows arent completely off the hook, but theyre far less guilty of contributing to global warming than humans and cars are. (7) The amount of methane produced by cows' adds up to about 3 percent of the total amount of greenhouse gases produced by people. (8) Getting a cow to change it's diet wo'nt solve the worlds warming problem.

■ EDITING REVIEW 2

(1) Some people are terribly annoyed by misplaced apostrophes, and some people are'nt. (2) In England, John Richards, a man whos annoyed by incorrect apostrophe placement, has founded an organization called the Apostrophe Protection Society to campaign for the correct use of

apostrophe's. (3) He has attracted dozen's of supporters who are infuriated by signs, menu's, and other notices in public places that contain apostrophe errors. (4) One woman who joined the society carries small apostrophes on sticky piece's of paper so that she can correct signs with missing punctuation. (5) She admits that her husbands view of punctuation is not as strict as her's, and she says that this sometimes causes arguments between them. (6) An article about the Englishman appeared in a major U.S. newspaper, and afterward the papers editors were flooded with letters related to the subject of apostrophes. (7) Although a few people thought Richards crusade shouldnt be taken seriously, the majority of letter writers supported his view, and one or two couldn't wait to start a chapter of the society in the United States. (8) It seems that no matter how relaxed some people get about punctuation, there will always be some other's who want to make sure that all the *i*s are dotted, all the *t*s are crossed, and all the apostrophe's are in their proper places.

EDITING REVIEW 3

(1) In March of 2001, the keyless entry systems of cars in Bremerton, Washington, suddenly stopped working, and no one knows why. (2) The cars locks were supposed to respond when their owner's pushed a button, and all at once they wouldnt. (3) After a few days wait, the entry systems began functioning again. (4) Many resident's of Bremerton, the home of a Navy shipyard, were convinced that the militarys technological activity had affected the cars, but Navy official's denied it. (5) Other people wondered if radio transmissions might have jammed the frequency and prevented the keyless systems' from functioning. (6) Fortunately, people whose cars have keyless entry systems were'nt locked out for those days. (7) These

owners simply had to resort to a backup system to open and lock their

car's—its called a "key."

■ PRACTICE 4   EDITING YOUR OWN WRITING FOR APOSTROPHES

As a final practice, edit a piece of your own writing for apostrophes. It can be a paper you are working on for this course, a paper you've already finished, a paper for another course, or a recent piece of writing from your work or everyday life.

38

Quotation Marks

" "

Understand What Quotation Marks Do

Quotation marks (" ") are punctuation marks with two common uses in college writing: They are used with some quotations, and they are used to set off titles. They always appear in pairs.

A **quotation** is the report of another person's words. There are two types of quotations: **direct quotations** (the exact repetition, word for word, of what someone said or wrote) and **indirect quotations** (a restatement of what someone said or wrote, not word for word). Quotation marks are used only for direct quotations.

■ To understand this chapter, you need to know what a sentence is. For a review, see Chapter 21.

DIRECT QUOTATION	George said, "I'm getting a haircut."
INDIRECT QUOTATION	George said that he was getting a haircut.

Practice Using Quotation Marks Correctly

Quotation Marks for Direct Quotations

When you write a direct quotation, you need to use quotation marks around the quoted words. These marks tell readers that the words used are exactly what was said or written.

1. "My license expires tomorrow," Gerri told me.

2. I asked, "Are you going to get it renewed?"

3. "Well, I should," Gerri admitted, "but I don't think I have time to get to the Registry of Motor Vehicles. What will happen if I'm late?"

4. "Probably nothing," I replied. "But you can renew it online."

5. After thinking for a moment, Gerri said, "Yes, but I want a new photograph."

Quoted words are usually combined with words that identify who is speaking, such as *Gerri told me* in the first example. The identifying words can come after the quoted words (example 1), before them (example 2), or in the middle (example 3). Here are some guidelines for capitalization and punctuation:

- Capitalize the first letter in a complete sentence that's being quoted, even if it comes after some identifying words (example 2).

- Do not capitalize the first letter in a quotation if it's not the first word in a complete sentence (*but* in example 3).

- If it is a complete sentence and its source is clear, you can let a quotation stand on its own, without any identifying words (example 4).

- Attach identifying words to a quotation; these identifying words cannot be a sentence on their own.

- Use commas to separate any identifying words from quoted words in the same sentence.

■ For more on commas with quotation marks, see page 566.

- Always put quotation marks after commas and periods. Put quotation marks after question marks and exclamation points if they are part of the quoted sentence.

Quotation mark   Quotation mark

I asked, "Are you going to get it renewed?"

Comma   Question mark

- If a question mark or exclamation point is part of your own sentence, put it after the quotation mark.

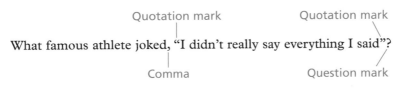

Quotation mark   Quotation mark

What famous athlete joked, "I didn't really say everything I said"?

Comma   Question mark

■ For information about how to use quotations in research papers, see Chapter 20.

When you are writing a paper in which you use outside sources, use quotation marks to indicate the exact words that you quote from a source. You'll then have to cite, or give credit to, the source.

The government needs to ensure that when a company fails, employees' pensions are protected. A recent article in the *Boston Globe* reported, "When Polaroid collapsed, pension funds and employee stock programs were suddenly worthless. At the same time, however, the chief financial officer walked away with a package worth more than $2 million." (Richardson B3)

■ For more on citing and documenting sources, see pages 313–19.

Setting Off a Quotation within Another Quotation

Sometimes you may directly quote someone who quotes what someone else said or wrote. Put **single quotation marks (' ')** around the quotation within a quotation so that readers understand who said what.

The student handbook said, "Students must be given the opportunity to make up work missed for excused absences."

Terry's entire quotation

Terry told his instructor, "I'm sorry I missed the exam, but I would like to take a makeup exam. Our student handbook says, 'Students must be given the opportunity to make up work missed for excused absences,' and I have a good reason."

Here, Terry is including a quotation from the student handbook.

■ PRACTICE 1   PUNCTUATING DIRECT QUOTATIONS

Edit the following sentences by adding quotation marks and commas where needed.

EXAMPLE: At a meeting of a self-help group, the leader, Brooke, stood up and said, "We are all here because each of us is suffering from an eating disorder."

1. Looking around the room, Allison said I thought only teenage girls had eating disorders. There are people here of all ages, including several men.

2. Yes, there are men here said Brooke. Only some of us are teenage girls.

3. I'm forty years old, not a teenager, and not a girl Patrick said. However, I have an eating disorder.

4. Allison said You don't look like you have an eating disorder. You are not super skinny.

5. I eat too much said Patrick. I'm a compulsive eater.

6. When you say I'm a compulsive eater I don't know what you mean said Allison.

7. The dictionary defines *compulsive* as related to a psychological obsession, said Brooke.

8. Evan suddenly shouted We're all doing this because we're trying to hurt our families and friends!

9. That is one myth we're going to talk about said Brooke. In fact, people with eating disorders are hurting themselves. They are usually upset that their families and friends are worried about them.

10. Why did it suddenly get quiet when Brooke said Does this ring true to any of you?

■ For more practice with quotation marks, visit Exercise Central at <bedfordstmartins .com/realessays>.

No Quotation Marks for Indirect Quotations

When you report what someone said or wrote but do not use the person's exact words, you are writing an indirect quotation. Do not use quotation marks for indirect quotations. Indirect quotations often begin with the word *that*.

INDIRECT QUOTATION	Sophie said that the exam was postponed.
DIRECT QUOTATION	Sophie said, "The exam was postponed."
INDIRECT QUOTATION	The boy asked me what time it was.
DIRECT QUOTATION	"What time is it?" asked the boy.
INDIRECT QUOTATION	Carolyn told me that she had an accident.
DIRECT QUOTATION	Carolyn told me, "I had an accident."

■ **PRACTICE 2   PUNCTUATING DIRECT AND INDIRECT QUOTATIONS**

Edit the following sentences by adding quotation marks where needed and crossing out quotation marks that are incorrectly used. If a sentence is already correct, put a "C" next to it.

> **EXAMPLE:** Sarita told me that ~~"~~she met her new boyfriend through an online dating service~~."~~

1. I never thought I would use the Internet for dating, but it really worked, she said.

2. Sarita remembered "how easy it was to look up profiles of men with her interests and to pick the best candidates."

3. She said, I could tell right away if I wasn't going to have anything in common with a person.

4. "I could also tell a lot about a guy's personality by the way he expressed himself," she added.

5. Sarita said the hardest part of the experience was going on trial dates to see if her original impressions of candidates were correct.

6. She knew that there was no future with one man when he showed up a half hour late for their date and told her, I had something else to do first.

7. "He apparently thought that I was happy to wait around for him forever," she said exasperatedly.

8. Sarita told me that "I should think about online dating."

9. I found a great person, she said, and you could too.

10. I told her that I appreciated the advice but that I'm happy being single right now.

Quotation Marks for Certain Titles

When referring to a short work such as a magazine or newspaper article, a chapter in a book, a short story, an essay, a song, or a poem, put quotation marks around the title of the work.

NEWSPAPER ARTICLE	"Mayor Warns of Budget Cuts"
SHORT STORY	"Everyday Use"
ESSAY	"Mother Tongue"

Usually, titles of longer works—such as novels, books, magazines, newspapers, movies, television programs, and CDs—are underlined or italicized. The titles of sacred books such as the Bible or the Koran are neither underlined, italicized, nor surrounded by quotation marks.

BOOK	The Chocolate War or *The Chocolate War*
NEWSPAPER	Washington Post or *Washington Post*

[Do not underline, italicize, or capitalize the word *the* before the name of a newspaper or magazine, even if it is part of the title: I saw that in the *New York Times*. But do capitalize *The* when it is the first word in titles of books, movies, and other sources.]

If you are writing a paper with many outside sources, your instructor will probably refer you to a particular system of citing sources. Follow that system's guidelines when you use titles in your paper.

NOTE: Do not put quotation marks around the title of a paper you write.

PRACTICE 3   USING QUOTATION MARKS FOR TITLES

Edit the following sentences by adding quotation marks around titles as needed. Underline any book, magazine, or newspaper titles.

EXAMPLE: As we rode the elevator to our meeting on the fortieth

floor, we had to listen to a piped-in instrumental version

of "Nine to Five.

1. At the meeting, an outside consultant tried to motivate us by quoting from an article in USA Today called How to Get the Job Done.

2. Then, he gave each of us a copy of a well-known CEO's autobiography and asked us to read Chapter 4, The Road to the Top.

3. Marta looked as if she were taking careful notes, but I knew that she was working on the final draft of an essay she was hoping to publish in Business Review, her favorite magazine.

4. When she had told me earlier that the essay would be called Why Meetings Are Usually Useless, I had volunteered to provide many personal examples to prove her point.

5. When the grueling meeting was over, Marta reminded me that Wallace Stevens, the poet who wrote Sunday Morning, had found a way to be creative while he spent his days working at an insurance company.

Edit Paragraphs and Your Own Writing

Edit the following paragraphs by adding quotation marks where needed and crossing out any incorrectly used quotation marks. Correct any errors in punctuation.

EDITING REVIEW 1

(1) On our way home from a Britney Spears concert, Nicole said that "she wanted to go out and get some of Britney's CDs as soon as possible." (2) The very next day, on our way to the record store, I said, Every time I listen to these songs, I'll see her performing them in my mind. (3) Nicole agreed and added that she "wanted to have recordings of some of Britney's especially moving songs." (4) At the store, she immediately found the CD called "In the Zone," which has two songs that Nicole loves. (5) At the concert, she had gone insane when Britney sang Everytime and Outrageous;

Nicole said that they were her favorite songs of all time. (6) I bought that CD too, as well as a Madonna CD called "American Life." (7) I explained that I love Madonna's singing, and I was also amazed by her performance in the movie "Evita." (8) While going home from the record store, I asked Nicole if "she would like to come over to my place and listen to music." (9) Not right now, she replied. I think I want to relive that fantastic concert alone for a while. (10) Is this what my mom meant when she used to say, Being at a live Beatles concert was one of the greatest experiences of my life?"

EDITING REVIEW 2

(1) "Did you know that people our age could experience a life crisis"? my twenty-five-year-old friend Beth asked as we browsed at the newsstand. (2) She showed me an article called The Trouble with Being 25 in a magazine she was looking at.

(3) I told her that "she was crazy." (4) You wait until midlife for your crisis, silly, I said. (5) I was imagining a middle-aged businessman suddenly buying an expensive sports car and driving around listening to Prince singing Little Red Corvette.

(6) Beth pointed out that she had plenty of anxiety about being twenty-five. (7) It's as if people look at me and think I'm still basically a teenager, yet I have a grown-up job and grown-up responsibilities to go with it, she said.

(8) I asked her "what kinds of responsibilities she was talking about." (9) I have rent and bills to pay, she said, and I'm trying to decide if I should take a couple of classes at night to get a better job. (10) She thought for a moment and then added, "And sooner or later I'll need to figure out

whether I want to get married and have children". (11) She picked up a newspaper and idly turned the pages until she found a headline that said Confusion Reigns among Young Singles.

(12) "Wow! You're right"! I blurted out. (13) It's a good thing you read those stupid magazines, I said to Beth. (14) I was only partly kidding when I added that "she and I would never have realized that we were supposed to be having a crisis if we hadn't read about it."

(15) Let's do something to celebrate, said Beth. (16) That's why we spent the rest of the afternoon sitting around my kitchen table drinking coffee, listening to Beck singing Loser, and reading out loud to each other from How to Tell If You're Ready to Settle Down in the new issue of Cosmopolitan.

■ PRACTICE 4   EDITING YOUR OWN WRITING FOR QUOTATION MARKS

As a final practice, edit a piece of your own writing for quotation marks. It can be a paper you are working on for this course, a paper you've already finished, a paper for another course, or a recent piece of writing from your work or everyday life.

39

Other Punctuation

; : ( ) — -

Understand What Punctuation Does

Punctuation helps readers understand your writing. If you use punctuation incorrectly, you send readers a confusing message—or, even worse, a wrong one. This chapter covers five marks of punctuation that people sometimes use incorrectly. Knowing what functions these marks serve can help you avoid such mistakes.

SEMICOLON ;   Joins two independent clauses into one sentence

Separates complete items in a list that already has commas within individual items

COLON :   Introduces a list

Announces an explanation or example

PARENTHESES ( )   Set off extra information that is not essential to the sentence

DASH —   Sets off words for emphasis

Indicates a pause

HYPHEN -   Joins two or more words that together form a single description

Shows a word break at the end of a line

■ To understand this chapter, you need to know what sentences and independent clauses are. For a review, see Chapters 21 and 23.

Practice Using Punctuation Correctly

Semicolon ;

Semicolons to Join Independent Clauses (Sentences)

Use a semicolon to join very closely related sentences and make them into one sentence.

> In an interview, hold your head up and don't slouch; it is important to look alert.

> Make good eye contact; looking down is not appropriate in an interview.

Semicolons When Items in a Series Contain Commas

■ For more on using semicolons to join sentences, see Chapter 29.

Use a semicolon to separate the items in a list that themselves contain commas. Otherwise, it is difficult for readers to tell where one item ends and another begins.

> I have a cousin who lives in Devon, England; another cousin who lives in Derry, New Hampshire; and a third cousin who lives in Freeport, Maine.

Colon :

Colons before Lists

Use a colon to introduce a list after an independent clause.

> In the United States, three ice cream flavors are the most popular: vanilla, chocolate, and strawberry.

> I have three stops to make on the way home: the grocery store, the post office, and the police station.

Colons before Explanations or Examples

Use a colon after an independent clause to let readers know that you are about to provide an explanation or example of what you just wrote. If the explanation or example is also an independent clause, capitalize the first letter after the colon.

> Sometimes, the choice of cereals is overwhelming: My supermarket carries at least five different types of raisin bran.

> I use one criterion to choose a cereal: price.

NOTE: A colon in a sentence must follow an independent clause. A common misuse is to place a colon after a phrase instead of an independent clause. Watch out especially for colons following the phrases *such as* or *for example.*

An independent clause contains a subject and a verb, and it expresses a complete thought. It can stand on its own as a sentence.

INCORRECT	The resort offers many activities, such as: snorkeling, golf, and windsurfing.
CORRECT	The resort offers many activities: snorkeling, golf, and windsurfing.
CORRECT	The resort offers many activities, such as snorkeling, golf, and windsurfing.
INCORRECT	Suzy has many talents. For example: writing, drawing, and painting.
CORRECT	Suzy has many talents: writing, drawing, and painting.

Colons in Business Correspondence

Use a colon after a greeting (called a salutation) in a business letter and after the standard heading lines at the beginning of a memorandum.

Dear Mr. Latimer:

To: Rob Senior

From: Susan Anker

Parentheses ( )

Use parentheses to set off information that is not essential to the meaning of a sentence. Parentheses are always used in pairs and should be used sparingly.

My grandfather's most successful invention (his first) was the electric blanket.

My worst habit (and also the hardest to break) is interrupting.

When people speak too slowly, I often finish their sentences (at least in my mind).

Dash —

Use dashes as you use parentheses: to set off additional information, particularly information that you want to emphasize.

> The essay question—worth 50 percent of the whole exam—will be open book.

> Your answers should be well developed, and points—2 per error—will be deducted for major grammar mistakes.

A dash can also indicate a pause, much as a comma does.

> My son wants to buy a car—more power to him.

Make a dash by typing two hyphens together. Do not leave any extra spaces around a dash.

Hyphen -

Hyphens to Join Words That Form a Single Description

Use a hyphen to join words that together form a single description of a person, place, or thing.

■ If you are unsure about whether or how to hyphenate a word or phrase, consult a dictionary or your instructor.

> The eighty-year-old smoker was considered a high-risk patient.

> I followed the company's decision-making procedure.

> I can't wait to see my end-of-the-year grade.

Hyphens to Divide a Word at the End of a Line

Use a hyphen to divide a word when part of the word must continue on the next line. Most word-processing programs do this automatically, but if you are writing by hand, you need to insert hyphens yourself.

> If you give me the receipt for your purchase, I will imme-
> diately issue a refund.

If you are not sure where to break a word, look it up in a dictionary. The word's main entry will show you where you can break the word: dic • tio • nary. If you still aren't confident that you are putting the hyphen in the right place, don't break the word; write it all on the next line.

Edit Paragraphs and Your Own Writing

Edit the following paragraphs by adding semicolons, colons, parentheses, dashes, and hyphens where needed. Keep in mind that more than one type of punctuation may be acceptable in some places.

■ **EDITING REVIEW**

(1) In his novel *Native Son* published in 1940, Richard Wright confronted the treatment of African Americans in a frank and, to some readers, shocking way in fact, the novel was so candid that some of its most powerful sections were omitted from its originally published version. (2) *Native Son,* which takes place in Chicago in the 1930s, recounts the last days of a twenty year old African American named Bigger Thomas. (3) The novel's disconcerting beginning Bigger is awakened by the screams of his mother and sister when they see a large rat that Bigger kills sets the tone for the story to come. (4) Bigger's anger toward the poverty and racism he experiences blinds him to rational action and leads to tragic consequences He accidentally kills a white heiress the daughter of his employer and later, in a rage, beats his girlfriend nearly to death. (5) Bigger's trial is extremely one sided, and he is convicted and sentenced to die in a dreadful way by electrocution.

(6) Blindness is a major theme in the novel it pertains both to Bigger's view of his situation and to the white society in which he struggles. (7) Bigger's pride and anger prevent him from seeing things as they really are, and the insensitivity of his well to do employer embodies white society's blindness to racism.

(8) With this book's publication and immediate commercial success, a new glimmer of awareness appeared in America an awareness of racial

■ For more practice with the punctuation covered in this chapter, visit <**bedfordstmartins .com/realessays**>.

injustice that had long been ignored. (9) It was not until 1991 with the first publication of *Native Son* in its complete, original form that many of the novel's strongest and most moving passages were included.

■ PRACTICE 1   EDITING YOUR OWN WRITING FOR OTHER PUNCTUATION MARKS

As a final practice, edit a piece of your own writing for semicolons, colons, parentheses, dashes, and hyphens. It can be a paper you are working on for this course, a paper you've already finished, a paper for another course, or a piece of writing from your work or everyday life. You may want to try more than one way to use these marks of punctuation in your writing.

40
Capitalization
Using Capital Letters

Understand Capitalization

There are three basic rules of capitalization: Capitalize the first letter of

- every new sentence.
- names of specific people, places, dates, and things.
- important words in titles.

If you can remember these three rules, you will avoid the most common errors in capitalization.

Practice Capitalization

Capitalization of Sentences

Capitalize the first letter in each new sentence, including the first word in a direct quotation.

Mary was surprised when she saw all the people.

She asked, "What's going on here?"

■ PRACTICE 1   **CAPITALIZING THE FIRST WORD IN A SENTENCE**

■ For more practice
with capitalization,
visit Exercise Central at
<bedfordstmartins
.com/realessays>.

Edit the following paragraph, changing lowercase letters to capital letters as needed. If a sentence is already correct, put a "C" next to it.

(1) Many fans of classic films point to 1939 as the greatest year in cinema history. (2) Moviegoers that year were mesmerized by Rhett Butler telling Scarlett O'Hara, "frankly, my dear, I don't give a damn." (3) the same year, audiences thrilled to the story of little Dorothy, who clicked her heels together and chanted, "there's no place like home." (4) the films of 1939 still make movie buffs shake their heads and mutter, "they don't make movies like that anymore!"

Capitalization of Names of Specific People, Places, Dates, and Things

Capitalize the first letter in names of specific people, places, dates, and things. Do not capitalize general words such as *college* as opposed to the specific name: *Lincoln College*. Look at the examples for each group.

People

■ The word *president* is not capitalized unless it comes directly before a name as part of that person's title: President George W. Bush.

Capitalize the first letter in names of specific people and in titles used with names of specific people.

SPECIFIC	NOT SPECIFIC
Carol Schopfer	my friend
Dr. D'Ambrosio	the physician
Professor Shute	your professor
Aunt Jane, Mother	my aunt, my mother

The name of a family member is capitalized when the family member is being addressed directly or when the family title is standing in for a first name.

Good to see you, Sister.

I see Mother is now taking classes.

In other instances, do not capitalize.

It is my sister's birthday.

My mother is taking classes.

Places

Capitalize the first letter in names of specific buildings, streets, cities, states, regions, and countries.

SPECIFIC	NOT SPECIFIC
Bolton Police Department	the police department
Washington Street	our street
Boston, Massachusetts	my hometown
Texas	this state
the West	the western part of the country
Italy	that country

■ Do not capitalize directions in a sentence: *Drive south for five blocks.*

Dates

Capitalize the first letter in the names of days, months, and holidays. Do not capitalize the names of the seasons (winter, spring, summer, fall).

SPECIFIC	NOT SPECIFIC
Monday	today
January 4	winter
Presidents' Day	my birthday

Organizations, Companies, and Groups

SPECIFIC	NOT SPECIFIC
San Antonio College	my college
Toys "R" Us	the toy store
Merrimack Players	the theater group

Languages, Nationalities, and Religions

■ The names of languages should be capitalized even if you aren't referring to a specific course: *I am taking nutrition and Spanish.*

SPECIFIC	NOT SPECIFIC
English, Greek, Spanish	my first language
Christianity, Buddhism	your religion

Courses

SPECIFIC	NOT SPECIFIC
English 100	a writing course
Nutrition 100	the basic nutrition course

Commercial Products

SPECIFIC	NOT SPECIFIC
Diet Coke	a diet cola
Hershey bar	a chocolate bar

PRACTICE 2   CAPITALIZING NOUNS

Edit the following sentences by adding capitalization as needed or removing capitalization where it is inappropriate.

EXAMPLE: My H̲igh S̲chool had a painting by Birger Sandzen on
display in an A̲rt classroom.

1. Lindsborg is a small town in McPherson county, Kansas, that calls itself
   "little sweden, U.S.A."

2. Lindsborg's Restaurant, the Swedish crown, serves Swedish Meatballs at
   its sunday smorgasbord.

3. The Town's most famous resident was probably a swedish immigrant
   Artist named Birger Sandzen.

4. He read a book by the founder of Bethany college in lindsborg and came to kansas to teach at the College in 1894.

5. Sandzen intended to stay in kansas for two or three years, but he loved the great plains and ended up remaining in lindsborg for the rest of his life.

6. Sandzen taught Art, but he also taught Languages, and he sang as a Tenor with the Bethany oratorio society.

7. Although Sandzen worked mainly in the midwest, the Rocky mountains, and other relatively unpopulated parts of The United States, he exhibited widely.

8. His show at the Babcock galleries in new york received an enthusiastic Critical response.

9. Sandzen's use of vivid color showed the beauty of the natural landscapes of the west.

10. Sandzen's name may not be familiar to every Art Lover, but his paintings and engravings—which are found in private collections, at Schools in Kansas, and at the Sandzen memorial gallery in Lindsborg—are quite valuable today.

Capitalization of Titles

Capitalize the first word and all other important words in titles of books, movies, television programs, magazines, newspapers, articles, stories, songs, papers, poems, legislation, and so on. Words that do not need to be capitalized (unless they are the first word) include articles (*the, a, an*); coordinating conjunctions (*and, but, for, nor, or, so, yet*); and prepositions.

■ For more on punctuating titles, see pages 585–86. For a list of common prepositions, see page 330.

The Apprentice is a very popular television program.

Newsweek and *Time* often have similar cover stories.

"Once More to the Lake" is one of Chuck's favorite essays.

■ **PRACTICE 3 CAPITALIZING TITLES**

Edit the following sentences by capitalizing titles as needed.

                                        I   N   E   B   G   T

EXAMPLE: Kermit the Frog sang "it's not easy being green" in *the*
muppet movie.

1. The television show *sesame street,* which began in 1969, brought innovative programming to children.

2. My favorite among the show's friendly puppets, known as the Muppets, was Ernie, who liked to sing "rubber ducky."

3. The popular Muppets Kermit the Frog and Miss Piggy starred in several films, including one based on Charles Dickens's classic *a christmas carol* and one based on Robert Louis Stevenson's *treasure island.*

4. The show contained no advertising, but magazines such as *sesame street parents* and toys based on the characters brought in huge amounts of money.

5. "Elmo's world," a segment added to the show in the 1990s, introduced the small red monster who would become one of the most popular toys in history.

Edit Paragraphs and Your Own Writing

Edit the following paragraphs by capitalizing as needed and removing any unnecessary capitalization.

■ **EDITING REVIEW**

    (1) Are Pennies necessary? (2) In 2001, representative Jim Knowles of arizona introduced legislation, the legal tender modernization act, to

require that prices be rounded up or down to the nearest nickel, eliminating the need for pennies. (3) according to the group Americans For Common cents, however, "pennies are a part of our culture and our economy." (4) Should the united states keep its least valuable coin?

(5) Opponents of the Copper coin—which has been made of Zinc with a Copper coating since 1982—say that people don't like to use Pennies. (6) Although many of us are familiar with the saying "find a penny, pick it up; All day long you'll have good luck," a majority of americans do not think that picking up a dropped penny is worth their time and effort. (7) many stores place Penny trays on the counter so that Customers can either leave unwanted pennies or pick a few up for the Cashier to avoid getting any pennies in change. (8) The U.S. mint says that there are over 130 Billion pennies in circulation, but in 2000 it had to produce 14 Billion more—70 Percent of the total number of coins minted—because people tend to throw loose change in a jar and leave it there.

(9) Yet the penny is undeniably a part of American History. (10) Pennies were the first coins minted in the united states, in 1793. (11) Only four of these original coins survive, and they are valued at more than a quarter of a Million dollars each. (12) Pennies were the first U.S. Coins to carry the image of a historical figure: They have featured the likeness of president abraham lincoln since 1909, the one hundredth anniversary of his birth. (13) fifty years later, the lincoln memorial was added to the reverse side, replacing the stalks of wheat on earlier Pennies.

(14) Pennies are part of the culture, too. (15) Everyone has heard the saying "a penny saved is a penny earned," and that idea is not likely to change even though a penny doesn't buy much today. (16) Music lovers may know the popular song "pennies from Heaven," which was a hit for

frank sinatra, and film buffs might have seen either the bing crosby or the steve martin movie with the same name. (17) finally, unlike the john f. kennedy half-dollar coin, which is no longer minted, people simply expect pennies to be there.

(18) Of course, other american coins have disappeared over the years, and perhaps the Penny has outlived its usefulness. (19) But many U.S. Citizens care about the fate of the penny and don't want it to disappear.

■ PRACTICE 4   EDITING YOUR OWN WRITING FOR CAPITALIZATION

As a final practice, edit a piece of your own writing for capitalization. It can be a paper you are working on for this course, a paper you've already finished, a paper for another course, or a recent piece of writing from your work or everyday life.

Part Eight

Readings for Writers

41

Introduction to the Readings

In this part of the book, you will find twenty essays (in Chapters 42–50) that demonstrate the types of writing you have studied: narration, illustration, description, process analysis, classification, definition, comparison and contrast, cause and effect, and argument. Chapter 51 presents a mini-casebook of readings on two themes ("Fitting In" and "Expanding Our Horizons").

These readings are more than just good models of writing. They also tell great stories, argue passionately about controversial issues, and present a wide range of perspectives and information. These essays can also provide you with ideas for your own writing, both in and out of school. Most important, they offer you a chance to become a better reader and writer by examining how others write.

How Can These Readings Help You?

Reading the essays in this part of the book will help you develop several different abilities.

Your Ability to Write

The essays in this section are good examples of the types of the writing you are doing in your writing course. By looking at how someone else states main ideas, provides supporting details, organizes ideas, and introduces and concludes an essay, you gain a better sense of how you might write a similar type of essay. The essays can also help you choose writing topics: As you react to an author's ideas, you may discover ideas of your own to explore. It's a good idea to keep a reading journal to record these ideas.

Your Ability to Read Critically

To get the most out of what you read, you need to read closely and critically. **Close reading** means that you pay attention to every word and every point in the essay. **Critical reading** means that you ask yourself why the author has made these points in this way and whether you agree. To help you read closely and critically, the essays in this section contain many notes and questions. Soon you will find that questioning, checking, and probing come naturally to you. For more advice on close, critical reading, see Chapter 1.

Your Ability to Understand Other Experiences and Points of View

The authors of these selections vary in age, gender, race, culture, and experience, and their writing reflects their many differences. In a rapidly changing world, your ability to understand, appreciate, and interact with people whose outlooks and experiences differ from your own is essential.

Increasingly, employers value social skills, communication skills, and the ability to work as part of a team. Being able to understand new and different viewpoints can help you work well in a group. Another benefit may be more personal: As you read more and learn to see things through other people's eyes, you may discover new perspectives on your own life.

Your Ability to Help Yourself

Much practical information about living in the modern world is contained in written form, either print or electronic. As a good reader, you will be able to find out whatever you need to know. The list of topics is endless: making money, investing, starting your own business, finding a job, raising a family, treating an illness, protecting yourself from unfairness, buying a car at the best price, and so on. When you read well, you can find help to get what you need, which means you can be independent.

42
Narration

Each essay in this chapter uses narration to get its main point across. As you read these essays, consider how they achieve the four basics of good narration that are listed below and discussed in Chapter 9 of this book.

▟ FOUR BASICS OF GOOD NARRATION

1. It reveals something of importance to you (your **main point**).
2. It includes all of the major events of the story (**primary support**).
3. It uses details to bring the story to life for your audience (**supporting details**).
4. It presents the events in a clear order, usually according to when they happened.

Chitra Banerjee Divakaruni
Spice of Life

Chitra Banerjee Divakaruni, born in 1956 in Calcutta, India, is a writer known for her portrayals of immigrant Indian women in the United States. In 1995, Divakaruni published her first collection of short stories, *Arranged Marriage,* which won an American Book Award. Since then, she has published articles in more than fifty magazines, written several books of poetry and short stories, and authored several novels, including *The Mistress of Spices* (1997), *Sister of My Heart* (1999), *The Vine of Desire* (2002), and *Queen of Dreams* (2004).

In "Spice of Life," Divakaruni shares the story of an abused woman she met while volunteering at an organization that helps victims of domestic violence. A year after the events detailed in this essay, Divakaruni founded a help line for South Asian women in abusive relationships. The essay, originally published by Salon.com, reveals the writer's desire to give readers a fuller view of battered women than the simplistic views often presented in other media.

GUIDING QUESTION

What does Divakaruni want readers to learn from this story?

PREDICT: Pause after you've finished the first paragraph. Why do you think the young woman might be afraid?

Seven years ago, soon after I started volunteering with an organization 1 against domestic violence, I was called one morning to come into the office of the Support Network for Women in Mountain View. There was a South Asian woman there, and they needed help talking to her. When I got there, I found, in one of the inner rooms, a young woman with a baby boy. She was a beautiful young woman. Her face, with its strikingly dark, long-lashed eyes and sculpted lips, would not have been out of place on the cover of a fashion magazine. From her designer-label clothes I could see that she, or at least her spouse, was well-to-do. But she was emaciated,[1] as though she hadn't eaten properly in months, and when later, in the course of our conversation, she raised her shirt, I could see that her back was completely lacerated,[2] as though she'd been dragged over a rough surface like a concrete patio. That day, sitting in that tiny room, I learned the smell of fear. It was an odor like rusting metal, rising from her skin. Every breath coming from her was laden with it.

The first thing she said to me was, "I've made a terrible mistake, leav- 2 ing home like this. My husband will kill me if he finds out, or worse. I've got to get back before he returns from work."

I told her she had been brave and right to leave a home where she was 3 obviously abused. The agency would place her in a safe shelter where her husband wouldn't find her.

"The writer's story of an abused woman really hit home for me. I enjoyed reading this piece."
—Roseann Castillo, student

She told me of her family back in India, how ashamed they would be 4 that she left her husband's home, that she couldn't make her marriage work. I asked her if they knew about the abuse. She shrugged her shoulders. It didn't matter, she said. What mattered was that she had a younger sister who wouldn't be able to find a good marriage-match if people came to know of her situation. "You have to think about yourself," I said. "You have to take care of yourself and your baby."

[1] **emaciated:** extremely thin

[2] **lacerated:** wounded by ripping or tearing

She started crying then. That was what was bothering her the most, she said. She'd deprived her son of a good home, all the love and opportunity his father could provide him with—for he was a good father, her husband, and rich also. How could she, who'd never been trained to work, provide for him in America? "There are programs to help you with money and training," I told her. "Your son will be safer and better off in a poorer home, if it is one without abuse." But I could see she wasn't convinced.

I told her how, in most cases of battering, the abuse gets worse if the woman goes back to the abuser. I told her of women who had died or been damaged for life. I urged her to report the case to the police and ask for a restraining order, but from her eyes I could see that the idea of turning her own husband over to the police was a horrifying one to her. "You have many other options," I said. "You can start a new life. We've seen hundreds of women do it."

But not me, her eyes said. It's hard for eyes to say otherwise, when for years they've seen hate and anger and lack of respect on the face of the man who's supposed to love them more than anyone in the whole world.

"At least think it over carefully before you make any hasty decisions," I said. "You can always go back, but once you're back, you may not be able to leave."

Finally she agreed to let us put her in a shelter. She agreed to think about options other than returning to her husband. That was the last time I saw her. Sometime the next day, she called her husband from a street phone, and he came and got her. Since she had not given us her name or an address, we never found out what happened after that.

I think of her often as I last saw her, climbing into the car that is to take her to the shelter. She clutches her baby tightly as she looks over her shoulder, her beautiful eyes full of fear and guilt and self-doubt and love and family duty and hopelessness.

Can you blame her for the choice she made, even as you see how wrong it was for her to go back to a violent home? Can you say that in her situation you could have done better? No matter what your ethnicity or background, can you say she is that different from you in wanting what she wanted: security, caring, a chance at happiness? I can't.

It is my hope that more people will think a little more about the place in which the battered woman finds herself: dark and cold and suffocating, like the bottom of a well. I hope they will look beyond the popular stereotypes of weakness, lack of education, and low self-esteem to see into her heart. I hope they will feel for themselves the many conflicting and confusing forces pulling her this way and that in the darkness as she tries to climb out. For some of us, that climbing out takes years, perhaps a lifetime. But it can happen. And it can, perhaps, happen a little sooner if people around us are a little slower to judge us.

5

6 **REFLECT:** Do you think the author gives the young woman good advice in paragraph 6? Why or why not?

_____

7 _____

_____

8 _____

9

10

11 **REFLECT:** How would you answer the questions in paragraph 11?

_____

12 _____

_____

_____

■ **SUMMARIZE AND RESPOND**

In your reading journal or elsewhere, summarize the main point of "Spice of Life." Then, go back and check off support for this main idea. Next, write a brief summary (three to five sentences) of the essay. Finally, jot down your initial response to the essay. How would you answer the questions posed in paragraph 11?

■ **CHECK YOUR COMPREHENSION**

1. Which of the following would be the best alternative title for this essay?

   a. "At the Bottom of the Well"

   b. "A Bad Choice"

   c. "Hasty Decisions"

   d. "Hopeless"

2. The main idea of this essay is that

   a. it is very difficult to counsel women who are victims of abuse.

   b. many victims of domestic abuse return to their abuser because they have low self-esteem or lack the education needed to support themselves.

   c. victims of domestic abuse should consider their children, not themselves, when deciding how to handle their situation.

   d. society needs to look beyond the stereotype of the battered woman to understand the difficult position she is in.

3. According to the author,

   a. the woman's lack of education and low self-esteem contributed to her abusive situation.

   b. the woman was unable to understand the pattern of repeated and escalating violence that could occur if she returned to her husband.

   c. the abuse victim was confused about the types of support that the agency could offer her.

   d. the woman was hesitant to leave her husband because he was a good father and provider.

4. If you are unfamiliar with the following words, use a dictionary to check their meanings: laden (para. 1); deprived (5); ethnicity (11); suffocating (12).

READ CRITICALLY

1. In paragraph 11, Divakaruni asks a series of questions. How do these questions help her achieve the essay's main purpose?

2. In paragraph 12, to what does Divakaruni compare the abused woman's situation? Why do you think she makes this comparison? Is it effective?

3. Why do you think the abuse victim returned to her husband? Support your answer with examples from the essay.

4. After meeting the woman in the story, how might the author have changed the way she counsels abuse victims?

5. Having read this essay, what suggestions would you make to domestic abuse counselors to help them improve the way they counsel abuse victims? Support your answer with specific examples from the essay.

WRITE AN ESSAY

Write a narration essay about a situation in which you made an important decision. You could write about a decision to attend a particular college, to change your major, to end a relationship, or to confront a serious problem at work. In paragraphs within your essay, explain how you gathered information to make the decision, how you presented the decision to others, and how your life has been affected by that decision.

Langston Hughes

Salvation

Langston Hughes was born in 1902 in Joplin, Missouri, and spent his high school years in Cleveland, Ohio. Later, he studied engineering at Columbia University, but he eventually dropped out, soon becoming a central figure in the Harlem Renaissance, a period of creative innovation by writers, artists, and musicians in the African American section of New York. Hughes died in 1967. While he is primarily known as a poet, he was also a prolific writer of stories, plays, and essays.

In this excerpt from his autobiography, *The Big Sea*, Hughes recounts a childhood struggle to fulfill others' expectations while remaining true to his own ideas about being "saved."

GUIDING QUESTION
Why does Hughes say in the second sentence that he was "not really saved"?

PREDICT: Based on the first paragraph, what do you expect this essay to be about?

I was saved from sin when I was going on thirteen. But not really saved. [1] It happened like this. There was a big revival at my Auntie Reed's church. Every night for weeks there had been much preaching, singing, praying, and shouting, and some very hardened sinners had been brought to Christ, and the membership of the church had grown by leaps and bounds. Then just before the revival ended, they held a special meeting for children, "to bring the young lambs to the fold." My aunt spoke of it for days ahead. That night I was escorted to the front row and placed on the mourners' bench with all the other young sinners, who had not yet been brought to Jesus.

My aunt told me that when you were saved you saw a light, and some- [2] thing happened to you inside! And Jesus came into your life! And God was with you from then on! She said you could see and hear and feel Jesus in your soul. I believed her. I had heard a great many old people say the same thing and it seemed to me they ought to know. So I sat there calmly in the hot, crowded church, waiting for Jesus to come to me.

The preacher preached a wonderful rhythmical sermon, all moans and [3] shouts and lonely cries and dire pictures of hell, and then he sang a song about the ninety and nine safe in the fold, but one little lamb was left out in the cold. Then he said: "Won't you come? Won't you come to Jesus? Young lambs, won't you come?" And he held out his arms to all us young sinners there on the mourners' bench. And the little girls cried. And some of them jumped up and went to Jesus right away. But most of us just sat there.

A great many old people came and knelt around us and prayed, old [4] women with jet-black faces and braided hair, old men with work-gnarled hands. And the church sang a song about the lower lights are burning, some poor sinners to be saved. And the whole building rocked with prayer and song.

Still I kept waiting to *see* Jesus. [5]

Finally all the young people had gone to the altar and were saved, but [6] one boy and me. He was a rounder's[1] son named Westley. Westley and I were surrounded by sisters and deacons praying. It was very hot in the church, and getting late now. Finally Westley said to me in a whisper: "God damn! I'm tired o' sitting here. Let's get up and be saved." So he got up and was saved.

Then I was left all alone on the mourners' bench. My aunt came and [7] knelt at my knees and cried, while prayers and songs swirled all around me

[1] **rounder:** man with a bad character

in the little church. The whole congregation prayed for me alone, in a mighty wail of moans and voices. And I kept waiting serenely for Jesus, waiting, waiting—but he didn't come. I wanted to see him, but nothing happened to me. Nothing! I wanted something to happen to me, but nothing happened.

I heard the songs and the minister saying: "Why don't you come? My dear child, why don't you come to Jesus? Jesus is waiting for you. He wants you. Why don't you come? Sister Reed, what is this child's name?"

"Langston," my aunt sobbed.

"Langston, why don't you come? Why don't you come and be saved? Oh, Lamb of God! Why don't you come?"

Now it was really getting late. I began to be ashamed of myself, holding everything up so long. I began to wonder what God thought about Westley, who certainly hadn't seen Jesus either, but who was now sitting proudly on the platform, swinging his knickerbockered[2] legs and grinning down at me, surrounded by deacons and old women on their knees praying. God had not struck Westley dead for taking his name in vain or for lying in the temple. So I decided that maybe to save further trouble, I'd better lie, too, and say that Jesus had come, and get up and be saved.

So I got up.

Suddenly the whole room broke into a sea of shouting, as they saw me rise. Waves of rejoicing swept the place. Women leaped in the air. My aunt threw her arms around me. The minister took me by the hand and led me to the platform.

When things quieted down, in a hushed silence, punctuated by a few ecstatic "Amens," all the new young lambs were blessed in the name of God. Then joyous singing filled the room.

That night, for the last time in my life but one—for I was a big boy twelve years old—I cried. I cried, in bed alone, and couldn't stop. I buried my head under the quilts, but my aunt heard me. She woke up and told my uncle I was crying because the Holy Ghost had come into my life, and because I had seen Jesus. But I was really crying because I couldn't bear to tell her that I had lied, that I had deceived everybody in the church, and I hadn't seen Jesus, and that now I didn't believe there was a Jesus any more, since he didn't come to help me.

[2] **knickerbockered:** wearing a pair of knee-length pants popular for boys in the early twentieth century

8 PREDICT: What do you think Hughes might do next?

9 _____

10 _____

11 _____

12

13

14

15

SUMMARIZE AND RESPOND

In your reading journal or elsewhere, summarize the main point of "Salvation." Then, go back and check off support for this main idea. Next, write a brief summary (three to five sentences) of the essay. Finally, jot down your initial response to the essay. What do you think Hughes wanted to communicate to readers by relating this story from his youth? What did you learn about Hughes as a young person?

■ **CHECK YOUR COMPREHENSION**

1. Which of the following would be the best alternative title for this essay?
   a. "Auntie Reed's Church"
   b. "The Power of Prayer"
   c. "Waiting for Jesus"
   d. "Westley and Me"

2. The main idea of this essay is that
   a. most religious people are hypocrites.
   b. a good preacher can stir a congregation to be saved.
   c. Hughes had a very religious upbringing that affected him throughout his lifetime.
   d. Hughes lost his faith because he didn't see Jesus when he pretended to be saved.

3. According to Hughes, his aunt
   a. deeply wanted him to be saved.
   b. raised him for most of his childhood.
   c. was herself saved when she was twelve years old.
   d. knew why Hughes was really crying after the revival meeting.

4. If you are unfamiliar with the following words, use a dictionary to check their meanings: escorted (para. 1); dire (3); gnarled (4); congregation, serenely (7); deacons (11); deceived (15).

■ **READ CRITICALLY**

1. How can you tell that Hughes truly wanted to be "brought to Christ" (para. 1)?

2. Why did Hughes finally join the other children who had been "saved"?

3. What does the fact that Hughes cried after the revival service tell you about him?

4. What is the purpose of the exclamation points after the first three sentences of paragraph 2?

5. Note where Hughes uses direct quotation in the essay. What is the effect of these quotations?

WRITE AN ESSAY

Write an essay about a time in your youth when you desperately wanted to experience or achieve something but failed to do so. In addition to narrating the events that occurred, share the thoughts and feelings you had at the time.

43

Illustration

Each essay in this chapter uses illustration to get its main point across. As you read these essays, consider how they achieve the four basics of good illustration that are listed below and discussed in Chapter 10 of this book.

▚ FOUR BASICS OF GOOD ILLUSTRATION

1. It has a point to illustrate.
2. It gives specific examples to show, explain, or prove the point.
3. It gives details to support these examples.
4. It uses enough examples to get the writer's point across.

Bob Greene

Foul Mouths Are Fair Game in Our Coarsening Culture

Bob Greene was born in Columbus, Ohio, in 1947. After graduating with a degree in journalism from Northwestern University, he began his writing career as a reporter for the *Chicago Sun-Times*. Greene quickly shifted from reporting to writing columns, and he joined the *Chicago Tribune* as a columnist in 1978. He resigned from the *Tribune* in 2002. In addition to publishing collections of his columns, Greene has written several full-length works: *Billion Dollar Baby* (1974), an account of his experiences touring with the rock band Alice Cooper; *Good Morning,*

Merry Sunshine (1984), a journal about his first year as a father; and *Duty* (2000), a memoir of his own father, a World War II veteran.

In "Foul Mouths Are Fair Game in Our Coarsening Culture," originally published as a column in the *Chicago Tribune,* Greene explores the issue of vulgar language. Note how he presents several specific incidents to illustrate his main point.

GUIDING QUESTION
Why do people use profanity so often, according to Greene?

We claim to want to change the world, but before we attempt anything quite that grandiose,[1] we ought to work on changing how we treat each other. 1

Here are two scenes from the lakefront in Chicago, from two recent sunny days: 2

A fellow who is out with his wife—apparently uncertain of the etiquette of the lake's bike-and-jogging path—tentatively[2] moves his bicycle away from the water fountain and horizontally across the path so that he can get in the proper lane. Another bicyclist is barreling along. He sees the crossing bicyclist too late, and slams into him. Both men hit the deck. 3

The man who has been speeding along picks himself up and screams at the top of his voice, "You (bleeping) idiot! You (bleeping) idiot! What is wrong with you, you (bleeping) idiot?" 4

The man who had been walking the bike across the path is humiliated; he tries to apologize, but the obscenities continue to bellow at him as people watch. His wife looks as if she is about to cry. 5

Here is the next scene: 6

Farther north on the trail, a line of six or seven men and women on bicycles is rolling, single file, in a southward direction. It's kind of narrow, and there isn't much extra room for people on one side or the other. 7

Walking north, by herself, is a woman considerably older than the bicyclists. She is not straddling the center line with her feet; she is where she is supposed to be. The bicyclists, as they speed past her, tell her to "Get over"—to move out of their way. As she is doing so, a female bicyclist, near the end of the line, pedals past the woman, whom she knows nothing about and has never met, and uses a vulgar reference to a female dog. 8

The expression on the older woman's face is startled, embarrassed, and sad at the same time. She has gone out for a walk—alone, unlike 9

PREDICT: What do you think Greene will do in the following paragraphs?

_____

_____

_____

_____

[1] **grandiose:** impressive, important

[2] **tentatively:** hesitantly

many people along the lake—and for no apparent reason she has been gratuitously[3] cursed by some younger woman rolling by.

REFLECT: Do you agree that using obscenities in this way allows people to take control?

Now in the first scenario, the man who repeatedly bellowed the obscenity at the crossing bicyclist in front of the crossing bicyclist's wife, had the right of way; the person he hit was inadvertently[4] in the wrong for trying to cross. In the second situation the older woman walking by herself was completely in the right. In both cases, though, the aggressors took control immediately with their foul language.   10

Why did they do this? They did it because they could. They did it because there is absolutely no value placed, in our current in-your-face culture, on the concept of restraint. If you don't refer to a man who has made a regrettable and unintentional mistake as "a (bleeping) idiot," you are somehow thought to have lost the upper hand. The same applies to the woman bicyclist's reaction to the elderly woman.   11

It's everywhere. At the Wimbledon tennis championships, the men's winner, Goran Ivanisevic, was telling reporters about a controversial point in the match, in which a female official called a foot fault on him.   12

"My first foot fault all tournament," Ivanisevic said. "That ugly, ugly lady, she was really ugly, very serious, you know. I was kind of scared."   13

How very, very gentlemanly and compassionate, after you've won the match, to publicly say that about the appearance of a woman whose only crime was to call a penalty against you that didn't even affect the outcome. Let the woman think of that in days after the tournament—let her think about what the new champion has told the world about her.   14

Of course, it won't make any difference in Ivanisevic's career. He's just doing what comes naturally in our society, in which strength is measured not by what is inside of you, but by the ferocity with which you choose to belittle others.   15

> "I agree that people have become more accepting of foul language in everyday conversation. Most people do not realize that changing society's behavior begins with changing our own."
> —Mark Coronado, student

[3] **gratuitously:** unnecessarily, without reason or cause

[4] **inadvertently:** unintentionally, by mistake

■ SUMMARIZE AND RESPOND

In your reading journal or elsewhere, summarize the main point of "Foul Mouths Are Fair Game in Our Coarsening Culture." Then, go back and check off support for this main idea. Next, write a brief summary (three to five sentences) of the essay. Finally, jot down your initial response to the essay. Do you agree with Greene that profanity is becoming increasingly common and accepted in our society? How often and in what situations are you likely to use coarse words or expressions? Why do you think people use profanity?

CHECK YOUR COMPREHENSION

1. Which of the following would be the best alternative title for this essay?

    a. "Dealing with Anger in Everyday Situations"

    b. "Territorial Aggression"

    c. "Poor Sportsmanship"

    d. "Verbal Restraint: A Need in Our Society"

2. The main idea of this essay is that

    a. the increasingly common use of vulgarity is a disturbing trend.

    b. women use vulgar language just as often as men.

    c. vulgarity helps relieve stress and anger.

    d. people should be fined for using vulgar language in public.

3. According to Greene, people are using coarse language more frequently because

    a. they want to demonstrate the depth of their anger.

    b. they have more reasons to be angry.

    c. they don't care about other people's feelings.

    d. it comes naturally in a culture that places little value on politeness.

4. If you are unfamiliar with the following words, use a dictionary to check their meanings: bellow (para. 5); ferocity, belittle (15).

READ CRITICALLY

1. Greene presents several examples of people using foul language. How do these examples support his main point?

2. How is the example about the tennis player different from Greene's first two examples? What is significant about this difference?

3. Find examples of Greene's use of sarcasm. Is his tone effective? Why, or why not?

4. What does Greene say about the relationship between foul language and the desire to control?

5. According to Greene, how does today's society measure a person's strength?

■   **WRITE AN ESSAY**

Write an essay illustrating one of the following main points:

- People generally treat each other with respect and kindness.
- People generally treat each other with very little respect.

Use examples of incidents you have recently witnessed to support your point.

Barbara Lazear Ascher
On Compassion

Barbara Lazear Ascher (b. 1946) worked as an attorney for several years before turning to writing full-time. She has published several books of essays, including *Landscape Without Gravity: A Memoir of Grief* (1993) and *Dancing in the Dark: Romance, Yearning, and the Search for the Sublime* (1999). Ascher has also been a columnist for the *New York Times* and *Elle* magazine and a contributing editor for *Self*.

This essay was first published in *Elle* in 1988 and later reprinted in Ascher's collection *The Habit of Loving*. Using several scenes witnessed in New York City, she illustrates the complexity of compassion.

GUIDING QUESTION
What two examples does Ascher present in this essay?

The man's grin is less the result of circumstance than dreams or mad-   1
ness. His buttonless shirt, with one sleeve missing, hangs outside the waist of his baggy trousers. Carefully plaited dreadlocks bespeak a better time, long ago. As he crosses Manhattan's Seventy-ninth Street, his gait is the shuffle of the forgotten ones held in place by gravity rather than plans. On the corner of Madison Avenue, he stops before a blond baby in an Aprica[1] stroller. The baby's mother waits for the light to change and her hands close tighter on the stroller's handle as she sees the man approach.

The others on the corner, five men and women waiting for the   2
crosstown bus, look away. They daydream a bit and gaze into the weak rays

---

[1] **Aprica:** an expensive brand of baby stroller

of November light. A man with a briefcase lifts and lowers the shiny toe of his right shoe, watching the light reflect, trying to catch and balance it, as if he could hold and make it his, to ease the heavy gray of coming January, February, and March. The winter months that will send snow around the feet, calves, and knees of the grinning man as he heads for the shelter of Grand Central or Pennsylvania Station.

But for now, in this last gasp of autumn warmth, he is still. His eyes fix   3
on the baby. The mother removes her purse from her shoulder and rummages through its contents: lipstick, a lace handkerchief, an address book. She finds what she's looking for and passes a folded dollar over her child's head to the man who stands and stares even though the light has changed and traffic navigates about his hips.

His hands continue to dangle at his sides. He does not know his part.   4
He does not know that acceptance of the gift and gratitude are what make this transaction complete. The baby, weary of the unwavering[2] stare, pulls its blanket over its head. The man does not look away. Like a bridegroom waiting at the altar, his eyes pierce the white veil.

The mother grows impatient and pushes the stroller before her, bear-   5
ing the dollar like a cross. Finally, a black hand rises and closes around green.

Was it fear or compassion that motivated the gift?   6

Up the avenue, at Ninety-first Street, there is a small French bread   7
shop where you can sit and eat a buttery, overpriced croissant[3] and wash it down with rich cappuccino. Twice when I have stopped here to stave hunger or stay the cold, twice as I have sat and read and felt the warm rush of hot coffee and milk, an old man has wandered in and stood inside the entrance. He wears a stained blanket pulled up to his chin, and a woolen hood pulled down to his gray, bushy eyebrows. As he stands, the scent of stale cigarettes and urine fills the small, overheated room.

The owner of the shop, a moody French woman, emerges from the   8
kitchen with steaming coffee in a Styrofoam cup, and a small paper bag of . . . of what? Yesterday's bread? Today's croissant? He accepts the offering as silently as he came, and is gone.

Twice I have witnessed this, and twice I have wondered, what compels   9
this woman to feed this man? Pity? Care? Compassion? Or does she simply want to rid her shop of his troublesome presence? If expulsion were her motivation she would not reward his arrival with gifts of food. Most proprietors do not. They chase the homeless from their midst with expletives and threats.

As winter approaches, the mayor of New York City is moving the   10
homeless off the streets and into Bellevue Hospital. The New York Civil

IDENTIFY: What is the purpose of this one-sentence paragraph (para. 6)?

_____

_____

_____

_____

SUMMARIZE: How would you summarize what Ascher has tried to communicate in the essay so far?

_____

_____

_____

_____

_____

[2] **unwavering:** not moving

[3] **croissant:** a flaky, crescent-shaped French roll

Liberties Union is watchful. They question whether the rights of these people who live in our parks and doorways are being violated by involuntary hospitalization.

I think the mayor's notion is humane, but I fear it is something else as well. Raw humanity offends our sensibilities. We want to protect ourselves from an awareness of rags with voices that make no sense and scream forth in inarticulate rage. We do not wish to be reminded of the tentative state of our own well-being and sanity. And so, the troublesome presence is removed from the awareness of the electorate.   11

Like other cities, there is much about Manhattan now that resembles Dickensian[4] London. Ladies in high-heeled shoes pick their way through poverty and madness. You hear more cocktail party complaints than usual, "I just can't take New York anymore." Our citizens dream of the open spaces of Wyoming, the manicured exclusivity of Hobe Sound.[5]   12

And yet, it may be that these are the conditions that finally give birth to empathy,[6] the mother of compassion. We cannot deny the existence of the helpless as their presence grows. It is impossible to insulate ourselves against what is at our very doorstep. I don't believe that one is born compassionate. Compassion is not a character trait like a sunny disposition. It must be learned, and it is learned by having adversity at our windows, coming through the gates of our yards, the walls of our towns, adversity that becomes so familiar that we begin to identify and empathize with it.   13

For the ancient Greeks, drama taught and reinforced compassion within a society. The object of Greek tragedy was to inspire empathy in the audience so that the common response to the hero's fall was: "There, but for the grace of God, go I." Could it be that this was the response of the mother who offered the dollar, the French woman who gave the food? Could it be that the homeless, like those ancients, are reminding us of our common humanity? Of course, there is a difference. This play doesn't end—and the players can't go home.   14

---

[4] **Dickensian:** related to the works of the nineteenth-century novelist Charles Dickens, who often wrote of the plight of London's poor

[5] **Hobe Sound:** an expensive waterfront community in Florida

[6] **empathy:** understanding of another's situation and feelings

---

SUMMARIZE AND RESPOND

In your reading journal or elsewhere, summarize the main point of "On Compassion." Then, go back and check off support for this main idea. Next, write a brief summary (three to five sentences) of the essay. Finally, jot down your initial response to the reading. How do you respond to the

---

IDENTIFY: Underline the topic sentence of paragraph 11.

"I enjoyed this selection because I strongly agree with Ascher that we learn how to become compassionate through many encounters (both good and bad)."
—Masataka Aita, student

REFLECT: Why does Ascher conclude her essay with these questions?

_____

_____

_____

_____

actions of the two homeless men and the women they encounter? Do you think the women act out of compassion or from some other motivation?

CHECK YOUR COMPREHENSION

1. Which of the following would be the best alternative title for this essay?

    a. "On the Streets of Manhattan"

    b. "Encounters with Homelessness"

    c. "A Problem We All Ignore"

    d. "The Act of Accepting a Gift"

2. The main idea of this essay is that

    a. homeless people make everyone, even babies, uncomfortable.

    b. homeless people can inspire others to compassionate behavior.

    c. homeless people should be hospitalized for their own good.

    d. not many people show compassion in modern society.

3. According to the author, the decision by the mayor of New York to hospitalize homeless people

    a. is partly intended to spare New Yorkers from having to face the homeless.

    b. violates the rights of homeless people and is therefore a mistake.

    c. is a good idea because most homeless people probably have health problems.

    d. will make it easier for homeless people to eventually find homes.

4. If you are unfamiliar with the following words, use a dictionary to check their meanings: bespeak, gait (para. 1); dangle, weary (4); expulsion, proprietors, expletives (9); humane, inarticulate, tentative, electorate (11); adversity (13).

READ CRITICALLY

1. What does Ascher mean when she writes in paragraph 4 that the homeless man "does not know his part"?

2. What does Ascher mean when she writes "We do not wish to be reminded of the tentative state of our own well-being and sanity" (para. 11)? Do you

agree that exposure to homelessness creates empathy and compassion, or might people fail to notice the homeless after regular exposure to them?

3. How, according to Ascher, can we learn compassion?

4. Why, in her final paragraph, does Ascher refer to Greek tragedy? What comparison is she making?

WRITE AN ESSAY

Write an essay in which you consider, on the basis of your own experiences and observations, how people respond to the misfortunes of others. Do most people respond similarly, or are there a variety of responses? Be sure to illustrate your main point with specific examples.

44

Description

Each essay in this chapter uses description to get its main point across. As you read these essays, consider how they achieve the four basics of good description that are listed below and discussed in Chapter 11 of this book.

▪▪ FOUR BASICS OF GOOD DESCRIPTION

1. It creates a main impression—an overall effect, feeling, or image—about the topic.
2. It uses specific examples to support the main impression.
3. It supports those examples with details that appeal to the senses: sight, hearing, smell, taste, and touch.
4. It brings a person, place, or physical object to life for the reader.

Rubén Martínez

Mexico to Mecca: The Flores Family

Rubén Martínez is an Emmy Award–winning journalist, writer, and musician. He is the author of *Crossing Over: A Mexican Family on the Migrant Trail* (2001) and an associate editor for the Pacific News Service. In addition to publishing articles in the *New York Times,* the *Washington Post,* and many other publications, he has appeared as a political commentator on *Frontline, Nightline,* and *All Things Considered.* He currently teaches creative writing at the University of Houston.

"Mexico to Mecca: The Flores Family" is from Martínez's *The New Americans,* a companion book to his PBS series of the same name. In it he describes the landscape and culture of an area of California recently settled by Mexican immigrants.

GUIDING QUESTION

What is life like for the families who live in Mecca, California?

SUMMARIZE: Summarize the main impression created by paragraph 1.

It is 95 degrees at nine o'clock in the evening in Mecca, California, not 1 unusual for the month of September. Ventura Flores, a woman of forty who looks closer to fifty, sits in the dim light on the front steps of her sister's thirty-foot trailer home, where she, her husband, Pedro, and five of their children, along with her sister and five of her children, live. It is a Friday night, and the kids are glued to the TV inside the stifling-hot trailer. In an effort to save money, the owner of the trailer, Ventura's sister Irma, does not turn on the cooler—not an air conditioner, but a contraption that works by dint of evaporating water, also known as a "swamp cooler." It gets its name from the fact that the evaporative system works wonders when the weather is hot and dry, but if there's even a tad of humidity in the air—such as during the "monsoon"[1] summer months, when towering thunderheads rise over the desert floor—the machine merely redoubles the moisture in the air, creating a "swamp" indoors. The Floreses didn't have any kind of cooler in Mexico, but they also lived not in the desert but in the temperate climes of the central part of the country.

Few people would consider Mecca, a small desert outpost about forty 2 miles southeast of Palm Springs, a paradise. It is some fifteen miles off the interstate; the only reason a tourist would wind up in Mecca is, perhaps, to visit the Salton Sea, a strange body of brackish water created when the Colorado River flooded at the turn of the last century. The river no longer floods, having been manipulated by human hands, dammed and diverted, for hydroelectric purposes—and agribusiness. The fortuitous[2] proximity of Mecca to the California Aqueduct[3] transformed the badlands into a booming agricultural region. That's the reason the immigrants are here. Once a place that attracted only a handful of desert rats, Mecca's population is now overwhelmingly Mexican. Increasing numbers of immigrants work in such out-of-the-way places—the economy pushes and pulls, from Third World to First, from city to suburb, from coast to interior, from factory to farmland.

[1] **monsoon:** in southern Asia, a season of heavy rainfall

[2] **fortuitous:** by chance

[3] **aqueduct:** a channel created to carry water from wet regions to more arid ones

There is no movie theater, no mall, only a couple of motels on the out- 3
skirts of town. "Downtown," in fact, is not much more than a gas station
and a convenience store. Not much for a teenager to do here—and there
are plenty of them, hauled in by their migrant parents. Many of them work
alongside the elders in the fields well before their eighteenth birthdays.
Many of them will not finish high school; if they're lucky, they will attend
a couple of night classes to learn basic English. Wound tight with nervous
energy—the tension between their desires and the reality of their station
in life—some of them turn to the "cholo" lifestyle, emulating the gang-
sters of East L.A. with oversize pants, bandanas, and badder-than-bad
shades. They cruise the dusty streets of town in their dilapidated mobiles
looking for action, but they find only the vastness of desert night, an in-
scrutable black mirror. By day, they take their place alongside everyone
else in the fields.

The five working adults of the Flores family (including Ventura's 4   **REFLECT:** What is
daughters Nora and Lorena, nineteen and eighteen years old, respectively)   your response to
all work for $6.75 an hour, just a cut above the minimum wage in Cali-   the working lives
fornia, but there are thirteen mouths to feed at home, rent for the trailer   of the people in
park space, and utility bills. The income is barely enough to cover these   Mecca?
expenses.

The air is dead without the slightest breeze. The heat radiates up from 5
the ground, from the walls of the trailers, from every solid surface that sat
under the white sun all day long. The only sound comes from a couple of
TVs and radios, but even these are turned down low. For most of the
American workforce, Friday night is time to cut loose, but not for the
Mexicans of Mecca. Most of them work six days a week. Saturday is just
another workday that will begin well before dawn.

I ask Ventura's daughter Nora, the eldest, what she usually does on a 6   **REFLECT:** How
Friday night. "Nada," she says, although she clearly wants to go some-   would you feel if
where, anywhere. When she comes home from a day in the fields, where   you were in Nora's
she crouches alongside her aunt from six-thirty in the morning to about   place?
three in the afternoon, she bathes, fixes her hair, and dons makeup, but
more often than not she remains in the trailer park, waiting for something
or someone that never comes.

The trailer park where the family lives is an unpaved slice of land 7
on the outskirts of town. Because most of the trailers are lit so dimly—
low-wattage bulbs mean cheaper electric bills—it is almost impossible
to tell that there is a community of about two dozen families here. You
can drive past it at night and not notice it, the tiny camp lost in the dusty
dark.

It is nearly ten o'clock now, bedtime for the Flores family and for most 8
of Mecca. Since they got off of work, they have bathed, cooked, cleaned,
watched TV, and chatted quietly on the steps of the trailer. There is nothing more to do, except sleep, and dream.

SUMMARIZE AND RESPOND

In your reading journal or elsewhere, summarize the main point of "Mexico to Mecca: The Flores Family." Then, go back and check off support for this main idea. Next, write a brief summary (three to five sentences) of the essay. Finally, jot down your initial response to the reading. What impression do you have of the Flores family? Why do you suppose they live as they do? What would you guess is in store for them in the future?

 CHECK YOUR COMPREHENSION

1. Which of the following would be the best alternative title for this essay?
   a. "Desert Heat"
   b. "A Day in the Fields with Farmworkers"
   c. "Snapshot of a Farmworkers' Community"
   d. "Friday Night Fun in Mecca, California"

2. The main idea of this essay is that
   a. the life of immigrant farmworkers requires a lot of travel.
   b. the farmworkers of Mecca live lives made up mostly of labor.
   c. immigrants from Mexico are drawn to the United States because of its many opportunities.
   d. Mecca is a desert community with an economy based on agriculture.

3. According to the essay, the members of the Flores family
   a. have lived in Mecca for many years.
   b. make barely enough money to cover their expenses.
   c. dream of moving from Mecca to someplace where there is more to do.
   d. are better off than most of their neighbors in the trailer park.

4. If you are unfamiliar with the following words, use a dictionary to check their meanings: contraption, dint, temperate (para. 1); brackish, proximity (2); dilapidated (3); crouches, dons (6).

 READ CRITICALLY

1. What do you think was Martínez's purpose in writing this essay? What might he have hoped readers would take away?

2. What descriptive details of the community of Mecca does Martínez include?

3. What do you think the young people of Mecca have to look forward to as they grow older?

4. How would you describe the effect of paragraph 7? What impression does it leave on you?

5. Martínez uses a comma between the two verbs (*sleep* and *dream*) in his final sentence. How does the comma affect your reading?

■ WRITE AN ESSAY

Write an essay in which you describe a community you know well—the neighborhood where you grew up, for example, or the community you occupy at school or at work. Focus on both the physical aspects of the community and the people there.

Nick Paumgarten
Lost and Found: One Glove

Nick Paumgarten was born in New York City in 1969. After completing a master's degree at Princeton University, he returned to Manhattan and worked as a reporter and editor for the *New York Observer*. He currently writes for the *New Yorker*.

"Lost and Found: One Glove" appeared in the *New Yorker*'s "Talk of the Town" section in 2004. In it, Paumgarten describes a scientist's search for lost gloves and catalogs her findings.

GUIDING QUESTION
Why do you suppose Paumgarten thought Alexandra Horowitz would be an interesting subject to write about?

The ratio of right-handed people to left-handed people is said to be about nine to one (and this dominance goes back more than a million years, apparently), so the lost-glove theory espoused by Alexandra Horowitz, a cognitive[1] scientist who taught at Hunter College last fall, either needs work or suggests that New York is more of a lefty town than most. Last winter, Horowitz began collecting the misplaced—trampled, forlorn,

[1] **cognitive:** related to the functions of the brain

PREDICT: After reading the first paragraph, what would you predict this essay is going to be about?

snot-slicked—mittens and gloves that she saw on the street, not for the sake of research or even, God forbid, art, but out of some deep-seated altruistic[2] urge to see them reunited with their other halves.

"It's an overweening[3] concern for lost objects," she said last week—a 2 very cold week, a great week for gloves. "The melancholy of a lost glove sitting in the middle of a sidewalk struck me as minorly tragic, for the glove and for its owner." Horowitz, who is tall and skinny and thirty-four years old, was in her family's apartment on Central Park West, with her collection in shopping bags on the kitchen counter: a hundred and eighteen mittens and gloves, in varying states of deformity and decay. Black wool dominated, but there was, semi-Arkishly,[4] one of everything: brown zippered faux[5] leather (Lower East Side), tan elbow-length nylon (Lincoln Center), a ludicrous boxing glove (center lane, Columbus Avenue). There were dozens of children's gloves, of course, including Horowitz's first find, a crusty blue mitten, and some thumbless things for infants (and even one for a dog). Central Park is full of little mittens, she said, especially on snowy nights, after the sledders head home. Storefronts, pay phones, subway stairs—O city of lost gloves!

IDENTIFY: What is the effect of the last sentence of paragraph 2?

Horowitz, whose work involves studying the behavior of animals and 3 making inferences about their minds, had done a breakdown—three to one, right hand to left—and come up with a hypothesis. "It's what I call active loss," she explained. "The glove isn't just falling away; the owner has removed it to do something with the dominant hand: dial a phone, dig for change, shake someone's hand. In the cognitive distraction of paying or meeting someone, the glove gets lost. Given that for most people the dominant hand is the right, they're more apt to lose the right glove." Horowitz has observed that, among pedestrians who have one glove off, it's usually the right hand that's bare.

SUMMARIZE: How would you summarize Horowitz's theory regarding single lost gloves?

Wearing colorful, hand-knit mittens and an elegant wool coat, Horo- 4 witz set out on a hunt. She headed for Broadway, scouring the gutters, slowing briefly for a hat that was trapped in a frozen puddle so filthy it looked like lard. A bitter wind kicked up cyclones of movie-ticket stubs and Christmas-tree needles. It soon became clear that lost gloves were one of those things that seem to be everywhere until you start looking for them. She acknowledged this but also worried that the temperature might be too severe. "When it's this cold, there are fewer lost gloves," she said. "People are aware of a lost glove in cold like this. The gloveless intervals

[2] **altruistic:** having others' interests at heart

[3] **overweening:** exaggerated, excessive

[4] **semi-Arkishly:** referring to the biblical Ark of Noah, which carried pairs of all earthly creatures to survive the Great Flood

[5] **faux:** fake

are shorter—the cognitive distraction of an activity is trumped by the extreme cold."

On Broadway, everyone was wearing gloves, but no one was dropping them. The sidewalk looked uncharacteristically clean, as though another glove-hunter had just passed through. Horowitz related some of her ground rules. She doesn't pick up work gloves or rubber kitchen gloves or gloves that have more or less disintegrated. Gloves that have been found by someone else and propped up—on a wrought-iron fence, for example—in the hope that the owner will come back for them, she leaves alone. Obviously, since her mission is pair restoration, she can't in good conscience claim fresh-fallen gloves or stalk someone who seems on the verge of dropping one. "A friend once accused me of eyeing a baby's mittens," she said. Her brother, who happened to lose a nice new leather glove as soon as she started collecting, has blamed her for spreading bad Karma.[6]

5 **REFLECT:** What do you think of Horowitz's "ground rules" for collecting gloves?

At Broadway and Seventy-second, a typically prolific intersection, lost-glove-wise—Gray's Papaya looked promising—there was nothing. While waiting to cross the avenue, though, Horowitz suddenly found that a cameraman was filming one of her mittens: a CBS News crew, prospecting for stories about the cold. The correspondent closed in with a microphone. "We're rolling," the cameraman said. Horowitz hurried off.

6

Two blocks up Broadway, in front of the Ansonia, she suddenly veered into the street and headed for what looked to the untrained eye like a patch of tar but was in fact prime booty: a brown cotton dress glove. Right beside it were two others, a canvas gardening glove and a flattened blue wool-and-nylon number. Here was a glove cluster,[7] a phenomenon that Horowitz had never encountered. There had to be a theory for this.

7

[6] **Karma:** from Hinduism and Buddhism, the belief that one's actions—good or bad—bring back on oneself inevitable related results

[7] **cluster:** in scientific research, a group of things of the same kind that may indicate a significant pattern or phenomenon

▮ SUMMARIZE AND RESPOND

In your reading journal or elsewhere, summarize the main point of "Lost and Found: One Glove." Then, go back and check off support for this main point. Next, write a brief summary (three to five sentences) of the essay. Finally, jot down your initial response to the reading. What do you think of Alexandra Horowitz and her interest in collecting lost gloves? Would you ever consider collecting lost items as she does?

■ **CHECK YOUR COMPREHENSION**

1. Which of the following would be the best alternative title for this essay?

   a. "Right-Handedness versus Left-Handedness"

   b. "A Winter Day in Manhattan"

   c. "The Story of a Missing Glove"

   d. "The Glove Lady of Manhattan"

2. The main idea of this essay is that

   a. Alexandra Horowitz is a cognitive scientist who has taught at Hunter College.

   b. Alexandra Horowitz is an unusual New Yorker who retrieves lost gloves as a hobby and comes up with theories about them.

   c. Alexandra Horowitz has collected shopping bags full of more than a hundred lost gloves and is running out of room.

   d. Alexandra Horowitz had trouble finding lost gloves the day the writer accompanied her on her search.

3. Horowitz tells the author that people are less likely to lose a glove

   a. when the weather is particularly cold.

   b. when the glove is an expensive leather one.

   c. on snowy nights in Central Park after sledding.

   d. when the gloves are work gloves or rubber kitchen gloves.

4. If you are unfamiliar with the following words, use a dictionary to check their meanings: espoused, forlorn (para. 1); melancholy, ludicrous (2); inferences (3); lard, trumped (4); prolific, prospecting (6); veered, booty, phenomenon (7).

■ **READ CRITICALLY**

1. What would you say is Paumgarten's attitude toward Alexandra Horowitz? Why do you feel as you do?

2. What would you point to as some particularly effective descriptive details in the essay?

3. What do you think of the theory regarding misplaced gloves summarized in paragraph 3 and referred to again at the end of paragraph 4?

4. What is Horowitz's purpose in collecting gloves? Do you think she achieves it? Why or why not?

5. Why do you suppose Paumgarten chose to end the essay as he does?

WRITE AN ESSAY

Write an essay describing someone you know who has an unusual hobby or who pursues an unusual interest. Like Paumgarten, focus on your subject's personality as well as his or her activities.

45

Process Analysis

Each essay in this chapter uses process analysis to get its main point across. As you read these essays, consider how they achieve the four basics of good process analysis that are listed below and discussed in Chapter 12 of this book.

▣ FOUR BASICS OF GOOD PROCESS ANALYSIS

1. It helps readers either perform the steps themselves or understand how something works.
2. It presents the essential steps in the process.
3. It explains the steps in detail.
4. It arranges the steps in a logical order (usually in chronological order).

Malcolm X

My First Conk[1]

Malcolm X was born Malcolm Little in Omaha, Nebraska, in 1925. When a teacher told Malcolm that he would never fulfill his dream of becoming a lawyer because he was black, Malcolm lost interest in school,

[1] **conk:** a method of straightening curly hair

dropped out, and spent several years committing drug-related crimes. Malcolm turned his life around, though, when he was sentenced to prison on burglary charges, using the time to further his education and to study the teachings of the Nation of Islam, the Black Muslim movement in America. He also changed his surname from Little to X, suggesting that he could never know his true name—the African name of his ancestors who were made slaves. Malcolm X became an important leader of the Nation of Islam soon after his release from prison, but he later left the group to form his own, less radical religious and civil rights group. In 1964, Malcolm X was assassinated while giving a speech.

"My First Conk" is an excerpt from *The Autobiography of Malcolm X,* which Malcolm cowrote with his friend Alex Haley. Using vivid details to bring the painful process to life, Malcolm takes readers step-by-step through his first "conk"—a process that straightens curly hair.

GUIDING QUESTION
What main point does Malcolm X make about the process he analyzes?

Shorty soon decided that my hair was finally long enough to be conked.[2]   1
He had promised to school me in how to beat the barbershop's three- and four-dollar price by making up congolene,[3] and then conking ourselves.

I took the little list of ingredients he had printed out for me, and went   2
to a grocery store, where I got a can of Red Devil lye,[4] two eggs, and two medium-sized white potatoes. Then at a drugstore near the poolroom, I asked for a large jar of vaseline, a large bar of soap, a large-toothed comb and a fine-toothed comb, one of those rubber hoses with a metal spray-head, a rubber apron and a pair of gloves.

"Going to lay on that first conk?" the drugstore man asked me. I   3
proudly told him, grinning, "Right!"

Shorty paid six dollars a week for a room in his cousin's shabby apart-   4
ment. His cousin wasn't at home. "It's like the pad's mine, he spends so much time with his woman," Shorty said. "Now, you watch me—"

He peeled the potatoes and thin-sliced them into a quart-sized Mason   5
fruit jar, then started stirring them with a wooden spoon as he gradually poured in a little over half the can of lye. "Never use a metal spoon; the lye will turn it black," he told me.

A jelly-like, starchy-looking glop resulted from the lye and potatoes,   6
and Shorty broke in the two eggs, stirring real fast—his own conk and dark face bent down close. The congolene turned pale-yellowish. "Feel the

[2] **conked:** straightened

[3] **congolene:** a product used to straighten hair

[4] **lye:** a strong alkaline substance used in soaps and cleaners

IDENTIFY: What is the main point of paragraphs 8–15?

_____

_____

_____

_____

jar," Shorty said. I cupped my hand against the outside, and snatched it away. "Damn right, it's hot, that's the lye," he said. "So you know it's going to burn when I comb it in—it burns *bad*. But the longer you can stand it, the straighter the hair."

He made me sit down, and he tied the string of the new rubber apron 7 tightly around my neck, and combed up my bush of hair. Then, from the big vaseline jar, he took a handful and massaged it hard all through my hair and into the scalp. He also thickly vaselined my neck, ears and forehead. "When I get to washing out your head, be sure to tell me anywhere you feel any little stinging," Shorty warned me, washing his hands, then pulling on the rubber gloves, and tying on his own rubber apron. "You always got to remember that any congolene left in burns a sore into your head."

The congolene just felt warm when Shorty started combing it in. But 8 then my head caught fire.

I gritted my teeth and tried to pull the sides of the kitchen table to- 9 gether. The comb felt as if it was raking my skin off.

My eyes watered, my nose was running. I couldn't stand it any longer; 10 I bolted to the washbasin. I was cursing Shorty with every name I could think of when he got the spray going and started soap-lathering my head.

He lathered and spray-rinsed, lathered and spray-rinsed, maybe ten or 11 twelve times, each time gradually closing the hot-water faucet, until the rinse was cold, and that helped some.

"You feel any stinging spots?" 12

"No," I managed to say. My knees were trembling. 13

"Sit back down, then. I think we got it all out okay." 14

The flame came back as Shorty, with a thick towel, started drying my 15 head, rubbing hard. *"Easy, man, easy,"* I kept shouting.

"The first time's always worst. You get used to it better before long. 16 You took it real good, homeboy. You got a good conk."

When Shorty let me stand up and see in the mirror, my hair hung 17 down in limp, damp strings. My scalp still flamed, but not as badly; I could bear it. He draped the towel around my shoulders, over my rubber apron, and began again vaselining my hair.

I could feel him combing, straight back, first the big comb, then the 18 fine-tooth one.

Then, he was using a razor, very delicately, on the back of my neck. 19 Then, finally, shaping the sideburns.

_____

_____

_____

_____

_____

_____

My first view in the mirror blotted out the hurting. I'd seen some 20 pretty conks, but when it's the first time, on your *own* head, the transformation, after the lifetime of kinks, is staggering.

The mirror reflected Shorty behind me. We both were grinning and 21 sweating. And on top of my head was this thick, smooth sheen of shining red hair—real red—as straight as any white man's.

How ridiculous I was! Stupid enough to stand there simply lost in ad- 22 miration of my hair now looking "white," reflected in the mirror in

Shorty's room. I vowed that I'd never again be without a conk, and I never was for many years.

This was my first really big step toward self-degradation:[5] When I en- 23 dured all of that pain, literally burning my flesh to have it look like a white man's hair. I had joined that multitude of Negro men and women in America who are brainwashed into believing that the black people are "inferior"— and white people "superior"—that they will even violate and mutilate their God-created bodies to try to look "pretty" by white standards.

[5] **self-degradation:** loss of moral character or honor

REFLECT: Do you think Malcolm X's ideas in this essay are still relevant today?

_____

_____

_____

_____

■ SUMMARIZE AND RESPOND

In your reading journal or elsewhere, summarize the main point of "My First Conk." Then, go back and check off support for this main idea. Next, write a brief summary (three to five sentences) of the essay. Finally, jot down your initial response to the essay. Did it surprise you that a well-known black activist leader once wanted to look more like a white man? What is something you have done to conform to a particular group?

■ CHECK YOUR COMPREHENSION

1. Which of the following would be the best alternative title for this essay?
   a. "The Pain of Conformity"
   b. "Why I Hated My First Conk"
   c. "Hairstyles of the Past"
   d. "Does Anyone Remember Congolene?"

2. The main idea of this essay is that
   a. most people regret something they have done to change their appearance.
   b. making a homemade conking solution is a dangerous process.
   c. when Malcolm X was younger, he wanted to straighten his hair.
   d. conking is a painful and degrading process that Malcolm X later regretted having gone through.

3. According to the author,
   a. he was very pleased when he first saw his straightened hair.
   b. Shorty helped him conk his hair the first time because he didn't have his family's approval.

c.   conking was such a painful experience that he never did it again.

d.   the conk didn't change the way he saw himself.

4. If you are unfamiliar with the following words, use a dictionary to check their meanings: shabby (para. 4); bolted (10); blotted, staggering (20); sheen (21); endured, brainwashed, inferior, mutilate (23).

READ CRITICALLY

1. What do you think is Malcolm X's purpose in analyzing the process of conking?

2. Reread paragraphs 6 through 11, underlining the details Malcolm X uses that appeal to the senses. How do these details support his main point?

3. Without going into too much detail, list the major steps in the conking process.

4. Describe the author's attitude toward conking when he was a teenager. How and why do you think this attitude changed as he grew older?

5. Are the essay's final two paragraphs a good example of an effective conclusion? Why or why not?

WRITE AN ESSAY

Write an essay about a process you have gone through to change your appearance (dieting, tattooing, body piercing, or bodybuilding, for example). In your essay, explain why you made the decision to change your appearance, and then explain the process. In your conclusion, examine how your perception of the experience has changed over time.

Kathleen Squires
Reading between the Lines

Kathleen Squires was born in Pequannok, New Jersey, and attended Lafayette College in Pennsylvania. Her articles have appeared in publications such as the *New York Times, Gourmet,* the *New York Post,* and *Paper* magazine. Before becoming a full-time writer, Squires was a book editor, and she is currently at work on her own novel, *Hot Corn.*

"Reading between the Lines" was published in the September 2004 issue of *Real Simple* magazine. In it Squires gathers the advice of ten experts—in subjects from legal contracts to gossip columns—on how to read in different situations.

GUIDING QUESTION

What does the title suggest about how people can learn to read the types of writing covered in this essay?

It's the too-much-information age. There are the phone book–thick newspapers we don't have time to slog through, the legalese-stuffed contracts we can't fathom, the real estate ads with nuances[1] and code words only insiders get. In the face of our confusion, it helps to understand that "language has meaning and function only in context," says Robin Lakoff, Ph.D., a linguistics[2] professor at the University of California, Berkeley, and the author of *The Language War.* "Focus on who is writing, to whom, where, and with what intentions." [In the following excerpts,] masters of some very different contexts describe how to read more effectively by identifying what is and is not important—and even revealing the secret meaning in the words themselves.

PREDICT: What do you think this selection will be about?

_____

_____

_____

A Menu

Anthony Bourdain, executive chef at Les Halles, in New York City, and author of Kitchen Confidential

Watch out for a menu that is too big, with too many dishes, or is trying to do too many things. It makes me ask, what are they *good* at? Or one that mixes in foreign words and phrases. If you can't sell the monkfish, give it a French name (*lotte*) and jack up the price. When a menu points out that something is "house made," it's just pretentious. Whether you make it or somebody else really good makes it, I don't care. The word *fresh* also rings a warning bell. I'm assuming it's fresh. Why lay it on so thick? Smacks of a guilty conscience. If the same ingredient pops up in various guises on the menu, it's often a sign of hard times. And when you see gimmicky big, lavish leather-bound menus with a lot of scrollwork, it's like seeing a guy in his fifties driving a spanking new Porsche—you know he's having erectile dysfunction. Give me a plain piece of white paper with information on it.

A Real Estate Ad

Barbara Corcoran, founder and chairman, the Corcoran Group

I find that all the truth lies between the lines in life, especially in real estate. The first thing you should do when reading ads is eliminate the adjectives. You'll be left with very little, but it will be much more realistic. The most important bits are location, because it can't be changed; size, because

[1] **nuances:** fine distinctions in meaning

[2] **linguistics:** the study of language

REFLECT: How do you respond to Corcoran's translations of brokers' "short-cut words"?

it's expensive to change; and price, because in today's market there's little room for negotiation. Keep an eye out for brokers' shortcut words. If a place is "cozy," it's too small. If it's "charming," it's too old. Words like "classic," "value," and "needs TLC" mean it's a fixer-upper. A "steal" is a dump. "Convenient" translates to "a little too close to Main Street." "Unique" equals "hard to sell," so bid low. "Asking price" means the broker thought it should be lower but the seller wouldn't have it. "A peek at the park" means if you angle the mirror just so, you'll see an inch of green.

A Wine Label

Olivier Flosse, sommelier, Café Boulud, New York City

The grape, the winemaker, and the vintage are the most important pieces 4 of information on a wine label—the grape because you can immediately decide whether it's the type of wine you want to drink, the winemaker because some are good and some are not, and the vintage because some years are better than others. (I always check to see that the vintage I'm served is the one I ordered—others may be more expensive or not as good.) Words like "reserve" and "private selection" basically mean nothing; they're just marketing. Same for bin or bottle numbers. "Table wine," in any language, is a blend of different grapes from different vintages; that doesn't mean it's not good. "California wine" can mean a blend of grapes from anywhere in the state, not just where they grow best. If a wine's from Napa or Sonoma, it will say so. Country-specific quality classifications may be given. France's best, for example, is labeled "AOC."

A Credit-Card Agreement

Rosetta Jones, director, Visa USA

IDENTIFY/ SUMMARIZE: Underline the main point of this paragraph and summarize the three pieces of advice the writer offers about this main point.

A credit-card agreement is similar to a contract, so you need to under- 5 stand all the nuances. Key terms are given in boldface. The most important thing to understand is the cost of ownership: Zero in on your annual percentage rate; any annual, cash-advance, or ATM fees; and what the late charges are. If you've gotten a promotional rate, make sure you're clear on when it ends and what rate you'll pay afterward. Check for details on fraud protection, resolution options for disputes with merchants, and perks and rewards. Don't be shy about calling the bank if you're unsure about any of the terminology. (Or check your card's Web site. Visa's www.practicalmoneyskills.com has a glossary of credit terms.) For example, people confuse the terms "authorized user" and "cosigner": If you make your daughter an authorized user, she can use the card but has no legal responsibility, whereas a cosigner does.

A Cookbook

Nigella Lawson, cooking-show host and author of Feast: Food to Celebrate Life

Sit down with a new recipe and read it a couple of times over a cup of tea, 6 then ask yourself: *How long is this going to take? Do I understand what I'm being told to do?* Figure out everything you'll need, including tools. If the ingredient list is too long, I know I'm going to be buying things I'll need one tablespoon of and never use again. But don't be deceived that a short recipe is a simple recipe — you want as much description of the method as possible. Generally, if a recipe says something like "combine," it won't matter too much if everything is stirred for ages or not, but it's more helpful if it says, "Listen, this will be very lumpy at this stage. Don't worry — it will get smoother later." And when you glance at a cookbook and know deep down that's not your sort of food, accept it. Don't force yourself to become someone you're not.

A Contract

Raoul Felder, celebrity attorney, New York City

Before you begin, have in front of you a piece of paper listing the key   7
elements to watch for: who the parties are, the duration of the contract, anything relating to payments, and how to prematurely end it. Read everything — including the small print — and highlight things that are unclear to you. Many states have passed a "plain English act," which means contracts have to be in language laymen can understand, but lawyers still often rely on archaic[3] language and protect themselves with double-talk. Look very carefully at anything to do with money and dates — like whether a contract becomes void if a delivery date isn't met. Key terms to watch out for: "nonrefundable" (it means what it says), "default" (are you given time to rectify it?), and "automatic renewal." When you see phrases like "time is of the essence" and "reasonable man standard" — which have an entire body of law defining them — that's your cue to call a lawyer.

A Gossip Column

Jeannette Walls, gossip columnist, MSNBC

When you read an item, think of who the source might be — whom it   8
would benefit. Usually people are trying to get back at an enemy, plug themselves, or divert attention from the real story. If somebody is described as "a major heartthrob," you know it's been leaked by the star's PR people. (If a couple is "blissfully happy," you know the marriage is in trouble.) Blind items — things we know but can't be specific about or name names because we'll get sued — tend to contain reliable information, because it hasn't been planted. The adjectives give clues (for example, someone who's "friendly" is probably from the cast of *Friends*). "Gal pal is often a euphemism for a lesbian lover. If someone is "looking much slimmer," it usually means "liposuction!" "Looking much younger": "facelift!" And to me a "no comment" is generally a confirmation. If it's not true, they'll usually deny it.

---

[3] **archaic:** used in an earlier period but not currently in wide use

IDENTIFY: How does the advice from Walls (p. 641) and Ibargüen, both journalists, differ?

_____

_____

_____

_____

_____

_____

_____

A Newspaper

Alberto Ibargüen, publisher, The Miami Herald

When you're short on time, remember that news stories are typically   9
structured so that "who, what, when, where, and how" go at the top. Read
the first two paragraphs. If you've gotten enough, move on. The front page,
above the fold, has the most important news of the day; the closer a story
is to the top of the page or the bigger its headline, the more important it
is. Headlines, information boxes, and summaries will give you the flavor of
the story. Great photography itself tells a story, and the caption should give
details to ground the photo. If you're not familiar with a particular newspaper, look for the index and a summary. That will point you to the sections of most interest to you and make your read more efficient. U.S.
papers usually take a neutral stance, politically, except in the editorials.
When reading a European paper, keep in mind that the news will generally be slanted toward the left, center, or right.

A Map

Jan Coyne, director, AAA Publishing, GIS/cartography division

REFLECT: What do you find useful about this advice on reading a map?

_____

_____

_____

_____

A good place to start is by checking out the legend,[4] the most overlooked   10
element of a map, to see how the mapmakers represent things like
parks, rest areas, and road classifications (U.S. highway, interstate, etc.—
typically, the brighter and thicker the line, the more major the road). Also
check the legend for the copyright year to be sure the map's not outdated.
Find streets or cities by looking them up in the index. It will give their co-
ordinates—what we call bingo keys—based on the grid numbers and letters at the edges of the map. Orient yourself by checking for an arrow
pointing north. Major U.S. east-west interstates have even numbers;
north-south interstates have odd ones. In most states, interstate exits are
no longer sequential (1, 2 . . .) but indicate mileage from state borders,
going west to east on even routes, south to north on odd.

A Repair Manual

Julie Sussman and Stephanie Glakas-Tenet, authors of Dare to Repair:
A Do-It-Herself Guide to Fixing (Almost) Anything in the Home

First read the instructions from beginning to end and make sure you have   11
all the tools, materials, and know-how you need. This is critical; otherwise
you may realize halfway through the process—like when you've taken
apart your toilet and turned off the plumbing—that you didn't purchase a
necessary part or can't interpret some of the instructions. Often manuals
take basic steps for granted. If you're a beginner, you may leave out those
steps and find yourself in trouble. And don't assume that the instructions
are right—many mistakes just keep getting passed on. It's always good

[4]**legend:** a chart on a map listing the symbols used and their meanings

to check other sources, such as a home-repair book. The manufacturer's customer-service line may be able to fax you more detailed instructions or walk you through the repair over the phone. Check its Web site too.

■ SUMMARIZE AND RESPOND

The opening paragraph describes why and how people need to read between the lines. Write a brief one- or two-sentence summary of this paragraph. Then, for two or three of the passages from experts, check off points of advice for such close reading. Next, summarize the basic advice in each of the passages you selected. Finally, jot down your response to the overall piece. What was some valuable information you learned from the selection? Were you surprised by any of the information presented by the experts? Do you think you will now be able to read some of the featured documents more effectively?

■ CHECK YOUR COMPREHENSION

1. Which of the following would be the best alternative title for this essay?
   a. "A Linguistics Professor's Approach to Reading"
   b. "Learning to Read Like the Experts"
   c. "How to Write to Impress Readers"
   d. "The World of Reading"

2. The main idea of this selection is that
   a. all pieces of writing can be read in basically the same way, regardless of the writer's intention.
   b. different kinds of writing require a different sort of understanding on the part of readers.
   c. readers should be careful in their reading because most public writing is basically dishonest.
   d. the best writing is clear, direct, and concerned primarily with the needs of readers.

3. Which of the following is *not* one of the important points made by one or more of the experts in this selection?
   a. Sometimes, it is important to read through a piece of writing completely before acting on it.
   b. In some cases, writers use words in a specialized sense or in a way not immediately familiar to readers outside of a particular field.

c.   There are many cases when only experts can read a document because average readers cannot understand the language.

d.   Sometimes, readers need to understand some key terms to comprehend a document as a whole.

4. If you are unfamiliar with the following words, use a dictionary to check their meanings: legalese, fathom (para. 1); pretentious, guises (2); vintage (4); promotional, perks, terminology (5); duration, prematurely, void, default (7).

READ CRITICALLY

1. Why is it sometimes important to be able to read between the lines?

2. Why might each particular expert have been chosen to provide advice for reading the documents featured in this selection?

3. What are some of the differences and similarities among the ten processes presented here?

4. Does it seem to you that each of the ten experts has the same kind of reader in mind? Why or why not?

5. What did you learn from these experts about the intentions of writers of the kind of documents included in this piece?

WRITE AN ESSAY

Write an essay describing how to read a certain document between the lines. For instance, you might choose a descriptive advertisement (a product or personal ad), an instruction manual, an interview in a celebrity magazine, a course description or syllabus, an article in a section of the newspaper you often read, or a political speech.

46

Classification

Each essay in this chapter uses classification to get its main point across. As you read these essays, consider how they achieve the four basics of good classification that are listed below and discussed in Chapter 13 of this book.

▪▪ FOUR BASICS OF GOOD CLASSIFICATION

1. It makes sense of a group of people or items by organizing them into meaningful categories.
2. It has a purpose for sorting the people or items.
3. It uses a single organizing principle.
4. It gives detailed examples or explanations of the people or items that fit into each category.

Scott Russell Sanders

The Men We Carry in Our Minds

Since 1971, Scott Russell Sanders (b. 1945) has been an English professor at Indiana University. His observations of the midwestern landscape have informed several of his works, including his latest essay collection, *The Force of Spirit* (2000). In addition to nonfiction, Sanders writes novels, short stories, and children's books, and he has been awarded, among many other honors, a Lannan Literary Award and a Guggenheim Fellowship.

In "The Men We Carry in Our Minds," which first appeared in the *Milkweed Chronicle* in 1984, Sanders looks back at the men he knew during his boyhood in Tennessee. He considers how the hard lives they led challenge some common assumptions of feminism.

GUIDING QUESTION

Into what three categories does Sanders classify the sorts of men he grew up with?

"This must be a hard time for women," I say to my friend Anneke. "They 1 have so many paths to choose from, and so many voices calling them."

"I think it's a lot harder for men," she replies. 2

"How do you figure that?" 3

"The women I know feel excited, innocent, like crusaders in a just 4 cause. The men I know are eaten up with guilt."

We are sitting at the kitchen table drinking sassafras tea, our hands 5 wrapped around the mugs because this April morning is cool and drizzly. "Like a Dutch morning," Anneke told me earlier. She is Dutch herself, a writer and midwife and peacemaker, with the round face and sad eyes of a woman in a Vermeer[1] painting who might be waiting for the rain to stop, for a door to open. She leans over to sniff a sprig of lilac, pale lavender, that rises from a vase of cobalt blue.

"Women feel such pressure to be everything, do everything," I say. 6 "Career, kids, art, politics. Have their babies and get back to the office a week later. It's as if they're trying to overcome a million years' worth of evolution in one lifetime."

"But we help one another. We don't try to lumber on alone, like so 7 many wounded grizzly bears, the way men do." Anneke sips her tea. I gave her the mug with owls on it, for wisdom. "And we have this deep-down sense that we're in the *right*—we've been held back, passed over, used— while men feel they're in the wrong. Men are the ones who've been discredited, who have to search their souls."

I search my soul. I discover guilty feelings aplenty—toward the poor, 8 the Vietnamese, Native Americans, the whales, an endless list of debts—a guilt in each case that is as bright and unambiguous as a neon sign. But toward women I feel something more confused, a snarl of shame, envy, wary tenderness, and amazement. This muddle troubles me. To hide my unease I say, "You're right, it's tough being a man these days."

[1] **Vermeer:** a seventeenth-century Dutch painter known for depictions of people in moments of contemplation

"Don't laugh." Anneke frowns at me, mournful-eyed, through the sassafras steam. "I wouldn't be a man for anything. It's much easier being the victim. All the victim has to do is break free. The persecutor has to live with his past."   9

How deep is this past? I find myself wondering after Anneke has left.   10
How much of an inheritance do I have to throw off? Is it just the beliefs I breathed in as a child? Do I have to scour memory back through father and grandfather? Through St. Paul?[2] Beyond Stonehenge[3] and into the twilit caves? I'm convinced the past we must contend with is deeper even than speech. When I think back on my childhood, on how I learned to see men and women, I have a sense of ancient, dizzying depths. The back roads of Tennessee and Ohio where I grew up were probably closer, in their sexual patterns, to the campsites of Stone Age hunters than to the genderless cities of the future into which we are rushing.

The first men, besides my father, I remember seeing were black con-   11
victs and white guards, in the cottonfield across the road from our farm on the outskirts of Memphis. I must have been three or four. The prisoners wore dingy gray-and-black zebra suits, heavy as canvas, sodden with sweat. Hatless, stooped, they chopped weeds in the fierce heat, row after row, breathing the acrid dust of boll-weevil[4] poison. The overseers wore dazzling white shirts and broad shadowy hats. The oiled barrels of their shotguns flashed in the sunlight. Their faces in memory are utterly blank. Of course those men, white and black, have become for me an emblem of racial hatred. But they have also come to stand for the twin poles of my early vision of manhood—the brute toiling animal and the boss.

When I was a boy, the men I knew labored with their bodies. They   12
were marginal farmers, just scraping by, or welders, steelworkers, carpenters; they swept floors, dug ditches, mined coal, or drove trucks, their forearms ropy with muscle; they trained horses, stoked furnaces, built tires, stood on assembly lines wrestling parts onto cars and refrigerators. They got up before light, worked all day long whatever the weather, and when they came home at night they looked as though somebody had been whipping them. In the evenings and on weekends they worked on their own places, tilling gardens that were lumpy with clay, fixing broken-down cars, hammering on houses that were always too drafty, too leaky, too small.

The bodies of the men I knew were twisted and maimed in ways   13
visible and invisible. The nails of their hands were black and split, the hands tattooed with scars. Some had lost fingers. Heavy lifting had given many of them finicky backs and guts weak from hernias. Racing against

[2] **St. Paul:** New Testament author who established strictures on the roles of husbands and wives

[3] **Stonehenge:** massive prehistoric monument in southern England

[4] **boll weevil:** parasite that destroys cotton plants

PREDICT: What do you expect that Sanders will do in the next few paragraphs of the essay?

_____

_____

_____

_____

SUMMARIZE: How would you summarize the life of the working men Sanders remembers from childhood?

_____

_____

_____

_____

conveyor belts had given them ulcers. Their ankles and knees ached from years of standing on concrete. Anyone who had worked for long around machines was hard of hearing. They squinted, and the skin of their faces was creased like the leather of old work gloves. There were times, studying them, when I dreaded growing up. Most of them coughed, from dust or cigarettes, and most of them drank cheap wine or whiskey, so their eyes looked bloodshot or bruised. The fathers of my friends always seemed older than the mothers. Men wore out sooner. Only women lived into old age.

REFLECT: Do you believe that soldiers have an easier life than do physical laborers?

As a boy I also knew another sort of men, who did not sweat and break down like mules. They were soldiers, and so far as I could tell they scarcely worked at all. During my early school years we lived on a military base, an arsenal in Ohio, and every day I saw GIs in the guardshacks, on the stoops of barracks, at the wheels of olive drab Chevrolets. The chief fact of their lives was boredom. Long after I left the arsenal I came to recognize the sour smell the soldiers gave off as that of souls in limbo.[5] They were all waiting—for wars, for transfers, for leaves, for promotions, for the end of their hitch—like so many braves waiting for the hunt to begin. Unlike the warriors of older tribes, however, they would have no say about when the battle would start or how it would be waged. Their waiting was broken only when they practiced for war. They fired guns at targets, drove tanks across the churned-up fields of the military reservation, set off bombs in the wrecks of old fighter planes. I knew this was all play. But I also felt certain that when the hour for killing arrived, they would kill. When the real shooting started, many of them would die. This was what soldiers were *for*, just as a hammer was for driving nails.

Warriors and toilers: Those seemed, in my boyhood vision, to be the chief destinies for men. They weren't the only destinies, as I learned from having a few male teachers, from reading books, and from watching television. But the men on television—the politicians, the astronauts, the generals, the savvy lawyers, the philosophical doctors, the bosses who gave orders to both soldiers and laborers—seemed as remote and unreal to me as the figures in tapestries. I could no more imagine growing up to become one of these cool, potent creatures than I could imagine becoming a prince.

A nearer and more hopeful example was that of my father, who had escaped from a red-dirt farm to a tire factory, and from the assembly line to the front office. Eventually he dressed in a white shirt and tie. He carried himself as if he had been born to work with his mind. But his body, remembering the early years of slogging work, began to give out on him in his fifties, and it quit on him entirely before he turned sixty-five. Even such a partial escape from man's fate as he had accomplished did not seem possible for most of the boys I knew. They joined the army, stood in line for jobs in the smoky plants, helped build highways. They were bound

[5] **limbo:** in Roman Catholic teaching, a region eternally occupied by souls assigned to neither heaven nor hell

to work as their fathers had worked, killing themselves or preparing to kill others.

A scholarship enabled me not only to attend college, a rare enough feat in my circle, but even to study in a university meant for children of the rich. Here I met for the first time young men who had assumed from birth that they would lead lives of comfort and power. And for the first time I met women who told me that men were guilty of having kept all the joys and privileges of the earth for themselves. I was baffled. What privileges? What joys? I thought about the maimed dismal lives of most of the men back home. What had they stolen from their wives and daughters? The right to go five days a week, twelve months a year, for thirty or forty years to a steel mill or a coal mine? The right to drop bombs and die in war? The right to feel every leak in the roof, every gap in the fence, every cough in the engine, as a wound they must mend? The right to feel, when the lay-off comes or the plant shuts down, not only afraid but ashamed? **17**

I was slow to understand the deep grievances of women. This was because, as a boy, I had envied them. Before college, the only people I had ever known who were interested in art or music or literature, the only ones who read books, the only ones who ever seemed to enjoy a sense of ease and grace were the mothers and daughters. Like the menfolk, they fretted about money, they scrimped and made-do. But, when the pay stopped coming in, they were not the ones who had failed. Nor did they have to go to war, and that seemed to me a blessed fact. By comparison with the narrow, ironclad days of fathers, there was an expansiveness, I thought, in the days of mothers. They went to see neighbors, to shop in town, to run errands at school, at the library, at church. No doubt, had I looked harder at their lives, I would have envied them less. It was not my fate to become a woman, so it was easier for me to see the graces. Few of them held jobs outside the home, and those who did filled thankless roles as clerks and waitresses. I didn't see, then, what a prison a house could be, since houses seemed to me brighter, handsomer places than any factory. I did not realize—because such things were never spoken of—how often women suffered from men's bullying. I did learn about the wretchedness of abandoned wives, single mothers, widows; but I also learned about the wretchedness of lone men. Even then I could see how exhausting it was for a mother to cater all day to the needs of young children. But if I had been asked, as a boy, to choose between tending a baby and tending a machine, I think I would have chosen the baby. (Having now tended both, I know I would choose the baby.) **18**

REFLECT: Why was Sanders "slow to understand the deep grievances of women"?

_____

_____

_____

_____

_____

_____

So I was baffled when the women at college accused me and my sex of having cornered the world's pleasure. I think something like my bafflement has been felt by other boys (and by girls as well) who grew up in dirt-poor farm country, in mining country, in black ghettos, in Hispanic barrios,[6] in the shadows of factories, in third world nations—any place **19**

---

[6]**barrios:** Spanish-speaking communities

where the fate of men is as grim and bleak as the fate of women. Toilers and warriors. I realize now how ancient these identities are, how deep the tug they exert on men, the undertow of a thousand generations. The miseries I saw, as a boy, in the lives of nearly all men I continue to see in the lives of many—the body-breaking toil, the tedium, the call to be tough, the humiliating powerlessness, the battle for a living and for territory.

 REFLECT: Why might Sanders have concluded his essay with these questions?

————————

————————

————————

————————

————————

————————

————————

————————

————————

When the women I met at college thought about the joys and privi-   20
leges of men, they did not carry in their minds the sort of men I had known in my childhood. They thought of their fathers, who were bankers, physicians, architects, stockbrokers, the big wheels of the big cities. These fathers rode the train to work or drove cars that cost more than any of my childhood houses. They were attended from morning to night by female helpers, wives and nurses and secretaries. They were never laid off, never short of cash at month's end, never lined up for welfare. These fathers made decisions that mattered. They ran the world.

The daughters of such men wanted to share in this power, this glory.   21
So did I. They yearned for a say over their future, for jobs worthy of their abilities, for the right to live at peace, unmolested, whole. Yes, I thought, yes yes. The difference between me and these daughters was that they saw me, because of my sex, as destined from birth to become like their fathers, and therefore an enemy to their desires. But I knew better. I wasn't an enemy, in fact or in feeling. I was an ally. If I had known, then, how to tell them so, would they have believed me? Would they now?

▰ SUMMARIZE AND RESPOND

In your reading journal or elsewhere, summarize the main point of "The Men We Carry in Our Minds." Then, go back and check off support for this main idea. Next, write a brief summary (three to five sentences) of the essay. Finally, jot down your initial response to the reading. To what extent do you believe that Sanders's categories of types of men still hold true today? To what extent do you feel that the positions held by men and women in society have changed (or remained the same) since this essay was written? How much sympathy do you have for the feelings Sanders expresses?

▰ CHECK YOUR COMPREHENSION

1. Which of the following would be the best alternative title for this essay?

   a.   "A Conversation with Anneke about Men and Women"

   b.   "My Childhood on a Tennessee Farm"

    c. "A Scholarship Student's Reflections on the Differences between Men and Women"

    d. "The 'Privileges' of Being a Man"

2. The main idea of this essay is that

    a. men control most of the power in society and, therefore, lead more comfortable lives than women.

    b. it is difficult for a young man who grew up poor to see men as having more power than women.

    c. the balance of power between men and women has shifted significantly over the years so that men and women are now more nearly equal.

    d. access to education can create a more level playing field for those who grow up poor and those who grow up rich.

3. According to Sanders,

    a. his childhood observations led him to believe that women led easier lives than men did.

    b. when he went away to college, he felt a great deal of sympathy for the grievances of the women he met there.

    c. the "warriors and toilers" he observed in childhood provided role models for him later in life.

    d. his father struggled throughout his life to provide a comfortable home environment for his family.

4. If you are unfamiliar with the following words, use a dictionary to check their meanings: midwife (para. 5); lumber (7); unambiguous, wary, muddle (8); persecutor (9); genderless (10); acrid (11); marginal (12); maimed, hernias (13); arsenal (14); tapestries (15); dismal (17); expansiveness, wretchedness (18); baffled, undertow, tedium (19).

■ READ CRITICALLY

1. In paragraphs 1–9, what point does Sanders's friend Anneke make about men and women in the United States at the time the essay was written in the early 1980s?

2. Why, in paragraph 8, does Sanders suggest that he chose to agree with Anneke about the place of men in relationship to women ("You're right, it's tough being a man these days") when this was not his true feeling?

3. What sorts of images of men did Sanders grow up with? How did these images affect his attitudes toward the position of women in society?

4. In what ways did the women he met in college challenge Sanders's views of the positions of men and women in society? Why does he think his viewpoint and that of the college women he met were so different? Why did he consider himself their "ally" rather than their "enemy"?

5. How does Sanders communicate a point about social class that goes beyond simply his own experiences?

◼ WRITE AN ESSAY

Write an essay titled "The _____ I Carry in My Mind," filling in the blank with a specific label referring to people: for example, *teachers, students, parents, bosses, coworkers, friends* (or *boyfriends, girlfriends*). Be sure that you have enough examples of the subject you choose so that you can classify them into at least three categories, each of which you can name concretely (as Sanders names "warriors" and "toilers"). In your essay, focus primarily on defining these categories, using specific examples (at least one per category) as illustrations.

Amy Tan
Mother Tongue

Amy Tan was born in Oakland, California, in 1952, several years after her mother and father immigrated from China. She studied at San Jose City College and later San Jose State University, receiving a B.A. with a double major in English and linguistics. In 1973, she earned an M.A. in linguistics from San Jose State. In 1989, Tan published her first novel, *The Joy Luck Club,* which was nominated for the National Book Award and the National Book Critics Circle Award. Tan's other books include *The Kitchen God's Wife* (1991) and *The Hundred Secret Senses* (1995). Her short stories and essays have been published in the *Atlantic, Grand Street, Harper's,* the *New Yorker,* and other publications.

   In the following essay, which was selected for *The Best American Essays 1991,* Tan discusses the different kinds of English she uses, from academic discourse to the simple language she speaks with her mother.

GUIDING QUESTION
In what ways did Tan's mother's "limited" ability to speak English affect Tan as she was growing up?

I am not a scholar of English or literature. I cannot give you much more than personal opinions on the English language and its variations in this country or others.

I am a writer. And by that definition, I am someone who has always loved language. I am fascinated by language in daily life. I spend a great deal of my time thinking about the power of language—the way it can evoke an emotion, a visual image, a complex idea, or a simple truth. Language is the tool of my trade. And I use them all—all the Englishes I grew up with.

Recently, I was made keenly aware of the different Englishes I do use. I was giving a talk to a large group of people, the same talk I had already given to half a dozen other groups. The nature of the talk was about my writing, my life, and my book, *The Joy Luck Club*. The talk was going along well enough, until I remembered one major difference that made the whole talk sound wrong. My mother was in the room. And it was perhaps the first time she had heard me give a lengthy speech, using the kind of English I have never used with her. I was saying things like "The intersection of memory upon imagination" and "There is an aspect of my fiction that relates to thus-and-thus"—a speech filled with carefully wrought grammatical phrases, burdened, it suddenly seemed to me, with nominalized forms, past perfect tenses, conditional phrases, all the forms of standard English that I had learned in school and through books, the forms of English I did not use at home with my mother.

Just last week, I was walking down the street with my mother, and I again found myself conscious of the English I was using, the English I do use with her. We were talking about the price of new and used furniture and I heard myself saying this: "Not waste money that way." My husband was with us as well, and he didn't notice any switch in my English. And then I realized why. It's because over the twenty years we've been together I've often used that same kind of English with him, and sometimes he even uses it with me. It has become our language of intimacy, a different sort of English that relates to family talk, the language I grew up with.

SUMMARIZE: What is Tan's central point in paragraph 4?

So you'll have some idea of what this family talk I heard sounds like, I'll quote what my mother said during a recent conversation which I videotaped and then transcribed. During this conversation, my mother was talking about a political gangster in Shanghai[1] who had the same last name as her family's, Du, and how the gangster in his early years wanted to be adopted by her family, which was rich by comparison. Later, the gangster became more powerful, far richer than my mother's family, and one day showed up at my mother's wedding to pay his respects. Here's what she said in part:

"Du Yusong having business like fruit stand. Like off the street kind. He is Du like Du Zong—but not Tsung-ming Island people. The local

[1] **Shanghai:** a major city in eastern China

people call putong, the river east side, he belong to that side local people. That man want to ask Du Zong father take him in like become own family. Du Zong father wasn't look down on him, but didn't take seriously, until that man big like become a mafia. Now important person, very hard to inviting him. Chinese way, came only to show respect, don't stay for dinner. Respect for making big celebration, he shows up. Mean gives lots of respect. Chinese custom. Chinese social life that way. If too important won't have to stay too long. He come to my wedding. I didn't see, I heard it. I gone to boy's side, they have YMCA dinner. Chinese age I was nineteen."

You should know that my mother's expressive command of English   7
belies how much she actually understands. She reads the *Forbes* report,[2] listens to *Wall Street Week,* converses daily with her stockbroker, reads all of Shirley MacLaine's[3] books with ease — all kinds of things I can't begin to understand. Yet some of my friends tell me they understand 50 percent of what my mother says. Some say they understand 80 to 90 percent. Some say they understand none of it, as if she were speaking pure Chinese. But to me, my mother's English is perfectly clear, perfectly natural. It's my mother tongue. Her language, as I hear it, is vivid, direct, full of observation and imagery. That was the language that helped shape the way I saw things, expressed things, made sense of the world.

IDENTIFY: In paragraphs 9–14, what evidence does Tan present to support her claim that others believed that her mother's English reflected a lack of intelligence?

———————————

———————————

———————————

———————————

———————————

———————————

———————————

Lately, I've been giving more thought to the kind of English my   8
mother speaks. Like others, I have described it to people as "broken" or "fractured" English. But I wince when I say that. It has always bothered me that I can think of no other way to describe it other than "broken," as if it were damaged and needed to be fixed, as if it lacked a certain wholeness and soundness. I've heard other terms used, "limited English," for example. But they seem just as bad, as if everything is limited, including people's perceptions of the limited English speaker.

I know this for a fact, because when I was growing up, my mother's   9
"limited" English limited *my* perception of her. I was ashamed of her English. I believed that her English reflected the quality of what she had to say. That is, because she expressed them imperfectly her thoughts were imperfect. And I had plenty of empirical[4] evidence to support me: the fact that people in department stores, at banks, and at restaurants did not take her seriously, did not give her good service, pretended not to understand her, or even acted as if they did not hear her.

My mother has long realized the limitations of her English as well. When   10
I was fifteen, she used to have me call people on the phone to pretend I was

[2] *Forbes* **report:** a financial publication geared toward investors

[3] **Shirley MacLaine:** actress whose works of autobiography have often referred to her past lives

[4] **empirical:** based on direct experience or observation

she. In this guise, I was forced to ask for information or even to complain and yell at people who had been rude to her. One time it was a call to her stockbroker in New York. She had cashed out her small portfolio and it just so happened we were going to go to New York the next week, our very first trip outside California. I had to get on the phone and say in an adolescent voice that was not very convincing, "This is Mrs. Tan."

And my mother was standing in the back whispering loudly, "Why he don't send me check, already two weeks late. So mad he lie to me, losing me money."   11

And then I said in perfect English, "Yes, I'm getting rather concerned. You had agreed to send the check two weeks ago, but it hasn't arrived."   12

Then she began to talk more loudly. "What he want, I come to New York tell him front of his boss, you cheating me?" And I was trying to calm her down, make her be quiet, while telling the stockbroker, "I can't tolerate any more excuses. If I don't receive the check immediately, I am going to have to speak to your manager when I'm in New York next week." And sure enough, the following week there we were in front of this astonished stockbroker, and I was sitting there red-faced and quiet, and my mother, the real Mrs. Tan, was shouting at his boss in her impeccable broken English.   13

We used a similar routine just five days ago, for a situation that was far less humorous. My mother had gone to the hospital for an appointment, to find out about a benign brain tumor a CAT scan[5] had revealed a month ago. She said she had spoken very good English, her best English, no mistakes. Still, she said, the hospital did not apologize when they said they had lost the CAT scan and she had come for nothing. She said they did not seem to have any sympathy when she told them she was anxious to know the exact diagnosis, since her husband and son had both died of brain tumors. She said they would not give her any more information until the next time and she would have to make another appointment for that. So she said she would not leave until the doctor called her daughter. She wouldn't budge. And when the doctor finally called her daughter, me, who spoke in perfect English—lo and behold—we had assurances the CAT scan would be found, promises that a conference call on Monday would be held, and apologies for any suffering my mother had gone through for a most regrettable mistake.   14

I think my mother's English almost had an effect on limiting my possibilities in life as well. Sociologists and linguists probably will tell you that a person's developing language skills are more influenced by peers. But I do think that the language spoken in the family, especially in immigrant families which are more insular, plays a large role in shaping the language of the child. And I believe that it affected my results on achievement tests, IQ tests, and the SAT. While my English skills were never judged as poor,   15

REFLECT: Have you or anyone you know not been taken seriously because of language, age, race, or some other trait?

_____

_____

_____

_____

[5] **CAT scan:** a form of X-ray used to produce internal images of the body

compared to math, English could not be considered my strong suit. In grade school I did moderately well, getting perhaps B's, sometimes B-pluses, in English and scoring perhaps in the sixtieth or seventieth percentile on achievement tests. But those scores were not good enough to override the opinion that my true abilities lay in math and science, because in those areas I achieved A's and scored in the ninetieth percentile or higher.

REFLECT: What has been your experience with the kinds of English tests that Tan writes about in paragraphs 16–17?

This was understandable. Math is precise; there is only one correct answer. Whereas, for me at least, the answers on English tests were always a judgment call, a matter of opinion and personal experience. Those tests were constructed around items like fill-in-the-blank sentence completion, such as "Even though Tom was _____, Mary thought he was _____." And the correct answer always seemed to be the most bland combinations of thoughts, for example, "Even though Tom was shy, Mary thought he was charming," with the grammatical structure "even though" limiting the correct answer to some sort of semantic⁶ opposites, so you wouldn't get answers like, "Even though Tom was foolish, Mary thought he was ridiculous." Well, according to my mother, there were very few limitations as to what Tom could have been and what Mary might have thought of him. So I never did well on tests like that.

The same was true with word analogies, pairs of words in which you were supposed to find some sort of logical, semantic relationship—for example, "*Sunset* is to *nightfall* as _____ is to _____." And here you would be presented with a list of four possible pairs, one of which showed the same kind of relationship: *red* is to *stoplight, bus* is to *arrival, chills* is to *fever, yawn* is to *boring.* Well, I could never think that way. I knew what the tests were asking, but I could not block out of my mind the images already created by the first pair, "*sunset* is to *nightfall*"—and I would see a burst of colors against a darkening sky, the moon rising, the lowering of a curtain of stars. And all the other pairs of words—red, bus, stoplight, boring—just threw up a mass of confusing images, making it impossible for me to sort out something as logical as saying: "A sunset precedes nightfall" is the same as "a chill precedes a fever." The only way I would have gotten that answer right would have been to imagine an associative situation, for example, my being disobedient and staying out past sunset, catching a chill at night, which turns into feverish pneumonia as punishment, which indeed did happen to me.

REFLECT: How do you think Tan might answer the questions she poses in paragraph 18?

I have been thinking about all this lately, about my mother's English, about achievement tests. Because lately I've been asked, as a writer, why there are not more Asian Americans represented in American literature. Why are there few Asian Americans enrolled in creative writing programs? Why do so many Chinese students go into engineering? Well, these are broad sociological questions I can't begin to answer. But I have noticed in

⁶**semantic:** related to the meaning of words

surveys—in fact, just last week—that Asian students, as a whole, always do significantly better on math achievement tests than in English. And this makes me think that there are other Asian American students whose English spoken in the home might also be described as "broken" or "limited." And perhaps they also have teachers who are steering them away from writing and into math and science, which is what happened to me.

Fortunately, I happen to be rebellious in nature and enjoy the challenge of disproving assumptions made about me. I became an English major my first year in college, after being enrolled as pre-med. I started writing nonfiction as a freelancer the week after I was told by my former boss that writing was my worst skill and I should hone my talents toward account management.

19 **REFLECT:** How do you respond when people make certain assumptions about you?

But it wasn't until 1985 that I finally began to write fiction. And at first I wrote using what I thought to be wittily crafted sentences, sentences that would finally prove I had mastery over the English language. Here's an example from the first draft of a story that later made its way into *The Joy Luck Club,* but without this line: "That was my mental quandary[7] in its nascent[8] state." A terrible line, which I can barely pronounce.

20

Fortunately, for reasons I won't get into today, I later decided I should envision a reader for the stories I would write. And the reader I decided upon was my mother, because these were stories about mothers. So with this reader in mind—and in fact she did read my early drafts—I began to write stories using all the Englishes I grew up with: the English I spoke to my mother, which for lack of a better term might be described as "simple"; the English she used with me, which for lack of a better term might be described as "broken"; my translation of her Chinese, which could certainly be described as "watered down"; and what I imagined to be her translation of her Chinese if she could speak in perfect English, her internal language, and for that I sought to preserve the essence, but neither an English nor a Chinese structure. I wanted to capture what language ability tests can never reveal: her intent, her passion, her imagery, the rhythms of her speech, and the nature of her thoughts.

21

Apart from what any critic had to say about my writing, I knew I had succeeded where it counted when my mother finished reading my book and gave me her verdict: "So easy to read."

22

[7]**quandary:** a state of uncertainty

[8]**nascent:** developing; beginning to come into existence

SUMMARIZE AND RESPOND

In your reading journal or elsewhere, summarize the main point of "Mother Tongue." Then, go back and check off support for this main idea. Next, write a brief summary (three to five sentences) of the essay. Finally, jot down your initial response to the reading. What do you think of Tan's relationship with her mother? Do you think that Tan's mother's "limited" English has affected their relationship for the better, for the worse, or in some more complex way? What impression do you have of Tan herself?

CHECK YOUR COMPREHENSION

1. Which of the following would be the best alternative title for this essay?
   a. "The Englishes I Grew Up With"
   b. "My Mother's Difficulties Communicating in English"
   c. "How to Communicate with an Immigrant Parent"
   d. "A Writer's Fascination with the English Language"

2. The main idea of this essay is that
   a. children of immigrant parents have difficulties communicating in English because of their parents' "limited" command of the language.
   b. there is no single, proper way to speak English because different people communicate in different ways.
   c. teachers believe that Asian American students necessarily do better in math and science than they do in English and writing.
   d. the kind of English one uses may change in different contexts.

3. Tan concludes that
   a. to become a successful writer, she had to work harder than would someone who grew up in a home where English was the native language.
   b. her mother found her book easy to read because her mother grew up speaking Chinese.
   c. in finding her voice as a writer, she called on the memory of her mother and their communication with each other.
   d. to prove her mastery of the English language, she had to write in a way that her mother would find impossible to understand.

4. If you are unfamiliar with the following words, use a dictionary to check their meanings: evoke (para. 2); keenly, wrought, burdened (3); intimacy (4); belies (7); fractured (8); guise (10); impeccable (13); benign (14); linguists, insular (15); associative (17); freelancer, hone (19); wittily (20).

READ CRITICALLY

1. Why, when speaking with her husband, does Tan sometimes switch to the kind of English her mother speaks? What does this tell you of her feelings about her mother's way of speaking?

2. Why does Tan dislike using labels such as "broken" or "limited" in referring to the English her mother speaks?

3. In what ways does Tan say that the language spoken within immigrant families can limit the possibilities of the children in such families? Do you agree with her?

4. What, exactly, does Tan classify in this essay? What are the specific classifications she writes about?

5. Tan divides her essay into three sections, indicated by the spaces between paragraphs 7 and 8 and paragraphs 17 and 18. What is the focus of each of these sections? Why do you suppose she chose to organize her essay in this way?

WRITE AN ESSAY

Write an essay classifying your use of language in different situations: at home with family members, with friends outside of home, at school, in your workplace, and elsewhere that your language may change because of the circumstances in which you find yourself. For each situation, give examples of the kind of language you use that differ from the language you use in other situations.

47

Definition

Each essay in this chapter uses definition to get its main point across. As you read these essays, consider how they achieve the four basics of good definition that are listed below and discussed in Chapter 14 of this book.

▪▪ FOUR BASICS OF GOOD DEFINITION

1. It tells readers what term is being defined.
2. It presents a clear basic definition.
3. It uses examples to show what the writer means.
4. It gives details about the examples that readers will understand.

Nancy Mairs

On Being a Cripple

In her essays, memoirs, and poetry, Nancy Mairs (b. 1943) often writes about multiple sclerosis and her experience, since 1993, of life in a wheelchair. Mairs attended Wheaton College and earned an M.F.A. and Ph.D. from the University of Arizona. Her essay collections include *Waist High in the World: A Life Among the Nondisabled* (1996) and *A Troubled Guest* (2002).

This essay, from the collection *Plaintext* (1986), addresses the words we use to talk about people with disabilities. Mairs makes a case for honesty in language and explains what she means when she calls herself a cripple.

GUIDING QUESTION
How would you describe Mairs's attitude toward her disability?

To escape is nothing. Not to escape is nothing. —LOUISE BOGAN

The other day I was thinking of writing an essay on being a cripple. I was   1
thinking hard in one of the stalls of the women's room in my office building, as I was shoving my shirt into my jeans and tugging up my zipper.
Preoccupied, I flushed, picked up my book bag, took my cane down from
the hook, and unlatched the door. So many movements unbalanced me,
and as I pulled the door open I fell over backward, landing fully clothed
on the toilet seat with my legs splayed in front of me: the old beetle-on-
its-back routine. Saturday afternoon, the building deserted, I was free to
laugh aloud as I wriggled back to my feet, my voice bouncing off the yellowish tiles from all directions. Had anyone been there with me, I'd have
been still and faint and hot with chagrin. I decided that it was high time
to write the essay.

REFLECT: Why might this incident in the women's room have prompted Mairs to write her essay?

First, the matter of semantics.[1] I am a cripple. I choose this word to   2
name me. I choose from among several possibilities, the most common of
which are "handicapped" and "disabled." I made the choice a number of
years ago, without thinking, unaware of my motives for doing so. Even
now, I'm not sure what those motives are, but I recognize that they are
complex and not entirely flattering. People—crippled or not—wince at
the word "cripple," as they do not at "handicapped" or "disabled." Perhaps I want them to wince. I want them to see me as a tough customer,
one to whom the fates/gods/viruses have not been kind, but who can face
the brutal truth of her existence squarely. As a cripple, I swagger.

But, to be fair to myself, a certain amount of honesty underlies my   3
choice. "Cripple" seems to me a clean word, straightforward and precise.
It has an honorable history, having made its first appearance in the Lind-
isfarne Gospel in the tenth century. As a lover of words, I like the accuracy
with which it describes my condition: I have lost the full use of my limbs.
"Disabled," by contrast, suggests any incapacity, physical or mental. And
I certainly don't like "handicapped," which implies that I have deliberately
been put at a disadvantage, by whom I can't imagine (my God is not a
Handicapper General), in order to equalize chances in the great race of
life. These words seem to me to be moving away from my condition, to be
widening the gap between word and reality. Most remote is the recently
coined euphemism[2] "differently abled," which partakes of the same semantic hopefulness that transformed countries from "undeveloped" to
"underdeveloped," then to "less developed," and finally to "developing"

[1] **semantics:** in general, the study of words; here, the choice of particular words
[2] **euphemism:** a word that puts a pleasant cover over an unpleasant condition

SUMMARIZE: Why
does Mairs dislike
the terms *disabled,*
handicapped, and
differently abled?

_____

_____

_____

_____

_____

_____

_____

_____

_____

nations. People have continued to starve in those countries during the shift. Some realities do not obey the dictates of language.

Mine is one of them. Whatever you call me, I remain crippled. But I 4 don't care what you call me, so long as it isn't "differently abled," which strikes me as pure verbal garbage designed, by its ability to describe anyone, to describe no one. I subscribe to George Owell's thesis that "the slovenliness[3] of our language makes it easier for us to have foolish thoughts." And I refuse to participate in the degeneration of the language to the extent that I deny that I have lost anything in the course of this calamitous disease; I refuse to pretend that the only differences between you and me are the various ordinary ones that distinguish any one person from another. But call me "disabled" or "handicapped" if you like. I have long since grown accustomed to them; and if they are vague, at least they hint at the truth. Moreover, I use them myself. Society is no readier to accept crippledness than to accept death, war, sex, sweat, or wrinkles. I would never refer to another person as a cripple. It is the word I use to name only myself.

I haven't always been crippled, a fact for which I am soundly grateful. 5 To be whole of limb is, I know from experience, infinitely more pleasant and useful than to be crippled; and if that knowledge leaves one open to bitterness at my loss, the physical soundness I once enjoyed (though I did not enjoy it half enough) is well worth the occasional stab of regret. Though never any good at sports, I was a normally active child and young adult. I climbed trees, played hopscotch, jumped rope, skated, swam, rode my bicycle, sailed. I despised team sports, spending some of the wretchedest afternoons of my life, sweaty and humiliated, behind a field-hockey stick and under a basketball hoop. I tramped alone for miles along the bridle paths that webbed the woods behind the house I grew up in. I swayed through countless dim hours in the arms of one man or another under the scattered shot of light from mirrored balls, and gyrated through countless more as Tab Hunter and Johnny Mathis gave way to the Rolling Stones, Creedence Clearwater Revival, Cream. I walked down the aisle. I pushed baby carriages, changed tires in the rain, marched for peace.

When I was twenty-eight I started to trip and drop things. What at first 6 seemed my natural clumsiness soon became too pronounced to shrug off. I consulted a neurologist, who told me that I had a brain tumor. A battery of tests, increasingly disagreeable, revealed no tumor. About a year and a half later I developed a blurred spot in one eye. I had, at last, the episodes "disseminated[4] in space and time" requisite for a diagnosis: multiple sclerosis. I have never been sorry for the doctor's initial misdiagnosis, however. For almost a week, until the negative results of the tests were in, I thought that I was going to die right away. Every day for the past nearly ten years, then, has been a kind of gift. I accept all gifts.

[3] **slovenliness:** sloppiness

[4] **disseminated:** spread over

Multiple sclerosis is a chronic[5] degenerative[6] disease of the central ner-   7
vous system, in which the myelin that sheathes the nerves is somehow eaten
away and scar tissue forms in its place, interrupting the nerves' signals. During its course, which is unpredictable and uncontrollable, one may lose vision, hearing, speech, the ability to walk, control of bladder and/or bowels,
strength in any or all extremities,[7] sensitivity to touch, vibration, and/or pain,
potency, coordination of movements — the list of possibilities is lengthy and,
yes, horrifying. One may also lose one's sense of humor. That's the easiest to
lose and the hardest to survive without. [. . .]

Like many women I know, I have always had an uneasy relationship   8
with my body. I was not a popular child, largely, I think now, because I was
peculiar: intelligent, intense, moody, shy, given to unexpected actions and
inexplicable notions and emotions. But as I entered adolescence, I believed myself unpopular because I was homely: my breasts too flat, my
mouth too wide, my hips too narrow, my clothing never quite right in fit
or style. I was not, in fact, particularly ugly, old photographs inform me,
though I was well off the ideal; but I carried this sense of self-alienation
with me into adulthood, where it regenerated in response to the depredations of MS. Even with my brace I walk with a limp so pronounced that,
seeing myself on the videotape of a television program on the disabled,
I couldn't believe that anything but an inchworm could make progress
humping along like that. My shoulders droop and my pelvis thrusts forward as I try to balance myself upright, throwing my frame into a bony S.
As a result of contractures, one shoulder is higher than the other and I
carry one arm bent in front of me, the fingers curled into a claw. My left
arm and leg have wasted into pipestems, and I try always to keep them
covered. When I think about how my body must look to others, especially
to men, to whom I have been trained to display myself, I feel ludicrous,
even loathsome.

At my age, however, I don't spend much time thinking about my ap-   9
pearance. The burning egocentricity of adolescence, which assures one
that all the world is looking all the time, has passed, thank God, and I'm
generally too caught up in what I'm doing to step back, as I used to, and
watch myself as though upon a stage. I'm also too old to believe in the accuracy of self-image. I know that I'm not a hideous crone, that in fact,
when I'm rested, well dressed, and well made up, I look fine. The self-
loathing I feel is neither physically nor intellectually substantial. What I
hate is not me but a disease.

I am not a disease.

And a disease is not — at least not singlehandedly — going to deter-   11
mine who I am, though at first it seemed to be going to. Adjusting to a

REFLECT: Why
might Mairs have
chosen to write this
one-sentence para-
graph (para. 10)?

[5] **chronic:** marked by a long duration; always present

[6] **degenerative:** having a worsening effect; causing deterioration

[7] **extremities:** limbs of the body

chronic incurable illness, I have moved through a process similar to that outlined by Elisabeth Kübler-Ross in *On Death and Dying*. The major difference—and it is far more significant than most people recognize—is that I can't be sure of the outcome, as the terminally ill cancer patient can. Research studies indicate that, with proper medical care, I may achieve a "normal" life span. And in our society, with its vision of death as the ultimate evil, worse even than decrepitude, the response to such news is, "Oh well, at least you're not going to *die*." Are there worse things than dying? I think that there may be.

I think of two women I know, both with MS, both enough older than   12
I to have served me as models. One took to her bed several years ago and has been there ever since. Although she can sit in a high-backed wheelchair, because she is incontinent she refuses to go out at all, even though incontinence pants, which are readily available at any pharmacy, could protect her from embarrassment. Instead, she stays at home and insists that her husband, a small quiet man, a retired civil servant, stay there with her except for a quick weekly foray[8] to the supermarket. The other woman, whose illness was diagnosed when she was eighteen, a nursing student engaged to a young doctor, finished her training, married her doctor, accompanied him to Germany when he was in the service, bore three sons and a daughter, now grown and gone. When she can, she travels with her husband; she plays bridge, embroiders, swims regularly; she works, like me, as a symptomatic-patient instructor of medical students in neurology. Guess which woman I hope to be.

[8] **foray:** trip, outing

SUMMARIZE AND RESPOND

In your reading journal or elsewhere, summarize the main point of "On Being a Cripple." Then, go back and check off support for this main idea. Next, write a brief summary (three to five sentences) of the reading. Finally, jot down your initial response to the selection. What impression of Mairs do you come away with? What did you learn from her description of her disease? If you could write a note to Mairs, what would you say to her?

CHECK YOUR COMPREHENSION

1. Which of the following would be the best alternative title for this essay?

   a.   "The Painfulness of a Disease"

   b.   "Surviving with Multiple Sclerosis"

    c. "Learning to Laugh at My Disability"

    d. "Coping with Others' Attitudes toward Disability"

2. The main idea of this essay is that

    a. multiple sclerosis is an incurable disease of the central nervous system that can affect movement, vision, hearing, and speech.

    b. many labels are used to describe disabled people, but most such people prefer the term *crippled*.

    c. one needs a strong sense of humor and a circle of supportive friends to live with a disability.

    d. being disabled presents many difficulties and obstacles, but one can learn to cope with these challenges.

3. Mairs makes the point that

    a. she is grateful to have the memory of being able-bodied as a young woman.

    b. the greatest drawback to her disability is that it makes her feel unattractive.

    c. she feels doctors are not doing enough to discover a cure for multiple sclerosis.

    d. she believes everyone should use the word *crippled* rather than *disabled* or *handicapped*.

4. If you are unfamiliar with the following words, use a dictionary to check their meanings: splayed, chagrin (para. 1); wince, swagger (2); incapacity, partakes, dictates (3); degeneration, calamitous (4); gyrated (5); neurologist (6); inexplicable, regenerated, depredations, contractures, ludicrous, loathsome (8); crone (9); decrepitude (11); incontinent (12).

READ CRITICALLY

1. How effective do you find Mairs's opening paragraph as an introduction to the essay as a whole?

2. Why do you think Mairs devotes her second through fourth paragraphs to discussing her use of the word *cripple* to describe herself? How do you respond to this section of the essay? Mairs also objects to terms like *differently abled,* which do not tell the full truth about a condition. Can you think of other such words? Why do you think such words come into the language?

3. How would you evaluate "On Being a Cripple" as an essay of definition? What have you learned from the essay that you did not know before?

4. Mairs writes at the end paragraph 11, "Are there worse things than dying? I think that there may be." What does she mean? How do this question and answer lead into the subject of paragraph 12?

5. What do you think of Mairs's closing sentence? What image of Mairs does it leave you with?

■ **WRITE AN ESSAY**

Write an essay defining an important aspect of yourself. This definition might relate to a challenge you face in life, or it might focus on another facet of your identity—your family heritage, your membership in a particular group, a personality or physical trait that you believe sets you apart from many others you know. Think about titling your essay "On Being _____" and, as Mairs does, relating experiences that help communicate your definition to readers.

Juliet B. Schor

Age Compression

Juliet B. Schor (b. 1955) is a professor of sociology at Boston College. Her research and writings focus on work and leisure activities and their relation to family life. Her books include the best-selling *The Overworked American: The Unexpected Decline of Leisure* (1993) and *The Overspent American: Why We Want What We Don't Need* (1999).

In this essay, Schor describes a marketing phenomenon in which products designed for adults or teenagers are pitched to younger kids. It is an excerpt from her most recent book, *Born to Buy* (2004), a study of the commercial pressures placed on today's children.

GUIDING QUESTION
What is Schor's attitude toward age compression as a marketing strategy?

One of the hottest trends in youth marketing is age compression—the   1
practice of taking products and marketing messages originally designed for older kids and targeting them to younger ones. Age compression includes

offering teen products and genres, pitching gratuitous violence to the twelve-and-under crowd, cultivating brand preferences for items that were previously unbranded among younger kids, and developing creative alcohol and tobacco advertising that is not officially targeted to them but is widely seen and greatly loved by children. "By eight or nine they want 'N Sync," explained one tweening expert to me, in the days before that band was eclipsed by Justin Timberlake, Pink, and others.

Age compression is a sprawling trend. It can be seen in the import of television programming specifically designed for one year olds, which occurred, ironically, with Public Broadcasting's *Teletubbies*. It includes the marketing of designer clothes to kindergartners and first graders. It's the deliberate targeting of R-rated movies to kids as young as age nine, a practice the major movie studios were called on the carpet for by the Clinton administration in 2000. It's being driven by the recognition that many children nationwide are watching MTV and other teen and adult programming. One of my favorite MTV anecdotes comes from a third-grade teacher in Weston, Massachusetts, who reported that she started her social studies unit on Mexico by asking the class what they knew about the country. Six or seven raised their hands and answered, "That's the place where MTV's Spring Break takes place!" For those who haven't seen it, the program glorifies heavy partying, what it calls "bootylicious girls," erotic dancing, wet T-shirt contests, and binge drinking.

A common argument within the marketing world is that age compression is being caused by social trends that make contemporary children far more sophisticated than their predecessors. These include the increased responsibilities of kids in single-parent or divorced families, higher levels of exposure to adult media, children's facility[1] with new technology, early puberty, and the fact that kids know more earlier. In the 1980s, Hasbro sold its GI Joe action figure to boys aged eleven to fourteen. Now, Joe is rejected by eight year olds as too babyish. Twenty years ago, *Seventeen* magazine targeted sixteen year olds; now it aims at eleven and twelves. In a telling gesture, the toy industry has officially lowered its upper age target from fourteen to ten.

Marketers have even coined an acronym to describe these developments. It's KAGOY, which stands for Kids Are Getting Older Younger. The social trends become part of the license for treating kids as if they were adults. Indeed, some advertisers are even arguing that current approaches are too protective of children. In a presentation at the 2001 annual Marketing to Kids Conference, executive Abigail Hirschhorn of DDB New York argued that it's time to stop talking down to kids and start "talking up" to them and that too much advertising denies kids what they really crave—the adult world. She argued for more "glamour, fashion, style, irony, and popular music."

[1] **facility:** ability to use easily

IDENTIFY: Put a check mark next to each example of age compression in paragraph 2.

REFLECT: Do you agree that the social trends described in paragraph 3 are leading to age compression? Can you think of other trends that are a factor?

SUMMARIZE: What is tweening, and how has it changed?

_____

_____

_____

_____

_____

_____

_____

_____

Nowhere is age compression more evident than among the eight- to twelve-year-old target. Originally a strategy for selling to ten to thirteen year olds, children as young as six are being targeted for tweening. And what is that exactly? Tweens are "in-between" teens and children, and tweening consists mainly of bringing teen products and entertainment to ever-younger audiences. If you're wondering why your daughter came home from kindergarten one day singing the words to a Britney Spears or Jennifer Lopez song, the answer is that she got tweened. Tween marketing has become a major focus of the industry, with its own conferences, research tools, databases, books, and specialty firms. Part of why tweening is so lucrative is that it involves bringing new, more expensive products to this younger group. It's working because tweens have growing purchasing power and influence with parents. The more the tween consumer world comes to resemble the teen world, with its comprehensive branding strategies and intense levels of consumer immersion, the more money there is to be made. 5

In some cases, it's the advertisers pushing the trend with their clients. But clients are also initiating the process. Mark Lapham (pseudonym),[2] president of a company that has focused almost exclusively on the teen market, says, "We're being asked all the time about it" by makers of school supplies, apparel manufacturers, cosmetics companies. Lapham explains how his clients are thinking: "Hey, we can actually sell a cosmetic, not just bubble gum lip gloss . . . we can sell foundation possibly . . . nail polish." 6

PREDICT: Based on the second sentence, what do you expect paragraph 7 will be about?

_____

_____

_____

_____

_____

_____

Abigail Hirschhorn's plea for industry change is well behind the times. Children are being exposed to plenty of glamour, fashion, style, irony, and popular music, that is, sex. Even the family-friendly Disney Channel is full of sexually suggestive outfits and dancing. One radio Disney employee explained to me that the company keeps a careful watch on lyrics but is hands-off with the other stuff. A stroll down the 6X–12 aisles of girls' clothing will produce plenty of skimpy and revealing styles. People in advertising are well aware of these developments. Emma Gilding of Ogilvy and Mather recounted an experience she had during an in-home videotaping. The little girl was doing a Britney Spears imitation, with flirting and sexual grinding. Asked by Gilding what she wanted to be when she grew up, the three year old answered: "A sexy shirt girl." As researcher Mary Prescott (pseudonym) explained to me in the summer of 2001, "We're coming out of a trend now. Girl power turned into sex power. A very sexy, dirty, dark thing. Parents were starting to panic." While Prescott felt that a reversal toward "puritanism" had already begun, other observers aren't so sure. Not long after Prescott's prediction, Abercrombie and Fitch came under fire for selling thong underwear with sexually suggestive phrases to seven to fourteen year olds. And child development expert Diane Levin alerted parents to the introduction of World Wrestling Entertainment action figures recommended for age four 7

[2] **pseudonym:** an assumed name, here to protect the identity of the speaker

and above, which include a male character with lipstick on his crotch, another male figure holding the severed head of a woman, and a female character with enormous breasts and a minimal simulated black leather outfit and whip. Four year olds are also targeted with toys tied to movies that carry PG-13 ratings.

Some industry insiders have begun to caution that tweening has gone too far. At the 2002 KidPower conference, Paul Kurnit spoke out publicly about companies "selling 'tude' to pre-teens and ushering in adolescence a bit sooner than otherwise." Privately, even more critical views were expressed to me. Mark Lapham revealed that he finds this "kind of an amazing thing . . . this is where personally my guilt comes out, like gosh, it's not really appropriate sometimes." But, he continues, "that's where society's going, what do you do?" Prescott, who is more deeply immersed in the world of tweening, confessed that "I am doing the most horrible thing in the world. We are targeting kids too young with too many inappropriate things. . . . It's not worth the almighty buck."

8 **REFLECT:** Do you believe that these members of the industry really feel guilty? Why or why not?

_____

_____

_____

■ SUMMARIZE AND RESPOND

In your reading journal or elsewhere, summarize the main point of "Age Compression." Then, go back and check off support for this main idea. Next, write a brief summary (three to five sentences) of the reading. Finally, jot down your initial response to the selection. Before reading this essay, had you already noticed instances of age compression in advertising and the entertainment media? Do you share Schor's concern over such practices? Do you agree or disagree that age compression is simply a reflection of the times we live in? Why or why not?

■ CHECK YOUR COMPREHENSION

1. Which of the following would be the best alternative title for this essay?

   a. "Growing Up with the Media"

   b. "Sex and Violence for Kids"

   c. "Capturing the Tween Consumer"

   d. "Are Kids Getting Older Younger?"

2. The main idea of this essay is that

   a. today more and more children are being treated as if they were adults.

   b. many marketers today focus on attracting young children to increasingly mature products.

   c. age compression is the result of contemporary children having more responsibilities than did children in the past.

d. some marketers are beginning to feel guilty about targeting inappropriate products to young children.

3. Schor suggests that one reason for age compression is

a. children today have increased exposure to teenage and adult media.

b. marketers now have more respect for children than they did in the past.

c. parents take too little responsibility for monitoring the shopping habits of their children.

d. contemporary children believe that most toys are just too babyish to play with.

4. If you are unfamiliar with the following words, use a dictionary to check their meanings: genres, gratuitous (para. 1); predecessors (3); irony (4); puritanism (7).

READ CRITICALLY

1. What would you describe as Schor's purpose in this essay? Who might her intended audience be?

2. On the basis of this essay, what would you say drives marketers to target younger children as they do?

3. Why do you suppose two of Schor's sources, Mark Lapham and Mary Prescott, agreed to be quoted only if their real names weren't used?

4. Evaluate Schor's use of examples in the essay. What do they tell us about age compression in marketing?

5. One researcher quoted in the essay suggests that "a reversal toward 'puritanism'" has begun (para. 7). In looking at marketing toward children today, do you see any evidence of such a reversal?

WRITE AN ESSAY

Write an essay in which you focus on the kinds of products and entertainment media targeted toward consumers ages thirteen to seventeen. You may wish to refer to television commercials, print ads in magazines, in-school advertising, advertising on Internet sites, film trailers, and the like, as well as to particular products. Do you find any evidence of age compression in marketing to this older group of consumers?

48

Comparison and Contrast

Each essay in this chapter uses comparison and contrast to get its main point across. As you read these essays, consider how they achieve the four basics of good comparison and contrast that are listed below and discussed in Chapter 15 of this book.

▟▘ FOUR BASICS OF GOOD COMPARISON AND CONTRAST

1. It uses subjects that have enough in common to be usefully compared and contrasted.
2. It serves a purpose — either to help readers make a decision or to understand the subjects.
3. It presents several important, parallel points of comparison and contrast.
4. It is organized either point-by-point or whole-to-whole (see pages 216–17).

Dave Barry
The Ugly Truth about Beauty

According to the *New York Times,* humorist Dave Barry is "the funniest man in America." Born in 1947 in Armonk, New York, Barry earned a B.A. from Haverford College. He then worked for several years as a newspaper reporter and a lecturer on business writing before discovering his talent as a humor columnist. The columns he now writes for the *Miami Herald* appear in newspapers nationwide, and his work has been collected in numerous books. Barry's hilarious observations on American life won him the Pulitzer Prize for commentary in 1988.

In "The Ugly Truth about Beauty," first published in the *Philadelphia Inquirer Magazine* in 1998, Barry compares and contrasts men's and women's beauty routines. The essay humorously highlights differences in the ways that men and women view themselves.

GUIDING QUESTION
Why do men and women think of their looks differently?

If you're a man, at some point a woman will ask you how she looks.   1

"How do I look?" she'll ask.   2

You must be careful how you answer this question. The best technique   3
is to form an honest yet sensitive opinion, then collapse on the floor with some kind of fatal seizure. Trust me, this is the easiest way out. Because you will never come up with the right answer.

PREDICT: Based on the first sentence of paragraph 4, how do you think Barry will go on to develop this essay?

_____

_____

_____

_____

The problem is that women generally do not think of their looks in the   4
same way that men do. Most men form an opinion of how they look in seventh grade, and they stick to it for the rest of their lives. Some men form the opinion that they are irresistible stud muffins, and they do not change this opinion even when their faces sag and their noses bloat to the size of eggplants and their eyebrows grow together to form what appears to be a giant forehead-dwelling tropical caterpillar.

Most men, I believe, think of themselves as average-looking. Men will   5
think this even if their faces cause heart failure in cattle at a range of three hundred yards. Being average does not bother them; average is fine, for men. This is why men never ask anybody how they look. Their primary form of beauty care is to shave themselves, which is essentially the same form of beauty care that they give to their lawns. If, at the end of his four-minute daily beauty regimen,[1] a man has managed to wipe most of the shaving cream out of his hair and is not bleeding too badly, he feels that he has done all he can, so he stops thinking about his appearance and devotes his mind to more critical issues, such as the Super Bowl.

Women do not look at themselves this way. If I had to express, in three   6
words, what I believe most women think about their appearance, those words would be: "not good enough." No matter how attractive a woman may appear to be to others, when she looks at herself in the mirror, she

[1] **regimen:** routine

thinks: woof. She thinks that at any moment a municipal animal-control officer is going to throw a net over her and haul her off to the shelter.

Why do women have such low self-esteem? There are many complex psychological and societal reasons, by which I mean Barbie. Girls grow up playing with a doll proportioned such that, if it were a human, it would be seven feet tall and weigh eighty-one pounds, of which fifty-three pounds would be bosoms. This is a difficult appearance standard to live up to, especially when you contrast it with the standard set for little boys by their dolls . . . excuse me, by their action figures. Most of the action figures that my son played with when he was little were hideous-looking. For example, he was very fond of an action figure (part of the He-Man series) called "Buzz-Off," who was part human, part flying insect. Buzz-Off was not a looker. But he was extremely self-confident. You could not imagine Buzz-Off saying to the other action figures: "Do you think these wings make my hips look big?"

7 IDENTIFY: What two subjects does Barry contrast in paragraph 7?

_____

_____

_____

_____

But women grow up thinking they need to look like Barbie, which for most women is impossible, although there is a multibillion-dollar beauty industry devoted to convincing women that they must try. I once saw an Oprah show wherein supermodel Cindy Crawford dispensed makeup tips to the studio audience. Cindy had all these middle-aged women applying beauty products to their faces; she stressed how important it was to apply them in a certain way, using the tips of their fingers. All the women dutifully did this, even though it was obvious to any sane observer that, no matter how carefully they applied these products, they would never look remotely like Cindy Crawford, who is some kind of genetic mutation.

8 SUMMARIZE: What is Barry's main point in paragraph 8?

_____

_____

_____

_____

_____

_____

_____

I'm not saying that men are superior. I'm just saying that you're not 9 going to get a group of middle-aged men to sit in a room and apply cosmetics to themselves under the instruction of Brad Pitt, in hopes of looking more like him. Men would realize that this task was pointless and demeaning.[2] They would find some way to bolster their self-esteem that did not require looking like Brad Pitt. They would say to Brad: "Oh YEAH? Well what do you know about LAWN CARE, pretty boy?"

Of course many women will argue that the reason they become obsessed 10 with trying to look like Cindy Crawford is that men, being as shallow as a drop of spit, WANT women to look that way. To which I have two responses:

1. Hey, just because WE'RE idiots, that does not mean YOU have to 11 be; and

2. Men don't even notice 97 percent of the beauty efforts you make 12 anyway. Take fingernails. The average woman spends 5,000 hours per year worrying about her fingernails; I have never once, in more than forty years of listening to men talk about women, heard a man say, "She has a nice set of fingernails!" Many men would not notice if a woman had upward of four hands.

---

[2] **demeaning:** degrading, lowering one's character

Anyway, to get back to my original point: If you're a man, and a   13
woman asks you how she looks, you're in big trouble. Obviously, you can't
say she looks bad. But you also can't say that she looks great, because she'll
think you're lying, because she has spent countless hours, with the help of
the multibillion-dollar beauty industry, obsessing about the differences between herself and Cindy Crawford. Also, she suspects that you're not qualified to judge anybody's appearance. This is because you have shaving
cream in your hair.

■ SUMMARIZE AND RESPOND

In your reading journal or elsewhere, summarize the main point of "The
Ugly Truth about Beauty." Then, go back and check off support for this
main idea. Next, write a brief summary (three to five sentences) of the
essay. Finally, jot down your initial response to the essay. Do you agree
with Barry's assessment of why there are differences in the ways men and
women view themselves? What examples from your experience do or do
not support his points?

■ CHECK YOUR COMPREHENSION

1. Which of the following would be the best alternative title for this essay?

    a. "Barbie versus He-Man"

    b. "Men and Women: What They See in the Mirror"

    c. "It's Kinder to Lie"

    d. "The Beauty Industry's Dark Secret"

2. The main idea of this essay is that

    a. men don't know how to respond when women ask about their ap-
        pearance.

    b. men don't care how much effort women put into their looks.

    c. because of society and the media, men and women view their physi-
        cal appearances differently.

    d. childhood toys influence the way men and women think about their
        looks.

3. According to Barry,

    a. most men are concerned with how women view their appearance.

    b. women want men to be honest about their looks.

   c. most women are dissatisfied with their appearance.

   d. a woman's perception of her appearance is influenced by her moods and her female friends.

4. If you are unfamiliar with the following words, use a dictionary to check their meanings: societal, proportioned (para. 7); mutation (8); bolster (9).

■ READ CRITICALLY

1. Who is Barry's intended audience, and what do you think is his purpose in writing this essay?

2. In paragraphs 7 and 8, Barry discusses children's toys. Why did he choose these particular toys, and how do they help him explain his points of contrast?

3. What is Barry's attitude toward Cindy Crawford and Brad Pitt? Explain how he uses these examples to support his main point.

4. Explain the significance of the title. What do you think Barry would say is the ugly truth about beauty?

5. Why do you think the beauty industry is so successful? Support your answer with examples from this essay.

■ WRITE AN ESSAY

Look through your family photographs, or use the Internet or magazines to view men's and women's fashions over the last fifty years. Think about how fashions have changed, and write an essay that compares and contrasts fashion trends from two different decades. Use concrete examples to show differences and similarities in the two time periods' styles.

Robb Walsh
The Inkblot Test

Robb Walsh has written food articles and reviews for a number of publications, including the *Houston Press, Natural History Magazine,* and the *Austin Chronicle.* In addition to essays, he has published several cookbooks and was nominated for a James Beard Cookbook Award for the *Legends of Texas Barbecue Cookbook* (2002).

"The Inkblot Test" first appeared in the *Houston Press* in 2001 and was reprinted in Walsh's essay collection *Are You Really Going to Eat That? Reflections of a Culinary Thrill Seeker* (2003). After comparing two very different diners, he considers how he developed a preference for one over the other.

GUIDING QUESTION
Which of the two diners does Walsh prefer, and why?

There are eight customers in the Triple A Restaurant at 10:30 in the morning. All of them are men, and four sport comb-overs.[1] The wood-grain Formica on the tables and the orange vinyl on the chairs are a little worn. There is a picture of a 1935 high school football team hanging on one wall. My waitress is named Betty; she grew up in the Heights and has been working at Triple A for eighteen years.

I am interested in a menu item that occupies almost half the page: "Two Farm Fresh Eggs (Any Style) with. . . ." The "with" options include a pork chop, a breakfast steak, chicken-fried steak with cream gravy, and bacon or ham or choice of sausage. The sausage choices constitute another sublist. All of the above includes grits or country-style potatoes and toast or biscuits. Betty describes the three kinds of sausage available: The home-made pan style is a free-form patty that's been spiced up hot; the country sausage is a big link like kielbasa; and the little links are the regular kind. I order two eggs with chicken-fried steak and hash browns and biscuits. And I get a side order of that homemade sausage, just out of curiosity.

REFLECT: Do you find this kind of breakfast appetizing? Why or why not?

_____

_____

_____

"How do you want your eggs?" Betty asks.

"Over easy and greasy," I smile.

"It's going to take a while," she says. "We batter the chicken-fried steak from scratch. It's not the frozen kind."

Neither are the crunchy potatoes; they are big pieces of fresh spuds fried crisp. The eggs are just right. The chicken-fried steak is piping hot with a wrinkly brown crust and a peppery tan cream gravy on the side. The biscuits are average. The biggest problem with Triple A's breakfast is the vehicle on which it is served: The oval platters are too small for the portions. I end up eating from three plates. I split my biscuits on the right-hand plate and pour a little cream gravy on them, while I eat the eggs, potatoes, and chicken-fried steak from the middle plate. From the left, I sample the homemade sausage, which is extremely spicy and fried extra brown.

[1] **comb-over:** an (unsuccessful) attempt to conceal baldness by letting one's hair grow long on one side and combing it over the top

Betty is gabbing with the other waitresses, and it takes a lot of gesturing to get my coffee refilled. But it's a sunny day outside, and from the window by my booth I can see the farmer's market next door. I also see an old black shoeshine man working on Triple A's front porch. His customer is sitting against the wall, so I can't see his face, just his brown brogues.[2] The shoeshine man is spreading the polish with his fingers. I linger over my coffee until 11:20 and leave just as the lunch crowd arrives.   7

If the scene above were an inkblot test,[3] how would you characterize it? Inviting? Depressing? Boring? Charming?   8

Before you answer, consider the following inkblot: 9

At 11 in the morning, almost all the tables are occupied at Century Diner on the corner of Main Street and Texas Avenue. There are some young, hip guys lingering over books and magazines, and a lot of downtown business folks in nice clothes eating lunch.   10

The vinyl booths by the window are two-tone, pastel green and off-white. The tables are covered with brand-new Formica in a bright pattern of circles and shapes, a design that was called "modern" forty years ago. The waiters wear black-and-white bowling shirts with slogans such as "Something Superior for Your Interior" on the back. The menu is sprinkled with little nuggets about old diner lingo, such as the fact that "Adam and Eve on a raft" once meant ham and eggs on toast.   11

But ham and eggs on toast is not on the menu. Instead, the place offers a contemporary take on diner food, including "The Total New Yorker," a bagel with Nova Scotia salmon and cream cheese, and "The Health Kick," an egg-white omelet. Although two eggs with ham, bacon, or sausage aren't offered, the menu does feature "Eggs N' Hash," two eggs with hash browns and New York–style corned-beef hash.   12

My waiter is a young guy with dyed black hair. He's too busy to chat, so I don't get his name. I order two eggs. They don't have hash browns at lunch, so I settle for french fries. The waiter doesn't know what the breakfast meats are, but he checks. I order the sausage and a side of biscuits and gravy.   13

"How do you want your eggs?" he asks.   14

"Over easy and greasy," I smile.   15

Coffee comes in a little stainless-steel Thermos, which is a nice touch. It reminds me of the little glass "hottle" you used to get at coffee shops in the 1960s. The eggs are just right. The french fries are excellent. The link sausage is precisely what you'd expect. The biscuits are huge, and the gravy has lots of bacon pieces in it. Unfortunately, it has been spooned over the top of unsplit biscuits. I try to break them up to soak up some of the gravy.   16

PREDICT: Based on paragraph 10, what would you guess Walsh is preparing to do?

_____

_____

_____

_____

REFLECT: What might the detail about the gravy being spooned over unsplit biscuits suggest?

_____

_____

_____

_____

_____

[2] **brogues:** heavy lace-up shoes

[3] **inkblot test:** a psychological test in which respondents are asked to describe what they see in undefined inkblots

At a table just across the divide from mine, two men and a woman in 17 conservative business suits are gossiping about somebody's chances in some election. The conversation is spirited, and the woman's eyes sparkle as she laughs at one of the men's observations. I can't hear what he said, but it must have been pretty funny. I pour myself some more coffee and copy down this quote from the big shiny menu: " 'The character of a diner builds up the way grime does'—Douglas Yorke."

My own reactions to these diner-shaped inkblots are not hard to pre- 18 dict. Breakfast at Triple A puts me in a warm and wonderful mood. And the retro-chic[4] at Century Diner feels phony. But I'm pretty much alone in this opinion.

One friend calls the breakfast at Triple A "a heart attack on a plate." 19 Another finds the dark wood paneling, worn-out furniture, and fat old guys with comb-overs "depressing." And she thinks the Century's decor and waiters' costumes are "precious."

What does the inkblot test tell you? 20

The same restaurant can feel entirely different to you and me. I can walk 21 into a truck stop alone and feel right at home. But a beautiful young woman walking in by herself might feel differently. My mother is obsessive about cleanliness; she'd rather eat at McDonald's than at a place with character if there's the threat of grime. And then there are deeper prejudices.

When I moved to Austin from Connecticut to start school at UT (the 22 University of Texas), I was seventeen years old, 2,000 miles away from my parents, and high on my newfound freedom. I drove my motorcycle all over town discovering funky places to eat. I loved little luncheonettes run by crazy old ladies, drugstore soda fountains, and old urban institutions like the Southern Dinette on East 11th Street in the heart of the black east side.

SUMMARIZE: What do paragraphs 22–23 tell you about the writer as a young man?

Why did I love these places? It wasn't always about the food. I was also 23 seeking a level of comfort. As a newcomer, I was fascinated by the characters in these old places and by the vestiges[5] of a disappearing Texas. As a long-haired geek from the East, I was scared of the rednecks and fraternity boys who prowled the trendy campus hangouts. Maybe I ate in eccentric dives and places on the wrong side of the tracks because I felt like an outcast myself.

Sometimes friends who grew up in Texas, people who are concerned 24 with healthy diets and whose families struggled with poverty in their childhood, don't find these funky joints nearly as endearing as I do. In another's eyes, these places are outdated, high-cholesterol slop houses, full not of colorful characters but of boring old farts. I understand these biases, and I want to be honest about my own.

[4] **retro-chic:** characterized by a trendy reinvention of a past style

[5] **vestiges:** traces or remains

It's still not always about the food with me. Sometimes I think a 25 restaurant review needs to stick closely to the subject at hand. But in other cases, I'm more interested in food as a reflection of culture, and so it is with this case. There are some differences in the food at Triple A and Century Diner. But having breakfast at an old diner one morning and a new retro diner the next brings up intriguing questions.

Like, do you prefer sanitized imitations of old institutions to grimy old 26 institutions themselves? And why does a retro-chic diner in the oldest part of Houston get its history lessons (and breakfast dishes) from New York? Does the architectural preservation downtown make any sense absent some cultural preservation?

IDENTIFY: What is Walsh's purpose in posing the questions in paragraph 26?

Several letters to the editor lately have complained about my ram- 27 blings—that my restaurant reviews are too personal and not focused enough on food. To this charge I proudly plead guilty.

When I began reviewing at the *Austin Chronicle* in 1991, I was influ- 28 enced by the very personal narratives of food writer John Thorne. Thorne's own inspiration was Mark Zanger, who under the pseudonym Robert Nadeau reviewed restaurants for the *Boston Phoenix* in the late 1970s. "He was teaching himself eating and drinking and simultaneously wondering out loud what he should be making of it, gnawing away at all pat assumptions," wrote Thorne. "He taught me that honesty means nothing if there's no real risk to it, no genuine self-examination."

Lofty aspirations for a restaurant reviewer, no doubt, but at least it's a 29 worthy goal. In that spirit, I offer you this nonreview. And I invite you to visit Triple A and Century Diner for some genuine self-examination of your own. Which one do *you* like better?

■ SUMMARIZE AND RESPOND

In your reading journal or elsewhere, summarize the main point of "The Inkblot Test." Then, go back and check off support for this main idea. Next, write a brief summary (three to five sentences) of the reading. Finally, jot down your initial response to the selection. How well does Walsh convey the atmosphere and food of each of the diners? Do you understand why he prefers one diner over the other? What impression do you have of Walsh himself?

■ CHECK YOUR COMPREHENSION

1. Which of the following would be the best alternative title for this essay?
    a. "Eating Out in Houston, Texas: There Are Many Choices"
    b. "The Art of Writing Restaurant Reviews"

c. "The Social Function of the Neighborhood Diner"

d. "Dining Tastes: A Reflection of Culture"

2. The main idea of this essay is that

a. the author likes the Triple A Restaurant and places like it because he sees their atmosphere and food as authentic and comfortable.

b. the Triple A Restaurant is not as clean or as sophisticated as the Century Diner, but it has better food.

c. the best restaurant reviews are ones that are highly personal and focus on many other matters in addition to food.

d. the author learned to love diners and luncheonettes when he first moved to Texas as a college student and was intimidated by the trendy campus hangouts.

3. One of Walsh's concerns is that

a. readers of the newspaper for which he writes have complained that his restaurant reviews are inaccurate.

b. sanitized imitations of old-style dining institutions could replace the old-style institutions themselves.

c. some people find the Triple A Restaurant depressing and the food there unappealing and unhealthy.

d. readers of his reviews will not always understand or appreciate his lofty goals as a writer.

4. If you are unfamiliar with the following words, use a dictionary to check their meanings: Formica (para. 1); constitute, kielbasa (2); eccentric (23); endearing (24); intriguing (25); simultaneously, pat (28).

READ CRITICALLY

1. What is the effect of Walsh's repeating his reply to the question of how he likes his eggs ("Over easy and greasy") in paragraphs 4 and 15?

2. What would you point to as the three main contrasts between the two diners Walsh describes?

3. In paragraph 21, Walsh writes, "The same restaurant can feel entirely different to you and me." Why do you suppose he makes this point?

4. Walsh begins paragraph 23 with the question "Why did I love these places?" What is his explanation? Do you find it sufficient and convincing?

5. How would you evaluate Walsh's two concluding paragraphs? What effect do they have on you as a reader?

WRITE AN ESSAY

Write an essay in which you use description to compare and contrast two specific places that have a similar function. These could be two eating establishments, as in Walsh's essay, or two other places that you have the opportunity to observe closely, such as work settings, school settings, retail stores, homes, or parks or playgrounds. Like Walsh's subjects, your subjects should be closely related but still reflect contrasts that will be of interest to readers. (Alternatively, you might focus on presenting surprising similarities between subjects that don't on the surface seem to be very closely related.)

49

Cause and Effect

Each essay in this chapter uses cause and effect to get its main point across. As you read these essays, consider how they achieve the four basics of good cause and effect that are listed below and discussed in Chapter 16 of this book.

▟ FOUR BASICS OF GOOD CAUSE AND EFFECT

1. The main point reflects the writer's purpose: to explain causes, effects, or both.
2. If the purpose is to explain causes, it presents concrete causes.
3. If the purpose is to explain effects, it presents actual effects.
4. It gives readers clear and detailed examples or explanations of the causes and/or effects.

Amy L. Beck
Struggling for Perfection

Amy L. Beck was born in 1979 in Greenwich, Connecticut. After graduating from Harvard University in 2000, Beck joined Teach for America, a program that places recent college graduates in inner-city or rural schools, and she taught first graders in Long Beach, California, for two years. She has also worked in France as a researcher for the travel guide

Let's Go and as an intern with the French Public Health Administration. Beck is currently a third-year medical student at the University of Connecticut School of Medicine.

In "Struggling for Perfection," which she wrote for the *Harvard Crimson* in 1998, Beck explores eating disorders and domestic abuse. How are these two problems linked? According to Beck, they are both partly caused by media images.

GUIDING QUESTION
How does the title of the essay relate to the cause/effect relationship that Beck writes about?

Sex sells. This truth is a boon[1] for marketing gurus and the pornography industry but a rather unfortunate situation for women. Every issue of *Playboy*, every lewd poster, and even the Victoria's Secret catalog transform real women into ornaments, valued exclusively for their outward appearance. These publications are responsible for defining what is sexy and reinforce the belief that aesthetic[2] appeal is a woman's highest virtue. **1**

Some argue that the proliferation[3] of pornography and other sexually explicit images of women is both harmless for society and inevitable. Just this point was made in a recent *Crimson* column titled "In Defense of Hooters and the St. Pauli Girl." In the tone of an expert, the author boldly claims that the objectification[4] of women in the media does not affect the way men treat the real women in their lives, nor does it give those with pathological[5] tendencies "the decisive nudge into misogyny."[6] Furthermore, the author says, those women who feel pressure to conform to beauty standards set by the media are suffering from a classic psychosis in which they "confuse fiction with reality." **2**

My first reaction was to ask how anyone could possibly believe that the pervasiveness[7] of pornography and sexually explicit depictions of women could fail to have any sort of effect on society. Having spent twelve weeks working in a psychiatric hospital last summer, I am writing from a starkly different perspective. **3**

PREDICT: After reading her second paragraph, what do you expect Beck will go on to do in her essay?

_____

_____

_____

_____

_____

_____

"The author made me feel the pain she felt while treating her patients. She made it clear how much women suffer just because they think they have to be perfect."
—*Peggy L. Gamble, student*

[1] **boon:** a welcome benefit

[2] **aesthetic:** having to do with beauty

[3] **proliferation:** rapid growth

[4] **objectification:** the treatment of a person as an object

[5] **pathological:** abnormal, diseased

[6] **misogyny:** hatred of women

[7] **pervasiveness:** the extension or spread of one thing throughout something else

During my first eight weeks at the hospital, I worked on an eating dis- 4 order unit in constant contact with anorexics and bulimics. Many patients on the unit were so emaciated[8] that I could never accustom myself to their appearance; every time I saw them I experienced the same shock. Most had been in and out of countless other hospitals and treatment programs, improving slightly each time but always sliding back into eating-disordered behavior when released.

IDENTIFY: Underline the sentence that best expresses the main point of paragraph 5.

These people were truly at rock bottom, considered by many to be in- 5 curable. Their eating disorders had consumed them entirely, leaving no trace of the vibrant, intelligent people that once inhabited their now skeletal bodies. Certainly, these people also had family problems, alcoholic parents, histories of abuse and clinical depression, to name a few, all of which contribute to feelings of worthlessness and extremely low self-esteem — cited by experts as a major cause of eating disorders. What I find significant, however, is not the root of their problems but that these women (there were a few men, but never more than five percent of the patient population) turned to their bodies as a means of expression and self-healing. Profoundly influenced by the depiction of women by the fashion industry, they had been convinced that the only way to attain love, respect, and personal fulfillment was through a relentless pursuit of physical perfection. Most were perfectly aware that they would never look like a supermodel, but it was inconceivable not to try to do so. They found that they were good at dieting and that they were praised and rewarded for their success. And by the time things had gone too far, they had lost all sense of perspective.

Convinced by the media and popular culture to believe that, as women, 6 they should look a certain way and that only if they looked that way would they be loved and respected, they turned to dieting as a means of personal fulfillment and self-definition. While cases as extreme as those I saw at the hospital are rare, many women experience milder but still debilitating[9] forms of eating disorders. They may never get sick enough to require hospitalization, but they nonetheless devote excessive mental and physical energy to diet and exercise, often jeopardizing their health in the process.

SUMMARIZE: What is the main point of paragraph 7?

_____

_____

_____

_____

_____

For my last four weeks at the hospital I transferred from eating disor- 7 ders to a general psychology unit. The diagnoses varied, but the number of patients with histories of abuse was astounding. After listening to and reading countless case histories, I began to recognize the patterns. In many cases, domestic battering was chronic, occurring weekly or daily whenever the victim broke some sort of household rule, such as serving dinner late or dressing "too sexy." The majority of the sexual abuse victims had been

[8] **emaciated:** extremely thin

[9] **debilitating:** weakening

raped by people close to them: relatives, ex-boyfriends, or family friends. In one particularly striking case, a patient's boyfriend made her have sex with five of his friends on a frequent basis.

The men who committed these heinous crimes were rarely pathological rapists or batterers. Few would even be deemed mentally ill or classically misogynistic. Rather, they are men who view the real women in their lives in the same manner that they would view a *Playboy* model, a waitress at Hooters or a prostitute—as objects that exist solely for their pleasure and convenience. These men are not genetically predisposed[10] to disrespect and abuse women. Their attitudes towards women were societally conditioned.

Some would argue that pornography did not contribute to these men's behavior towards women. I disagree. Rape and battery are not new problems, and objectification of women by the media reinforces historically entrenched beliefs that a woman's main reason for existence is procreation and the sexual pleasure of her mate. Pornographic magazines and lewd posters reduce women to a commodity[11] that can be purchased and owned, divorcing the physical manifestation[12] from the person within. The power of popular culture to affect how we eat, how we dress, and how we behave is enormous. Conceptions of gender are in no way immune to this phenomenon.

Certainly some of us are more affected by the media than others. Not all teenage girls develop anorexia, nor do all men who read *Playboy* abuse their wives. Nonetheless, the prevalence of both eating disorders and various forms of domestic and sexual abuse indicate major societal trends. The American Anorexia/Bulimia Association reports that 5 percent of women will develop a full-fledged eating disorder, while 15 percent have "substantially disordered eating." The Family Violence Prevention Program documents that 4 million American women were battered last year. And, yes, I am absolutely convinced that the objectification of women by the media is an integral part of both of these problems, presenting women with unrealistic role models while encouraging men to think of women solely in terms of their sexuality.

Women are up against a long history of devaluation and oppression, and, unfortunately, the feminist movements have been only partially successful in purging[13] those legacies. Sexually charged images of women in the media are not the only cause of this continuing problem, but they certainly play a central role.

8

9

10 **REFLECT:** How are you and others you know affected by media images?

_____

_____

_____

11

[10] **predisposed:** susceptible, inclined to something in advance

[11] **commodity:** a thing of use, value, or advantage

[12] **manifestation:** visible presence, outward show

[13] **purging:** removing something unwanted

■ **SUMMARIZE AND RESPOND**

In your reading journal or elsewhere, summarize the main point of "Struggling for Perfection." Then, go back and check off support for this main idea. Next, write a brief summary (three to five sentences) of the essay. Finally, jot down your initial response to the essay. Do you agree or disagree with Beck's points? What else do you think causes eating disorders and domestic abuse?

■ **CHECK YOUR COMPREHENSION**

1. Which of the following would be the best alternative title for this essay?

   a.   "The Alarming Growth of Eating Disorders"

   b.   "The Causes and Effects of Eating Disorders"

   c.   "The Media's Influence on Eating Disorders and Domestic Abuse"

   d.   "Pressure to Conform"

2. The main idea of this essay is that

   a.   media images of women are not the only cause of eating disorders.

   b.   publications such as *Playboy* and the Victoria's Secret catalog transform women into sexual objects.

   c.   low self-esteem is a major cause of eating disorders.

   d.   media images of women contribute to eating disorders and violence against females.

3. According to the author,

   a.   women who try to look like supermodels are unable to tell the difference between fiction and reality.

   b.   many of the women she met while working in the hospital had backgrounds that included abuse, family problems, and depression.

   c.   patients with eating disorders are often incurable.

   d.   feminist movements have been very successful in their attempts to lessen the prevalence of eating disorders and abuse against women.

4. If you are unfamiliar with the following words, use a dictionary to check their meanings: gurus, lewd (para. 1); inevitable, psychosis (2); anorexics, bulimics (4); depiction (5); chronic (7); heinous, genetically (8); entrenched, procreation (9); integral (10); devaluation, legacies (11).

█ READ CRITICALLY

1. Why do you think Beck begins her essay by discussing the column "In De-fense of Hooters and the St. Pauli Girl"?

2. Media images of women lead to what two major problems, according to Beck? How are these problems linked?

3. Describe Beck's attitude toward men who commit domestic abuse. What examples from the essay support your response?

4. Does Beck provide clear links between media images of women and the effects of those images? Discuss some of the supporting details she uses to show these links.

5. Beck presents some statistics about eating disorders and domestic abuse. How does she use these statistics to make a further observation about her main point?

█ WRITE AN ESSAY

Beck acknowledges the fact that sexually charged media images of women are not the only cause of eating disorders and abuse. Write an essay about a different possible cause of one of these problems. You could also choose to write about a similar problem (what causes some men to take steroids, for example). If you addressed other causes of eating disorders and abuse for the Summarize and Respond section above, feel free to use those ideas.

Brent Staples

Just Walk on By: Black Men and Public Space

Brent Staples was born in 1951 in Chester, Pennsylvania. After graduating from Widener University, he earned a Ph.D. in psychology from the University of Chicago. He is a member of the editorial board of the *New York Times,* writing commentary on politics and culture. In 1995, he published a memoir, *Parallel Time: Growing Up in Black and White* (1994).

In "Just Walk on By," Staples observes how people, particularly women, react to him when he goes out for a walk. This essay was first published in *Ms.* magazine.

GUIDING QUESTION
How does Staples use examples to make his point?

PREDICT: After reading the title and the first paragraph, what do you expect Staples to write about in the rest of the essay?

My first victim was a woman—white, well dressed, probably in her early 1 twenties. I came upon her late one evening on a deserted street in Hyde Park, a relatively affluent neighborhood in an otherwise mean, impoverished section of Chicago. As I swung onto the avenue behind her, there seemed to be a discreet, uninflammatory[1] distance between us. Not so. She cast back a worried glance. To her, the youngish black man—a broad six feet two inches with a beard and billowing hair, both hands shoved into the pockets of a bulky military jacket—seemed menacingly close. After a few more quick glimpses, she picked up her pace and was soon running in earnest. Within seconds she disappeared into a cross street.

That was more than a decade ago, I was twenty-two years old, a grad- 2 uate student newly arrived at the University of Chicago. It was in the echo of that terrified woman's footfalls that I first began to know the unwieldy inheritance I'd come into—the ability to alter public space in ugly ways. It was clear that she thought herself the quarry[2] of a mugger, a rapist, or worse. Suffering a bout of insomnia, however, I was stalking sleep, not defenseless wayfarers. As a softy who is scarcely able to take a knife to a raw chicken—let alone hold one to a person's throat—I was surprised, embarrassed, and dismayed all at once. Her flight made me feel like an accomplice in tyranny.[3] It also made it clear that I was indistinguishable from the muggers who occasionally seeped into the area from the surrounding ghetto. That first encounter, and those that followed, signified that a vast, unnerving[4] gulf lay between nighttime pedestrians—particularly women—and me. And I soon gathered that being perceived as dangerous is a hazard in itself. I only needed to turn a corner into a dicey situation, or crowd some frightened, armed person in a foyer somewhere, or make an errant[5] move after being pulled over by a policeman. Where fear and weapons meet—and they often do in urban America—there is always the possibility of death.

[1] **uninflammatory:** unlikely to cause fear

[2] **quarry:** one that is pursued, as in a hunt

[3] **tyranny:** the abuse of power

[4] **unnerving:** upsetting

[5] **errant:** stray, unintended

In that first year, my first away from my hometown, I was to become thoroughly familiar with the language of fear. At dark, shadowy intersections, I could cross in front of a car stopped at a traffic light and elicit the *thunk, thunk, thunk, thunk* of the driver—black, white, male, or female—hammering down the door locks. On less traveled streets after dark, I grew accustomed to but never comfortable with people crossing to the other side of the street rather than pass me. Then there were the standard unpleasantries with policemen, doormen, bouncers, cabdrivers, and others whose business it is to screen out troublesome individuals *before* there is any nastiness.

I moved to New York nearly two years ago and I have remained an avid night walker. In central Manhattan, the near-constant crowd cover minimizes tense one-on-one street encounters. Elsewhere—in SoHo, for example, where sidewalks are narrow and tightly spaced buildings shut out the sky—things can get very taut indeed.

After dark, on the warrenlike⁶ streets of Brooklyn where I live, I often see women who fear the worst from me. They seem to have set their faces on neutral, and with their purse straps strung across their chests bandolier-style, they forge ahead as though bracing themselves against being tackled. I understand, of course, that the danger they perceive is not a hallucination. Women are particularly vulnerable to street violence, and young black males are drastically overrepresented among the perpetrators of that violence. Yet these truths are no solace against the kind of alienation that comes of being ever the suspect, a fearsome entity with whom pedestrians avoid making eye contact.

It is not altogether clear to me how I reached the ripe old age of twenty-two without being conscious of the lethality nighttime pedestrians attributed to me. Perhaps it was because in Chester, Pennsylvania, the small, angry industrial town where I came of age in the 1960s, I was scarcely noticeable against a backdrop of gang warfare, street knifings, and murders. I grew up one of the good boys, had perhaps a half-dozen fistfights. In retrospect, my shyness of combat has clear sources.

As a boy, I saw countless tough guys locked away; I have since buried several, too. They were babies, really—a teenage cousin, a brother of twenty-two, a childhood friend in his mid-twenties—all gone down in episodes of bravado played out in the streets. I came to doubt the virtues of intimidation early on. I chose, perhaps unconsciously, to remain a shadow—timid, but a survivor.

The fearsomeness mistakenly attributed to me in public places often has a perilous flavor. The most frightening of these confusions occurred in the late 1970s and early 1980s, when I worked as a journalist in Chicago. One day, rushing into the office of a magazine I was writing for with a deadline story in hand, I was mistaken for a burglar. The office manager

---

⁶**warrenlike:** narrow and having many blind spots

REFLECT: In paragraph 3, what do you suppose Staples means by "standard unpleasantries"?

_____

_____

_____

_____

_____

SUMMARIZE: What point is Staples making about himself in paragraphs 6 and 7?

_____

_____

_____

_____

_____

3

4

5

6

7

8

called security and, with an ad hoc[7] posse, pursued me through the labyrinthine halls, nearly to my editor's door. I had no way of proving who I was. I could only move briskly toward the company of someone who knew me.

Another time I was on assignment for a local paper and killing time   9
before an interview. I entered a jewelry store on the city's affluent Near North Side. The proprietor excused herself and returned with an enormous red Doberman pinscher straining at the end of a leash. She stood, the dog extended toward me, silent to my questions, her eyes bulging nearly out of her head. I took a cursory look around, nodded, and bade her good night.

Relatively speaking, however, I never fared as badly as another black   10
male journalist. He went to nearby Waukegan, Illinois, a couple of summers ago to work on a story about a murderer who was born there. Mistaking the reporter for the killer, police officers hauled him from his car at gunpoint and but for his press credentials would probably have tried to book him. Such episodes are not uncommon. Black men trade tales like this all the time.

IDENTIFY: In paragraph 11, put a check mark next to each of the precautions Staples says he takes to appear less threatening.

Over the years, I learned to smother the rage I felt at so often being   11
taken for a criminal. Not to do so would surely have led to madness. I now take precautions to make myself less threatening. I move about with care, particularly late in the evening. I give a wide berth to nervous people on subway platforms during the wee hours, particularly when I have exchanged business clothes for jeans. If I happen to be entering a building behind some people who appear skittish,[8] I may walk by, letting them clear the lobby before I return, so as not to seem to be following them. I have been calm and extremely congenial[9] on those rare occasions when I've been pulled over by the police.

REFLECT: How do you respond to the image, in paragraph 12, of Staples whistling classical music as he walks at night?

And on late-evening constitutionals[10] I employ what has proved to be   12
an excellent tension-reducing measure: I whistle melodies from Beethoven and Vivaldi and the more popular classical composers. Even steely New Yorkers hunching toward nighttime destinations seem to relax, and occasionally they even join in the tune. Virtually everybody seems to sense that a mugger wouldn't be warbling bright, sunny selections from Vivaldi's *Four Seasons*. It is my equivalent of the cowbell that hikers wear when they know they are in bear country.

---

[7] **ad hoc:** made up of whatever is available (Latin, *for this purpose*)

[8] **skittish:** nervous, jumpy

[9] **congenial:** pleasant, agreeable

[10] **constitutionals:** walks taken for one's health

■ SUMMARIZE AND RESPOND

In your reading journal or elsewhere, summarize the main point of "Just Walk on By: Black Men and Public Space." Then, go back and check off support for this main idea. Next, write a brief summary (three to five sentences) of the reading. Finally, jot down your initial response to the selection. Did you find any of what Staples relates surprising, or do his observations match your own experience? Did reading about Staples's experiences change your attitudes in any way? What impression do you have of the writer himself?

■ CHECK YOUR COMPREHENSION

1. Which of the following would be the best alternative title for this essay?

    a. "Walking the Streets after Dark"

    b. "The Burdens of Racial Identity"

    c. "Being Mistaken for a Criminal Because of One's Skin"

    d. "How to Avoid Muggers and Other Street Criminals"

2. The main idea of this essay is that

    a. the author had to learn how to make himself appear less threatening to others.

    b. the author recognizes that strangers may be unjustifiably afraid of him because he is a black man.

    c. the author believes that people should try to see black men as individuals and not stereotype them as muggers.

    d. the author knew criminals as he was growing up but wants readers to understand that he himself is not one.

3. An important point that Staples makes in this essay is that

    a. the police and other authorities often stop black men for questioning for no good reason.

    b. he felt angry because of strangers' behavior toward him but found ways to suppress his anger.

    c. people in large cities like Chicago and New York are more likely than others to fear black men.

    d. he was once almost arrested because he was mistaken for a murderer he was writing a story about.

4. If you are unfamiliar with the following words, use a dictionary to check their meanings: menacingly (para. 1); unwieldy, insomnia, wayfarers, dismayed, indistinguishable, dicey (2); hallucination, perpetrators, solace, alienation, entity (5); lethality, retrospect (6); bravado (7); perilous, posse, labyrinthine (8); affluent, cursory (9); credentials (10); warbling (12).

READ CRITICALLY

1. What, specifically, is the cause-and-effect relationship that Staples is describing in the essay? How well do you think he shows this relationship? What is the effect of the situation on Staples himself?

2. Why do you suppose Staples opens his essay by referring to "[m]y first victim"? What is the effect of this language?

3. Who would you say Staples imagined as his audience for this essay? What vision of himself does he seem to want his readers to come away with?

4. Why do you think Staples refers to the experience of another black man in paragraph 10, when all of his other examples are drawn from his own experience?

5. What is your response to Staples's final two paragraphs? To his final sentence? How would you evaluate this conclusion?

WRITE AN ESSAY

Write an essay, based on your own experiences, about the causes and effects of stereotypes and mistaken perceptions. You might focus on mistaken perceptions others have had of you or on mistaken perceptions you have had of others—or on both kinds of mistaken perceptions. You might also focus on instances of mistaken perceptions and stereotyping that you have witnessed. Be sure to establish clear cause-and-effect relationships.

50
Argument

The essays in this chapter use argument to get their main point across. We have provided a pro and con essay for each of two topics — reinstatement of the military draft and legalization of same-sex marriage. This will allow you to compare and contrast the argumentative strategies used. As you read the essays in each pair, decide which essay you find stronger and why.

As you read these essays, consider how they achieve the four basics of good argument that are listed below and discussed in Chapter 17 of this book.

▞ FOUR BASICS OF GOOD ARGUMENT

1. It takes a strong and definite position on an issue or advises a particular action.
2. It gives good reasons and supporting evidence to defend the position or recommended action.
3. It considers opposing views.
4. It has enthusiasm and energy from start to finish.

The Military Draft
William Broyles Jr.
A War for Us, Fought by Them

William Broyles Jr. (b. 1944) served in the U.S. Marine Corps in Vietnam. A graduate of Rice University, he pursued a career in journalism after the war, becoming a founding editor of *Texas Monthly* magazine and, later, editor-in-chief of *Newsweek.* Broyles has also written for movies and television. His screenplays include *Apollo 13* and *Castaway.* He also wrote *Brothers in Arms* (1986), a book based on his experiences in Vietnam.

The following column appeared in the *New York Times* in May 2004. In an argument for reinstating the draft, he condemns the willingness of politicians to let "Other People's Children" fight the war.

GUIDING QUESTION

Who, according to Broyles, makes up the bulk of the current military, who is underrepresented, and why is this a problem?

REFLECT: Why do you suppose Broyles refers to Bill Clinton, George W. Bush, and Dick Cheney in this opening paragraph?

The longest love affair of my life began with a shotgun marriage.[1] It was the height of the Vietnam War and my student deferment had run out. Desperate not to endanger myself or to interrupt my personal plans, I wanted to avoid military service altogether. I didn't have the resourcefulness of Bill Clinton, so I couldn't figure out how to dodge the draft. I tried to escape into the National Guard, where I would be guaranteed not to be sent to war, but I lacked the connections of George W. Bush, so I couldn't slip ahead of the long waiting list. My attitude was the same as Dick Cheney's: I was special, I had "other priorities."[2] Let other people do it. 1

When my draft notice came in 1968, I was relieved in a way. Although I had deep doubts about the war, I had become troubled about how I had angled to avoid military service. My classmates from high school were in the war; my classmates from college were not — exactly the dynamic that exists today. But instead of reporting for service in the Army, on a whim I joined the Marine Corps, the last place on earth I thought I belonged. 2

My sacrifice turned out to be minimal. I survived a year as an infantry lieutenant in Vietnam. I was not wounded; nor did I struggle for years with post-traumatic stress disorder. A long bout of survivor guilt was the price I paid. Others suffered far more, particularly those who had to serve after the war had lost all sense of purpose for the men fighting it. I like to think that in spite of my being so unwilling at first, I did some small service to my country and to that enduring love of mine, the United States Marine Corps. 3

SUMMARIZE: What is the writer's main point in paragraph 4?

To my profound surprise, the Marines did a far greater service to me. In three years I learned more about standards, commitment, and, yes, life than I did in six years of university. I also learned that I had had no idea 4

---

[1] **shotgun marriage:** a marriage forced by the bride's family

[2] **"other priorities":** Vice President (and former Secretary of Defense) Dick Cheney has been quoted as telling a *Washington Post* reporter, "I had other priorities in the sixties than military service."

of my own limits: when I was exhausted after humping up and down jungle mountains in 100-degree heat with a 75-pound pack, terrified out of my mind, wanting only to quit, convinced I couldn't take another step, I found that in fact I could keep going for miles. And my life was put in the hands of young men I would otherwise never have met, by and large high-school dropouts, who turned out to be among the finest people I have ever known.

I am now the father of a young man who has far more character than 5 I ever had. I joined the Marines because I had to; he signed up after college because he felt he ought to. He volunteered for an elite unit and has served in both Afghanistan and Iraq. When I see images of Americans in the war zones, I think of my son and his friends, many of whom I have come to know and deeply respect. When I opened this newspaper yesterday and read the front-page headline, "9 G.I.'s Killed," I didn't think in abstractions. I thought very personally.

The problem is, I don't see the images of or read about any of the young 6 men and women who, as Dick Cheney and I did, have "other priorities." There are no immediate family members of any of the prime civilian planners of this war serving in it—beginning with President Bush and extending deep into the Defense Department. Only one of the 535 members of Congress, Senator Tim Johnson of South Dakota, has a child in the war— and only half a dozen others have sons and daughters in the military.

The memorial service yesterday for Pat Tillman, the football star killed 7 in Afghanistan, further points out this contrast. He remains the only professional athlete of any sport who left his privileged life during this war and turned in his play uniform for a real one. With few exceptions, the only men and women in military service are the profoundly patriotic or the economically needy.

It was not always so. In other wars, the men and women in charge 8 made sure their family members led the way. Since 9/11, the war on terrorism has often been compared to the generational challenge of Pearl Harbor,[3] but Franklin D. Roosevelt's[4] sons all enlisted soon after that attack. Both of Lyndon B. Johnson's[5] sons-in-law served in Vietnam.

This is less a matter of politics than privilege. The Democratic elites 9 have not responded more nobly than have the Republican; it's just that the Democrats' hypocrisy is less acute. Our president's own family illustrates the loss of the sense of responsibility that once went with privilege. In three generations the Bushes have gone from war hero in World War II, to war

[3] **Pearl Harbor:** location of the attack that led to the United States's entry into World War II

[4] **Franklin D. Roosevelt:** U.S. president during much of World War II

[5] **Lyndon B. Johnson:** U.S. president during the escalation of the war in Vietnam

evader in Vietnam, to none of the extended family showing up in Iraq and Afghanistan.

SUMMARIZE: What does the writer think would result from putting the children of the nation's elites into combat?

Pat Tillman didn't want to be singled out for having done what other 10 patriotic Americans his age should have done. The problem is, they aren't doing it. In spite of the president's insistence that our very civilization is at stake, the privileged aren't flocking to the flag. The war is being fought by Other People's Children. The war is impersonal for the very people to whom it should be most personal.

If the children of the nation's elites were facing enemy fire without 11 body armor, riding through gauntlets of bombs in unarmored Humvees, fighting desperately in an increasingly hostile environment because of arrogant and incompetent civilian leadership, then those problems might well find faster solutions.

The men and women on active duty today—and their companions in 12 the National Guard and the reserves—have seen their willingness, and that of their families, to make sacrifices for their country stretched thin and finally abused. Thousands of soldiers promised a one-year tour of duty have seen that promise turned into a lie. When Eric Shinseki, then the Army chief of staff, told the president that winning the war and peace in Iraq would take hundreds of thousands more troops, Mr. Bush ended his career. As a result of this and other ill-advised decisions, the war is in danger of being lost, and my beloved military is being run into the ground.

This abuse of the voluntary military cannot continue. How to ensure 13 adequate troop levels, with a diversity of backgrounds? How to require the privileged to shoulder their fair share? In other words, how to get today's equivalents of Bill Clinton, George W. Bush, Dick Cheney—and me—into the military, where their talents could strengthen and revive our fighting forces?

IDENTIFY: What two opposing arguments does the writer acknowledge in paragraph 14?

The only solution is to bring back the draft. Not since the nineteenth 14 century has America fought a war that lasted longer than a week with an all-volunteer army; we can't do it now. It is simply not built for a protracted[6] major conflict. The arguments against the draft—that a voluntary army is of higher quality, that the elites will still find a way to evade service—are bogus. In World War II we used a draft army to fight the Germans and Japanese—two of the most powerful military machines in history—and we won. The problems in the military toward the end of Vietnam were not caused by the draft; they were the result of young Americans being sent to fight and die in a war that had become a disaster.

One of the few good legacies of Vietnam is that after years of abuses we 15 finally learned how to run the draft fairly. A strictly impartial lottery, with no deferments, can ensure that the draft intake matches military needs. Chance, not connections or clever manipulation, would determine who serves.

[6]**protracted:** drawn out

If this war is truly worth fighting, then the burdens of doing so should   16
fall on all Americans. If you support this war, but assume that Pat Tillman
and Other People's Children should fight it, then you are worse than a
hypocrite. If it's not worth your family fighting it, then it's not worth it, period. The draft is the truest test of public support for the administration's
handling of the war, which is perhaps why the administration is so dead
set against bringing it back.

▇ SUMMARIZE AND RESPOND

In your reading journal or elsewhere, summarize the main point of "A War
for Us, Fought by Them." Then, go back and check off support for this
main idea. Next, write a brief summary (three to five sentences) of the
reading. Finally, jot down your initial response to the selection. Does
Broyles offer a convincing argument? Does he raise any issues you hadn't
thought about before? What is your reaction to the writer himself? What
would you say if you could speak to him directly?

▇ CHECK YOUR COMPREHENSION

1. Which of the following would be the best alternative title for this essay?
   a. "The Hypocrisy of War"
   b. "Sharing the Burdens of War"
   c. "The Lessons of the War in Vietnam"
   d. "The Problems of Achieving a Fair and Impartial Draft"

2. The main idea of this essay is that
   a. only through a draft can the United States ensure that citizens from
       all walks of life serve proportionately in the military.
   b. during the war in Vietnam, those who were clever or had family con-
       nections were in a position to avoid the draft.
   c. in earlier wars, family members of government officials served in the
       military, but few government officials today have family in the military.
   d. the draft should be brought back because the author was drafted and
       benefited greatly from serving in the Marines.

3. Which of the following is *not* a concern expressed by the author?
   a. His son is serving in the Marines and could possibly be killed in
       action.

b. The resources of the men and women currently on active duty in the military are being stretched thin.

c. The war in Iraq could be lost because of ill-advised decisions by the Bush administration.

d. If the children of the country's elites were serving in the military, there would be more public support for the war.

4. If you are unfamiliar with the following words, use a dictionary to check their meanings: deferment, resourcefulness (para. 1); dynamic (2); elite, abstractions (5); profoundly (7); hypocrisy (9); arrogant (11); bogus (14); manipulation (15).

READ CRITICALLY

1. Why do you suppose Broyles opens his essay by writing about being drafted during the Vietnam conflict and serving in the Marines?

2. Why does it bother Broyles that none of the planners of the war in Iraq and only a few members of Congress have family members serving in the military? What purpose does this point serve in his argument? Do you find this an effective strategy?

3. What is Broyles's point in introducing the example of football star Pat Tillman (para. 7)? What role does this paragraph play in his argument?

4. Do you think Broyles successfully deals with the arguments against the draft acknowledged in paragraph 14? Why or why not?

5. How do you respond to Broyles's final paragraph? Do you find it an effective closing? What is he implying in his final sentence? What does this sentence suggest about his attitude toward the Bush administration?

WRITE AN ESSAY

Write an essay arguing for or against a law requiring that all young people perform at least two years of mandatory government service—with the option of serving in the military or in some other capacity that would benefit the country. (A bill proposing such service was introduced in Congress in 2003. You might want to do some research about how such service would work.) Alternatively, you might focus your argument on community service requirements that have been established by a number of school districts and colleges as a prerequisite for graduation. In developing your argument, be sure to consider both sides of the issue.

Nathaniel Fick

Don't Dumb Down the Military

After graduating with honors from Dartmouth College in 1999, Nathaniel Fick joined the U.S. Marine Corps. He served in both Afghanistan and Iraq and earned a Navy Commendation Medal. Honorably discharged in November 2003, he is currently working on a memoir of his experiences in the military.

Fick published the following essay in the *New York Times* in July 2004. Using his firsthand knowledge of combat, he argues that a draft would only hurt today's military, in which extensive training is necessary.

GUIDING QUESTION
What two opposing views does the author acknowledge in this essay, and how does he address them?

I went to war as a believer in the citizen-soldier. My college study of the classics idealized Greeks who put down their plows for swords, returning to their fields at the end of the war. As a Marine officer in Afghanistan and Iraq, however, I learned that the victors on today's battlefields are long-term, professional soldiers. Thus the increasing calls for reinstating[1] the draft—and the bills now before Congress that would do so—are well intentioned but misguided. Imposing a draft on the military I served in would harm it grievously for years.

IDENTIFY: What does Fick do in this opening paragraph to establish himself as an authority on his subject?

I led platoons of volunteers. In Afghanistan, my marines slept each night in holes they hacked from the rocky ground. They carried hundred-pound packs in addition to their fears of minefields and ambushes, their homesickness, loneliness and exhaustion. The most junior did it for $964.80 per month. They didn't complain, and I never wrestled with discipline problems. Each and every marine wanted to be there. If anyone hadn't, he would have been a drain on the platoon and a liability[2] in combat.

In Iraq, I commanded a reconnaissance[3] platoon, the Marines' special operations force. Many of my enlisted marines were college-educated; some had been to graduate school. All had volunteered once for the Marines, again for the infantry, and a third time for recon. They were proud to serve as part of an elite unit. Like most demanding professionals, they were their own harshest critics, intolerant of their peers whose performance fell short.

[1] **reinstating:** restoring, putting into effect again

[2] **liability:** someone or something that puts others at a disadvantage

[3] **reconnaissance:** referring to troops who examine potential battle sites in advance

The dumb grunt[4] is an anachronism.[5] He has been replaced by the strategic corporal. Immense firepower and improved technology have pushed decision-making with national consequences down to individual enlisted men. Modern warfare requires that even the most junior infantryman master a wide array of technical and tactical skills. 4

SUMMARIZE: What is Fick's main point in paragraph 5?

———————————

———————————

———————————

———————————

Honing these skills to reflex, a prerequisite for survival in combat, takes time—a year of formal training and another year of on-the-job experience were generally needed to transform my young marines into competent warriors. The Marine Corps demands four-year active enlistments because it takes that long to train troops and ensure those training dollars are put to use in the field. One-or two-year terms, the longest that would be likely under conscription,[6] would simply not allow for this comprehensive training. 5

Some supporters of the draft argue that America's wars are being fought primarily by minorities from poor families who enlisted in the economic equivalent of a Hail Mary pass.[7] They insist that the sacrifices of citizenship be shared by all Americans. The sentiment is correct, but the outrage is misplaced. There is no cannon-fodder underclass in the military. In fact, front-line combat troops are a near-perfect reflection of American male society. 6

Yes, some minority men and women enlist for lack of other options, but they tend to concentrate in support jobs where they can learn marketable skills like driving trucks or fixing jets, not throwing grenades and setting up interlocking fields of machine gun fire. African-Americans, who comprise nearly 13 percent of the general population, are overrepresented in the military at more than 19 percent—but they account for only 10.6 percent of infantry soldiers, the group that suffers most in combat. Hispanics, who make up 13.3 percent of the American population, are underrepresented at only 11 percent of those in uniform. 7

REFLECT: From what you have read and seen of U.S. forces in combat, do they appear to reflect a cross-section of the United States?

———————————

———————————

———————————

———————————

The men in my infantry platoons came from virtually every part of the socio-economic spectrum. There were prep-school graduates and first-generation immigrants, blacks and whites, Muslims and Jews, Democrats and Republicans. They were more diverse than my class at Dartmouth, and far more willing to act on their principles. 8

The second argument most often advanced for a renewed draft is that the military is too small to meet its commitments. Absolutely true. But the armed forces are stretched thin not from a lack of volunteers but because Congress and the Pentagon are not willing to spend the money to expand the force. Each of the services met or exceeded its recruiting goals in 2003, and the numbers have increased across the board so far this year. Even the Army National Guard, often cited as the abused beast of burden in Iraq, 9

[4]**grunt:** slang for foot soldier

[5]**anachronism:** something no longer relevant to the present

[6]**conscription:** compulsory enrollment in military service

[7]**Hail Mary pass:** in football, a long pass made in desperation

has seen reenlistments soar past its goal, 65 percent, to 141 percent (the figure is greater than 100 because many guardsmen are reenlisting early).†

Expanding the military to meet additional responsibilities is a matter of structural change: If we build it, they will come. And build it we must. Many of my marines are already on their third combat deployment in the global war on terrorism; they will need replacing. Increasing the size of the active-duty military would lighten the burden on every soldier, sailor, airman and marine. Paradoxically,[8] a larger military becomes more sustainable than a smaller one: Fewer combat deployments improves service members' quality of life and contributes to higher rates of enlistment and retention. For now, expanding the volunteer force would give us a larger military without the inherent liabilities of conscription.

10 **SUMMARIZE:** Why does Fick believe it is important to "lighten the burden" on the military?

And while draft supporters insist we have learned the lessons of Vietnam and can create a fair system this time around, even an equitable draft would lower the standards for enlistees. Defense Secretary Donald Rumsfeld was chastised[9] for saying Vietnam-era draftees added no value to the armed forces. But his error was semantic;[10] the statement was true of the system, if not of the patriotic and capable individuals who served.

11

The current volunteer force rejects applicants who score poorly on its entrance aptitude exam, disclose a history of significant drug use, or suffer from any of a number of orthopedic[11] or chronic injuries. Face it: Any unwilling draftee could easily find a way to fail any of these tests. The military, then, would be left either to abandon its standards and accept all comers, or to remain true to them and allow the draft to become volunteerism by another name. Stripped of its volunteer ideology, but still unable to compel service from dissenters, the military would end up weaker and less representative than the volunteer force—the very opposite of the draft's intended goals.

12

Renewing the draft would be a blow against the men and women in uniform, a dumbing down of the institution they serve. The United States military exists to win battles, not to test social policy. Enlarging the volunteer force would show our soldiers that Americans recognize their hardship and are willing to pay the bill to help them better protect the nation. My view of the citizen-soldier was altered, but not destroyed, in combat. We cannot all pick up the sword, nor should we be forced to—but we owe our support to those who do.

13

† In February 2005, the regular Army missed its recruiting goal—the first time this has happened since 2000. Recent data also suggest that the National Guard is missing recruiting goals.

[8] **paradoxically:** seemingly—but not really—contradictory

[9] **chastised:** criticized

[10] **semantic:** a matter of word choice

[11] **orthopedic:** in this sense, crippling

SUMMARIZE AND RESPOND

In your reading journal or elsewhere, summarize the main point of "Don't Dumb Down the Military." Then, go back and check off support for this main idea. Next, write a brief summary (three to five sentences) of the reading. Finally, jot down your initial response to the selection. How well do you think Fick makes his case? Do you find his argument convincing, or are there parts of it that you question? Why do you feel as you do?

■ **CHECK YOUR COMPREHENSION**

1. Which of the following would be the best alternative title for this essay?

   a. "A Case against the Military Draft"

   b. "The Importance of the Citizen-Soldier"

   c. "My Experiences as a Marine Commander"

   d. "Expanding Our Volunteer Military Force"

2. The main idea of this essay is that

   a. current U.S. military forces are stretched too thin and should be expanded.

   b. every citizen should volunteer for some type of military service.

   c. reinstating a draft would have negative consequences for the U.S. military.

   d. the current U.S. military reflects the diverse makeup of the country as a whole.

3. According to the author,

   a. the size of the U.S. military is adequate to meet its commitments.

   b. a draft would mean that fewer young people would volunteer for military service.

   c. current warfare requires troops to have extensive training in a variety of skills.

   d. volunteer members of the military would be unhappy working alongside those who were drafted.

4. If you are unfamiliar with the following words, use a dictionary to check their meanings: misguided (para. 1); infantry (3); strategic, tactical (4); prerequisite (5); cannon-fodder (6); spectrum (8); deployment, retention, inherent (10); equitable (11); chronic, dissenters (12).

READ CRITICALLY

1. Why, in Fick's view, would a draft "dumb down" the U.S. military? Do you think he makes a strong case for this view? Why or why not?

2. Why does Fick open and close his essay by referring to the idea of the "citizen-soldier"? In what ways did his experiences in the military change his view of this classic ideal?

3. What would you identify as Fick's most convincing point in the essay? Can you find any weaknesses in his argument?

4. How well do you think Fick deals with the two arguments in favor of a draft that he acknowledges in paragraphs 6 and 9? Would people who make these claims likely have their minds changed by Fick's assertions? Can you think of other arguments in favor of a draft that he should have dealt with?

5. While arguing against a draft, what change is Fick arguing in favor of in the essay?

WRITE AN ESSAY

Write an essay in which you take a stand on a current political, cultural, or social issue about which you have strong feelings. If necessary, do some reading so that you can acknowledge opposing arguments. Be sure to provide enough background so that readers understand the terms of the controversy and why it is of concern. In developing your essay, keep in mind that you need to express your own viewpoint clearly.

Same-Sex Marriage

Anna Quindlen

Desecration? Dedication!

Anna Quindlen was born in 1953 in Philadelphia, Pennsylvania. She joined the *New York Times* in 1977 and began writing her nationally syndicated column "Public and Private" for the op-ed page in 1981. Her columns were compiled into the acclaimed book *Living Out Loud* (1989). In 1992, Quindlen was awarded a Pulitzer Prize for commentary.

Quindlen left the *New York Times* in 1995 to write novels. Her novels *Object Lessons* (1992) and *Black and Blue* (1999), and the children's book *Happily Ever After* (1999), were all best sellers. Quindlen is currently a columnist for *Newsweek*.

In this essay, originally published in *Newsweek* in 2004, Quindlen argues that gay couples and straight couples are held to different standards when it comes to marriage.

GUIDING QUESTION
What is Quindlen's point in comparing gay men and lesbians who wish to marry with immigrants who become citizens of the United States?

And now for a short quiz: 1

- How many amendments are there in the Constitution?
- How many times may a senator be reelected?
- Which president was the first commander in chief of the U.S. military?
- What do the stripes on the flag stand for?

You got the flag one, didn't you? But what about the other three? These 2
are just a few of the questions people may be asked to answer if they are taking the test to become citizens of the United States. That's a good thing. A working knowledge of the governing processes and the history of our country can be reasonably expected of those who want to share in the benefits and responsibilities of being American.

The problem is that most native-born citizens probably can't pass the 3
test. Americans are remarkably casual about their citizenship, not voting in sufficient numbers, not following the critical political issues. Those of us to the Star-Spangled Banner born aren't tested in the same way converts are. In fact the United States seems to have a bad case of what you might call natalism, privilege conferred by accident of birth, high or low. (Although there is still no privilege like the privilege of wealth. Who knew that National Guard service was so flexible that you could duck out nearly a year early because, as President Bush said in his ill-advised interview with Tim Russert, "I was going to Harvard Business School and worked it out with the military.")

PREDICT: After reading paragraph 4, what do you expect the focus of Quindlen's argument to be?

The latest citizens to be required to perform, as gadfly[1] feminist 4
politico Charlotte Whitton once said of women, twice as well to be thought half as good are gay men and lesbians. All these people want is what we hetero types take for granted: the opportunity to drop to one knee in a

_____

[1] **gadfly:** a persistent critic

white-tablecloth restaurant and pledge eternal fealty[2] in the eyes of the waiters and the world. But if gay people persist in this wild-eyed determination to marry, it's clear they will be held to that higher standard that outsiders have learned to expect.

In a recent sermon, Cardinal Edward Egan of New York, who somehow managed for a long time to contain his public outrage at pedophiles[3] in the priestly ranks, decried the notion of same-sex marriage and referred to "the desecration[4] of something sacred." The marriages we're talking about are civil marriages, which are so short of being sanctified in the eyes of the church that it will scarcely recognize their existence if you are Roman Catholic. And in a secular nation, why should church leaders be required to acknowledge civil marriage — or, for that matter, be attended[5] to when they pass judgment on what they will not acknowledge? Let them police the rites they have the right to regulate.

One of the chief arguments opponents have against same-sex marriage is that marriage is designed first and foremost to produce and shelter children. Naturally, we straight people don't have to conform to that standard. Infertile people, people who don't want to have kids, women who are past childbearing age: all of us get married as a matter of course, no questions asked. Unfortunately for those who rely on that argument, the barrenness of gay unions isn't accurate. In a soon-to-be-published book, *Gay Marriage: Why It Is Good for Gays, Good for Straights, and Good for America,* Jonathan Rauch reports that the most recent Census found 28 percent of gay couples had kids. And that's probably an undercount. Opponents might also argue that the children of gay couples are not the sort of biological fruit of marriage to which we are accustomed. They might try telling that to straight people who have used IVF[6] or a sperm bank, who are stepparents or adoptive parents.

Comedians have made jokes about the gay-marriage controversy along predictable lines: Why shouldn't they have the same right to be miserable that the rest of us have? Rauch's book turns that offhanded ridicule[7] of the institution on its head. In few books about matrimony will you read descriptions that so powerfully evoke the married state as a blessing for human beings. It is the yearning of the exile, the hunger of the disenfranchised.[8] Even the dedication packs a wallop: "For Michael. Marry me,

5

6

SUMMARIZE: What two opposing arguments does Quindlen acknowledge in paragraph 6?

_____

_____

_____

_____

_____

7

_____

_____

_____

_____

[2] **fealty:** devotion

[3] **pedophiles:** child abusers

[4] **desecration:** violation of something holy

[5] **attended:** listened

[6] **IVF:** in vitro fertilization; joining egg and sperm outside of the human body

[7] **ridicule:** mockery

[8] **disenfranchised:** those deprived of basic rights

when we can." To characterize this sort of devotion as desecration is reprehensible.[9] Anyone who defines marriage largely in terms of what happens in bed has never been married. Which may explain the Catholic Church's official reaction.

Like the naturalized citizens who are expected to know more about   8 America than those of us born here, gay couples are being held to a standard the denizens[10] of Vegas chapels and divorce courts have never had to meet: to justify the simple human urge, so taken for granted by the rest of us, to fully and legally come together. Just as it's common to see an immigrant take the oath and then kiss the ground, the result of all this enforced soul-searching may well be a fervor that will honor an embattled institution. Gay people are being asked to form a more perfect union. In the process, perhaps they can teach us something that we casual citizens and spouses badly need to learn.

[9]**reprehensible:** deserving of the strongest criticism

[10]**denizens:** frequent visitors

◼ SUMMARIZE AND RESPOND

In your reading journal or elsewhere, summarize the main point of "Desecration? Dedication!" Then, go back and check off support for this main idea. Next, write a brief summary (three to five sentences) of the reading. Finally, jot down your initial response to the selection. What were your thoughts on the issue before you read the essay? Did any of the points Quindlen makes help solidify your prior opinion or make you rethink your position in any way? Why or why not?

◼ CHECK YOUR COMPREHENSION

1. Which of the following would be the best alternative title for this essay?
   a. "Same-Sex Marriage and the Catholic Church"
   b. "Same-Sex Marriage and the Question of Children"
   c. "Marriage: A Higher Standard for Same-Sex Couples"
   d. "The Devotion of Same-Sex Couples Who Long to Be Married"

2. The main idea of this essay is that
   a. same-sex couples shouldn't be held to a higher standard than heterosexual couples when it comes to marriage rights.

b. in a secular nation, same-sex marriages are civil marriages that need not be recognized by the Catholic Church.

c. same-sex couples who have children should be allowed to marry.

d. same-sex partners tend to be more devoted to each other than heterosexual partners are.

3. According to Quindlen, Jonathan Rauch's book *Gay Marriage: Why It Is Good for Gays, Good for Straights, and Good for America* makes the point that

a. straight people do not have to conform to the standard that marriage is designed primarily to produce and nurture children.

b. many same-sex couples long for marriage because they regard it as a blessing for human beings.

c. same-sex couples who wish to be married are comparable to immigrants who wish to become U.S. citizens.

d. marriage is not defined mainly in terms of what two people do in bed.

4. If you are unfamiliar with the following words, use a dictionary to check their meanings: converts (para. 3); sanctified, secular (5); infertile, barrenness (6); offhanded, institution, exile (7); naturalized, fervor, embattled (8).

READ CRITICALLY

1. Why does Quindlen open her essay with the four questions of her "short quiz"? What connection does she make between being able to answer these questions and the issue of same-sex marriage?

2. What point is Quindlen making in paragraph 5 about the opposition of church leaders to same-sex marriage? Do you accept her conclusions?

3. Quindlen acknowledges two opposing arguments to same-sex marriage in paragraph 6. How does she address these arguments? Do you find her points convincing? Why or why not?

4. How do you respond to Quindlen's references to Jonathan Rauch's book *Gay Marriage: Why It Is Good for Gays, Good for Straights, and Good for America*? What do you expect she hopes these will contribute to her argument? Do you think she succeeds in her purpose?

5. How would you evaluate Quindlen's final paragraph? Her final sentence? Do you find these an effective conclusion to her essay? Why or why not?

WRITE AN ESSAY

Write an essay in which you argue for your own definition of what constitutes a family. Be sure to acknowledge and address alternative definitions and to use specific examples to help readers understand your definition.

Charles Colson and Anne Morse

Societal Suicide

Charles Colson (b. 1931) served as special counsel to President Richard Nixon during the Watergate scandal that led to Nixon's resignation in 1974. After serving seven months in prison for obstruction of justice in the Watergate case, Colson founded Prison Fellowship Ministries, which provides support to both prisoners and crime victims. Colson has published many books, including the autobiographies *Born Again* (1976) and *Life Sentence* (1979), *Justice That Restores* (2001), and *Science and Evolution: Developing a Christian Worldview of Science and Evolution* (with Nancy Pearcey, 2001). He is also a contributing editor of *Christianity Today* and a commentator on the Christian radio program *BreakPoint*. Anne Morse is a senior writer for *Christianity Today*.

In this essay, published in *Christianity Today* in 2004, the authors argue in support of a proposed Federal Marriage Amendment, which defines marriage strictly as a union between a man and a woman.

GUIDING QUESTION
What evidence do the authors cite in support of their argument?

PREDICT: After reading the title and the first two paragraphs, what do you expect this essay to argue?

_____

_____

_____

_____

Is America witnessing the end of marriage? The Supreme Judicial Court   1
of Massachusetts has ordered that the state issue marriage licenses to same-sex couples. (By late March, the Massachusetts legislature voted to recognize same-sex civil unions instead.) An unprecedented period of municipal lawlessness has followed, with officials in California, New York, Oregon, and New Mexico gleefully mocking their state constitutions and laws. The result: Thousands of gays rushed to these municipalities to "marry," while much of the news media egged them on.

In the midst of the chaos, President Bush announced his support for   2
a Federal Marriage Amendment, which assures that this contentious[1] issue will be debated in every quarter of American life. It should be, because the

[1] **contentious:** causing argument

consequences of having "gay marriage" forced on us by judicial (or mayoral) fiat[2] will fall on all Americans—not just those who embrace it.

As a supporter of the amendment, I'm well aware of the critical arguments. As the president noted, "After more than two centuries of American jurisprudence,[3] and millennia[4] of human experience, a few judges and local authorities are presuming to change the most fundamental institution of civilization. Their action has created confusion on an issue that requires clarity."   3

He's right. Here's the clarity: Marriage is the traditional building block of human society, intended both to unite couples and bring children into the world.   4

Tragically, the sexual revolution led to the decoupling[5] of marriage and procreation;[6] same-sex "marriage" would pull them completely apart, leading to an explosive increase in family collapse, out-of-wedlock births—and crime. How do we know this?   5

In nearly thirty years of prison ministry, I've witnessed the disastrous consequences of family breakdown—in the lives of thousands of delinquents. Dozens of studies now confirm the evidence I've seen with my own eyes. Boys who grow up without fathers are at least twice as likely as other boys to end up in prison. Sixty percent of rapists and 72 percent of adolescent murderers never knew or lived with their fathers.   6

Even in the toughest inner-city neighborhoods, just 10 percent of kids from intact families get into trouble, but 90 percent of those from broken families do.   7

Girls raised without a father in the home are five times more likely to become mothers while still adolescents. Children from broken homes have more academic and behavioral problems at school and are nearly twice as likely to drop out of high school.   8

Critics agree with this but claim gay "marriage" will not weaken heterosexual marriage. The evidence says they're wrong.   9

Stanley Kurtz of the Hoover Institution writes: "It follows that once marriage is redefined to accommodate same-sex couples, that change cannot help but lock in and reinforce the very cultural separation between marriage and parenthood that makes gay marriage conceivable to begin with."   10

SUMMARIZE: What point are the authors making in paragraphs 6–8?

_____

_____

_____

_____

_____

---

[2] **fiat:** command that forces something to happen

[3] **jurisprudence:** a system or body of law

[4] **millennia:** thousands of years

[5] **decoupling:** separation

[6] **procreation:** the bringing forth of offspring

IDENTIFY: What cause-and-effect relationship are the authors suggesting in paragraph 11?

_____

_____

_____

_____

He cites Norway, where courts imposed same-sex "marriage" in 11 1993—a time when Norwegians enjoyed a low out-of-wedlock birth rate. After the imposition of same-sex "marriage," Norway's out-of-wedlock birth rate shot up as the link between marriage and childbearing was broken and cohabitation[7] became the norm.

Gay "marriage" supporters argue that most family tragedies occur be- 12 cause of broken *heterosexual* marriages—including those of many Christians. They are right. We ought to accept our share of the blame, repent, and clean up our own house. But the fact that we have badly served the institution of marriage is not a reflection on the institution itself; it is a reflection on us.

REFLECT: What is your response to the statement, in paragraph 13, that "there is a natural moral order for the family"?

_____

_____

_____

As we debate the wisdom of legalizing gay "marriage," we must re- 13 member that, like it or not, there is a natural moral order for the family. History and tradition—and the teachings of Jews, Muslims, and Christians—support the overwhelming empirical evidence: The family, led by a married mother and father, is the best available structure for both child-rearing and cultural health.

This is why, although some people will always pair off in unorthodox 14 ways, society as a whole must never legitimize any form of marriage other than that of one man and one woman, united with intention of permanency and the nurturing of children.

Marriage is not a private institution designed solely for the individual 15 gratification of its participants. If we fail to enact a Federal Marriage Amendment, we can expect, not just more family breakdown, but also more criminals behind bars and more chaos in our streets.

[7]**cohabitation:** living together unmarried

■ **SUMMARIZE AND RESPOND**

In your reading journal or elsewhere, summarize the main point of "Societal Suicide." Then, go back and check off support for this main idea. Next, write a brief summary (three to five sentences) of the reading. Finally, jot down your initial response to the selection. What were your beliefs about this issue before you read the essay? Did the authors offer any evidence that supported your initial opinions or caused you to change your mind in any way? Why or why not?

■ **CHECK YOUR COMPREHENSION**

1. Which of the following would be the best alternative title for this essay?

   a. "Why We Must Pass the Federal Marriage Amendment"

b. "Marriage: The Traditional Building Block of Human Society"

c. "The Negative Effects of Family Breakdown on the Lives of Children"

d. "The Natural Moral Order for the Family"

2. The main idea of this essay is that

a. the Massachusetts Supreme Court decision allowing same-sex marriage created national chaos.

b. the sexual revolution led to an increase in the number of children growing up in broken homes.

c. same-sex couples should not be allowed to raise children because a family should be led by a mother and father.

d. same-sex marriage should be prohibited because it will break the link between marriage and childbearing.

3. Which of the following is *not* offered as evidence by the authors in supporting their argument?

a. Children who grow up in broken homes are more likely than others to commit crime.

b. In Norway, the allowing of same-sex marriage was followed by an increase in out-of-wedlock births.

c. Most family tragedies occur because of the breakdown of heterosexual marriages.

d. Married families led by a mother and father provide the best structure for raising children.

4. If you are unfamiliar with the following words, use a dictionary to check their meanings: unprecedented, municipal, gleefully (para. 1); chaos (2); clarity (3); disastrous, delinquents (6); imposition (11); empirical (13); unorthodox (14).

READ CRITICALLY

1. Why do you suppose the authors chose to put forms of the word *marriage* in quotation marks when referring to same-sex unions? How did this usage affect your reading of the essay?

2. What purpose is served by quoting President Bush in paragraph 3 of the essay?

3. How strong do you find the evidence presented by the authors of the essay? Do you think the evidence is sufficient? Why or why not?

4. The authors point to a "natural moral order for the family" (para. 13). Do you think that Colson, having been imprisoned after a political scandal, is qualified to make statements about moral behavior? Why or why not?

5. How would you evaluate the final two paragraphs? Do they provide an effective conclusion? Why do you feel as you do?

▮ WRITE AN ESSAY

Write an essay in which you make an argument about an issue related to marriage or child rearing. You might focus on same-sex marriage or another issue, such as the high rate of divorce in the United States, out-of-wedlock births, adoption of children by gay men and lesbians, or support for single-parent households. In drafting your essay, be sure to acknowledge and respond to opposing positions. (If necessary, do some reading to discover such opposing positions.)

51

Mini-Casebook of Readings

This chapter presents readings (and refers to earlier readings) on two themes: "Fitting In" and "Expanding Our Horizons." "Fitting In" focuses on the lessons we learn as we try to fit into social groups, while "Expanding Our Horizons" describes how reading and education can and should shape us and our sense of the possibilities for our lives.

Each set of readings is followed by assignments that ask you to draw on multiple selections while using writing strategies covered in Part Two of this book. At the end of the chapter is a final set of assignments that ask you to take a wider view of both themes, again drawing on multiple selections.

As you read the selections, you might want to annotate them or note your reactions in a journal, using the advice in Chapter 1.

Fitting In

At various times in our lives, most of us feel pressured to fit in with a certain group, even when doing so may come at great cost to us personally. Certainly, we feel this as children and teenagers, but we also may feel the pressure as adults in a whole range of situations: in the workplace, in a neighborhood, in a family, as part of a community, and so on. Sometimes fitting in is a good thing, but it is important to think carefully before attempting to do so. The essays that follow, as well as some others in this book, show different kinds of people trying to fit into different circumstances. Reading, thinking, and writing about these experiences may help us deal more easily with our own situations.

Roger Hoffmann

The Dare

Roger Hoffmann began his school years in Atlanta as a good kid who was always first to finish his homework. As he got older, however, he learned that in order to fit in he'd have to, as he says, "dirty up [his] act."

His first test came in the form of a dare from one of his friends. In this essay, published in the *New York Times Magazine* in 1986, Hoffmann recalls the incredible risk he took to avoid being called a teacher's pet.

The secret to diving under a moving freight train and rolling out of the other side with all your parts attached lies in picking the right spot between the tracks to hit with your back. Ideally, you want soft dirt or pea gravel, clear of glass shards[1] and railroad spikes that could cause you instinctively, and fatally, to sit up. Today, at thirty-eight, I couldn't be threatened or baited enough to attempt that dive. But as a seventh grader struggling to make the cut in a tough Atlanta grammar school, all it took was a dare.

I coasted through my first years of school as a fussed-over smart kid, the teacher's pet who finished his work first and then strutted around the room tutoring other students. By the seventh grade, I had more A's than friends. Even my old cronies,[2] Dwayne and O.T., made it clear I'd never be one of the guys in junior high if I didn't dirty up my act. They challenged me to break the rules, and I did. The I-dare-you's escalated:[3] shoplifting, sugaring teachers' gas tanks, dropping lighted matches into public mailboxes. Each guerrilla act won me the approval I never got for just being smart.

Walking home by the railroad tracks after school, we started playing chicken with oncoming trains. O.T., who was failing that year, always won. One afternoon he charged a boxcar from the side, stopping just short of throwing himself between the wheels. I was stunned. After the train disappeared, we debated whether someone could dive under a moving car, stay put for a 10-count, then scramble out the other side. I thought it could be done and said so. O.T. immediately stepped in front of me and smiled. Not by me, I added quickly, I certainly didn't mean that I could do it. "A smart guy like you," he said, his smile evaporating, "you could figure it out easy." And then, squeezing each word for effect, "I . . . DARE . . . you." I'd just turned twelve. The monkey clawing my back was Teacher's Pet. And I'd been dared.

[1] **shards:** sharp fragments

[2] **cronies:** close friends

[3] **escalated:** rose, increased

As an adult, I've been on both ends of life's implicit[4] business and social   4
I-dare-you's, although adults don't use those words. We provoke[5] with body
language, tone of voice, ambiguous[6] phrases. I dare you to: argue with the
boss, tell Fred what you think of him, send the wine back. Only rarely are the
risks physical. How we respond to dares when we are young may have something to do with which of the truly hazardous male inner dares—attacking
mountains, tempting bulls at Pamplona?[7]—we embrace or ignore as men.

For two weeks, I scouted trains and tracks. I studied moving boxcars   5
close up, memorizing how they squatted on their axles, never getting used
to the squeal or the way the air felt hot from the sides. I created an imag-
inary, friendly train and ran next to it. I mastered a shallow, head-first dive
with a simple half-twist. I'd land on my back, count to ten, imagine wheels
and, locking both hands on the rail to my left, heave myself over and out.
Even under pure sky, though, I had to fight to keep my eyes open and my
shoulders between the rails.

The next Saturday, O.T., Dwayne, and three eighth graders met me   6
below the hill that backed up to the lumberyard. The track followed a slow
bend there and opened to a straight, slightly uphill climb for a solid third
of a mile. My run started two hundred yards after the bend. The train
would have its tongue hanging out.

The other boys huddled off to one side, a circle on another planet, and   7
watched quietly as I double-knotted my shoelaces. My hands trembled.
O.T. broke the circle and came over to me. He kept his hands hidden in
the pockets of his jacket. We looked at each other. BB's[8] of sweat appeared
beneath his nose. I stuffed my wallet in one of his pockets, rubbing it
against his knuckles on the way in, and slid my house key, wired to a red-
and-white fishing bobber, into the other. We backed away from each other,
and he turned and ran to join the four already climbing up the hill.

I watched them all the way to the top. They clustered together as if I were   8
taking their picture. Their silhouette resembled a round shouldered tomb-
stone. They waved down to me, and I dropped them from my mind and sat
down on the rail. Immediately, I jumped back. The steel was vibrating.

The train sounded like a cow going short of breath. I pulled my shirt-   9
tail out and looked down at my spot, then up the incline of track ahead of
me. Suddenly the air went hot, and the engine was by me. I hadn't pic-
tured it moving that fast. A man's bare head leaned out and stared at me.
I waved to him with my left hand and turned into the train, burying my
face into the incredible noise. When I looked up, the head was gone.

[4]**implicit:** understood but not directly stated

[5]**provoke:** cause anger

[6]**ambiguous:** having more than one meaning

[7]**Pamplona:** city in the north of Spain

[8]**BB's:** pellets used in air guns

I started running alongside the boxcars. Quickly, I found their pace, 10 held it, and then eased off, concentrating on each thick wheel that cut past me. I slowed another notch. Over my shoulder, I picked my car as it came off the bend, locking in the image of the white mountain goat painted on its side. I waited, leaned forward like the anchor in a 440-relay, wishing the baton up the track behind me. Then the big goat fired by me, and I was flying and then tucking my shoulder as I dipped under the train.

A heavy blanket of red dust settled over me. I felt bolted to the earth. 11 Sheet-metal bellies thundered and shook above my face. Count to ten, a voice said, watch the axles and look to your left for daylight. But I couldn't count, and I couldn't find left if my life depended on it, which it did. The colors overhead went from brown to red to black to red again. Finally, I ripped my hands free, forced them to the rail, and, in one convulsive jerk, threw myself into the blue light.

I lay there face down until there was no more noise, and I could feel 12 the sun against the back of my neck. I sat up. The last ribbon of train was slipping away in the distance. Across the tracks, O.T. was leading a cavalry charge down the hill, five very small, galloping boys, their fists whirling above them. I pulled my knees to my chest. My corduroy pants puckered wet across my thighs. I didn't care.

Jeri Becker

Fitting In

After being sent to prison as an accomplice to murder, Jeri Becker kicked a drug addiction and developed some strong relationships in and outside of jail, including an acquaintance with the judge who convicted her. Paroled after twenty-four years, Becker moved to a rural part of northern California. She works as an educator for a community service organization.

Becker contributed the following piece to a special section on "Fitting In" published in the *Sun* magazine in September 2004. In it, she describes how she became involved in a world of drugs and violence.

In my formative years, my mother hoped to make me perfect by remind- 1 ing me of how imperfect I was. This, of course, made me nervous, anxious, and insecure. Having failed miserably at perfecting me, my mother unceremoniously[1] tossed me out.

[1] **unceremoniously:** without fuss or hesitation

At the age of fifteen, I was sent to San Francisco to find my big ²
brother, who lived on a houseboat in an "alternate-lifestyle community."
Maybe I would fit in there.

But my brother was mostly indifferent to my presence, and I found ³
myself a misfit among misfits, just as insecure as ever. Looking to others
in this hedonistic² community for an example, I wound up having sex with
a lot of men to whom I wasn't the least bit attracted. I eventually turned
to alcohol and drugs. I still didn't fit in, but I didn't mind so much.

It all came to a tragic end when, during a disagreement over a heroin ⁴
deal, my boyfriend shot another man. Caught in the middle, I went to
prison. At twenty-nine, I began serving a sentence of twenty-five years to life.

I was nothing like the tattooed, illiterate, uneducated inmates around ⁵
me, and for once, I wasn't interested in trying to fit in. I was sent to soli-
tary³ for a year. With no one to compare myself to, I had to confront who
I really was. And I realized that I was the person I had been running from.
I decided to stop running.

Now I am about to be released into the society I left more than two ⁶
decades ago. The old anxiety has returned: Will I fit in?

²**hedonistic:** emphasizing pleasure

³**solitary:** short for "solitary confinement" in prison

Larry Lane's "Showing Off" (p. 126) also addresses the theme of fitting
in. Read that selection now if you haven't already. If you read it earlier,
skim it now to refresh your memory.

▉ WRITING ASSIGNMENT 1   FITTING IN

"The Dare," "Fitting In," "Showing Off" (p. 126), "My First Conk" (p. 634),
and the report on *The Bluest Eye* (p. 285) all focus on how pressures to fit
in cause people to do things that are unwise, often dangerous, and—in the
case of Jeri Becker—dramatically life-changing. Using evidence from at
least two of these pieces, write an essay that

- recounts a time or an incident when you felt the pressure to fit in and
  acted unwisely, relating the authors' experiences to your own.

- compares/contrasts the experiences of the authors.

- argues against the pressure to fit in. Perhaps address the essay to a
  younger relative or friend. Give examples from the readings.

Expanding Our Horizons

Although we sometimes want to fit in, at other times we want to grow beyond what is familiar and comfortable. For all of you, going to college is one of those times, as you are exposed to new ideas, situations, and expectations. The essays that follow emphasize the importance of expanding your horizons and learning new things. Like the readings about fitting in, these essays may help you see and experience new things more comfortably.

Barbara Kingsolver

How Mr. Dewey Decimal
Saved My Life

Barbara Kingsolver was born in 1955 in eastern Kentucky. She studied biology and ecology, earning a B.A. from DePauw University and an M.S. from the University of Arizona in Tucson. She began her writing career as a journalist, writing features and science articles for various newspapers and journals. Later, she became a novelist and essayist. Her works include *The Poisonwood Bible* (1998), *Prodigal Summer* (2000), and *Small Wonder* (2002).

"How Mr. Dewey Decimal Saved My Life" was published in Kingsolver's essay collection *High Tide in Tucson* (1995). Remembering some of the books she read as a young woman, Kingsolver talks about how reading can be a form of rebellion and a means to justice.

The most important thing about the books I read in my rebellion is that they were not what I expected. I can't say I had no previous experience with literature; I grew up in a house full of books. Also, I'd known my way around the town's small library since I was tall enough to reach the shelves (though the town librarian disliked children and censored us fiercely) and looked forward to the Bookmobile as hungrily as more urbane children listened for the ice cream truck. So dearly did my parents want their children to love books, they made reading aloud the center of our family life, and when the TV broke, they took about two decades to get around to fixing it.

It's well known, though, that when humans reach a certain age, they identify precisely what it is their parents want for them and bolt in the opposite direction like lemmings[1] for the cliff. I had already explained to my classmates, in an effort to get dates, that I was raised by wolves, and I really

[1] **lemmings:** rodents that migrate in packs, sometimes leaping into the ocean together

had to move on from there. If I was going to find a path to adult reading, I had to do it my own way. I had to read things I imagined my parents didn't want me looking into.

What snapped me out of my surly[2] adolescence and moved me on were books that let me live other people's lives. I got to visit the Dust Bowl[3] and London and the Civil War and Rhodesia. The fact that Rhett Butler[4] said "damn" was a snoozer to me—I had hardly noticed the words that mothers worried about. I noticed words like *colour bar,* spelled "colour" the way Doris Lessing[5] wrote it, and eventually I figured out it meant racism. It was the thing that had forced some of the kids in my county to go to a separate school—which wasn't even a school but a one-room CME[6] church—and grow up without plumbing or the hope of owning a farm. When I picked up *Martha Quest,* a novel set in southern Africa, it jarred open a door that was right in front of me. I found that I couldn't close it.

If there is danger in a book like *Martha Quest,* and the works of other authors who've been banned at one time or another, the danger is generally that they will broaden our experience and blend us more deeply with our fellow humans. Sometimes this makes waves. It made some at my house. We had a few rocky years while I sorted out new information about the human comedy, the human tragedy, and the ways some people are held to the ground unfairly. I informed my parents that I had invented a new notion called justice. Eventually, I learned to tone down my act a little. Miraculously, there were no homicides in the meantime.

Now with my adolescence behind me and my daughter's still ahead, I am nearly speechless with gratitude for the endurance and goodwill of librarians in an era that discourages reading in almost incomprehensible ways. We've created for ourselves a culture that undervalues education (compared with the rest of the industrialized world, to say the least), undervalues breadth of experience (compared with our potential), downright discourages critical thinking (judging from what the majority of us watch and read), and distrusts foreign ideas. "Un-American," from what I hear, is meant to be an insult.

Most alarming, to my mind, is that we the people tolerate censorship in school libraries for the most bizarre and frivolous of reasons. Art books

---

[2] **surly:** angry, defiant

[3] **Dust Bowl:** parts of the central United States devastated by dust storms in the 1930s

[4] **Rhett Butler:** character in the Civil War novel and movie *Gone with the Wind.* He is well known for saying to heroine Scarlett O'Hara, "Frankly, my dear, I don't give a damn."

[5] **Doris Lessing:** British novelist and short story writer

[6] **CME:** Christian Methodist Episcopal

that contain (horrors!) nude human beings, and *The Wizard of Oz* because it has witches in it. Not always, everywhere, but everywhere, always something. And censorship of certain ideas in some quarters is enough to sway curriculums at the national level. Sometimes profoundly. Find a publishing house that's brave enough to include a thorough discussion of the principles of evolution in a high school text. Good luck. And yet, just about all working botanists, zoologists, and ecologists will tell you that evolution is to their field what germ theory[7] is to medicine. We expect our kids to salvage a damaged earth, but in deference[8] to the religious beliefs of a handful, we allow an entire generation of future scientists to germinate[9] and grow in a vacuum.

7   The parents who believe in Special Creation[10] have every right to tell their children how the world was made all at once, of a piece, in the year 4,004 B.C. Heaven knows, I tell my daughter things about economic justice that are just about as far outside the mainstream of American dogma.[11] But I don't expect her school to forgo teaching Western history or capitalist economics on my account. Likewise, it should be the job of Special Creationist parents to make their story convincing to their children, set against the school's bright scenery of dinosaur fossils and genetic puzzle-solving, the crystal clarity of Darwinian[12] logic, the whole glorious science of an evolving world that tells its own creation story. It cannot be any teacher's duty to tiptoe around religion, hiding objects that might raise questions at home. Faith, by definition, is impervious[13] to fact. A belief that can be changed by new information was probably a scientific one, not a religious one, and science derives its value from its openness to revision.

8   If there is a fatal notion on this earth, it's the notion that wider horizons will be fatal. Difficult, troublesome, scary—yes, all that. But the wounds, for a sturdy child, will not be mortal. When I read Doris Lessing at seventeen, I was shocked to wake up from my placid, color-blind coma into the racially segregated town I called my home. I saw I had been a fatuous[14] participant in a horrible thing. I bit my nails to the quick, cast nets of rage over all I loved for a time, and quaked to think of all I had—still

---

[7] **germ theory:** The theory that infectious diseases are caused by germs

[8] **deference:** giving in to the opinion of others

[9] **germinate:** to sprout

[10] **Special Creation:** the belief (generally running counter to the theory of evolution) that life, especially human life, is the special creation of God

[11] **dogma:** belief or principle

[12] **Darwinian:** referring to British naturalist Charles Darwin (1809–1882), who described the process of natural selection central to the theory of evolution

[13] **impervious:** not affected by

[14] **fatuous:** unconsciously foolish

have — to learn. But if I hadn't made that reckoning, I would have lived a smaller, meaner life.

The crossing is worth the storm. Ask my parents. Twenty years ago I 9 expect they'd have said, "Here, take this child, we will trade her to you for a sack of limas."[15] But now they have a special shelf in their house for books that bear the family name on their spines. Slim rewards for a parent's thick volumes of patience, to be sure, but at least there are no motorcycles rusting in the carport.

My thanks to Doris Lessing and William Saroyan[16] and Miss Truman 10 Richey, my librarian. And every other wise teacher who may ever save a surly soul like mine.

[15] **limas:** lima beans

[16] **William Saroyan:** American fiction writer, essayist, and playwright

Martin Luther King Jr.
The Purpose of Education

Martin Luther King Jr. was a dominant figure in the American civil rights movement and an advocate of nonviolent resistance. He was born in Atlanta in 1929 and followed in his father's footsteps by attending seminary and becoming a Baptist minister. King led some of the most important demonstrations in the fight for civil rights, including the Montgomery bus boycott and the March on Washington for Jobs and Freedom, at which he delivered his famous "I Have a Dream" speech. King was assassinated on April 4, 1968.

In "The Purpose of Education," King expresses his hope that education will not only enable people to distinguish fact from fiction but also give them values on which to judge their actions. He delivered this speech at Morehouse College in 1948.

As I engage in the so-called "bull sessions"[1] around and about the school, 1 I too often find that most college men have a misconception of the purpose of education. Most of the "brethren" think that education should equip them with the proper instruments of exploitation[2] so that they can forever trample over the masses. Still others think that education should furnish them with noble ends rather than means to an end.

[1] **bull sessions:** informal conversations

[2] **exploitation:** taking advantage of others

It seems to me that education has a two-fold function to perform in   2
the life of man and in society: The one is utility, and the other is culture.
Education must enable a man to become more efficient, to achieve with
increasing facility[3] the legitimate goals of his life.

Education must also train one for quick, resolute, and effective think-   3
ing. To think incisively[4] and to think for one's self is very difficult. We are
prone to let our mental life become invaded by legions of half-truths, prejudices, and propaganda.[5] At this point, I wonder whether or not education
is fulfilling its purpose. A great majority of the so-called educated people
do not think logically and scientifically. Even the press, the classroom, the
platform, and the pulpit in many instances do not give us objective and
unbiased truths. To save man from the morass of propaganda, in my opinion, is one of the chief aims of education. Education must enable one to
sift and weigh evidence, to discern the true from the false, the real from
the unreal, and the facts from the fiction.

The function of education, therefore, is to teach one to think inten-   4
sively and to think critically. But education which stops with efficiency
may prove the greatest menace to society. The most dangerous criminal
may be the man gifted with reason, but no morals.

The late Eugene Talmadge,[6] in my opinion, possessed one of the bet-   5
ter minds of Georgia, or even America. Moreover, he wore the Phi Beta
Kappa[7] key. By all measuring rods, Mr. Talmadge could think critically
and intensively; yet he contends that I am an inferior being. Are those the
types of men we call educated?

We must remember that intelligence is not enough. Intelligence plus   6
character—that is the goal of true education. The complete education
gives one not only power of concentration, but worthy objectives upon
which to concentrate. The broad education will, therefore, transmit to one
not only the accumulated knowledge of the race but also the accumulated
experience of social living.

If we are not careful, our colleges will produce a group of close-   7
minded, unscientific, illogical propagandists, consumed with immoral
acts. Be careful, "brethren"!? Be careful, teachers!

[3] **facility:** ease

[4] **incisively:** clearly, sharply

[5] **propaganda:** persuasive information that is often one-sided

[6] **Eugene Talmadge:** Georgia politician who opposed the civil rights movement in the 1940s

[7] **Phi Beta Kappa:** prestigious academic honor society that gives a golden key to its members

WRITING ASSIGNMENT 2   EXPANDING OUR HORIZONS

"How Mr. Dewey Decimal Saved My Life," "The Purpose of Education," "A Return to Education" (p. 121), and "Crossing Frontiers: Scenes from a Summer with Casa Alianza" (p. 139) all focus on how reading and education help people grow and improve themselves. Choose at least two of these pieces, and refer to them as you write an essay that

- recounts your own experience with reading, learning, or seeing something that opened up your view of the world or your place in it.

- defines what it means to be educated or well read.

- makes an argument for not just accepting things.

- discusses how reading and education can make people better human beings.

- discusses how reading can empower individuals.

- describes something that inspired you by expanding your perspective.

WRITING ASSIGNMENT 3   WIDENING THE PERSPECTIVE

1. While rebelling against adults and authority in general can have damaging consequences (see Larry Lane's "Showing Off" and Jeri Becker's "Fitting In"), Barbara Kingsolver, in "How Mr. Dewey Decimal Saved My Life," suggests that such rebellion is a natural—and healthy—part of our development. How would you define *healthy* versus *unhealthy* rebellion? To make your point, use examples from your own experiences and from those of the authors in this casebook.

2. Taken together, the readings in this casebook suggest two types of education: that obtained through personal, often difficult, experiences, and that drawn from books and classroom lessons. Write an essay considering the two types of education, using the following suggestions as a guide.

   - Discuss what type of education has been more valuable up until now, providing examples. If both types have been equally important, indicate why and give examples.

   - How do both types of education contribute to our growth? Draw examples from the essays and from your own experiences.

   - If you believe that one type of education has become less valued (or emphasized) than the other, support this point in an essay, and draw examples from the casebook essays if you can. Should anything be done about this? If so, what?

■ You may use summary, analysis, synthesis, and evaluation to complete these final assignments. For advice on these strategies, see Chapter 1.

Appendix A

Problem Solving in Writing

Some writing assignments, both in English and in other subjects, will require you to use problem-solving skills. Such assignments will ask you to read and analyze a problem in order to develop possible solutions, often by synthesizing information from various sources.

Problem-solving skills are necessary not only in college but also — and even more so — in the work world. Often, managers assign a team to work on and pose possible solutions to a problem that the organization faces. Also, problem-solving skills will help you in your everyday life when you run into a situation that you want to change.

Each of the chapters in Part Two includes problem-based writing assignments ("Writing to Solve a Problem"). These assignments offer you the opportunity to solve real-world problems by working alone or as a part of a team. Use the following section to complete those assignments or to address any problem you may face in college, at work, or in your everyday life.

Problem Solving

Problem solving is the process of identifying a problem and figuring out a reasonable solution.

Problems range from minor inconveniences like finding a rip in the last clean shirt you have when you're running late to more serious problems such as being laid off from your job. While such problems disrupt our lives, they also give us opportunities to tackle difficult situations with confidence.

Too often, people are paralyzed by problems because they don't have strategies for attacking them. However, backing away from a problem rarely helps solve it. When you know how to approach a challenging situation, you are better able to take charge of your life.

Problem solving consists of five basic steps, which can be used effectively by both individuals and groups of people.

725

THE PROBLEM-SOLVING PROCESS

Understand the problem.

You should be able to say or write it in a brief statement or question.

EXAMPLE:
Your ten-year-old car needs a new transmission, which will cost at least $750. Do you keep the car or buy a new one?

Identify people or information that can help you solve the problem (resources).

EXAMPLES:
- Your mechanic
- Friends who have had similar car problems
- Car advice from print or Web sources

List the possible solutions.

EXAMPLES:
- Pay for the transmission repair.
- Buy a new car.

Evaluate the possible solutions.

1. Identify the steps each solution would require.
2. List possible obstacles for each solution (like money or time constraints).
3. List the advantages and disadvantages of the solutions.

EXAMPLES (considering only advantages and disadvantages):
- Pay for the transmission repair.
  Advantage: This would be cheaper than buying a new car.
  Disadvantage: The car may not last much longer, even with the new transmission.
- Buy a new car.
  Advantage: You'll have a reliable car.
  Disadvantage: This option is much more expensive.

Choose the most reasonable solution, one that is realistic—the simpler the better. Be able to give reasons for your choice.

Solution: Pay for the transmission repair.

Reasons: You do not have money for a new car, and you don't want to assume more debt. Opinions from two mechanics indicate that your car should run for three to five more years with the new transmission. At that point, you'll be in a better position to buy a new car.

Appendix B

How to Make an Oral Presentation

Five Surefire Strategies

■ Two additional appendices—on writing e-mail and memos and preparing résumés and letters of application—are posted at <**bedfordstmartins .com/realessays**>.

In college, at work—sometimes even in your everyday life—you will need to make oral presentations. Most people rate public speaking as one of life's most stressful experiences. A number of practical strategies, however, can help you cope with the anxiety that may be caused by this task. Knowing how to prepare for an oral presentation will help you feel confident and in control of the situation.

You have probably witnessed an embarrassing oral presentation, a situation in which the speaker fell apart and the audience felt as uncomfortable as the speaker. The following is an example of such an occurrence.

SITUATION: Jean is in the middle of reviewing her presentation notes when she hears herself being introduced. Startled, she gathers her materials into a messy stack of notes and papers, apologizes for not being ready, and walks quickly to the front of the room.

Obviously flustered, she tries to reorganize her notes, shuffling papers, frowning, and sighing loudly. She begins reading her presentation with her head down, speaking quickly and softly. Several people call out, "I can't hear you" or "Speak up."

Jean clears her throat and starts from the beginning. She's so rattled that her voice quivers and then breaks. She looks up, red in the face, and says, "Sorry. I'm really nervous."

She continues but moves too quickly from one point to the next because she doesn't want to bore people. She forgets to introduce or summarize any of her points, so the audience finds it difficult to follow her speech. People start to tune out.

Aware that she's not doing very well, Jean nervously fiddles with her hair while speaking. She reads quickly and with no emphasis, thinking that the sooner she gets through this, the sooner she can sit down. The words that looked so good when she wrote them sound stupid and awkward when she says them aloud.

As Jean turns to the second page, she realizes that her papers are out of order. There is an awkward silence as she searches desperately for the right page. She finally finds it and begins again. Soon she comes to a word that she can't read, and she has to stop again to figure it out. Still fiddling with her hair, she now looks as if she's about to pull it out.

Jean skips the word and continues. Her only goal now is to finish. But she's run out of time because of her fumbling and because her presentation was too long to begin with. The warning signal goes off, indicating that one minute remains.

This is the last straw for Jean. She looks up, bright red and nearly in tears, and says, "I guess I've run out of time. I only got through one of my points. I don't have time for what I really wanted to say." She grabs her papers and returns to her seat.

Jean sits in total misery, sure that everyone is looking at her. She can't listen to anyone else's presentation. All she can do is stare at the floor and wait impatiently for the moment she can escape from the room.

ANALYSIS: Jean's presentation was not successful because of some common pitfalls she could easily have avoided. She wasn't adequately prepared, she was obviously very nervous, she hadn't structured her presentation to make her points clear to her audience, she hadn't practiced reading her presentation aloud, and she fled at the end. If she had practiced five simple strategies for making an oral presentation, her experience would have been much less painful, and her presentation would have been much better.

Strategy 1. Be Prepared

Jean's first mistake was not being well prepared. She wasn't psychologically ready to speak, and she hadn't organized the materials for her presentation properly. Because she was busy reviewing her notes at the last minute, she was caught off guard. Her papers got messed up, she was startled, and she was off to a bad start.

Organize Your Notes

Before you go into the room where you are giving your presentation, make sure all of your notes are in order. Number all pages or notecards so you can quickly reorganize them if they get mixed up, and carry all of your materials in a folder.

Keep Your Notes in Order

If you want to review your key points while waiting to make your presentation, try to run through them in your head. Leave the folder closed. If you need to refresh your memory on a particular point, open the folder and carefully go through your notes until you find the answer.

Use Your Energy

Be aware of when your turn is coming, and focus on being calm. Tell yourself that you're prepared and you know what you're doing. Breathe deeply. Don't worry if your heart is beating hard and fast; that's normal. Nervous energy before a performance of any sort is natural and can make you a more engaging speaker. You just need to learn to channel that energy and make it work *for* you. Use that adrenaline to fuel your enthusiasm for your topic.

Build Yourself Up

Keep breathing normally. However silly it may seem, remind yourself of your strengths and repeat them in your head as your turn to speak approaches: "I know what I'm talking about." "I look good today." "I have a good voice." Remember that your audience isn't waiting for you to fail. Most people understand the stress of oral presentations and are sympathetic. Your audience wants you to do well.

Carry Yourself Like Royalty

When it's your turn, take a deep breath, calmly pick up your folder, and walk to the front of the room. Walk slowly, stand straight, and focus on projecting a confident image. Remember that you're in control.

Strategy 2. Act with Confidence

Jean's second mistake was not acting with confidence and authority. She was visibly upset as she tried to get her notes in order, and when she did start, she spoke too softly to be heard. When her voice broke, she apologized to the audience and announced her nervousness. Practicing several techniques would have made her appear confident and in control.

Take Your Time

After you've walked to the front of the room, take a few moments to calmly arrange your notes and papers before you begin. Relax. The timing of your presentation won't start until you begin speaking, so make sure your materials are where you need them before beginning. Remember that even professional speakers need a few moments to lay out their notes and compose themselves.

Take Command and Greet Your Audience

When you're ready to begin, stand up straight and look up and out at the audience. Remember that you are in command of the room. Pause for a few seconds to let people know you're about to begin, and wait for them to give you their attention. When you have their attention, take a deep breath and begin.

Smile and greet the audience, surveying the room as you do so. Your greeting should be simple, like "Good morning and thank you all for coming." If some people in the audience don't know you, be sure to introduce yourself. Don't forget to smile: It will relax you as well as your audience.

Slow Down and Speak Up

Make sure that you speak slowly, clearly, and loudly. If you're nervous, you will tend to speak too quickly, so try to slow down your speech a bit. Try to project your voice so that the people in the last row can hear you. It may feel as if you're shouting, but you won't be. Don't be embarrassed to ask if everyone can hear you. Experienced speakers often break the ice by encouraging an audience to tell them if they need to speak up.

Strategy 3. Structure Your Presentation

Jean's third mistake was not giving her presentation a clear structure, which would have made it easy for her audience to follow her key points. Your presentation should include lots of verbal cues that let people know when you're making a point, what it is, and when you're moving to another point. The structure of an oral presentation must be much more obvious than the structure of a written paper so that people can understand as they are listening.

Limit Your Topic

Choose a manageable topic for the time allotted, and limit the number of points you plan to make. Listening is hard work, and most people can absorb only a few key points from a speech. In any presentation, try to limit yourself to three key points, and be sure to support each of them with concrete examples. When you give more complex presentations, you may need to use visual aids—such as transparencies or slides—that will allow you to illustrate and reinforce your points.

State Your Thesis and Preview Your Key Points

Let your audience know what your topic is and the main point you are going to make about it. State your thesis (your main point) slowly so that people understand the purpose of your presentation. Tell them: "My topic today is _____," and "I will be arguing [or showing, or explaining] _____."

Tell your audience about the structure of your presentation by giving them a preview of your key points. You might say: "There are three major points I'd like to make about _____. First I'll present _____. Second I'll discuss _____. And my third point will be _____. This presentation should take approximately three minutes, and there will be time for questions at the end."

Use Transitions to Move from Point to Point

Use transitions to let your audience know when you're finished with one point and are about to make another. In your preview, you told the audience what your key points would be. As you speak, you should give clear verbal cues when introducing and summarizing each point. Here is one way to do so.

- My first point is _____.
- Give examples/explanation.
- Repeat or summarize the first point (to remind the audience of what it is and to let them know you're about to move to another point).
- My second point is _____.

- Give examples/explanation.
- Repeat or summarize second point.
- My third and final point is ＿＿＿＿＿＿＿.
- Give examples/explanation.
- Repeat or summarize third point.

Conclude by Reviewing Your Key Points

Let people know when you're coming to the end of your presentation by using a verbal cue such as *in conclusion, to summarize,* or *to review.* Then, review your key points. Conclude with a simple, strong sentence that restates the overall purpose of your presentation—the main point you want to make.

Strategy 4. Practice Your Presentation

Like many people, Jean made the mistake of not adequately practicing her presentation. The right kind of practice would have helped her avoid the following problems: fidgeting with her hair, writing a presentation that sounded awkward when presented orally, losing her place in the middle of her talk, being unable to read her handwriting, and running out of time.

Even professional speakers practice their speeches. You should allow plenty of time to practice giving your oral presentation.

Practice Aloud

Phrases and sentences that sound good in writing often sound awkward when spoken. Read your presentation aloud—several times—to make sure that it sounds right. You'll feel silly, but do it anyway. Stop and make changes when a sentence sounds awkward. Be aware of any distracting habits you may have, such as interrupting your speech with expressions like "uh," or "you know."

Practicing aloud will also help you remember your key points. Practice your speech again and again until you feel comfortable with it. Be sure to practice aloud a final time on the day of your presentation.

Practice in Front of a Mirror

You need to see what you look like as you give your presentation, so try practicing in front of a mirror. This may make you feel even sillier than just saying the speech aloud, but it will also make you feel much more confident when you actually give the presentation.

- Stand straight and look up at the mirror frequently. Pretend you are looking out at an audience.
- Be aware of any distracting habits you have while speaking, such as fidgeting with your hair, as Jean did. Some people shift their weight from one leg to another, or sway back and forth, or stand with their legs far apart in a military stance.
- Practice keeping your hands still, except when you want to gesture or point to something for emphasis. You can hold your notes at your side or in front of you, or you can place them on a table or podium.
- Practice keeping your feet slightly apart and your weight evenly distributed. Don't shift back and forth or rock.
- If you know you will be seated when giving your presentation, you should sit in a chair while practicing. Don't jiggle your feet or swing your legs. Keep your feet flat on the floor.

Practice Working with Your Material

Figure out in advance how you will handle your notes and papers. After you've made your presentation aloud a couple of times to get the wording right, decide whether you will work with the whole presentation written out, an outline, or notecards.

THE WHOLE PRESENTATION: If you think you need to read from the whole presentation—written out word for word—that's fine, but you still have to practice. You have to be comfortable enough with the written version to be able to deliver it naturally, not as if you're reading, and to look up at your audience without fear of losing your place. If your eyes are glued to the page, you'll lose your audience's attention.

In addition to practicing, you should format your presentation so that it will be easy for you to find your place.

- Highlight your key points in color or by obvious underlining so that you'll be able to find your place quickly if you get lost.

- Double-space between the lines of your presentation so that you won't have trouble reading it.

- Use a large type size. If you must handwrite your presentation, make sure that you can read your handwriting.

- Write the numbers of your key points in the margin (next to the paragraphs where you introduce those points), write "conc." next to your conclusion, and so on.

- Make sure your pages are clearly numbered so that you can easily put them in order if you mix them up.

OUTLINE: Instead of writing out your entire presentation word for word, you may want to write your key points in outline form. An outline should include all of the major points you want to make, with examples or explanations. It should also include the points to be made in the introduction and conclusion.

NOTECARDS: Some people prefer to work from 3" × 5" notecards rather than pieces of paper. They prepare a separate notecard for each major point, listing the point and an example. If you use notecards, be sure to number them in the top right corner so that you can easily reassemble them if they get out of order.

Time Yourself

As you practice aloud, time yourself. You need to be sure that you can finish your presentation within the time limit you've been given.

If you find that you don't have enough time to make your major points, don't just speak more quickly. Go back and revise your presentation. Keep the points simple and the examples clear. If necessary, cut back on the number of points you are making, keeping only the strongest ones.

Be sure to time yourself at least twice after you have your presentation in final form.

Strategy 5. Create a Good Final Impression

Jean's last mistake was that when she ran short on time, she panicked and ended on a bad note. Practicing aloud and timing yourself will help you avoid this problem, but if you do run short on time, don't panic.

Usually speakers are given a warning signal of some sort to let them know that they need to finish. If you get a warning signal before you've said all you wanted to, remember that it's a warning. You have a little time left to conclude your presentation.

You may have enough time to finish your speech as planned, but if you know you can't cover all of it in the time remaining, you will need to condense it. Reduce the details about your points, and move to a very brief conclusion. You may need to move to your final point and give it without an example. Then say, "Again, here are the major points," repeat them briefly, and conclude.

When the time is over, look up, smile at your audience, thank them for their attention, and ask if they have any questions. Give the audience time to respond. It may take them a while to start asking questions. Wait calmly, and look around the room. If there are no questions, thank the audience again and return to your seat.

Answers to Odd-Numbered Editing Exercises

CHAPTER 21: THE BASIC SENTENCE

Practice 22-1, page 330
Answers:
1. Subject: people; prepositional phrase: around the country
3. Subject: Ronald; prepositional phrases: in a program called Puppies Behind Bars **5.** Subject: Cooper; prepositional phrases: in the cell; with him **7.** Subject: Ronald; prepositional phrases: before the start; of Cooper's formal guide dog training **9.** Subject: Cooper; prepositional phrase: with a blind person

Practice 21-2, page 334
Answers:
1. Subject: family; action verb: moved **3.** Subject: Miguel; helping verb + main verb: was learning **5.** Subject: he; linking verb: was **7.** Subject: plan; helping verb + main verb: had been **9.** Subject: family; linking verb: is

Practice 21-3, page 335
Answers and possible edits:
1. I (incomplete thought); He walked down the red carpet, smiling broadly as the cameras flashed all around him. **3.** I (incomplete thought); The man who lives in the big brick house on Valley Street is my new boss. **5.** C (complete thought) **7.** I (incomplete thought); Sandra had her appendix removed, which explains why she missed class last week. **9.** C (complete thought)

CHAPTER 22: FRAGMENTS

Practice 22-2, page 340
Answers and possible edits:
1. Preposition: with. With their technical talents, hackers try to break into computer systems. **3.** Preposition: with. Some hackers offer excuses for meddling with computer systems. **5.** Preposition: from. Sometimes, hackers are kids looking for something different from the routines of school, chores, and ordinary play. **7.** Preposition: Upon. Upon catching a hacker doing something illegal, the government may try to send him or her to jail. **9.** Preposition: with. For example, one former hacker founded a computer security company that got many contracts with the U.S. government and several large companies.

Practice 22-3, page 342
Answers and possible edits:
1. Dependent word: Because. Because we are considering a future human mission to Mars, these questions are more important now than ever before. **3.** Dependent word: After. After enough bone tissue is lost, bones become dangerously thin and fragile. **5.** Dependent word: that. Another solution may be the use of the drugs that people on Earth use to help maintain bone mass. **7.** Dependent word: unless. One astronaut said that he felt isolated unless he could speak with his family more than once a week. **9.** Dependent word: Although. Although all of these problems are serious, most scientists believe they can be addressed.

Practice 22-4, page 345
Answers and possible edits:
1. *-ing* verb: living. My grandmother spent her entire life living on a farm in eastern Wyoming. **3.** *-ing* verb: creating. She was a natural seamstress. My grandmother created shirts and dresses more beautiful than anything available in a store. **5.** *-ing* verb: using. The quilting circle made quilts for special occasions using scraps of cloth left over from other sewing projects. **7.** *-ing* verb: Celebrating. Celebrating the birth of her first child, my father, the quilting circle gave my grandmother a baby quilt that is now a treasured heirloom. **9.** *-ing* verb: Looking. Looking at each bit of cloth in that quilt, my grandmother could still describe, years later, the garment she had made from it.

Practice 22-5, page 347
Answers and possible edits:
1. *To* + verb: To lift weights. To lift weights, bodybuilders then met at the Muscle Beach of Santa Monica in Los Angeles. **3.** *To* + verb: to lift. Muscle Beach had become known as Venice by then, but bodybuilders still went there to lift railroad ties and buckets filled with concrete. **5.** *To* + verb: To get. To get the best possible workout, Arnold Schwarzenegger regularly went to Gold's Gym in Venice. **7.** *To* + verb: To have. To have a realistic setting for the 1977 movie *Pumping Iron,* the filmmaker selected Gold's Gym. **9.** *To* + verb: to sell. In the early 1970s, however, Joe Gold made a decision to sell his original business along with the name *Gold's Gym* to another company.

Practice 22-6, page 349
Possible edits:
1. Many parents believe that they would know if their daughters were being abused, either physically or emotionally.   **3.** A young man can be abusive without laying a finger on his girlfriend. He might monitor her actions and keep her from spending time with other friends.   **5.** Around her parents, a teenager's boyfriend may act like a perfect gentleman. He may be polite, attentive, and kind to the young woman.   **7.** A young woman with an abusive boyfriend may develop psychological problems that will be difficult to treat, such as low self-esteem.   **9.** Friends who think that a young woman is involved in an abusive relationship should try to be supportive of her, not turn away even if she refuses to leave her boyfriend.

Editing Reviews, pages 351–53
Possible edits:
1. (1/2) Genetically modified foods are being marketed as the foods of the future. (3) Correct (4) Correct (5/6) A gene from a fish may be found to make tomatoes more resistant to disease. (7/8/9) Of course, genetic modification may have unintended effects, as in the case of genetically modified corn, which may harm monarch butterfly caterpillars. (10/11) Arguing that the long-term effects of genetic modification may not be known for years to come, some scientists urge caution before marketing genetically modified foods.   **3.** (1/2) The term *organic* means different things to different people. (3/4) Organic foods are supposed to be grown without pesticides, a method that reduces a farm's impact on the environment. (5) Correct (6) Correct (7/8) They pay premium prices for organic products because they think the food is good for their own well-being, not just that of the environment. (9) Correct (10/11) The label merely means that the ingredients meet a certain government standard, while guaranteeing nothing about the nutritional content or health benefits of the food.   **5.** (1) Correct (2/3) Doctors have begun to explain to their patients that antibiotics are useful only for certain kinds of infections and that patients must finish every course of antibiotics they start. (4/5) Antibiotic use in agriculture, however, has continued to increase. (6/7) The government does not even keep records of antibiotic use in farm animals. (8/9) Many cattle, pigs, and chickens get antibiotics for economic reasons, such as to keep them healthy and to make them grow faster. (10) Correct (11) Correct

CHAPTER 23: RUN-ONS
Practice 23-2, page 358
Answers and possible edits:
1. FS (fused sentence). The invention of cell phones made telephoning from a car possible. People could telephone for help if they were stranded on the highway.   **3.** CS (comma splice). Some communities in the United States have banned drivers from talking on handheld cell phones; a driver must stop the car to place a call legally in those areas.   **5.** FS (fused sentence). No one debates that drivers can be distracted by cell phones. Some people wonder, however, whether the problem is really the fact that a driver is holding the phone.   **7.** FS (fused sentence). Some people worry that drivers are distracted not by holding the telephone, but by holding a conversation. A tense discussion with the boss or good news from a relative can take the driver's attention from traffic.   **9.** CS (comma splice). There are differences, however, between talking on a cell phone and listening to music in the car. The telephone requires interaction from the driver, but the radio calls for passive listening.

Practice 23-3, page 361
Answers and possible edits:
1. Subjects: penguins; birds. Verbs: live; have been. Fairy penguins, a small breed of penguin, live in Tasmania, and these birds have often been the victims of oil spills.   **3.** Subjects: attempts; oil. Verbs: can be; is. Unfortunately, the penguins' attempts to clean off their feathers can be fatal, for crude oil is poisonous to penguins.   **5.** Subjects: One; volunteers; Verbs: created; knitted. One of the conservationists created a pattern for a sweater for the penguins, and volunteers from around the world knitted these unusual sweaters.   **7.** Subjects: Most; some. Verbs: were made; were sent. Most of the sweaters were made by elderly nursing-home residents in Tasmania, but some were sent from as far away as Japan.   **9.** Subjects: knitters; few. Verbs: made; have. Some creative knitters made tuxedo-patterned sweaters, and a few of these penguin suits even have bow ties.

Practice 23-4, page 363
Answers and possible edits:
1. Subjects: phenomenon; it. Verbs: is; may be changing. Although this phenomenon is something we take for granted, it may be changing.   **3.** Subjects: change; materials. Verbs: happened; pointed. Such a change happened before in the earth's history, when magnetic materials pointed south instead of north for long periods.   **5.** Subjects: change; satellites. Verbs: has affected; have been. The change in magnetism has affected some satellites, which have been damaged.   **7.** Subjects: bees, pigeons, salmon, turtles, whales, newts, bacteria; they. Verbs: need; will adjust. Because bees, pigeons, salmon, turtles, whales, newts, and even bacteria need the magnetic field to navigate, they will have to adjust to the magnetic change.   **9.** Subjects: processes, change. Verbs: may unfold; may occur. The processes affecting magnetism may unfold much more slowly, so that the magnetic change may not occur for millions of years.

Editing Review 1, page 366

1. (1) Correct (2) It's often easy to forget things when you want desperately to remember them. (3) You have probably had the experience of forgetting an acquaintance's name, which comes to your mind only when it's too late. (4) You have also probably been unable to find your keys once in a while because you put them down somewhere without thinking. (5) At other times, however, you may find it difficult to forget some things even though you wish you could never think of them again. (6) Correct (7) Sometimes you may find yourself forced to relive your most embarrassing moment over and over again in your mind; your memory won't let you leave that part of your past behind. (8) Some scholars believe that these annoying habits of memory evolved for a reason. It's hard to imagine, though, any good reason for developing the ability to forget where you left your keys.

CHAPTER 24: PROBLEMS WITH SUBJECT-VERB AGREEMENT

Practice 24-2, page 373

Answers:

1. Subject: I; verb: was   3. Subject: I; verb: have   5. Subject: games; verb: are   7. Subject: incidents; verb: do   9. Subject: Children; verb: do

Practice 24-3, page 373

Answers:

1. Subject: students; verb: are   3. Subject: computer; verb: does   5. Subject: program; verb: has   7. Subject: teachers; verb: are   9. Subject: computer; verb: does

Practice 24-4, page 375

Answers:

1. Prepositional phrase: with hearing loss; verb: have   3. Prepositional phrase: with words; verb: comes   5. Prepositional phrase: in this country; verb: feel   7. Prepositional phrase: in a deaf household; verb: resembles   9. Prepositional phrase: to the hearing world and the deaf world; verb: pull

Practice 24-5, page 376

Answers:

1. Dependent clause: which is a job applicant's first contact with many prospective employers; verb: contains   3. Dependent clause: who held a previous job for two months; verb: claims   5. Dependent clause: who never received a college degree; verb is OK   7. Dependent clause: who like a résumé; verb: check   9. Dependent clause: who invent material on a résumé; verb: forget

Practice 24-6, page 378

Answers:

1. Subject joined by: and; verb: do   3. Subject joined by: or; verb: is   5. Subject joined by: and; verb: contain   7. Subject joined by: and; verb: contribute   9. Subject joined by: nor; verb: are

Practice 24-7, page 380

Answers:

1. Subject: anyone; verb: needs; dependent clause: who wants to take college courses   3. Subject: some; verb: offer; prepositional phrase: of the hundreds of accredited colleges in the United States   5. Subject: everyone; verb: has; dependent clause: who takes online courses   7. Subject: someone; verb: is; dependent clause: who learns best by listening   9. Subject: anybody; verb: needs; dependent clause: who is considering an online class

Practice 24-8, page 382

Answers:

1. Where are the corporation's main offices located?   3. How well does the average employee abroad speak English?   5. How many languages is the manual written in?   7. There are some machines that can do translation.   9. OK

Editing Reviews, pages 383–85

Answers:

1. (1) School systems around the country are embracing educational standards. (2) The idea of standards sounds reasonable. (3) Correct (4) A national standard for all American students has many supporters, too. (5) If the requirements for graduation in Oregon and Tennessee are the same, everyone with a high school diploma gets a similar education. (6) Correct (7) Correct (8) Mathematics and writing are important, but so are music and physical education. (9) How are parents, teachers, and administrators ever going to find standards that everyone accepts?   3. (1) Correct (2) Most school districts that have a testing program use tests that can be scored by a computer. (3) Computers cannot read, so the tests that they grade usually offer multiple-choice questions. (4) A multiple-choice test in science or mathematics does not allow students to demonstrate critical thinking. (5) How do students show their writing ability on such a test? (6) There are tricks to answering multiple-choice questions that many students learn. (7) Correct (8) Nevertheless, the quick results and low cost of a computer-graded multiple-choice test mean that this imperfect testing system is used in many school systems.   5. (1) Many parents who send their children to public school fear that the schools are not teaching the students adequately. (2) As these fears increase, the number of states that require tests rises as well. (3) But there have been some teachers and

parents willing to resist standardized testing. (4) A few parents have kept their children home on test days. (5) In rare cases, teachers who oppose testing have refused to administer standardized tests to their students. (6) In the places that require students to pass tests in order to graduate, rebellion against tests has serious consequences for the student. (7) Correct (8) People who believe that standardized testing is not the answer are still trying to change this growing national trend.

CHAPTER 25: VERB PROBLEMS

Practice 25-2, page 389
Answers:
1. Subject: Golfers; verb: decide   3. Subject: Some; verb: use   5. Subject: golfer; verb: walks   7. Subject: RoboKaddy; verb: stops   9. Subject: golfers; verb: want

Practice 25-3, page 391
Answers:
1. Helping verb: is; main verb: starting   3. Helping verb: is; main verb: gathering   5. Helping verb: are; main verb: helping   7. Helping verb: is; main verb: pitching   9. Helping verb: is; main verb: sharing

Practice 25-4, page 392
Answers:
1. Helping verb: has; past participle: forced   3. Helping verb: have; past participle: attended   5. Helping verb: have; past participle: objected   7. Helping verb: have; past participle: traveled   9. Helping verb: has; past participle: liked

Practice 25-5, page 393
Answers:
1. decided   3. cared   5. engaged   7. participated; stopped   9. charged   11. died

Practice 25-6, page 394
Answers:
1. have increased   3. have attempted   5. raised   7. violated   9. have started

Practice 25-7, page 396
Answers:
1. Helping verb: was; main verbs: studying; working   3. Helping verb: was; main verb: walking   5. Helping verb: was; main verb: heading   7. Helping verb: was; main verb: laughing   9. Helping verb: was; main verb: smiling

Practice 25-8, page 397
Answers:
1. got   3. had heard   5. had just learned   7. raised   9. had warned

Practice 25-9, page 399
Answers:
1. will begin   3. will involve   5. will be working   7. will discuss   9. will need

Practice 25-10, page 401
Answers:
1. am   3. has   5. are   7. has   9. are

Practice 25-11, page 403
Answers:
1. were; were   3. was; were   5. was; was   7. was   9. were; were

Practice 25-12, page 406
Answers:
1. built   3. wrote   5. struck   7. began   9. left; stood

Practice 25-13, page 407
Answers:
1. Two years ago, my high school set up a student court to give students a voice in disciplining rule breakers.   3. Some of us served as members of juries, and others became advocates or even judges.   5. Then, last spring, my friend Dewayne appeared before the student court after he lost his temper and struck a fellow student.   7. I told the jury that he knew his violent reaction was a mistake.   9. After hearing the verdict, Dewayne shook hands with all the jurors and thanked them for their fairness.

Practice 25-14, page 408
Answers:
1. Helping verb: had; past participle: taken   3. Helping verb: had; past participle: begun   5. Helping verb: had; past participle: been   7. Helping verb: had; past participle: bought   9. Helping verb: had; past participle: sold

Practice 25-15, page 410
Possible edits:
1. The *Queen Mary 2* has a grand lobby and an old-style three-story restaurant.   3. The ship's computer systems can automatically correct the effects of the wind, waves, and ocean currents.   5. He said he would probably use the joystick more in the future.

Practice 25-16, page 411
Answers:
1. Verbs: want, needed; corrected verb: need   3. Verbs: makes, caused; corrected verb: causes   5. Verbs: wore, snap; corrected verb: wear   7. Verbs: chose, knows; corrected verb: chooses   9. Verbs: kept, eases; corrected verb: keeps

Editing Reviews, pages 412–13
Answers:
1. (1) Since 1835, trapeze artists have considered the triple somersault the most dangerous maneuver. (2) That year, a performer tried to do a triple somersault on a trapeze for the first time and died in the attempt. (3) Only one person managed to do the trick successfully in the next sixty-three years. (4) That man, a trapeze artist named Armor, did a triple somersault in 1860 and was afraid to try it again. (5) According to circus legend, the second person to survive the triple, Ernie Clarke, once did a quadruple somersault in private. (6) Correct (7) Circus historians now believe that Alfredo Codona, a performer in the 1920s and 1930s, was the greatest master of the triple somersault. (8) He has gone down in history as the King of Trapeze. 3. (1) The Olympic Games first let women compete in swimming events in 1912, and with that, the swimsuit revolution began. (2) Correct (3) Before that year, women had only been able to wade at the beach in bathing costumes with long, baggy legs. (4) The 1913 suits, designed by Carl Jantzen, were ribbed one-piece outfits that allowed actual swimming. (5) An engineer, Louis Réard, came up with the next major development in swimwear in 1946 while working in the lingerie business. (6) He called it the "bikini," after a Pacific island used for testing the atomic bomb. (7) In the 1950s, few Americans dared to wear bikinis, which were considered scandalous. (8) Two-piece swimsuits caught on in the 1960s and 1970s. (9) The bikini lost some popularity in the last decades of the twentieth century, but it has made a triumphant return in the new millennium.

CHAPTER 26: PRONOUNS
Practice 26-1, page 419
Answers:
1. Pronoun: they; noun: people 3. Pronoun: it; noun: microlending 5. Pronoun: them; noun: owners 7. Pronoun: her; noun: woman 9. Pronoun: his or her; noun: entrepreneur

Practice 26-2, page 422
Answers:
1. his or her 3. their 5. himself or herself 7. they need 9. their

Practice 26-3, page 424
Answers:
1. its 3. their 5. its 7. its 9. its

Practice 26-4, page 425
Possible edits:
1. In a psychology study, volunteers who watched a video of two basketball teams had to count the number of passes.

3. Later, when meeting with the researchers, many of the volunteers asked, "What gorilla?" 5. The way the human brain processes visual information may keep people from using that information wisely. 7. A stop sign appearing at an intersection cannot prevent an accident if drivers do not see the sign. 9. However, the study indicates that drivers make mistakes because they may not see problems ahead.

Practice 26-5, page 427
Answers:
1. Robots have been part of many science-fiction classics, from *The Jetsons* to *Star Wars*. 3. In some industries, robots are already part of the workforce. 5. A factory might use robots to handle substances that are dangerous for humans to touch. 7. Some children who wanted a robot friend have already gotten their wish. 9. The robot dog was first on many holiday and birthday gift lists for children in the past few years.

Practice 26-6, page 430
Answers:
1. However, a TV program on dental health started making her and me rethink our soda-drinking habit. 3. Dr. Summers asked Ian to place a tooth in a bottle of soda, and she and he observed what happened to the tooth. 5. The result of the experiment surprised her and me. 7. They and we said "Wow" at the same time. 9. Megan and I learned that each can of soda we drink contains about ten teaspoons of sugar, which creates even more tooth-dissolving acid and contributes to weight gain.

Practice 26-7, page 431
Answers:
1. My mother and father had a garden in their backyard, but she spent much more time there than he. 3. The garden was filled with tomatoes because my mother loved no other vegetable as much as them. 5. C 7. He made sure that each plant was free of slugs, for few other garden pests are as destructive as they. 9. I spend just as much time as he working in the garden, however.

Practice 26-8, page 433
Answers:
1. whom 3. whom 5. who

Practice 26-9, page 434
Possible edits:
1. Experts agree that the percentage of people with allergies to foods is rising, but they don't know why. 3. If a person has a severe allergy to a food and unknowingly eats even a small amount of that food, he or she could die. 5. When children have severe allergies, their parents can be extremely

cautious.   **7.** He carries an adrenaline pen that can save his life if he goes into shock from a food allergy.   **9.** My mother will not take my brother to any public place where she can even smell peanuts.

Editing Review 1, page 435
Possible edits:
1. (1) More and more people are using videoconferencing, for good reason. (2) Anyone who has a video camera hooked up to a home computer can connect, via networking technology, to someone else with a similar setup. (3) A person simply sits in front of the camera and talks; a person or group of people on the other end is able to see and hear him or her. (4) Videoconferencing has been wonderful for both businesses and families. (5) In the new global economy, a company often has its offices all over the world. (6) Once, a businessperson might have had to travel a great deal to keep in touch with his or her clients, suppliers, and fellow employees around the globe. (7) Today, much business can be done with videoconferencing. (8) People can attend a meeting and see their clients face to face while remaining on a different continent. (9) The technology has improved so that anyone can transmit high-quality images and sound, and the cost of videoconferencing continues to drop. (10) And of course, a videoconferencing businessperson with competitors who travel the world will save much more money than they on airfare and accommodations. (11) Correct (12) A family today may find that they often must spend time apart. (13) A parent traveling for business may not see his or her spouse or children for days at a time. (14) People move across the country from where they grew up, leaving parents and siblings behind. (15) Parents sometimes divorce, and sometimes one starts a new job far away from the children. (16) Today, however, people who cannot be present to kiss their children goodnight or wish their sister a happy birthday can see family members across the miles through videoconferencing. (17) Divorced parents whom judges have allowed to move to another state have actually been required by law to buy videoconferencing technology to keep in touch with their children. (18) Most people do not feel that videoconferencing can replace being physically present with family members and clients, but videoconferences cost less than regular visits while offering more intimacy than a telephone call. (19) If the eyes are the windows of the soul, videoconferencing helps people look into those windows and stay connected.

CHAPTER 27: ADJECTIVES AND ADVERBS
Practice 27-1, page 440
Answers:
1. *Easy* modifies *jobs*.   **3.** *Frequently* modifies *employ*.   **5.** *Interesting* modifies *work*.   **7.** *Responsibly* modifies *behaving*.   **9.** *Financially* modifies *independent*.

Practice 27-2, page 443
Answers:
1. biggest   **3.** fonder   **5.** healthiest   **7.** higher   **9.** purer

Practice 27-3, page 444
Answers:
1. *Well* modifies *known*.   **3.** *Well* modifies *contrasts*.   **5.** *Good* modifies *tale*.   **7.** *Well* modifies *lives*.   **9.** *Well* modifies *jump*.

Practice 27-4, page 445
Answers:
1. better   **3.** worst   **5.** worst   **7.** best   **9.** worse

Editing Review 1, page 447
Answers:
1. (1) For an average European in the Middle Ages, wearing stripes was not simply a fashion mistake. (2) According to Michel Pastoureau, a scholar of the medieval period, wearing stripes was one of the worst things a European Christian could do in the thirteenth and fourteenth centuries. (3) Stripes might be taken as a sign that the wearer was sillier than other people; jesters, for example, often wore them. (4) Prostitutes also wore striped clothes, so stripes might be seen as an indication that the person was more sinful than others. (5) Wearing stripes was most dangerous for clergymen. (6) At least one clergyman in fourteenth-century France was executed because he had been foolish enough to wear striped clothes. (7) Carmelite monks who wore striped cloaks were frequently attacked, and several popes insisted that the monks change to a simpler costume. (8) People in medieval Europe certainly took their clothing seriously. (9) Correct

CHAPTER 28: MISPLACED AND DANGLING MODIFIERS
Practice 28-1, page 452
Possible edits:
1. Are there energy fields in a human body that can be touched by trained professionals?   **3.** According to believers in therapeutic touch, an energy field that is out of alignment can cause pain and illness.   **5.** After a session of therapeutic touch, many patients report that they just felt better without knowing why.   **7.** In her experiment, practitioners who could not see Emily were supposed to use the invisible energy field to determine when her hands were near theirs.   **9.** Anyone who can demonstrate the ability to detect a human energy field in a similar experiment can claim a million-dollar prize.

Practice 28-2, page 453
Possible edits:
1. Trading in a used car, a seller will get a better price if the car is clean.   **3.** With the used car looking like new, the

owner can get the best price for a trade-in or a resale. **5.** Approved as safe and drivable by a reputable mechanic, a used car may still have minor mechanical problems that do not have to be fixed. **7.** By deducting the cost of repairing minor problems from the asking price, the owner can be fair with a buyer. **9.** With higher than usual mileage, a used car might need a reduced asking price.

Editing Review 1, page 454
Possible edits:
1. (1) Shipping and handling costs can make or break a business that sells online. (2) By charging too much, a site may force customers to abandon their order. (3) A customer who feels that shipping and handling charges are too high may never return to the site. (4) Most people have shipped packages at least occasionally, so they know how much shipping costs. (5) Going too far in the other direction, some online sites offer their customers free shipping and handling. (6) The sites that offer free shipping lose money and may have to either close down for good or start charging shipping fees. (7) Correct (8) Using these shippers, the online sites must either charge a flat fee, which may be too much or too little, or make the customer wait until the order is complete to find out the shipping fee. (9) Neither option is perfect, so a business that wants to keep expanding its customer base must choose the least unattractive solution.

CHAPTER 29: COORDINATION AND SUBORDINATION
Practice 29-1, page 460
Possible edits:
1. and **3.** yet **5.** so **7.** and **9.** for

Practice 29-2, page 461
Possible edits:
1. Gasoline prices are lower in the United States than in many other industrialized countries, but most Americans do not find this news comforting. **3.** European drivers pay more than five dollars a gallon for gasoline, and gas prices in Asia have been triple those in the United States. **5.** Few people would argue that gasoline prices in the United States are too low, but the reason for these relatively cheap prices is that gasoline is not heavily taxed. **7.** Gasoline taxes can help to pay for roads, or they can raise money for research into fuel efficiency. **9.** Many Americans do not want to pay gas taxes of even two or three cents per gallon, nor do most want to spend tax money on mass transit systems.

Practice 29-3, page 463
Answers:
1. Graphology involves identifying personality features on the basis of a person's handwriting; these features include honesty, responsibility, and loyalty. **3.** An owner of a jew-

elry business says that an increase in employee theft made him use a graphology consultant; he says that handwriting analysis helped to identify the thieves. **5.** Nevertheless, even some job seekers are beginning to use graphology to help them find work; one says he submitted his handwriting analysis report along with his résumé and got the job he wanted.

Practice 29-4, page 464
Possible edits:
1. Two inventors believed that Americans would welcome the opportunity to have a gas mask; as a result, they invented one that is part of a baseball cap. **3.** The new baseball-cap gas mask is small and lightweight; in fact, it can fit in the corner of a drawer, in a coat pocket, or in a briefcase. **5.** The wearer slips a thin sheet of transparent plastic attached to the hat over his or her head; then, the plastic sheet can be tied shut at the back of the neck. **7.** The inventors say that the plastic sheet allows the wearer to see clearly; also, it does not make the wearer feel too closed in. **9.** The goal is to allow the wearer to get out of the contaminated area quickly; consequently, the wearer can simply slip on the mask and then move into fresh air.

Practice 29-5, page 466
Possible edits:
1. because **3.** after **5.** so that **7.** where **9.** if

Practice 29-6, page 467
Possible edits:
1. Although toddlers do not get to make many decisions, they want to have some power over their own lives. **3.** If parents want to avoid power struggles with their toddlers, they should learn to pick their battles. **5.** Parents should not let a child do anything dangerous even though the child may want to. **7.** Although adolescents need to establish their independence from their parents, they also want their parents to set some limits. **9.** Food, sleep, clothes, and grooming are often battlefields for children and parents unless parents remember their own rebellious phases and try to understand what their children are feeling.

Editing Review 1, page 468
Possible edits:
1. (1/2) Lyme disease, which is carried by deer ticks, appears most frequently in the northeastern United States. (3) No change (4/5) After people venture into tall grass or brush against other foliage, they should inspect any exposed skin carefully for the minuscule ticks. (6) No change (7/8) Limiting exposed skin by wearing socks, long pants, and long sleeves gives ticks fewer chances to attach themselves; so does washing exposed skin within about ninety minutes of being outdoors. (9) No change

CHAPTER 30: PARALLELISM
Practice 30-1, page 472
Answers and possible edits:
1. Parts that should be parallel: remain safe/so that assistance will come quickly. When your car breaks down on the road, you should follow simple rules to remain safe and get assistance quickly.   **3.** Parts that should be parallel: open the hood/put on emergency flashers/you could tie a handkerchief to the antenna. All of the cars in a parking lot look similar, so a mechanic may have trouble finding your car unless you open the hood, put on emergency flashers, or tie a handkerchief to the antenna.   **5.** Parts that should be parallel: sees no obviously broken-down car/he or she has other calls to deal with. A mechanic who sees no obviously broken-down car and has other calls to deal with may simply go on to the next customer.   **7.** Parts that should be parallel: about problems/if there are delays. Most pay phones nowadays do not receive incoming calls, so the garage may not be able to call you back on a pay phone to let you know about problems or delays.   **9.** Parts that should be parallel: sitting in a car/if you stand behind it. Sitting in a car or standing behind it can be very dangerous when a breakdown occurs on the side of the highway.

Practice 30-2, page 474
Answers and possible edits:
1. Parts that should be parallel: getting the household electric bill/to pay the rent each month. For many people, getting the household electric bill is more worrisome than paying the rent each month.   **3.** Parts that should be parallel: saving money/to use less electricity. Saving money appeals to many consumers more than using less electricity.   **5.** Parts that should be parallel: running the refrigerator/the use of all other appliances. In most households, running the refrigerator uses more energy than using all other appliances.   **7.** Parts that should be parallel: an energy-efficient new refrigerator/running an inefficient older model. However, running an energy-efficient new refrigerator uses much less electricity than running an inefficient older model.   **9.** Parts that should be parallel: to buy an efficient new refrigerator/it would take to run the old one for another five years. Householders might spend less money to buy an efficient new refrigerator than to run the old one for another five years.

Practice 30-3, page 475
Answers and possible edits:
1. Paired words: both/and. Parts that should be parallel: pressed for time/have gotten used to convenient but fattening foods. People in the United States are both pressed for time and used to convenient but fattening foods.   **3.** Paired words: rather/than. Parts that should be parallel: look thinner/

to stay the same size and get in better shape. Being overweight can be unhealthy, but many Americans would rather look thinner than stay the same size and get in better shape.   **5.** Paired words: both/and. Parts that should be parallel: overweight people/it even influences people of normal weight. The idea that thinner is better affects both overweight people and people of normal weight.   **7.** Paired words: either/or. Parts that should be parallel: surgical procedures to remove fat/they have died from dangerous diet drugs. Dozens of healthy, average-sized Americans in the past ten years have died from either surgical procedures to remove fat or dangerous diet drugs.   **9.** Paired words: not only/but also. Parts that should be parallel: in good health/can be physically fit. Some people who are larger than average are not only in good health but also physically fit.

Practice 30-4, page 476
Possible edits:
1. but also leadership experience.   **3.** nor allows flexibility.
5. and from other students.

Editing Review 1, page 477
Possible edits:
1. (1) Some employees who want to advance their careers would rather transfer within their company than look for a new job elsewhere. (2) In-house job changes are possible, but employees should be sure that they both meet the criteria of the job and avoid making their present boss angry. (3) Because businesses invest money in each person they hire, many companies would rather hire from within than bring an outsider into a position. (4) By hiring an employee from another department, a company neither needs to make an investment in a new employee nor loses a current employee. (5) Transfers usually go more smoothly now than in the past; however, an in-house job move can still require diplomacy and honesty. (6) Experts caution employees who are considering an in-house transfer to tell their current manager the truth and to discuss their wish to transfer with the potential new manager. (7) Employees should neither threaten to quit if they do not get the new job nor spread the word around the department that they are anxious to leave their present job. (8) Employees' goals for in-house transfers should be advancing their careers and making sure that they create no bad feelings with the move.

CHAPTER 31: SENTENCE VARIETY
Practice 31-1, page 482
Answers:
1. Annually, harsh weather takes a toll on sandy beaches.
3. Eventually, the ocean washed the ground out from under it.   **5.** Now it is going to be demolished.

Practice 31-2, page 482
Possible edits:
1. Once   3. Overnight,   5. Later,

Practice 31-4, page 484
Possible edits:
1. Paying attention to role models, some children—maybe even Sean—learn aggression from people at home, at school, or on television.   3. Acting violently under stress, his favorite television characters do not model good behavior, either.   5. Punishing my son for his angry outbursts, I used to take away his toys and privileges.   7. Giving him something to focus on before lashing out, I taught my son concrete ways to react to his anger.   9. Counting to ten when he gets angry, Sean now gives himself time to cool off.

Practice 31-5, page 485
Possible answers:
1. Switching   3. Earning   5. Preventing

Practice 31-7, page 487
Possible edits:
1. Many New Yorkers refused to believe in the existence of an alligator spotted in a pond in Central Park in New York City.   3. Believed by some gullible people, the rumors about giant sewer alligators were untrue.   5. Reported by several New Yorkers, the Central Park alligator sightings were confirmed when a television news crew filmed a reptile in the pond.   7. Surrounded by news cameras and curious onlookers, the pond in Central Park was brightly lit just before 11:00 p.m. on the day the alligator wrestler arrived.   9. Surprised to find that the caiman was only two feet long, some New Yorkers may have felt a bit foolish for expecting to see a giant alligator in the park.

Practice 31-8, page 488
Possible edits:
1. Trained   3. Treated   5. Asked

Practice 31-10, page 490
Possible edits:
1. Shakespeare, the son of a former town leader, grew up in Stratford, England.   3. In 1582, Shakespeare, just eighteen, married twenty-six-year-old Anne Hathaway, a farmer's daughter.   5. Young Shakespeare, once a simple country boy, soon became involved in acting, writing, and managing for one of London's theater companies.   7. Greene's publisher soon printed a public apology for the criticism, proof that Shakespeare had won the respect of some influential figures.   9. Eventually, Shakespeare returned to Stratford and purchased a large home, New Place, where he lived until his death in 1616.

Practice 31-11, page 491
Possible edits:
1. *Love and Desire*   3. an aging but reliable machine   5. a pile over two feet high

Practice 31-12, page 492
Possible edits:
1. Cats produce a protein that keeps their skin soft.   3. Some cat lovers who are allergic to cats can control their allergies with medication.   5. Scientists have successfully cloned mice that have been genetically engineered for scientific study.   7. According to cat experts, more than 10 percent of those people who have allergic reactions to cats are allergic to something other than the skin-softening protein.   9. However, owning a genetically engineered cat would allow an allergic person to avoid taking allergy medications, which can sometimes cause dangerous side effects.

Practice 31-13, page 493
Possible edits:
1. that receive hundreds or thousands of hits each day   3. , which is becoming rarer every day,   5. , which companies use to target potential customers,

Editing Review, page 494
Possible edits:
(1) Lotteries, which were illegal until recently in most U.S. states, have now been legalized in most parts of this country. (3) Run by state governments in many places, lotteries allow the governments to raise money without raising taxes. (5) The money can help fund education and other projects that are necessary and expensive. (7) Many citizens who consider lotteries an ideal way to raise funds reason that no one is forced to buy a lottery ticket. (9) No change

(10/11) Many experts on gambling worry about the increasing numbers of state lotteries, which are difficult for many people to resist. (12/13) Offering prizes of millions of dollars, lotteries make people fantasize about easy wealth. (14/15) Costing very little, lottery tickets are sold in grocery stores and shops in every neighborhood. (16/17) Unfortunately, the people least able to afford lottery tickets spend the most money on them, convinced that they will strike it rich someday. (18/19) In many impoverished areas, large numbers of people regularly buy several lottery tickets each week, hoping to escape boring, low-paying jobs.

(20) No change (21) Many people addicted to gambling do not consider the nearly impossible odds of winning a lottery jackpot. (23/24) Hooked by occasional small payoffs of two or three dollars, addicted gamblers will keep buying tickets until they have no money left.

(25/26) Promising a big payoff for a little investment, lotteries bring vast amounts of money into state treasuries.

(27/28) But lottery supporters, believing that lotteries save everyone money, seldom think about the victims of lotteries. (29) No change (31) No change

CHAPTER 32: ESL CONCERNS
Practice 32-1, page 498
Answers:
1. I (incorrect); Sara likes sports a lot.   **3.** C (correct)   **5.** I (incorrect); She will try to stay in touch with them.

Practice 32-2, page 501
Answers:
1. Sometimes, doctors will ask questions that seem odd, like "Do you wear a seat belt?"   **3.** For example, if you do not wear a seat belt, you are more likely to be injured in a car accident.   **5.** They may also ask you questions like "Can you think of a recent time when you have been depressed?"   **7.** Not everybody feels happy all the time, but serious depression should be treated.   **9.** Don't be embarrassed if your answers are not what you think the doctor will want to hear.

Practice 32-3, page 503
Answers:
1. there are   **3.** Is there   **5.** there are

Practice 32-4, page 504
Answers:
1. the   **3.** a; an   **5.** a; the   **7.** the   **9.** the

Practice 32-5, page 508
Answers:
1. the   **3.** The   **5.** the   **7.** The   **9.** no article

Practice 32-6, page 509
Answers:
1. I am a waitress at a restaurant four days a week.   **3.** There is a university close by, so many college students eat at my restaurant because it serves cheap food.   **5.** They seem to think that it is okay to be rude to the person serving them.   **7.** I do not make a high salary, so I need the tips from my customers to make a good living.   **9.** However, I think that people who cannot afford to leave a tip should not eat in a restaurant.

Practice 32-7, page 510
Possible edits:
1. The first thing to do is to put the right plants in the right places.   **3.** Also, it is a good idea to test the soil before planting to make sure the plants will have enough of the right nutrients.   **5.** They come with charts that help amateur gardeners interpret the results.   **7.** Adding compost is an especially good way to enrich the soil.

Practice 32-8, page 513
Answers:
1. Marlene and Agnetha wanted to see a certain movie after they saw the advertisement for it in the newspaper.   **3.** The two women did not want to miss seeing the film at their neighborhood theater, so they arranged their schedules carefully.   **5.** After they saw the movie, they were very angry that they had wasted their time and money.   **7.** Then, Marlene read in a different newspaper that the movie studio had admitted to inventing David Manning.   **9.** Therefore, the studio executives had decided to publish advertisements that contained a made-up quotation saying that the film was wonderful.

Practice 32-9, page 515
Answers:
1. During World War II, more than 120,000 Japanese Americans were locked up in internment camps.   **3.** These soldiers often had to fight against prejudice as well as the enemy.   **5.** After the war, many Japanese Americans who had been interned were ashamed of their experience.   **7.** They wanted to make other Americans aware of the sacrifices of Japanese Americans during World War II.   **9.** For the center of the memorial park, the designers picked out a sculpture by a Japanese American artist, Nina Akamu, featuring two cranes tangled in barbed wire.

Practice 32-10, page 516
Answers:
1. Students who are anxious about mathematics take fewer math classes and perform worse in them than students who do not have math anxiety.   **3.** It turns out that worry prevents students from understanding mathematics as well as they could.   **5.** Starting at about the age of twelve, students with math anxiety become less able to compensate for the loss of working memory.   **7.** Students who once thought they would never be able to understand math may someday find out that they can conquer their anxiety and cope with numbers.

Practice 32-11, page 518
Possible edits:
1. We found a faded lace handkerchief lying in the drawer.   **3.** During the restoration, builders added a massive new marble stairway to the entrance.   **5.** I put several delicious red New Jersey tomatoes in the salad.

CHAPTER 33: WORD CHOICE
Practice 33-1, page 523
Answers and possible edits:
1. Vague or abstract words: little; good. My four-year-old sister cleans up her room, puts away her toys and books, and helps my parents and me with simple chores.   **3.** Vague or

abstract words: fun. My sister and I enjoy playing board games and reading books together.   **5.** Vague or abstract words: nicest. My grandmother hugs me enthusiastically and has been encouraging me to try to get a dance scholarship.   **7.** Vague or abstract words: one of my uncles; a little crazy. My uncle Mahmoud wears loud purple suits and spikes his hair straight up.   **9.** Vague or abstract words: treats me; very young. He pinches my cheeks as if I were a kindergartner instead of a college student.

Practice 33-2, page 524
Answers and possible edits:
1. Slang: fab. I wanted to express my appreciation for the wonderful new benefits package.   **3.** Slang: biggie. Now that my wife and I are starting a family, insurance is a major factor.   **5.** Slang: no way. Without the company paying for this leave, I would not be able to afford the time off.   **7.** Slang: cake. I know that adjusting to fatherhood will not be easy.   **9.** Slang: give me a shout. If I can do anything to make my absence easier on my coworkers, please let me know.

Practice 33-3, page 526
Answers and possible edits:
1. Wordy language: At this point in time. That may be changing, thanks to four Japanese inventors.   **3.** Wordy language: become dimmer and then grow brighter in an expressive fashion. The patent application describes a car with an antenna that wags, headlights that dim and brighten expressively, and ornaments that look like eyebrows, eyelids, and tears.   **5.** Wordy language: In order to have the vehicle. To express anger, the car's hood would glow red as the eyebrows light up.   **7.** Wordy language: In the event that. If the driver wants the car to "cry," he or she could make the hood dark blue, shade the headlights, and show a blinking "tear" light.   **9.** Wordy language: could also be taken advantage of for. The inventors say that their ideas could be applied not just to cars but also to motorcycles, ships, or aircraft.

Practice 33-4, page 528
Answers and possible edits:
1. Cliché: eyes in the back of their heads. People with young children need to be constantly alert.   **3.** Cliché: have their heads examined. Parents of a toddler should rethink their safety policies if they do not lock cabinets containing household chemicals.   **5.** Cliché: in the nick of time. Parents sometimes recognize dangers moments before a mishap and stop their children from injuring themselves.   **7.** Cliché: mortal fears. Parents worry about their young children running into traffic to chase a ball.   **9.** Cliché: keep their hands to themselves. Children must be taught that if they find a gun in someone's home, they should not touch the weapon and they should leave the area immediately.

Editing Review, page 529
(1) Being the chief executive officer at a major American corporation almost always pays extremely well. (2) CEOs earn millions of dollars each year, and most also get stock options. (3) Even if the company performs poorly and the CEO gets fired, he (and it is almost always a man) often gets a severance package that is worth additional millions. (4) A CEO's salary in the United States is usually several hundred times larger than the average company worker's salary. (5) This ratio is enormous compared with the ratios in other industrialized countries. (6) In Japan, for example, a CEO's salary is at most about ten times that of a worker. (7) Are American CEOs really exceptional? (8) Are they worth what they are paid?

(9) In fact, highly paid CEOs can rarely do what corporate directors hope. (10) They may have earned huge profits at a previous corporation, but every business is different. (11) There is no guarantee that these men will be able to make another business succeed. (12) If a company promoted a worker from within, he or she probably would not only know the company thoroughly but also work for a smaller salary than a successful current CEO. (13) Then, the corporation would be able to spend a few million dollars less on its chief officer. (14) Why, then, are corporations willing to pay millions to recruit expensive outsiders as CEOs?

(15) The problem with promoting a CEO from within the company is that few companies want to take risks. (16) For a decade or more, hiring a CEO has meant finding the CEO of another company and paying him enough to get him to leave his current position. (17) Company directors think that their stockholders expect the company to bring in a highly paid outsider. (18) The directors are afraid that an insider might fail and disappoint stockholders. (19) Of course, most CEOs brought in from elsewhere also fail to satisfy the shareholders, but the corporate boards can at least reassure themselves that their choice has a track record when he arrives. (20) Corporations claim to want leaders who are original thinkers. (21) However, few corporate boards of directors are willing to look anywhere other than conventional places for their next leaders. (22) This conventional thinking will eventually hurt business; perhaps only then will the trend toward hiring expensive CEOs change.

CHAPTER 34: COMMONLY CONFUSED WORDS
Practice 34-1, page 541
Answers:
1. their   **3.** find   **5.** an; except   **7.** write   **9.** though; effect

Editing Review 1, page 542
Answers:
1. (1) Most people know that Americans love to drive their cars. (2) However, many people may not be conscious of

how much the government does to support our car culture. (3) For instance, the United States would never have had so many good highways without federal and state assistance for road construction and maintenance. (4) New highways are usually paid for mainly by tax money. (5) It is rare for a new road to be paid for with tolls, which would come exclusively from the people driving on it. (6) Americans also expect their roads to be well maintained, and they may write to their representatives to complain about potholes and aging road surfaces. (7) The government is even responsible for keeping gas prices lower here than in most other industrialized nations. (8) Few people mind that the government assists drivers in these ways. (9) Some would argue that it's a government's job to help pay for transportation. (10) However, other forms of transportation in this country are often passed over when Congress hands out funds. (11) Amtrak, the U.S. railroad, may soon lose virtually all government funds, even though many government officials are skeptical of its ability to keep operating without government assistance. (12) Except for a few places like New York and San Francisco, most U.S. cities do not have good mass transit systems. (13) Americans whose travels have taken them to certain parts of the world praise the national train systems and city transit systems they find there. (14) As traffic gets worse in our nation's urban and suburban areas, some people find it odd that the United States does not invest more in transportation that would allow people to leave their cars at home.

CHAPTER 35: SPELLING
Practice 35-1, page 546
Spelling errors/corrections:
oportunity/opportunity, excellant/excellent, promiseing/promising, referances/references

Editing Review 1, page 553
Answers:
1. (1) Anyone interested in weird events should visit New York City on October 31, when the biggest Halloween parade in the country takes place. (2) Everyone in the city, it seems, marches in the parade, yet there are still an estimated two million people watching from the sidewalks. (3) The parade had its beginnings in Greenwich Village, and original parade-goers walked though the small, winding streets of that old New York neighborhood. (4) By now, the parade has gotten so large that it has to go down one of the city's broad avenues. (5) The Halloween parade surprises a lot of people who see it for the first time. (6) The merriment begins early in the evening, as costumed paraders line up. (7) You're likely to see a huge group of friends dressed as one hundred and one dalmatians or perhaps some comically exaggerated versions of government officials. (8) Every kind of costume is permitted in the parade, and some people attend skimpily dressed, apparently without embarrassment, in spite of the October chill. (9) For a fascinating look at how strangely people can behave on Halloween, the New York City Halloween parade is the place to be.

CHAPTER 36: COMMAS
Practice 36-1, page 558
Answers:
1. C   3. A recent study of sixty-eight dollar bills found five carrying germs that could infect healthy people, fifty-nine harboring bacteria that could sicken people with depressed immune systems, and only four that were free of dangerous infectious agents.   5. Of course, this study involved a very small, localized, and not necessarily representative sample of bills.   7. Once, when I was attempting to open my purse, accept a receipt from a cashier, and hold my change at the same time, I stuck some dollar bills in my mouth for a moment.   9. Although the study of the sixty-eight dollar bills did not reveal whether germs can survive for long periods on money, transfer from bills to people, or otherwise contribute to human illness, reading about it made me realize that my mother had been right to be worried.

Practice 36-2, page 559
Answers:
1. Working in a nursing home is a difficult job, for elderly patients can seldom do much for themselves.   3. Few trained nurses and nurse's aides want nursing-home jobs, for the pay is also usually lower than that offered by hospitals.   5. More workers will be needed as the baby boomers become elderly, yet there is already a shortage of people willing to do the tough and often unpleasant work.   7. C   9. Solving these problems will be difficult, for long-term care for the elderly is already very expensive.

Practice 36-3, page 561
Answers:
1. Along roadsides all across this country, drivers see the bodies of animals hit by cars.   3. Of course, hitting a deer is not only disturbing but also potentially harmful or fatal to the occupants of a car.   5. On the other hand, drivers in wilderness areas may accidentally kill endangered species.   7. Maintaining the world's largest network of roads, the U.S. Forest Service tries to balance the needs of humans and wildlife.   9. Unfortunately, wilderness roads may isolate populations of animals that will not cross them and kill animals that make the attempt.

Practice 36-4, page 563
Answers:
1. Road rage, as most people have heard, occurs when an angry driver overreacts.   3. One famous air rage incident, a confrontation between a drunken businessman and a

flight attendant, ended with the passenger tied to his seat for the rest of the flight.   **5.** Ground rage, as the name suggests, occurs in the terminal, not in the air.   **7.** Oversold seats, a common occurrence in air travel, can mean that some passengers are forced to miss a flight.   **9.** Some delayed or bumped passengers take out their anger on the gate agent, a convenient target.

Practice 36-5, page 565
Answers:
1. C   **3.** C   **5.** C   **7.** Such people, who may never love clowns, will still be able to tolerate having them around.   **9.** Few adults admit to having coulrophobia, which is most effectively treated when the sufferer confronts the fear.

Practice 36-6, page 567
Answers:
1. My sister asked, "James, do you get a lot of telemarketing calls?"   **3.** C   **5.** My address, which is 21 Highland Road, Binghamton, New York, has now been added to the state registry.   **7.** I simply replied, "No, I have news for you."   **9.** "As you probably know," I told my unwanted callers, "it is illegal for you to contact me in this way."

Editing Review 1, page 568
Answers:
1. (1) Everyone who uses cleaning products at home has probably seen warning labels on those products, for most household cleaners contain harsh chemicals. (2) The warnings, which are required by law, are so common that many users probably ignore them. (3) However, all cleaning products should be used with care, and some of them can seriously injure children or anyone else who misuses them. (4) Drain cleaners, toilet bowl cleaners, and chlorine bleach can all cause serious damage to skin, eyes, and other sensitive tissue. (5) Glass cleaners can react with bleach to produce toxic fumes. (6) Alternative cleansers, nontoxic products that can be made from items in an average kitchen, are cheaper than brand-name cleaning products and usually work just as well. (7) For most cleaning jobs, a solution of vinegar and water or baking soda and water is effective. (8) A plunger can often fix a clogged drain as well as a drain cleaner can, and club soda cleans windows nicely. (9) As for air fresheners, one expert advises, "Open your windows." (10) Economy, efficiency, and safety are three excellent reasons for choosing homemade cleansers.

CHAPTER 37: APOSTROPHES
Practice 37-1, page 573
Answers:
1. A thermometer's indicator mark at 98.6 degrees is supposed to show a person's normal body temperature.   **3.** Fevers help the body combat viruses and stimulate the immune system.   **5.** A fever's appearance is not necessarily a reason to take fever-reducing medications, which can lower a body's temperature without doing anything to fight the infection.   **7.** Many doctors do not recommend using any drugs to treat a fever if it's lower than 102 degrees.   **9.** Some parents' fears of fever are so intense that they suffer from "fever phobia" and overreact to their children's symptoms.

Practice 37-2, page 575
Answers:
1. Those who do often say they're using these drugs because their competitors are probably using them too.   **3.** Most athletes taking steroids and other substances say they wouldn't use these drugs if they could be certain that their opponents aren't using them.   **5.** If sports organizations don't eliminate drug use, we all know who's the loser.   **7.** When even one athlete gets away with using drugs, we can't trust that any athletic competition has been won fairly.   **9.** Let's eliminate performance-enhancing drugs now.

Practice 37-3, page 576
Answers:
1. Next month's schedule is less busy, so I think I'll be able to keep my blog current then.   **3.** His blog is a little hard to read because he always leaves out certain letters, such as *a*'s, *e*'s, and *o*'s.   **5.** When Manny's computer was stolen, he lost notes for his blog and two years' work on his novel.

Editing Reviews, pages 577–78
Answers:
1. (1) Some of the first discussions of global warming focused attention on one of the gases that contributes to the greenhouse effect: methane. (2) Like other greenhouse gases, methane helps to keep the earth's heat trapped in our atmosphere, and the temperature of the earth goes up as a result. (3) Humans aren't the only producers of methane; it's also a by-product of cows' digestion of their food. (4) For a while, many Americans' knowledge of global warming didn't go much further than cow jokes. (5) As scientists have become more convinced that global warming is real and a potential threat to humans, our knowledge of the causes of the greenhouse effect has expanded. (6) Cows aren't completely off the hook, but they're far less guilty of contributing to global warming than humans and cars are. (7) The amount of methane produced by cows adds up to about 3 percent of the total amount of greenhouse gases produced by people. (8) Getting a cow to change its diet won't solve the world's warming problem.   **3.** (1) C (2) The cars' locks were supposed to respond when their owners pushed a button, and all at once they wouldn't. (3) After a few days' wait, the entry systems began functioning again. (4) Many residents of Bremerton, the home of a Navy shipyard, were

convinced that the military's technological activity had affected the cars, but Navy officials denied it. (5) Other people wondered if radio transmissions might have jammed the frequency and prevented the keyless systems from functioning. (6) Fortunately, people whose cars have keyless entry systems weren't locked out for those days. (7) These owners simply had to resort to a backup system to open and lock their cars—it's called a "key."

CHAPTER 38: QUOTATION MARKS
Practice 38-1, page 582
Answers:

1. Looking around the room, Allison said, "I thought only teenage girls had eating disorders. There are people here of all ages, including several men." **3.** I'm forty years old, not a teenager, and not a girl," Patrick said. "However, I have an eating disorder." **5.** "I eat too much," said Patrick. "I'm a compulsive eater." **7.** "The dictionary defines *compulsive* as 'related to a psychological obsession,'" said Brooke. **9.** "That is one myth we're going to talk about," said Brooke. "In fact, people with eating disorders are hurting themselves. They are usually upset that their families and friends are worried about them."

Practice 38-2, page 584
Answers:

1. "I never thought I would use the Internet for dating, but it really worked," she said. **3.** She said, "I could tell right away if I wasn't going to have anything in common with a person." **5.** C **7.** C **9.** "I found a great person," she said, "and you could too."

Practice 38-3, page 585
Answers:

1. At the meeting, an outside consultant tried to motivate us by quoting from an article in USA Today called, "How to Get the Job Done." **3.** Marta looked as if she were taking careful notes, but I knew that she was working on the final draft of an essay she was hoping to publish in Business Review, her favorite magazine. **5.** When the grueling meeting was over, Marta reminded me that Wallace Stevens, the poet who wrote "Sunday Morning," had found a way to be creative while he spent his days working at an insurance company.

Editing Review 1, page 586
Answers:

1. (1) On our way home from a Britney Spears concert, Nicole said that she wanted to go out and get some of Britney's CDs as soon as possible. (2) The very next day, on our way to the record store, I said, "Every time I listen to these songs, I'll see her performing them in my mind." (3) Nicole agreed and added that she wanted to have recordings of some of Britney's especially moving songs. (4) At the store, she immediately found the CD called In the Zone, which has two songs that Nicole loves. (5) At the concert, she had gone insane when Britney sang "Everytime" and "Outrageous"; Nicole said that they were her favorite songs of all time. (6) I bought that CD too, as well as a Madonna CD called American Life. (7) I explained that I love Madonna's singing, and I was also amazed by her performance in the movie Evita. (8) While going home from the record store, I asked Nicole if she would like to come over to my place and listen to music. (9) "Not right now," she replied, "I think I want to relive that fantastic concert alone for a while." (10) Is this what my mom meant when she used to say, "Being at a live Beatles concert was one of the greatest experiences of my life"?

CHAPTER 39: OTHER PUNCTUATION
Editing Review, page 593
Possible edits:

(1) In his novel *Native Son* (published in 1940), Richard Wright confronted the treatment of African Americans in a frank—and, to some readers, shocking—way; in fact, the novel was so candid that some of its most powerful sections were omitted from its originally published version. **Note:** Some students might hyphenate *African American,* which is acceptable according to some of style guides. (2) *Native Son,* which takes place in Chicago in the 1930s, recounts the last days of a twenty-year-old African American named Bigger Thomas. (3) The novel's disconcerting beginning (Bigger is awakened by the screams of his mother and sister when they see a large rat that Bigger kills) sets the tone for the story to come. (4) Bigger's anger toward the poverty and racism he experiences blinds him to rational action and leads to tragic consequences: He accidentally kills a white heiress—the daughter of his employer—and later, in a rage, beats his girlfriend nearly to death. (5) Bigger's trial is extremely one-sided, and he is convicted and sentenced to die in a dreadful way: by electrocution.

(6) Blindness is a major theme in the novel; it pertains both to Bigger's view of his situation and to the white society in which he struggles. (7) Bigger's pride and anger prevent him from seeing things as they really are, and the insensitivity of his well-to-do employer embodies white society's blindness to racism.

(8) With this book's publication and immediate commercial success, a new glimmer of awareness appeared in America: an awareness of racial injustice that had long been ignored. (9) It was not until 1991—with the first publication of *Native Son* in its complete, original form—that many of the novel's strongest and most moving passages were included.

CHAPTER 40: CAPITALIZATION
Practice 40-1, page 596
Answers:

(1) C (3) The same year, audiences thrilled to the story of little Dorothy, who clicked her heels together and chanted, "There's no place like home."

Practice 40-2, page 598
Answers:

1. Lindsborg is a small town in McPherson County, Kansas, that calls itself "Little Sweden, U.S.A." 3. The town's most famous resident was probably a Swedish immigrant artist named Birger Sandzen. 5. Sandzen intended to stay in Kansas for two or three years, but he loved the Great Plains and ended up remaining in Lindsborg for the rest of his life. 7. Although Sandzen worked mainly in the Midwest, the Rocky Mountains, and other relatively unpopulated parts of the United States, he exhibited widely. 9. Sandzen's use of vivid color showed the beauty of the natural landscapes of the West.

Practice 40-3, page 600
Answers:

1. The television show *Sesame Street*, which began in 1969, brought innovative programming to children. 3. The popular Muppets Kermit the Frog and Miss Piggy starred in several films, including one based on Charles Dickens's classic *A Christmas Carol* and one based on Robert Louis Stevenson's *Treasure Island*. 5. "Elmo's World," a segment added to the show in the 1990s, introduced the small red monster who would become one of the most popular toys in history.

Editing Review, page 600
Answers:

(1) Are pennies necessary? (3) According to the group Americans for Common Cents, however, "Pennies are a part of our culture and our economy." (5) Opponents of the copper coin—which has been made of zinc with a copper coating since 1982—say that people don't like to use pennies. (7) Many stores place penny trays on the counter so that customers can either leave unwanted pennies or pick a few up for the cashier to avoid getting any pennies in change. (9) Yet the penny is undeniably a part of American history. (11) Only four of these original coins survive, and they are valued at more than a quarter of a million dollars each. (13) Fifty years later, the Lincoln Memorial was added to the reverse side, replacing the stalks of wheat on earlier pennies. (15) Everyone has heard the saying "A penny saved is a penny earned," and that idea is not likely to change even though a penny doesn't buy much today. (17) Finally, unlike the John F. Kennedy half-dollar coin, which is no longer minted, people simply expect pennies to be there. (19) But many U.S. citizens care about the fate of the penny and don't want it to disappear.

Acknowledgments, continued from page iv

Amy L. Beck. "Struggling for Perfection." From the *Harvard Crimson*, March 19, 1998. Reprinted by permission.

Jeri Becker. Excerpt from *The Sun*, September 2004. Reprinted by permission of Jeri Becker.

Kathleen S. Berger. Excerpt from *The Developing Person Through the Life Span*, Sixth Edition, by Kathleen S. Berger. Copyright © 2005. Reprinted by permission of W. H. Freeman and Company/Worth Publishers.

Kenneth Blanchard. Excerpts from *Exploring the World of Business* by Kenneth Blanchard. Copyright © 1996. Reprinted by permission of Worth Publishers.

William Broyles Jr. "A War for Us, Fought by Them." From the *New York Times*, May 4, 2004, p. A29. Copyright © 2004 by the New York Times Company. Reprinted with permission.

Perry W. Buffington. "Get the Raise You Deserve." From *Cheap Psychological Tricks: What to Do When Hard Work, Honesty, and Perseverance Fail*, by Perry W. Buffington, Ph.D., illustrated by Mitzi Carter and published by Peachtree Publishers. Copyright © 1996 by Perry W. Buffington, Ph.D. Reprinted by permission of Peachtree Publishers, Atlanta, GA.

Traci E. Carpenter. "I Cannot Be Charted." From *Newsweek*, July 12, 2004. © Newsweek, Inc. Reprinted by permission of Newsweek. All rights reserved.

Charles Colson and Anne Morse. "Societal Suicide." From *Christianity Today*, June 16, 2004. Copyright © 2004. Reprinted by permission of Prison Fellowship, www.pfm.org.

Chitra Banerjee Divakaruni. "Spice of Life." Copyright © 1997 by Chitra Divakaruni. Copyright © 1997 by Chitra Divakaruni. First appeared on Salon.com. Reprinted by permission of the author and the Sandra Dijkstra Literary Agency.

Nathaniel Fick. "Don't Dumb Down the Military." From the *New York Times*, July 20, 2004, p. A19. Copyright © 2004 by the New York Times Company. Reprinted with permission.

Gabrielle Glaser. Sidebar from "Past Scents," *Health*, July/August 2001, pp. 128–33. Copyright © 2001 *Health*. Reprinted by permission.

Bob Greene. "Foul Mouths Are Fair Game in Our Coarsening Culture." Published July 22, 2001. © Tribune Media Services, Inc. All Rights Reserved. Reprinted with permission of the publisher.

Don H. Hockenbury and Sandra E. Hockenbury. "Anosmia" (p. 81), "Defining Eating" (p. 283), "Anorexia nervosa" (pp. 288–89), and Key Terms, Review Questions, Critical Thinking Questions (p. 345). Excerpts from *Discovering Psychology*, Second Edition. Copyright © 2001 Worth Publishers. Reprinted by permission of Worth Publishers.

Roger Hoffmann. "The Dare." From the *New York Times*. Copyright © 1986 by the New York Times Company.

Langston Hughes. "Salvation." From *The Big Sea* by Langston Hughes. Copyright © 1940 by Langston Hughes. Copyright © 1940 by Langston Hughes. Copyright renewed 1968 by Ama Bontemps and George Houston Bass. Reprinted by permission of Hill and Wang, a division of Farrar, Straus & Giroux, LLC.

Martin Luther King Jr. "The Purpose of Education." Speech given at Morehouse College (1948). Copyright 1963 Martin Luther King Jr., copyright renewed 1991 Coretta Scott King. Copyright 1968 Martin Luther King Jr., copyright renewed 1996 Coretta Scott King. Reprinted by arrangement with the Estate of Martin Luther King Jr., c/o Writers House as agent for the proprietor New York, NY.

Barbara Kingsolver. "High Tide in Tucson." From *High Tide in Tucson: Essays from Now or Never* by Barbara Kingsolver. Copyright © 1995 by Barbara Kingsolver. Reprinted by permission of HarperCollins Publishers, Inc.

"Literacy and Health." From *Parade*, January 18, 2004, p. 16. © 2004 Parade Publications, Inc. Reprinted by permission. All rights reserved.

Nancy Mairs. "On Being a Cripple." From *Plaintext* by Nancy Mairs. © 1986 by The Arizona Board of Regents. Reprinted by permission of the University of Arizona Press.

Malcolm X. "My First Conk." Originally titled "Hair" from *The Autobiography of Malcolm X* by Malcolm X and Alex Haley. Copyright © 1964 by Alex Haley and Malcolm X. Copyright © 1965 by Alex Haley and Betty Shabazz. Used by permission of Random House, Inc.

Rubén Martínez. "Mexico to Mecca: The Flores Family." From *The New Americans* by Rubén Martínez. Copyright © 2004 by Rubén Martínez. First published in The New Press in 2004. Reprinted by permission of Susan Bergholz Literary Services. All rights reserved.

Wesley Morris. "Delay Gives 'Damage' a Fighting Chance." From the *Boston Globe*, February 8, 2002. "Survey Finds Many Firms Monitor Staff." From the *Boston Globe*, April 29, 2001. Copyright 2001 by Wesley Morris. Reprinted by permission of Wesley Morris.

Vidhya Murugesan and Katie Smith. From the *New York Times Upfront Online: Scholastic*. www.scholastic.com. Copyright © 2004 by Scholastic, Inc. Reprinted by permission of Scholastic, Inc.

Nick Paumgarten. "Lost and Found: One Glove." From the *New Yorker*, January 19, 2004. Copyright © 2004 by Condé Nast Publications, Inc. Reprinted by permission. All rights reserved.

Anna Quindlen. "Desecration? Dedication!" Originally published in *Newsweek*, February 23, 2004, volume 143, issue 8, p. 68. Copyright © 2004 by Anna Quindlen. Reprinted by permission of International Creative Management, Inc.

Scott Russell Sanders. "The Men We Carry in Our Minds." First appeared in *Milkweed Chronicle*. Copyright © 1984 by Scott Russell Sanders. Reprinted by permission of author and the author's agents, the Virginia Kidd Agency, Inc.

Juliet B. Schor. "Age Compression." From *Born to Buy* by Juliet B. Schor. Copyright © 2004 by Juliet B. Schor. Reprinted with the permission of Scribner, an imprint of Simon & Schuster Adult Publishing Group.

Kathleen Squires. "Reading between the Lines." © Time, Inc. All rights reserved. Reprinted by permission.

Brent Staples. "Just Walk on By: Black Men and Public Space." Originally published in *Ms. Magazine*. Reprinted by permission of the author.

Amy Tan. "Mother Tongue." Copyright © 1990 by Amy Tan. First appeared in the *Threepenny Review*. Reprinted by permission of the author and the Sandra Dijkstra Literary Agency.

Robb Walsh. "The Inkblot Test." From *Are You Really Going to Eat That?* by Robb Walsh. Copyright © 2003 by Robb Walsh. Reprinted by permission of Counterpoint Press, a member of Perseus Books, L.L.C.

Stanley Weil. Excerpt from "Health Bulletin." First published in *Men's Health*, June 2004. Copyright © 2004. Reprinted by permission of Stanley Weil.

Art Credits

Page 1: Bob Deammrich/The Image Works, Inc.

Page 15: Don H. Hockenbury and Sandra E. Hockenbury. From *Discovering Psychology*, Second Edition. Copyright © 2001 Worth Publishers. Reprinted by permission of Worth Publishers.

Page 39: Google Inc.

Page 113: Gary Conner/Photo Edit

Page 115: Frederick M. Brown/Getty Images

Page 129: © Scott Roper/CORBIS

Page 133: Richard Ambo/*The Honolulu Advertiser*

Page 146: Gary Brookins

Page 150: Courtesy Want Ad Publications, Inc.

Page 161: Amy Eckert

Page 177: © Daniel Aubry NYC/CORBIS

Page 181: Zappos.com

Page 192: Jason Reblando

Page 197: © The 5th Wave, www.the5thwave.com

Page 208: Andrew Scott/*Columbia College Chronicle*

Index

Correction Symbols

This chart lists typical symbols that instructors use to point out writing problems. The explanation of each symbol includes a step you can take to revise or edit your writing. Included also are suggested chapters to check for more help and information. If your instructor uses different symbols for some errors, write them in the lefthand column for future reference.

YOUR INSTRUCTOR'S SYMBOL	STANDARD SYMBOL	HOW TO REVISE OR EDIT (Numbers in boldface are chapters where you can find help)
	adj	Use correct adjective form **27**
	adv	Use correct adverb form **27**
	agr	Correct subject-verb agreement or pronoun agreement **24; 26**
	awk	Awkward expression: edit for clarity **8**
	cap	Use capital letter correctly **40**
	case	Use correct pronoun case **26**
	cliché	Replace overused phrase with fresh words **33**
	coh	Revise paragraph or essay for coherence **8**
	combine	Combine sentences **31**
	con t	Correct the inconsistent verb tense **25**
	coord	Use coordination correctly **29**
	cs	Comma splice: join the sentences correctly **23**
	d or dic	Diction: edit word choice **33**
	dev	Develop your paragraph or essay more completely **5; 7**
	dm	Revise to avoid a dangling modifier **28**
	frag	Attach the fragment to a sentence or make it a sentence **22**
	fs	Fused sentence: join the two sentences correctly **23**
	intro	Add or strengthen your introduction **7**
	ital	Use italics **38**
	lc	Use lowercase **40**
	mm	Revise to avoid a misplaced modifier **28**
	pl	Use the correct plural form of the verb **25**
	ref	Make pronoun reference clear **26**
	ro	Run-on sentence: join the two sentences correctly **23**
	sp	Correct the spelling error **34; 35**
	sub	Use subordination correctly **29**
	sup	Support your point with details, examples, or facts **5**
	tense	Correct the problem with verb tense **25**
	trans	Add a transition **8**
	ts	Add or strengthen your topic sentence or thesis statement **4**
	u	Revise paragraph or essay for unity **8**
	w	Delete unnecessary words **33**
	?	Make your meaning clearer **8**
	,	Use comma correctly **36**
	; : ( ) - —	Use semicolon/colon/parentheses/hyphen/dash correctly **39**
	" "	Use quotation marks correctly **38**

Useful Lists, Checklists, and Charts